RESOLUTION
AND
E-DISCOVERY
2013

By

DANIEL B. GARRIE

and

YOAV M. GRIVER

For Customer Assistance Call 1-800-328-4880

Mat #98765432

To Sabrina and Sarah
Thanks for everything.

Summary of Contents

Table of Contents

CHAPTER 9. E-DISCOVERY IN AAA ARBITRATION

CHAPTER 10. JAMS AND E-DISCOVERY

CHAPTER 11. E-DISCOVERY UNDER THE LONDON COURT OF INTERNATIONAL ARBITRATION

Chapter 1

Introduction: Welcome and Remarks

> **KeyCite**[R]: Cases and other legal materials listed in KeyCite Scope can be researched through the KeyCite service on Westlaw[R]. Use KeyCite to check citations for form, parallel references, prior and later history, and comprehensive citator information, including citations to other decisions and secondary materials.

*by Daniel Garrie, Yoav M. Griver & Candice Lang**

§ 1:1   Introduction

This book is for practitioners and written by practitioners. Today, lawyers, neutrals, Judges, and clients all confront the ad-

---

*Mr. Garrie is a Partner at Law & Forensics (www.lawandforensics.com) and is a renowned e-discovery special master and thought leader in the fields of information security, forensics, e-discovery, information governance, and digital privacy. Quoted in Forbes and profiled in the Los Angeles Daily Journal, he is a member of the International Institute for Conflict Prevention and Resolution (CPR) Panel of Distinguished Neutrals; a Neutral on the Hong Kong International Arbitration Centre; Chair of the Forensic and E-Discovery Panel at Alternative Resolution Centers; and an Arbitrator with the London Court of International Arbitration neutrals. Mr. Garrie has published over 100 articles and been recognized by several U.S. Supreme Court Justices for his legal scholarship. In addition, Mr. Garrie has served as an electronically stored information liaison, E-Mediator, Neutral and Expert for the L.A. Superior Courts, 2nd Circuit, 3rd Circuit, 7th Circuit, New York Supreme Court, and Delaware Supreme Court. Mr. Garrie is admitted to practice law in New York, New Jersey, and Washington State. You can reach Daniel at Daniel@lawandforensics.com.

Yoav M. Griver, Esq. is a Partner in the New York office of Zeichner Ellman & Krause LLP (www.zeklaw.com) where he concentrates his practice on complex commercial litigation where he litigates commercial and intellectual property matters for clients in the banking, credit, insurance, software, and pharmaceutical industries. An adjunct professor at NYU, Yoav writes and lectures frequently on legal issues for the *Los Angeles Daily Journal, The Deal.com,* and various law journals, including on the offensive and defensive use of electronic discovery in dispute resolution. The thoughts expressed herein are solely the authors' own and not those of ARC or ZEK.

ditional costs and time spent on electronic discovery. And increasingly, these parties must face the challenge of electronic discovery outside the federal and state court systems, as new methods of dispute resolution—arbitration, mediation, special masters—are chosen with increasing frequency.

While each dispute resolution forum has its strengths and weaknesses (as summarized in the following chart), they are all concerned with determining facts and reaching a resolution to whatever dispute is at hand. Accordingly, it is no surprise that many of the issues that arise in litigation with respect to electronically-stored information, or ESI, parallel issues arising in arbitration or mediation. Yet, there is little law or commentary on the topic of electronic discovery outside the courts. This book, which is updated yearly, hopes to provide a one-stop guide for counsel, arbitrators, judges and jurists seeking to develop a better grasp of electronic discovery and its application to mediation, arbitration, special master proceedings, or other dispute resolution forums. It also provides "practitioner points," to help the reader better navigate the often contentious and costly process of discovery that arises in arbitration, mediation, and litigation.

Candice Lang is Senior Associate Counsel with Law & Forensics. Ms. Lang's practice focuses on working with large companies and firms on complex e-discovery, privacy, and forensic investigations and disputes. Prior to joining Law & Forensics, Ms. Lang worked in Central Asia and advised on complex legal and business issues. Ms. Lang is based out of our New York City office and can be reached at clang@lawandforensics.com

AREAS	ARBITRATION	MEDIATION	LITIGATION
Authority	Parties agree to submit their dispute to arbitration	Parties agree to mediation or court by mandate	Jurisdiction determined by law
	Arbitrator decides submitted disputes	Mediator decides to take submitted case	Court is limited by its jurisdiction
	Parties choose the location for the arbitration	Parties choose the location for the mediation	Jurisdiction determined by the type of case and amount in dispute
	Decision made by arbitrator(s)	Decision made by parties	Decisions made by judge or jury
	Appeal rights are limited	Option not to settle	Appealable Judgment
Procedure	Confidential	Confidential	Open to the public
	Adversarial	Cooperative	Adversarial
	Flexible process	Flexible process	Procedural Rules
	Parties choose "Rules" which are enforced by arbitrator(s)	Parties and mediator determine ground rules	Statutory Rules
The Fact-Finder	Selected by parties	Parties select mediator	Appointed Judge
	Arbitrator may have industry expertise	Mediator is an expert in process	Judges may lack technical expertise
	Panels can include partial or non-partial arbitrators	Mediator is neutral	Judges are a neutral third party

AREAS	ARBITRATION	MEDIATION	LITIGATION
Results	Parties can determine end date	Cooperative agreement may be reached, or not	Controlled by precedent and/or statute; Possible Appeal
	Win-lose solution	Win-win solutions or No Result	Win-lose solution
Enforcement	National or International regulations; Entered as court order	Implementation depends on the parties' good will	Court Order enforced by established mechanism
	Award conclusive, final and binding (limited appeal)	No appeal—parties either reach solution or they do not	Decision subject to appeal
Cost	Parties pay for arbitrator(s) and may pay for staff	Parties pay for mediator and may pay for staff	Judge and court staff are free to parties; there may be various court fees
	Expensive to very expensive: Rules may be available that limit expense	Usually least expensive option	Very expensive; usually most expensive option
Time	Can be lengthy; Parties determine schedule with arbitrator(s); Limited appeal rights	Quickest form of ADR; From couple of hours to couple of weeks; no appeal	Potentially most lengthy; Months to years, plus appeal

Below is a brief summary of each of the chapters and the chapter authors. We were indeed fortunate in that each chapter author is a recognized authority and practitioner in the particular topic of his or her chapter.

The 2013 edition you hold in your hands (or are reading on the screen) is updated from the 2012 edition. Among other things, it contains expanded discussions regarding AAA and JAMS Arbitration, and a new chapter on E-Discovery in International Chamber of Commerce (ICC) Arbitrations. Next year, we hope to include chapters covering FINRA, the Hong Kong Rules, the Singapore Rules, and others.

The second chapter, "Electronic Discovery Overview," is written by Deborah Baron, Vice President, Legal and Compliance at Autonomy Inc., where she is responsible for advanced electronic discovery, assisting clients with electronic discovery strategy and workflow, and developing industry standards and best practices. Deborah uses her expertise and experience to provide the reader with an introduction to electronic discovery with a focus on the law, industry standards, and best practices. Deborah also provides a summary of some of the current technologies tied to different aspects of electronic discovery.

The third chapter, "Mediation and Discovery," is written by Simeon Baum, President of Resolve Mediation Services, Inc., where he has successfully mediated roughly 700 disputes, including the highly publicized mediation of the Studio Daniel Libeskind-Silverstein Properties dispute over architectural fees relating to the redevelopment of the World Trade Center site, and Donald Trump's $1 billion suit over the West Side Hudson River development. Simeon uses his expertise and experience to introduce the reader to mediation from the mediator's viewpoint, so that the practitioner can better understand the mediator across the table and the strengths and weakness of mediation.

The fourth chapter, "Mediation and Electronic Discovery," is written by Daniel Gelb, a partner at Gelb & Gelb, where Mr. Gelb represents clients in federal and state court litigation, arbitration and regulatory proceedings. Daniel is a member of The Sedona Conference Working Group on Electronic Document Retention and Production, the National Association of Criminal Defense Lawyers' Electronic Discovery Task Force, and the Massachusetts Bar Association's Implementation of Technology Task Force. Daniel uses his expertise and experience in electronic discovery and mediation to introduce practitioners to best practices when mediating electronic discovery issues, and presents various tools and strategies practitioners can employ when engaged in electronic discovery mediation.

The fifth chapter, "Using Key Word Mediation To Facilitate Efficient and Effective Electronic Discovery," is written by ourselves. Daniel Garrie is Senior Managing Partner at Law & Forensics LLC, chairs the Alternative Resolution Center's (ARC) Electronic Discovery and forensic panel, and is a member of several Sedona Conference Working Groups. Daniel has overseen 500+ electronic discovery disputes as a special master, neutral, arbitrator or expert and is a thought leader in the areas of electronic discovery, computer forensics, data leak prevention and detection, computer software, mobile and cyber security. Yoav M. Griver is a partner in Zeichner, Ellman and Krause LLP's litigation group where he specializes in representing clients in complex commercial matters. Yoav was a pioneer in the offensive and defensive use of electronic discovery in both State and Federal litigation. We use this chapter to explain to the practitioner how keywords are understood by a machine; explore different keyword search methodologies; and provide both the practitioner, Judge and meditator with a roadmap on how to handle keyword disputes. Daniel and Yoav were assisted in the preparation of this chapter by Siddartha Rao, an attorney at Zeichner Ellman & Krause LLP.

In the sixth chapter, "The Role of Special Master in Electronic Discovery," Daniel Garrie, Michael Sherman and Jeffrey Rosenfeld address the ways courts, arbitrators, and parties to litigation are increasingly turning to Special Masters to provide analysis and make recommendations—which can range from how to resolve discovery disputes to the question of whether to issue terminating sanctions—on complicated e-discovery issues. The chapter provides an overview of the role of a Special Master, including case studies and practitioner tips on how to effectively use a Special Master. Daniel Garrie is a partner and co-founder at Law & Forensics LLC and is a frequently appointed e-discovery neutral and special master in state and federal courts. Michael Sherman is a partner at Bingham McCutchen, and an accomplished trial lawyer. Named to the "Daily Journal" list of top 100 Lawyers in the State of California in 2009, he has handled a number of cases involving e-discovery disputes. Jeffrey Rosenfeld is Counsel at Bingham McCutchen, where his practice focuses on complex business litigation. Mr. Rosenfeld is a member of Bingham McCutchen's Electronic Document Retention and Discovery group, which helps clients navigate the complexities of electronic discovery and use it to their strategic advantage in litigation.

The seventh chapter, "Arbitration and Discovery Overview: Potential Minefields and Dispute Resolution Strategies," is written by Maura Grossman, Of Counsel at Wachtell, Lipton, Rosen & Katz, where she focuses exclusively on advising lawyers and clients on issues involving electronic discovery and information management, and on matters of legal ethics. Maura is a member of The Sedona Conference Working Group 1 on Best Practices for Electronic Document Retention and Production, and Working Group 6 on International Electronic Information Management, Discovery, and Disclosure. Maura uses her expertise and experience to provide practitioners, arbitrators and Judges with an overview of electronic discovery in arbitration, providing insightful practices tips to the fact-finder and to counsel.

The eighth chapter, " Electronic Discovery Under The Federal Arbitration Act," is written by Michael Davis and Anthony I. Giacobbe, Jr., partner and counsel respectively at Zeichner Ellman and Krause LLP. Mike has over 35 years of experience litigating and arbitrating commercial disputes. He frequently appears before arbitration panels on behalf of his clients and also serves as an ARIAS arbitrator hearing complex insurance disputes. Tony is a commercial litigator and is a member of the Sedona Conference's Electronic Document Retention and Production Working Group and was appointed to the NYS Unified Court System's Electronic Discovery Working Group. They focus their chapter on providing the practitioner with a roadmap to the Federal Arbitration Act (FAA), with a specific focus on the application and use of electronic discovery in arbitrations governed by the FAA.

The ninth chapter, "E-Discovery in AAA Arbitration ," is written by Steven Bennett. Steven Bennett is a partner at Jones Day LLP whose practice focuses on domestic and international commercial litigation and arbitration. Steven is a qualified arbitrator for the American Arbitration Association (AAA) and the CPR Institute, chairs the Firm's e-Discovery Committee, cofounded the Sedona Conference Working Group on International E-Discovery, and teaches a course on electronic discovery at New York Law School. The chapter discusses AAA arbitration and examines electronic discovery issues unique to AAA, and includes practitioner tips for arbitrators and counsel engaged in AAA arbitration.

The tenth chapter, "JAMS and E-Discovery," is written by Richard Chernick, Esq. and Hon. Carl J. West (Ret.). Richard Chernick, Esq. is Vice President and Managing Director of JAMS' Arbitration Practice, and is a nationally recognized expert in the resolution of complex and multi-party matters. Mr. Chernick has conducted hundreds of large and complex arbitrations and mediations employing various rules and before all major administering institutions, both nationally and internationally. He was recently named by the Daily Journal as one of California's top neutrals for 2012. Hon. Carl J. West (Ret.) joined JAMS following eighteen years on the bench, spending the most recent ten years as a judge with the Los Angeles County Superior Court's complex litigation panel. Judge West held hundreds of settlement conferences for disputes that spanned the legal spectrum, often working closely with parties to bring them together and foster resolution of even the most complex and difficult cases. Judge West is highly regarded as a tech-savvy and hands-on innovator in complex case management, e-discovery, and civil procedure, and is a frequent speaker and lecturer on these topics. The Daily Journal recently named Judge West as one of California's top neutrals for 2012. The chapter discusses JAMS arbitration and electronic discovery issues unique to JAMS, and includes practitioner tips for arbitrators and counsel engaged in JAMS arbitration.

The eleventh chapter, "E-Discovery Under The London Court of International Arbitration," is written by Richard Gelb, a partner at Gelb & Gelb, where Mr. Gelb tries jury and non-jury cases in federal and state courts, and business and securities cases in both domestic and international arbitrations. Richard uses his expertise and experience to present an overview of the rules and procedures of arbitrations before the London Court of International Arbitration (LCIA), focusing on the process and rules governing electronic discovery in the LCIA.

The twelfth chapter, "E-Discovery in International Chamber of Commerce (ICC) Arbitrations" is written by Antonio Tavares Paes Jr., a partner at Costa, Waisberg & Tavares Paes Advogados in Sao Paulo, Brazil. He was assisted in the preparation of this chapter by his associate Claudia Helena Poggio Cortez. Antonio is a member of the Brazilian and New York State Bars and has over 30 years of experience working in the field of international law and finance, during which he has successfully represented clients in many disputes under ICC rules. Antonio is fluent in Portuguese, English, French and Spanish. The chapter discusses ICC arbitration as a forum, and examines electronic discovery issues under ICC rules. The chapter also provides practitioner tips for arbitrators and counsel engaged in ICC arbitration.

The thirteenth and final chapter, "Additional Resources in ADR and Electronic Discovery," is written by Candice Lang, Associate Counsel at Law & Forensics LLC, and Amy Newman, president of Alternative Resolution Centers (ARC), one of the West Coast's most successful full-service conflict resolution firms. ARC over the past several decades has heard and resolved tens of thousands of disputes and is a leader in the field of electronic discovery dispute resolution both in the United States and abroad, Amy and Candice were assisted in the preparation of this chapter by Jovi Federici, Esq. and Jerry Levine, Esq., and thank both of these individuals for their substantial contribution to this chapter. Further resoures are available for purchasers of this book and can be obtained by emailing either Daniel Garrie (daniel@lawandforensics.com) or Yoav M. Griver (ygriver@zeklaw.com).

Finally, the editors gratefully recognize the herculean efforts of Jovi Federici, Esq., who spent many weeks proofing the hundreds of footnotes contained in each of these chapters.

In authoring and editing this book, it has become even more evident that whatever the dispute resolution mechanism, introducing electronic discovery into the mix without a firm understanding of the law, technology, and applicable rules and procedures is an invitation to disaster. Similarly, it is critical that the special master or court appointed neutral selected is savvy in the law and the technologies. All too often arbitrators, mediators, or neutrals selected by parties lack the *technical* and *legal* aptitudes necessary to really delivery substantive value to the proceedings.

Accordingly, this book provides pragmatic guidance to parties and fact-finders in arbitration, mediation or trial discovery disputes. It is our hope that by using the lessons and tools presented in this book, your clients will pay less money, receive quicker justice, and enjoy more effective representation.

We trust you will find this book of significant use. As always, please do not hesitate to email either of us, Yoav M. Griver (ygriver@zeklaw.com) or Daniel Garrie (daniel@lawandforensics.com), with feedback or suggestions.

Chapter 2

Electronic Discovery Overview

Deborah Baron[*]

> KeyCite®: Cases and other legal materials listed in KeyCite Scope can be researched through the KeyCite service on Westlaw®. Use KeyCite to check citations for form, parallel references, prior and later history, and comprehensive citator information, including citations to other decisions and secondary materials.

§ 2:1   Introduction

The basic principles that resolve legal disputes have changed little since Roman times. Parties in a dispute still come before a judge or panel to present evidence in support of their claims and defense where an adjudicator weighs the facts and makes a decision. All that has changed is the form of the evidence.

While evidence in Roman times was entirely tangible, including livestock and hard currency, evidence today is dominated by electronic data. These sources include electronic documents and multimedia such as email, text documents, spreadsheets, PDFs, audio recordings, Facebook postings, Tweets and, even YouTube

---

[*]Deborah Baron is Vice President, Legal and Compliance at Autonomy Inc. where she is responsible for advanced information governance and eDiscovery, assisting clients with strategy and workflow, as well as developing industry standards and best practices. Ms. Baron is on the Advisory Board of the Electronic Discovery Reference Model (EDRM) and is an active member of The Sedona Conference® WG1 on Information Management and WG6 on Cross-border eDiscovery. She conducts MCLE courses nationally, and writes and speaks on best practices including governance and discovery in Cloud-based systems and Social Networking sites.

videos.[1] Whether or not you were born in the digital age, the facts critical to your case require some level of comfort with digital data.

The process of gathering and reviewing digital evidence is called electronic discovery, or e-discovery. Fueled by the interplay of law and technology and attracting some of the brightest minds in the bench, bar, and business communities, electronic discovery is one of the most dynamic areas of law. In practice, lawyers and executives must assess the merits and risks of a legal dispute or regulatory investigation using facts that are increasingly based in the digital domain.[2]

E-discovery can be cumbersome, expensive, and laden with risk.[3] In large part, it has earned this reputation because of the extensive volume and complexity of modern information sources which increases the associated cost of disclosure.[4] Unprepared organizations and untrained practitioners often generate massive costs when faced with electronic disclosure obligations. These costs, in conjunction with high risk mistakes leading to fines and sanctions for discovery mishaps, are the unintended but likely consequences of ill-informed participants.[5]

There is a common misconception that e-discovery is the domain of the rich and therefore limited to large, complex matters. In reality, e-discovery costs and risks impact small cases

---

[Section 2:1]

[1]*See, e.g.,* Viacom Intern. Inc. v. Youtube Inc., 253 F.R.D. 256, 87 U.S.P. Q.2d 1170 (S.D. N.Y. 2008) (restricting discovery of the content of YouTube videos).

[2]In Cynergy Ergonomics, Inc. v. Ergonomic Partners, Inc., 2008 WL 2064967 (E.D. Mo. 2008), the court took notice of certain facts presented on websites; but in Mackelprang v. Fidelity National Title Agency of Nevada, Inc., 2007 WL 119149 (D. Nev. Jan. 9, 2007), the electronic discovery sought was highly attenuated from the facts of the case.

[3]*See,* Rodriguez-Torres v. Government Development Bank of Puerto Rico, 265 F.R.D. 40 (D.P.R. 2010) (noting that the volume of information and the way it is stored makes privilege determinations more expensive and time-consuming).

[4]*See,* Ameriwood Industries, Inc. v. Liberman, 2007 WL 496716 (E.D. Mo. 2007) (applying the seven factors listed in the Committee Note to Rule 26(b)(2) to limit the volume of electronic discovery).

[5]In CBT Flint Partners, LLC v. Return Path, Inc., 676 F. Supp. 2d 1376 (N.D. Ga. 2009), vacated, 654 F.3d 1353, 99 U.S.P.Q.2d 1610 (Fed. Cir. 2011), the court imposed sanctions for one party's discovery abuse in requesting a large volume of electronic discovery.

too.[6] E-discovery also affects non-parties to a case,[7] and may involve public document and FOIA requests.[8] The breadth of e-discovery helps explain why billions of dollars are spent each year on e-discovery.[9] It is also why disputes are often won and lost in discovery.

For most organizations, searching and analyzing electronic information is nearly unavoidable in resolving disputes. Not only is e-discovery often inevitable, but it can be the cornerstone of a successful legal or business practice. Ultimately, efforts spent preparing systems for electronic discovery, no matter how unpredictable legal disputes and discovery may seem, is the best use of resources for optimizing legal strategies and protecting business interests.

This chapter will outline the basic principles of e-discovery and introduce technical considerations for efficient, cost-effective, and defensible methods to optimize e-discovery.

§ 2:2 E-discovery rules and regulations

A. Purpose and Professional Obligations

In the United States, the primary purpose of e-discovery in legal disputes is to identify, preserve, and analyze the electronically stored information (ESI) needed to support a party's claims or defenses. When faced with a legal dispute, whether in a federal or state court or in the various alternative dispute resolution (ADR) venues, it is more likely than not that ESI will be requested and will need to be preserved and produced. To do so, parties must act reasonably to produce ESI that is potentially responsive to the adverse party.

---

[6]In Starbucks Corp. v. ADT Sec. Servs., Inc., No. 08-02620 (W.D. Wash. Apr. 30, 2009), a small employment matter, defendants mishandled their approach to email collection and were required to produce the ESI at their own expense.

[7]*See,* Guy Chemical Co., Inc. v. Romaco AG, 243 F.R.D. 310 (N.D. Ind. 2007) (nonparty subpoenaed under Federal Rule 45 to provide electronic discovery); Integrated Service Solutions, Inc. v. Rodman, 2008 WL 4791654 (E.D. Pa. 2008) (seeking discovery of the laptop computer of a nonparty); Gulfstream Worldwide Realty, Inc. v. Philips Electronics North America Corp., 2007 WL 5685128 (D.N.M. 2007) (requesting protective order for nonparty's electronic information).

[8]*See,* Miller v. Holzmann, 2007 U.S. Dist. LEXIS 2987 (D.D.C. Jan. 17, 2007) (finding government's failure to preserve FOIA request in electronic form was unreasonable).

[9]See George Socha & Tom Gelbmann, *"Climbing Back,"* Law Technology News Aug. 2010; *Worldwide Search and Discovery Software 2010–2014 Forecast* (IDC #222715, April 2010).

In e-discovery, the reasonableness standard is meant to reflect fairness in conduct. This is highlighted by the American Bar Association's (ABA) use of the standard in Rule 3.4 on the "fairness to opposing party and counsel."[1] To ensure professional conduct that meets ethical obligations, the ABA requires that a lawyer must not "fail to make reasonably diligent effort to comply with legally proper discovery request by an opposing party."[2] Furthermore, a party must not "unlawfully obstruct another party's access to evidence or unlawfully alter, destroy or conceal a document or other material having potential evidentiary value."[3] Without a doubt, this standard of conduct applies to ESI.

B. **Federal Rules of Civil Procedure and Evidence**

In the United States, the Federal Rules of Civil Procedure (FRCP) further reflect the importance and purpose of discovery in litigation with increasing attention paid to electronic discovery. In December 2006, amendments to the FRCP went into effect that codified the emerging de-facto standard that ESI is discoverable.[4] In many other countries the purpose of discovery is similar to the U.S., with the intent of locating information quickly, efficiently and in a manner that complies with the rules for data protection and laws for personal privacy that differ by jurisdiction.

Some of the most important FRCP rules to consider when formulating legal stratagem for e-discovery include:

1. FRCP 16 defines pretrial conferences, scheduling and case management.[5]
2. FRCP 26 defines general provisions governing discovery and duty of disclosure.[6]
   a. FRCP 26(a)(1)(A) requires that all documents and ESI that may be responsive and are within a party's "possession, custody or control" must be provided to the requesting party, or a description by category and locations.[7]
   b. FRCP 26(a)(1)(C) requires that parties make initial

[Section 2:2]

[1]ABA Model Rules of Prof'l Conduct R. 3.4 (Discussion Draft 1983).

[2]ABA Model Rules of Prof'l Conduct R. at 3.4(d).

[3]ABA Model Rules of Prof'l Conduct R.. at 3.4(a).

[4]FED. R. CIV. P. RULE 34

[5]Fed. R. Civ. P. at 16.

[6]Fed. R. Civ. P. at 26.

[7]Fed. R. Civ. P. at 26(a)(1)(A).

disclosures within 14 days of the Rule 26(f) conference or at a time agreed upon by the parties or ordered by the court.[8]

c. FRCP 26(b)(2)(B) provides that a party need not disclose ESI that is not reasonably accessible because of undue burden or cost.[9]

d. FRCP 26(b)(2)(C) requires the court limit the frequency and extent of discovery if information sought is either unreasonably cumulative or duplicative.[10] FRCP 26(b)(2)(C) also applies where information is more easily obtained elsewhere such as when the requesting party has had ample opportunity to obtain the information.[11] Finally, this rule imposes a limit when the burden or expense of production outweighs the likely benefit when considering the needs of the case, the importance of the issue, and the importance of the discovery in resolving the issue.[12]

e. FRCP 26(b)(5)(B) is the "claw-back" provision: if information produced is claimed to be privileged then the receiving party must promptly return, sequester, or destroy the information. The producing party must preserve the information until the claim of privilege is resolved.[13]

f. FRCP 26(f) requires the parties to meet at least 21 days prior to the scheduling conference and develop a discovery plan, which must be submitted to the court within 14 days of the Rule 26(f) meeting.[14]

g. FRCP 26(g) provides for certification of discovery completeness. It also requires that a discovery request, response, or objection not be imposed for an improper purpose.[15]

3. FRCP 33 governs the service of interrogatories to parties. Each party may serve no more than 25 interrogatories relat-

---

[8]Fed. R. Civ. P. at 26(a)(1)(C).

[9]Fed. R. Civ. P. at 26(b)(2)(B).

[10]Fed. R. Civ. P. at 26(b)(2)(C).

[11]Fed. R. Civ. P. at 26(b)(2)(C).

[12]Fed. R. Civ. P. at 26(b)(2)(C).

[13]Fed. R. Civ. P. at 26(b)(5)(B).

[14]Fed. R. Civ. P. at 26(f).

[15]Fed. R. Civ. P. at 26(g).

ing to any matter that may be inquired into under Rule 26(b).[16]

4. FRCP 34 pertains to producing ESI, physical documents, and other tangible things.[17]

   a. FRCP 34(b) provides that the request for production may specify the form or forms in which ESI is to be produced.[18]

5. FRCP 37(e) provides the ESI "safe harbor."[19] It was included to mitigate spoliation sanctions for inadvertent losses of ESI.

6. FRCP 45 governs the use of subpoenas, which can be used to compel discovery from third parties and nonparties.[20]

The Federal Rules of Evidence (FRE) also provide a wealth of useful rules to improve discovery efficiency. Some of the most pertinent include:

1. Federal Rule of Evidence (FRE) 502 pertains to the disclosure of a communication or information covered by the attorney-client privilege or work-product protection and was enacted to reduce litigation costs typically arising in the process of privilege review and production.[21] FRE 502(b) addresses when inadvertent disclosure does not operate as a waiver.[22]

2. FRE 502(d) addresses the controlling effect of a court order: a Federal court may order that the privilege or protection is not waived by disclosure connected with the litigation pending before the court—in which event the disclosure is also not a waiver in any other Federal or State proceeding.[23]

3. FRE 901 addresses authentication and admissibility. It requires that authentication or identification as a condition precedent to admissibility is satisfied by evidence sufficient to support a finding that the matter in question is what its proponent claims.[24]

---

[16]Fed. R. Civ. P. at 33.

[17]Fed. R. Civ. P. at 34.

[18]Fed. R. Civ. P. at 34(b).

[19]Fed. R. Civ. P. at 37(e).

[20]Fed. R. Civ. P. at 45.

[21]Fed. R. Evid. 502.

[22]Fed. R. Evid. at 502(b).

[23]Fed. R. Evid. at 502(d).

[24]Fed. R. Evid. at 901.

C. State Rules

Three quarters of the states have adopted changes to civil procedure rules dealing with e-discovery. Over 50% have adopted some form of the basic provisions in the 2006 amendments to the FRCP for use in state civil courts.[25] In New York, for example, Commercial Division Uniform Rule 8(b) and Uniform Trial Court Rule 202.12(c)(3) were adopted so that parties would meet and confer prior to the preliminary discovery conference to work out ESI related issues.[26] In California, the 2009 Electronic Discovery Act amended the California Code of Civil Procedure to bring California in line with the 2006 amendments to the FRCP and create new, more specific rules that address the unique issues related to ESI.[27]

D. Discovery Outside the United States: Data Protection, Privacy, and Disclosure Rules

Generally, disclosure, privacy, and data protection obligations and regulations are stricter outside the US, but these rules vary by country. Where rules are stricter, the result is narrower, and therefore more restrictive, disclosure that is less burdensome and disruptive to a party's daily operation. However the restrictive, protective nature of these rules and laws adds another layer of complexly in cross-border discovery. Naturally, there is a lack of understanding of non-U.S. law and rules by U.S. courts, lawyers, and parties.[28] The reverse is also true. This can be problematic for parties that conduct business operations and transactions in the U.S. because they are subject to U.S. rules and laws within the relevant jurisdiction and violation can lead to hefty sanctions and fines.[29]

---

[25]See The Sedona Conference ® *"State E-Discovery Today: An Update on Rulemaking in light of the 2006 Federal Amendments"* 2011, by Thomas Y. Allman, Cincinnati, Ohio, and *see generally* Thomas Y. Allman, ARTICLE: *The Impact of the Proposed Federal E-Discovery Rules*, 12 RICH. J.L. & TECH 13 (Spring, 2006).

[26]The New York Unified Court System, *Electronic Discovery in the New York Courts: A Report to the Chief Judge and Chief Administrative Judge* (February 2010).

[27]Electronic Discovery Act, ASSEMBLY BILL No. 5 (2010).

[28]*E.g.*, Volkswagen, A.G. v. Valdez, 909 S.W.2d 900 (Tex. 1995) (finding abuse of discretion in trial court's entire disregard of Germany's privacy laws).

[29]*See*, Samsung Electronics Co., Ltd. v. Rambus, Inc., 439 F. Supp. 2d 524 (E.D. Va. 2006), vacated, 523 F.3d 1374, 86 U.S.P.Q.2d 1604 (Fed. Cir. 2008) (imposing sanctions for spoliation of electronic evidence outside of the US) (rev'd on other grounds); In re Societe Nationale Industrielle Aerospatiale, 782 F.2d 120, 3 Fed. R. Serv. 3d 1275 (8th Cir. 1986), judgment vacated, 482 U.S. 522,

European rules on discovery are some of the most restrictive. For example:

1. In the European area, discovery requests in international cases are vetted through the Hague Convention for Continental Europe. The Hague Convention regulates the transfer of evidence located abroad through national legal proceedings.[30]
2. The Civil Procedure Rules (CPR) in the UK establishes a far more narrow scope of data for disclosure as compared to the United States' FRCP.[31] Part 31.6 of the CPR holds that a party is required to disclose documents on which it relies, those which adversely affect its case, and those which support or adversely affect another party's case.[32] Relevancy is not the test. The expectation of the CPR is to focus parties on finding and disclosing the essential facts.

§ 2:3   The impact of volume and diversity of data on legal disputes

In the United States, a party is obligated to preserve all evidence potentially relevant to a legal dispute.[1] The evidence at issue includes relevant documents and electronic data associated

---

107 S. Ct. 2542, 96 L. Ed. 2d 461, 7 Fed. R. Serv. 3d 1105 (1987) (discussing Petitioner's contention that compliance with the court's discovery requests would subject Petitioners to criminal liability under France's "Blocking Statute").

[30]*See, The Sedona Conference® International Overview of Discovery Data Privacy and Disclosure Requirements* (2009).

[31]*See generally* Gavin Foggo, et al., *Comparing E-Discovery in the United States, Canada, the United Kingdom, and Mexico,* WWW.MCMILLAN.CA (last visited Mar. 28, 2011) (comparing e-discovery rules in the U.S. with those of the U.K.).

[32]*See,* Earles v Barclays [2009] All ER (D) 179 (Oct); [2009] EWHC 2500 [QB]; *see also* Andrew M. Kanter & Deborah Baron, *When Good Faith is Not Good Enough,* 3(10) INT'L IN-HOUSE COUNSEL JOURNAL. 1 (Winter, 2010) ("There are several layers to a decision whether a document or class of documents is worth troubling opponents or the court with. The first is whether it is actually disclosable as part of standard disclosure under Part 31.6 CPR, and the test for that is NOT relevance.").

[Section 2:3]

[1]Union Pacific R. Co. v. U.S. Environmental Protection Agency, 2010 WL 2560455 (D. Neb. 2010) (enjoining the EPA and its employees from deleting or destroying any potentially relevant electronic information); Genworth Financial Wealth Management, Inc. v. McMullan, 267 F.R.D. 443 (D. Conn. 2010) (holding that defendant unreasonably refused plaintiff access to potentially relevant electronic information); Maggette v. BL Development Corp., 2009 WL 4346062 (N.D. Miss. 2009) (noting defendant's failure to search all sources of potentially relevant electronic information); Zubulake v. UBS Warburg LLC, 229 F.R.D.

with key players and data systems. This ESI can be difficult to locate, access, search, and preserve. The discoverable data may amount to tens of thousands on up to millions of files. For example, an employee can generate over 1.25 GB of email in a year on average, or roughly 93,000 printed pages. A typical custodian collection, including email and other files, ranges from 2GB to 10GB or from 150,000 up to half a million pages.[2] If the pages were printed, they would fill between 60 to 300 banker's boxes for *each* custodian.

Disclosure of ESI is a rapidly changing arena. The norms, procedures and rules impacting a party's e-discovery obligations are evolving by jurisdiction and accessibility of data. The evolution of e-discovery has also expanded what is discoverable. E-discovery is no longer confined to data stored on hard drives, such as downloaded email or documents. New media, including audio, video and social networking content, if relevant and within the parties' possession, custody and control are also discoverable.[3] The sheer number of texts, recordings, Tweets, LinkedIn, wiki and FB postings, and YouTube videos is staggering and the rate at which they are increasing is exponential. While rich media is still relevant in many matters, not all ESI is created equal. The relevance, proportionality, accessibility, and richness of data that differentiates one type of ESI from another will be addressed later in this chapter.

It is the ever increasing quantity of data that escalates the costs because the volume of data makes it challenging and time consuming to find and prioritize the key facts for review. Because of this, it should be clear that the party with the most data does not necessarily win. Even so, preserving all potentially relevant

---

422, 94 Fair Empl. Prac. Cas. (BNA) 1, 85 Empl. Prac. Dec. (CCH) P 41728 (S.D. N.Y. 2004); *see also* WHITE PAPER: *Reshaping the Rules of Civil Procedure for the 21st Century: The Need for Clear, Concise, and Meaningful Amendments to Key Rules of Civil Procedure*, DUKE LAW SCHOOL 39 (May 2, 2010) ("The duty to preserve evidence relevant to litigation is not a new concept in our legal jurisprudence.").

[2]This volume of email is based on industry averages and an analysis of actual volume across Autonomy clients who archive email in the Autonomy's private cloud. Data on industry averages can be found at www.e-discoveryteam. com.

[3]*See*, Equal Opportunity Comm'n v. Simply Storage Mgmt., Case No. 1:09-cv-1223-WTL-DML (S.D. Ind. May 11, 2010) (requiring, by discovery order, the plaintiff to produce relevant data, including photos and videos, from social media sites, such as Facebook and MySpace).

information mitigates risk of spoliation sanctions.[4] Ultimately, the party that has the right data, at the right time, has the advantage and therefore stands the best chance of achieving their desired outcomes.

A. e-Discovery Surprises: Litigation Profile and Costs

The uninitiated believe they have little chance of encountering the pitfalls of ESI disclosure because the organization's litigation profile is modest, or they, and their outside counsel, are simply avoiding it. Closer inspection of the frequency of disclosure searches and the manual nature of current practices should give senior legal and IT executives pause. For example, a modest litigation profile may include a half dozen labor and employment matters, a few internal investigations, a handful of government, regulatory audits, or third-party subpoenas a year, and a larger matter, such as product liability, IP or securities litigation every other year. This adds up to an average of 12–15 matters per year.

Each of these matters is associated with a certain scope of disclosure. Normally, email correspondence between key players is the first target of discovery. In the landmark case, *Zubelake v. UBS*, mishandling of email in this employment matter contributed to costly distractions, sanctions, and a multimillion-dollar settlement.[5]

Apart from email, custodians often have relevant data on their PCs and on the organization's servers.[6] Outside these servers, cloud-based social networking sites may be pertinent, particularly in employment and family law cases. There is a growing body of case law involving social media that span disability and other employment claims, unfair competition, libel, and divorce.[7]

What is the cost of e-discovery? A realistic estimate of cost takes an organization's litigation profile and assumptions about the scope of its matters into account. Take for example an organization with a modest litigation profile of 12–14 small matters per

---

[4]Spoliation sanctions were imposed in Victor Stanley, Inc. v. Creative Pipe, Inc., 269 F.R.D. 497 (D. Md. 2010) because the defendant company's president intentionally deleted thousands of files weeks after the preservation order for relevant ESI.

[5]Zubulake v. UBS Warburg LLC, 220 F.R.D. 212, 92 Fair Empl. Prac. Cas. (BNA) 1539 (S.D. N.Y. 2003) ("Zubulake IV").

[6]*See,* R & R Sails Inc. v. Insurance Co. of State of PA, 251 F.R.D. 520 (S.D. Cal. 2008) (defendant repeatedly failed to identify relevant "claims data" on the custodian's PC and on the "claims server").

[7]*E.g.* Crispin v. Christian Audigier, Inc., 717 F. Supp. 2d 965 (C.D. Cal. 2010) involving Facebook and MySpace; Leduc v Roman, ¶ 23 (2009 CanLI6838 (ON S.C.) "366 people have been granted access to the private site."

year and one large case every other year. Assuming a small matter involves three to four custodians and a larger matter involves 20, the organization is conducting search and disclosure of approximately 55 to 75 custodian's ESI each year. That is an average of at least once a week for a modest litigation profile.

Assuming the organization collects on average 2 GB per custodian[8] 50 times a year, the data volume mushrooms to 100GB a year. With an average of 75,000 pages per GB,[9] organizations are burdened with a minimum of 7.5 million pages to process, search and potentially review for privilege before production.

Review is the largest portion of e-discovery costs. This cost is driven by the volume of data. To reduce the volume going into review, parties are adopting a new practice to cull out nonresponsive ESI.[10] Applied to the above example, a party that culls the data will likely reduce the total volume by 25%. Assuming a blended average review fee of $100 per hour and a review rate of 50 to 100 documents per hour, e-discovery processing and review costs alone amount to $1.5 to $2M each year.

The final cost also includes internal legal and technology staff resources spent on labor intensive tasks, disjointed tools, storage, and consulting fees for remote custodian collection. Executives in legal and IT recognize that e-discovery is a significant business expense that recurs annually. Worse yet, these activities do not, on their face, contribute to business development but they do increase risk exposure. Risks include claims by opposing parties of insufficient disclosure, spoliation, and faulty review. Adversaries use these tactics to derail proceedings with discovery sanctions that can generate unfortunate media attention that impacts brand reputation and shareholder value.[11] More importantly, parties with significant deficits in production may be faced with a presumption of bad faith and therefore a default judgment. In such cases, third parties with claims will be encouraged to bring

---

[8]This volume of email is based on industry averages and an analysis of actual volume across Autonomy clients who archive email in the Autonomy's private cloud. Data on industry averages can be found at www.e-discoveryteam. com.

[9]For a list of devices and their respective data capacities see the table entitled "HOW MUCH DATA DO YOU HAVE?" at the webpage http://e-discover yteam.com/?s=gigabyte.

[10]John M. Facciola, Sailing on Confused Seas: Privilege Waiver and the New Federal Rules of Civil Procedure, FED. CTS. L. REV. at 6 (Sept. 2006).

[11]A significant body of case law examining e-discovery issues are available on with world wide web and suggested reading. See for example the K&L Gates digest of e-discovery case law available at http://www.e-discoverylaw.com/article s/case-summaries/.

these claims knowing their litigation costs will be low and their outcome favorable due to likely default judgments. This spiral could, very easily, bring down an unassuming organization.

B. **Right-Sizing e-Discovery for Maximum Efficiency**

Being prepared for e-discovery requests and being able to conduct it efficiently is fundamental to achieving desired outcomes.[12] It is equally important to controlling litigation by ensuring manageable discovery cost and reducing risk of delays, sanctions and inadvertent disclosure. This allows the party to maintain their footing in settlement negotiations long other parties fearful of production. While this sounds sensible, many organizations are still woefully unprepared. Instead, these organizations rely on manual methods and disparate tools to handle the volume of data and many steps in the process. They take it on faith that their employees will follow policy.[13]

To illustrate this point, consider an example timeline of a typical policy. When faced with a dispute or investigation, a case manager normally sends an email to the relevant custodians notifying them of the duty to preserve. The email informs them that they are under a legal hold and thus obligated not to delete relevant email and files, within some parameters such as a date range. The custodians are asked to respond and confirm that they understand and agree to comply. In turn, the responsible parties rely on respondents to preserve evidence when they may be under the false impression that they can conceal their destruction or that custodians will not accidentally delete information, even if acting in good faith.

In parallel an email is sent to IT or Legal/IT to request that the custodians' email files are restored and copied off the drives along with relevant folders from shared servers. Custodians may also be asked to save and turn over the files from their PC that they believe to be responsive. Organizations generally trust their employees to follow instructions and ask them to verify their understanding and actions. This method to meet the duty to preserve is based on the assumption that employees will act in

---

[12]*See,* Ross v. Abercrombie & Fitch Co., 2010 WL 1957802 (S.D. Ohio 2010) (ordering the parties to meet and confer on e-discovery issues before the court made a ruling).

[13]*See,* Wachtel v. Health Net, Inc., 239 F.R.D. 81 (D.N.J. 2006) (". . .many of these specific employee-conducted searches managed to exclude inculpatory documents that were highly germane to Plaintiffs' requests.").

good faith.[14] Even where employees are acting in good faith, employees with a lack of technological expertise could create the impression of bad faith.

Eventually, the technology team collects and delivers the custodian's data to the legal team who copies the email onto their servers to search for relevance and privilege. They use their own email system to walk through the custodians' mailbox and files one by one. Some use keywords to search for specific topics and privilege documents. However, the attorney may not be aware that some email systems will miss keywords in files attached to email because the system does not search the attachments or that encrypted files may contain full terms.

The legal team may not be aware that some interactions with data, such as copying or opening, will change the metadata of the email and files. Metadata must also be preserved.[15] Finally, when finished with the in-house process, the selected ESI is copied to media and sent to outside counsel where another review process takes place. With data changing hands so often and under the control of so many, the potential for losing critical information and therefore creating the impression of impropriety is great.

In an era of instant information anywhere, this process seems antiquated. It is labor intensive, ad hoc, reactive, inefficient and fraught with risk of human error that can result in data spoliation and sanctions that could derail proceedings.[16] Proactive steps are needed to streamline the process and implement smart, effective e-discovery that reduces both risk and cost.

The end game is to right-size discovery to that which is in proportion to the amount in controversy. How do practitioners do this? By planning for the inevitable, establishing and using smart, well documented methods and tools to manage ESI and

---

[14]*See*, Wachtel v. Health Net, Inc., 239 F.R.D. 81 (D.N.J. 2006).

[15]Metadata is data about the data or the document. There are two types of metadata: file metadata and system metadata. *See*, Aguilar v. Immigration and Customs Enforcement Div. of U.S. Dept. of Homeland Sec., 255 F.R.D. 350 (S.D. N.Y. 2008). Metadata has been called "the electronic equivalent of DNA" and it can shed light on the origins, context, authenticity, and distribution of electronic evidence.

[16]*See*, Samsung Electronics Co., Ltd. v. Rambus, Inc., 439 F. Supp. 2d 524 (E.D. Va. 2006), vacated, 523 F.3d 1374, 86 U.S.P.Q.2d 1604 (Fed. Cir. 2008) (imposing sanctions for spoliation of electronic evidence) (rev'd on other grounds).

quickly access and analyze the facts critical to the case. This is fundamental to controlling cost and risk.[17]

§ 2:4   The main components of e-discovery

Electronic discovery is a multifaceted discipline that includes both legal and technical processes.[1] People, policies and technology are engaged to enable an organization to produce ESI in response to disclosure requests. An organization is expected to make reasonable good faith efforts to respond to ESI disclosure requests,[2] including:

- Managing and organizing ESI to support timely responsiveness
- Identifying and notifying custodians or data stewards of preservation duties
- Identifying and preserving all potentially responsive electronic evidence (for matters in the U.S.)
- Identifying and preserving all data that support or adversely affect a party's claims or that of another party (for matters in the U.K.)[3]
- Searching and collecting potentially responsive ESI
- Further analyzing and prioritizing collected ESI
- Processing and culling data to reduce the amount going into review
- Reviewing the ESI for responsiveness, privilege and confidentiality
- Quality checking review for accuracy and defensibility
- Producing the data in accordance with agreed upon forms of production

A. Preliminary Processes: Meet and Confer

Although the overall timeline of the discovery process will vary

---

[17]*See,* Browning Marean, Jay E. Grenig & Mary Pat Poteet, *"Electronic Discovery and Records Management"* 262 (Thompson Reuters 2009) (proper planning in advance of possible discovery can greatly reduce the costs and burden of complying with discovery requests).

[Section 2:4]

[1]*See,* In re Seroquel Products Liability Litigation, 244 F.R.D. 650 (M.D. Fla. 2007) (discussing technical problems of e-discovery).

[2]ABA Model Rules of Prof'l Conduct R. 3.4 (Discussion Draft 1983).

[3]*See generally Gavin Foggo, et al., Comparing E-Discovery in the United States, Canada, the United Kingdom, and Mexico,* www.mcmillan.ca (last visited Mar. 28, 2011) (comparing e-discovery rules in the U.S. with those of the U.K.).

for each matter, case law and federal rules provide a framework to plan for the 'meet and confer' process under FRCP 26(f).[4] The meet and confer process helps parties narrow the legal issues and negotiate e-discovery elements such as date range, custodians, data sources, search terms and forms of production. The bench and bar believe this process materially reduces risk of e-discovery disputes and sanctions.[5] The diagram below is an illustration of the e-discovery timeline.[6]

1. The process begins when litigation or an investigation is "reasonably anticipated." This triggers the duty to preserve.[7]
2. When a complaint is served the "Meet and Confer," the gate is open to:
   - Prepare the legal issues and scope the matter
   - Identify key players and sources of ESI for the matter
   - Implement legal hold notification and preservation
   - Conduct an early assessment of the case based on the merits
   - Estimate litigation budget
   - Set case strategy
3. The meet and confer is scheduled no later than 21 days prior to the "Scheduling Conference"[8]
   - E-discovery tasks are well underway
   - Implement legal hold preservation and notification processes and document methods
   - Prepare search protocol
   - Conduct collections as needed
4. The FRCP 26(f) scheduling conference is within 120 days of the complaint, unless the court orders differently[9]

---

[4]Fed R. Civ. P. 26(a) (governing early disclosures, "meet and confer" and identification).

[5]*See*, The Sedona Conference ® Cooperation Proclamation, 10 SEDONA CONF. J. 331, 332 92009 Sup.).

[6]The diagram can be found: http://www.jdsupra.com/post/documentViewer. aspx?fid=53ef2627-e048-4c30-8cfb-e4c853dce4a5.

[7]*See*, Beard Research, Inc. v. Kates, 981 A.2d 1175, 1185 (Del. Ch. 2009) ("A party in litigation or who has reason to anticipate litigation has an affirmative duty to preserve evidence that might be relevant to the issues in the lawsuit.") (citing Triton Const. Co., Inc. v. Eastern Shore Elec. Services, Inc., 2009 WL 1387115 (Del. Ch. 2009), judgment aff'd, 988 A.2d 938 (Del. 2010)).

[8]Fed R. Civ. P. 26(f) (requiring the "meet and confer" to be scheduled no later than 21 days prior to the Scheduling Conference).

[9]Fed R. Civ. P. 16(b) (requiring that the scheduling conference be set within 120 days of the compliant filing, unless court orders differently).

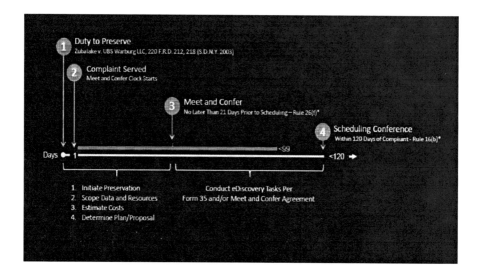

* Unless otherwise directed by the court

B. **Electronic Discovery Reference Model**

The "Electronic Discovery Reference Model" ("EDRM") diagram below provides a graphical overview of the e-discovery process end-to-end. The reference model displayed in the diagram below was developed by the industry forum of the same name. The diagram includes the core tasks along the e-discovery continuum. The arrows show iterative data flows where ESI may be re-analyzed and new data added as a case unfolds, reflecting the repetitive nature of e-discovery tasks.[10]

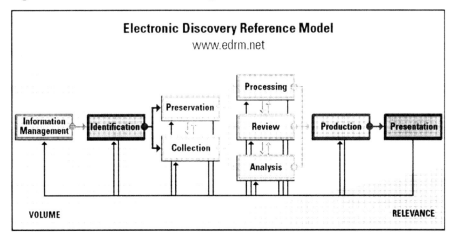

---

[10]This diagram is made available at http://edrm.net/.

The EDRM is comprised of nine major sections pertaining to discovery of ESI including:

- **Information Management**: Similar to organizing paper documents in stacks, file folders and filing cabinets, this is organizing electronic documents and files in an orderly fashion.
- **Identification**: Locating potential sources of ESI such as custodian PCs, email and file servers, and in what form it is available, and determining the scope, breadth, and depth.
- **Preservation**: Ensuring that ESI is protected against inappropriate alteration or destruction.
- **Collection**: Gathering ESI for further use in the electronic discovery process (processing, review, etc.).
- **Analysis:** Evaluating ESI for content and context, including key patterns, topics, people and discussion.
- **Processing**: Reducing the volume of ESI and converting it, if necessary, to forms more suitable for review and analysis.
- **Review**: Evaluating ESI for relevance and privilege.
- **Production:** Delivering ESI to others in appropriate forms and using appropriate delivery mechanisms.
- **Presentation**: Displaying ESI before audiences (at depositions, hearings, trials, etc.), especially in native and near-native forms.

C. Preparation: Information Management

Information management practices are utilized to prepare for disclosure requests. Usually, this is the part of a discovery plan where organizations identify sources of ESI that are repeatedly accessed for discovery, such as email, before discovery arises.[11] Email correspondence is a common source of data and may be managed in an archive to support search and retrieval. This reduces the cost of maintaining ESI while also enabling far more efficient and effective compliance with legal and regulatory requests. Technology teams use methods such as archiving email and indexing ESI in place, in the system of record, including shared file servers, document and records management systems, collaboration systems and PCs, to support the organizations goals for improved compliance and lower cost and risk in discovery.

D. Legal Hold of ESI

The legal hold process is intended to support an organization's

---

[11]The Sedona Conference® Journal, *An overview of ESI Storage and Retrieval,* Volume 11, 2010.

efforts to meet their preservation obligation and identify and collect ESI. It begins when the duty to preserve attaches. This occurs when litigation or investigation is "reasonably anticipated."[12] The duty to preserve arises from the common law duty to preserve and protect from spoliation relevant evidence that supports a party's claims and defenses.[13] While it is not addressed directly by the Federal Rules of Civil Procedure, this process ensures compliance and is based on good faith efforts.

Two of the most important issues for any legal department trying to identify, preserve and produce relevant custodian data are spoliation and the protection of privacy rights of individuals.[14] These are even more challenging overseas, at least in the U.K. and much of mainland Europe, where privacy and data protec-

---

[12]Pension Committee of University of Montreal Pension Plan v. Banc of America Securities, 685 F. Supp. 2d 456 (S.D. N.Y. 2010) (abrogated by, Chin v. Port Authority of New York & New Jersey, 685 F.3d 135, 115 Fair Empl. Prac. Cas. (BNA) 720, 95 Empl. Prac. Dec. (CCH) P 44555 (2d Cir. 2012)); Beard Research, Inc. v. Kates, 981 A.2d 1175, 1185 (Del. Ch. 2009) ("A party in litigation or who has reason to anticipate litigation has an affirmative duty to preserve evidence that might be relevant to the issues in the lawsuit.") (citing Triton Const. Co., Inc. v. Eastern Shore Elec. Services, Inc., 2009 WL 1387115 (Del. Ch. 2009), judgment aff'd, 988 A.2d 938 (Del. 2010)); Acierno v. Goldstein, 2005 WL 3111993 (Del. Ch. 2005); see also Brandt v. Rokeby Realty Co., 2004 WL 2050519 (Del. Super. Ct. 2004) ("A party, anticipating litigation, has an affirmative duty to preserve relevant evidence."); Positran Mfg., Inc. v. Diebold, Inc., 2003 WL 21104954 (D. Del. 2003) (citations omitted); Zubulake v. UBS Warburg LLC, 220 F.R.D. 212, 216, 92 Fair Empl. Prac. Cas. (BNA) 1539 (S.D. N.Y. 2003); John B. v. Goetz, 531 F.3d 448 (6th Cir. 2008) (concluding that defendants had a duty to preserve ESI from the beginning of the litigation); Convolve, Inc. v. Compaq Computer Corp., 223 F.R.D. 162, 175 (S.D. N.Y. 2004), order clarified, 2005 WL 1514284 (S.D. N.Y. 2005) ("The obligation to preserve evidence arises when the party has notice that the evidence is relevant to the litigation or when a party should have known that the evidence may be relevant to future litigation.").

[13]Where state law is silent on duty to preserve the court may turn to federal law. See, Einstein v. 357, LLC, Index No. 604199/07 (N.Y. Sup. Ct. Nassau Cty. Nov. 4, 2009).

[14]See generally Stengart v. Loving Care Agency, Inc., 201 N.J. 300, 990 A.2d 650, 108 Fair Empl. Prac. Cas. (BNA) 1558, 30 I.E.R. Cas. (BNA) 873, 93 Empl. Prac. Dec. (CCH) P 43853 (2010) (discussing the expectation of privacy of emails); Gucci America, Inc. v. Curveal Fashion, 2010 WL 808639 (S.D. N.Y. 2010) (enforcing subpoena to compel production of ESI finding that interest in protecting privacy rights was not superior to that of enforcing a judgment against the defendants); see also Quon v. Arch Wireless Operating Co., Inc., 445 F. Supp. 2d 1116, 25 A.L.R.6th 649 (C.D. Cal. 2006), aff'd in part, rev'd in part, 529 F.3d 892, 27 I.E.R. Cas. (BNA) 1377, 91 Empl. Prac. Dec. (CCH) P 43233, 155 Lab. Cas. (CCH) P 60628 (9th Cir. 2008), rev'd and remanded, 130 S. Ct. 2619, 177 L. Ed. 2d 216, 30 I.E.R. Cas. (BNA) 1345, 93 Empl. Prac. Dec. (CCH) P 43907, 159 Lab. Cas. (CCH) P 61011 (2010) (discussing a police officer's rea-

tion rules are far more restrictive than in the U.S.[15] Of the
hundreds of cases involving e-discovery issues since the amended
rules went into effect, dozens have included fines and sanctions
for failure to identify or preserve relevant data[16] and for spoliation, where data is destroyed.[17]

A legal hold lifecycle is made up of four main phases: notification and acknowledgment, identification and preservation, collection, and release. These typically translate into notifying
custodians and data stewards, interviewing key players, searching to identify and preserve any and all potentially responsive evidence and collecting a targeted subset for further analysis,
review and production.[18] The last phase of the legal hold lifecycle
is the release of documents and other ESI when a case is closed
and no further actions are expected.

Throughout the legal hold lifecycle two interrelated cost
considerations must be accounted for. The first is that e-discovery
disputes and sanctions, monetary and non-monetary, frequently
stem from failures in the legal hold process. Second, document
review is the dominant cost driver in discovery due to the volume
of data generated in collection which has a direct and sizeable
impact on review costs. If either of these are ignored, costs are
likely to skyrocket and may inhibit resolution of the matter on
the facts.

1. Notification and Acknowledgment

During this stage of a litigation hold, parties notify custodians
and data stewards of the obligation to preserve potentially relevant documents and data when the duty to preserve attaches.

---

sonable expectation of the privacy of text messages sent from a cell phone issued by the police department).

[15]*See generally* The Sedona Conference® Framework for Analysis of Cross-
Border Discovery Conflicts: A Practical Guide to Navigating the Competing
Currents of International Data Privacy & e-Discovery—Public Comment Version
(Aug. 2008).

[16]*See,* R & R Sails Inc. v. Insurance Co. of State of PA, 251 F.R.D. 520 (S.D.
Cal. 2008), defendant repeatedly failed to identify relevant "claims data" on the
custodian's PC and on the "claims server."

[17]*See,* Mattel, Inc. v. MGA Entertainment, Inc., 616 F.3d 904, 30 I.E.R.
Cas. (BNA) 1812, 96 U.S.P.Q.2d 1012 (9th Cir. 2010), as amended on denial of
reh'g, (Oct. 21, 2010) (the "Bratz Case") (defendant used the Window Washer
program knowing his PC was to be searched for discovery); Zubulake v. UBS
Warburg LLC, 220 F.R.D. 212, 92 Fair Empl. Prac. Cas. (BNA) 1539 (S.D. N.Y.
2003) ("Zubulake IV").

[18]*See generally* U.S. v. O'Keefe, 537 F. Supp. 2d 14, 69 Fed. R. Serv. 3d
1598 (D.D.C. 2008) (discussing the role of information custodians in electronic
discovery).

Little has changed in regard to what triggers a legal hold. The preservation obligation arises when a party receives notice of a legal dispute or regulatory investigation, or reasonably anticipates one.[19] Some triggers are obvious and some are subtle. Some prominent examples include repeated complaints, past claims, complaints against a party filed with a federal agency or commission, contractual disputes, and industry wide investigations.[20]

Once the triggering event has occurred, it is important to issue notifications of such litigation hold to relevant custodians. Failure to timely issue a written notice can have costly consequences, such as sanctions or adverse inferences.[21] The Sedona Conference® Commentary on Legal Holds recommends that organizations fully document the notification process and its implementation, including acknowledgments, and monitor and report on it to provide counsel status for pre-trial conferences.[22] This will also provide validation of a party's good faith, routine efforts to meet the preservation obligation, and a record for audit and defensibility purposes.[23]

There are, however, exceptions to notifying custodians of the duty to preserve. One possible exception includes internal

---

[19]*See*, Convolve, Inc. v. Compaq Computer Corp., 223 F.R.D. 162, 175 (S.D. N.Y. 2004), order clarified, 2005 WL 1514284 (S.D. N.Y. 2005) ("The obligation to preserve evidence arises when the party has notice that the evidence is relevant to the litigation or when a party should have known that the evidence may be relevant to future litigation.").

[20]Some courts take no chances with preservation compliance. In In re National Security Agency Telecommunications Records Litigation, 2007 WL 3306579 (N.D. Cal. 2007), the court required senior counsel to file a statement conforming to Rule 11 regarding their preservation efforts. See also John J. Isaza, Esq. & John Jablonski, Esq. "*7 Steps for Legal Holds of ESI and Other Documents*" 2009 ARMA International (If an event occurs where an organization anticipates that litigation may follow, the organization has a duty to preserve evidence. Such an event is commonly called a trigger event.).

[21]*E.g.*, Pension Committee of University of Montreal Pension Plan v. Banc of America Securities, LLC, 592 F. Supp. 2d 608 (S.D. N.Y. 2009) (amended twice) (finding multiple plaintiffs failed to issue timely written legal hold notices and that the parties acted with either negligence or gross negligence in relation to "contemporary standards" for discovery, and applying severe sanctions).

[22]The Sedona Conference® Commentary on Legal Holds (Sept. 2010) available for download at thesedonaconference.org.

[23]In Anadarko Petrol. Corp. v. Davis, 2006 U.S. Dist. LEXIS 93594 (S.D. Tex. Dec. 28, 2006), the court ordered a forensic audit of defendant's computers in response to allegations of bad faith.

investigations where ESI is analyzed before key players are notified.[24]

Even after initiating the hold, new custodians and search terms can turn up or be identified through analysis of initial facts. New custodians should be notified and tracked in a manner consistent with the original custodians placed on litigation holds. Doing all of this manually and keeping track in spreadsheets is very time consuming. Organizations are rapidly adopting automated methods to manage the full legal hold lifecycle to improve efficiency and reduce the risk.

2. **Identification and Preservation:**

While notifications are being sent, parties must undertake reasonable efforts to determine where responsive ESI might be located across custodian and organization data sources. During this phase of the legal hold lifecycle, the potential data sources are analyzed pre-collection for relevance, format, accessibility, security, etc wherever this is possible. Any and all ESI found that is potentially responsive is preserved.

The potential sources of ESI are diverse and may include email, custodian PCs, office files, PDFs, TIFFS, content management system files, databases, audio and video recordings, spreadsheets, etc.[25] When applicable third-party data is relevant, such as email in the cloud, wikis, blogs, social networking content, and text messages, parties may request it. If found relevant courts may agree to require disclosure, as in *Graves v. Doe*[26] where the court served FRCP 45 subpoenas seeking documents and ESI. For

---

[24]*But see*, Board of Regents of University of Nebraska v. BASF Corp., 2007 WL 3342423 (D. Neb. 2007) in which defendant sought sanctions against the plaintiff for violating a court order compelling document production, deposition testimony established that a key custodian had not been instructed to search electronic files. Internal investigations raise additional concerns. In In re Intel Corp. Microprocessor Antitrust Litigation, 258 F.R.D. 280 (D. Del. 2008), the defendant waived attorney-client privilege by asserting a human error defense in discovery dispute while engaging in a critical self-evaluation of discovery compliance.

[25]*See, e.g.*, In re Genetically Modified Rice Litigation, 2007 WL 1655757 (E.D. Mo. 2007) (ordering preservation of ESI with great specificity).

[26]*See* Graves v. Doe, 2010 U.S. Dist. LEXIS 41376 (D. Utah Apr. 27,2010) (regarding private email allegedly accessed and reviewed by unknown defendants, the court held that good cause exists "in cases where physical evidence may be consumed or destroyed with the passage of time" and "relevant electronic evidence in the possession of third parties may be altered, erased, or destroyed." The court granted plaintiffs' motion and permitted immediate discovery on Yahoo! Inc., Microsoft Corporation, and others.).

third-parties, FRCP 45 governs duties regarding production of ESI.[27]

The breadth and depth ESI that must be preserved is influenced by the scope and amount in controversy.[28] A common practice is to preserve broadly to mitigate risk of spoliation and collect narrowly to reduce the burden of downstream review costs. In either case, readily accessible data that is responsive, such as custodian files and email on PCs and servers, must be preserved in a routine, good faith manner. ESI can be copied for preservation in a forensically sound manner where it may be filtered before collection.[29] If the ESI is in a system that can accept legal hold policies to prevent deletion or alteration, such as an email archive or document or records management system, then it may be preserved-in-place rather than copied to a preservation server.

In contrast, data that is not readily accessible but is potentially responsive, such as legacy email and files on backup tapes and other media must also be preserved but will not necessarily be searched depending upon availability of the same data from other sources. It is important to quickly identify backup media that meets the preservation criteria and suspend recycling to avoid inadvertent spoliation.

These topics should be discussed at pretrial discovery conferences to avoid disputes later on. Because this stage is so critical, it is important that key players and knowledgeable IT personnel meet with counsel as soon as possible to assist in this identification and preservation process and avoid unintended data destruction and spoliation.

For any given matter, there are a variety of preservation models and methods that can be used to ensure optimal results. Some of the most influential include:

a. **Custodian self-preservation: aka Custodian Preservation-in-Place (PIP):**

This method of preservation is low cost but can be disruptive

---

[27]Fed. R. Civ. P. 45.

[28]One factor to consider when ordering discovery of ESI is the cost of production in light of the total amount in controversy. *See,* Zubulake v. UBS Warburg LLC, 217 F.R.D. 309, 91 Fair Empl. Prac. Cas. (BNA) 1574 (S.D. N.Y. 2003).

[29]*See,* Covad Communications Co. v. Revonet, Inc., 258 F.R.D. 5 (D.D.C. 2009) (court reserving its decision regarding forensic examination of the servers until after the production of the forensic copy); In re Weekley Homes, L.P., 295 S.W.3d 309 (Tex. 2009) (reversing lower court ordering employees of the defendant to turn over hard drives for forensic copying).

and time consuming for custodians. It is also high risk. Human error, such as forgetting to not delete, results in lost, altered or deleted data and metadata, and other, both good and bad faith actions can be sanctioned.[30] Intended or unintended deletion of data by a custodian can result in severe sanctions such as an adverse inference jury instruction and even jail. There is a significant and growing body of case law on this topic.[31]

b. **Repository Preservation-in-Place (PIP):**

This method can be very cost effective with relatively low risk if the repository supports the ability to apply policy changes that prevent deletion and altering of data. Note that many email or messaging systems DO NOT support this ability. If an email system contains responsive ESI that is not available on another readily accessible source then it is imperative to act quickly to collect data from a messaging server. The same may be true for shared folders on file servers.

The cost of preservation is dramatically lower when the data in the repository is managed by a retention plan, indexed and can be accessed by automated tools. Costs are higher and cycle time longer when manual methods and proprietary access and search must be used. If a repository is frequently identified for disclosure then consider indexing the content and automating the processes to access, search, filter, preserve and collect.

Repositories that support preservation-in-place (PIP) include some email archives, document and records management systems and media backups. Check with IT that these support file reten-

---

[30]*See,* Wachtel v. Health Net, Inc., 239 F.R.D. 81 (D.N.J. 2006) ("Wachtel II") (holding that employee conducted searches were "utterly in adequate."); Mattel, Inc. v. MGA Entertainment, Inc., 616 F.3d 904, 30 I.E.R. Cas. (BNA) 1812, 96 U.S.P.Q.2d 1012 (9th Cir. 2010), as amended on denial of reh'g, (Oct. 21, 2010) (the "Bratz Case") (using the Window Washer program while knowing his PC was to be searched for discovery).

[31]In *Victor Stanley, Inc. v Creative Pipe, Inc., 269 F.R.D. 497 (D. Md. 2010)* ,based on the willful, bad faiththe defendant company's president intentionally deleted thousands of files weeks after the preservation order for relevant ESI and was sentenced to jail. In *Hawaiian Airlines, Inc. v. Mesa Air Grp., Inc.* (In re Hawaiian Airlines, Inc., 49 Bankr. Ct. Dec. (CRR) 11, 2007 WL 3172642 (Bankr. D. Haw. 2007), an executive received a legal hold notice, agreed to comply with the notice, and subsequently intentionally deleted relevant evidence. An adverse inference instruction (the jury can infer that the evidence lost was adverse to the party) was issued against the company because it "simply told [the custodian] to preserve all evidence and trusted him to comply," rather than taking reasonable steps to prevent spoliation. More recently, in the case of Green v. Blitz U.S.A., Inc., 2011 WL 806011 (E.D. Tex. 2011), through discovery in a subsequent litigation plaintiffs discovered that defendants failed to produce and preserve relevant ESI and moved for sanctions.

tion and deletion policy changes and can be programmatically accessed and searched to automate manual discovery tasks.

c. **Preservation via Collection:**

This is the opposite of PIP. It is a common method and the root cause of over-collection. Many parties choose to preserve broadly to reduce risk of spoliation. In the absence of advanced tools to cull preserved data down in an efficient and defensible manner, this preservation method is a major driver to runaway review costs due to data volumes.[32] It also raises risk of confidential data leaving the organization.

However this method can be very cost effective and reduce risk if it is automated and well integrated with legal hold policies and early case assessment tools. ESI that is responsive can be identified and collected for preservation purposes in a manner that ensures the integrity of the data, including metadata. The collected data is typically copied to a secure preservation/collection area.

Once in the preservation area the ESI can be further searched, analyzed, organized and prioritized before sending on for processing and review. Failure to preserve by plaintiff or defendant can lead to sanctions, including severe sanctions such as multimillion dollar fines and adverse inference.[33] In Pension Committee severe sanctions were based on findings of negligence including failure to supervise preservation and collection of employee records from key players and submitting false and misleading declarations regarding document collection and preservation efforts.[34]

---

[32]*See, e.g.*, Oracle Corp. v. SAP AG, 566 F. Supp. 2d 1010 (N.D. Cal. 2008) (the discovery of the documents of 165 key custodians will cost the defendant an estimated $16.5 million and take more than a year).

[33]In re Nat'l Century Fin. Enterprises, Inc. Fin. Inv. Litig., 2009 WL 2160174 (S.D. Ohio July 16, 2009) (considering the imposition of sanctions under its inherent power and holding that federal common law governed and that only "egregious" conduct warranted the extreme sanction of dismissal and that only "bad faith" warranted an adverse inference instruction").

[34]In Pension Committee of University of Montreal Pension Plan v. Banc of America Securities, LLC, 592 F. Supp. 2d 608 (S.D. N.Y. 2009) (amended twice), severe sanctions were based on findings of Legal Hold failures including failure to supervise preservation and collection of employee records from key players and submitting false and misleading declarations regarding document collection and preservation efforts.

In *Zubelake IV*, failure to preserve email and resulting spolia-tion lead to sanctions.[35] The defendant should have known that documents were relevant to future litigation when a former em-ployee filed a complaint with the Equal Employment Opportunity Commission.[36]

Custodian self-collection has the same issues of human error as self-preservation. Custodians can be directed to manually copy responsive data to a designated preservation/collection server. While this is a low cost method, there are inherent risks with it including potential to alter metadata when files and computers are opened, viewed, copied, and sent. It is not a recommended preservation or collection method due to the high risk of human error and spoliation.

3. Collection

The third phase of the Legal Hold life cycle is collection of ESI and its associated metadata. ESI is searched and collected from data sources on the organizations' network as well as custodian PCs, including those that are remote from the organization's network. Parties search for and collect ESI from responsive data sources based upon preservation and collection policies. The col-lection policies may describe custodians, date range, data formats, key terms and phrases, as well as ESI to be excluded. If a party has an ongoing requirement to preserve and collect responsive ESI, preservation and collection policies must run continuously to meet the duty to preserve.

> ◆ *Practice Tip 1* When faced with a dispute or investigation the first steps are typically to talk with the players central to the matter and identify the key legal issues. The legal issues and exposure to risk guide the scope and content of discovery.
>
> Before you figure out what facts you need to locate, or select which search terms narrow your data sets, you need to analyze what the legal issues are in the case," said The Hon. David J. Waxse, U.S. Magistrate Judge. "Too often I see attorneys just start trying to find the sources of information and what information is available, without trying to narrow it by looking at what issues the case involves.[37]

Conducting collection in a routine, good faith, consistent, and auditable manner is critical. Further it is paramount that a

---

[35]Zubulake v. UBS Warburg LLC, 220 F.R.D. 212, 217, 92 Fair Empl. Prac. Cas. (BNA) 1539 (S.D. N.Y. 2003) ("Zubulake IV").

[36]Zubulake v. UBS Warburg LLC, 220 F.R.D. 212, 217, 92 Fair Empl. Prac. Cas. (BNA) 1539 (S.D. N.Y. 2003) ("Zubulake IV").

[37]Hon. David J. Waxse, et al., *Upfront Assessments Lead to Downstream Savings,* AUTONOMY (2009).

party's search and collection method and tools find all potentially relevant data.[38] Finally, the party must fully preserve and protect the data and metadata from change or destruction.[39] These are fundamental to defensibility, and to control cost and risk. Overlooking or simply missing critical files in ESI due to inadequate search methods or tools creates significant risk.[40]

Amended Rule 26(a) requires the, "search for and identification of sources of discoverable electronically stored information, regardless of form, including email and voice content for disclosure."[41] Voice content is growing in organizations, for example in call centers due to increased regulation and in email repositories due to use of integrated voicemail and email systems. *In re Vioxx Litigation* Merck was ordered to preserve all voicemails. In *Nursing Home v. Oracle* the court ruled that although defendants were not in physical possession of the audio recordings, the files were under their control and therefore the preservation order extended to the ESI.[42]

Unfortunately conventional methods of custodian self-preservation and collection do not meet the standard of Rule 26. With so much case law exposing the risk of manual, do-it-yourself methods many organizations have come to accept that these are not tenable. Relying on conventional approaches it risky, in effect, "Good faith is not good enough."

To reduce cost and mitigate risk parties are encouraged to give collection early attention and negotiate to narrow scope as much as possible at pre-trial conferences.[43] The results of the negotiations will drive the preservation and collection policies, which

---

[38]*See* U.S. v. O'Keefe, 2007 WL 1239204 (D.D.C. 2007), subsequent determination, 537 F. Supp. 2d 14, 69 Fed. R. Serv. 3d 1598 (D.D.C. 2008), By his Order of April 27, 2007, Judge Friedman required the government to conduct a thorough and complete search of both its hard copy and electronic files in "a good faith effort to uncover all responsive information in its 'possession custody or control.' " (D.D.C. April 27, 2007) (quoting Fed. R. Crim. P. 16(a)(1)(E)); *Disabilities Rights Counsel of Greater WDC v. WDC MTA* U.S. Magistrate Judge Facciola required the parties to meet and confer and present him with an agreed search protocol for ESI.

[39]*See Victor Stanley, Inc. v Creative Pipe, Inc., 269 F.R.D. 497 (D. Md. 2010)* (sanctions for destruction of electronic evidence).

[40]*See,* R & R Sails Inc. v. Insurance Co. of State of PA, 251 F.R.D. 520 (S.D. Cal. 2008).

[41]Fed R. Civ. P. 26(a), Identification.

[42]*See generally* Nursing Home Pension Fund v. Oracle Corp., 254 F.R.D. 559 (N.D. Cal. 2008). *In re Vioxx Litigation*, 2006 WL 2950622.

[43]*See generally* Fed. R. Civ. P. 16 *and* Fed. R. Civ. P. 26 (providing procedures for pretrial conferences).

may need to change as the proceedings unfold so it is important to have flexible collection tools and methods. The number of remote collections, particularly when the PC is off the organization's network, will rapidly drive up cost if these are done manually. Look for technology that can automate access to data sources on and off the organization's network.

ESI collection methods:

a. Manual Imaging of Custodians' Pcs

Manual imaging of custodians' PCs to preserve and collect ESI is similar to making a copy of all of the paper files in a custodian's office and file cabinets without first sorting and searching for potentially relevant information. In general far more data is preserved and collected with this method than is relevant to the matter. However over-collection greatly reduces risk of data spoliation stemming from overlooking a file. It is highly disruptive to the custodians, especially to senior executes who are frequently custodians. It's also expensive. The cost of manual collection by trained professionals of remote custodians is on average hundreds of dollars per collection, plus travel expense.

b. Snapshot Collection

A snapshot collection of ESI is like taking a photo at the scene of a crime, or copying all the documents in a custodians' office at the moment. An ESI snapshot collects all of the information that is at hand and accessible over the organizations' network.[44] It can use date range and other filters to narrow the data volume. This method can relieve much of the cost burden of manual collection.

However the snapshot method of collecting to preserve contributes to over collection because little filtering is done and new snapshots are often needed when the scope or search terms change. If the scope of a matter changes and or custodians are frequently traveling then the snapshot method may prove inadequate and expensive.

c. Spidering

Spidering an organization's network is similar to running an Internet keyword search on the web. It typically brings back a

---

[44]*See, e.g.*, In re Intel Corp. Microprocessor Antitrust Litigation, 258 F.R.D. 280 (D. Del. 2008) (creating a company-wide snapshot of email and other electronic documents).

very large volume of responses with widely varying relevance.[45] Spidering the organization's network is done to search for relevant ESI on servers and custodian PCs connected to the organization's network. It's a more automated method to collect data than the cumbersome and manual methods typically used to reach and search desktop and laptop PCs, and servers. While this approach addresses some of the issues of expensive manual methods, it is not without its shortcomings.

Spidering technology cannot access PCs if they are not connected to the organization's network. If a custodian is traveling spidering technology cannot reach their PC. Like snapshots, if scope or key terms change, the spidering has to be done again and duplicates will be collected. Also it relies on simple keyword searching much like internet keyword searches that return a large number of non-relevant results. This contributes to over-collection.

d. Policy-based and Network Independent

Policy-based collection utilizes a rules engine and advanced search techniques to reduce the volume of ESI collected. It automates the change process when scope or search terms change, and can implement the changes immediately. If new ESI is received that matches the criteria, a real-time policy based system will detect it and collect it to meet the preservation obligation and prevent spoliation.

A network independent, policy-based system can access PCs NOT connected to the organization's network. In this way remote collection is more automated and cost effective. These are newer systems and technologies that cost more than conventional collection tools.

4. Legal Hold Release

The fourth and final phase of the Legal Hold lifecycle is the release of ESI from litigation hold. This is the Holy Grail—the unlocking of data to return to standard retention cycles, with hope of moving some or all of the data into the disposition process. Before releasing ESI verify and document that it is not under legal hold in another matter, including regulatory, government, or internal investigation.

---

[45]*See*, George L. Paul & Jason R. Baron, *Information Inflation: Can the Legal System Adapt?*, 13 RICH. J.L. & TECH. 10, 22–24 (2007); The Sedona Conference® Best Practices Commentary on the Use of Search and Information Retrieval Methods in E-Discovery (Aug. 2007).

5. Legal Hold Landmines: Additional Challenges and Recommended Practices

Take care when defining policies and procedures for the legal hold component of your e-discovery plan. Identify processes and tasks that have the greatest impact on risk, cost and timeline. Consider the following practice tips:

◆ *Practice Tip 2*   Early identification of e-discovery issues: if the other party(s) does not discuss e-discovery or raise questions or issues, beware. It is highly recommended that the parties establish an agreed protocol for search and forms of production to facilitate the just, speedy and inexpensive conduct of discovery of ESI, and to promote the resolution of disputes regarding it without court intervention.

◆ *Practice Tip 3*   ESI is more than email: Does the dispute warrant more than email in disclosure? Discuss with parties and counsel the range of data sources and formats that are reasonable and accessible, as well as forms of production. A good faith effort to find all forms of potentially responsive content is the standard of professional conduct.

◆ *Practice Tip 4*   Importing and searching email in an email program: This is generally not recommended due to the risk of changing the metadata and deficiencies in email search technology, such as not searching the attachments. Email and other ESI must be extracted, copied and collected carefully. One can easily change electronic evidence by copying office files and forwarding email, which changes the metadata. Although done inadvertently, these actions can put a party at high risk of spoliation.

◆ *Practice Tip 5*   Remote custodians: How frequently does an organization have to collect from remote and traveling custodians that are often disconnected from the enterprise network? If frequently then consider an automated collection method that can handle remote collection for custodians that are frequently not connected to the corporate network.

◆ *Practice Tip 6*   Suspending data recycling processes: What are the retention, backup and deletion cycles for target e-discovery data sources, and how are they changed to preserve ESI? Are the deletion cycles suspended quickly and correctly?

◆ *Practice Tip 7*   Departing employees: What is the policy regarding employee data on PCs and servers when an employee leaves the organization? Is there a policy and process to check if the employee is under legal hold and the protocol to preserve (e.g. freezing their IT assets)?

◆ *Practice Tip 8*   Preserved computer equipment: Does the

legal dispute require computer equipment such as PCs and servers to be preserved? If so, do not turn them on or off. This can and will likely directly alter system information which may be needed in the matter. Consider engaging a computer forensics expert.

◆ *Practice Tip 9* An efficient and defensible legal hold system will include all phases of the lifecycle and integrate directly with downstream discovery tasks such as culling, review and or production. This level of integration supports chain of custody and avoids costly hand offs and conversions, eliminating time wasted copying data from one place to another.

◆ *Practice Tip 10* Plan to right-size the legal hold system to scale to support all of your matters and enable a 360o view to monitor custodians and data source across all legal hold activities globally. This will enable consistency checking across matters and over the complete legal hold lifecycle.

E. **Review and Production**

Review and production of ESI are the final stages in responding to disclosure requests. Review is conducted to identify privileged and confidential information. This information may be withheld or redacted. All other ESI that is determined to be potentially responsive to the legal document request may be produced to the requesting party. In regulatory and government requests parties may be less able to negotiate scope of discovery resulting in production of a larger portion of collected ESI.

1. **Review**

In restating the obvious, the largest cost driver in a legal dispute is attorney review.[46] In this segment of the e-discovery

---

[46]*Compare* High Voltage Beverages, LLC v. Coca-Cola Co., 2009 WL 2915026 (W.D. N.C. 2009) (allowing defendant to avoid review of supplemental information) *with* John B. v. Goetz, U.S. Dist. LEXIS 8821 (M.D. Tenn. Jan. 28, 2010) (granting plaintiff's motion to compel in light of, among other things, defendant's exaggeration of review costs).

continuum, efficiency is king.[47] The variables impacting review costs[48] include:

- The total number of documents or files reviewed
- The review rate—that is the number of documents reviewed per hour
- The cost per hour of review

The illustration of review costs presented earlier in this chapter reflects how expensive review is, even for an organization with a modest litigation profile and number of files per matter. Estimating review cost is extremely useful in determining proportionality, and thus case strategy. In *Hopson v. City of Baltimore* the courted noted that e-discovery, which may include "millions of documents" and "record-by record pre-production privilege review, on pain of subject matter waiver, would impose upon parties costs of production that bear no proportionality to what is at stake in the litigation."[49]

These considerations are recognized by the bench, bar and Congress to have bearing on the reasonableness of a producing party's efforts to respond to disclosure requests.[50] Reasonableness is evaluated on a matter by matter basis relative to the importance of a matter to the party and the amount in controversy. Federal Rule of Evidence (FRE) 502 was enacted in 2008 in an effort to address the burden of privilege review and production. It seeks to help parties reduce litigation costs related to privilege review and production in a reasonable and defensible manner.

One of the main purposes of FRE 502 is to respond to, "the widespread complaint that litigation costs necessary to protect against waiver of attorney-client privilege or work product have become prohibitive due to the concern that any disclosure (however innocent or minimal) will operate as a subject matter

---

[47]*See generally* Daniel B. Garrie, Esq., *Indirect Costs of Electronic Discovery (e-discovery)*, HTTP://LTRM.ORG, (February 8, 2008), http://ltrm.org/wp/ltrmblog/2010/02/08/indirect-costs-of-electronic-discovery-e-discovery/ (noting that indirect costs of e-discovery include diverting critical resources and decreased job satisfaction, which impacts the overall bottom line).

[48]*See generally* Suzanne Barlyn, *Call My Lawyer . . . in India*, NEW.STJOHNS. EDU (Apr. 3, 2008) (discussing the costs of document review at US firms as compared to overseas legal service providers).

[49]Hopson v. Mayor and City Council of Baltimore, 232 F.R.D. 228, 244, 97 Fair Empl. Prac. Cas. (BNA) 617, 63 Fed. R. Serv. 3d 582 (D. Md. 2005) *available at* http://www.fowlerlaw.com/blog/wp-content/uploads/2008/08/hopson-v-mayor-of-baltimore.pdf.

[50]Fed. R. Evid. 502 (advisory committee notes, Feb. 27 2008, Congressional Record—Senate).

waiver of all protected communications or information. This concern is especially troubling in cases involving electronic discovery."[51]

In an effort to reduce attorney review costs, parties are outsourcing legal work and support services to offshore locations. This emerging practice is known as legal process outsourcing (LPO). It is a rapidly growing field and a strategy used by law firms and corporations to reduce operating costs.[52]

◆ **Practice Tip 11** FRE 502 Advisory Committee Notes discuss the use of advanced technology to assist lawyers in conducting privilege review.

> Depending on the circumstances, a party that uses advanced analytical software applications and linguistic tools in screening for privilege and work product may be found to have taken "reasonable steps" to prevent inadvertent disclosure. The implementation of an efficient system of records management before litigation may also be relevant

2. Production

Production of ESI has evolved from producing stacks of paper to producing files in a semi-structured format. Typically the receiving party loads the files into review software to search and analyze key documents. E-discovery disputes can arise out of forms of production. For example, if the documents are not produced in a form that is readily searchable by the receiving party then the party may take issue and motion to compel production in a form that is searchable.

For example in *National Day Laborer Organizing Network v U.S. Immigration & Customs Enforcement Agency* the plaintiffs moved to compel production of documents because the original production files were not searchable in the form produced. The court ordered the government to produce according to a specification that made the files searchable. The court also noted that the discovery dispute could have been avoided if the parties "had the good sense to 'meet and confer,' . . . .. and to 'communicate' as to the form in which ESI would be produced."[53]

---

[51]Fed. R. Evid. 502 (advisory committee notes, Feb. 27 2008, Congressional Record—Senate).

[52]*See,* R. Suskind, *"The End of Lawyers? Rethinking the Nature of Legal Services"* (New York: Oxford University Press, 2008); *see generally* Suzanne Barlyn, *Call My Lawyer . . . in India,* NEW.STJOHNS.EDU (Apr. 3, 2008) (discussing the costs of document review at US firms as compared to overseas legal service providers).

[53]*National Day Laborer Organizing Network v U.S. Immigration & Customs Enforcement Agency,* 2011 WL 381625 (S.D.N.Y. Feb. 7, 2011) (plaintiff alleged

FRCP 34(b) address forms of production, specifically:[54]

- 34(b)(2)(D) Responding to a Request for Production of Electronically Stored Information. The response may state an objection to a requested form for producing electronically stored information. If the responding party objects to a requested form—or if no form was specified in the request—the party must state the form or forms it intends to use.

- 34 (b)(2)(E) Producing the Documents or Electronically Stored Information. Unless otherwise stipulated or ordered by the court, these procedures apply to producing documents or electronically stored information:

  (i)   A party must produce documents as they are kept in the usual course of business or must organize and label them to correspond to the categories in the request;

  (ii)   If a request does not specify a form for producing electronically stored information, a party must produce it in a form or forms in which it is ordinarily maintained or in a reasonably usable form or forms; and

  (iii) A party need not produce the same electronically stored information in more than one form.

The final step in the process is to conduct quality assurance on productions to check for privilege and confidential information. Failures in this step can lead to inadvertent disclosure. For example in *Victor Stanley, Inc. v Creative Pipe I* (*"VSI I"*) defendants claimed inadvertent production of documents in spite of an extensive privilege review. Plaintiffs claimed faulty review and the court agreed, finding that defendants were vague in describing their search protocol and failed to adequately conduct quality controls on their production set.[55]

◆ *Practice Tip 12*   To make review more efficient and effective seasoned practitioners are focusing on:
- Review structure: linear and non-linear review
- Prioritized review using advanced technology
- Single review tool for all types of ESI
- Reasonable, consistent and defensible methodology, end-to-end

---

the electronic documents produced pursuant to its FOIA request were "stripped of all metadata" that should have been produced in the original production).

[54]Fed. R. Civ. P. 34(b).

[55]Victor Stanley, Inc. v. Creative Pipe, Inc., 250 F.R.D. 251, 70 Fed. R. Serv. 3d 1052 (D. Md. 2008).

- Quality controls

§ 2:5 Advanced concepts

A. Proportionality

Proportionality is not simple to assess. Courts consider whether "the burden or expense of the proposed discovery outweighs its likely benefit, considering the needs of the case, the amount in controversy, the parties' resources, the importance of the issues at stake in the action, and the importance of the discovery in resolving the issues."[1]

In *Rimkus Consulting Group v. Cammarata*, U.S. Magistrate Lee Rosenthal notes that the parties' obligation to preserve information is proportional to the case at hand, "Whether preservation or discovery conduct is acceptable in a case depends on what is reasonable and that in turn depends on whether what was done—or not done- was proportional to that case and consistent with clearly established applicable standards."[2]

In *Mancia v Mayflower Textile Servs.*, U.S. Magistrate Judge Paul Grimm highlights the excessive costs of overly broad disclosure requests and equally vague, boiler plate objections. Judge Grimm applied the proportionality standard to resolve the issues in this matter.[3] Case law prompts parties and adjudicators to question overly broad requests as well as vague, unsubstantiated claims of burden. Both behaviors put parties at risk of sanction under FRCP 26(g).[4]

Rule 26(g) requires that every discovery request, response and objection NOT be imposed for an improper purpose, such as to harass or needlessly increase the cost of litigation, and neither unreasonable nor unduly burdensome or expensive, considering the needs of the case, prior discovery in the case, the amount in

---

[Section 2:5]

[1]Fed. R. Civ. P. 26(b)(2)(C)(iii).

[2]Rimkus Consulting Group, Inc. v. Cammarata, 688 F. Supp. 2d 598 (S.D. Tex. 2010).

[3]Mancia v. Mayflower Textile Servs. Co., 253 F.R.D. 354 (D. Md. 2008) (highlighting Federal Rule 26(g) related to curbing discovery abuse and applying the proportionality standard of Federal Rule 26(b)(2)(C) to require that the parties meet and confer to work out the remainder of the discovery issues).

[4]*See*, Cartel Asset Management v. Ocwen Financial Corp., 2010 WL 502721 (D. Colo. 2010) (discussing the interplay between Federal Rules 26(b)(2) (B), 26(c)(1), and (26(g)); *but see*, Cherrington Asia Ltd. v. A & L Underground, Inc., 263 F.R.D. 653 (D. Kan. 2010) (not imposing sanctions under Federal Rule 26(g) because no signed certification was at issue).

controversy, and the importance of the issues at stake in the action.[5] If a lawyer or party violates this rule without substantial justification the court must impose a sanction, including ordering the payment of reasonable attorneys' fees and expenses.[6]

Proportionality is even more elusive when the organization is not a party to a legal dispute, or is obligated as a regulated entity or a public agency to respond to a legal document request. For example *In re Fannie Mae Securities Litigation*, a third-party organization was subpoenaed for documents. In a hearing an agreement was made for the third-party to use 400 search terms. The search produced hundreds of thousands of documents and cost millions of dollars to review. All costs were born by the third-party, paid out of taxpayer dollars.[7]

Other examples include regulatory audits, public document and Freedom of Information Act requests.[8] It's worth noting that social networking sites and other public cloud based repositories and services receive a continuous stream of legal document requests from their customers and government agencies. Given these conditions it's not surprising that organizations are actively seeking smart e-discovery options to reduce burden and right-size the activity.

Reasonableness and proportionality are linked.[9] What is a reasonable amount to spend on e-discovery in a dispute, and is it proportionate to the amount in controversy? Parties struggle to

---

[5]*See, e.g.*, CE Design Ltd. v. CY's Crabhouse North, Inc., 2010 WL 3327876 (N.D. Ill. 2010) (claiming that plaintiff engaged in improper discovery tactics). *See*, Schubert v. Pfizer Inc., 2010 WL 3672215 (S.D. Iowa 2010), subsequently aff'd, 459 Fed. Appx. 568 (8th Cir. 2012) (court urging parties to use cooperation and proportionality to save time and money).

[6]Parties should avoid inefficient and costly discovery practices or risk sanctions: while the responding party must make reasonable inquiry before responding, the requesting party is also required to act judiciously. *See*, Fed. R. Civ. P. 26(g).

[7]In re Fannie Mae Securities Litigation, 552 F.3d 814 (D.C. Cir. 2009).

[8]*See*, Miller v. Holzmann, 2007 U.S. Dist. LEXIS 2987 (D.D.C. Jan. 17, 2007) (finding government's failure to preserve FOIA request in electronic form was unreasonable).

[9]*See*, SEC v. Collins & Aikman Corp., 2009 U.S. Dist. LEXIS 3367 (S.D.N.Y. Jan. 13, 2009) (noting the proportionality provisions of FRCP 26(b)(2) (C), the court observed that the requests "seem particularly reasonable in an action initiated by the SEC").

analyze whether the benefits outweigh the burden.[10] Does this case put at risk millions of dollars of future revenue, the reputation of a leading brand or shareholder value? If a trivial matter, how does the estimated cost of e-discovery stack up to the estimated price of an early settlement?

For example if the amount in controversy is under $50,000 and the requesting party demands broad disclosure across custodians, data sources and time frame the cost to the responding party could be large. A responding party that has a handle on their information sources and e-discovery process is in a stronger position to assess the burden versus the benefit of the disclosure requests. The party can better prepare to negotiate an alternative scope of discovery that is in proportion to the amount in controversy.[11]

Defining the scope of a dispute and potentially relevant ESI is essential to right-sizing the e-discovery activity.[12] The legal issues in the matter will impact the timeframe, breadth of custodians and key terms to search on.[13] The legal issues provide direction to prioritize custodians, date range, types and sources of information and search criteria.[14]

◆ *Practice Tip 1* Draw up a list of potential custodians and the relevant time period. Two to three individuals are at the center of most legal disputes. Discuss and agree to the date

---

[10]*See*, Young v. Pleasant Valley School Dist., 2008 WL 2857912 (M.D. Pa. 2008) (discussing whether burdens associated with a search of ESI outweighed the benefits).

[11]*See*, Helmert v. Butterball, LLC, 16 Wage & Hour Cas. 2d (BNA) 559, 2010 WL 2179180 (E.D. Ark. 2010) (citing Zubulake v. UBS Warburg LLC, 217 F.R.D. 309, 91 Fair Empl. Prac. Cas. (BNA) 1574 (S.D. N.Y. 2003)) (listing "amount in controversy" as a factor to be considered when determining whether a production request is unduly burdensome).

[12]*See*, Siemens Aktiengesellschaft v. Jutai 661 Equipamentos Electronicos, Ltda., 2009 WL 800143 (S.D. Fla. 2009) (establishing reasonable limitations on the scope of plaintiff's obligation to produce responsive ESI); Simon Property Group, Inc. v. Taubman Centers, Inc., 2008 WL 205250 (E.D. Mich. 2008), aff'd, 2008 WL 906271 (E.D. Mich. 2008) (ordering the parties to negotiate a narrower scope to the request to avoid undue burden on the nonparty); Benton v. Dlorah, Inc., 2007 WL 3231431 (D. Kan. 2007) ("Benton II") (plaintiff objecting to production of hard drive claiming that it contained personal information beyond the scope of discovery).

[13]*See*, Board of Regents of University of Nebraska v. BASF Corp., 2007 WL 3342423 (D. Neb. 2007) (arguing for sanctions where a key custodian had not been instructed to search electronic files).

[14]*See*, Wixon v. Wyndham Resort Development Corp., 2009 WL 3075649 (N.D. Cal. 2009) (finding that a party ignored significant logistical obstacles to its proposed custodian-based search).

range and primary custodians, the secondary and tertiary. This will be valuable during the 'meet and confer' phase, when negotiating scope, to right-size discovery to be in proportion to the amount in controversy.

B. **Early Case Assessment (ECA)**

Early analysis of key documents to assess the merits of a case is a long standing best practice in resolving legal disputes. Early analysis of key digital documents is a relatively new practice. It is harder to do than pulling paper documents from file folders and cabinets because ESI is locked in a digital straight jacket. It takes time and money to extract it properly and process it before you begin.

Analyzing, culling and filtering ESI early in a matter, and well before review, is referred to as Early Case Assessment (ECA). A survey reported that conducting thorough early case assessment reduced expenses by 28–50% and was found to assist attorneys in their ability to prepare a more accurate litigation budget.

The practice of culling non-responsive documents from the collection to reduce the volume of data and cost of review is recognized by the bench and bar. United States Magistrate Judge Facciola put a fine point on this topic in an article in the Federal Courts Law Review:

> It is hard to imagine a greater waste of money than paying a lawyer $250 an hour to look at recipes, notices of the holiday party, and NCAA Final Four pool entries while doing a privilege review. A company that permits that situation to occur is wasting its share holders' money as surely as if it were burning it in the parking lot.[15]

Early attention to responsive ESI is essential in understanding what happened in a dispute. The sooner one can access the most relevant facts in the case the earlier one can assess the merits, risk and amount in controversy. Is this a trivial matter or 'bet the company' case?

> "If you have a case that you've analyzed that has a risk of $100,000, and you have an estimate that it will cost much more to process that data, that has to be a really important principle for you to litigate," Judge Waxse said. "Too often the focus of counsel is to get the data to try the case, when in reality you need this data to as-

---

[15]John M. Facciola, *Sailing on Confused Seas: Privilege Waiver and the New Federal Rules of Civil Procedure*, FED. CTS. L. REV. at 6 (Sept. 2006).

sess the chance of success in the case and whether to settle, which is what happens to the vast majority of cases."[16]

The size of the corpus of electronic evidence collected and the diversity of the data is one of the main challenges in discovery. Right-sizing e-discovery for a particular matter is the practice of reasonably narrowing down the corpus of data to reduce costs and bring it in line with the amount in controversy. In the diagram below a funnel is used to illustrate the recommended practices and techniques for winnowing down electronic evidence. The recommended practices include:

- Combining all data types including text, images, audio and video into one funnel or processing platform
- Removing duplicates and system files
- Culling non-responsive data in a reasonable and defensible manner
- Reviewing data in native form rather than TIFFing up front
- TIFFing files after determining they are responsive for production

Right-sizing: The E-discovery Funnel

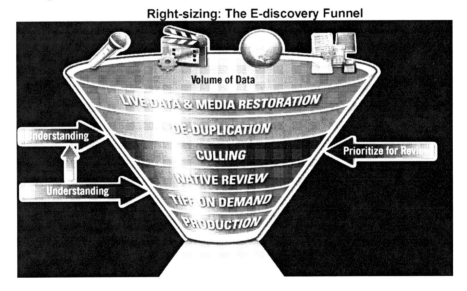

---

[16]Honorable David J. Waxse, et al., *Upfront Assessments Lead to Downstream Savings,* AUTONOMY (2009).

§ 2:6　Conclusion

E-discovery is a dynamic area of law that is directly impacted by emerging technology and new case opinions. E-discovery is neither a walk in the park nor an endurance race. A well-studied, thoughtful approach is the recommended practice. There is no easy street or short cut. E-discovery is distinctly NOT for dummies. It's a critical cornerstone to resolving legal disputes and investigations, and responding to regulatory inquiries, public disclosure and FOIA requests. It fully requires an engaged mind and a systematic approach.

From the outset the purpose and focus of e-discovery is to fully and fairly meet our obligations to respond to document requests. This requires a reasonable process with effective quality controls that will produce responsive documents and protect privilege as well as confidential information. A well-prepared practitioner will:

- Study relevant federal, state and or international rules and laws, as well as case law.
- Conduct an assessment of the range of disclosure activities to form a profile for the organization, including time, expense and risk.
- Take an inventory of the volume of data and range of formats involved in discovery, identifying the most prevalent types and sources.
- Learn the fundamental components of e-discovery and the iterative workflow between the various tasks.
- Learn about best practices and advanced methods to address cost, risk, cycle time, and defensibility.
- Be cognizant of reasonableness, proportionality, and quality with each disclosure request.

An upfront assessment of the organization's litigation profile, inventory of data and frequency of disclosure will guide and assist you in preparedness and right-sizing your e-discovery operations. While the specific timing of any legal document request is as unpredictable as the dispute or inquiry it stems from, the certainty that requests will occur, repeatedly, is high. The first step, and a fundamental principle of e-discovery, is to get prepared and proactively manage ESI in anticipation of legal document requests to reduce risk and cost.

Chapter 3

Mediation and Discovery

*by Simeon H. Baum**

---

*Simeon H. Baum, litigator, and President of Resolve Mediation Services, Inc. (www.mediators.com), has successfully mediated roughly 1,000 disputes. He has been active since 1992 as a neutral in dispute resolution, assuming the roles of mediator, neutral evaluator and arbitrator in a variety of cases, including the highly publicized mediation of the Studio Daniel Libeskind-Silverstein Properties dispute over architectural fees relating to the redevelopment of the World Trade Center site, and Trump's $ 1 billion suit over the West Side Hudson River development. For two decades, he has played a leadership role in the Bar relating to ADR, including service as founding Chair of the Dispute Resolution Section of the New York State Bar Association, and chairing the ADR Section of the Federal Bar Association and ADR Committee of the New York County Lawyers Association. He has served on ADR Advisory Groups to the New York Court system and is President of the SDNY Chapter of the Federal Bar Association. He was selected for the 2005–2012 "Best Lawyers" and "New York Super Lawyers" listings for ADR, and as the Best Lawyers' "Lawyer of the Year" for ADR in New York for 2011. He teaches on the ADR faculty at Benjamin N. Cardozo School of Law and is a frequent speaker and trainer on ADR.

KeyCite[R]: Cases and other legal materials listed in KeyCite Scope can be researched through the KeyCite service on Westlaw[R]. Use KeyCite to check citations for form, parallel references, prior and later history, and comprehensive citator information, including citations to other decisions and secondary materials.

§ 3:1 Introduction

There is nothing like a book focused on e-discovery to give the reader a sense of the complexity and expense of litigation. Over the last two decades, as cases have grown increasingly complex and expensive, there has been growing interest in alternative dispute resolution ("ADR") mechanisms, like arbitration and mediation, as a possible means of reducing the cost, formality, complexity and disruption of litigation. Arbitration is a process in which one or more neutral experts make factual findings and determinations, under legal and other norms, that are binding on the parties. Historically, it was seen as fair, fast, flexible, final and, if not free, then inexpensive. Over the last decade or more, increased complexity, forum, satellite litigation, the use of U.S. litigation style discovery[1] in that forum have magnified costs and delays in arbitration. Nevertheless, arbitration has continued to thrive, particularly on the international scene, where parties seek a neutral forum offering no "home court" advantage.

Mediation has emerged as another available process for resolving disputes to the satisfaction of the parties. At its best, media-

---

[Section 3:1]

[1]In 2008, Bernice Leber, then chair of the New York State Bar Association ("NYSBA") charged this author, who then served as Chair of NYSBA's newly formed Dispute Resolution Section, with addressing the problem of uncertainty, lack of control, rising costs, and conversely the risk of unfairness through arbitrary limits on discovery in the arbitration forum. Ms. Leber posed the problem with two scenarios: (1) the arbitrator who permits wide open discovery way beyond party or counsel's initial expectations or preferences; and (2) the arbitrator who bars necessary discovery adversely impacting the fairness of the proceeding or outcome. Recognizing that norms might vary depending on the arbitral context, the Section broke this challenge down into different types of arbitration and the forum involved. In 2009, a task force led by Carroll Neesemann, John Wilkinson and Sherman Kahn published a Report on Arbitration Discovery in Domestic Commercial Cases. See, http://www.nysba.org/Conte nt/NavigationMenu42/April42009HouseofDelegatesMeetingAgendaItems/Discov eryPreceptsReport.pdf. That report proposed a list of factors to be considered by arbitrators in making discovery decisions. The following year, NYSBA's Dispute Resolution Section prepared a set of Guidelines for the Arbitrator's Conduct of the Pre-Hearing Phase of International Arbitration. See, http://www.nysba.org/ Content/NavigationMenu42/November62010HouseofDelegatesMeetingAgendaIt ems/internationalguidelines.pdf.

tion enables parties to focus on the core issues, interests and information needed, cutting time and cost and leading to an expedited resolution of the matter tailored to the parties' needs and circumstances. Mediation offers truncated disclosure in a confidential setting that can cut through many of litigation's tangles. This chapter will explore the nature and uses of mediation, consider its benefits and limitations, and investigate the relationship of mediation and discovery.

Discovery in the litigation context serves two core purposes: developing the strengths and weaknesses of one's own case and developing the strengths and weaknesses of the adverse party's case.[2] Mediation, as will be more fully discussed below, is essentially a facilitated negotiation. Information has a broader use in negotiation and mediation than litigation. In negotiation and mediation, information is developed not only for case assessment, but also to understand and address the underlying causes of a dispute, to understand and modulate the parties relationship, and to arrive at and judge the value, feasibility and durability of a deal. Information is the currency of mediation. One of the unique features of the mediation process is the freedom and creativity that infuses it. Litigation follows established rules of evidence and civil practice and procedure. Mediation by contrast is informal and an extension of party choice. In mediation, parties and the mediator can adjust to develop information in a flexible way, for disclosure in a confidential setting. Freedom of process creation enables parties and the mediator directly to address some of the secondary aspects of information development that attend litigation. While the ostensible reason for discovery in litigation is case development, the cost and burden of discovery can often become a problem by itself, and can be used by one party as leverage against the other. Mediation permits parties to pare down information sought and disclosed to that which is essential to reach a deal. Thus, in mediation, not only outcome and information, but even the process itself can be considered, crafted and negotiated. We can ask the questions: Is this working? Is this information, and the process of obtaining information, worth the cost? What is the best way for us to proceed? This chapter will

---

[2]While it might seem counterintuitive, litigators know that it is important to understand the weaknesses of one's own case and the strengths of the adversary's case as well. Knowledge of this information can help the advocate think ahead to develop the best spin for his weaknesses, to introduce the weaknesses himself in order to draw its poison, to work to find ways to exclude that information from introduction into evidence, to dig deeper and find flaws with the weakness itself, and to find legal arguments that make the weakness immaterial or irrelevant.

take a closer look at how information and the process of information gathering, assessment, use and disclosure is handled in mediation.

§ 3:2 Nature of mediation

General Definitions

Over the last 20 years, the mediation field has generated divergent views on the nature of mediation and the role and purpose of the mediator. A classic definition of mediation is found in the ABA/AAA/SPIDR Standards of Conduct for Mediators:

> Mediation is a process in which an impartial third party—a mediator—facilitates the resolution of a dispute by promoting voluntary agreement (or "self-determination") by the parties to the dispute. A mediator facilitates communications, promotes understanding, focuses the parties on their interests, and seeks creative problem solving to enable the parties to reach their own agreement.[1]

In addition to focusing parties on their own interests, the mediator can also encourage parties to consider the alternatives to deal proposals that are under consideration. Among these alternatives can be economic and non-economic costs, risks, and probable outcomes of litigation

Riskin's Grid and the Evaluative-Directive/Facilitative Debate

Over the last two decades, particularly in the 1990s, there was lively discussion concerning the scope, function and purpose of the mediator's role. In his seminal article, *Understanding Mediators' Orientations, Strategies, and Techniques: A Grid for the Perplexed,* Professor Len Riskin mapped out what he saw to be a variety of approaches and orientations demonstrated by mediators,[2] using contrasting concepts of "broad/narrow," and "evaluative-and-directive/facilitative" to create spectrums framing the map. Some mediators, for example, might see themselves

---

[Section 3:2]

[1]Standards of Conduct for Mediators (Joint Committee of Delegates from the American Arbitration Association, American Bar Association Sections of Dispute Resolution and Litigation, and the Society of Professionals in Dispute Resolution 1994); cited in KK Kovach & LP Love, *Mapping Mediation: The Risks of Riskin's Grid,* 3 Harv. Neg. L. Rev. 71 (hereinafter *"Riskin's Risks"*), at 74, n. 23.

[2]*See,* Leonard L. Riskin, Understanding Mediators' Orientations, Strategies, and Techniques: A Grid for the Perplexed, 1 HARV. NEG. L. REV. 7, 25 (1996) hereinafter Riskin, Grid]. The Grid was first published in 1994. *See also* Leonard L. Riskin, Mediator Orientations, Strategies and Techniques, 12 Alternatives to High Cost Litig. 111 (1994).

as mini-judges, holding a discussion in which the chief focus is legal issues. Toward the end of this discussion, the mediator might provide an evaluation of the case and strongly urge the parties to come to a settlement under terms that this mediator proposed. This extreme example would be deemed "narrowly focused, evaluative and directive" in the Riskin Grid.

Other mediators might see their job as facilitating the parties' own decision making. These mediators would use elicitive means—through questioning, reflecting back the parties own communications and meanings, and encouragement—to help the parties through their own decision making process, offering assistance in keeping communications effective and constructive, and helping parties seek clarity and maintain stability throughout this process. In this example, the mediators would foster discussion on any topic the parties find meaningful. This could include business interests, personal and community values, emotions generated by the conflict, principles, economic limitations, hierarchical pressures, the negotiation process itself, goals, visions, aspirations,[3] and a wide range of other topics, as well as strengths and weaknesses of the legal case. This latter approach to mediation would fit in the "broadly focused, facilitative" quadrant of the Riskin Grid.

Riskin's Grid sparked passionate and thoughtful discussion in the field. Professors Lela Love and Kim Kovach, both now past Chairs of the ABA Dispute Resolution Section, declared "evaluative mediation" to be an oxymoron.[4] To them, and many others in the field, the mediator's role is purely facilitative. While there might be a separate and legitimate role for a neutral evaluator or arbitrator, Love and Kovach assert that labels, transparency and consumer choice matter and that mediators should be clear on their own role; they are not a practice "rent-a-judge." This is not to say that the mediator is simply a "message bearer." Love and Kovach point out a variety of actions a mediator might perform which are far more active, such as shifting the agenda, prodding parties to reconsider a position and, perhaps in caucus, challeng-

---

[3]*See,* Love, L, *Training Mediators to Listen—Deconstructing Dialogue and Constructing Understanding, Agendas and Agreements,* 38 Fam. & Concil. Cts. Rev. 27 (Jan. 2000 Sage Publications, Inc.), reprinted in LEXIS/NEXIS.

[4]*See, Riskin's Risks, supra;* Kovach & Love, *Evaluative Mediation is an Oxymoron,* 14 Alternatives to High Cost Litig. 31 (1996).

ing an unworkable or misleading proposal.[5] There are many tasks performed by a facilitative style mediator to activate the parties' own reflection, enhance the quality of their communication, and engage and keep them in a process that leads to change and resolution. Love and Kovach's central point is that it is up to the parties to arrive at their own decision and evaluation, and it is the mediator's role simply to help them do that, not to tell the parties what is fair, the likely legal outcome, or the right deal for them.

It should be noted that nothing prevents the broadly focused, facilitative mediator from also engaging the parties and their counsel in a thoughtful consideration of the strengths and weaknesses of their own case and the other party's case. The difference is that it is the parties and their counsel, rather than the mediator who openly engage in this evaluation.

Mediation as Facilitated Negotiation & the Problem Solving Model

While case analysis is thus not alien to the process, a hallmark of the broad, facilitative mediation approach is joint, mutual gains problem solving. A centrist view of mediation casts the process as a facilitated negotiation. To be effective, mediators must understand the negotiation process and grease the wheels of negotiation to enable all parties to be most effective in arriving at a deal that resolves their dispute. The Harvard Negotiation project and other literature in the field has informed the mediation process. Fisher and Ury's "Getting to Yes"[6] popularized the recognition that greater gains can be achieved for all negotiators through cooperation than through competition. This notion was captured by the Italian economist, Vilfredo Pareto, who posited the optimal deal as one that maximizes achievement of the interests of all parties.[7] Fisher and Ury advise negotiators on how best to achieve the Pareto optimum, or the *"win/win"* result in five essential points.

First, they recommend that negotiators "separate the people from the problem." They observe that where relationships become part of the negotiation, or even drive the negotiation, conflict and inefficiencies can arise. One example given is that of the negotia-

---

[5]*Riskin's Risks, supra,* n. 37, citing Joseph B. Stulberg, *Facilitative Versus Evaluative Mediator Orientations: Piercing the "Grid" Lock,* 24 FLA. ST. U. L. REV. 985 (1997).

[6]Fisher, Roger and Ury, William, Getting to Yes: Negotiating Agreement Without Giving In (New York, NY: Penguin Books, 1983).

[7]Pareto, Vilfredo, *Cours d'Economie Politique* (1896–97).

tor in the *shuk* or Arab marketplace. If the lamp merchant knows the purchaser's family and is seen as overcharging, he may be perceived as having no care for that family. Similarly if the purchaser is seen as offering too little, he might be showing a lack of concern for the wellbeing of the merchant's family. A lowball offer might offend the integrity of the merchant, the value of his wares, and his status in society. Offers or demands that do not reflect the "real" or "objective" value of the item might be seen as an insult to the intelligence of the party on the other side. Perceived slights can escalate into use of mutually insulting or threatening language. Before parties know it, *ad homina* are being launched and their relationship is not simply part of the issue, it is seriously at risk.

Fisher and Ury therefore advise negotiators to be "soft on the people and hard on the problem." Casting negotiation as problem solving, they recommend that negotiators use their tough analytic skills to identify the issues and find solutions to the problem. By being "soft" on the people, using encouraging forms of communication, active listening skills, and acknowledgment, negotiators cultivate a smoother, richer, and more complete flow of the information that is needed to perform this problem solving.

The next step in this problem solving model is to move from "positions to interests." Returning to the *shuk*, we can imagine a negotiation in which the seller makes an absurdly high demand and the buyer makes an equally implausibly low offer. Each party takes a "position" and holds firm. The seller swears that the lamp is worth every penny demanded and stakes his honor on not taking a penny less, and *vice versa*. In litigation, this can be seen in lawyer-negotiators insisting on the complete validity of their claims or defenses and the certainty of a favorable outcome, and, accordingly, demanding 100% payment or insisting on not paying a dime or making any other concession. What Fisher and Ury observe is that positional bargaining, like relationship based bargaining, generates inefficiencies and conflict. Where each party holds firm to a position, no deal can be done. Once strong positions have been staked out, with claims of truth and moral superiority attached, the only way to arrive at a deal is for the parties to prove themselves to be liars or reprobates. Loss of face is inevitable with positional approaches to bargaining.

Fisher and Ury suggest another way. Each party candidly describes his own interests and learns the interests of the other. There is no risk of apparent dishonesty when the lamp seller states that he needs to make a profit, feed his family and maintain his business—or any other need he might have. Similarly, there is no harm in the buyer's expressing his need for light, quality interior design, love of antiques, need to preserve the family fortune, financial limitations, or any other set of needs or interests.

Indeed, by identifying interests, the parties prepare themselves for step three in this problem solving model: developing options for mutual gain, to maximize satisfaction of the interests of all parties—*i.e.*, the Pareto optimum. In a classic example, two sisters are described as fighting over a dozen oranges. Each girl takes the *position* that she is entitled to the full dozen. A distributive approach to solving this problem might be to split the oranges, giving each girl six. Along comes their Uncle Sol, who wisely asks the sisters why they want the oranges. He discovers that Susie wants to make orange cake and Sally wants to make orange juice. Thus, Susie needs the rinds and Sally needs the pulp. Armed with this knowledge of *interests*, Uncle Sol can give each girl 100% of what she wants. One sister gets all rinds and the other gets all pulp. Critical to solving this problem is using the word "why" to learn the interests of each party. By learning their interests, Uncle Sol can arrive at an integrative approach generating greater potential gains than that available with a distributive approach.

Fisher and Ury's fourth piece of advice is to use standards in negotiation. By finding a standard that all parties might find acceptable, the negotiations shift from a battle of wills to an objective dimension. Standards might be that which is objectively verifiable, a common principle, or a shared or recognized value, method or approach. One frequently cited example is using the "Kelly Blue Book" as a standard for arriving at the value of a used car in a negotiation with one's automobile insurer. Standards can be of great help in distributive as well as integrative approaches in allocating value in a negotiation.

Finally, in their appendix, Fisher and Ury coin the now much used acronym, BATNA: the "best alternative to a negotiated agreement." By considering what will happen if one chooses not to take a given deal, one is put in a better position for evaluating that proposal. Say, for example, one is making $150,000 as an associate in a law firm. One has been there for several years, has a good likelihood of making partner, but is not very interested in the firm's specialty—insurance coverage litigation. Along comes an offer from an entertainment law firm, at $140,000. The offer is $10,000 lower than one's BATNA, *i.e.*, one's existing salary. Nevertheless, applying non-economic factors, one might choose to take a $10,000 hit on the theory that greater job satisfaction is worth more than $10,000; let us say for this example that one attended Julliard before law school and has always hoped to work in a job associated with the arts. Other factors could be comparing chances of partnership at each firm and comparing firm culture and lifestyle. The BATNA offers a point of comparison on all fronts, enabling one to develop a standard by which to judge the proposed deal. In negotiations concerning cases that are in, or might go to, court, the probable court outcome and associated transaction costs[8]—including noneconomic factors like adverse publicity and disruption—are often seen as the legal BATNA against which the value of a given settlement proposal might be judged.

Other Models of Mediation—Transformative, Understanding Based, and Protean (or 360 Degree) Mediation

Mediators who adopt the problem solving model of negotiation see their chief job as helping the parties engage constructively in a problem solving process. The view of mediator as problem-solver was challenged in the mid 1990s, by the ultra-facilitative "Transformative" school of mediation popularized by Baruch Bush and Joseph Folger in a book entitled "The Promise of Mediation."[9] The electrifying premise of transformative mediation is that the mediator's purpose is not to solve a problem or settle a case. Rather, the mediator has the dual purpose of fostering empowerment and recognition. The focus of the mediator is not so much on the parties' deal as it is on the quality of their relationship and their mode of communication. Moreover, the transformative mediator does not seek to see the big picture, figuring out the core issues, identifying interests, generating options to meet interests, using standards to help with valuation, distribution or decision making, or even comparing deals to alternatives. Rather, the mediator applies a moment to moment microfocus, reflecting back what each party does or says, following the parties as a passenger in the back seat of a car is driven where the driver takes him.

This approach is rooted in the transformatives' understanding

---

[8]Transaction costs include fees that will be spent on lawyers and experts, as well as the associated costs and disbursements that make their way into the typical retainer agreement. One of the greatest transaction costs can be those associated with the activity that is the subject of this book: e-discovery. Related factors can include present value of the proposed deal and possible interest. Collectability of a judgment is another factor to be considered in this type of analysis.

[9]Bush, Robert A. Baruch and Folger, Joseph P., The Promise of Mediation: Responding to Conflict Through Empowerment and Recognition (Jossey-Bass Publishers, San Francisco 1994) ("Promise of Mediation"). A good synopsis of this book is found at: http://www.colorado.edu/conflict/transform/bushbook.htm.

of the nature of conflict and of the self. Transformatives see people as being uncomfortable in conflict. We can even feel ugly in that role, and urgently want to be out of it. We lash out and become defensive, shoring up protective walls around ourselves and focusing on our own feelings, views, interests, rights and entitlements. In this state, we have difficulty seeing the other's perspective. When parties see that they have some control over themselves and the situation, they can relax a bit and open up to the perspective of the other. In short, empowerment leads to the growth of empathy, and empathy is the moral transformation that gives "Transformative" mediation its name. Resolution is more a natural outgrowth of this change than the goal of the mediator. In turn, empowerment is fostered by the mediator's raising up for parties opportunities to make choices concerning not only the deal terms but also the host of available process choices, including, *inter alia*, whether to speak or not, what to say, how to respond, and whether or not to make a deal. Bush and Folger adopt a view of self that is neither individualistic nor organic (collectivist), but rather a "both/and" view that focuses on relationship[10] and the choice of how and in which mode one relates to the other. Conflict is seen as a crisis in relationship and, thus, transformative focus is on the quality of relationship.[11]

Mediators Jack Himmelstein and Gary Friedman have for years promoted an "understanding based" approach to mediation.[12] For them, conflict is based on misunderstanding and unwillingness to accept reality. As parties come to a better understanding of each other and of their compelling contexts and circumstances, they can dig beneath the "v." in a litigation or dispute and come to a resolution through understanding. The understanding based approach posits that the parties are already in relationship in the broader world. The mediator's job is to bring peace, not conflict, into the room. Accordingly Himmelstein

---

[10]*See,* Promise of Mediation, Ch. 9. While Bush cites to the work of a mid-20th century social scientist in connection with this work, the modern Jewish existentialist thinker, Martin Buber, sets for a groundbreaking work on relationship as essential to one's true self in I and Thou (Kaufman, W. trans., Charles Scribner's Sons 1970).

[11]From a transformative vantage point, Fisher and Ury's advice to be soft on people, and to separate the people from the problem, can be seen as an instrumental approach to relationships from an individualistic sense of self. Transformatives, by contrast, give high value to the quality of relationship as essential to the nature of being fully human. In their defense, Fisher and Ury could argue that their first injunction simply liberates relationship from entanglement in an independently solvable problem.

[12]*See,* Friedman, G, Himmelstein, J., Challenging Conflict: Mediation Through Understanding (ABA Dispute Resolution Section 2009).

and Friedman train mediators to use joint session only. Private, confidential meetings between mediator and fewer than all parties—known as caucuses—are rarely, if ever, held in this model of mediation.

Development of mediation theory and schools over the last two decades has been good for the field. It creates greater clarity, promotes discipline and enables practitioners and users to make sharper choices in mediator selection, process design, and use of opportunities in the mediation process itself. Distinctions increase recognition of possibilities. Yet, for many mediators, what Peter Adler says about negotiators in his piece "Protean Negotiation"[13] can apply to mediators themselves. Many mediators do not fit a particular mold or school and do not necessarily limit themselves by being purely facilitative, or evaluative, directive, transformative or understanding based. A phrase used by mediator Lori Matles—"the 360 mediator"—might apply to the mediator who, while generally seeking to fulfill the central role of facilitating the parties negotiation or dialogue, will also do what seems appropriate under the circumstances. Whether these choices to depart from the facilitative role are error or highly effective is what makes mediation an art. Tact, appropriateness, knowing when rapport has been developed, understanding when humor will help or offend, and a host of subtle interpersonal skills that come with emotional intelligence can guide the mediator's choices of variation from the common theme.

§ 3:3   Uses of mediation

Court-Annexed, Public and Private Mediation
The use of mediation has grown extensively over the last two decades and is now being used to resolve disputes in nearly every conceivable substantive area. In the early 1990s, the federal district courts began pilot programs utilizing mediation. Those programs have grown into regular panels of mediators applied to nearly every type of civil case found in those courts.[1] Similarly, state courts around the country have developed mediation

---

[13]Adler, P.S., *Protean Negotiation,* in The Negotiator's Fieldbook, The Desk Reference for the Experienced Negotiator, Kupfer Schneider, A., Honeyman, C., editors (ABA Section of Dispute Resolution 2006).

[Section 3:3]

[1]The Alternative Dispute Resolution Act of 1998 formalized these pilot programs, directed all district courts to devise and implement some form of ADR program, and empowered federal courts to mandate arty participation in mediation or neutral evaluation. 28 U.S.C.A. §§ 651 to 658 (1998).

programs for a variety of case types. California, Texas, Florida, New Jersey, and Maryland feature widely used mandatory mediation programs, or multi-door ADR approaches. In New York, for example, mediation programs began at the community dispute level with referrals to Community Dispute Resolution Centers ("CDRCs") from family courts, Civil Court, and criminal courts. Mediation and neutral evaluation programs next appeared in New York's matrimonial courts. In the late 1990s, New York's Commercial Division, which handles its large, complex business cases, formed panels of neutrals offering a broad array of ADR options, including mediation.

Mediation has been embraced by the federal government as well.[2] Congress passed the Administrative Dispute Resolution Act of 1990,[3] which was renewed without a sunset provision in 1996.[4] Implementation of these ADR Acts gained strength in 1996, when President Clinton issued an Executive Order directing federal agencies to develop ADR programs for intra-agency, interagency, and even agency-public disputes. Today, a wide array of ADR, and in particular mediation, programs exist within the federal government. Quasi public organizations, like the U.S. Postal Service, have implemented mediation programs, like the USPS's REDRESS. Similarly Self Regulating Organizations (SROs), like the National Association of Securities Dealers (NASD), now called the Financial Industry Regulatory Association (FINRA), have mediation programs. FINRA, which manages approximately 85% of all customer-broker disputes nationwide,[5] in addition to broker-broker dealer disputes, handles nearly 1,000 mediations a year.[6]

In the private sector, acceptance of mediation is also widespread. The Center for Public Resources ("CPR"), now known as the International Center for Conflict Prevention and Resolution (still "CPR"), promoted a "pledge," adopted by many Fortune 500 corporations, in which corporations commit to utilizing ADR

---

[2]A helpful synopsis of the expansion of the use of ADR in the federal government can be found at http://www.dot.gov/ost/ogc/CADR/policy.htm#_edn 23.

[3]Pub. L. No. 101-552, 104 Stat. 2736 (codified at 5 U.S.C.A. § 571).

[4]Pub. L. No. 104-320, 110 Stat. 3870 (codified at 5 U.S.C.A. § 571).

[5]FINRA's annual intake of arbitrations pursuant to mandatory arbitration clauses numbers in excess of 8,000.

[6]Statistics on FINRA arbitration and mediation filings and resolutions can be found at: http://www.finra.org/ArbitrationMediation/AboutFINRADR/Statisti cs/. During one of its more busy years, the NASD (FINRA's precursor) had 1,300 mediations pending.

mechanisms before resorting to litigation. Mediation or other ADR clauses can be found in many tailored and garden variety agreements across the board. Some particularly favored areas[7] include insurance[8] and reinsurance[9]—both first party and third party claims[10]—employment discrimination, securities, general business, family and matrimonial, and the commercial matrimonial (partnership or other business form dissolutions or general disputes), franchising, intellectual property, and real estate.[11]

Matching the Mediator to the Mess

As demonstrated above, mediation is a flexible process that can address a variety of different concerns. Depending on the participants' needs and the posture of a particular dispute or case, one mode of mediation might be more suitable than another.

Let us imagine, for example, an embedded employment dispute, where the parties have an ongoing workplace relationship and where the greatest source of conflict is less a monetary issue than the manner in which an employee is being treated or a manager is being perceived. For that dispute, a transformative model might be the most appropriate. The transformative mediator will focus on the quality of the parties' relationship and their communication. If effective in fostering empowerment and recognition, the transformative approach might repair, restore or enhance the relationship, making for a better tone in the workplace after completion of the mediation session.

Now, let us imagine an accounting proceeding between busi-

---

[7]The Dispute Resolution Section of the New York State Bar Association has published a series of White Papers elaborating on mediation in a variety of substantive areas. See 13 White Papers displayed at: http://www.nysba.org/AM/Template.cfm?Section=Section__Reports__and__White__Papers=/TaggedPage/TaggedPageDisplay.cfm=55=47287.

[8]Policies offering coverage in areas where the use of mediation has grown include disability, life, and health, as well as the more typical property and casualty policies. Directors and Officers ("D&O") or Errors and Omissions ("E&O") coverage, Employment Practices Liability Insurance ("EPLI"), and even Title Insurance policies generate disputes that are commonly being mediated today. For further details on Insurance and Reinsurance industry mediation, *see,* Platto, C., Scarpatto, P., and Baum, S., White Paper on Insurance and Reinsurance Industry Mediation (New York State Bar Association Dispute Resolution Section 2011).

[9]One well regarded panel of reinsurance industry neutrals is ARIAS.

[10]Both coverage issues and underlying claims are excellent areas for mediation.

[11]The Dispute Resolution Section of the New York State Bar Association has published a series of White Papers elaborating on mediation in a variety of substantive areas.

ness partners, now pending in a state court's Commercial Division or its equivalent. Perhaps there, a facilitative style mediator with a broad focus might be ideal. That mediator could address the parties' relationship, elicit their interests and creatively explore options to meet the parties' interests. This mediation might commence with a view that the plaintiff is in the dark on bookkeeping and needs information to determine just how much additional money he is owed. The cost of a full blown accounting proceeding might be monumental, and, if there are serious bookkeeping deficiencies, the outcome might still be inconclusive. A dissolution of the partnership might kill the proverbial goose that lays the golden egg. It is quite possible that, in this scenario, interest development might reveal that one partner is domestically focused and would like to run the retail operation and the other partner would like to go global, exploiting the brand on the international market. This discovery could lead to a restructuring of the business and licensing arrangements that separates out the partners' functions and domains, preserves, or even augments, value for both parties, and obviates the original need for an accounting.

Imagine a third, insurance oriented scenario, say a personal injury matter between strangers. The bulk of key discovery has been completed, but development of experts, not to mention a lengthy trial and possible appeal, have not yet occurred. There is thus no ongoing relationship. Here a facilitative mediator who is capable of running the parties through an effective risk and transaction cost analysis might be optimal. Comprehending the strengths and weaknesses of a case might make it easier for the parties, including the insurance claims representative, to come to a monetary deal that makes sense in light of the possible court outcome and its ancillary costs. Effective management of the negotiation can help parties, counsel and experienced claims representatives as they approach the last phase of negotiations. In this phase emotions even among professionals can hit higher valences as people test each other's commitment level, seek to ascertain that value is not being left behind or overpaid, and offer concessions beyond their original goals for the endgame. This mediator can foster, or in caucus engage in, empathetic discussion with the injured party, providing understanding and acknowledgement which provides satisfaction beyond mere monetary relief.

In sum, it pays for counsel to be alert to the various modes of, and possibilities available in, mediation to maximize client satisfaction. Counsel should use the process in a way that takes full advantage of what it has to offer, not only for outcome but also for the route to that end and management of the people involved.

§ 3:4 Preparation for mediation

In some forums, little, if any, preparation is undertaken prior to participating in the mediation session. This is a mistake. For most substantial matters going into mediation—whether it is an employment, insurance, securities, business, intellectual property, or any other matter that might make its way into Court—it makes a significant difference to prepare for mediation. While an entire chapter could be written on preparation, for purposes of this chapter, where our focus is discovery and mediation, we will give a brief overview of preliminary considerations and preparation for the mediation session.

The first steps in mediation preparation are the threshold questions of whether and when to mediate, and selection of the mediator. While much can be said about this, for purposes of this Chapter, we would urge that the sooner one mediates, the better. As will be discussed further, to the extent there is a concern that certain information is needed before a party can make a rational decision to settle a case, that information can be obtained in a much more direct and speedy manner through mediation. The sooner resources are committed to resolving the matter the greater the resources that will be available for the settlement pot.

On mediator selection, sophisticated counsel should consider the process needs, client needs, relationship issues (including relationship with adverse counsel), case assessment needs, and other factors referenced in the above discussion of the nature of mediation and matching the mediator to the mess. Mediators tend to be selected based on prior experience of counsel or parties with that mediator, or on reputation—essentially the prior experience of others. Counsel might ask colleagues, reach out to Court ADR Administrators, or inquire from other known mediators or ADR experts about the reputation, style and approach of a given mediator; or generally, seek a mediator who fits the particular bill. It is not out of the norm for experienced counsel to contact a potential mediator to learn of that mediator's availability and experience with mediating matters of the type in question. It is entirely appropriate for counsel during the mediator selection phase to ask not only about substantive background, but also about the mediator's style. This is a chance to learn if the mediator is facilitative, gives evaluative feedback, shares process choices with parties and counsel or is more directive, follows an understanding based model—including the degree to which the mediator uses joint session or caucuses—whether the mediator is transformative, or whether he or she takes a protean, or 360 degree approach. Not only are these questions appropriate, but they send a positive message to the mediator about counsel's familiarity with, and support of, the mediation process.

Counsel might go further still in this initial interview and seek the mediator's views on what approach might work best from a holistic perspective to satisfy the parties' needs—ranging from case risk and transaction cost analysis, through party dynamics, emotional issues, business issues, economic limitations, reputational and public relations issues, discovery and other informational needs, or any other process issue that might exist. Of course, this is also an opportunity to learn whether the mediator has any conflicts. Unlike binding evaluative processes like arbitration or litigation, prior experience or even relationships with the parties or counsel does not preclude the mediator's participation. Rather, those relationships should be disclosed, and the parties are free to waive any perceived conflicts. Indeed, some sophisticated counsel actually prefer finding a mediator who has worked with, and has a good relationship with the counterparty, on the theory that feedback from this mediator will be very credible to the party that already knows and trusts him or her.

After mediator selection, three general areas for preparation include (a) further communications with the mediator and with the other parties or their counsel, (b) preparation of pre-mediation statements, and (c) communications with one's own client.

Pre-Mediation Conference Calls

In advance of mediation, particularly in matters that merit counsel's retention, once the mediator has been selected or appointed, it is advisable to participate in a pre-mediation conference call with the mediator. This can be done as a joint call, with all counsel (or parties) participating, or in separate calls that are essentially equivalent to confidential pre-mediation caucuses. Since the mediator is not a decision-maker, there is not the same bar against "ex parte" communications with the neutral third party as one finds in arbitration or litigation.[1]

One key point to cover during this call is who will be attending

---

[Section 3:4]

[1]See ABA/ABA/SPIDR Standards of Conduct for Mediators (1994), revised 2005, Standard 2 on "Impartiality" (requiring that a mediator decline an appointment if that mediator cannot act with impartiality—a subjective standard

the mediation—both from one's own group as well as from the counterparties. It is important to establish that people with full authority will attend the mediation, and, where applicable, that there will not be hierarchical imbalances that will create interparty issues. It can be awkward and time consuming to begin a mediation with one party's feeling insulted that he or she chose to put down other business to prepare for and attend the mediation, while the other party's equivalent level representative did not deign to do the same.

Most pertinent to the focus of this chapter, the most central task of the first pre-mediation conference call, is to provide the mediator with a "nutshell" overview of the dispute and associated case for the purpose of clarifying what, if anything, needs to be done before the first mediation session, so that when the parties do get together they have a fully productive session. This is the opportunity for all concerned—mediator, counsel, and any participating parties—to be sure that they will have pertinent information in hand to discuss and consider during their mediated negotiation. In this regard, the mediator might check whether formal discovery is outstanding, whether document production or interrogatory responses are needed, whether depositions need to be conducted, damages need to be developed, or expert reports exist or need to be exchanged or provided. A pivotal balance here is whether core information that will be needed for a productive negotiation has already been made available to all concerned parties or can be provided at less cost and expense than might be required by full blown, pretrial discovery. This balance of cost, effectiveness and need is a major advantage of the pragmatic and flexible approach that may be taken in mediation.

The first pre-mediation conference call is also a good opportunity to be clear on what the mediator can use in, and attached to, the pre-mediation statement.

Pre-Mediation Statements

Pre-mediation statements are very helpful in bringing the

---

determined by the mediator); and Standard 3 on Conflicts of Interest (requiring the mediator to determine whether a conflict or the appearance of a conflict exists and to disclose this, but permitting the mediator to continue with the mediation if there has been disclosure and waiver. Standard 3.C.). A limitation to this disclose and waive rule is expressed in Standard 3.E: "If a mediator's conflict of interest might reasonably be viewed as undermining the integrity of the mediation, a mediator shall withdraw from or decline to proceed with the mediation regardless of the expressed desire or agreement of the parties to the contrary." *Id.* The 2005 revision was adopted by SPIDR's successor, ACR, *i.e.,* the Association for Conflict Resolution, which is a merged organization of the Academy of Family Mediators, the Conflict Resolution Education Network and the Society of Professionals in Dispute Resolution (SPIDR).

mediator up to speed with parties and counsel. Advance review of these statements enables the mediator to concentrate at the mediation session on interparty dynamics and facilitating the parties' negotiation, rather than playing informational "catch up" at that session. To encourage candor, these statements are typically presented to the mediator in confidence. Some counsel, parties and mediators might prefer an exchange of these statements between the parties, to begin the process of bringing all parties onto the same page. Some recommend a hybrid approach, in which statements are exchanged, but additional confidential submissions are made exclusively to the mediator, for information that the parties would prefer not to share. Confidential information in this latter scenario might include, *inter alia*, thoughts on settlement proposals; observations about interparty dynamics; information on a party's economic limitations; insurance coverage limits or concerns; strategic thoughts for structuring the mediation process, including the use of caucus or joint session, settlement history, and even case weaknesses.

Pre-mediation statements are typically presented in letter form, rather than as formal briefs. They generally include the core facts, information on inter-party dynamics and the history of the dispute, settlement posture, settlement challenges, thoughts for settlement, thoughts for the mediation process, and identification of the parties who will be attending the mediation. Law is not typically included in great detail, except to the extent it involves a point of law that is likely to be pivotal in the negotiations or in the parties' assessment of the strength and value of their legal BATNA (*i.e.,* their case). Law is also included where there is a sense that the mediator needs to be brought up to speed on a legal schema or framework with which he or she might not be familiar.

Counsel are encouraged to attach key documents to pre-mediation statements, such as contracts, invoices, insurance policies, documents that relate to damages, or any other document that the mediator should see in order to be up to speed with counsel and the parties on the pivotal issues and background. Expert reports, medicals, tax returns, deposition transcripts, key correspondence, invoices, change orders, and summary spreadsheets are some of the wide range of documents that might be useful for a mediator to review in advance of the first mediation session.

Client Preparation

In advance of the mediation, it is wise for counsel to spend time preparing the client. This includes describing the mediation

process and developing a clear understanding of the roles of parties and counsel in that process. Because it is the parties' dispute
and an excellent opportunity for the party to obtain non-economic
satisfaction through expression and understanding, or to develop
business solutions, parties are encouraged to talk in the mediation process. Counsel may work out in advance a system in which
the party might comfortably talk until counsel signals that the
discussion is entering rough waters or that counsel would like to
take the floor.

Counsel should learn not only the facts from the client, but
also what the client's needs and interests are. Together, counsel
and client can develop a set of goals. This can be an aspirational
best deal, then a reasonable deal, and finally the "walk away,"
i.e., the proposal below (or above) which that party is not willing
to go. Of course, it is wise for attorneys to advise their parties to
keep an open mind, and to note that these provisional goals might
change as more information is developed over the course of the
mediation. To aid in the development of these goals, counsel
might discuss with the client the strengths and weaknesses of
the case and the transaction costs in going forward. This can
include a disciplined risk and transaction cost analysis.[2]

§ 3:5 Benefits and limitations of mediation

In considering, recommending or suggesting mediation, sophisticated counsel should know its benefits and limitations.

Time Savings
Mediation saves time. The typical litigation takes years, from
commencement through trial or appeal. Preparation for trial
takes years, if one includes the discovery phase. By contrast,
some mediations are held with virtually no preparation or communication in advance with the mediator, and resolved in sessions lasting one day or less. The REDRESS transformative
mediation program, dealing with embedded US Postal Service
claims of employment discrimination, is an example of this
approach. The majority of REDRESS mediations are resolved in
several hours.[1] Commercial mediations, like those associated

---

[2]*See,* www.treeage.com for a useful downloadable software program for
carrying out a formal decision tree analysis for consideration of probable case
outcomes, risks, costs, and values.

[Section 3:5]

[1]*See* results of study performed by Lisa Bingham on the USPS REDRESS
Program, Nabatchi, T. and Bingham, L. B., *From Postal to Peaceful: Dispute*

with federal district court or a Commercial Division or held privately with a professional mediation services provider, generally do involve some limited preparation by the mediator and the parties. Indeed, preparation is essential to effective representation of clients in many mediations.[2] That said, time savings remains a benefit in all mediations.

Cost Savings

Where attorneys are paid on an hourly basis, savings in time generate savings in cost. Many cases that might take years in litigation can be resolved in a single mediation session. That session might last a few hours or go into the wee hours of the morning. In other instances, if the matter is not resolved in the first session, the mediator can follow up by conducting telephone conferences—effectively continuing telephonic caucuses with parties or counsel—and bring the matter to closure through this route. There might also be multiple mediation sessions. Sometimes, despite best efforts to prepare and bring all necessary party representatives to the table, some parties might need to discuss what has been learned at the first mediation session with people who did not attend. Particularly in matters involving municipalities that need board approval, large corporations, and out of state or overseas insurers, there might be a need to seek greater settlement authority from those who were not present at the first session.

In addition, there are times when, despite initial efforts to have all information present at the mediation session, new information is learned for the first time in mediation or it becomes apparent that further information is needed. The mediator can help create a forum where the needed information can be developed as expeditiously as possible, even without formal discovery. Nevertheless, time might be required to obtain certain documents, conduct a deposition, develop numbers for a damages assessment, or consider the viability of a proposed deal. The mediator can follow up during interstitial time as parties process information to maintain momentum and assist in moving the parties to resolution.

Systems Design in the USPS REDRESS(R) Program DOI: 10.1177/ 0734371X09360187, available online at: http://pubget.com/search?q=authors%3 A%22Lisa%20Bingham%22; Bingham, L., *Mediation at Work: Transforming Workplace Conflict at the United States Postal Service*; Report to the IBM Center for The Business of Government (2003); Nabatchi, T., and Bingham, L. *Transformative Mediation in the USPS Redress Program: Observations of ADR Specialists,* Vol. 18 Hofstra Labor and Employment Law Journal, p. 399 (2001).

[2]Preparation for mediation could be the subject of its own chapter.

Whether it is in a single session or after multiple mediation sessions, with or without pre-mediation or post-mediation conference calls, the time spent in mediation and the consequent cost is a fraction of that spent by parties and counsel in full blown litigation, with fulsome discovery; procedural, substantive, pretrial and post trial motions; pre-trial preparation; jury selection; trial; and appeal.

Party Control of Process

Litigation is governed by formal rules of civil procedure. The manner in which parties wend their way to closure is determined well in advance by the rules of the forum. This is true at all stages of the proceedings: pleadings, discovery, motions, trial, and appeal. Rules of evidence and procedure govern not only how information is developed but also how it is introduced at the adjudicative hearing. Any issue on how the parties must proceed at any given juncture is ultimately decided by the judge, magistrate or arbitrator. While counsel might seek an adjournment, it is up to the court whether the request will be granted.

Mediation is a very different process indeed. At critical junctures mediators will take the opportunity to learn what parties and counsel feel is the most constructive way to approach the problems posed by the dispute. A facilitative mediator will ask parties and counsel from the start whether they feel a particular procedural approach would be helpful. Parties and counsel have a say in whether and how to hold pre-mediation communications or provide pre-mediation statements, and whether to participate in joint sessions or caucuses. Parties and counsel are also actively involved in identifying issues and setting the agenda on the order and content of the parties' discussions. To the extent certain information is seen as confidential, beyond the general umbrella of confidentiality that covers the entire mediation process, parties are free to choose what, when and to whom they will make disclosure. They might choose to disclose information to the mediator only in caucus. They might withhold disclosure of certain information until it is obviously needed or until they have greater assurance that the other party is genuinely engaged in deal making. They might decide that it might be helpful to have a meeting of parties only—with or without the mediator—or of counsel only. They might decide it is time to take a break, whether for a brief respite or to adjourn or even terminate the mediation session itself. And, of course, parties have control of what proposals they will make or accept, in short, how to resolve their dispute.

Party Control of Outcome

Litigation or arbitration are binding adjudicative processes in which a third party—judge, jury, or arbitrator—decides the outcome. By contrast, in mediation, it is the parties who decide how their dispute is resolved. Decisions by third parties often please no one. At other times, they produce a winner and a loser, certainly leaving the losing party in far worse position than would have been achieved in a settlement.

In mediation, there is no binding outcome other than one to which the parties agree. Each party is able to avoid the risk of outright loss. Each party may work hard to design a deal that best meets that party's interests—of course, keeping in mind that there can be no deal unless all parties find it acceptable. If no deal is mutually acceptable, the parties are still free to resort to their BATNA, whether it is litigation or not.

Flexibility of Remedy

Many, if not most, civil cases involve claims for damages where no injunctive relief is possible, due to money damages being deemed an adequate remedy at law. Even in cases where injunctive relief is possible, courts tend to be constrained in the scope of the relief that may be had, or the range of factors that might be considered when fashioning this relief.

In mediation, the only limit to possible relief is the imagination, will and capacity of parties and counsel and the structure of reality. Courts do not typically issue damages awards payable over time. Structured settlements are a regular occurrence in mediation, where real economic circumstances may legitimately influence the parties' deal. Courts do not mandate apologies. Parties in mediation may apologize, give letters of reference or recommendation, and generally acknowledge the human consequences and emotional significance of circumstances surrounding or producing a dispute. Courts cannot typically restructure a business, but parties in mediation can.

Building Understanding

Court determinations do not tend to generate either great enthusiasm in the losing party or a sense of greater understanding between the parties. In mediation, by contrast, as Himmelstein and Friedman emphasize, there is a possibility of growth in understanding through dialogue.[3] Parties are able to come to a greater understanding of not only the other party's perspective but also their own interests, motivations and goals, of the legal and business risks and possibilities, and of the surrounding cir-

---

[3]*See* Friedman, G., Himmelstein, J., Challenging Conflict Mediation Through Understanding (ABA Dispute Resolution Section 2009).

cumstances and realities affecting all parties. Mediation offers a possibility of having all parties leave the room with the sense that "we are all in this together," in lieu of the isolating and alienating sense that there is a winner and a loser.

Relationship Preservation or Repair

The ink of a judgment can etch an indelible rift in the parties' relationship. The recognition and joint decision making possible in mediation can support restoration of interparty harmony.

Reducing Reputational Risk

Many a nasty allegation gets filed in pleadings and motions in court or is aired during trial or publicized with an appellate decision. These same allegations are available to the press, competitors, potential customers, family members, or any party who wishes to review the record.

Mediation, by contrast, is a confidential process. Mediated settlement agreements often contain confidentiality terms, as well.

It is not unusual for certain defendants to express concern that if they settle a case involving one employee or a single transaction, the settlement would set a precedent encouraging future litigation by other employees or in connection with other similar transactions. In fact, the converse is a greater risk: an adverse judgment might truly publicize exposure and encourage future litigation. Adverse judgments can affect entire industries. Confidential settlement in mediation can dramatically limit the risk of a bad, publicized precedent.

Limiting Disruption

Beyond eliminating or reducing public exposure of preferably private disputes, mediation offers the chance to limit other forms of disruption that attend litigation. Officers, employees, customers and vendors need not be served with subpoenas, forced to gather massive quantities of documents or electronic data, or pulled from their workplace to attend depositions or trial. As a consequence, a company's participation in mediation can still the water cooler chatter and lessen anxieties among peripherally interested parties. It can keep key personnel focused on productive work and constructive relations.

Confidentiality and Information Disclosure

There is one added benefit of the confidential character of mediation. As noted above, each party controls the flow of information it chooses to communicate to the mediator or the other parties. In litigation, discovery obligations must be met, court orders must be obeyed, and opposing or rebuttal evidence must be adduced to avoid adverse consequences. Mediation permits much greater flexibility in the timing, content, and audience for disclosures. The insulting fact that might enrage the counterparty may be tactfully withheld rather than produced in discovery or raised in defense. Negative facts that might emerge later in discovery can be kept confidential through a reasonable settlement proposal. The existence of a business interest—e.g., in exploiting a patent, tradename or brand, developing a territory, obtaining capital, or acquiring a new line, market, or business unit—can be disclosed only to the mediator until it grows clear that there is a deal to be made. Similarly, a settlement option or possibility might be raised first just with the mediator until it has been sufficiently analyzed or the time is right for its communication. That same proposal might be a damaging admission in court, but even when communicated to the counterparty remains entirely confidential.

Another unique benefit of mediation confidentiality is the ability to use the mediator as a double blind to protect trade secrets, customer lists or other information that would not typically be shared with a competitor. Where there is a concern over generating informational asymmetry by providing a disclosure without a corresponding disclosure from the other party, the mediator can be used to confirm to each party that information has been provided before the information is jointly shared.

Limitations of Mediation

Mediation is is no panacea. If a governmental unit or other party seeks to establish a legal precedent that will affect the social fabric or a given industry, some might prefer to do this through a published judgment or order, rather than by confidential agreement that will not have precedential impact on others.[4] In addition, while most matters are resolved in dramatically less

---

[4]Of course, if sufficient interested parties participate in the mediation, it can more effectively address ongoing problems comprehensively and in a manner that truly and flexibly addresses the interests of all stakeholders. For example, groups like the Environmental Protection Agency have initiated facilitated regulatory negotiations with a wide range of stakeholders to address a complex set of problems that affects a broad and diverse group. *See, e.g.*, Reg03, Encourage Consensus-Based Rulemaking, http://govinfo.library.unt.edu/npr/library/reports/reg03.html. For an interesting review of the question of whether regulatory negotiated rulemaking is effective and can be conducted more effectively, *see*, Fairman, D. *Evaluating Consensus Building Efforts: According To Whom? And Based On What?*, Jan. 1999 Consensus, a joint publication of the Consensus Building Institute and the MIT-Harvard Public Disputes

time in mediation than in litigation, there is no guaranty that mediation will produce a final and binding result. If the need for finality trumps concerns with cost, disruption and outcome, and if there is a strong sense that mediated settlement talks will be futile,[5] counsel and parties might opt to continue in litigation. The question of whether mediation is a preferred process for developing information, some of which might otherwise be sought through litigation discovery, is addressed later in this Chapter.

One misunderstanding that is occasionally raised is that mediation is best where the parties can "get past" emotions and move constructively into deal making. The notion that emotional parties need to be bound by the leash of litigation misapprehends mediation's potential for understanding, empowerment, and recognition. There is a special satisfaction in participating in a process where a party's emotion is not excluded as subjective and irrelevant. Indeed, while instrumental approaches may be disapproved by transformative mediation theorists, the observation still holds that highly emotional parties can find satisfaction in mediation discussions that do enable them to vent and then move on to constructive deal making.

§ 3:6 Discovery and information

There are a variety of reasons we seek discovery in litigation. Discovery develops information on the strengths and weaknesses of one's case, and the strengths and weaknesses of the adversary's case. It reveals what information exists, corrals evidence to present at trial, and, also critically, nails down the absence of evidence on any given point. As noted in the Introduction to this Chapter, the process of discovery itself is an independent force. It can be intrusive; can, through third party discovery, threaten to harm client, friend, or family relationships; can impose tremendous cost on both the party seeking and the party providing disclosure; and can be disruptive to the businesses and people involved.

All of the general reasons for obtaining information in litigation can apply to mediation as well, to the extent that participants

---

Program, *republished at* http://www.mediate.com/articles/evaluateconsensusC. cfm.

[5]One *caveat* is that most mediators have a number of stories—particularly in the court-mandated context—of parties or counsel initially expressing certainty that the matter cannot be resolved but ending the mediation with a deal.

in that process "bargain in the shadow of the law."[1] Transformative mediators might urge that the focus is on the parties, their communication and their relationship. Nevertheless, context—including the legal framework—matters in a problem solving approach, where the alternative to an unresolved mediation is litigation. In order to understand the legal BATNA, development of information can be critical.

§ 3:7   The mediation discovery paradox: more information in less time

Information development in mediation presents a paradox. A much wider range of categories of information are developed and significant in mediation than in litigation. We consider more than the legal BATNA and the legal "story" that is woven into the dispute. In addition to the legal shadow, other significant areas for development of information include the parties' interests—business, familial, relational; the business context; economic constraints; emotional issues; principle, goals, aspirations, visions; even deeper questions of identity. All of these can influence whether, how, and in what form a resolution might emerge. The seeming paradox is that, despite this richly varied and nuanced cloud of information, which includes the legal BATNA, much less time and cost is typically spent in mediation than in litigation, not only on trial and appeal, but especially on discovery.

Bypassing Entanglement—Informational Aikido

There is more than one reason that a greater range of information can be developed in a shorter period of time through mediation. One explanation comes from an analogy to martial arts. Litigants can identify a single issue over which counsel might spend months developing competing information and arguments. In a construction case, for example, expert opinions might vary widely on whether work on a neighboring building now requires a multimillion dollar foundation reconstruction, or

---

[Section 3:6]

[1]*See,* Mnookin, R.H. and Kornhauser, L., *Bargaining in the Shadow of the Law: The Case of Divorce,* The Yale Law Journal, Vol. 88, No. 5, Dispute Resolution (Apr., 1979), pp. 950–997, published by: The Yale Law Journal Company, Inc.; Stable URL: http://www.jstor.org/stable/795824; Mnookin, R.H., Cooter, R. & Marks, S. *Bargaining in the Shadow of the Law: A Testable Model of Strategic Behavior,* 11 Journal of Legal Studies 225 (1982). For a critical review of the question of whether law frames, overshadows, is subject to, or need have no meaningful bearing on parties' bargaining, *see, e.g.,* Jacob, H., *The Elusive Shadow of the Law,* Law & Society Review, Vol. 26, No. 3, 1992.

simply a several thousand dollar repair to cracks in the building's façade. This question can lead to multiple depositions, review of extensive documents, including daily logs, job records, plans and blueprints, Building Department filings, approvals and inspection records, photographs and sketches, not to mention extensive expert reports.

For court, all of this information would be mustered and, to the extent the jury remains awake, the information will be presented to make one or the other of the competing points. During mediation, the same case might be developed through pre-mediation statements, during the initial joint session, and through subsequent caucuses. The form of presentation, however, permits parties more quickly to get to the essence of the matter. Beyond this, there might come a point when parties, claims representatives, and counsel might—with or without the mediator's prodding—wake up. They might conclude that each group could spend hours, if not days, developing, demonstrating, and arguing its point without getting the other group materially to change its perspective or demand. They then might change the game to developing settlement proposals that meet the parties' interests of reducing cost, risk and disruption and finding resolution.

The martial arts analogy here can be to Aikido,[1] and the moves known as *iriminage*[2] or *tenkan*.[3] The gist of these moves is that, instead of directly confronting force with equal or greater opposing force, the practitioner (a) sidesteps the aggressive force and

---

[Section 3:7]

[1]Aikido is the most recently developed classical Japanese martial art. It is derived from judo, jujitsu and Iaido (the live sword technique). Its founder, Morihei Ueshiba chose the term "Ai" for its association with love and harmony. "Ki," ("chi" in Chinese) is seen as universal life force and is related to breath. "Do" means "Way." Both spiritual path and martial practice, Aikido fundamentally seeks unification of the practitioner with the universe, non-opposition. Aikido posture is a stable equilateral tetrahedron (like a pyramid) when stationary, and circular movements when in action. In lieu of the sword hilt of *Iaido* is the attacker's hand and wrist. Philosophically and functionally similar to *Tai Chi*, the basic approach of this defensive, non-competitive art is the use of circular movements to go with, and then redirect, the attacker's force, leading to a throw or pin. Ueshiba's view was that an orientation of great love or unity with the universe meant that not speed or force was needed, but that the attacker—whose hostility departs from harmony with the universal—was defeated from the time he initiated hostilities. *See,* Ueshiba, K., Aikido (Hozansha Pub. distributed by Kodansha America, Inc. through Oxford University Press 1985); Ueshiba, M, and Stevens, J. (trans. and compiler), The Essence of Aikido: Spiritual Teachings of Morihei Ueshiba (Kodansha Int'l 1999).

[2]This is also known as the "entering move" or the "twenty year move," due to the time needed for mastery of this fundamentally simple movement.

then enters (*irimi*) or (b) permits the force to stay where it is by pivoting from the point of confrontation to face the same direction as the aggressor (*tenkan*) and then leads the aggressor even slightly further forward in his path of aggression before redirecting the aggressive movement into a more constructive path—one which brings the aggressor under the practitioner's control. The lesson from Aikido is that there are times when it is better to avoid direct engagement with an issue. Many a mediation has been resolved by changing topics. Thinking about damages and transaction costs in a case such as the above construction example can obviate the need to spend a day developing the liability picture. Similarly, where one party cannot pay the bill that a judgment might represent, focusing on that party's economic condition and developing a workable deal for some form of payment, with time terms and security, might be far more productive than discussing either liability or damages. Facts, theories, arguments, legal imbroglios, and discovery battles can pile up around an issue like myriad metal filings drawn to a magnet. Mediation utilizes a neutral professional who can spot this, or encourage parties and counsel to consider this and shift the agenda to the most productive discussion.[4]

Hashing it Out—Directly or with Experts

Another discovery shortcut available in mediation is holding discussions during joint session or even through caucuses. Using the construction example again, in lieu of lengthy discovery, parties could appear at the mediation with their architect, engineer or construction professional, together with pertinent plans, specifications, drawings, photos and contract documents. In short order, under the umbrella of confidentiality provided by mediation, the Owner's architect might hash out with the general contractor, subcontractor or professional engineer associated with another party, what was or was not included in the contract,

---

[3]A snapshot demonstration of *irimi* and *tenkan* can be found online at: htt p://www.youtube.com/watch?v=N7Euz2MFg9U&feature=related.

[4]This is akin to the classic Buddhist tale of a student, Malunkyaputta, who refused to find relief from psychic pain until he had answers to all of life's metaphysical and ontological questions. The Buddha compared this student to a man on a battlefield dying from a poison arrow, refusing to take medicine or permit the arrow's removal until he had learned all details of the shooter, the arrow, and the manner in which he had been shot. By the time he could obtain answers, he would be dead. *Culamalunkya Sutta* of the *Majjhima Nikaya*, Discourse 63, *see* Warren, H. C. (trans.) Buddhism in Translation, Henry C. Warren, ed. (Cambridge; Harvard Univ., 1896) pp. 117–122, passim. Reprinted in Andrea, A. J. and Overfield, J. H. eds., The Human Record: Sources of Global History, 3rd ed., Vol. 1, (New York; Houghton Mifflin, 1998) pp. 77–79.

whether the work conformed to the specifications, or whether a particular installation met code or was reasonable under applicable quality standards.

While working on this problem, parties from both sides of the litigation "v" might sit or stand by the same side of the table, poring over plans or drawings. As one party's expert takes one view, immediately it can be questioned by the other party's expert. Through an iterative process a great deal of information can emerge quickly, potentially and literally ensuring that parties are on the same page. The differences from litigation are apparent with this approach. Rather than conduct an information tug of war, the parties in this scenario take a collaborative approach. This significantly reduces the time, cost and form of information development. In addition, as detailed below, this approach levels informational asymmetry.[5]

Reducing Information Asymmetry

Negotiation theorists make much of the impact informational asymmetry might have on the ability of parties to arrive at a deal. As parties share information in mediation, the domain of their common knowledge increases. The more knowledge they share, the less likely they will disagree over facts relating to the commonly shared knowledge. In addition, lack of knowledge might keep a party from seeing ways to satisfy that party's own interests or to meet the interests of the other party. A more common understanding of the deal or legal BATNA can also reduce the spread in what options for resolution will satisfy all parties.

One clear opportunity for reducing informational asymmetry involves expert reports. There are differences in the degree to which expert reports are required to be produced, depending on whether one is in state or federal court, and depending on whether the expert will testify or not. In addition, some expert reports are more revealing than others. Putting aside cynical interpretations of experts as professionals hired to say what furthers the hiring party's case, it is common for each party, guided by its experts, to have a different view of the science associated with a particular proposition. Having experts speak at a

---

[5]Asymmetry of information in the bargaining context has been a significant area of study in game theory and is of interest to negotiators in general. *See, generally,* Nash, J., *The Bargaining Problem,* 18 Econometrica 155 (1950); Camerer, C., *Behavioral Studies of Strategic Thinking in Games,* 7 Trends in Cognitive Science 225, 227 (2003); Sally, D.F. & Jones, G.T., *Game Theory Behaves,* The Negotiator's Fieldbook: The Desk Reference for the Experienced Negotiator (Kupfer Schneider, A., and Honeyman, C. editors, ABA Section of Dispute Resolution 2006) pp. 87–94.

mediation can dramatically reduce the knowledge gap between parties. Where parties have legitimately differing views of the risk in a case, it undoubtedly increases the likelihood of a deal to have them close that information gap through the discussions that can be had in mediation.

Going for the Gold: Efficiently Selecting Key Discovery

A repeated theme in studying mediation is that mediation is pragmatic, flexible and holistic. At any given phase, the process can involve meticulous reflection on a single consideration or, conversely, can jump past an isolated entanglement and consider the fundamental questions of what the parties need and how to get the matter comprehensively and finally resolved. With the mediator primarily acting as facilitator, there is no need conclusively to prove a case to anyone. Case assessment must simply satisfy the parties themselves, to the extent they choose to have that satisfaction. There might be times in mediation when it pays to go step by step in the consideration of facts and issues until each party comprehends where all parties stand on a given set of facts and issues and their implications, with the hope that thereafter values might be attributed to each group of facts and issues and a bargain might be struck. At any time, however, the parties are free to agree on an issue without going through the time, burden, and cost of amassing each piece of reliable evidence in admissible form. They have no one to prove it to other than themselves. With the gist of an issue, sophisticated parties can often predict how it will be factually developed and its likely outcome.

Accordingly, parties can shortcut discovery and information development in mediation through focusing on the essential message of a point of fact or issue. They can also identify a core piece of evidence that is likely to be pivotal and focus on obtaining that core evidence. If commercial trial evidence is a mosaic art, established tile by tile, mediation disclosure can, at times, be a Zen drawing—an instantly summoned image that captures the whole.

Plain Inquiry, Plain Talk

Just as the contents of disclosures can be abbreviated, so too the forms by which they are obtained and produced can be simplified in mediation. During a pre-mediation conference call with all counsel, the mediator might seek to get a read of the parties' discovery status, primarily to learn whether the parties have sufficient information to conduct a meaningful negotiation. It is not unusual for a mediator to ask whether, in lieu of formal discovery, the parties might save time and cost by simply listing the core information needed in a letter, and encouraging the parties to produce the core documents and information needed to put the parties in a position to assess the case and negotiate. Dotting of "i"s and crossing of "t"s might not be essential where the task is getting to the nitty gritty heart of a case.

Greasing the Wheels of Discovery

The mediator is not typically a Special Master appointed by the Court to resolve discovery disputes. Nevertheless, the atmosphere created by the mediation process—which includes not only the mediator but also the attitude and expectation of parties and counsel—tends to be conducive to resolving discovery issues. There is little point in proving the other counsel to be obstructionist where the mediator has no power, will make no ultimate decision (let alone a sanctions decision), and is not tasked with stacking up merits and demerits to be assessed against counsel and their respective parties. Indeed, the mediator's job is to smooth the path to getting to the core point. To the extent parties or counsel think there is benefit in currying favor with this neutral, all indicators suggest that any favor would be found in speeding the plow, candor, collaboration and pragmatism.[6] Thus, the unstated social influence, as well, supports collaborative and efficient sharing of information in mediation.

During the pre-mediation conference call, or at any time during the mediation process, it might develop that counsel believe the matter unripe for mediation. They might, for example, conclude that certain information should be nailed down before a meaningful negotiation can be held. There might be concern that the free ranging and open discussions in joint session, or even through the "telephone" game of inter-caucus communications— where messages are conveyed by the mediator from one room to the next—could empower the other party and counsel with insight into case strategy that might influence future deposition or trial testimony if the case does not settle. Alternatively, counsel might need to consult with management, a Board, or an insurance representative, prior to the mediation, to assess the "BATNA," set a

---

[6]Of course, the central ethical principle in mediation is party self-determination. *See* ABA/ABA/SPIDR Standards of Conduct for Mediators (1994), revised 2005, Standard 1 (Self-Determination). Particularly when coupled with Standard 2 (Impartiality), a mediator should not be susceptible to favoring any party regardless of whether that party chooses to make greater or lesser disclosure or prefers more or less formality in the means and manner by which information is exchanged. The point above goes to the parties' and counsel's own perceptions and tendencies in the mediation "atmosphere."

reserve, or arrive at a plan of action for the mediation. Counsel might understand the decision makers will be unable to arrive at a meaningful assessment without certain discovery and information in place.

Whatever the reason, the mediator's initial inquiry will likely be whether the information is really seen as necessary or whether from a cost/benefit analysis counsel or the party might prefer to dispense with it. Once it becomes apparent that counsel perceives a need for this information as a threshold matter before mediating, the mediator may facilitate a discussion on timing and logistics. At this juncture, the mediator can help speed the discovery process through setting dates, encouraging effective disclosure by underscoring its utility for reaching a deal, and by keying the discovery schedule to the date of pre-mediation statements and the mediation session. Likewise, even during or after a first mediation session, it might appear that further discovery will enable parties to move past a point of contention. The mediator can similarly help with discussions to arrange for the conduct and swift completion of this discovery.

Forgiveness and Accepting the Unknown

Worthy of brief mention is a topic that has gained traction in the mediation community. Justice based resolutions tend to require information—and hence disclosure—in order to produce assessments that support judgments, either by the parties or to anticipate the outcome of the legal shadow. An alternative solution that can obviate the need for information is forgiveness.[7] It is true that some information can be required to generate the

---

[7]*See, e.g.,* Sandlin, J.W., *Forgiving in Mediation: What Role?* (Advanced Solutions Mediation & Conflict Management Services, Charleston, South Carolina 29402) http://www.apmec.unisa.edu.au/apmf/2003/papers/sandlin.pdf; Braskov, S. & Neumann, A., *On Guilt, Reconciliation And Forgiveness—A Case Story About Mediation, Dilemmas And Interventions In A Conflict Among Colleagues* (Lipscomb University Institute for Conflict Management), http://www.mediate.com/articles/BraskovNeumann1.cfm; Schmidt, J. P., *Mediation and the Healing Journey Toward Forgiveness*, Conciliation Quarterly, 14:3 (Summer 1995), pp.2-4; Della Noce, D. J., *Communication Insight*, ConflictInzicht, Issue 1, February 2009; Luskin, F, Forgive for Good: A Proven Prescription for Health and Happiness (HarperCollins 2002), used in trainings on forgiveness in mediation, *see, e.g.,* http://danacurtismediation.com/dcm/forgivenessyrslater.html; and Waldman, E. & Luskin, F., *Unforgiven: Anger and Forgiveness*, The Negotiator's Fieldbook: The Desk Reference for the Experienced Negotiator (Kupfer Schneider, A., and Honeyman, C. editors, ABA Section of Dispute Resolution 2006) (hereinafter "Negotiator's Fieldbook") pp. 435–443.

apology[8] that might prompt forgiveness. Yet, for other information, we might apply the old adage: to forgive is to forget.

Similarly, even without forgiveness, negotiators can reach a point where they accept the fact that they will not or cannot know every detail pertinent to an assessment of a case, to understanding the root causes and circumstances pertaining to a dispute, or to the value or feasibility of a deal. Nevertheless, they take a deep breath and accept a deal despite a recognized lack of information. Thus, as a corollary to reducing informational asymmetry, simple acceptance of the unknown, and acceptance of the attendant risk, permits many parties to reap the reward of a resolution. This, too, ends the need for further discovery.

§ 3:8 Developing information in mediation

While we have focused on the way in which mediation expedites and truncates the process of obtaining discovery, there are circumstances when more time is afforded to a particular informational need. Take our earlier example of the construction mediation and a dialogue of experts. During the course of discussions, a question might arise concerning the roof of the building in question. It can be quite constructive to take a break to schedule a site visit by the experts, with the understanding that the mediation will reconvene soon thereafter with discussions clarified as a result of the visit. There is any number of good reasons to adjourn a mediation session in order to permit the development of information. These can include: retaining an expert who might or might not attend the next mediation session; taking the deposition of a key witness; impleading and obtaining discovery from another potentially liable party; obtaining tax or other financial information relating to an economically challenged party; developing further information on liability or damages; and developing information on the value or feasibility of a proposed deal. The decision to adjourn and seek further information is typically preceded with some type of cost/benefit analysis. We have stressed that there are times when it pays to accept the unknown or to overlook an issue. Nevertheless, mediation is not a

---

[8]*See, e.g.,* Gerarda Brown, J. & Robbennolt, J.K., *Apology in Negotiation,* Negotiator's Fieldbook, pp. 425–434; Schneider, C.D., *"I'm Sorry": The Power of Apology in Mediation,* (Association for Conflict Resolution Oct. 1999), http://www.mediate.com/articles/apology.cfm; Kichaven, J., *Apology in Mediation: Sorry To Say, It's Much Overrated,* (International Risk Management Institute Sept. 2005), http://www.mediate.com/articles/kichavenJ2.cfm; *and also see,* Garzilli, J.B., Bibliography of articles on apology in mediation, http://www.garzillimediation.com/pg247.cfm.

one note Johnny. As an expression of party self-determination and to promote understanding, the mediation process should be held at the ready to serve the parties' legitimate needs for further information.

Collaborative Information Development

Furthering the previous observation, mediation ideally can foster the collaborative approach to negotiation lauded by Fisher and Ury.[1] Thus, in mediation, parties are encouraged to share information, while respecting their freedom to control their own acts of disclosure and their strategic assessments. Fuller disclosure means that parties are making decisions with their eyes wide open. This reduces anxiety and generates a greater sense of fair dealing. Some helpful approaches to reduce informational asymmetry, and to provide all parties with the ability to make clear choices, include: preparing and exchanging binders with key documents; preparing damages spreadsheets with backup; sharing videotapes or DVDs of key facts[2]; sharing key emails; and sharing mirrored hard drives with software rendering the data searchable.[3]

§ 3:9   Confidentiality and disclosure

One hallmark of mediation is that it is a confidential process.[1] The purpose of this protection is to encourage parties and counsel to speak freely and foster open discussions aimed at understanding, reconciliation, problem solving, and resolution. It is intended to diminish the chilling affect on candor and creativity that attends the fear that admissions will be used against a party in court if the matter is not resolved in mediation. Apart from these general benefits, confidentiality in mediation affords parties some unique opportunities for handling disclosure.

[Section 3:8]

[1] *See* Fisher, Roger and Ury, Willliam, Getting to Yes: Negotiating Agreement Without Giving In (New York, NY: Penguin Books, 1983).

[2] Videos could show: a plaintiff in a personal injury case performing tasks which he claims he is disabled to do; a detailed walk through of the building site in question in a construction case; a walk-through of a ship in an admiralty case; the scene of a fire or flood loss; any number of imaginable damaged or defective goods; etc.

[3] The parties can agree to share the cost of this discovery. They might also defer the question of cost sharing until later in negotiations, to be wrapped up in a comprehensive settlement.

[Section 3:9]

[1] *See* ABA/ABA/SPIDR Standards of Conduct for Mediators (1994), revised 2005, Standard 5 (Confidentiality).

Skimming Cream from the Milk: Using Confidentiality to Draw Benefit from Information without Risky Disclosure

There are times when parties are simply uncomfortable sharing information with the other party. A recurring case of this discomfort arises in unfair competition cases. One party might accuse the other of taking a customer list or of doing business with customers who are off limits under the terms of a non-compete agreement. While each competitor refuses to show its list of customers to the other, they might be willing to share their list with the mediator. The mediator can commit not to disclose the names of customers or other sensitive information, such as pricing, profit margins, or the size of a piece of business. Nevertheless, armed with this information, and subject to the disclosing party's approval, the mediator might, for instance, be able to share his or her observation that there are no, or just a limited number of, overlapping customers. This observation can work wonders in getting parties past a standoff in an unfair competition case. Another common use of this mechanism is financial disclosure. One party may share financial information with the mediator to demonstrate inability to pay, the uncollectiblity of a judgment, or lack of resources to support a hefty punitive damage award. At times, the mediator might be able generally to confirm that there is a difficulty without all of the confidential information making its way into the hands of the other party.

Disclosures Made Solely for the Purpose of Mediation

There might also be times when parties are willing to make disclosures in the resolution focused mediation context, but are unwilling to do so in litigation. The development of financial information concerning a debtor, discussed immediately above, provides a good example. Solvency information is typically not a part of discovery during the case in chief, but rather awaits entry of a judgment and supplementary proceedings to enforce that judgment. Nevertheless, some debtors might be willing to permit the creditor to jump the line within mediation and see this information, with the understanding that this information may not be used for any other purpose if the case is not resolved. The one caveat is that once this information has been disclosed, if the mediation terminates without resolution, nothing prevents a party from serving a discovery demand or asking questions in a deposition which are designed to elicit this information.

Far Broader Range of Information

The range, depth, texture, and type of information that is pertinent to the parties and can be developed legitimately in mediation is far greater than that traditionally sought in discovery. Thus, it is good for counsel and party representatives to keep in mind that they are seeking to develop this wider assortment of information in mediation; mediation-based disclosure is not just an adjunct to litigation discovery.

Mediation is a facilitated negotiation. Therefore, the information sought is that which will help parties be effective in negotiation. Certainly, that information includes the legal BATNA. But beyond this, information should be developed, where possible, to help each party understand the other party's perspective, interests, feelings, values, goals, principles, sense of self (or identity) circumstances, position in impinging hierarchies, leverage, financial condition, and any other type of information that will aid one's party in making a deal. At its heart, the process involves a search for ways to meet the interests of all parties—to fashion options that might approximate the Pareto optimum, if possible.

Discussions in mediation will include brainstorming sessions to generate these options. During brainstorming, to enhance creativity, parties put aside judgment and willingly suspend disbelief. These sessions can be followed by more carefully evaluative sessions, where the various options are tested against reality for feasibility, and where their value is judged against legal or business alternatives. If a proposed deal involves a license grant, the feasibility of that license's being effectively and productively exploited can be tested. If it is a license to develop a certain territory, parties can seek market studies, can test the validity of the intellectual property rights, and can consider economic figures for any business unit that might be bought or sold in connection with the deal.

In short, a wealth of information other than what is typically developed in discovery may be uncovered in mediation.

§ 3:10 The spigot of disclosure

We have seen that information is the currency of mediation. The greater one's information, the greater one's power to find common ground, identify interests, see deal possibilities, understand the degree to which the other party might have flexibility, assess and apply leverage, and judge the value and feasibility of a proposed deal. The universal recognition that information is power tends to make parties wary when making disclosures, whether the disclosure is of case related information or of pure negotiation related elements. In short, people hesitate not only to disclose case weaknesses, but they also hesitate to disclose their own wants and needs out of concern that these are personal weaknesses in the bargaining arena. Ironically, just as Uncle Sol could not have arrived at the Pareto optimal division of 12 orange rinds and 12 orange pulps for Susie and Sally, negotiators cannot generate options that meet the other party's needs if those needs are not disclosed.

Similarly, lawyers are often hesitant to reveal the "smoking gun"—that surprise fact which will dramatically advance the ball in support of their case. They fear that the other side will counteract this evidence more effectively if it is revealed in advance of trial. Yet, without sharing this piece of the other party's legal BATNA, the party whom this evidence favors loses the ability to demonstrate that a proposed deal is a good one in light of the negative impact this information has on the adverse party's legal alternative.

One further challenge in disclosure is the lack of knowledge of just how much value the other party is willing to concede in order to make a deal. The term "zone of possible agreement" (ZOPA)[1] can be used to represent the range of the greatest concession of each party to a potential deal. The risk that there is a large ZOPA, generates reluctance to be the first to communicate a proposal, for fear that one is cutting off the chance of reaching a higher level of concession from the other party. Conversely, if there is a narrow ZOPA, failure to make disclosure might lead to a standoff as each party rightly perceives that the proposed deals are falling outside that party's possible concession range.

The examples above demonstrate the challenges in determining whether, when, and to what degree a party should be willing to make a disclosure. It is a psychological truism that self-disclosure builds intimacy, and that disclosure by one party increases the likelihood of disclosure by the other party. Essentially, one must give to get. At each juncture negotiators can engage in a cost/benefit analyses to assess whether disclosure, or nondisclosure, is worth the risk.

§ 3:11 Mediating discovery disputes

The focus of this Chapter, consistent with the focus of mediation itself, has been on the development of information within the

---

[Section 3:10]

[1]This term, as "zone of potential agreement," was likely coined in Lewicki, R.J., Minton, J., and Saunders, J., in Negotiation (3rd Edition. Burr Ridge, IL: Irwin-McGraw Hill, 1999). *See, also,* http://www.beyondintractability.org/essay/zopa/.

mediation context, both of the litigation discovery type and of the broader range of information that is expressed and significant in negotiation. The pragmatic and holistic nature of mediation tends to recognize that each piece of a discussion is not simply compartmentalized, but can be related to a much larger whole. Therefore, if a discovery dispute arises, it is natural for a problem solving mediator to look at the broader picture and wonder whether this is really essential, or whether it also provides an opportunity for shifting focus to resolution of the overall dispute itself. A transformative mediator will be inclined to see not only the statement being made about the discovery, but also to recognize the tone and choice involved in the communication as indicative of the quality of the parties' relationship at that moment. An understanding based mediator will see opportunities for understanding of persons and context well beyond the confines of the particular discovery dispute. Essentially, to lift a pebble in mediation is to embrace, and be embraced by, the world.

Despite this wonderful quality of mediation, nothing prevents parties or a mediator from being able to mediate a narrow set of issues, such as a discovery dispute within the litigation context. The mediator may apply the same skills of facilitating dialogue, aiding the parties in communicating their interests in the discovery, or nondisclosure, in question, helping them work to find options that meet their interests, supporting them in applying standards to work through the choice of how to resolve the dispute, and aiding them in the consideration of alternatives to proposed deals. Consideration of the BATNA in the discovery dispute can range from asking about the costs of litigating the discovery battle, the costs of discovery itself, the way the trial judge or magistrate might be predicted to rule, the impact on the judge of being presented with this problem, risk of sanctions, and the consequences of getting more or less of the discovery sought.

Mediators can be used to help resolve discovery disputes at any juncture. They can be called in well in advance of the mediation, can be engaged in connection with preparation for the mediation, can address a discovery dispute during the course of a mediation session, and can even be brought in to help the parties work through a discovery dispute after a mediation has been adjourned or put into hiatus during a subsequent substantial period of discovery.

Fortunately, because of the holistic and pragmatic nature of mediation, at any point during any of these discovery disputes, the mediator can also test to see whether the parties are open to having broader and more end game conclusive settlement discussions. As a function of party empowerment, if the answer is that parties prefer to focus the discussion on the discovery dispute itself, the discovery dispute will be the focus of that mediation session.

§ 3:12 Use of evidence and proof in mediation

We can here underscore what has been said throughout this Chapter. Mediation is a flexible, informal process, in which it is not necessary meticulously to lay out a case with each properly introduced and admitted mosaic tile of evidence. By contrast, we have also seen that information, including discovery and even evidence, can play a very meaningful role in mediation. All participants in mediation seek quickly and directly to get to the point, to the heart of a matter. In this regard, there are a variety of ways in which evidence, and the use of evidence, comes into play.

Evidence can be found in virtually all stages of mediation. It can be annexed to the pre-mediation statement. It can be shared in the opening joint session. Throughout the balance of the mediation session—both in joint session and in caucus—evidence can be considered and reconsidered, and new evidence can be introduced.

At any juncture the parties might discuss and consider the weight, credibility, implications, and significance of a piece of evidence. Even though admissibility is not a bar to discussing evidence or information in mediation, it might be a very significant topic of its own concerning a certain piece of information in mediation. For instance, the question of whether a 30 year old bordereaux in a reinsurance liquidation case will be admissible at trial as a hearsay exception under the ancient documents rule might have tremendous significance in discussion of a multimillion dollar claim that will rise or fall on the strength of the bordereaux.

As mentioned earlier, where one party considers a piece of evidence to be a smoking gun, that evidence might be discussed with the mediator alone in caucus. This can place the mediator in the awkward position of being authorized to tell the other party, in separate caucus, that the mediator has seen evidence which has a negative impact on that party's case, but that the mediator is not at liberty to elaborate about the sum, substance or provenance of the evidence. Many a party or counsel might respond by saying that they can give this no weight without further detail. Therefore, the mediator's reality testing with the party who possesses the smoking gun might be critical to assessing whether and when that evidence can be used to advance the negotiation ball.

One pattern that can emerge is increasing disclosure and assessment of evidence as the mediation proceeds, followed in the latter portion of the mediation, with a greater focus on deal making. Where one party initially believes that the other party has not been forthcoming with evidence, that party might seek to hold certain evidence pending provision of evidence by the other party. A corollary phenomenon is the expression of concern by one party that the other party is simply using mediation as "free discovery." In each instance, one value the mediator brings is finding ways to encourage parties to take modest risks to get the disclosure ball rolling. Observing that disclosure breeds disclosure and supporting parties' engagement in cost/benefit analyses can be helpful here.

It is helpful to keep in mind that resolution in mediation is achieved by the parties themselves. Sharing significant evidence with the other party, and using it in a meaningful way to demonstrate that power of the shadow of the law, can be well worth the effort because it may create the impetus to bring the matter to closure.

§ 3:13 Conclusion

Mediation is a flexible, party driven process that enables participants to address problems of minor and major magnitude. Parties may use it to address a discovery dispute within a litigation; to handle the development of information—both related to the case and related to the parties, their circumstances and their deal; and to resolve the underlying dispute that prompts counsel's discovery efforts. Whether, and when, the parties and counsel choose to use a microscope or a telescope is entirely their own decision. Mediation not only helps with the use of these tools, but also helps parties recognize and reflect on the value of the choice of which tool to use.

Chapter 4

Mediation and Electronic Discovery

*Daniel K. Gelb, Esq.**

KeyCite®: Cases and other legal materials listed in KeyCite Scope can be researched through the KeyCite service on Westlaw®. Use KeyCite to check citations for form, parallel references, prior and later history, and comprehensive citator information, including citations to other decisions and secondary materials.

---

*Daniel K. Gelb, Esq. is a partner at Gelb & Gelb LLP where he handles white collar and general criminal defense matters in state and federal court, complex civil litigation, arbitration, and regulatory proceedings. Prior to joining Gelb & Gelb LLP, Dan was an Assistant District Attorney in Massachusetts. Dan is a member of The Sedona Conference® Working Group on Electronic Document Retention and Production and an Advisory Board Member for Bloomberg BNA's *White Collar Crime Report*. He is also a member of the National Association of Criminal Defense Lawyers' ("NACDL") White Collar Crime Committee where he is the Massachusetts District Chair. Dan is a member of the Massachusetts Bar Association's Criminal Justice Section, the Massachusetts Academy of Trial Attorneys, the Massachusetts Association of Criminal Defense Lawyers, and the Criminal Law Section of the Boston Bar Association. Dan is a *Louis D. Brandeis Fellow* of the Massachusetts Bar Foundation, has been named a "Rising Star" by *Massachusetts Super Lawyers*, and is a recipient of Massachusetts Lawyers Weekly's "Excellence in the Law" award in the category of "Up & Coming Lawyers." Dan is a frequent author and lecturer on electronic evidence and discovery, civil and criminal trial practice and procedure, and is a co-author of the book *Massachusetts E-Discovery and Evidence: Preservation through Trial* (2d. ed.) (©2011) published by Massachusetts Continuing Legal Education, Inc.

§ 4:1   Introduction

As information proliferates, the burdens and costs of discovery during civil litigation and arbitration continue to increase.[1] Unfortunately, lawyers that are not familiar with how technology has greatly impacted discovery interchange in general are placing their clients at a great disadvantage. Practitioners must understand that as technology continually redefines how individuals communicate and businesses operate, electronic discovery ("e-discovery") has become inextricably tied with nearly every legal dispute.[2] Mobile communications such as cell phones and smart phones are unquestionably inundating daily life, progressively replacing the traditional landline.[3] Moreover, a new generation of business market participants—on a macro level—rely more heavily upon short messaging services ("SMS" or "text messaging") and free email services which have rapidly grown in the last couple of years.[4] The reality is that the traditional notion of the hard copy documents is becoming obsolete.[5] The volume of potential discovery is a function of the ease of use computers, Palm Pilots, smart phones and tablets (e.g., Apple's iPad) afford **both** individuals and businesses to generate electronically-stored information ("ESI"). Therefore, disputes concerning e-discovery

---

[Section 4:1]

[1]Elizabeth Chamblee Burch, Esq. *Litigating Together: Social, Moral, and Legal Obligations*, 91 B.U.L. Rev. 87, 145 (2011) *citing* Joe Nocera, "Forget Fair; It's Litigation as Usual," N.Y. Times, Nov. 17, 2007 (discussing costs of complex plaintiff's products liability class action are estimated to be between $1 million and $1.5 million to develop in order to create a path of subsequent suits at approximately $200,000); *see also* Nate Raymond, "More Attorneys Exploring Third-Party Litigation Funding," *Law.com* (ALM Media Properties, LLC) (June 4, 2010).

[2]*See* Munshani v. Signal Lake Venture Fund II, LP, 60 Mass. App. Ct. 714, 805 N.E.2d 998 (2004); Charm v. Kohn, 27 Mass. L. Rptr. 421, 2010 WL 3816716 (Mass. Super. Ct. 2010); U.S. v. Warshak, 631 F.3d 266 (6th Cir. 2010).

[3]*See* Stephen J. Blumberg, Ph.D., and Julian V. Luke, *Wireless Substitution: Early Release of Estimates From the National Health Interview Survey, July-December 2009* (Center for Disease Control & Division of Health Interview Statistics, National Center for Health Statistics) http://www.cdc.gov/nchs/data/nhis/earlyrelease/wireless201005.htm.

[4]Jefferson Graham, "E-mail carriers deliver gifts of nifty features to lure, keep users" April 16, 2008 (citing ComScore Media Metrix figures for February 2008, the article indicates Microsoft webmail with 256.2 million users, Yahoo! with 254.6 million users, Google with 91.6 million users, and AOL with 48.9 million users).

[5]*See* "Windows Live Hotmail Fact Sheet" Sept. 30, 2010 (*Windows Live Hotmail* has more than 355 million active email accounts) (found at http://www.microsoft.com/presspass/presskits/windowslive/materials.aspx).

have begun to infiltrate legal disputes, and therefore, have become a substantial factor in discovery trends and will continue as such in future legal disputes.[6]

The enactment of the amendments relating to ESI in the Federal Rules of Civil Procedure ("FRCP") on December 1, 2006, revolutionized the discovery process, making "e-discovery" central to the judicial process in *all* civil litigation in Federal Court across the United States.[7] Procedural rules relating to the exchange of ESI are the response to the growing concern that e-discovery has become a significant source of expense, time and delay on both litigants and the courts. The rapid increase of computerized data and advent of email demanded that reactive procedural mechanisms be incorporated into the FRCP which not only impacts how the parties approach discovery, but also how the Court manages it.[8] The ease of use and accessibility of documents and mobile communications are not the sole factors responsible for placing the heavy burden of cost and time on parties who must undertake e-discovery cases. Most notably, inexperienced practitioners and the diminishing numbers of trial attorneys appears to substantially contribute to litigation over discovery rather than the underlying merits of the legal dispute because trial issues are not identified and defined during discovery.

With individual and corporate litigants routinely confronting tight ligation budgets—particularly in a down economy—parties are forced to reconcile the ultimate dilemma concerning e-discovery: the possibility of compromising meritorious claims and/or defenses due to the burdens and expense of e-discovery. This dilemma is a systemic problem that should not be the con-

---

[6]*See* PRACTICE TIPS: THE DUTY TO PRESERVE ELECTRONIC EVIDENCE: WHEN IT IS TRIGGERED AND HOW TO SATISFY IT, 51 B.B.J. 13, March/April, 2007.

[7]FRCP 16 (Pre-Trial Conferences; Scheduling; Management); FRCP 26 (General Provisions Governing Discovery; Duty of Disclosure); FRCP 33 (Interrogatories to Parties); FRCP 34 (Production of Documents, ESI, and Things and Entry Upon Land for Inspection and Other Purposes); FRCP 37 (Failure to Make Disclosures or Cooperate in Discovery; Sanctions); and FRCP 45 (Subpoenas). Form 35 (Report of Parties' Planning Meeting) amends the discovery plan to include the handling of the disclosure or discovery of ESI and claims of assertion of privilege or protection as trial preparation material after production.

[8]*See generally Civil Litigation Management Manual (2d Edition)* (2010) published by The Judicial Conference of the United States Committee on Court Administration and Case Management (found at http://www.fjc.gov/public/pdf.nsf/lookup/CivLit2D.pdf/$file/CivLit2D.pdf).

trolling factor in whether or not to pursue a claim or defense.[9] Litigation decisions driven by costs rather than the merits have become the norm. However, in reality the process has become enveloped by e-discovery taking on a life of its own, thereby often becoming the driving factor when parties and counsel formulate their case strategy.

Although litigation can become unreasonably expensive, there are alternative dispute resolution ("ADR") mechanisms (i.e. arbitration and mediation) whose objectives are to simplify the dispute process, reduce costs and adjudicate matters expeditiously. This chapter discusses, among other issues, two driving concepts: (1) as e-discovery becomes more complex, expensive and time consuming, parties are utilizing mediation as a cost-effective means of making the discovery process more fluid; and (2) an alternative dispute resolution tool with the ability to reach a universal settlement by making the role ESI will likely play during litigation more tangible to the disputants.

§ 4:2 The mediation process

The mediation process is most successful when its participants *buy into it*—both literally and figuratively.[1] *Mediation* has been defined as the "[i]ntervention; interposition; the act of a third person who interferes between two contending parties with a view to reconcile them or persuade them to adjust or settle their dispute. In international law and diplomacy, the word denotes the friendly interference of a state in the controversies of others, for the purpose, by its influence and by adjusting their difficulties, of keeping the peace in the family of nations."[2] This definition was developed by Henry Campbell Black, the founder of *Black's Law Dictionary*, who saw the applicability of mediation to international legal disputes. Extrapolating the concept to modern-day disputes, mediation has certainly evolved into a process where an informal setting has the capability of producing a formal, mutually respected result.

With respect to e-discovery, mediation has been extrapolated

---

[9]*See* 33 Harv. J.L. & Pub. Pol'y 607, 611 ("Consequently, the decisions of the plaintiffs' attorneys may be driven by concern over litigation costs and personal gain rather than by an interest in obtaining the best result for class members.").

[Section 4:2]

[1]11 Harv. Negotiation L. Rev. 1, Spring, 2006.

[2]*Black's Law Dictionary*, (2nd Ed.) (1910); *see also Black's Law Dictionary*, West Publishing (9th Ed.) (2010).

into various forms and purposes. Mediation—a process which began as a mechanism to reach settlement of a legal dispute in its entirety—has developed into a niche market for parties to address the factors that come into play in complex business litigation such as securities, mass tort, and class action disputes.[3] Due to the growing expense of litigating discovery disputes, mediation of the exchange of ESI as a stepping stone towards a comprehensive resolution of the entire litigation is indicative of the economic threat e-discovery poses if it is not tamed by a neutral. The "neutral" could be a judge during the judicial process; however, should the parties wish to embark on a more discrete, cost-effective approach to complex e-discovery including the use of legal experts with expertise in technology or computer forensics experts, the best avenue may be mediation.

PRACTITIONER'S TIP: PRACTICAL ROLES OF COUNSEL

Agree to Mediate

↓

Delegate Tasks between Counsel of Record

↓

Select Mediator with Opposing Counsel and Discuss with Client

↓

Prepare Client for Mediation and Identify Necessary Data/Documents

↓

Respectfully Assist Communication between Mediator and Client

↓

Identification of Issues and Resolution(s)

---

[3]*See generally,* Robert J. Niemic, et als., *Guide to Judicial Management of Cases in ADR,* Section III, Part C (©Federal Judicial Center 2001) ("Parties may decide that the case will require such a long trial and will present such complicated legal issues and facts that jury confusion is a real possibility, making the outcome of the case difficult to predict even when the parties have great confidence in their legal positions.").

The crux of mediation is to place decision-making authority completely in the hands of the participating parties.[4] In addition to providing facilitation for resolving disputes, mediation affords to the parties legal protections when participating in the process (e.g., confidentiality).[5] However, the ultimate goal is resolution of the legal dispute at hand;[6] and, in order to reach such a result, there are five well-settled principles upon which the alternative dispute resolution community typically relies:[7]

1. *All parties must provide informed consent.* Litigants must be aware of their absolute right to information about the mediation process, the rights of the parties in the process, and the options available before agreeing to engage in mediation and possibly consenting to terms incorporated into any mediation agreement.

2. *The process must be confidential.* The mediation process must promise its participants that any information divulged to the mediator will be kept in confidence. Confidentiality not only ensures the integrity of the process, it also provides security that participants will be comfortable in discussing legal issues and facts with the mediator without waiving the attorney-client privilege and work product protection in an effort to reach a resolution.

3. *The process must be neutral and impartial.* It is crucial for the parties to feel equal in the process in order to ensure "buy-in." The very same concept is applicable the mediator who cannot appear persuaded by or biased to a party.

4. *The process must be voluntary.* It is the parties' right to consensually participate in mediation so that any agreement reached will be due the parties alone and not as a result of outside influences. Should a party feel uncomfortable or dis-

---

[4]*See, e.g.,* Marc Galanter & Mia Cahill, "Most Cases Settle": Judicial Promotion and Regulation of Settlements, 46 Stan. L. Rev. 1339, 1339–40 (1994).

[5]*See* Wagshal v. Foster, 28 F.3d 1249, 1250 (D.C. Cir. 1994) (granting immunity to a court-appointed mediator sued for an alleged breach of his confidentiality obligation).

[6]JAMS—The Resolution Experts®, "Mediation Defined" (found at http://www.jamsadr.com/adr-mediation/) ("The mediator does not decide what is "fair" or "right," does not assess blame nor render an opinion on the merits or chances of success if the case were litigated. Rather, the mediator acts as a catalyst between opposing interests attempting to bring them together by defining issues and eliminating obstacles to communication, while moderating and guiding the process to avoid confrontation and ill will. The mediator will, however, seek concessions from each side during the mediation process.").

[7]*See generally Association for Conflict Resolution* (http://www.acrnet.org/).

interested in the process, there is an absolute right to withdraw at any given point in time without consequence.

5. *Self-determination and independence.* Parties to a litigation—or potential litigation—have the opportunity to define their own issues as a party-opponent free from any outside influences or from the mediator him or herself. This independence is crucial to the parties' ultimate input into the terms of any resolution accomplished through mediation.

The abovementioned five principles of mediation are applicable to a mediation confined to e-discovery disputes. Litigants aided by counsel and e-discovery experts familiar with industry best practices can only facilitate the cost-benefit analysis of reaching a comprehensive settlement where large volumes of data are at stake. As with all expense analyses in complex litigation, it is crucial to determine the level of importance large volumes of ESI will be relative to the burden and cost of acquiring and reviewing it.[8] Therefore, litigants—or potential litigants if a complaint has not yet been filed in court—should develop a greater appreciation for the opportunities mediation affords in order to resolve e-discovery disputes in a manner other than through what may develop into protracted motion practice over pretrial discovery.[9]

For individuals and businesses, mediation is an ideal forum for exploring solutions to e-discovery matters without the risk of an uncertain result in court. Since the mediation process is confidential which enables the parties to be more forthcoming and candid about the merits and weaknesses of their positions than would be expected in an adversary proceeding in a court.[10] Moreover, the American legal system continues to develop metrics

---

[8]*See* Rander & Rozdeiczer, *Matching Cases and Dispute Resolution Procedures: Detailed Analysis Leading to a Mediation Centered Approach*, 11 Harv. Negotiation L. Rev. 1 (Spring, 2006).

[9]West Coast Life Ins. Co. v. Longboat, 2010 WL 4942146 (M.D. Fla. 2010) ("[Defendant's] assertion as to the inconvenience and burden of attending mediation is unpersuasive. Each party (whether *pro* se or represented by counsel) bears the cost of litigation. Court-ordered mediation is the most effective method-short of a privately negotiated settlement-of reducing a party's legal expenses and expediting the conclusion of litigation.").

[10]*See* Bishop v. U.S. Dept. of Homeland Sec., 2010 WL 5392897 (D.N.J. 2010) (Plaintiff alleges that DHS breached both the employment agreement and the agreement to keep confidential information disclosed during mediation. The harm connected to the latter purported "breach" is that the information may have been an element in the decision to terminate him. Thus this second purported "breach" does not supply an independent cause of action . . . [t]he law is well settled that, public employment does not . . . give rise to a contractual relationship in the conventional sense."). Bishop v. U.S. Dept. of Homeland Sec., 2010 WL 5392897 (D.N.J. 2010) citing Shaw v. U. S., 226 Ct.

to promote value in mediation through ethical standards and codes of conduct.[11] The more progressive mediation becomes in facilitating parties to incorporate e-discovery into settlement discussions, the more likely e-discovery will become a factor—and not the controlling one—during civil litigation. This is particularly the case where the United States Federal Court system, on average, dedicates approximately two years to reach and complete trials across all the jurisdictional circuits.[12]

§ 4:3 Use of mediation to structure e-discovery

One of the most import aspects of modern-day litigation is for counsel to formulate and informed approach e-discovery to determine the magnitude it will have as a case proceeds. However, notwithstanding counsel's proactive approach to e-discovery, it is one area most vulnerable to protracted litigation.[1] Notably, counsel's ability to appreciate the level of involvement ESI will have in a given case is far from perfunctory.[2] Notably, one of the great risks for parties is if counsel fail effectively com-

---

Cl. 240, 640 F.2d 1254, 1260 (1981) (quoting Urbina v. U. S., 192 Ct. Cl. 875, 428 F.2d 1280 (1970)).

[11]*See* Prof. Carrie Menkel-Meadow, *Are There Systemic Ethics Issues in Dispute System Design? And What We Should [Not] Do About It: Lessons from International and Domestic Fronts*, 14 Harv. Negotiation L. Rev. 195 (2009) citing ABA Section of Dispute Resolution, Task Force on Improving the Quality of Mediation (April 2006-March 2007) "Final Report" ("convened to consider a national credential in mediation, concluding that market conditions made it not feasible and suggesting other indicators of mediator quality to be further studied").

[12]*See Federal Judicial Caseload Statistics 2010* (Table C-05: "U.S. District Courts—Median Time Intervals From Filing to Disposition of Civil Cases Terminated, by District and Method of Disposition, During the 12-Month Period Ending March 31, 2010") (http://www.uscourts.gov/uscourts/Statistics/FederalJu dicialCaseloadStatistics/2010/tables/C05Mar10.pdf).

[Section 4:3]

[1]*See* "How to Control Litigation Costs with In-House E-Discovery" (eWeek. com) (August 8, 2009) found at http://www.eweek.com/c/a/Enterprise-Applicatio ns/How-to-Control-Litigation-Costs-with-InHouse-EDiscovery/ ("According to the Federal Judiciary, pre-trial discovery expenses alone now represent 50 percent of litigation costs in an average case. In situations where discovery is actively used, it could represent as much as 90 percent of litigation costs, approaching and perhaps exceeding $1 million on a single case.").

[2]For example, the State of New York promulgated N.Y. CPLR §§ 202. 10(b), 202.70(g) mandating that counsel must present themselves ". . . sufficiently versed in matters relating to their clients' technological systems to discuss competently all issues relating to electronic discovery . . . ." Furthermore, the rule directs counsel to seek assistance from an e-discovery consultant if necessary.

municate during the initial disclosure process to be most prepared for a court's scheduling conference.[3] Therefore, mediation can be leveraged to provide structure in otherwise complex discovery. Not only is the process more organized and productive, it is more palatable that the unpredictable litigious alternative of myopic e-discovery contests—which in the long run—have little or no impact on the dispute as a whole.

Practice Tips: How Mediation Can Provide Structure to E-Discovery

- Coordinate multi-party automatic disclosures and Fed. R. Civ. P. 26(f) conferences relieving pressure placed on litigants to pursue what can otherwise be protracted and irrelevant discovery.
- Determine mutually agreeable preservation, harvesting, review, and production protocols.
- Facilitate agreements on search terms, format of production, cost-allocation and collaborating on review tool platforms.
- Discuss scope of accessibility to opposing party's information systems, production of network schematics and investigate claims of burdensomeness and cost.
- Work with parties in drafting claw-back and quick-peeks agreements for FRE 502 safe arbor protection of privilege where applicable.
- Assist parties with protocol for compliance with state, federal and international data protection and privacy laws.
- Provide analysis and explanation of claims for spoliation (e.g., determining likelihood of establishing intent vs. negligence).
- Drafting mutually agreeable protective order language and forensics services for determining cost-effective and informal exchanges of information for preparation of mediation statements and negotiations.

Parties should also consider soliciting the assistance of a mediator in early case assessment and document review where the scope of ESI is substantial. For example, cases involving large-scale multi-district litigation and class actions claims are the kinds of disputes warranting the early-intervention of discovery mediation.

A proactive approach to the e-discovery process will enable parties to pragmatically project the impact e-discovery will have on the claims or defenses in a given dispute. In the context of media-

---

[3]Fed. R. Civ. P. 26; Fed. R. Civ. P. 16.

tion readiness, the ECA process enables counsel to determine the amount of ESI at stake, presenting a the sobering opportunity for parties to analyze what evidence is likely not readily accessible and other potential evidentiary risks.[4] In other words, ECA can act as a catalyst in engaging parties to a dispute in the mediation process.

Many complex business disputes involve intellectual property such as patents (technological and/or business method), copyrights, trademarks, service marks, trade secrets, etc. In a competitive business market where the integrity of secrecy is constantly placed at risk, organizations are less inclined to interject their propriety information into a public court record. First, protective orders that completely prevent *any* proprietary knowledge from being disclosed in litigation are difficult to ascertain.[5] This is especially the case in modern litigation where many complex business disputes arise out of technology patents and business methods protected by non-competition agreements. Therefore, prior to taking a particular position on the viability of mediation concerning a particular matter, counsel should confront the client on the comfort level of divulging at certain aspects of confidential business information into the public record.[6]

Another litigation risk—and expense—surfaces for parties involved in the potential disclosure of statutorily protected or

---

[4]*See* Helmert v. Butterball, LLC, 2010 U.S. Dist. LEXIS 60777 (E.D. Ark. May 27, 2010) *citing* Moses v. Halstead, 236 F.R.D. 667, 671 (D. Kan. 2006) ("A request for discovery should be allowed 'unless it is clear that the information sought can have no possible bearing' on the claim or defense of a party.").

[5]*See* Fed. R. Civ. P. 26(c); *see also* Phillip M. Adams & Assocs., L.L.C. v. Dell, Inc., 2008 U.S. Dist. LEXIS 96897, *18–19 (D. Utah Nov. 19, 2008) *citing* 8 Charles Alan Wright, Arthur R. Miller & Richard L. Marcus, Federal Practice & Procedure § 2043 n. 12 (2d. ed. 1994 and Supp. 2008) ("The matter was well put by the Advisory Committee on Rules of Evidence: 'The need for accommodation between protecting trade secrets, on the one hand, and eliciting facts required for full and fair presentation of a case, on the other hand, is apparent. Whether disclosure should be required depends upon a weighing of the competing interests involved against the background of the total situation, including consideration of such factors as the dangers of abuse, good faith, adequacy of protective measures, and the availability of other means of proof.'"). Wright & Miller allude to the Advisory Note to Rule 508 of proposed Federal Rules of Evidence; however, Rule 508was not ultimately adopted. *See* 26 Charles Alan Wright, Arthur R. Miller & Richard L. Marcus, Federal Practice & Procedure §§ 5641 to 5652 (2d. ed. 1994 and Supp. 2008).

[6]Federal Rules of Civil Procedure permit litigants ". . . obtain discovery regarding any matter, not privileged, that is relevant to the claim or defense of any party." Fed. R. Civ. P. 26(b)(1). Information subject to e-discovery may be proprietary and not covered by a legal privileged during the judicial process.

otherwise regulated private information.[7] Such information may be covered by statute, placing the responsibility of non-disclosure on the party responding to the discovery requests. In addition, an emerging issue in modern-day dispute resolution—including mediation—is determining risk and cost associated with cases where the ESI being pursued by the parties resides *outside* of the United States.[8] Various forums outside of the United States, such as the European Union, have directives which govern the manner in which ESI is transmitted to non-European Union countries.[9] Since electronic data is volatile and subject to alteration, potential litigants should balance the investment that will be made into cross-border disputes against the benefit of potential settlement when engaging in the ECA process.

In addition to the privacy issues addressed above, parties to any complex business legal dispute must consider any collateral regulatory consequences. Many federal and state regulators initiate proceedings—or at least investigations—where a particular legal dispute raises public concern. Although drawing the attention of regulators should not be a concern relegated to the securities industry, one example is that of a corporate defendant in a securities matter that could benefit from ECA practices that contemplate preparation for the mediation process should a defalcation on managing ESI be uncovered.

---

[7]Examples of such private information may include telecommunication and other electronically stored records (18 U.S.C.A. §§ 2510 to 2522 (Wiretap Statute); 18 U.S.C.A. §§ 2701 et seq. (Electronic Communications Privacy Act ("ECPA"); Stored Communications Privacy Act ("SCA")); and 18 U.S.C.A. §§ 3121 to 3127 (Pen/Trap Statute); for medical records: Health Insurance Portability and Accountability Act ("HIPAA") of 1996 (P.L.104-191); for financial records: Gramm—Leach—Bliley Acta/k/a Financial Services Modernization Act of 1999, (Pub. L. 106-102, 113 Stat. 1338); Right to Financial Privacy Act of 1978 (12 U.S.C.A. §§ 3401 to 3422) provides individuals with a privacy interest in their banking records held by a financial institution.

[8]Marissa L. P. Caylor, *Modernizing the Hague Evidence Convention: A Proposed Solution to Cross-Border Discovery Conflicts During Civil and Commercial Litigation*, 28 B.U. Int'l L.J. 341, 387 *citing* Keith Y. Cohan, Note, *The Need for a Refined Balancing Approach when American Discovery Orders Demand the Violation of Foreign Law*, 87 Tex. L. Rev. 1009, 1011–12 (2009) ("By establishing different standards for litigants who have information abroad and litigants who have all of their information in the United States, courts could potentially create an unlevel playing field. Companies with all of their information in the United States would face higher risks in litigation and the higher insurance premiums that attach to those risks.").

[9]*See* European Union's *Data Protection Directive* 95/46/EC.

§ 4:4 Choosing a mediator and what to expect

A mediator should be well educated, well trained, experienced and well respected. However, these qualifications are the starting point when selecting a mediator for e-discovery disputes. The mediator may have to work with the parties in a complex case with large volumes of ESI residing in various locations.

The mediator should be interviewed in person or by telephone in order to obtain a fuller understanding of the mediator's style and approach before making a selection. The mediator's orientation must be understood (i.e., facilitative, evaluative or a combination thereof), and a determination must be made as to whether the mediator is the right person to resolve the e-discovery issues to be presented. Facilitative mediators foster communications between and among parties with the hope that by doing so the parties themselves will reach common ground. Evaluative mediators attempt to bring the parties together by commenting on the strengths and weaknesses of the positions they take. Mediators who have the timing and sensitivity to apply the most effective techniques at given points during the mediation will likely have the greatest chance of success. Therefore, it is important that the mediator be creative and flexible. Additionally, acceding to the selection of the mediator proposed by the opponent party may further the mediation when the mediator favors the position of the party that did not select him or her (i.e. it is more difficult to criticize a mediator chosen by the critic).

The mediator must appreciate the context in which the mediation will occur (i.e. arbitration as opposed to litigation). First, arbitration has as its primary objectives providing a forum where disputes are resolved more efficiently, expeditiously and less expensively than in litigation. Second, the rules of the arbitration forums are far less formal than in litigation and do not contain the detail provided for in litigation to guide the parties through the e-discovery process. Third, the body of authority relating to e-discovery issues available through court rules and case law is geared to discovery where information is obtained by the use of document requests, interrogatories, requests for admissions and depositions. In contrast, e-discovery issues in arbitration arise in the context of document requests which may be the only discovery tool available to the parties absent discovery provisions in their arbitration agreement. Moreover, the litigation leverage of bring spoliation motions will not available in arbitration absent agreement of the parties otherwise. Fourth, the mediator must be able to deal with cultural differences between parties, especially if one party comes from a *common law* tradition and the other from a *civil law* tradition. Parties from the United Kingdom may have a tradition of automatic disclosure which differs from the American style of litigation. Therefore, it is important that the mediator possesses skills necessary to identify the differences and nuances between litigants, finding ways to bridge "gaps" that could have otherwise been avoided through informed cooperation between the parties. Fifth, the mediator must be a good listener and communicator, especially if there are language barriers between the parties and with the parties and the arbitral tribunal. Issues collateral to the ESI such as privacy of information may differ in the countries from which the parties and arbitral tribunal reside, and therefore, the mediator must be aware of issues to incorporate into the mediation process.

The mediator should be well organized and detail oriented. He or she should require the parties to submit mediation statements and those documents which may assist the mediator when preparing for the mediation (e.g. document retention policies; computer systems schematics). In mediating e-discovery issues, the exchange of mediation statements between the parties may move the process forward inasmuch are there are likely no issues or facts that will provide an advantage in the case if hidden. Employing a computer forensics expert to assist the mediator may be prudent in certain circumstances (e.g. the mediator does not have sufficient knowledge of technology; alternative methods for obtaining ESI should be explored).

The mediator should also be goal oriented. The parties may have to work long hours and tempers may flair during the mediation sessions. The mediator must maintain control of the process. The parties should keep in mind that even if the mediator cannot fully resolve all of the e-discovery issues, reaching resolution with respect to at least to some of the issues will likely save the time and expense for the parties which makes the mediation process worthwhile.

The mediator should discuss with counsel who will be in attendance and how the mediation will proceed. Foregoing opening statements and plenary meetings may be warranted based on the nature of the case and the relationship of the parties. At the mediation, the mediator should explain to the parties and their counsel what he or she will attempt to achieve and what ground rules will apply to the mediation sessions (e.g. confidentiality; the mediator will not be called as a witness in the case). The use of e-mediation (i.e. over the internet) where the parties are not proximate to one another should be considered.

The mediator must have a clear understanding of the facts and legal issues to be able to determine the importance of the ESI which is at issue (i.e. proportionality). The mediator must also be able to explain to the parties and counsel his or her thought processes so the reasonableness of the mediator's suggestions can be appreciated. The mediator will have to guide the parties and counsel in balancing the relevance and materiality of the ESI with the burden and expense of obtaining the ESI. For example, metadata may be of no import in a breach of contract case when the parties agree which version of the contract is final and operative. However, metadata contained in spreadsheet cells may be significant in securities cases when data has been altered prior to disclosure of the information.

The mediator must know when and how to close an agreement between the parties. A memorandum of understanding should be prepared, even if handwritten, to record the parties' agreement subject to a formal writing. The mediator should set a deadline for the completion of the final written agreement which should then be submitted to the arbitral tribunal in accordance with its rules in order to bind the parties to their agreement. Finally, the mediator should not have tunnel vision. He or she should seize every opportunity for attempting to reach a global settlement of the parties' dispute.

§ 4:5   E-discovery challenges may be avoided through mediation

The ultimate goal of mediation is to settle legal disputes. However, the process by which the mediator assists the parties in reaching a formal settlement or compromise may depend on addressing issues not directly related to the merits of the case. Therefore, "opportunity cost" should be a threshold issue in mediating complex litigation matters involving e-discovery.[1] For example, opportunity cost in litigation may be a significant factor for a plaintiff who is more concerned about the *cost of pursuing a claim* than the risk of losing at trial. However, in order to avoid the expense of high volume discovery, a party may opt not to proceed with the claim—or settle for much less. Alternatively, a defendant may deduce that settlement of a litigation demand is a better decision than defending the claim and incurring e-discovery costs. Therefore, it is important for parties and their counsel to

---

[Section 4:5]

[1]*See* Maskaev v. World Boxing Council, 2007 WL 2825728 (S.D.N.Y. Sept. 24, 2007) (granting a motion to stay litigation pending non-binding mediation, and if necessary, binding arbitration).

evaluate using mediation rather than simply deciding that litigating would be throwing "good money after bad," when e-discovery issues come into play.

Given e-discovery frequently impacts a litigant's analysis of its opportunity costs, mediation is a productive means to determine whether e-discovery should function as a quantifiable factor in reaching settlement or whether it is collateral to the dispute and at risk of being improperly leveraged to drive up costs. Additionally, parties to a transaction should decide whether mediation should be made compulsory by including such a provision in their contract. The mediation terms should provide for an approach to e-discovery protocol and the exchange of information for the parties—and the mediator—to make an informed decision about the merits of the dispute. Moreover, the exchange of ESI during the mediation process may obviate unnecessary litigation over e-discovery should the matter not reach settlement during mediation.

Compulsory mediation not only provides the parties with a more discrete mechanism to address their dispute, it is a form of alternative dispute resolution courts are disinclined to find waived absent certain factors being met.[2] First, courts will likely support compulsory mediation provided for in a contract if the process may avoid the courts having to address the issues through motion practice. Second, e-discovery, as a general proposition, will continue to evolve in synch with the progression of computer technology and remain a permanent component of the judicial process because mediators are able to devote the time necessary to remain current. Third, the parties will be able to vet e-discovery issues a reach a known result rather than having the court decide

---

[2]Maskaev v. World Boxing Council, 2007 WL 2825728 (S.D.N.Y. Sept. 24, 2007) ("Courts consider three factors in determining whether a party has waived its right to arbitration: "(1) the time elapsed from when litigation was commenced until the request for arbitration; (2) the amount of litigation to date, including motion practice and discovery; and (3) proof of prejudice."); Louis Dreyfus Negoce S.A. v. Blystad Shipping & Trading Inc., 252 F.3d 218, 229, 2001 A.M.C. 1939 (2d Cir. 2001) (citing Leadertex, Inc. v. Morganton Dyeing & Finishing Corp., 67 F.3d 20, 25 (2d Cir. 1995)). "An inquiry into whether an arbitration right has been waived is factually specific and not susceptible to bright line rules." Cotton v. Slone, 4 F.3d 176, 179, Fed. Sec. L. Rep. (CCH) P 97748 (2d Cir. 1993). "Generally, waiver is more likely to be found the longer the litigation goes on, the more a party avails itself of the opportunity to litigate, and the more that party's litigation results in prejudice to the opposing party." Thyssen, Inc. v. Calypso Shipping Corp., S.A., 310 F.3d 102, 105, 2002 A.M.C. 2332 (2d Cir. 2002).

how they should proceed.[3] In other words, building compulsory mediation into the parties' contracts may be the most effective means by which individuals and businesses can maintain control over their "e-discovery destiny."[4]

There are many issues that can be addressed with the mediator with respect to ESI; however, it is very important for counsel to effectively communicate the following issues in the client's mediation statement. The below list is not all-inclusive, but it should facilitate in framing the scope of the role ESI will play in a particular matter:

- Should a neutral computer forensics expert be retained?
- What document retention polices do the parties follow?
- What computer systems do the parties use?
- Where is the ESI located?
- Is the ESI reasonably accessible?
- What ESI must be preserved?
- What methods will be used to preserve the ESI (e.g., hold notices)?
- What is the scope of the search for the ESI based on the importance the ESI bears on the issues of the case?
- Can the information contained in the ESI be obtained from any other sources?

---

[3]*See* Swartz v. Westminister Services, Inc., 2010 WL 3522141 (M.D. Fla. 2010) ("Here, granting a stay to require the parties to negotiate and mediate in good faith concerning Plaintiff's claims is a more appropriate remedy than dismissal without prejudice. Plaintiff claims mediation will cause a delay to the proceedings in this case but the Court concludes that mediation can be coordinated amongst the parties swiftly, with nominal delay to the entirety of the proceedings. In addition, public policy is fostered by enforcing the mediation provision within the Residency Agreement, where the stay, pending mediation, will further the intent of the parties, as evidenced in the Residency Agreement, and foster the possibility for a settlement before the attorneys' fees and costs associated with this litigation grow to a point where the option of settling is rendered futile.").

[4]*See American Arbitration Association,* "Commercial Arbitration Rules and Mediation Procedure (Including Procedures for Large, Complex Commercial Disputes)," Rules Amended and Effective June 1, 2009 (http://www.adr.org/sp.asp?id=22440#A4) stating the following:

If the parties want to adopt mediation as a part of their contractual dispute settlement procedure, they can insert the following mediation clause into their contract in conjunction with a standard arbitration provision:

If a dispute arises out of or relates to this contract, or the breach thereof, and if the dispute cannot be settled through negotiation, the parties agree first to try in good faith to settle the dispute by mediation administered by the American Arbitration Association under its Commercial Mediation Procedures before resorting to arbitration, litigation, or some other dispute resolution procedure.

- What are the identities of the creators and custodians of the ESI?
- What date ranges should be used for the ESI search?
- Should the disclosure of ESI be staged?
- What, if any, metadata will be produced?
- What technology (i.e. software tools) should be used to harvest the ESI?
- How will the ESI be de-duplicated?
- Will there be data sampling?
- How will ESI which is privileged be identified?
- Will there be a claw back for inadvertently produced ESI?
- In what format should the ESI be produced (e.g. native files)?
- Are any specialized tools necessary to review the ESI, and if so, how will they be provided?
- If necessary, will legacy software be made available?
- What search terms will the parties use?
- Will an inspection facility be needed?
- Should a neutral electronic depository be used to host the ESI?
- Should the e-discovery costs be shared (even in the context of mediation), and if so, how will the costs be allocated?

Counsel should proactively address all the above issues as well as those pertaining to a specific case when comprising a mediation statement where ESI is central to the case or controversy.

§ 4:6 Utilization of technology to prepare for mediation

Mediation demands creativity from the parties in order to prevent costly disputes which, more often than not, are the consequence of the parties' lack of understanding of their *own* e-discovery.[1] In order to avoid such e-discovery disputes—should mediation not succeed and litigation ensue—it is incumbent upon

---

[Section 4:6]

[1]*See Marian Riedy, Suman Beros & Kim Sperduto, Mediated Investigative E-Discovery*, 2010 Fed. Cts. L. Rev. 1 (April, 2010) (discussing, among other issues, how e-discovery has become ". . . increasingly contentious and expensive . . . often centered over the search and retrieval methodology, the resolution of which is a substantial drain on judicial resources").

practitioners to familiarize themselves with those technological resources available in the e-discovery industry.[2]

Counsel should be able to readily cull through large volumes of data in order to identify key documents that support a settlement position. However, counsel should not become isolated in counsel's own client's e-discovery, developing strategic approaches that embrace best practices for cooperating with opposing counsel to achieve a productive discovery process.[3] Technology can be leveraged in mediation as a mechanism to control cost and cooperate on reaching productive outcomes through compromise and cooperation during the discovery process.[4]

In essence, cooperative e-discovery in the litigation context is in and of itself a mediative process, and therefore, there generally is no excuse for the parties not to evaluate whether the exchange of information can be addressed in mediation. The ability of counsel to communicate effectively about how to evaluate, exchange and host ESI is paramount. A better understanding of technological resources for e-discovery can facilitate case management for all parties involved—especially if the matter cannot be successfully mediated. Moreover, addressing e-discovery in a pragmatic and cooperative manner will only promote judicial economy in complex litigation.[5] In other words, the process is only as efficient and economical as its participants.

The following are some tools counsel may wish to consider in

---

[2]For an analysis and breakdown of current trends and certain e-discovery review and management tools, *see* "E-Discovery: *The New Order,*" (Clearwell Systems featuring research from Gartner) (©2011) ("Table 3: Information Governance and E-Discovery Vendor Taxonomy").

[3]The Sedona Conference® WG1, The Sedona Conference® Best Practices Commentary on the Use of Search & Information Retrieval Methods in E-Discovery, 8 Sedona Conf. J. 189, 215 (2007).

[4]*See* The Sedona Conference®'s Cooperation Proclamation (2008) found at http://www.thesedonaconference.org/content/tsc_cooperation_proclamation/pro clamation.pdf) ("With this Proclamation, The Sedona Conference® launches a national drive to promote open and forthright information sharing, dialogue (internal and external), training, and the development of practical tools to facilitate cooperative, collaborative, transparent discovery. This Proclamation challenges the bar to achieve these goals and refocus litigation toward the substantive resolution of legal disputes.").

[5]*See* Civil Litigation Management Manual (2d Edition) (2010) published by The Judicial Conference of the United States Committee on Court Administration and Case Management, p. 120 fn. 129 (found at http://www.fjc.g ov/public/pdf.nsf/lookup/CivLit2D.pdf/$file/CivLit2D.pdf) *citing* Emery G. Lee III & Thomas E. Willging, National, Case-Based Civil Rules Survey: Preliminary Report to the Judicial Conference Advisory Committee on Civil Rules (Fed. Judicial Ctr. 2009) (presenting findings from a national survey of attorneys, including findings on the incidence and cost of cases with electronic discovery).

determining whether mediation could assist the parties in the e-discovery process:

- *Legal Holds/Preservation Notices.* Legal hold software applications are most effective for larger organizations with multiple custodians of potentially relevant ESI. There are certain legal hold resources that track and audit litigation hold efforts and data preservation protocols. These software tools are not only extremely effective in providing the custodian of the ESI with peace of mind that preservation obligations have been employed, it also provides a sense of good faith to an opposing party that may not be as anxious to file suit upon learning a status quo has been accomplished vis-à-vis ESI.

- *Early Case Assessment.* ECA software applications to determine the volume and scope of a parties own ESI. Many e-discovery service providers are making ECA software available online as an "out-of-the-box" software as a service.

- *Hosted Document Review.* Remote document review tools are increasingly popular alternatives to in-house e-discovery review software applications where data hosting charges are affordable, and access to the information is anywhere the user can get on to the Internet.

- *Digital Forensics.* Digital forensics software, most routinely used by certified forensics experts, enables parties to harvest ESI no longer accessible in *active files* on a parties computer or media storage device (e.g., server, external hard drive, USB/flash drive, etc.). Digital forensics software may also be helpful in determining the data mining efforts a party may have to embark on should the dispute not reach a resolution through mediation.

By leveraging technology in the context of mediation preparation, a party can simultaneously prepare for litigation should the mediation process not reach the desired result. Litigation readiness and mediation readiness do not have to be mutually exclusive concepts. Furthermore, parties may utilize the assistance of mediation to reach mutually agreeable protocols for the exchange of information, claw-back and/or "quick peek" agreements.[6]

For example, Federal Rule Evidence 502 not only provides certain protections for parties at against the threat of inadvertent disclosure of legally privileged communications, it also: (1) eliminates "automatic" subject matter waiver (with the exception

---

[6]*See* Fed. R. Evid. 502.

of very unusual circumstances); (2) clarifies the consequences of inadvertent disclosure; (3) Limits the consequences of the inadvertent disclosure of an otherwise privileged document in a prior state court action; and (4) permits parties to limit expenses associated with pre-production privilege review by entering into claw-back agreements which will protect against the consequences of inadvertent disclosure. Counsel should consider reviewing the protections Fed. R. Evid. 502 contemplates but in the context of the mediation process in order to benchmark the disclosure risks a party has before becoming entrenched in litigation.

§ 4:7 Utilization of experts through the mediation

E-discovery experts are extremely valuable resources for parties to assist in mediation preparation. Whenever possible, parties should cooperate on permitting experts to attend mediation which helps the flow of technical discussion should ESI become a sticking point in negotiation of settlement.

In an effort to avoid concern that parties will attempt to leverage mediation to embark on expert discovery "fishing expeditions," counsel should agree that any information provided to the expert in mediation (including attorney-client communications) are not discoverable should the case not settle. If counsel is concerned that the client will not be protected, a consulting expert for mediation should be retained independently of a testifying expert and communication between each must be separate and independent with counsel.

In the course of researching an e-discovery expert to assist in mediation, counsel should consider some of the following factors which are not all-inclusive as additional credentials may be required (or preferred) depending on the case:

- Resume (including publications and speaking engagements)
- Online marketing and promotional activity (e.g., webinars, social media, white papers, etc.)
- Academic credentials and professional certifications/licenses
- Communication and presentation style
- Experience with courtroom testimony and susceptibility to *Daubert* challenges
- Familiarity with industry landscape and best practices
- Training and experience with digital forensic tools/software (e.g., EnCase, Forensic Toolkit, etc.)
- Rate structure and cost allocation for services rendered

The above metrics—in addition to several others important to the specific matter at hand—are useful when determining the best expert to join a mediation proceeding. In addition to assisting in the technical aspects of e-discovery mediation, digital forensics service providers can also work with counsel to assess the complexity of future work beyond mediation, and the likelihood of e-discovery expert costs being taxed if the moving party prevails.[1]

§ 4:8 Conclusion

It should be clear from the discussion above that mediation of e-discovery issues has great upside potential that outweighs any potential downside risk. Therefore, counsel's perspective should not be fear that mediation will be perceived as a sign of weakness. Rather, counsel should develop the knowledge and skills necessary to make mediation, including the resolution of e-discovery issues, a significant tool of in the adversary process.

[Section 4:7]

[1]*See* Calder v. Blitz U.S.A., Inc., 2011 U.S. Dist. LEXIS 36945 (D. Utah, Apr. 5, 2011) ("Plaintiff admits that there is a division of opinion as to whether his e-discovery vendor costs are recoverable as taxable costs. Under the circumstances and facts of this case, the court has determined that the costs sought by Plaintiff relate to tasks ordinarily undertaken by attorneys or legal assistants. Consequently, the court is not persuaded that such costs are recoverable by Plaintiff in this case as taxable costs. Accordingly, this portion of Plaintiff's motion is denied.").

Chapter 5

Using Key Word Mediation to Facilitate Efficient and Effective Electronic Discovery

*by Daniel Garrie & Yoav M. Griver**

---

*Mr. Garrie is a partner at Law & Forensics (www.lawandforensics.com) and is a renowned e-discovery special master and thought leader in the fields of information security, forensics, e-discovery, information governance, and digital privacy. Quoted in Forbes and profiled in the Los Angeles Daily Journal, he is a member of the International Institute for Conflict Prevention and Resolution (CPR) Panel of Distinguished Neutrals; a Neutral on the Hong Kong International Arbitration Centre; Chair of the Forensic and E-Discovery Panel at Alternative Resolution Centers; and an Arbitrator with the London Court of International Arbitration neutrals. Mr. Garrie has published over 100 articles and been recognized by several U.S. Supreme Court Justices for his legal scholarship. In addition, Mr. Garrie has served as an Electronically Stored Information Liaison, E-Mediator, Neutral and Expert for the L.A. Superior Courts, 2nd Circuit, 3rd Circuit, 7th Circuit, New York Supreme Court, and Delaware Supreme Court. Mr. Garrie is admitted to practice law in New York, New Jersey, and Washington State. You can reach Daniel at Daniel@lawandforensics.com.

Yoav M. Griver, Esq. is a partner in the New York office of Zeichner Ellman & Krause LLP (www.zeklaw.com) where he concentrates his practice on complex commercial litigation where he litigates commercial and intellectual property matters for clients in the banking, credit, insurance, software, and pharmaceutical industries. An adjunct professor at NYU, Yoav writes and lectures frequently on legal issues for the *Los Angeles Daily Journal, The Deal.com,* and various law journals, including on the offensive and defensive use of electronic discovery in dispute resolution. The thoughts expressed herein are solely the authors' own and not those of ARC or ZEK.

§ 5:1 Introduction

Today's litigator confronts a discovery process that threatens to consume substantial litigation resources and poses a minefield of risk for the unwary attorney. As more data goes digital, the amount of electronically-stored information ("ESI") subject to discovery obligations has grown to enormous proportions. As a rough estimate, 10 terabytes of hard drive space (roughly contained in 10 to 15 standard desktop computers) can hold more information than the printed material in the Library of Congress.[1] While attorneys are generally aware of the recent efforts of legislators and the courts to confront this discovery hydra,[2] few are aware of strategies such as key word mediation, and how to leverage this process to make electronic discovery efficient and effective.

Traditional review techniques involving hard copy documents are neither practical nor financially feasible when reviewing enormous volumes of ESI. Thus, counsel has little choice but to use search terms or "key words" in a threshold effort to isolate

---

[Section 5:1]

[1]Jessen, J., *An Overview of ESI Storage & Retrieval*, 11 SEDONA CONF. J. 237, 237 (2010).

[2]Letters from John Roberts to Nancy Pelosi and Joseph R. Biden, Jr. dated April 28, 2010, submitting to the Congress the amendments to the Federal Rules of Civil Procedure adopted by the Supreme Court of the United States pursuant to Section 2072 of Title 28, United States Code, *available at*: http://www.supremecourt.gov/orders/courtorders/frcv10.pdf; Ashcroft v. Iqbal, 556 U.S. 662, 129 S. Ct. 1937, 1945, 1950, 173 L. Ed. 2d 868, 2009-2 Trade Cas. (CCH) ¶ 76785, 73 Fed. R. Serv. 3d 837 (2009) (noting "concern at the prospect of subjecting [petitioners] . . . to the burdens of discovery . . .," and holding that "Rule 8 . . . does not unlock the doors of discovery for a plaintiff armed with nothing more than conclusions"); Bell Atlantic Corp. v. Twombly, 550 U.S. 544, 559, 127 S. Ct. 1955, 167 L. Ed. 2d 929, 2007-1 Trade Cas. (CCH) ¶ 75709, 68 Fed. R. Serv. 3d 661 (2007) (". . . it is only by taking care to require allegations that reach the level suggesting conspiracy that we can hope to avoid the potentially enormous expense of discovery in cases with no reasonably founded hope that the [discovery] process will reveal relevant evidence . . . .") (internal quotations omitted).

the pertinent wheat from the electronic chaff.[3] Counsel (or the court) must then identify the right search terms and apply them to the proper databases and files.[4] Disputes over search methodology can result in the court deciding how the search will be conducted, requiring prolonged litigation and expending valuable judicial resources on issues ancillary to the merits of a case.[5]

An alternative to selection of terms by a party or the court is "key word mediation." This is a process by which the parties jointly select a mediator, neutral, or special master who possesses a thorough understanding of the legal elements of the case, the procedural aspects of electronic discovery, and most importantly, the information technology systems that will be subject to key word search. The mediator can then facilitate the selection of key words and resolve issues regarding the databases and files to be searched. This process benefits all parties as well as the court because (1) the parties maintain control over the key word selection process, and (2) a mediator can expedite an agreement. Such cooperative measures were contemplated in the landmark case,[6] in which Judge Sheindlin notes that "it might be advisable to solicit a list of search terms from the opposing party for [the purpose of preservation], so that [opposing counsel] could not later complain about which terms were used."[7]

§ 5:2 Differences between electronically-stored information and traditional documents

ESI is fundamentally different from traditional paper documents in many ways which make traditional document review and discovery techniques inapplicable. Among other differences,

---

[3]Victor Stanley, Inc. v. Creative Pipe, Inc., 250 F.R.D. 251, 257, 70 Fed. R. Serv. 3d 1052 (D. Md. 2008) ("it is universally acknowledged that keyword searches are useful tools for search and retrieval of ESI . . . .").

[4]See, Northington v. H & M Intern., 2011 WL 663055 (N.D. Ill. 2011), report and recommendation adopted, 2011 WL 662727 (N.D. Ill. 2011) (failure to search minor misspellings held sanctionable); Nycomed U.S. Inc. v. Glenmark Generics Ltd., 2010 WL 3173785 (E.D. N.Y. 2010) (finding failure to identify and search appropriate electronic databases sanctionable).

[5]See e.g., Laethem Equipment Co. v. Deere & Co., 261 F.R.D. 127, 80 Fed. R. Evid. Serv. 692 (E.D. Mich. 2009) (action sidetracked for 20 months in electronic discovery disputes); William A. Gross Const. Associates, Inc. v. American Mfrs. Mut. Ins. Co., 256 F.R.D. 134, 135 (S.D. N.Y. 2009) (parties who could not agree on key word search left the court in the "uncomfortable position" of crafting and imposing its own search methodology).

[6]Zubulake v. UBS Warburg LLC, 229 F.R.D. 422, 94 Fair Empl. Prac. Cas. (BNA) 1, 85 Empl. Prac. Dec. (CCH) P 41728 (S.D. N.Y. 2004).

[7]229 F.R.D. at 432 n. 75.

unlike traditional paper documents, ESI is volatile, portable, distributed, persistent, and high volume.

A. ESI is Volatile

The vast majority of ESI is "volatile," meaning it is stored for short periods of time and then vanishes when the storage device's power source is cut off. Nonetheless, this volatile ESI is increasingly coming within the purview of electronic discovery obligations.[1]

B. ESI is Portable

Digital evidence is portable; it can be stored on mobile or portable devices such as mobile phones, thumb drives, and laptops. Such decentralized storage practices present risks to counsel, and counsel and their clients are increasingly subject to sanctions for failure to preserve evidence on portable mobile devices.[2]

C. ESI is Distributed

Besides being portable, ESI is distributed, and may be found across a variety of media and platforms. Thus, ESI could take the form of, *inter alia*, e-mail and attachments, instant messages, document metadata, voicemail and unified messaging data, or portal and web content such as blogs, wikis, and social media content. Moreover, ESI could be found in a variety of locations and storage media, for example in a client's corporate headquarters on-premises, in backup tapes or archives, online, in thumb drives, or disks, in a client's branch offices on servers, in laptops or desktops, backups or mobile devices, or in a home office on mobile devices or personal computers.

D. ESI is Persistent

ESI (that is not volatile) is also "persistent," in that it is not as

---

[Section 5:2]

[1]*See e.g.*, Columbia Pictures, Inc. v. Bunnell, 245 F.R.D. 443, 69 Fed. R. Serv. 3d 173 (C.D. Cal. 2007) (ordering defendants to capture and preserve Internet Protocol addresses that servers stored in volatile memory and did not otherwise permanently log).

[2]*See e.g.*, Kvitka v. Puffin Co., L.L.C., 2009 WL 385582 (M.D. Pa. 2009) (Court struck plaintiff's complaint and granted adverse inference to defendant where plaintiff discarded laptop allegedly used to send emails at issue.); Moreno v. Ostly, 2011 WL 598931 (Cal. App. 1st Dist. 2011), unpublished/noncitable (Court sanctioned plaintiff and plaintiff's counsel where they hid plaintiff's disposal of laptop and cell phones from the court, rejecting counsel's explanation that he was torn between "competing duties" of candor to the court and zealous representation of his client.).

easily destroyed as a paper document, which can be shredded or burnt. Judge Scheindlin explored this issue in the *Zubulake* opinion stating:

> "Deleting" a file does not actually erase that data from the computer's storage devices. Rather, it simply finds the data's entry in the disk directory and changes it to a "not used" status—thus permitting the computer to write over the "deleted" data. Until the computer writes over the deleted data, however, it may be recovered . . . Deleted data may also exist because it was backed up before it was deleted.

Zubulake, 217 F.R.D. at 313 n. 19 (internal quotations and citations omitted).

Similarly, Magistrate Judge Facciola noted "e-mails, even if deleted, may be recoverable from other places within [a] computer, such as its 'slack space.' "[3]

E. ESI is Voluminous

ESI frequently presents challenges fundamentally different to traditional evidence in the sheer volume of discoverable data. This volume exacerbates existing challenges of locating relevant evidence, preserving the evidential weight, chain of custody and defensibility of evidence, maintaining the transparency and validation of the discovery process, ensuring accuracy and completeness of electronic evidence, and proving the reliability and trustworthiness of evidence.

For example, in *U.S. v. Philip Morris USA, Inc.,*[4] *two hundred million* emails were searched by key word mechanism to narrow the document set down to two hundred thousand emails. Of these, only one hundred thousand were found relevant, resulting in a privilege review of all one hundred thousand emails. Eighty thousand emails were produced while twenty thousand were noted in privilege logs. After the dust settled over this extensive discovery effort, only *five* of these emails were used at trial.

The *Phillip Morris* case and other cases referenced above illustrate three problems posed by electronic discovery: (1) time,

---

[3]Peskoff v. Faber, 2006 WL 1933483 (D.D.C. 2006), subsequent determination, 240 F.R.D. 26, 67 Fed. R. Serv. 3d 760 (D.D.C. 2007), subsequent determination, 244 F.R.D. 54 (D.D.C. 2007), citing U.S. v. Triumph Capital Group, Inc., 211 F.R.D. 31, 46 n.7 (D. Conn. 2002) (" 'Slack space' is the unused space at the logical end of an active file's data and the physical end of the cluster or clusters that are assigned to an active file. Deleted data, or remnants of deleted data can be found in the slack space . . . .").

[4]U.S. v. Philip Morris USA, Inc., 396 F.3d 1190, R.I.C.O. Bus. Disp. Guide (CCH) P 10815 (D.C. Cir. 2005).

i.e. the problem of searching for a needle in a haystack, especially where that haystack is portable and distributed; (2) litigation resources, i.e. the process of culling the wheat from the electronic chaff can tie up counsel's and the court's resources with issues ancillary to the merits of the case, particularly where technical issues related to information storage, volatility, or persistence lead to discovery disputes; and (3) money, i.e. the immense cost of complying with discovery obligations to avoid disputes ancillary to the merits. This three-headed electronic discovery Cerberus has the potential to trap unwary counsel in the netherworld of discovery litigation, exposing counsel to risks of sanctions while the merits of a case remain unresolved.

§ 5:3   Challenges of effectively searching electronically-stored information

Courts have acknowledged the "challenge of overseeing discovery at a time when potential access to [ESI] is virtually limitless, and when the costs and burdens associated with full discovery could be more outcome-determinative, as a practical matter, than the facts and substantive law."[1] Indeed the technicalities of the subject can be daunting even for experienced attorneys and judges:

> Whether search terms or "keywords" will yield the information sought is a complicated question involving the interplay, at least, of the sciences of computer technology, statistics and linguistics. . . . . Given this complexity, for lawyers and judges to dare opine that a certain search term or terms would be more likely to produce information than the terms that were used is truly to go where angels fear to tread.[2]

These challenges can lead to extended litigation over the technical and specialized areas of electronic search and the precise obligations of counsel in preserving, collecting, searching,

---

[Section 5:3]

[1]Cache La Poudre Feeds, LLC v. Land O'Lakes, Inc., 244 F.R.D. 614, 620, 68 Fed. R. Serv. 3d 1181 (D. Colo. 2007).

[2]U.S. v. O'Keefe, 537 F. Supp. 2d 14, 24, 69 Fed. R. Serv. 3d 1598 (D.D.C. 2008) (internal citations omitted); *see also*, Equity Analytics, LLC v. Lundin, 248 F.R.D. 331, 333 (D.D.C. 2008), ("determining whether a particular search methodology, such as keywords, will or will not be effective certainly requires knowledge beyond the ken of a lay person (and a lawyer) and requires expert testimony . . . .").

retrieving and reviewing ESI.[3] Failure to use the right key words or search proper databases can result in sanctions litigation with possible adverse consequences to counsel and their clients.[4]

Counsel and the courts should be aware of the many search techniques applicable to ESI. These include, in addition to key word searching: "fuzzy" searching, which returns documents containing words with spelling similar to the search term; "Boolean" searching, allowing the exclusion or inclusion of certain terms using Boolean operators; concept searching, which seeks documents related by concept to a word; "latent semantic indexing," which uses indexing based on co-occurrence or clustering of terms; "text clustering," which relates documents that have many terms in common; and "Bayesian search," which applies Bayesian statistics in searching. Counsel faced with this bewildering array of search methodologies may be ill-equipped to properly navigate electronic discovery disputes relating to adequacy of search.[5] Acknowledging the possibilities for error, one court imposed a requirement on counsel analyzing privilege issues of testing a key word search for accuracy by further sampling a subset of documents: "The only prudent way to test the reliability of the keyword search is to perform some appropriate sampling of the documents determined to be privileged and those determined not to be in order to arrive at a comfort level that the categories are neither over-inclusive nor under-inclusive."[6]

Indeed, there are many possible sources of error when conducting a key word search. "Digital" words are merely strings of ones

---

[3]*See e.g.*, Peskoff v. Faber, 2006 WL 1933483 (D.D.C. 2006), subsequent determination, 240 F.R.D. 26, 67 Fed. R. Serv. 3d 760 (D.D.C. 2007), subsequent determination, 244 F.R.D. 54 (D.D.C. 2007) (questions regarding adequacy of search of emails of former employees email account required parties to file "detailed" affidavits and an evidentiary hearing requiring testimony of "employees and other witnesses").

[4]Diabetes Centers of America, Inc. v. Healthpia America, Inc., 2008 WL 336382 (S.D. Tex. 2008) (in discussing discovery sanctions motion, noting that a junior associate worked with "little supervision or direction" and that the search terms used by associate were "inadequate"); Victor Stanley, 250 F.R.D. at 257 ("all keyword searches are not created equal; and there is a growing body of literature that highlights the risks associated with conducting an unreliable or inadequate keyword search or relying exclusively on such searches for privilege review") (finding privilege waived as to 165 documents inadvertently produced due to faulty key word search); 2010 WL 3173785, at *1 (party required to pay $125,000 for failure to identify and search appropriate electronic databases).

[5]Indeed, new search methodologies continue to be developed, for example, Gene Zyrl Ragan's "content-based implicit search query" (U.S. Patent Application No. 11/139131, Publication No. 20,060,271,520 (published Nov. 30, 2006)).

[6]*Victor Stanley,* 250 F.R.D. at 257.

and zeroes and do not contain within them the rich layers of contextual meaning which is the stuff of ordinary language.[7] Even in lay usage the same word may take on different meanings and connotations. References, usage, or dictionary definitions can all yield different answers to the question "what does that word mean." For example, the word "issue" could refer to any number of concepts including a question, a problem, a pet peeve, an inheriting descendant, or as a verb in which a judge may "issue" a judgment. Yet a basic key word search algorithm returns results merely based on the ones and zeroes which represent the string "issue" regardless of such contextual meanings. Moreover, language usage changes depending on the medium of communication,[8] and an idea communicated through email or text message will take a different form when communicated in a more formal writing or a more informal voicemail.[9] This can lead to both under and over inclusive results returned by any search method.

Questions and "issues" confronting counsel include double quoting, i.e. statements referring to other actions or statements, "noise" or "filler" words, such as "a," "and," "the," etc., Boolean operators that appear in natural language, and case sensitivity (i.e. "a" versus "A"). These issues require counsel to adequately define the scope of their searches, search appropriate headers, and use correct operators and syntax. Technical issues need careful consideration, including target data sources, character coding of the text, e.g. UTF-8, UTF-16, or CP1252, and special character sets. Even savvy counsel who consult a client's Information Technology (IT) department to gain a basic understanding of their client's systems would be unlikely to know, for example, the differences involved in recovering data from an AS400 or an OS390W machine.

The technical nature of these tasks often leads courts to ap-

---

[7]*William A. Gross Const. Associates, Inc.,* 256 F.R.D. at 136 ("'[K]eyword searches do not reflect context. They can also miss documents containing a word that has the same meaning as the term used in the query but is not specified.'") quoting, Grenig, et al., ELECTRONIC DISCOVERY & RECORDS MANAGEMENT GUIDE: RULES, CHECKLISTS & FORMS (2009 ed.), § 15:15.

[8]Describing the close interconnection between medium and content, in the coinage of communications theorist Marshall McLuhan, "the medium is the message." McLuhan, M., UNDERSTANDING MEDIA: THE EXTENSIONS OF MAN (Mentor Press, New York NY 1964), reissued (MIT Press, Cambridge, Massachusetts 1994).

[9]The availability of ESI in non-text forms, such as voicemail or video, raises a host of additional issues regarding search methodology and adequacy of search.

point experts where the parties cannot agree.[10] Key word mediation can bring in expertise early on, facilitating more efficient, cooperative resolution of discovery issues rather than adversarial
and prolonged motion practice and court involvement.

§ 5:4 Key word mediation: an overview

Before going into key word mediation, as with any mediation,
counsel should have a clear idea of timeline, budget and scope of
the mediation. In addition, counsel should have some idea of the
IT systems their clients use, including how clients manage information and what systems may be impacted. Counsel should
consider bringing an IT person and/or a technical document such
as a data map, to assist the mediation. Finally, counsel should
provide the mediator with a concise statement of the case, a
proposed list of key words sought and the reasoning behind this
selection, a summary of the internal cost breakdown of performing the search and a brief summary of the search method sought
(e.g. Boolean, Bayesian, etc.). Selection of an appropriate mediator is as important as this preparation by counsel. Counsel should
consider selecting mediators specifically qualified in the technical
aspects of electronic search and electronic discovery, rather than
mediators solely qualified in a certain aspect of industry or the
law relevant to the case (e.g. an ARIAS mediator with extensive
experience in insurance).

Once the parties have selected a mediator and made preliminary arrangements, the mediation is ready to begin.[1] Usually a
mediator will give an opening speech explaining the process and
any guidelines specific to that mediator or mediation. A good
mediator should explain that he or she acts as a neutral and will
not advocate for any party or take on decision-making authority.
Moreover, the mediator should maintain strict confidentiality in
his or her discussions with the parties. After these preliminaries,
the mediator will allow opening statements by the parties.
Because this is often the first forum where parties can fully hear
each other's side of a discovery dispute, this airing out of issues

---

[10]See, e.g. *Equity Analytics, LLC,* 248 F.R.D. at 331 (appointing computer
forensics expert at cost to the parties to resolve discovery issues); William A.
Gross Const. Associates, Inc. v. American Mfrs. Mut. Ins. Co., 256 F.R.D. 134
(S.D. N.Y. 2009) (crafting a search methodology based on keywords produced by
the parties where the parties could not agree on proposed keyword search of
nonparty's ESI).

[Section 5:4]

[1]Riskin, L., *Understanding Mediators' Orientations, Strategies, and
Techniques: A Grid for the Perplexed,* 1 HARV. NEGOT. L. REV. 7, 24 (1996).

can itself lead to a quick resolution of discovery disputes. After these opening statements, the parties will then caucus individually with the mediator. The mediator should help the parties understand the BATNA/WATNA, or "best alternative to a negotiated agreement" and "worst alternative to a negotiated agreement," so counsel can intelligently stake out their negotiating positions. The mediator should at all times maintain confidentiality and attempt to articulate even contentious and aggressive positions in a neutral manner, thus reaching an agreement on key words and databases to be searched.

Having facilitated this agreement, the mediator should insist that the parties test these proposed key words against a sample subset of the ESI. This step is crucial as it allows for early detection of inadequate or ineffective key word searches, preventing later disputes.[2] Finally, as the mediator does not retain decision making authority, the mediator should assist the parties in documenting the agreement as a stipulation to be so ordered or as a proposed discovery order. Done properly, key word mediation facilitates a mutually-agreed discovery protocol based on a full airing of relevant issues, leading to efficient and effective electronic discovery.

§ 5:5 Conclusion

Because of the unique nature of ESI, electronic discovery presents a three pronged problem of time, resources and money. Moreover the technical nuances involved in preserving, collecting, searching, retrieving and reviewing ESI can lead even experienced attorneys and judges into confusion. Key word mediation is a powerful method for efficiently and effectively cutting through the quagmire of electronic discovery. It should be in every attorney's toolkit, so counsel and courts can devote their scarce time and resources to the merits of a case.

---

[2]In re Seroquel Products Liability Litigation, 244 F.R.D. 650, 662 (M.D. Fla. 2007) (". . . key word searching . . . must be a cooperative and informed process . . . . Common sense dictates that sampling and other quality assurance techniques must be employed to meet requirements of completeness").

Chapter 6

The Role of Special Master in Electronic Discovery

*by Daniel B. Garrie, Jeffrey Rosenfeld, and Michael Sherman**

---

*Mr. Garrie is a Partner at Law & Forensics (www.lawandforensics.com) and is a renowned e-discovery special master and thought leader in the fields of information security, forensics, e-discovery, information governance, and digital privacy. Quoted in Forbes and profiled in the Los Angeles Daily Journal, he is a member of the International Institute for Conflict Prevention and Resolution (CPR) Panel of Distinguished Neutrals; a Neutral on the Hong Kong International Arbitration Centre; Chair of the Forensic and E-Discovery Panel at Alternative Resolution Centers; and an Arbitrator with the London Court of International Arbitration neutrals. Mr. Garrie has published over 100 articles and been recognized by several U.S. Supreme Court Justices for his legal scholarship. In addition, Mr. Garrie has served as an Electronically Stored Information Liaison, E-Mediator, Neutral and Expert for the L.A. Superior Courts, 2nd Circuit, 3rd Circuit, 7th Circuit, New York Supreme Court, and Delaware Supreme Court. Mr. Garrie is admitted to practice law in New York, New Jersey, and Washington State. You can reach Daniel at Daniel@lawandforensics.com.

Jeffrey Rosenfeld is counsel at Bingham McCutchen. His practice focuses on complex litigation involving securities, bankruptcy, intellectual property, corporate governance and other business disputes. He has been listed as a "Rising Star" in Super Lawyers Magazine since 2005. Mr. Rosenfeld is a member of Bingham McCutchen's Electronic Document Retention and Discovery group, which helps clients navigate the complexities of electronic discovery and use it to their strategic advantage in litigation.

Michael Sherman is a partner at Bingham McCutchen. He is an accomplished trial lawyer in high-stakes, "bet-the-company" litigation, and was named to the "Daily Journal" list of top 100 Lawyers in the State of California in 2009, and one of his trial victories in 2009 was named to the "Daily Journal" list of top defense verdicts of 2009. He has handled a number of cases involving e-discovery disputes.

> **KeyCite**ʀ: Cases and other legal materials listed in KeyCite Scope can be
> researched through the KeyCite service on Westlawʀ. Use KeyCite to check
> citations for form, parallel references, prior and later history, and comprehen-
> sive citator information, including citations to other decisions and secondary
> materials.

§ 6:1   Introduction

As discussed in Chapter 2, changes in technology, litigation
best practices, case law, and state and federal rules of civil procedure all drive a need for increased expertise in electronic
discovery. Practitioners must work with their clients and experts
to institute methods to identify, collect, preserve, process, and
disclose sometimes massive amounts of electronically stored information ("ESI").[1] Some of this information, such as e-mails between the parties before litigation, is easily accessible and likely
relevant.[2] Other information, such as deleted files,[3] metadata,[4]

[Section 6:1]

[1]*E.g.*, Whitlow v. Martin, 263 F.R.D. 507, 509 (C.D. Ill. 2009) (sustaining
and overruling Lower Court's granting of plaintiff's requested ESI during
discovery due to massive quantity); Young v. Pleasant Valley School Dist., 2008
WL 2857912 (M.D. Pa. 2008) (denying plaintiff's request to search through millions of emails); High Voltage Beverages, LLC v. Coca-Cola Co., 2009 WL
2915026 (W.D. N.C. 2009) (ruling defendant's production of over three million
documents in electronic form satisfied their burden); In re Hecker, 430 B.R. 189,
194, 197, 53 Bankr. Ct. Dec. (CRR) 76 (Bankr. D. Minn. 2010) (ruling defendant's production of an external hard drive with approximately one million
files and folders was not sufficient because the information was scrambled and
ordering sanctions); *see also Survey of Legal Holds Practices in Global 1000
Companies Released by CGOC and Huron Consulting Group*, BUSINESS WIRE, 2
(last visited Feb. 7, 2011) *available at*: http://op.bna.com/dde.nsf/r?Open=cleu-7k
fkkn ("Today, managing legal holds involves thousands of matters with tens of
thousands of custodians and millions of gigabytes of collected information.").

[2]*See. e.g.*, Petcou v. C.H. Robinson Worldwide, Inc., 2008 WL 542684 (N.D.
Ga. 2008) (discussing testimony that undeleted emails are easily acceptable,
and deleted emails may be recovered at a higher cost).

[3]A "deleted file" is "[a] file with disc space that has been designated as
available for reuse; the deleted file remains intact until it is overwritten." THE
SEDONA CONFERENCE® GLOSSARY: E-Discovery & Digital Information

and operating system information,[5] may also be relevant, but not as readily accessible.[6]

Disputes about ESI can become a determinative and expensive part of any case.[7] The sheer volume of data that must be processed, its malleability, the risks of intentional manipulation

---

Management (2nd ed.); A Project of The Sedona Conference® Working Group on Electronic Document Retention & Production (Dec., 2007 version).

[4]"Metadata" is "[d]ata typically stored electronically that describes characteristics of ESI, found in different places in different forms. It can be supplied by applications, users or the file system. Metadata can describe how, when and by whom ESI was collected, created, accessed, modified and how it is formatted. It can be altered intentionally or inadvertently. Certain metadata can be extracted when native files are processed for litigation. Some metadata, such as file dates and sizes, can easily be seen by users; other metadata can be hidden or embedded and unavailable to computer users who are not technically adept. Metadata is generally not reproduced in full form when a document is printed to paper or electronic image. *See also* Application Metadata, Document Metadata, Email Metadata, Embedded Metadata, File System Metadata, User-Added Metadata, and Vendor-Added Metadata. For a more thorough discussion, see The Sedona Guidelines: Best Practice Guidelines & Commentary for Managing Information & Records in the Electronic Age (Second Edition)." *Id.*

[5]An "Operating System" ("OS") ". . . provides the software platform that directs the overall activity of a computer, network or system, and on which all other software programs and applications can run. In many ways, choice of an operating system will effect which applications can be run. Operating systems perform basic tasks, such as recognizing input from the keyboard, sending output to the display screen, keeping track of files and directories on the disc and controlling peripheral devices such as disc drives and printers. For large systems, the operating system has even greater responsibilities and powers—becoming a traffic cop to makes sure different programs and users running at the same time do not interfere with each other. The operating system is also responsible for security, ensuring that unauthorized users do not access the system. Examples of operating systems are UNIX, DOS, Windows, LINUX, Macintosh, and IBM's VM. Operating systems can be classified in a number of ways, including: multi-user (allows two or more users to run programs at the same time—some operating systems permit hundreds or even thousands of concurrent users); multiprocessing (supports running a program on more than one CPU); multitasking (allows more than one program to run concurrently); multithreading (allows different parts of a single program to run concurrently); and real time (instantly responds to input-general-purpose operating systems, such as DOS and UNIX, are not real-time)." *Id.*

[6]*See generally* Daniel B. Garrie & Bill Spernow, *Legally Correct But Technologically Off the Mark*, 9 Nw. J. TECH. & INTELL. PROP. 1 (Oct., 2010) *available at* http://www.law.northwestern.edu/journals/njtip/v9/n1/1/ (discussing the different levels of accessibility and potential relevance of data).

[7]*See, e.g.*, Newman v. Borders, Inc., 257 F.R.D. 1, 3–4 (D.D.C. 2009) (noting that potential legal fees associated with electronci discovers may dwarf potential recovery and ordering questions about email systems to be answered by affidavit instead of deposition); Oracle Corp. v. SAP AG, 566 F. Supp. 2d 1010 (N.D. Cal. 2008) (noting that discovery of ESI could cost as much as $16.5

and inadvertent spoliation of evidence, combine to create traps for the unwary practitioner.[8] Increasingly, litigants, courts, arbitrators and mediators face arguments about ESI that can eclipse the underlying issues in the case.[9] In response, parties and courts increasingly are turning to special masters to provide analyses and make recommendations in this area.[10]

§ 6:2   What is a special master

A special master (also known as a master or referee) is a person appointed by a court, arbitrator, or other decision-making body to make factual determinations in complicated cases.[1] In e-discovery disputes, special masters may be tasked with reviewing technical compliance with discovery requests,[2] routing out attempts to

---

million); *Young, 2008 WL 2857912, at *1* (asserting that a single search of documents would initially cost $10,000).

[8]*See, e.g.,* Qualcomm Inc. v. Broadcom Corp., 2008 WL 66932 (S.D. Cal. 2008), vacated in part, 88 U.S.P.Q.2d 1169, 2008 WL 638108 (S.D. Cal. 2008) ("Qualcomm II") (imposing sanctions for intentionally or recklessly failing to meet electronic discovery obligations); Telequest Intern. Corp. v. Dedicated Business Systems, Inc., No. 06-5359 (PGS), 2009 U.S. Dist. LEXIS 19546, at *14–15 (D.N.J. Mar. 11, 2009) (discussing that to incur sanctions, spoliation must be intentional or negligent); World Courier v. Barone, 2007 WL 1119196 (N.D. Cal. 2007) (discussing and partially granting monetary sanctions and adverse jury instruction where electronic evidence was intentionally destroyed by defendant's husband).

[9]*See,* Mark A. Fellows & Roger S. Haydock, *Federal Court Special Masters: A Vital Resource in the Era of Complex Litigation,* 31 Wm. Mitchell L. Rev. 1269, 1295 (2005), *available at* http://www.courtappointedmasters.org/Articles/F ellowsHaydock.pdf ("[J]udges are increasingly aware of the effect of litigation complexity on the tractability of discovery and recognize Special Master appointments as a curative option."). *See also* Moody v. Tuner Corp., No. 1:07-cv-692, at *2 (S.D. Ohio Sept. 9, 2010).

[10]Paul v. USIS Commercial Services, Inc., 2007 WL 2727222 (D. Colo. 2007) (discussing use of special masters when electronic discovery is highly disputed). *See* Correy E. Stephenson, *Use of Special Masters in E-Discovery Disputes on the Rise,* www.newenglandinhouse.com (Mar. 31, 2008), http://ne wenglandinhouse.com/2008/03/31/use-of-special-masters-in-ediscovery-disputes-on-the-rise/ (discussing the perceived increase in use of special masters in e-discovery disputes).

[Section 6:2]

[1]Fed. R. Civ. P. 53(a)(1)(C) (notes of advisory committee on 2003 amendments to rules) ("The appointment of masters to participate in pretrial proceedings has developed extensively over the last two decades as some district courts have felt the need for additional help in managing complex litigation.").

[2]Board of Regents of University of Nebraska v. BASF Corp., 2007 WL 3342423 (D. Neb. 2007) (appointing a computer forensics expert to assist in fur-

avoid compliance,[3] opining on intentional or reckless spoliation of evidence,[4] and determining whether discovery orders are being followed.[5] Recently, Courts have appointed special masters to determine whether predictive coding is an appropriate method of culling through large amounts of data to find relevant and responsive information.[6]

Courts and arbitrators may be unfamiliar with the latest methods of storing, processing, copying, retaining or hiding ESI, and often do not have the resources to devote to learning them.[7] That is why technically proficient special masters, sometimes working in concert with computer forensics experts, are needed to resolve complex e-discovery issues.[8] Special masters have the

---

ther discovery when plaintiff did not meet the obligation to affirmatively direct complete compliance with the order in objective good faith); Wachtel v. Health Net, Inc., 239 F.R.D. 81 (D.N.J. 2006) ("Wachtel II") (appointing special master in light of a lengthy pattern of repeated and gross non-compliance with discovery).

[3]*E.g.*, Maggette v. BL Dev. Corp., No. 2:07CV181-M-A, 2010 U.S. Dist. LEXIS 91647, *13 (N.D. Miss. Sept. 2, 2010) (discussing Special Master's finding of bad faith when appointed to investigate allegations of concealing responsive documents).

[4]*E.g.*, Medcorp, Inc. v. Pinpoint Technologies, Inc., 2010 WL 2500301 (D. Colo. 2010) (reviewing Special Master's decision on sanctions for spoliation in the form of an adverse jury instruction *de novo*).

[5]*E.g.*, Wixon v. Wyndham Resort Development Corp., 2009 WL 3075649 (N.D. Cal. 2009) (rejecting SM's conclusion that defendant was not required to produce documents on a certain drive, and rejecting SM's conclusion that defendant should not be sanctioned).

[6]Da Silva Moore v. Publicis Groupe, 2012 WL 607412 (S.D.N.Y. Feb. 24, 2012) ("This judicial opinion now recognizes that computer-assisted review is an acceptable way to search for relevant ESI in appropriate cases.").

[7]*See*, Victor Stanley, Inc. v. Creative Pipe, Inc., 250 F.R.D. 251, 259–62, 70 Fed. R. Serv. 3d 1052 (D. Md. 2008) *citing* U.S. v. O'Keefe, 537 F. Supp. 2d 14, 24, 69 Fed. R. Serv. 3d 1598 (D.D.C. 2008) ("Whether search terms or 'keywords' will yield the information sought is a complicated question involving the interplay, at least, of the sciences of computer technology, statistics and linguistics . . . . Given this complexity, for lawyers and judges to dare opine that a certain search term or terms would be more likely to produce information than the terms that were used is truly to go where angels fear to tread.").

[8]*See, e.g.*, Gipson, et al. v. Southwestern Bell Tel. Co., No. 08-2017-EFM-DJW, 2008 U.S. Dist. LEXIS 103822, at *6 (D. Kan. Dec. 23, 2008) (recommending a special master appointment in a complex case involving 115 motions in just one year); Costello v. Wainwright, 387 F. Supp. 324, 325 (M.D. Fla. 1973) (appointing a special master where evidence likely to be highly technical).

expertise to analyze case specific facts and circumstances, and confirm compliance or unearth devious acts done, to hide ESI.[9]

Special masters may be appointed with or without the consent of the parties or pursuant to a motion.[10] The scope of the special master's authority may be limited by the appointment or reference order,[11] the statutory basis,[12] or the rules of due process.[13]

---

[9]*See, e.g.*, Eastman Kodak Co. v. Sony Corp., 2006 WL 2039968 (W.D. N.Y. 2006) (adopting Special Master's recommendation that Eastman Kodak had complied with Sony's discovery request notwithstanding Sony's objection as to the form of production); Maggette, 2010 U.S. Dist. LEXIS 91647, at *11, 60–63 (imposing sanctions where the Special Master found in just minutes information that defendant, "a sophisticated corporation with very significant financial resources, had repeatedly and stridently insisted did not exist for close to five years").

[10]Fed. R. Civ. P. 53(a)(1)(A) (notes of advisory committee on 2003 amendments to rules) ("Subparagraph (a)(1)(A) authorizes appointment of a master with the parties' consent."). *See*, Schwimmer v. U.S., 232 F.2d 855, 865, 56-2 U.S. Tax Cas. (CCH) P 9711, 50 A.F.T.R. (P-H) P 644 (8th Cir. 1956) ("Beyond the provisions of [Fed. R. Civ. P. 53] for appointing and making references to Masters, a Federal District Court has 'the inherent power to supply itself with this instrument for the administration of justice when deemed by it essential.' ").

[11]Fed. R. Civ. P. 53(b)(2) (requiring that the appointment order state the scope of a Special Master appointment); *see, e.g.*, In re New York Bextra and Celebrex Prod. Liab. Litig., Index No. 560001/2005, Case Management Order No. 10 (June 21, 2006) (appointment of the honorable Fern M. Smith as Special Master) *available at* http://www.nycourts.gov/supctmanh/Mass%20Tort%20PDF s/Bextra%20Cel%20CMO%2010.pdf (appointing a special master and defining scope of authority under N.Y. Comp. Codes R. & Regs. tit. 22, § 202.14 (2006)); *see generally* Mark A. Fellows & Roger S. Haydock, *Federal Court Special Masters: A Vital Resource in the Era of Complex Litigation*, 31(3) WM. MITCHELL L. R. 1269, 2004 *available at* http://www.courtappointedmasters.org/Articles/Fel lowsHaydock.pdf (discussing the revised Rule 53(2)(b)).

[12]Fed. R. Civ. P. 53(a)(1) (providing for the scope of the appointment of a Special Master "[u]nless a statute provides otherwise . . . ."). *See*, Cobell v. Norton, 334 F.3d 1128, 1143–44 (D.C. Cir. 2003) (overruling District Court's appointment of a special master where appointment was in conflict with "28 U.S.C. § 455(a): A judicial officer must be disqualified from 'any proceeding in which his impartiality might reasonably be questioned,' that is, questioned by one fully apprised of the surrounding circumstances.") *citing* Sao Paulo State of Federative Republic of Brazil v. American Tobacco Co., Inc., 535 U.S. 229, 232–33, 122 S. Ct. 1290, 152 L. Ed. 2d 346 (2002) (*per curiam*).

[13]Fed. R. Civ. P. 53(b)(1) (requiring that parties received notice and opportunity to be heard prior to the appointment of a Special Master); *see*, McGraw-Edison Co. v. Central Transformer Corp., 308 F.2d 70, 135 U.S.P.Q. 53, 6 Fed. R. Serv. 2d 959 (8th Cir. 1962) (arguing that unnecessary appointment of a special master could amount to denial of due process of law); *see, e.g.*, Cobell v. Norton, Case No. 1:96CV01285, at 1–2 (D.D.C. Oct. 2, 2002) (Special Master-Monitor Joseph S. Kieffer, III) (presenting due process challenge to the appointment of a special master).

When the appointment order is broad enough, a special master may hold hearings, entertain legal argument, subpoena records from third parties, review information produced by parties to the litigation, question witnesses, work with client information-technology representatives, and take nearly any other steps to resolve factual questions. Generally, proceedings before a special master are more fluid than those before a court.[14] A special master may act as mediator over certain disputes, providing a neutral perspective that allows for practical resolutions.[15]

By appointing a special master a court can conserve judicial resources.[16] In turn, however, a special master may tax the resources of the parties. Unlike a judge, a special master is typically paid by the hour.[17] They must be briefed on the factual and legal issues in the underlying case, so that they are aware of the significance of the particular dispute they are tasked with resolving.[18] They may require third party consultants,[19] travel ex-

---

[14]*See, Civil Litigation Management Manual*, THE JUDICIAL CONFERENCE OF THE UNITED STATES THE COMMITTEE ON COURT ADMINISTRATION AND CASE MANAGEMENT (2001) http://www.scribd.com/doc/8763686/CIVIL-LITIGATION-MANAGEMENT-MANUAL ("Masters can be useful adjuncts for a variety of tasks in the management of complex or large-scale litigation: supervising discovery, finding facts in complicated controversies, performing accountings, organizing and coordinating mass tort litigation, mediating settlements, and monitoring compliance with complex remedial orders."); *e.g.*, U.S. v. Microsoft Corp., 147 F.3d 935, 954, 1998-1 Trade Cas. (CCH) ¶ 72188, 41 Fed. R. Serv. 3d 216 (D.C. Cir. 1998) (appointing a special master to oversee discovery and also to propose findings of fact and conclusions of law).

[15]*See generally* THE SEDONA PRINCIPLES: BEST PRACTICES RECOMMENDATIONS & PRINCIPLES FOR ADDRESSING ELECTRONIC DOCUMENT PRODUCTION 40 (Jonathan M. Redgrave, Esq. et al. eds., July 2005) ("One immediate benefit of using such a court appointed 'neutral' third party is the probable elimination of privilege waiver concerns with respect to the review of information by that person.").

[16]*See generally* Martin Well, *How to Reduce E-Discovery Costs*, WWW.ASSOCIATEDCONTENT.COM, (Oct 28, 2010) http://www.associatedcontent.com/article/5944822/how_to_reduce_ediscovery_costs.html?cat=15 (discussing how hiring an expert to provide early case assessment can save money and time in the discovery process).

[17]*See, e.g.*, Capital Records Inc. v. Jammie Thomas-Rasset, No. 06-cv-1497 (D. Minn. June 18, 2010) *available at* http://www.scribd.com/doc/33247217/Order-appointing-special-master-in-Capitol-v-Thomas-Rasset (appointing a Special Master at the rate of $400 per hour).

[18]*E.g.*, 3D Systems, Inc. v. Envisiontec, INC., Case 2:05-cv-74891-AC-RSW, Document 64 (E. D. Mich. S. Div. Feb. 20, 2007) (appointment and order of reference to special master) *available at* http://ftp.resource.org/courts.gov/recop/pacer/ecf.mied/09711078635.pdf ("The Special Master shall confer with the parties to arrange a schedule for briefing and other matters.").

penses, and assistants to thoroughly analyze the problems.[20] The costs of a special master can also multiply due to uncooperative witnesses, parties, and counsel. If the order appointing the special master so allows, the special master may make recommendations as to which party ought to bear the costs related to the appointment.[21] Attorneys should understand the costs and the benefits of appointing a special master before advocating for or against one.

Acting as mediator, investigator, technologist, finder of fact and advisor to the judge or arbitrator, who will ultimately make decisions in the case, the special master has considerable latitude to follow leads and open areas of investigation that might not otherwise be practical for an arbitrator or court.[22] Since special masters usually work closely with the parties and ultimate decision-maker, a proficient special master can dissuade parties from taking the types of actions that frustrate the purposes of discovery.[23] For example, a special master may advise a party to take steps to preserve relevant data or advise parties on how to retained experts to focus their analysis.[24]

E-discovery proceedings before a special master end with the

---

[19]*See* Multiven, Inc. v. Cisco Systems, Inc., 2010 WL 2813618 (N.D. Cal. 2010) (suggesting that parties hire a third party vendor to assist in document review and a special master to resolve discovery disputes).

[20]*See generally* David I. Levine, *Calculating Fees of Special Masters*, 37 HASTINGS L. J. 141 (1985) (discussing the nature of Special Masters' fees and issues that can arise in fee calculation).

[21]*See, e.g.*, REV 973, LLC v. John Mouren-Laurens, Case No. CV98-10690 AHM (ex) (C.D. Cal. Jan. 7, 2003) (order adopting, as modified, report and recommendation of Special Master) *available at* http://rev973vsmloc.com/020204do cs/order111202.pdf (recommending that cost sharing of Special Master's fee not be extended to new parties joining litigation).

[22]*See generally, Appointing Special Masters and Other Judicial Adjuncts a Handbook for Judges and Lawyers*, ACAD. OF COURT-APPOINTED MASTERS, 1–7 (2009), http://www.fjc.gov/public/pdf.nsf/lookup/ACAM2009.pdf/$file/ACAM2009. pdf (providing detailed explanation of the many types of Special Masters available for appointment).

[23]*See, e.g.*, Key Equip. Fin., Inc. v. Americap Credit, LLC, Case No. 4:2005cv00585 (D.C. S.D. Tex, Houston Div. Feb. 22, 2005) (J. Hughes) (imposing sanctions where, notwithstanding computer forensic expert's speech dissuading parties from deleting files, finding evidence of a trail of deleted evidence).

[24]*See generally* Shira A. Scheindlin & Jonathan M. Redgrave, *Special Masters and E-Discovery: The Intersection of Two Recent Revisions to the Federal Rules of Civil Procedure*, 30 CARDOZO L. REV. 347, 383–84 (Nov., 2008) http://w ww.cardozolawreview.com/content/30-2/SCHEINDLIN.30.2.pdf (discussing the facilitative role of e-discovery special masters).

issuance of a final report.[25] Interim reports may also be submitted, both by the parties and the special master, to the court or arbitrator.[26] The special master's report should contain a detailed analysis of the methods used, the relevant law, problems encountered, solutions offered, and factual findings.[27]

As technologies for storing, copying, and moving ESI multiply, special masters will be needed more often to resolve discovery disputes.[28] Opinions by prominent jurists, including Honorable Judge Shira A. Scheindlin,[29] Honorable Judge John M. Facciola,[30] and Honorable Judge Andrew J. Peck,[31] place the burden on attorneys to know how to properly and effectively advise their clients to preserve, manage and produce ESI in an efficient and effective manner. The penalties for failing to do so can be harsh.[32]

---

[25]*See*, Fed. R. Civ. P. 53(e) ("A master must report to the court as required by the appointing order."); Benjamin v. Fraser, 343 F.3d 35, 45 (2d Cir. 2003) (overruled by, Caiozzo v. Koreman, 581 F.3d 63 (2d Cir. 2009)) ("The master's responsibilities typically culminate in a report. If the report includes findings of fact, they are binding in non-jury actions unless clearly erroneous. Fed.R.Civ.P. 53(e)(2).").

[26]*E.g.*, State of Nebraska v. State of Wyoming, 515 U.S. 1, 9, 115 S. Ct. 1933, 132 L. Ed. 2d 1 (1995) (special master submitting multiple interim reports).

[27]*E.g.*, Montana v. Wyoming, 130 S. Ct. 1753, 176 L. Ed. 2d 210 (2010) (first interim report of the special master) *available at* http://www.askaspecialm aster.com/downloads/Original-No.-137-Montana-v.-Wyoming-and-North-Dakot a.pdf (detailing a complex case involving multiple states' water rights).

[28]Barbara J. Rothstein & Thomas E. Willging, MANAGING CLASS ACTION LITIGATION: A POCKET GUIDE FOR JUDGES, FEDERAL JUDICIAL CENTER, at 39 (3rd ed. 2010) ("The emergence of electronic discovery and of a new industry of party experts on electronic discovery may increase the need for the court to appoint a discovery master.").

[29]*E.g.*, Zubulake v. UBS Warburg LLC, 229 F.R.D. 422, 94 Fair Empl. Prac. Cas. (BNA) 1, 85 Empl. Prac. Dec. (CCH) P 41728 (S.D. N.Y. 2004) (J. Scheindlin).

[30]*E.g.*, U.S. v. O'Keefe, 537 F. Supp. 2d 14, 69 Fed. R. Serv. 3d 1598 (D.D.C. 2008) (J. Facciola).

[31]*E.g.*, Anti-Monopoly, Inc. v. Hasbro, Inc., 1995-2 Trade Cas. (CCH) ¶ 71218, 1995 WL 649934 (S.D. N.Y. 1995) (J. Peck).

[32]*See, e.g.*, Qualcomm Inc. v. Broadcom Corp., Case No. 05cv1958-B (BLM), 2008 U.S. Dist. Lexis 911, at *71 (S.D. Cal. Jan. 7, 2008) (finding that Qualcomm intentionally withheld tens of thousands of decisive documents the court orders Qualcomm to pay Broadcom $8,568,633.24); Victor Stanley, Inc. v. Creative Pipe, Inc., No. MJG-06-2662, 2008 U.S. Dist. LEXIS 42025 (D. Md. Jan. 24, 2011) (awarding $1,049,850.04 in attorney's fees and costs as sanctions for discovery abuse).

Valuable claims or defenses can be lost due to a client's failure to properly preserve and produce evidence.[33]

Proceedings before a special master can lead to discovery of critical information. In egregious cases, where one side in the litigation has destroyed, failed to preserve, or otherwise made information unavailable, a special master's report can lead to termination of litigation or default judgments.[34]

§ 6:3   History of appointing special masters

Special masters, masters, or referees, have been appointed for hundreds of years to assist judicial bodies in resolving complicated factual disputes.[1] An early case by the California Supreme Court explains that a reference may be ordered "[w]hen the trial of an issue of fact requires the examination of a long account on either side."[2]

The length of special master appointments, as well as the scope and subjects can vary widely. The longest appointment on record is that of Tennessee attorney, Walter Armstrong. Armstrong was appointed by the United States Supreme Court in 1969, in a case

---

[33]*See,* Innis Arden Golf Club v. Pitney Bowes, Inc., 257 F.R.D. 334, 335, 70 Env't. Rep. Cas. (BNA) 1045 (D. Conn. 2009) (precluding any evidence based on destroyed soil samples); Asher Assoc., LLC v. Baker Hughes Oilfield Operations, Inc., Civil Action No. 07-cv-01379-WYD-CBS, 2009 U.S. Dist. LEXIS 40136, at *21 (D. Colo. May 12, 2009) (precluding certain testimony due to plaintiff's failure to preserve evidence); *see also* Richard H. Agins, Comment, *An Argument for Expanding the Application of Rule 53(b) to Facilitate Reference of the Special Master in Electronic Data Discovery,* 23 PACE L. REV. 689, 710 ("failure to employ qualified technical experts can seriously impair one's own case and can result in substantial damage to the opposing party's operations").

[34]In *Jane Doe v. Smith Corp. et al. (Super. Ct. Cal.),* a special master was appointed "to hear evidence and make recommendations to the court with respect to the issue of compliance" with the court's previous order. The case was settled and dismissed soon after the Special Master issued his report on the matter.

[Section 6:3]

[1]*See,* Shira A. Scheindlin & Jonathan M. Redgrave, *Special Masters and E-Discovery: The Intersection of Two Recent Revisions to the Federal Rules of Civil Procedure,* 30 CARDOZO L. REV. 347, 350 n.18 (Nov., 2008) *available at* http://www.cardozolawreview.com/content/30-2/SCHEINDLIN.30.2.pdf ("As early as 1917, Judge Learned Hand found such an appointment to be permissible. *See* Pressed Steel Car Co. v. Union Pac. R. Co., 241 F. 964, 967 (S.D. N.Y. 1917) (stating that most convenient way to conduct discovery would be for the parties to agree upon a master).").

[2]Williams v. Benton, 24 Cal. 424, 425, 1864 WL 594 (1864); *see also* Gunter v. Sanchez, 1 Cal. 45, 46, 1850 WL 588 (1850) (upholding decision by referees before enactment of statute allowing for reference).

to determine the seaward boundaries of states along the Gulf of Mexico.[3] Mr. Armstrong did not complete his duties until 1990.[4] The use of special masters in e-discovery disputes follows logically from the history of courts turning to special masters to solve a wide variety of complex disputes.[5]

The Honorable Judge Shira Scheindlin, U.S. District Court for the Southern District of New York has guided courts throughout the country with her decision in *Zubulake*.[6] She has said that special masters can be appointed in e-discovery "for a narrow dispute, such as a privilege review, or a broader task like supervising all discovery."[7]

§ 6:4   History of appointing special masters—Statutory basis for appointing special masters

1. Federal

Rule 53 of the Federal Rules of Civil Procedure governs the appointment of special masters in federal courts. The rule provides that, unless a statute provides otherwise, a court may only appoint a special master only to "(A) perform duties consented to by the parties; (B) hold trial proceedings and make or recommend findings of fact on issues to be decided without a jury if appointment is warranted by: (i) some exceptional condition; or (ii) the need to perform an accounting or resolve a difficult computation of damages; or (C) address pretrial and posttrial matters that

---

[3]U.S. v. Louisiana, 394 U.S. 11, 35–36, 89 S. Ct. 773, 22 L. Ed. 2d 44, 1969 A.M.C. 1019 (1969), decision supplemented, 394 U.S. 836, 89 S. Ct. 1614, 23 L. Ed. 2d 22 (1969), decision supplemented, 525 U.S. 1, 119 S. Ct. 313, 142 L. Ed. 2d 1 (1998) ("[W]e have decided to refer to a Special Master the task of resolving in the first instance several of the particularized disputes over the precise boundary . . . .").

[4]U.S. v. Louisiana, 498 U.S. 9, 15, 111 S. Ct. 377, 112 L. Ed. 2d 269 (1990) ("After his final accounting has been approved and any balance due him has been paid, the Special Master shall be deemed discharged with the thanks of the Court.").

[5]*See In re Oil Spill by the Deepwater Horizon,* CASE 2:10-MD-02179-CJB-SS, DOCUMENT 349 (Sept. 24, 2010) *available at* http://www.masstortdefense.com/uploads/file/BP.pdf ("Because of the complex nature of [this case], notably the numerous and varied defendants and issues, the Court has determined that appointment of a special master is warranted.").

[6]Zubulake v. UBS Warburg LLC, 229 F.R.D. 422, 94 Fair Empl. Prac. Cas. (BNA) 1, 85 Empl. Prac. Dec. (CCH) P 41728 (S.D. N.Y. 2004).

[7]*E.g.* Correy E. Stephenson, *New niche for e-discovery: Special Masters,* WWW.ALLBUSINESS.COM (Jan. 28, 2008), http://www.allbusiness.com/legal/trial-procedure-pretrial-discovery-electronic/8891805-1.html.

cannot be effectively and timely addressed by an available district judge or magistrate judge of the district."[1]

Before appointing a special master the court must give the parties notice and the opportunity to be heard.[2] The order appointing the special master must set forth:

(A) the master's duties, including any investigation or enforcement duties, and any limits on the master's authority under Rule 53(c); (B) the circumstances, if any, in which the master may communicate ex parte with the court or a party; (C) the nature of the materials to be preserved and filed as the record of the master's activities; (D) the time limits, method of filing the record, other procedures, and standards for reviewing the master's orders, findings, and recommendations; and (E) the basis, terms, and procedure for fixing the master's compensation under Rule 53(g).[3]

Furthermore, the order appointing the special master must set forth the master's hand.

Additionally, the proposed master must file an affidavit, disclosing any grounds for disqualification under 28 U.S.C.A. § 455, such as circumstances in which his or her impartiality may be questioned.[4] The parties then have the opportunity to move for disqualification.[5] Failure to move for disqualification based on disclosures constitutes a waiver.[6]

Once appointed, under the federal rules, a special master may

---

[Section 6:4]

[1]Fed. R. Civ. P. 53; *Jordan v. Jordan,* Nos. 09-FM-1152, 09-FM-1337, 10-FM-375 (D.C. Ct. App. Mar. 10, 2011) *available at* http://scholar.google.com/scholar__case?case=12950623124568316849&q=%22Rule+53+governs%22&hl=en&as__sdt=2,33 ("Rule 53 governs the use of 'special masters . . .' "); *but see* Constant v. Advanced Micro-Devices, Inc., 848 F.2d 1560, 1566, 7 U.S.P.Q.2d 1057 (Fed. Cir. 1988) *citing* In re Peterson (State Report Title: Ex Parte Peterson), 253 U.S. 300, 312, 40 S. Ct. 543, 64 L. Ed. 919 (1920) (arguing that a federal courts has the inherent power to appoint persons unconnected with the court to aid judges in the performance of specific duties); Glover v. Udren, 2012 WL 1436564 (W.D. Pa. Feb. 16, 2012) ("There is no legal authority supporting plaintiff's position that a magistrate judge cannot appoint a special master.").

[2]Fed. R. Civ. P. 53(b)(1); *see, e.g.,* In re Vioxx Products Liability Litigation, 501 F. Supp. 2d 789, 791–92 (E.D. La. 2007) (giving parties notice and opportunity to be heard on the issue of whether to appoint a special master).

[3]Fed. R. Civ. P. 53(b)(2).

[4]Fed. R. Civ. P. 53(b)(3)(A). *See* Cobell v. Norton, 334 F.3d 1128, 1143–44 (D.C. Cir. 2003) (overruling District Court's appointment of a special master where appointment was in conflict with 28 U.S.C.A. § 455(a)).

[5]Fed. R. Civ. P. 53(b)(3)(B).

[6]First Iowa Hydro Elec. Co-op. v. Iowa-Illinois Gas & Elec. Co., 245 F.2d 613, 627 (8th Cir. 1957) ("Failure to make timely objection to the appointment

exercise certain authority, as outlined in the Federal Rules of Civil Procedure.[7] These include regulating the proceedings and exercising their discretion in what measures are appropriate, such as evidentiary hearings and imposition of sanctions.[8]

The special master is required to file his or her report with the court, and serve copies on the parties.[9] The court then must give the parties notice and an opportunity to be heard on the report or recommendations of the master.[10]

The order appointing a special master should address whether the special master is permitted to communicate ex parte with the

of a Master either at the time of the order or promptly thereafter constitutes a waiver of error . . .").

[7]Fed. R. Civ. P. 53(c)(1) ("(A) regulate all proceedings; (B) take all appropriate measures to perform the assigned duties fairly and efficiently; and (C) if conducting an evidentiary hearing, exercise the appointing court's power to compel, take, and record evidence."); see, Ballard v. Consolidated Steel Corp., 61 F. Supp. 996, 1006 (S.D. Cal. 1945) (authorizing a special master, under Rule 53(c), to take evidence, review documents introduced into evidence, and to make findings and conclusions).

[8]Fed. R. Civ. P. 53(c)(2) ("The master may by order impose on a party any noncontempt sanction provided by Rule 37 or 45, and may recommend a contempt sanction against a party and sanctions against a nonparty."); see, e.g., E.I. DuPont de Nemours & Co. v. Waters, 287 Ga. 235, 695 S.E.2d 265, 266 (2010) (appointing a special master with the auhtoirty to impose sanctions); Chesa Intern., Ltd. v. Fashion Associates, Inc., 425 F. Supp. 234, 238, 193 U.S.P.Q. 506 (S.D. N.Y. 1977), aff'd, 573 F.2d 1288 (2d Cir. 1977) (upholding sanctions ordered by Special Master for defendant's failure to comply with production request); Denton v. Mr. Swiss of Missouri, Inc., 564 F.2d 236, 195 U.S.P.Q. 609, 1977-2 Trade Cas. (CCH) ¶ 61667, 24 Fed. R. Serv. 2d 431 (8th Cir. 1977) (upholding monetary sanctions imposed by Special Master as part of discovery dispute).

[9]Fed. R Civ. P. 53(e); e.g., In re Bridgestone/Firestone, Inc., ATX II, & Wilderness Tires Prod. Liab. Litig., MASTER FILE NO. IP 00-9373-C-B/S, MDL No. 1373, at 5 (S.D. Ind. Nov. 1, 2000) available at http://www.askaspecialmast er.com/wp-content/uploads/downloads/2010/12/In-re-BRIDGESTONE-FIRESTO NE-INC.-ATX-Hon.-Sarah-Evans-Barker-Chief-Judge.pdf (order of appointment of special master) (ordering that, pursuant to Rule 53(e), at the completion of duties, other than those of assisting, advising or consulting with the Court, "the Special Master shall promptly file a report upon the matters submitted to her and shall serve a copy of the report on each party").

[10]Fed. R Civ. P. 53(f)(1). In the Knott case the district court, "without notifying the parties or giving them an opportunity to object, took the full evidentiary record and made findings of fact and conclusions of law based upon the record taken before the special master." Henry A. Knott Co., Div. of Knott Industries, Inc. v. Chesapeake and Potomac Telephone Co. of West Virginia, 772 F.2d 78, 80, 3 Fed. R. Serv. 3d 945 (4th Cir. 1985). In reversing, the Fourth Circuit noted the fact that the Special Master's report, and the Court's resulting findings and conclusions, involved determinations of credibility. See, Id.

parties or the court.[11] The 2003 advisory committee notes provide as follows:

> Ex parte communications between a master and the court present troubling questions. Ordinarily the order should prohibit such communications, assuring that the parties know where authority is lodged at each step of the proceedings. Prohibiting ex parte communications between master and court also can enhance the role of a settlement master by assuring the parties that settlement can be fostered by confidential revelations that will not be shared with the court. Yet there may be circumstances in which the master's role is enhanced by the opportunity for ex parte communications with the court. A master assigned to help coordinate multiple proceedings, for example, may benefit from off-the-record exchanges with the court about logistical matters. The rule does not directly regulate these matters. It requires only that the court exercise its discretion and address the topic in the order of appointment.
>
> Similarly difficult questions surround ex parte communications between a master and the parties. Ex parte communications may be essential in seeking to advance settlement. Ex parte communications also may prove useful in other settings, as with in camera review of documents to resolve privilege questions. In most settings, however, ex parte communications with the parties should be discouraged or prohibited. The rule requires that the court address the topic in the order of appointment.

In some cases, the ability of a special master to communicate ex parte will change throughout his or her appointment. When a special master is appointed to analyze a factual dispute and make recommendations, it may be appropriate for the special master to have ex parte communications with the trier of fact without the knowledge of the parties. In other cases, the Court may limit ex parte communications to matters which do not concern the merits of the matter in dispute.[12]

If, for example, the Court later finds it desirable to use the

---

[11]*E.g., In re Chinese Mfd. Drywall Prod. Liab. Litig.*, MDL No. 2047, SECTION L, at 3 (E.D. La. Nov. 29, 2009) *available at* http://www.askaspecialmaster.com/wp-content/uploads/downloads/2011/01/UNITED-STATES-DISTRICT-COURT-E ASTERN-DISTRICT-OF-LOUISIANA-IN-RE-CHINESE-MANUFACTURED-D RYWALL-PRODUCTS-LIABILITY-LITIGATION-JUDGE-FALLON-MAG-JUD GE-WILKINSON.pdf (authorizing the Special Master to communicate ex parte with the Court and parties, without notice, as he deems appropriate).

[12]In EEOC v. United States Steel Corp., 2012 U.S. Dist. LEXIS 49167 (W.D. Pa. Apr. 5, 2012), defendant U.S. Steel sought to disqualify a special master and avoid the results of her report on the grounds improper ex parte communications purportedly in violation of such an order. The Court analyzed the substance of the communications, and determined that it did not concern the merits because "it would not cause an objective, reasonable layperson to believe that the Special Master's impartiality or her Reports and Recommendations had been tainted." *See also* In re FEMA Trailer, 2011 WL 5038849 (E.D.

special master as a mediator regarding the merits of a particular dispute, which mediation would require disclosure of information by the parties to the special master that the parties would prefer to keep from a final adjudicator, the Court may redefine the scope of allowed ex parte communications with the Court regarding that dispute.[13]

A party may file objections to a special master's report, or seek to modify or adopt it, within 21 days of after service, unless the court sets a different time.[14] Legal conclusions of the special master are reviewed de novo, and procedural matters are reviewed for abuse of discretion.[15] The court must decide on all objections to the report, including findings of fact,[16] unless the parties stipulate that the findings will be reviewed only for clear error, or that they will be final.

Where the special master is appointed by the consent of the parties, pursuant to Rule 53(a)(1)(A), or to address post-trial matters under Rule 53(a)(1)(C), the special master's findings of fact are final, subject to the same type of review as findings by a jury.[17]

Lastly, an order appointing a special master must set forth the terms of the special master's compensation.[18] However, the court may, at its discretion or by petition, change the terms, or order

---

La. Oct. 24, 2011) ("The Special Master may communicate ex parte with any party or his attorney, as the Special Master deems appropriate, for the purposes of ensuring the efficient administration and management of this MDL as set forth above, including the making of informal suggestions to the parties to facilitate compliance with Orders of the Court; such ex parte communications may, for example, address procedural issues and preference as to form of submissions and other data. Such ex parte communications shall not, however, address the merits of any substantive issue.").

[13]*E.g., In re Oral Sodium Phosphate Solution-Based Prods. Liab. Action*, Case No. 1:09-sp-80000,(MDL Docket No. 2066), 2009 U.S. Dist. LEXIS 81560, at *13–14 (N.D. Ohio Aug. 24, 2009) (allowing ex parte communications, but reserving the right to limit those communications as circumstances change).

[14]Fed. R. Civ. P. 53(f)(2). *See*, Connecticut Importing Co. v. Frankfort Distilleries, 42 F. Supp. 225, 227 (D. Conn. 1940) (requiring objections to Special masters report within 20 days after the filing of the report).

[15]Fed. R. Civ. P. 53(f)(4) and (5).

[16]In 2003, Federal Rule 53 was amended to provide for de novo review, unless otherwise agreed to by the parties, of a special master's findings of fact. Fed. R. Civ. P. 53(g)(3) (notes of advisory committee on 2003 amendments to rules).

[17]Fed. R. Civ. P. 53(f)(3)(B).

[18]Fed. R. Civ. P. 53(g)(1). Sample order. Appendix B.

that the compensation be paid by whichever party is more responsible for the reference to the master.[19]

2. California State Law

In California, special masters (or referees) may be appointed under either § 638 (with the consent of the party) or § 639 (on a motion) of the California Code of Civil Procedure. Prior to serving as a referee, a person appointed under either statute must make certain disclosures and filings. First, the proposed referee must "certify in writing that he or she consents to serve as provided in the order of appointment and is aware of and will comply with applicable provisions of canon 6 of the Code of Judicial Ethics and with the California Rules of Court."[20] Any grounds for disqualification under the Code of Judicial Ethics must be disclosed. In addition, the referee must disclose "[a]ny significant personal or professional relationship the referee has or has had with a party, attorney, or law firm in the current case, including the number and nature of any other proceedings in the past 24 months in which the referee has been privately compensated by a party, attorney, law firm, or insurance company in the current case for any services. The disclosure must include privately compensated service as an attorney, expert witness, or consultant or as a judge, referee, arbitrator, mediator, settlement facilitator, or other alternative dispute resolution neutral."[21]

In California, parties have the absolute right, one time, to disqualify a referee or special master upon showing that the person "is prejudiced against a party or attorney or the interest of a party or attorney appearing in the action or proceeding." Cal. Civ. Proc. Code § 170.6(a)(1). The necessary showing may be made "by an oral or written motion without prior notice supported by affidavit or declaration under penalty of perjury, or an oral statement under oath." *Id.* § 170.6(a)(2). If challenge is made timely, and supported by a declaration, the referee may be replaced "without any further act or proof." *Id.* § 170.6(a)(4). A referee may also be disqualified based on his or her required disclosures, or failure to make required disclosure, in the same way that a judge may be disqualified. *See Id.* § 170.5 ("For the purposes of Sections 170 to 170.5 . . . 'Judge' means . . . referees.").

While, there is no requirement that the referee be an attorney, if the referee is an attorney, he or she cannot be an inactive

---

[19]Fed. R. Civ. P. 53(g)(3).

[20]Cal. R. Ct. § 3.924(a).

[21]Cal. R. Ct. § 3.924(b)(2).

member of the bar. This is because Title 2, Rule 2.30(B) of the Rules and Regulations of the California State Bar provides that "[n]o member practicing law . . . or occupying a position wherein he or she is called upon in any capacity to give legal advice or counsel or examine the law or pass upon the legal effect of any act, document or law, shall be enrolled as an inactive member." The State Bar's website cites that rule, and warns inactive members that "transferring to inactive status: . . . precludes a member from engaging in certain activities in California, including but not limited to working as a private arbitrator, mediator, referee or other dispute resolution provider . . . . This is based on the presumption that these activities call upon a member to give legal advice or counsel or examine the law or pass upon the legal effect on any act, document or law."[22] Attorneys who serve as Special Masters or Referees are subject to discipline by the State Bar, and members of other professions may be subject to discipline by their own licensing authorities.[23]

a. Appointments under § 638

Appointments under § 638 are voluntary. Parties to a contract or litigation, may agree to the appointment of a referee or special master "to hear and determine any or all of the issues in an action or proceeding, whether of fact or of law, and to report a statement of decision."[24] A referee may also be appointed, with the consent of the parties, "to ascertain a fact necessary to enable the court to determine an action or proceeding."[25] The Courts in California, however, have discretion to refuse to enforce a pre-dispute agreement to have disputes resolved by a referee.[26]

Currently, it is uncommon for special masters to be appointed in ESI disputes by the voluntary consent of the parties. This is because contracting parties generally do not anticipate having electronic discovery disputes at the time of contract formation. As litigation regarding ESI and the costs associated therewith

---

[22]*See* http://calbar.ca.gov/state/calbar/calbar__sections__generic.jsp?cid=13726&id=1029

[23]Rand v. Board of Psychology, 206 Cal. App. 4th 565, 578 (2012) ("Rand proffers no reason why attorneys acting as special masters can be subject to discipline by their licensing authority (the State Bar), but psychologists acting as special masters cannot be subject to discipline by their licensing Board.").

[24]Cal. Civ. Proc. Code § 638(a).

[25]Cal. Civ. Proc. Code § 638(b).

[26]Tarrant Bell Property, LLC v. Superior Court, 51 Cal. 4th 538, 540 (2011) (holding that a court has the discretion to refuse to enforce a pre-dispute agreement to refer matters to a referee under Section 638 of the California Code of Civil Procedure).

increases, however, parties are likely to begin contracting for ESI special masters as part of their dispute resolution provisions.

An unambiguous voluntary reference under § 638, like an agreement to arbitrate, functions as a waiver of a jury trial;[27] therefore, decisions of a § 638 referee are final and "the decision of the referee must be attacked in the same manner as one made by the court, and an order vacating the decision and directing a rehearing is properly appealable as an order granting a new trial."[28][29] However, trial courts have the power to set aside a referee's report,[30] where the report is not supported by evidence.[31]

b. Appointments Under § 639

Appointments under § 639 are involuntary. They may be made on the motion of any party to litigation, or by a motion of the court. The statute provides five broad categories of circumstances under which a motion for involuntary reference may be granted:

(1) When the trial of an issue of fact requires the examination of a long account on either side, In such cases the referees may be directed to hear and decide the whole issue or report upon any specific question of fact involved therein;

(2) When the taking of an account is necessary for the information of the court before judgment, or for carrying a judgment or order into effect;

(3) When a question of fact, other than upon the pleadings, arises upon motion or otherwise, in any stage of the action;

(4) When it is necessary for the information of the court in a special proceeding [such as enforcing a search warrant on an attorney, which will require review of documents that may be privileged];

(5) When the court in any pending action determines that it is

---

[27]Woodside Homes of California, Inc. v. Superior Court, 142 Cal. App. 4th 99, 104, 47 Cal. Rptr. 3d 683 (3d Dist. 2006).

[28]In re Bassi's Estate, 234 Cal. App. 2d 529, 536–537, 44 Cal. Rptr. 541 (1st Dist. 1965).

[29]See Cal. Civ. Proc. Code § 644(a) ("In the case of a consensual general reference pursuant to Section 638, the decision of the referee or commissioner upon the whole issue must stand as the decision of the court, and upon filing of the statement of decision with the clerk of the court, judgment may be entered thereon in the same manner as if the action had been tried by the court.").

[30]Cal. Civ. Proc. Code § 645; see also SFPP, L.P. v. Burlington Northern & Santa Fe Ry. Co., 121 Cal. App. 4th 452, 466, 17 Cal. Rptr. 3d 96, 34 Envtl. L. Rep. 20066 (5th Dist. 2004) (explaining that motions to set aside or vacate judgments are available, "[t]he decision of the referee appointed pursuant to § 638 . . . may be excepted to and reviewed in like manner as if made by the court.").

[31]See, e.g., Cappe v. Brizzolara, 19 Cal. 607, 1862 WL 634 (1862).

necessary for the court to appoint a referee to hear and determine any and all discovery motions and disputes relevant to discovery in the action and to report findings and make a recommendation thereon.[32]

Decisions of a referee or special master appointed under § 639 are advisory. "The court may adopt the referee's recommendations, in whole or in part, after independently considering the referee's findings and any objections and responses thereto filed with the court."[33] Thus, "in the case of a special reference, the referee's report is only the first step. The court must determine 'the facts and the law by rendering its decision containing its findings of fact and conclusions of law which serves as the basis for the judgment which shall be entered; and the judgment thus entered is in nowise dependent upon the report of the referee for support but is grounded on the decision of the court.' "[34]

3. New York State Law

In New York, the appointment and duties of a referee are governed by Article 43 of the New York Civil Practice Law and Rules. "A referee to determine an issue or to perform an act shall have all the powers of a court in performing a like function; but he shall have no power to relieve himself of his duties, to appoint a successor or to adjudge any person except a witness before him guilty of contempt."[35]

An order of reference shall direct the referee to determine the entire action or specific issues, to report issues, to perform particular acts, or to receive and report evidence only. It may specify or limit the powers of the referee and the time for the filing of his report and may fix a time and place for the hearing.[36]

As in California, a reference or appointment of special master may be either voluntary or involuntary. Voluntary references are governed by New York Civil Practice Law and Rules § 4317(a).[37] Rule 4317(a) allows the parties to stipulate that any issue shall be determined by a referee. However, leave of court and designation by it of the referee is required for references in matrimonial actions.

---

[32]Cal. Civ. Proc. Code § 639(a).

[33]Cal. Civ. Proc. Code § 639(b).

[34]Yeboah v. Progeny Ventures, Inc., 128 Cal. App. 4th 443, 450, 27 Cal. Rptr. 3d 150 (2d Dist. 2005), as modified on denial of reh'g, (May 5, 2005).

[35]NY CLS CPLR § 4301.

[36]NY CLS CPLR § 4311.

[37]NY CLS CPLR § 4317(a), (b).

Involuntary references are made upon a motion of the parties or the court, subject to New York Civil Practice Law and Rules § 4317(b).[38] Subdivision (b) provides that on motion of any party or on its own initiative, the court may order a reference to determine a cause of action or an issue where the trial will require the examination of a long account. A referee to determine an issue has all of the powers of the court in performing a like function. However, he has no power to relieve himself of his duties, appoint a successor or to adjudge any person except a witness before him guilty of contempt.

§ 6:5 Reasons for seeking a special master in an e-discovery dispute

Special masters may be useful in complex cases to hear and determine e-discovery disputes:[1]

> Complex cases invariably involve complex discovery disputes and, unless managed, a case with many separately represented parties has the potential for burdensome and duplicative discovery. It is therefore appropriate for the case management order to provide for the appointment of a discovery referee under Code of Civil Procedure § 639. Such a referee assists the trial judge in resolving discovery disputes. However, even in the unlikely absence of disputes, the referee will work with the attorneys in developing a discovery plan, scheduling discovery in the most efficient, rational and least oppressive manner.[2]

The appointment of a special master is the exception, and not the rule. Courts at the state level may be reluctant to arrogate powers to a special master, or impose those costs on litigants. The appointment is generally a result of unique circumstances that make it necessary:

> Implicit in the statutory requirement that the reference be 'necessary' is the Legislature's acknowledgment of a litigant's right of access to the courts without the payment of a user's fee, and the concomitant notion that there ought to be a finding of something

---

[38]NY CLS CPLR § 4311(b).

[Section 6:5]

[1]Shira Sheindlin & Jonathan M. Redgrave, Special Masters and E-Discovery: The Intersection of Two Recent Revisions to the Federal Rules of Civil Procedure, 30 CARDOZO L. REV. 347, 364 n.84 (2008).

[2]Lu v. Superior Court, 55 Cal. App. 4th 1264, 1269, 64 Cal. Rptr. 2d 561 (4th Dist. 1997) (finding that a Referee can be appointed in complex litigation before an actual dispute. In fact, the court assumes "complex cases invariably involve complex discovery disputes" and recommends routine references as part of case management in complex litigation).

out of the ordinary before the services of a referee are forced upon a nonconsenting party.[3]

At the federal level, the presence of magistrate judges tasked with supervising discovery disputes also builds a bias against appointment:

> Since service as a special master is one of the duties specifically authorized for United States magistrates under 28 U.S.C. § 636(b)(1), it is necessary to consider both Fed. R. Civ. P. 53 and the Federal Magistrates Act of 1968, 28 U.S.C. § 631 et seq., and their history to determine whether [a reference is proper].[4]

There are a number of federal cases that have historically built a bias against appointment of special masters, many of which predate the explosion of ESI and computer forensics cases.[5]

While some judges are developing familiarly with ESI related issues, special masters may offer greater expertise. Properly qualified special masters may provide a level of expertise not possessed by judicial officers, and provide these services in an environment where the special master is able to provide a more thorough analysis of the facts and the technologies involved in a specific case. Much of the time that the parties may need to educate the court with respect to specific technologies may be avoided

---

[3]Hood v. Superior Court, 72 Cal. App. 4th 446, 449, 85 Cal. Rptr. 2d 114 (2d Dist. 1999); McMillan v. Superior Court, 57 Cal. Rptr. 2d 674 (App. 2d Dist. 1996); Marathon Nat. Bank v. Superior Court, 19 Cal. App. 4th 1256, 24 Cal. Rptr. 2d 40 (2d Dist. 1993); DeBlase v. Superior Court, 41 Cal. App. 4th 1279, 49 Cal. Rptr. 2d 229 (2d Dist. 1996).

[4]C. A. B. v. Carefree Travel, Inc., 513 F.2d 375, 379 (2d Cir. 1975).

[5]*See e.g.*, La Buy v. Howes Leather Company, 352 U.S. 249, 259, 77 S. Ct. 309, 1 L. Ed. 2d 290 (1957) ("we believe [the need for complicated legal and factual determinations] is an impelling reason for trial before a regular, experienced trial judge rather than before a temporary substitute appointed on an ad hoc basis and ordinarily not experienced in judicial work"); Graffis v. Woodward, 96 F.2d 329, 332, 37 U.S.P.Q. 374 (C.C.A. 7th Cir. 1938) ("references are to be used very sparingly, in view of the possible hardships they may create"); In re Irving-Austin Bldg. Corp., 100 F.2d 574, 577, 1 Fed. R. Serv. 570 (C.C.A. 7th Cir. 1938) ("References to masters are attended by dangerous and unhappy consequences . . . . The evils of delay and added expense are both inherent in references."); Helene Curtis Industries v. Sales Affiliates, 199 F.2d 732, 733, 95 U.S.P.Q. 172 (2d Cir. 1952) ("reference to a master should be the exception; delay, expense, and the postponement of judicial consideration all so suggest"); C. A. B. v. Carefree Travel, Inc., 513 F.2d 375, 379–380 (2d Cir. 1975) ("The exercise of the power of reference, at least in the days before full-time paid federal magistrates, resulted in a number of difficulties. Foremost, perhaps, was expense, stemming from the fact that generally the masters charged fees and were in effect paid by the piece . . . . References, moreover, often entailed considerable delay since many of the special masters were attorneys who gave their private practice precedence.").

if the parties choose a special master that is already familiar with e-discovery issues.

Special masters also provide parties to litigation greater flexibility in the collection, analysis, and interpretation of ESI.[6] Discovery without a special master can take far longer to produce results, especially where motion practice is required.[7] A special master can order parties to respond to discovery quicker. For example, a special master can perform (depending on the skill set) or appoint a data forensics specialist to perform, collections of ESI, searches for relevant documents, and analysis[8] data integrity. The appointment of a special master often leads to a more focused discovery plan, and resolution of disputes.[9]

Since special masters do not have the caseloads and time constraints of judicial offers, they may devote more time to e-discovery disputes. Special masters may conduct extended hearings, and take testimony and argument from computer forensic experts for the parties to understand and evaluate e-discovery issues.[10]

Federal and state court orders appointing special masters have allowed special masters to review documents in camera, without

---

[6]Cordoza v. Pacific States Steel Corp., 320 F.3d 989, 995, 54 Fed. R. Serv. 3d 1076 (9th Cir. 2003) ("[I]n this era of complex litigation, special masters may, subject to judicial review, be called upon to perform a broad range of judicial functions [including] supervising discovery."); *see also* Shira A. Scheindlin, E-Discovery: The Newly Amended Federal Rules of Civil Procedure, MOORE'S FEDERAL PRACTICE, 14–15 (2006).

[7]Thomas E. Willging, et al., *Special Masters' Incidence and Activity Report to the Judicial Conference's Advisory Committee on Civil Rules and its Subcommittee on Special Masters*, FEDERAL JUDICIAL BUREAU, 9 (2000) http://ftp.resource.org/courts.gov/fjc/specmast.pdf ("Several judges who appointed masters for pretrial and trial-related purposes, such as supervising discovery-related conflicts or assisting the court with complex issues, reported that the Special Master helped them understand the complex issues, saved the parties' money, made the case settle faster, or saved the appointing judge's time.").

[8]CITE sample order; *See* Shira A. Scheindlin & Jonathan M. Redgrave, *Special Masters and E-Discovery: The Intersection of Two Recent Revisions to the Federal Rules of Civil Procedure*, 30 CARDOZO L. REV. 347, 384 (Nov., 2008) *available at* http://www.cardozolawreview.com/content/30-2/SCHEINDLIN.30.2.pdf (a special master's role "may involve providing technical specifications for discovery or actually conducting discovery investigations and searches in a neutral capacity").

[9]Rodriguez-Torres v. Government Development Bank of Puerto Rico, 265 F.R.D. 40, 43–44 (D.P.R. 2010) (referencing ESI a description of the process and benefit derived from the ESI Specialist Report submitted for this matter).

[10]*See*, Fed. R. Civ. P. 53(c). CITE reference orders.

waiving privilege.[11] While controversial, this practice saves time and effort, because it allows discovery disputes to be addressed and resolved before a privilege review has been completed. Moreover the special master's ability to review privileged documents makes hiding potentially responsive documents under the guise of privilege less plausible.

As noted in the preceding paragraph, the subject of *in camera* review of potentially privileged documents is not free from controversy. The U.S. Supreme Court held that federal district courts may order in camera reviews in privilege disputes, and that "a lesser evidentiary showing is needed to trigger in camera review than is required ultimately to overcome the privilege."[12] In contrast, in 2009, the California Supreme Court held that a trial court erred by directing a referee to conduct such a review, because the "directions and order violated the attorney-client privilege, and violated as well the statutory prohibition against requiring disclosure of information claimed to be subject to the attorney-client privilege in order to rule on a claim of privilege."[13] Depending on jurisdiction, federal or state, there may be grounds for a party to object to a special master's review of potentially privileged documents.[14]

---

[11]*See, e.g.*, MSC.Software Corp. v. Altair Engineering, Inc., 2009 WL 4726588 (E.D. Mich. 2009) (adopting Special Master Hollaar's report and recommendation including "Recommendation #5: that the individual Defendants' request to see MSC source code that they may have authored, be denied, because the protective order says 'information designated as Highly Confidential/ Attorneys' Eyes Only shall be viewed only by outside Counsel and their expert witnesses and expert consultants retained by Counsel' ").

[12]U.S. v. Zolin, 491 U.S. 554, 572, 109 S. Ct. 2619, 105 L. Ed. 2d 469, 89-1 U.S. Tax Cas. (CCH) P 9380, 27 Fed. R. Evid. Serv. 833, 63 A.F.T.R.2d 89-1483 (1989) (holding in camera may be ordered in limited circumstances, such as determining the applicability of the crime-fraud exception).

[13]Costco Wholesale Corp. v. Superior Court, 47 Cal. 4th 725, 730, 101 Cal. Rptr. 3d 758, 219 P.3d 736 (2009).

[14]*Compare* Fed. R. Civ. P. 26(b)(5) (allowing a party to withhold privileged information) *and* Fed. R. Civ. P. 26(c) (allowing a party to request a protective order limiting the scope of discovery) *with* Cal. Civ. Proc. Code § 2017.010 (". . . any party may obtain discovery regarding any matter, not privileged, that is relevant . . . .") *and* Cal. Civ. Proc. Code § 2017.720 (providing that the use of technology in discovery does not "diminish[ ] the rights and duties of the parties regarding discovery, privileges, procedural rights, or substantive law.").

While special masters typically bill hourly, the costs of a special master should be considered in light of the likelihood of faster resolution of issues.[15]

The costs of appointing a special master may be outweighed by the benefits a special master can bring to the court and the parties. By having a special master involved throughout the discovery process, parties can save time and money on litigating discovery disputes in a court, while achieving their objectives fairly and effectively.[16] Special masters have the ability to recommend that the court impose sanctions for failure to cooperate with e-discovery demands and for spoliation or failure to preserve evidence.[17] Sanctions can range from monetary sanctions,[18] evidentiary sanctions,[19] or, in extreme cases, terminating sanctions.[20]

♦ **Practitioner Tip:** Special masters may be appointed with or without the consent of the parties or pursuant to a motion. The scope of the special master's authority may be limited by

---

[15]*See* Fed. R. Civ. P. 53(a)(3) ("In appointing a master, the court must consider the fairness of imposing the likely expenses on the parties and must protect against unreasonable expense or delay.").

[16]Daniel B. Garrie, Esq., *Indirect Costs of Electronic Discovery (E-Discovery)*, HTTP://LTRM.ORG, (February 8, 2008), http://ltrm.org/wp/ltrmblog/2010/02/08/ind irect-costs-of-electronic-discovery-e-discovery/ (noting that indirect costs of e-discovery include diverting critical resources and decreased job satisfaction, which impacts the overall bottom line); Martin Well, *How to Reduce E-Discovery Costs*, WWW.ASSOCIATEDCONTENT.COM, (Oct 28, 2010) http://www.associatedconte nt.com/article/5944822/how_to_reduce_ediscovery_costs.html?cat=15 (discussing how hiring an expert to provide early case assessment can save money and time in the discovery process).

[17]Wm. T. Thompson Co. v. General Nutrition Corp., Inc., 593 F. Supp. 1443, 1456–1457, 1985-1 Trade Cas. (CCH) ¶ 66325, 39 Fed. R. Serv. 2d 1187 (C.D. Cal. 1984) (discussing special master imposed sanctions of $453,312.56 due to defendant's failure to instruct employees to preserve electronic records).

[18]*E.g.*, In re Seroquel Products Liability Litigation, 244 F.R.D. 650, 660 (M.D. Fla. 2007) (sanctioning defendant and explaining that electronic discovery is a "cooperative undertaking, not part of the adversarial give and take").

[19]*E.g.*, Smith v. Slifer Smith & Frampton/Vail Associates Real Estate, LLC, 2009 WL 482603 (D. Colo. 2009) (opting for an adverse jury instruction as opposed to default judgment).

[20]Fed. R. Civ. P. 37(b)(2)(v) provides that if a party fails to obey a discovery order the court may "dismiss the action or proceeding in whole or in part"; *see, e.g.*, Arista Records LLC v. Usenet.com, Inc., 633 F. Supp. 2d 124, 158, 91 U.S.P.Q.2d 1744, 79 Fed. R. Evid. Serv. 1480, 73 Fed. R. Serv. 3d 1797 (S.D. N.Y. 2009) (granting terminating sanctions to the plaintiffs based on the defendant's discovery misconduct in wiping hard drives, reassigning computers to employees without preserving the relevant data for litigation, deleting relevant emails, and sending employees to Europe to keep them from being deposed).

the appointment or reference order, the statutory basis, or the rules of due process.

§ 6:6   Selecting a special master

a. The Court May Appoint a Special Master Subject to Parties' Objections

Special masters are typically appointed by a court, arbitrator, mediator, or other neutral. In most jurisdictions, the parties to the dispute have the ability to influence the process, or object to the appointment.[1]

In seeking a special master, attorneys often favor retired judicial officers or experienced attorneys. That may not always be appropriate for a special master tasked with making e-discovery decisions because practicing attorneys are not always up to date on the latest technology, and the technology of ESI changes rapidly. It can be time consuming to have to educate a special master that does not know of the latest data storage, gathering, and collection techniques. The parties, moreover, may look to the special master to provide examples of the type of e-discovery that will be appropriate for the case.

The ideal special master will have a solid background in both technology and law.[2] This will help the parties negotiate the boundaries of ESI collection, and understand the limits and advantages to the various collection and review methods.

§ 6:7   Case studies

b. In re Seroquel

- *Special masters may be appointed to assist parties and direct them in ways of complying with requirements of e-discovery in an efficient and reasonable manner.*

[Section 6:6]

[1]*Compare* Fed. R. Civ. P. 53(b)(1), providing that "[b]efore appointing a master, the court must give the parties notice and an opportunity to be heard [and] [a]ny party may suggest candidates for appointment" *with* Cal. Civ. Proc. Code § 641(a) to (g) listing seven independent grounds upon which a party may object to the appointment of a special master.

[2]For example *see* In re Vioxx Products Liability Litigation, 501 F. Supp. 2d 789, 792 (E.D. La. 2007), for the Court's discussion of the technical and legal expertise of its appointed Special Master.

In re Seroquel Products Liability Litigation, was a multidistrict federal case heard in the Central District of Florida.[1] The case related to injuries alleged to have been caused from ingesting the anti-psychotic medication Seroquel, which plaintiffs claimed can cause diabetes and related disorders. The defendants sought sanctions due to the plaintiff's failure to respond to discovery as ordered, including failure to identify and produce relevant databases, failure to identify appropriate custodians of records, and failure to produce readable electronic data.

A special master was appointed "to *assist* and, when necessary, *direct* the parties in completing required discovery of electronically stored information with reasonable dispatch and efficiency."[2] The Court required counsel for each of the parties to designate a lead attorney and a lead technical individual with "sufficient authority and knowledge to make commitments and carry them out to allow the Special Master to accomplish his duties."[3] It required the parties to each submit a "job description" of the special master's duties, which it then used to shape its order.[4] The order appointing the special master in *Seroquel* was designed to address past and future discovery issues. The court ordered that the special master "should obtain sufficient information from both sides as to the procedures used and problems encountered to determine whether past discovery is reasonably complete and, if not, what steps are needed to make it so. To the extent past or on-going difficulties involve technical issues, the [Special Master] shall assist the parties in reaching cost effective solutions. The parties are directed to provide access to any documents and personnel (including technical staff and vendors) necessary to these tasks."[5]

The special master kept the Court informed about the progress of discovery throughout the litigation. In one order, the Court found that "[w]ith the assistance of the [Special Master], the

---

[Section 6:7]

[1]In re Seroquel Products Liability Litigation, 244 F.R.D. 650 (M.D. Fla. 2007).

[2]*In re Seroquel Prods. Liab. Litig.*, CASE No. 6:06-md-01769-ACC-DAB, DOCUMENT 511, at 2 (Sept. 27, 2007) (order).

[3]*In re Seroquel Prods. Liab. Litig.*, CASE No. 6:06-md-01769-ACC-DAB, DOCUMENT 511, at 2 (Sept. 27, 2007) (order).

[4]*In re Seroquel Prods. Liab. Litig.*, CASE No. 6:06-md-01769-ACC-DAB, DOCUMENT 511, at 3 (Sept. 27, 2007) (order).

[5]*In re Seroquel Prods. Liab. Litig.*, CASE No. 6:06-md-01769-ACC-DAB, DOCUMENT 546, at 2 (Oct. 5, 2007) (order).

defendants were largely able to get production of electronically-stored documents back on track."[6]

c. Hohider v. UPS

- **Special masters may be appointed to make recommendations about sanctions for destruction of ESI**

Hohider was a class action filed in the Western District of Pennsylvania for alleging a pattern or practice of unlawful discrimination against employees under Title I of the Americans with Disabilities Act of 1990 (ADA), 42 U.S.C.A. §§ 12101 to 12117.[7] The plaintiff alleged that the defendant, UPS, had failed to preserve electronic information relevant to the dispute.[8] The court issued a detailed order, requiring the special master to examine UPS's computer systems, back up data, and make recommendations as to sanctions or remedies.[9]

The court ordered the special master to determine whether UPS had "withheld, deleted, destroyed or permitted to be destroyed" relevant information, and whether UPS had a duty to preserve the data.[10] The areas of the special master's investigation included plaintiffs' pre-litigation communications about their claims, and whether they had put defendant on notice to preserve ESI.[11]

d. Medtronic Sofamor Danek, Inc. v. Michelson

- **Special masters may be appointed to oversee electronic discovery and make decisions about which party is to bear the costs**

---

[6]*In re Seroquel Prods. Liab. Litig.*, CASE No. 6:06-md-01769-ACC-DAB, DOCUMENT 1640, at *10 (May 13, 2010).

[7]Hohider v. United Parcel Service, Inc., 574 F.3d 169, 22 A.D. Cas. (BNA) 133 (3d Cir. 2009); *see also* J.B. Hunt Transport, Inc. v. Bentley, 207 Ga. App. 250, 256–57, 427 S.E.2d 499 (1992) (upholding jury instruction that destruction of logbook supported a reasonable presumption that the logbook showed that the driver was compelled by Hunt to drive with insufficient rest).

[8]*See* Hohider v. United Parcel Serv., No. 04-363 (W.D. Pa. Dec. 19, 2007) (appointing special master).

[9]*See* Hohider v. United Parcel Serv., No. 04-363, at 2–3 (W.D. Pa. Dec. 19, 2007) (appointing special master).

[10]*See* Hohider v. United Parcel Serv., No. 04-363, at 3 (W.D. Pa. Dec. 19, 2007) (appointing special master).

[11]*See* Hohider v. United Parcel Serv., No. 04-363, at 3 (W.D. Pa. Dec. 19, 2007); *see also* Shira A. Scheindlin & Jonathan M. Redgrave, *Special Masters and E-Discovery: The Intersection of Two Recent Revisions to the Federal Rules of Civil Procedure*, 30 CARDOZO L. REV. 347, 371 (Nov., 2008) http://www.cardoz olawreview.com/content/30-2/SCHEINDLIN.30.2.pdf (discussing the facilitative role of e-discovery special masters).

Medtronic[12] "involved trade secrets, patents, and trade information in the field of spinal fusion medical technology."[13] The plaintiff objected to defendant's request for the production of data from backup tapes because, it claimed, extracting the data and reviewing it for privilege would have been "astronomically costly."[14] In response, the defendants sought appointment of a "Special Master to help the parties establish a discovery protocol."[15]

The defendant in *Medtronic* had propounded very broad discovery requests that included backup tapes. While the parties did not dispute that the information on the tapes would be relevant, they disagreed about the need for recovering the information, and who should bear the costs.

The court found that, "[g]iven the amount of electronic data at issue, the court finds that the appointment of a special master to oversee discovery is warranted and that the special master should be a technology or computer expert."[16] The court ordered that "[t]he special master's duties will include making decisions with regard to search terms; overseeing the design of searches and the scheduling of searches and production; coordinating deliveries between the parties and their vendors; and advising both parties, at either's request, on cost estimates and technical issues."[17]

e. Jane Doe v. Smith Corp.et. al.

- **Special masters may be appointed to determine whether parties have complied with court orders regarding ESI**

In *Jane Doe v. Smith Corp.*,[18] a case filed in California state

---

[12]Medtronic Sofamor Danek, Inc. v. Michelson, 229 F.R.D. 550, 56 Fed. R. Serv. 3d 1159 (W.D. Tenn. 2003).

[13]Medtronic Sofamor Danek, Inc. v. Michelson, 229 F.R.D. 550, 552, 56 Fed. R. Serv. 3d 1159 (W.D. Tenn. 2003).

[14]Medtronic Sofamor Danek, Inc. v. Michelson, 229 F.R.D. 550, 56 Fed. R. Serv. 3d 1159 (W.D. Tenn. 2003).

[15]Medtronic Sofamor Danek, Inc. v. Michelson, 229 F.R.D. 550, 56 Fed. R. Serv. 3d 1159 (W.D. Tenn. 2003).

[16]Medtronic Sofamor Danek, Inc. v. Michelson, 229 F.R.D. 550, 559, 56 Fed. R. Serv. 3d 1159 (W.D. Tenn. 2003).

[17]Medtronic Sofamor Danek, Inc. v. Michelson, 229 F.R.D. 550, 56 Fed. R. Serv. 3d 1159 (W.D. Tenn. 2003).

[18]For the reasons discussed in this case summary, Jane Doe and Smith Corp. settled Doe's claims shortly after the issuance of the special master's report, with various terms of confidentiality binding the parties. Out of respect for those agreements, pseudonyms are used.

court, a special master was appointed to determine whether the plaintiff had complied with previous orders requiring her to divest herself of data and information she was not permitted to use in litigation.

In the underlying case, the plaintiff alleged she was deprived of profits made in connection with a sale of an extraordinarily valuable business. Plaintiff alleged her former partners devised a complicated scheme, using a number of off-shore companies, to keep details of the transaction, and the profits, away from her. Plaintiff had been terminated from a related company for copying large amounts of data, which termination Plaintiff claimed was pre-textual in furtherance of her former partners' wrongful conduct. Litigation was pursued by the parties, as well as subsidiaries and related companies, in multiple jurisdictions at the same time.

Several different tribunals ordered the plaintiff to return documents and electronic data she took prior to being terminated. Doe made numerous excuses for not returning documents, including lost passwords to accounts, lost hard drives, lost USB drives, and the contention that she could not search an account at a nonprofit, which she founded and ran at the time, because she did not own the account. All the while, plaintiff claimed to have complied with the court's order that she divest herself of stolen documents.

Perhaps frustrated with Doe's seeming lack of cooperation, one arbitrator issued an order that plaintiff was not to use any of the data or documents that she had taken "for any purpose." A state court in the action by Doe to recover the allegedly wrongful profits then held that, in light of the arbitrator's award, the plaintiff's existing attorneys and experts could no longer represent her. The state court judge's reasoning was that it was impossible for Doe's attorneys and experts to separate what they learned from their analysis of the data that she provided to them from their analysis of information that she could legitimately retain and possess. The state court did, however, give Doe a "second chance". If she obtained new counsel and divested herself of all documents, data, and derivative works, then she would be permitted to continue the litigation. The remedy fashioned by the state court judge required that Doe to swear in a declaration of her divestiture, to put her on the path of her "fresh start."

Faced with conflicting declarations as to whether Doe had faithfully complied with the court order of divestiture, the Court appointed a special master to resolve the issue of whether Doe had complied with the order to divest herself of all materials. The order provided that "[t]he Special Master shall hold evidentiary hearings, permit such discovery that he deems reasonable and necessary, supervise such discovery, issue any discovery requests and subpoenas that he deems reasonable and necessary on all issues related to compliance, and shall make a detailed recommendation, supported by findings and conclusions, to the Court as to whether the Court should find that" Doe had fully complied with the Court's order to divest herself of all relevant data and information.

> ◆ **Practitioner Tip:** Where the issue is whether information exists on a hard drive or other data storage device, digital forensics can reveal such information or rule out the possibility that it exists. A Special Master can assist in facilitating access to data storage devices and in identifying the information relevant to the inquiry.

To address Doe's claims that discovery into the question of whether she complied with the Court's divestment order would infringe upon attorney-client privilege or the work product doctrine, the Court allowed that "[t]he evidence reviewed by the Special Master shall include any document as to which Doe claims any privilege, such as the attorney-client privilege and the work product doctrine, and all communications between Doe to her attorneys and advisors, in order to determine whether Doe complied with the requirement that she list all derivative works that she authored, regardless of whether such documents were sent to her counsel or consultants. Review of any document by the Special Master shall not constitute a waiver of any privilege."

Hearings before the special master lasted for nearly a year. The special master subpoenaed internet service providers, cellular telephone companies, electronics retails stores, forensic data consultants, and others to trace the evidence. He reviewed evidence, and worked with forensic experts, and issued a finding that led to the resolution of the case.

Although Doe had initiated legal proceedings against her former business partners at Smith Corp., and alleged wrongdoing by her former business partners designed to deprive her of a valuable investment opportunity, in the end her wrongdoing—rather than the allegations of her complaint—was the focus of litigation. Her former business partners had licensed the subject technology to an Internet company in a substantial financial transaction. Doe wanted a piece of that pie. And but for the expertise and hard work of a dedicated special master, Doe might have gotten away with stolen intellectual property, blackmail, and corporate espionage. Doe dismissed her claims.

§ 6:8 Trends in appointment of special masters to supervise e-discovery

As the costs involved with processing, reviewing, evaluating, and producing ESI increase, special masters are being used more frequently to facilitate e-discovery.[1] With the amount of data that is currently being stored, it is becoming increasingly difficult to find a cost-effective way to produce all documents and data responsive to certain discovery requests.[2]

The use of a neutral special master with access to the technical personnel of the parties can help the parties limit e-discovery costs. A special master can monitor discovery compliance and report to the decision-maker.[3] He or she can also adjudicate issues of fact,[4] technical compliance,[5] privilege,[6] and work product.[7] The increased use of technical special masters in e-discovery may allow the parties to complete discovery and focus on the merits of

---

[Section 6:8]

[1]*See generally* Daniel B. Garrie, Esq., *E-discovery Costs and Benefits*, LOS ANGELES DAILY JOURNAL (Dec. 29, 2009) http://www.arc4adr.com/e____discovery ost%20And%20Benefits.html (explaining why costs can reach unexpectedly high levels, e.g. one major Fortune 500 corporation found that an average litigation discovery request produced 100–150 GB, c.f. 6.5–9.75 million pages, of information); RALPH C. LOSEY, INTRODUCTION TO E-DISCOVERY: NEW CASES, IDEAS, AND TECHNIQUES, 228 (American Bar Association, 2009) (discussing the coming trend of special masters in e-discovery cases).

[2]*See, e.g.,* Mobil Oil Corp. v. Altech Industries, Inc., 117 F.R.D. 650, 652 (C.D. Cal. 1987) (appointing master in order to supervise discovery due to large number of documents and anticipated addition of new parties); In re Agent Orange Product Liability Litigation, 94 F.R.D. 173, 174, 33 Fed. R. Serv. 2d 1544 (E.D. N.Y. 1982) (appointing Special Master because discovery involved production of millions of documents).

[3]*See, e.g.,* Wachtel v. Health Net, Inc., 239 F.R.D. 81, 111–12 (D.N.J. 2006) (appointing a Special Master to supervise compliance with discovery orders in a case involving over 160 opinions and orders resolving discovery disputes).

[4]*See, e.g.,* RGIS, LLC v. A.S.T., Inc., 2008 WL 186349 (E.D. Mich. 2008) (appointing Special Master to review parties' source codes to determine whether substantial similarities exist and staying discovery of defendant's source code until Special Master submits a report of his findings).

[5]*See, e.g.,* D & P Painting & Const., Inc. v. Azteca Enter., No. 04-07205 (Dist. Ct. Dallas County 2005) (directing the Special Master to examine defendant's hard drives in order to evaluate the origin of certain email messages and determine the form in which they were sent to plaintiff).

[6]*See, e.g.,* In re Ampicillin Antitrust Litigation, 81 F.R.D. 377, 380, 202 U.S.P.Q. 134, 1978-1 Trade Cas. (CCH) ¶ 62043, 25 Fed. R. Serv. 2d 1248 (D.D.C. 1978) (adopting, in part, recommendations of Special Master appointed to review complicated privilege claims involving over 700 documents); In re Intel Corp. Microprocessor Antitrust Litigation, 258 F.R.D. 280 (D. Del. 2008) (special master determining that defendant had waived attorney-client privilege

litigation.[8] Where a party engages in misconduct a special master can issue appropriate sanctions.[9]

There is no reason to limit the use of special masters to the courts. E-discovery can be as complex in arbitration as it sometimes is in the courts.[10] Arbitrations, mediations, and other alternative dispute processes can benefit from the appointment of a special master.[11] An e-discovery special master can (i) review claims of privilege or work product; (ii) provide guidance on preservation of ESI, production, and cost control; (iii) make determinations of issues related to spoliation of evidence and prejudice; and (iv) provide technical assistance to the parties and the ADR official in completing discovery.[12]

E-discovery can potentially side-track an entire case. This is especially true where litigants have failed to preserve data, regardless of whether the failure to preserve has been intentional. A judicial officer may become overwhelmed with e-discovery issues, or the technology, and lose sight of the underlying dispute. A special master appointment isolates e-discovery issues from

---

by asserting human error defense in discovery dispute and engaging in a critical self-evaluation of discovery compliance).

[7]*See, e.g.*, U. S. v. American Tel. & Tel. Co., 461 F. Supp. 1314, 1346–49, 1978-2 Trade Cas. (CCH) ¶ 62247, 26 Fed. R. Serv. 2d 984 (D.D.C. 1978) (appointing master to make preliminary rulings on all claims of work product and other privilege asserted during discovery).

[8]*See*, Mark A. Fellows & Roger S. Haydock, *Federal Court Special Masters: A Vital Resource in the Era of Complex Litigation*, 31 WM. MITCHELL L. REV. 1269, 1295 (2005), *available at* http://www.courtappointedmasters.org/Articles/FellowsHaydock.pdf ("[J]udges are increasingly aware of the effect of litigation complexity on the tractability of discovery and recognize special master appointments as a curative option.").

[9]Fed. R. Civ. P. 53(c)(2);Wm. T. Thompson Co. v. General Nutrition Corp., Inc., 593 F. Supp. 1443, 1456–1457, 1985-1 Trade Cas. (CCH) ¶ 66325, 39 Fed. R. Serv. 2d 1187 (C.D. Cal. 1984) (discussing special master imposed sanctions of $453,312.56 due to defendant's failure to instruct employees to preserve electronic records).

[10]*See*, Daniel Garrie, *Defining Discovery in Arbitration*, PERSPECTIVE DAILY JOURNAL, at 5 (Feb. 3, 2010) (discussing the importance of selecting a technologically savvy arbitration panel).

[11]*See generally* Daniel B. Garrie, Esq., *E-discovery Costs for Corporate Litigants*, DAILY JOURNAL (Nov. 18, 2009) (discussing the benefit of selecting outside experts to assist in the e-discovery process).

[12]*See generally* Shira A. Scheindlin & Jonathan M. Redgrave, *Special Masters and E-Discovery: The Intersection of Two Recent Revisions to the Federal Rules of Civil Procedure*, 30 CARDOZO L. REV. 347, 383–84 (Nov., 2008) *available at* http://www.cardozolawreview.com/content/30-2/SCHEINDLIN.30.2.pdf (discussing the facilitative role of e-discovery special masters).

the rest of the case, which allows the trier of fact to focus on the merits.[13]

§ 6:9 Final reports

The special master's appointment ends with the issuance of a report.[1] The report should include, at minimum, the following things: (1) a history of the litigation and the reason for the appointment; (2) the order appointing the special master, as well as any limits on the special master's authority; (3) the method of investigation used by the special master, as well as any experts retained; (4) the number of hearings held, and the reasons for the hearings; (5) the record of the proceedings, including reference to transcripts and briefs; (6) any interim decisions, as well as challenges to interim decisions and their resolution; (7) the issues that were investigated; (8) any issues of disputed fact resolved by the special master, as well as issues of fact with respect to which the parties agreed were not in dispute; (9) any disputed issues of law resolved by the special master, as well as issues of law with respect to which the parties were not in dispute; (10) the special master's findings and recommendations; (11) reasons for the recommendations; (12) whether there was a prevailing party; and (13) the reasons, if applicable, why one party ought to be responsible for cost associated with the appointment.[2]

◆ **Practitioner Tip:** Require the Special Master to address these points in the order appointing the Special Master.

Special masters may request that the parties draft reports, which the special master can adopt or alter.[3] These are usually the final opportunity for counsel to advocate their positions to the special master.

The time periods and grounds on which a special master's

---

[13]*Aguilar v. EMI Resorts, Inc.*, CASE 1:09-cv-20526-ASG, DOCUMENT 956, at 1 of 35 (S.D. Fla. Feb. 11, 2010) *available at* http://www.flsd.uscourts.gov/wp-co ntent/uploads/2010/07/09cv20526__956.pdf (Commenting that "[w]hile most civil actions focus on the merits of the underlying dispute, this case has been inundated with ancillary issues . . . .").

[Section 6:9]

[1]Fed. R. Civ. P. 53(e) ("A master must report to the court as required by the appointing order.").

[2]Federal Rule of Civil Procedure 53(e) requires only that the master file a report as required by the appointing order.

[3]The parties in *Jane Doe v. Smith Corp. et al.* submitted numerous drafts to the Special Master, which he altered and selectively adopted in his lengthy report.

report can be appealed vary from jurisdiction to jurisdiction.[4] It is critical, however, that the reviewing court has a record to review. Where there is no transcript of proceedings, reviewing courts will often assume that the parties presented facts sufficient to support the special master's conclusion.[5]

There are at least three things that counsel can do to prepare for an appeal related to a special master's report:

1. First, have a court reporter transcribe all proceedings before a special master. This, of course, presumes that all proceedings were reported. A party's success on appeal will likely be seriously compromised if there is no record. A transcript gives the parties the ability to show the court precisely what issues and arguments were covered. If only parts of the proceedings were transcribed, then it is difficult to convince a court or appellate body what issues were raised during the untranscribed portions.

2. Second, put critical arguments in writing. When the parties disagree about important issues, request the opportunity to brief them. Also, request that the special master put his or her decisions in writing including the reasons for each decision.

3. Third, challenge important interim findings of the special master. Do not wait for the final report. Challenging rulings that are wrong can have the effect of making the court or judicial body doubt the ultimate report. There is risk in making a challenge. If the legal or factual analysis is not compelling, the court may discount future challenges, or challenges to the report.

---

[4]*Compare* Fed. R. Civ. P. 53(f)(2) ("A party may file objections to—or a motion to adopt or modify—the master's order, report, or recommendations no later than 21 days after a copy is served, unless the court sets a different time.") *with* Cal. Civ. Proc. Code § 643(c) ("Any party may file an objection to the referee's report or recommendations within 10 days after the referee serves and files the report, or within another time as the court may direct.").

[5]*See, e.g.*, U.S. v. Lothridge, 324 F.3d 599, 601 (8th Cir. 2003) ("Solely within the context of a referral to a special master (whether a magistrate judge or not), Rule 53(e)(2) specifies that in non-jury actions, the district court 'shall accept the master's findings of fact unless clearly erroneous.' ") *citing* Calvin Klein Cosmetics Corp. v. Parfums de Coeur, Ltd., 824 F.2d 665, 670, 3 U.S.P. Q.2d 1498, 8 Fed. R. Serv. 3d 580 (8th Cir. 1987); Bynum v. Baggett Transp. Co., 228 F.2d 566, 569 (5th Cir. 1956) ("the testimony heard by the Master never having been transcribed and included as a part of the record, we must, in the very narrow review of a Master's Report, abide by his fact findings since there is no way to test them under the scrutiny of 'clearly erroneous' ").

§ 6:10 Conclusion

Special masters appointed to resolve e-discovery disputes should be proficient with the technologies at issue. The benefits of using a special master may be lost if the parties are forced to spend time and money educating him or her on the systems in place and the methods of data storage. While special masters will often hire their own independent experts to perform analysis of data, they should be directing that analysis throughout their term.

A special master is more than an e-discovery technology expert. He or she must also be proficient in the law. Procedurally, the special master must understand how to conduct hearings, rule on objections, and receive evidence. Substantively, the special master should understand the issues in the case, so that he or she can know what is likely to be relevant.

Chapter 7

Arbitration and E-discovery Overview: Potential Minefields and Dispute Resolution Strategies

Maura R. Grossman[1]

KeyCite[R]: Cases and other legal materials listed in KeyCite Scope can be researched through the KeyCite service on Westlaw[R]. Use KeyCite to check citations for form, parallel references, prior and later history, and comprehensive citator information, including citations to other decisions and secondary materials.

---

§ 7:1   Introduction

Little law or authoritative commentary currently exists on the topic of electronic discovery in arbitration. But because of the nature of electronically stored information ("ESI"), and the volume of ESI that is typically reviewed and produced in many

---

[1]Maura R. Grossman is Counsel at Wachtell, Lipton, Rosen & Katz in New York City. She is co-chair of the E-Discovery Working Group advising the New York State Unified Court System, and a member of the Steering Committee of The Sedona Conference Working Group 1 on Electronic Document Retention and Production. The Author is a coordinator of the Legal Track of the National Institute of Standards and Technology's Text Retrieval Conference ("TREC"), and an adjunct faculty member at Columbia Law School and Rutgers School of Law–Newark, where she teaches courses on e-discovery. The Author gratefully acknowledges law clerk, Stephanie H. Lee, for her invaluable assistance in updating this overview chapter. The views expressed herein are solely those of the Author and should not be attributed to her firm or its clients.

disputes, many of the same issues that arise with respect to ESI in litigation also arise in arbitration. The primary difference is that arbitration allows the parties greater flexibility and creativity in dealing with these issues.[1]

The six issues to be discussed in this overview chapter to arbitration and e-discovery are as follows: (i) preservation of ESI; (ii) scope and proportionality in electronic discovery; (iii) cost allocation; (iv) the use of search terms and advanced search methodologies; (v) form of production of ESI; and (vi) privilege issues. Each section will address some of the key considerations for both the parties and the arbitrator who is tasked with resolving a dispute between the parties. Some of these issues also will be discussed in greater detail in subsequent chapters.

Most of these issues should be amenable to resolution by the parties themselves if they address them early and cooperatively. Others may require the assistance or intervention of the arbitrator or another neutral party. The best way for parties to avoid pitfalls is to discuss and negotiate these issues early, and to raise them promptly with the arbitrator when the parties cannot resolve the issues themselves.[2]

§ 7:2   Preservation of ESI

In the litigation context, the obligation to preserve evidence arises when a party is on notice that the evidence is relevant to litigation, or when the party knows or should know that the evi-

---

[Section 7:1]

[1]John Range & Jonathan Wilan, *Techniques for Obtaining Efficient and Economical E-Disclosure Despite Arbitral Resistance to U.S.-Style Discovery*, E-Discovery in Arbitration: Leading Lawyers on Recovering Electronic Evidence, Meeting New Disclosure Guidelines, and Implementing Measures to Streamline the Proceedings (Feb. 2010) ("The same issues respecting the volume and cost of ESI present themselves in both civil litigation and arbitration, but in arbitration, the parties have a right to expect that their arbitrator will devote the time and attention necessary to ensure that e-disclosure will be designed and implemented in a manner that is proportionate and appropriate to their dispute.").

[2]*See, e.g.*, Valecia McDowell, *Arbitration in the Digital Age: Synchronizing Your E-Discovery Plan With Your Arbitration Strategy*, E-Discovery in Arbitration: Leading Lawyers on Recovering Electronic Evidence, Meeting New Disclosure Guidelines, and Implementing Measures to Streamline the Proceedings (Feb. 2010) ("[W]hen it comes to electronic discovery in arbitration, you have to be both thoughtful and pragmatic" and "[y]ou have to plan.").

dence may be relevant to future litigation.[1] It is immaterial whether the party is the initiator or the target of the litigation, although the initiator will typically have knowledge earlier than the target. The duty to preserve is typically said to arise from a common law duty to avoid spoliation of relevant evidence for use at trial,[2] the inherent power of the court to control the judicial process and to prevent conduct which impedes the administration of justice,[3] and the court's power to impose sanctions under the Federal Rules of Civil Procedure.[4] Preservation obligations may also be imposed by statute or regulation, such as 18 U.S.C.A. § 1519, which provides penalties for the destruction of records with intent to impede an investigation.

The preservation duty applies with equal force in arbitration proceedings, although it is less clear from where the obligation derives in the arbitration context.[5] The primary difference between litigation and arbitration is that the *scope* of the preserva-

---

[Section 7:2]

[1]*See, e.g.*, Zubulake v. UBS Warburg LLC, 220 F.R.D. 212, 92 Fair Empl. Prac. Cas. (BNA) 1539 (S.D. N.Y. 2003) ("The duty to preserve attache[s] at the time that litigation [i]s reasonably anticipated."); Micron Technology, Inc. v. Rambus Inc., 645 F.3d 1311, 1320, 98 U.S.P.Q.2d 1693 (Fed. Cir. 2011) ("When litigation is 'reasonably foreseeable' is a flexible fact-specific standard that allows a district court to exercise the discretion necessary to confront the myriad factual considerations inherent in the spoliation injury . . . . This standard does not trigger the duty to preserve documents from the mere existence of a potential claim or the distant possibility of litigation . . . . However, it is not so inflexible as to require that litigation be 'imminent, or probable without significant consequences' . . . ." (internal citations omitted)); *Hynix Semiconductor, Inc. v. Rambus, Inc.*, 645 F.3d 1336 (Fed Cir. 2011) (adopting the "reasonable foreseeability standard described in *Silvestri* [*v. General Motors Corp.*, 271 F.3d 583, 51 Fed. R. Serv. 3d 694 (4th Cir. 2001)]").

[2]*See* Pension Committee of University of Montreal Pension Plan v. Banc of America Securities, 685 F. Supp. 2d 456 (S.D. N.Y. 2010) (abrogated by, Chin v. Port Authority of New York & New Jersey, 685 F.3d 135, 115 Fair Empl. Prac. Cas. (BNA) 720, 95 Empl. Prac. Dec. (CCH) P 44555 (2d Cir. 2012)) ("The common law duty to preserve evidence relevant to litigation is well recognized.").

[3]*See* Silvestri v. General Motors Corp., 271 F.3d 583, 589, 51 Fed. R. Serv. 3d 694 (4th Cir. 2001) ("The right to impose sanctions for spoliation arises from a court's inherent power to control the judicial process . . . .").

[4]F.R.C.P. 37.

[5]*See* John Range & Jonathan Wilan, *Techniques for Obtaining Efficient and Economical E-Disclosure Despite Arbitral Resistance to U.S.-Style Discovery*, E-Discovery in Arbitration: Leading Lawyers on Recovering Electronic Evidence, Meeting New Disclosure Guidelines, and Implementing Measures to Streamline the Proceedings (Feb. 2010) ("In theory, the same general principles respecting spoliation of evidence that apply in civil litigation apply in national (as opposed to international) arbitration."); Irene Warshauer, *Electronic Discovery in*

tion obligation will generally be narrower in arbitration than it is in civil litigation. With respect to timing, there is no question that the obligation to preserve relevant information is triggered when a party receives a notice of intent to arbitrate. But the duty also may arise before that point. Deciding when a duty to preserve is triggered is a fact-intensive determination that requires consideration of a number of factors, including, but not limited to: the level of knowledge within the organization about the claim; the level of risk to the organization posed by the claim; the risk of losing information if a legal hold is not implemented; and the number and complexity of the sources in which information is reasonably likely to be found.[6] This fact-intensive inquiry should be undertaken by someone who is reasonably experienced and who is in a position to make an informed judgment based on consideration of all the relevant facts and circumstances.

As a general proposition, a reasonable anticipation of arbitration arises when a party is on notice of a credible threat that it will become involved in arbitration, or it anticipates taking actions to initiate an arbitration proceeding. The mere possibility of arbitration, standing alone, does not trigger the preservation duty.[7]

As the party receives additional information, it should reevaluate its determination of whether arbitration is reasonably anticipated. This may require the party to revise an earlier determination that arbitration was not reasonably anticipated, thereby triggering the preservation duty. But the availability of new information can also work the other way, leading the party to

---

Arbitration: Privilege Issues and Spoliation of Evidence, 61 Disp. Resol. J. 9, 12 (Jan. 2007) ("[P]arties have an obligation to preserve evidence that may be relevant to matters at issue in an arbitration as well as a litigation.").

[6]*See* In re Enron Corp. Securities, Derivative & ERISA Litigation, 761 F. Supp. 2d 504 (S.D. Tex. 2011) (citing National Tank Co. v. Brotherton, 851 S.W.2d 193, 204 (Tex. 1993) ("[T]o determine when a party reasonably anticipates or foresees litigation, trial courts must look at the totality of the circumstances and decide whether a reasonably person in the party's position would have anticipated litigation and whether the party actually did anticipate litigation.").

[7]*See, e.g., The Sedona Conference Commentary on Legal Holds: The Trigger & the Process*, 11 Sedona Conf. J. 265, 269 (Fall 2010) ("A reasonable anticipation of litigation arises when an organization is on notice of a credible probability that it will become involved in litigation, seriously contemplates initiating litigation, or when it takes specific actions to commence litigation."); Zubulake v. UBS Warburg LLC, 220 F.R.D. 212, 217, 92 Fair Empl. Prac. Cas. (BNA) 1539 (S.D. N.Y. 2003) ("Merely because one or two employees contemplate the possibility that a fellow employee might sue does not generally impose a firmwide duty to preserve.").

conclude that the preservation obligation is no longer necessary because it now anticipates the dispute will be resolved amicably.[8]

Preservation issues may come before an arbitrator when one party seeks to question or challenge the timing of the other party's legal hold determination. An evaluation of a party's legal hold decision should be based on the reasonableness of the decision and the good faith of the party at the time the decision was made. Over the past few years, courts have often second-guessed these decisions in litigation, holding that the parties should have known more, and done more, than they did, at an earlier point in time.[9] There is a similar risk that arbitrators will attribute to a party a greater level of certainty than would be fair to conclude at that particular point in time. It is important to convince the arbitrator that the reasonableness of the determination to preserve or not to preserve should be examined in light of the facts and circumstances known to the party at the time of its decision, not based on hindsight or information acquired after the decision was made.

One common challenge in civil litigation arises when one party gives notice of its intent to sue another, and that notice is accompanied by a boilerplate preservation demand that is extremely broad in terms of the ESI it seeks the opposing party to preserve. This strategy is inappropriate in the arbitration context because it imposes exactly the kinds of costs and burdens that arbitration is designed to avoid.[10] When a party receives that kind of communication, it should consider trying to engage in a dialogue

---

[8]*The Sedona Conference Commentary on Legal Holds: The Trigger & the Process*, 11 Sedona Conf. J. 265, 270 (Fall 2010) ("[L]ater information may require an organization to reevaluate its determination and may result in a conclusion that litigation that previously had not been reasonably anticipated (and consequently did not trigger a preservation obligation) is then reasonably anticipated. Conversely, new information may enable an organization to determine that it should no longer reasonably anticipate a particular litigation, and that it is consequently no longer subject to a preservation obligation.").

[9]*See, e.g.*, Majors Tours, Inc. v. Colorel, 2009 U.S. Dist. LEXIS 68128 (D.N.J. 2009) (finding that defendants should have anticipated litigation as early as 2003 but failed to start preserving evidence until 2005); Zimmerman v. Poly Prep Country Day School, 2011 U.S. Dist. LEXIS 40704 (E.D.N.Y. 2011) (finding that private school "should have anticipated possible future litigation" because there was "ample evidence that numerous . . . children had been sexually abused" by the school's football coach).

[10]*See* John Range & Jonathan Wilan, *Techniques for Obtaining Efficient and Economical E-Disclosure Despite Arbitral Resistance to U.S.-Style Discovery*, E-Discovery in Arbitration: Leading Lawyers on Recovering Electronic Evidence, Meeting New Disclosure Guidelines, and Implementing Measures to Streamline the Proceedings (Feb. 2010) ("Most arbitrators and arbitral organizations

with its adversary. Alternatively, it can respond to the demand in writing with a statement of what it is willing to preserve and an explanation that if the other party wants more, it will have to absorb the cost. The most challenging situation arises when a party must make a unilateral decision about preservation because the other party has not yet stated whether it intends to bring suit or to initiate the arbitration process. In this instance, the party must make its own determination about whether there is a credible threat of litigation or arbitration, and if so, how much ESI should be preserved.

The scope of the duty to preserve involves the question of how much should be preserved once the party has decided to implement a legal hold. In civil litigation, the duty to preserve generally extends to information that is relevant to any party's claim or defense, or to the subject matter involved in the action, phrases that are very broadly construed.[11] In arbitration, the scope of the preservation duty should generally be narrower and limited to information that is material and necessary to resolve the dispute at hand. Unlike civil litigation, in which the parties often go on expensive "fishing expeditions," the whole point of arbitration is to narrow the issues and to focus on resolving the dispute. A duty to preserve that is unfocused and overly-broad in scope does not foster this goal.

There is no one-size-fits-all approach when it comes to implementing a legal hold. The proper strategy will depend on the unique aspects of the organization's IT systems, its data sources, the nature of the dispute, and the parties' roles in the dispute. But best practices usually suggest that in-house counsel, outside counsel, and the organization's IT and/or records management personnel should work together to define the appropriate scope.[12]

When a duty to preserve arises, reasonable steps must be taken

---

maintain that arbitration is, or at least should be, a faster, more private, less expensive, and less contentious method of dispute resolution. As a result . . . the 'leave no stone unturned' image often associated with 'U.S.-style discovery' is viewed by many arbitrators as a negative characteristic of litigation. The absence of broad 'discovery' in arbitration is one of the important characteristics that distinguish arbitration from litigation . . . .").

[11]Pippins v. KPMG LLP, 18 Wage & Hour Cas. 2d (BNA) 532, 2011 WL 4701849 (S.D. N.Y. 2011) ("In the context of discovery, relevance 'is to be interpreted broadly' and includes 'any matter that bears on, or that . . . reasonably could lead to other [information] that could bear on, any issue that is or may be the case.' ") (internal citations omitted). See also F.R.C.P. 26(b)(1).

[12]Valecia M. McDowell, *Arbitration in the Digital Age: Synchronizing Your E-Discovery Plan With Your Arbitration Strategy*, E-Discovery in Arbitration:

to identify and preserve information that is material and necessary to resolve the dispute, as soon as practicable. Under most circumstances, this will entail sending a written legal hold notice to custodians and others who may have such information.[13] With the proliferation of cloud computing, and the outsourcing of many IT functions and storage services, material and necessary information may increasingly be maintained outside the four walls of the organization. Therefore, it is important to consider whether there is information that is in the possession or custody of a third-party agent, that is subject to contractual or other factors that would place it within the control of the party. Examples would include an outsourced service provider, a storage facility operator, and services and storage "in the cloud" or in third-party databases like Bloomberg. In the arbitration context, information in the hands of a true, arm's-length third-party should not be sought unless that information is critical to resolving the dispute. Because the goal in arbitration is to avoid imposing unnecessary costs and burdens, preservation obligations should not be required for information held by third-parties that is not material and necessary for resolving the dispute.

Like the timing of the duty to preserve, the scope of the legal hold is also an area that is ripe for dispute and that an arbitrator may be asked to consider. In determining what information should be preserved, an arbitrator should consider various factors, weighing and balancing the usefulness of the information against the cost and burden of preserving that information. Factors to be considered include: the nature of the issues that are raised in the matter; the value of the matter in controversy; the types of information in dispute (e.g., whether the hold pertains to active data, historical data, or ongoing/future data); and the accessibility of the data. In arbitration, the goal is to narrow the scope and to focus on what is genuinely necessary to resolve the dispute. With proper motivation, it should be possible to do this

---

Leading Lawyers on Recovering Electronic Evidence, Meeting New Disclosure Guidelines, and Implementing Measures to Streamline the Process (Feb. 2010) ("[E]nsuring that your client's IT staff is part of the document hold process is *fundamental* to cost containment, as well as effective advocacy." (emphasis in original)).

[13]John Range & Jonathan Wilan, *Techniques for Obtaining Efficient and Economical E-Disclosure Despite Arbitral Resistance to U.S.-Style Discovery*, E-Discovery in Arbitration: Leading Lawyers on Recovering Electronic Evidence, Meeting New Disclosure Guidelines, and Implementing Measures to Streamline the Proceedings (Feb. 2010) ("[W]e recommend in arbitration, as we do in civil litigation, that counsel send a notice both to its own client and to the opposing party to preserve documents.").

and to generate cost savings in ways that are harder to accomplish in civil litigation.

One of the most common causes of later disputes over spoliation—the destruction or material alteration of evidence and the failure to preserve it for another's use in litigation—is the failure of the parties to engage in meaningful discussions about preservation early in the process. It is preferable for the parties to reach these decisions, rather than the arbitrator, since the arbitrator is typically in an inferior position to understand the IT systems of the parties and can inadvertently impose excessive costs and burdens without fully appreciating what he or she is doing. The best approach is for the parties to have a focused and frank discussion about the claims and defenses, to identify the sources of ESI that are most likely to contain relevant information, and to focus on preserving only the most material and necessary information.[14]

Another issue that sometimes arises in arbitration is determining whether there is a need to preserve metadata.[15] Metadata, which is data about data, is quickly and easily lost. Because it may be inadvertently altered or overwritten, the parties need to have a discussion about metadata early in the process to determine whether it is necessary for the resolution of any disputed issues, or for other purposes.[16] Otherwise, metadata may be lost by the time the arbitration takes place.

Failing to preserve relevant information (including metadata) can result in spoliation. Whenever evidence is not preserved, the integrity of the fact-finding or truth-seeking process is harmed and the tribunal (regardless of type) typically has to fashion a

---

[14]Valecia M. McDowell, *Arbitration in the Digital Age: Synchronizing Your E-Discovery Plan With Your Arbitration Strategy*, E-Discovery in Arbitration: Leading Lawyers on Recovering Electronic Evidence, Meeting New Disclosure Guidelines, and Implementing Measures to Streamline the Process (Feb. 2010) ("Reaching an agreement with your opposing counsel with respect to some or all of the outstanding e-discovery issues ahead of time prior to involving your arbitrators is often an important component of the overall e-discovery plan.").

[15]*The Sedona Conference Glossary: E-Discovery & Digital Information Management* (3d ed. Sept. 2010) (defining "Metadata" as "Data typically stored electronically that describes characteristics of ESI, found in different places in different forms . . .. Metadata can describe how, when, and by whom ESI was collected, created accessed, modified, and how it is formatted.").

[16]*See* Irene Warshauer, *Electronic Discovery in Arbitration: Privilege Issues and Spoliation of Evidence*, 61 Disp. Resol. J. 9, 13 (Jan. 2007) ("Metadata includes the computer system's automatic alteration of documents. Thus, information can be lost or changed. And when that happens in a litigation or arbitration, a claim for spoliation can result.").

remedy.[17] Parties in arbitration should earnestly strive to avoid this outcome, since sanctions defeat the goal of achieving a quick and economical resolution of the dispute on its merits. To avoid this pitfall, the parties should seek to have a timely and cooperative discussion about their preservation efforts, with the assistance of the arbitrator, if necessary, to ensure that those efforts are proportional to what is at stake and limited to what is truly material and necessary to resolve the dispute.

§ 7:3 Scope and proportionality in e-discovery

As discussed above, scope questions typically revolve around what needs to be preserved and produced. In civil litigation, the so-called "proportionality rule" requires courts to limit the extent of discovery if the burden or expense of the proposed discovery outweighs its likely benefit.[1] This rule has received much attention of late in the federal courts. In arbitration, the biggest risk is that the scope of e-discovery will not be appropriately circumscribed, which can eliminate the benefits that arbitration is intended to provide—speed and reduced cost.

Much of the ESI produced in civil litigation is redundant or of marginal relevance. A significant part of what drives cost in civil litigation is that the parties often request everything under the sun,[2] often because they have not taken the time to figure out what the dispute is truly about, they have not determined what they really need to resolve the dispute, or they suspect that their adversary will withhold information that is important. It is therefore critical in the arbitration context that parties spend

---

[17]*See* Robert Davidson & Margaret Shaw, *Arbitrators Hold Significant Power Over Discovery*, The National Law Journal (Nov. 27, 2006) (Both the JAMS and American Arbitration Association rules provide for sanctions "for a discovery abuse involving spoliation or the failure to disclose emails or other ESI."); Valecia McDowell, *Arbitration in the Digital Age: Synchronizing Your E-Discovery Plan With Your Arbitration Strategy*, E-Discovery in Arbitration: Leading Lawyers on Recovering Electronic Evidence, Meeting New Disclosure Guidelines, and Implementing Measures to Streamline the Proceedings (Feb. 2010) ("[T]he consequences of a party's failure to meet its e-discovery obligations in arbitration are very similar to those it might face in state or federal court.").

[Section 7:3]

[1]F.R.C.P. 26(b)(2)(C).

[2]Ethan Berghoff, *E-Discovery Invades International Arbitration*, E-Discovery in Arbitration: Leading Lawyers on Recovering Electronic Evidence, Meeting New Disclosure Guidelines, and Implementing Measures to Streamline the Proceedings (Feb. 2010) ("[F]ar-reaching and invasive discovery . . . is treated as a matter of course in the United States.").

time up front figuring out exactly what is in dispute, what evidence would most expeditiously resolve that dispute, who is most likely to have that evidence, and where it is most likely to be located. Each additional custodian, and each additional source of data that needs to be searched, reviewed, and produced adds to cost and delay. Because of asymmetries in knowledge about the existing ESI, this process may require the parties to be more transparent, and to work in a more collaborative fashion than that to which they have become accustomed in the adversarial system. For the requesting party, this means that it may need to reveal more about precisely what information it needs to prove (or to defend) its case. For the producing party, this may mean that it will need to be more transparent about the evidence to which it has access.

When assessing the proper scope of e-discovery, the arbitrator should consider whether the burden or expense of producing a source of evidence outweighs its likely benefit in resolving the dispute. In making this proportionality determination, the arbitrator will need to evaluate a number of factors. For example, he or she should consider the needs of the case and what is necessary to prove each element of the claim(s) or defense(s). The arbitrator needs to take into account the amount in controversy and the importance of any nonmonetary factors that may be at stake. He or she should evaluate the uniqueness and the probative value of the ESI that has been requested, as well as the resources of the respective parties.[3]

In weighing these factors, an arbitrator must make subjective determinations regarding the credibility of the parties. Parties can lose credibility when they do not come armed with accurate and detailed information about costs and burdens and, as a result, take unreasonable positions that do not end up being factually supportable. When this happens, arbitrators are likely to get frustrated and question further representations made by the parties. Accordingly, it is crucial to obtain accurate estimates and information about how difficult it is to preserve and produce the requested ESI and how much these efforts are likely to cost.

---

[3]In general, these factors parallel the proportionality test as set forth in F.R.C.P. 26(b)(2)(C). With respect to nonmonetary issues, the Advisory Committee Note to F.R.C.P. 26(b)(2)(C)(iii) encourages courts to consider "the significance of the substantive issues, as measured in philosophic, social, or institutional terms" and states that "many cases in public policy spheres, such as employment practices, free speech, and other matters, may have importance far beyond the monetary amount involved." *See generally* The Sedona Conference Commentary on Proportionality in Electronic Discovery, 11 Sedona Conf. J. 289 (Oct. 2010).

§ 7:4 Cost allocation in e-discovery

Cost allocation issues center around which party should pay, and for what. In the federal civil litigation system, the producing party pays for the cost of producing ESI that is reasonably accessible.[1] There are opportunities for cost-shifting with respect to ESI that is considered not reasonably accessible. In arbitration, there is even more flexibility for the arbitrator to shift and share costs between the parties, particularly the incremental costs for preserving and producing ESI that is not central to the issues in dispute.

There are various types of e-discovery costs that can be shared or shifted in arbitration. These include the cost of preservation, the cost of collecting and processing ESI, the cost of attorney review for responsiveness and privilege, the cost of production, and the costs associated with searching and producing inaccessible ESI. As with preservation and scope, the parties should have a frank discussion about whether there are costs that should be shifted or shared. Reasons for shifting or sharing might include consideration of the parties' respective resources, their relative ability or motivation to control costs, and the relative benefits to each party of obtaining the information.

Federal courts have generally used a seven-factor test for making cost-shifting determinations.[2] These are reasonable factors for the parties or arbitrator to consider, and they are set forth below in decreasing order of importance. The first consideration is the extent to which the request is specifically tailored to discover relevant information. Next is the availability of the information from other, more accessible sources. If the information can be easily obtained from another source, it does not make sense to go down an expensive e-discovery path. The third factor

---

[Section 7:4]

[1]"A party need not provide discovery of electronically stored information from sources that the party identifies as not reasonably accessible because of undue burden or cost." F.R.C.P. 26(b)(2)(B).

[2]*See, e.g.*, Zubulake v. UBS Warburg LLC, 217 F.R.D. 309, 91 Fair Empl. Prac. Cas. (BNA) 1574 (S.D. N.Y. 2003); Wood v. Capital One Servs., LLC, 2011 WL 2154279 (N.D.N.Y. Apr. 15, 2011); Universal Del., Inc. v. Comdata Corp., 2010 1381225 (E.D. Pa. Mar. 31, 2010); P&G Co. v. S.C. Johnsom & Son, Inc., 2009 U.S. Dist. LEXIS 13190 (E.D. Tex. Feb. 19, 2009); John B. v. Goetz, 2010 U.S. Dist. LEXIS 8821 (M.D. Tenn. Jan. 28, 2010); Hagemeyer North America, Inc. v. Gateway Data Sciences Corp., 222 F.R.D. 594 (E.D. Wis. 2004); Helmert v. Butterball, LLC, 2010 U.S. Dist. LEXIS 60777 (E.D. Ark. May 27, 2010); Advante Int'l Corp. v. Mintel Learning Tech., 2006 U.S. Dist. LEXIS 45859 (N.D. Cal. June 29, 2006).

is the total cost of production relative to the amount in controversy (this, as previously discussed, is the proportionality analysis). Next is the total cost of production compared to the resources available to each party. The fifth consideration is the relative ability of each party to control costs and its incentive to do so. It has been argued by some that a rule requiring the requesting party to pay for production will serve as a limit on e-discovery because a party will presumably be more circumspect about what it requests if it is required to pay for it. The sixth factor is the importance of the issues at stake in the litigation. The seventh factor is the relative benefits to the parties of obtaining the information. Sometimes the same information benefits both sides, and sometimes it benefits only one side.

Generally speaking, arbitrators should try to ensure fairness and restore any imbalance or asymmetry in the matter to make sure that the requesting party is neither advantaged nor disadvantaged in seeking discovery.[3] Arbitrators should not enable requesting parties to bludgeon their adversaries by asking for too much, but arbitrators should also avoid putting requesting parties in a position in which they cannot prove or defend their case because they are small or indigent. By shifting (or threatening to shift) costs, arbitrators can impose discipline on the parties and can encourage greater compromise between them.

§ 7:5 The use of search terms and advanced search methodologies

Significant cost savings can be achieved by using proper search strategies.[1] The most likely scenario in which an arbitrator will become involved with search issues is when the parties are un-

---

[3]The Recommended Arbitration Discovery Protocols promulgated by JAMS provides the following guideline: "Where the costs and burdens of e-discovery are disproportionate to the nature and gravity of the dispute or to the amount in controversy, or to the relevance of the materials requested, the arbitrator will either deny such requests or order disclosure on condition that the requesting party advance the reasonable cost of production to the other side, subject to the allocation of costs in the final award." JAMS Recommended Arbitration Discovery Protocols, *available at* http://www.jamsadr.com/arbitration-discovery-protocols/.

[Section 7:5]

[1]Valecia M. McDowell, *Arbitration in the Digital Age: Synchronizing Your E-Discovery Plan With Your Arbitration Strategy*, E-Discovery in Arbitration: Leading Lawyers on Recovering Electronic Evidence, Meeting New Disclosure Guidelines, and Implementing Measures to Streamline the Process (Feb. 2010) ("The designation of search terms is often the most strategically significant of [the discovery-related] agreements.").

able to reach agreement either on the search terms, or on the search methodology that should be applied to identify potentially responsive documents. Typically, the requesting party will propose a long list of general search terms and the producing party will want to apply a short list of narrow search terms. The producing party may test the requesting party's search terms by using something often referred to as a "hit list," to see how many documents are identified by each search term. The producing party will typically argue that the requested terms will result in an inordinate number of documents for review, with a high proportion that are irrelevant. On the other hand, the requesting party typically has limited knowledge of, and no access to, his or her adversary's data, so it is distrustful and does not want to give ground on any request. This can result in an impasse between the parties.

How should arbitrators resolve this problem? Whose search term list should apply? Or, should the arbitrator generate his or her own search term list, or "split the difference" between the parties' lists? It is important to understand that there is generally an asymmetry in knowledge about ESI.[2] Consequently, the producing party (who has the data) is generally in the best position to select the most appropriate search strategy because they know what language (or code words) would have been used.[3] Therefore, producing parties should typically generate the initial search term list, as long as they are operating reasonably and in good faith.

It is important to have a cooperative, iterative, and informed process if the parties are to identify quickly and cheaply the ESI that is most likely to resolve the dispute. If the parties do not spend time talking to the custodians that created the ESI, and reviewing samples of ESI from the "hits" and "misses" piles generated as a result of the application of the proposed search terms,

---

[2]*See generally* Jason R. Baron, *E-Discovery and the Problem of Asymmetric Knowledge*, Symposium: Ethics and Professionalism in the Digital Age, 60 Mercer L. Rev. 863 (2009); *see also* Baron, Law in the Age of Exabytes: Some Further Thoughts on "Information Inflation" and Current Issues in E-Discovery Search, XVII Rich. J.L. & Tech. 9, 17-24 (2011), *available at* http://jolt.richmond.edu/v17i3/article9.pdf.

[3]It is also important to point out that "many arbitrators . . . are not computer savvy, do not understand the terminology, the technology, or the process used to conduct searches for ESI," and therefore are not the best parties to produce search term lists. John Range & Jonathan Wilan, *Techniques for Obtaining Efficient and Economical E-Disclosure Despite Arbitral Resistance to U.S.-Style Discovery*, E-Discovery in Arbitration: Leading Lawyers on Recovering Electronic Evidence, Meeting New Disclosure Guidelines, and Implementing Measures to Streamline the Proceedings (Feb. 2010).

they are likely to have a poor outcome. A frequently-cited study by Blair and Maron evaluated the efficacy of searches performed by experienced paralegals and attorneys using a Boolean search engine on a large database of legal documents.[4] The study concluded that while the searchers thought they had retrieved approximately 75% of the relevant documents in the database, they in fact had only recovered approximately 20%.[5] This study underscores the fact that without an iterative, informed process, the parties can miss important evidence and can waste significant amounts of time and money gathering irrelevant ESI. One of the best ways to generate search terms, and one that is frequently overlooked by counsel, is to talk to the people who created or who maintain the documents about the terms that were used. Also, sometimes, an hour or two spent with a subject-matter expert, such as a linguist or statistician, can save a tremendous amount of money later on in the process by helping to derive an effective and efficient strategy to sift through the data and quickly get to the essence of what is needed to resolve the dispute.[6]

Obtaining an index of the words and the domain names or addresses that appear in the document collection, ranked from most frequent to least frequent in appearance, may also be helpful. This index can assist the parties in identifying items such as

---

[4]*See* David Blair & M. Maron, *An Evaluation of Retrieval Effectiveness for a Full Text Document Retrieval System*, 28 Communications of the ACM 289 (1985).

[5]David Blair & M. Maron, *An Evaluation of Retrieval Effectiveness for a Full Text Document Retrieval System*, 28 Communications of the ACM 289, 293 (1985). Even though search algorithms and search strategies have improved since 1985, the Blair and Maron study is often referenced because "there has been little in the way of peer-reviewable research establishing the efficacy of various methods of automated content analysis, search, and retrieval as applied to a legal discovery context." *The Sedona Conference Best Practices Commentary on the Use of Search and Information Retrieval Methods in E-Discovery*, 8 Sedona Conf. J. 189, 215 (Aug. 2007). *But see* Maura R. Grossman and Gordon V. Cormack, Technology-Assisted Review in E-Discovery Can Be More Effective and More Efficient Than Exhaustive Manual Review, XVII Rich. J.L. & Tech. 13 (2011), *available at* http://jolt.richmond.edu/v17i3/article11.pdf; Herbert L. Roitblat, Anna Kershaw & Patrick Oot, Document Categorization in Legal Electronic Discovery: Computer Classification vs. Manual Review, 61 J. Am. Soc'y for Info. Sci. & Tech. 70 (2010).

[6]*See* Ethan Berghoff, *E-Discovery Invades International Arbitration*, E-Discovery in Arbitration: Leading Lawyers on Recovering Electronic Evidence, Meeting New Disclosure Guidelines, and Implementing Measures to Streamline the Proceedings (Feb. 2010) (commenting that experts are "essential tools in the e-discovery process" because of their knowledge, their ability to communicate with the client's IT employees and their ability to testify at trial as an independent party regarding the rigor of the search process).

search terms that may retrieve too many irrelevant documents, possible misspellings, code names that might otherwise be overlooked, and people who may have used multiple email addresses or aliases. Additionally, this index may be useful in eliminating false positive or "noise" documents. For example, if the index reveals many documents from domain names like "wallstreetjournal.com" or "amazon.com," and the parties know that such documents would not likely be relevant, they can remove these documents from the set to be reviewed for production.

How should parties test or sample their search-term lists? Parties may be tempted to assume that a word that gets a very high number of search-term "hits" is less useful than a word that gets fewer search-term "hits," but the number of "hits" does not say anything about whether those "hits" are retrieving relevant documents.[7] To make that determination, parties need to review a random sample of the documents to see whether their search terms are effective or not, and they need to do sampling on both the "hits" and the "misses." Sampling the "hits" can help the parties to deal with the problem of over-inclusiveness (i.e., documents that are picked up by the search terms but are not relevant). For example, if a transaction was referred to by the code name "patriot," a search using the word "patriot" might find documents about the Patriot Act that have nothing to do with the dispute. If parties can learn this through sampling, they can tweak the search to retrieve "patriot," but not "act," thereby identifying only the documents related to the transaction. It is also important to sample the "misses," because if a substantial amount of relevant information is found in the "misses" pile," the parties will know that the search terms are not effective.[8] Thus, by sampling both search-term "hits" and "misses," parties can deal with the problems of over-inclusion and under-inclusion.[9] With respect to sample size, as a general rule of thumb, a set of

---

[7]Parties are often interested in the "precision" of the search terms, defined as "an information retrieval performance measure that quantifies the fraction of retrieved documents which are known to be relevant." Ricardo Baez-Yates & Berthier Ribeiro-Neto, Modern Information Retrieval 437–455 (1999) (glossary).

[8]Sampling on "misses" will help the parties measure the "recall" of the search terms, defined as "an information retrieval performance measure that quantifies the fraction of known relevant documents which were effectively retrieved." Ricardo Baez-Yates & Berthier Ribeiro-Neto, Modern Information Retrieval 437–455 (1999) (glossary).

[9]The Sedona Conference Best Practices Commentary on the Use of Search and Information Retrieval Methods in E-Discovery, 8 Sedona Conf. J. 189, 215 (Aug. 2007) ("Reviewing samples of information that include selected search

400 to 700 randomly selected documents should be sufficient for most very large document collections.

Parties can also tweak their searches in various ways. They can use Boolean restrictors (like "and," "or," and "but not"), proximity searches ("X" within so many words of "Y"), and wildcards (for example, "teach!" will pick up "teacher," "teachers," and "teaching"). Parties should consider performing at least one iteration to test the search terms so they can be tweaked as necessary. Research conducted in connection with the National Institute of Standards and Technology's Text Retrieval Conference ("TREC") suggests that the first search iteration generally provides the highest return, and while further iterations can help, there is generally declining marginal utility for these efforts.[10]

There are various advanced search technologies available to help the parties improve their search efforts. For example, early case assessment ("ECA") tools allow an organization to take large amounts of data, load it into a repository at a relatively modest per-gigabyte price, and use sophisticated search tools to cull the dataset while it is in the repository. These tools can assemble communications among the same groups of people, or ESI related to the same subject matter. One problem with some of these tools is that unless the user is fairly knowledgeable, it can be easy to remove documents early in the process that never get considered because they do not get placed in the queue for review. Consequently the parties need to be confident that they are well-informed when working with early case assessment tools.

A party can also use "concept search" and "clustering" tools. These tools apply statistical and linguistic models to help identify documents that are related in content.[11] For example, if the party does a search for "cup" using one of these tools, it will also find documents that concern glasses, coffee mugs, wine goblets, water

---

terms or concepts and ranking their relative value based on their efficacy in retrieving relevant information (recall) and their efficiency in excluding non-relevant information (precision) can help the review team to focus the selection of the terms.").

[10]*See* F.C. Zhao, D.W. Oard & J.R. Baron, *Improving Search Effectiveness in the Legal E-Discovery Process Using Relevance Feedback* (paper presented at the DESI III Global E-Discovery/E-Disclosure Workshop at the 12th International Conference on Artificial Intelligence and Law (2009).

[11]Maura R. Grossman & Terry Sweeney, What lawyers need to know about search tools, Nat'l L. J. (Aug. 23, 2010).

tumblers, champagne flutes, etc.[12] One challenge associated with these tools is that they are often proprietary and may prove difficult for the average attorney to understand, to explain, and to determine how well they work. Therefore, it may be difficult for a party to defend the use of such tools without hiring an expert, particularly if they are challenged by opposing counsel. This should not pose an issue if the parties reach agreement on, or the arbitrator approves, their use.

Parties can also use machine learning tools that are capable of what is commonly referred to as "technology-assisted review" or "predictive coding." If a party has a good set of exemplar documents that are relevant, these tools are capable of finding more documents in the collection that are like the "seed" or "training" documents. While this technology is not foolproof, it is quite promising and can be a more efficient and cost-effective approach than manual document review.[13] Machine learning approaches require sampling and testing, but they can be effective ways for parties to manage large data sets in arbitration. If the parties plan to use automated approaches to search and review of ESI, it is important that they put in place a clawback agreement or obtain a Federal Rule of Evidence 502(d) order providing that privilege is not waived by inadvertent disclosure (see below on privilege for more detail).

Research conducted by TREC has shown that, as of yet, no single approach to search is significantly better than all other approaches, under all circumstances.[14] Different approaches often yield different result sets, and some information is simply easier to find than others. For example, if a dispute concerns a specific patent or a drug, it may be much easier to find the relevant documents than if the dispute were to involve an accusation of accounting fraud. In the latter circumstance, it may be far less clear what language would have been used, and the facts may be

---

[12]In like manner, if a "labor lawyer were searching for evidence that management was targeting neophytes in the union, she might miss the term 'n00b' (a neologism for 'newbie')." The Sedona Conference Best Practices Commentary on the Use of Search and Information Retrieval Methods in E-Discovery, 8 Sedona Conf. J. 189, 203 (Aug. 2007).

[13]Maura R. Grossman & Gordon V. Cormack, Technology-Assisted Review in E-Discovery Can Be More Effective and More Efficient Than Exhaustive Manual Review, XVII Rich. J.L. & Tech. 11 (2011), http://jolt.richmond.edu/v17i 3/article11.pdf; see also Law By The Numbers: Efficient E-Discovery, ABA Journal (Apr. 2012), at 31.

[14]See generally, Overview of the TREC 2008 Legal Track, available at htt p://trec-legal.umiacs.umd.edu/; Overview of the TREC 2009 Legal Track, available at http://trec-legal.umiacs.umd.edu/.

more ambiguous and difficult to parse. In most cases, a hybrid search strategy will likely be the best approach. Parties can come to a reasonable agreement about what technology they will use, recognizing that it is not necessary to retrieve every single potentially relevant document, and that search results do not have to be perfect in order to resolve the dispute fairly.

The above discussion should serve to reinforce the point that search generally needs to be a relatively collaborative and iterative process if it is going to be successful. It should be well-planned, with substantial human input in the initial stages to determine what information the parties are looking for, how they are going to locate it, and where they are going to find it.[15] Some degree of testing, sampling, and feedback is generally important to make sure that the party's search terms are actually identifying the documents it seeks. Parties also need to focus on proportionality considerations, recognizing that what they need are the "key" documents that are going to help resolve the dispute quickly and inexpensively. They do not need every possible document, however marginally related.

Document review is typically the most expensive part of e-discovery, sometimes consuming 80% or more of the total cost, thus enormous savings can result from effective search strategies.[16] The more the strategy can distill the document population down to what is truly probative, the greater the savings will be. Parties should obtain specific estimates and consider staged approaches, starting with the highest-yielding ESI and expanding from there if a broader search is necessary.

§ 7:6 Forms of production of ESI

Form of production is another area where parties can get into

---

[15]The Sedona Conference Best Practices Commentary on the Use of Search and Information Retrieval Methods in E-Discovery, 8 Sedona Conf. J. 189, 215 (Aug. 2007) ("[T]o maximize the chances of success in terms of finding responsive documents, a well-thought out strategy capitalizing on 'human knowledge' available to a party should be put into action at the earliest opportunity.").

[16]*See Interview with Randall Burrows, A Major Leap Forward in E-Discovery*, The Metropolitan Corporate Counsel (Dec. 2010), available at http://www.metro corpcounsel.com/current.php?artType=view&EntryNo=11700 ("General wisdom is that 80 percent of all litigation costs come in the discovery phase and 80 percent of those costs stem from document review."); Chris May, *The Leading Edge of Document Review: The Content-Based Review Process*, Discovery Management Digest (Q4 2010), *available at* http://www.iediscovery.com/news-ev ents/newsletter.aspx?nsid=30&articleid=133&articletype=article ("[T]he document review phase . . . accounts for between 60 and 80 percent of discovery costs.").

trouble if they do not engage in early dialogue (and often they do not). There are many possible forms in which ESI can be produced. One possible form is paper; however, hardcopy production may or may not be reasonable depending on the volume of documents. If the dispute is not document-intensive, exchanging paper may be a perfectly reasonable approach.

Another common form of production is digital images, which are typically produced in either PDF or TIFF form. These are essentially a picture or rendering of the document, and they can be produced with or without something called a "load file."[1] A load file is an accompanying file that provides certain metadata and other information that enables the receiving party to search and classify, or otherwise make better use of the ESI. For example, a load file might include information indicating where documents begin and end, and what attachments, if any, were appended to them. Because digital images are generally unsearchable without additional information, whenever feasible, the parties should extract the text from the document and provide it in the load file in order to preserve the capacity to search the documents for particular keywords.[2] Load files also often include header information that makes email more useful, such as the sender, the date and time sent, the recipients (including both ccs and bccs), and the subject line.

For non-email electronic files, load files can also include information such as the names of the custodian(s) who retained the file, and a link or file path to a native version of the document. For example, voice mail that is stored in a WAV file and sent via email would be useless if produced only as a digital image, because the image would not allow the recipient to listen to the message. So, in addition to the image, the producing party would

---

[Section 7:6]

[1]*The Sedona Conference Glossary: E-Discovery & Digital Information Management* (3d ed. Sept. 2010) (defining a "Load File" as "A file that relates to a set of scanned images or electronically process files, and indicates where individual pages or files belong together as documents, to include attachments, and where each document begins and ends. A load file may also contain data relevant to the individual documents, such as selected metadata, coded data, and extracted text.").

[2]John Barkett, *E-Discovery for Arbitrators*, Dispute Resolution International 129, (Dec. 2007) ("Parties that want to be able to perform electronic searches will want data in a searchable format. In addition, there may be reasons to obtain electronically stored information in different formats. For example, word-processed documents could be imaged with word search capabilities while spreadsheets may be produced in native format to view the formulae used in the spreadsheet.").

need to provide a link to the WAV file so that the requesting party could listen to the message. The same considerations can apply to spreadsheets with formulas; the formulas are not available when the spreadsheets are produced as static images without native links.

The final form of production is "native" format. This is the form in which the document was created, and the form in which it is generally maintained on the IT system of the party that produced it, with the metadata intact. There are several types of metadata, which may or may not be relevant to the dispute. System metadata is not part of the file itself, but may be thought of as the "demographics" of the document, including information about when it was created, when it was last modified, who the author was, where it is stored on the system, who edited it, and the total editing time. Application metadata is embedded in the file and travels with the file. Examples would include the fonts used and other formatting features, track changes, spreadsheet formulas, and speaker notes in PowerPoint presentations. As previously mentioned, it is important for the parties to discuss up front whether the metadata is necessary to resolve the dispute or make the ESI useable. If it is not, they should not waste money to preserve and produce it.

As a general matter, it costs money and takes time to take data in its native format and convert it into digital images with load files, so producing in native format is generally cheaper than TIFFs or PDFs with load files. But depending on the number and types of files and software applications, native files can be more expensive to search and review because the parties need to have all the different software applications, or have to load the data into some kind of review platform. Native format may be perfectly adequate for small productions in arbitration, but it will generally not be the preferred form if significant document review or redaction will be required. If it is necessary to redact particular words or sections, the parties may prefer digital image files because redacting portions of the actual native file is infeasible. Additionally, if there is a need to maintain the integrity or prove the authenticity of ESI, the parties may prefer a digital image format because native files can be easier to alter.

The mechanics set forth by the Federal Rules of Civil Procedure provide that the requesting party may specify the form of production, allowing for different forms for different types of ESI.[3] Under Federal Rule 34(b), if the requesting party fails to specify

---

[3]F.R.C.P. 34(b)(1)(C).

a particular form, or if the producing party objects to the form, the producing party may propose an alternative form to the requesting party.[4] If the proposed alternative is acceptable to the requesting party, then there is no further discussion. But if the requesting party does not agree with the alternative form, the parties must meet and confer and try to resolve the disagreement. If they cannot, they issue will be resolved by the court.

There is no reason to employ a different process in the arbitration context. It behooves the requesting party to make clear its preferred form of production, and if there is disagreement, it behooves the producing party to explain why that form is unacceptable and/or too costly. If the parties cannot reach a satisfactory resolution, they should promptly raise the dispute with the arbitrator for resolution. The default position in the Federal Rules of Civil Procedure is either to produce the information as it is ordinarily maintained on the system (this usually means in native form), or in a reasonably useable form (this usually means in a searchable form).[5]

§ 7:7 Privilege issues

Privilege issues are the final potential minefield in e-discovery. With parties dealing with such high volumes of electronic information in short timeframes, exacerbated by the fact that most organizations and their attorneys do not properly label or segregate privileged ESI, it is inevitable that some privileged documents will slip through the cracks.[1] A related issue that arises in connection with privilege review is privilege logs, which are typically one of the most expensive and least useful aspects of e-discovery. Arbitration offers unique opportunities to address privilege issues in a flexible and creative fashion. While the parties do not always seek to do this, there are meaningful opportunities for significant cost savings in this area.

Perhaps the most important step is to implement a clawback or non-waiver agreement that provides for the return of inadvertently produced privileged documents and specifies that inadver-

---

[4]F.R.C.P. 34(b)(1)(D).

[5]F.R.C.P. 34(b)(2)(E)(ii).

[Section 7:7]

[1]See Irene Warshauer, Electronic Discovery in Arbitration: Privilege Issues and Spoliation of Evidence, 61 Disp. Resol. J. 11, 13 (Jan. 2007) ("[T]he massive amount of electronic documents potentially subject to discovery greatly increases the number of documents that must be reviewed for privilege. It also makes the inadvertent production of a privileged document more likely.").

tent production, alone, does not constitute a waiver of privilege or work product. The problem with such an agreement in arbitration is that it may only protect the parties to the arbitration at hand; it does not protect either party from a third-party that may seek to obtain the inadvertently produced documents in other litigation in federal or state court. In the federal litigation context, Federal Rule of Evidence 502(d) allows the parties to obtain an order stating that inadvertent production of a privileged document does not constitute a waiver of privilege in any other state or federal proceeding.[2] Moreover, Federal Rule of Evidence 502(f) provides that these orders apply to federal court-annexed and court-mandated arbitration.[3] Accordingly, parties who are engaged in such arbitrations should take advantage of this rule to obtain the maximum possible protection against waiver of privilege or work product due to inadvertent disclosure.

Finally, the parties should engage in a cooperative dialogue early on to seek ways they can reduce the burden of privileged logging, such as by using categories or "buckets" instead of doing an itemized privileged log.[4]

§ 7:8 Key take-away points

Finally, the practitioner should bear in mind these six key take-aways from this overview chapter.

- *First*, the importance of early, thoughtful, and targeted planning with respect to e-discovery cannot be underestimated. Parties need to determine the information they *really* need to prove or defend their case, which party or third-party controls that information, where they would best be able to find that information, and in what form they need it.

- *Second*, parties need to meet and confer with their adversary early and often. Cooperation and transparency—or at least translucency—can reduce cost and delay.

- *Third*, if parties cannot reach a satisfactory resolution about an ESI-related issue, they should promptly reach out for help

---

[2]Fed. R. Evid. 502(d).

[3]Fed. R. Evid. 502(f).

[4]*See* John Facciola & Jonathan Redgrave, Asserting and Challenging Privilege Claims in Modern Litigation: The Facciola-Redgrave Framework, 4 Fed. Cts. L. Rev. 19, 19 (2009) ("[T]he majority of cases should reject the traditional document-by-document privilege log in favor of a new approach that is premised on counsel's cooperation supervised by early, careful and rigorous judicial involvement."). This source provides helpful ideas about sampling, bucketing and other creative approaches that may work well to reduce costs in arbitration.

from the arbitrator. They should avoid engaging in "self-help" or gamesmanship, both of which contribute to cost and delay and subvert the goals of arbitration.

• *Fourth*, parties to arbitration should be reasonable and narrow the scope of e-discovery as much as possible. They should strive to apply the more stringent "material and necessary" standard, rather than the "relevant" or "reasonably calculated" standards applicable in civil litigation.

• *Fifth*, parties should use available technology to appropriately reduce the burden of search. Volume is a key driver of cost, so if the parties can use technology to reduce volume reasonably and defensibly, they should do so.

• *Sixth*, parties should try to be creative and flexible. They should take advantage of the opportunities presented by arbitration, and strive to reduce cost and time in areas in which arbitration allows creative alternatives that are not necessarily available in federal or state court. For example, parties may do this by agreeing amongst themselves, or convincing the arbitrator, that a streamlined privilege log will suffice.

Chapter 8

Electronic Discovery under the Federal Arbitration Act

By Michael S. Davis and Anthony I. Giacobbe, Jr.[*]

> **KeyCite®:** Cases and other legal materials listed in KeyCite Scope can be researched through the KeyCite service on Westlaw®. Use KeyCite to check citations for form, parallel references, prior and later history, and comprehensive citator information, including citations to other decisions and secondary materials.

§ 8:1   What is arbitration?

Arbitration is a binding form of alternative dispute resolution, where the parties entrust resolution of their dispute to others. Parties to a contract may agree that disputes will be resolved by one or more arbitrators instead of by a judge or a jury in a court

---

[*]Michael S. Davis is a partner in the New York office of Zeichner Ellman & Krause LLP with extensive experience in arbitration. He has been appointed by parties, by the American Arbitration Association, and by the New York Supreme Court to serve as an arbitrator for numerous disputes, and is a certified by ARIAS-US as an arbitrator. He has participated in scores arbitration hearings as counsel or as an arbitrator, and has represented clients in many court proceedings concerning arbitration matters.

Anthony I. Giacobbe, Jr. is Of Counsel in the New York office of Zeichner Ellman & Krause LLP, where his practice focuses on commercial litigation and arbitration. He is a member of the Sedona Conference's Electronic Document Retention and Production Working Group, is an appointed member of the NYS Unified Court System's E-Discovery Working Group and has frequently lectures and writes on e-discovery issues.

of law. Although as a general rule, a party has a right to seek redress in an appropriate court (subject to specific jurisdictional requirements in different courts), arbitration is available to parties who mutually agree not to have courts decide their disputes.

Arbitration represents several tradeoffs. The fundamental tradeoff is that parties agree on who shall resolve their dispute. Rather than non-specialized courts of general jurisdiction, arbitration allows mariners to submit their disputes to other seafarers, mining companies to submit their disputes about assays to experienced chemists, builders and architects to submit their disputes to construction professionals, and even allows major league baseball teams to submit their disputes to baseball professionals.

While plainly arbitration affords this very important right, a party who agrees not to use the court gives up certain other rights in return. All courts have a set of rules, procedural and substantive, that are applicable to disputes within their respective jurisdictions. These rules are further clarified and amplified by court decisions interpreting them, as well as by legislative histories, commentaries and articles. Many of these rules concern discovery—which of course is the subject of this Treatise—and, in recent years, as this book outlines, there have been many new rules and court rulings concerning electronic discovery. By agreeing to arbitrate, a party may trade informality and discretion for some burden and expense that comes with the established and evolving rules of e-discovery. Under the FAA, arbitrators are expected and required to attend due process of law but parties usually agree to an arbitration format that is less formal than court.

Another important right that is surrendered when parties agree to arbitrate is the right to appeal. This right may protect litigants against arbitrary decisions and is designed to ensure consistency among trial courts in applying legal rules. Arbitration decisions are subject to very limited review by the trial court in the jurisdiction where the arbitration takes place. Arbitrators can be given wide discretion by the parties' agreement to decide cases. Often an agreement provides that arbitrators are not bound to follow the "strict rule of law." Under FAA Section 10 (9 U.S.C. § 10), even if an arbitrator declines to rule in accordance with otherwise applicable law, that arbitration award is binding and should be confirmed by the trial court absent extraordinary circumstances such as evident partiality, corruption or fraud, or other "misconduct" that may amount to a denial of due process.[1] Thus, not only is the arbitrator given authority to decide the dispute in accordance with the contract, but the arbitrator is given broader discretion than a court to interpret and apply fact and law. Because arbitration is a function of the parties' agreement, an award can also be vacated if the "arbitrators exceeded their powers" (9 U.S.C. § 10(a)(4)) as set forth in the arbitration agreement.

The parties to an arbitration agreement not only gain the right to designate the qualifications of the arbitrators, but also gain the right to control their proceeding and thus can agree to flexibility and efficiency. Thus, when agreeing to arbitrate, the parties can also agree to rules governing their arbitration. They can agree to the number of arbitrators, the method of selection of arbitrators, the discovery rules that will govern, the conduct of the hearing, the type of arbitration award and any other terms they choose. This flexibility even allows the parties to reach new agreements during the arbitration or to change the prior rules.

For example, if there is one specific issue in dispute, the parties or the arbitration tribunal can tailor the discovery specifically to that issue without investing time or resources on other issues or processes that might be required in a court proceeding. This process can also be more efficient than courts because arbitrators typically are not overburdened with cases like courts are and thus can devote the time and attention necessary to deal with disputes and bring the case to conclusion. These elements of control, flexibility and efficiency can be particularly useful in the context of electronic discovery, where the time and expense of complying with court rules or rulings can in some instances exceed the value of the entire controversy.

§ 8:2   The Federal Arbitration Act

Congress enacted the Federal Arbitration Act ("FAA"), 9 U.S.C. §§ 1 et seq., in 1925 "in response to widespread judicial hostility

---

[Section 8:1]

[1]Ovitz v. Schulman, 133 Cal. App. 4th 830, 35 Cal. Rptr. 3d 117 (2d Dist. 2005) (upholding lower court's orders vacating the arbitration award and denying reconsideration); Truck Drivers Local No. 164 v. Allied Waste Systems, Inc., 512 F.3d 211, 183 L.R.R.M. (BNA) 2420, 155 Lab. Cas. (CCH) P 10951 (6th Cir. 2008) (reversing District Court's order vacating arbitrator's award).

to arbitration agreements."[1] The FAA is, in effect, a congressional instruction to courts that they should enforce private arbitration agreements as they do other written agreements between private parties. Given its genesis, the FAA does not afford courts discretion in deciding whether or not to order arbitration; rather, the FAA establishes a federal policy in favor of arbitration and requires that courts enforce written agreements to arbitrate involving interstate commerce.

Section 2 of the FAA provides:

> A written provision in any maritime transaction or a contract evidencing a transaction involving commerce to settle by arbitration a controversy thereafter arising out of such contract or transaction, or the refusal to perform the whole or any part thereof, or an agreement in writing to submit to arbitration an existing controversy arising out of such a contract, transaction, or refusal, **shall be valid, irrevocable, and enforceable,** save upon such grounds as exist at law or in equity for the revocation of any contract.

9 U.S.C. § 2. (Emphasis added.) The Supreme Court has unambiguously upheld this provision.[2] The Supreme Court has also directed that any doubt concerning whether a dispute is subject to arbitration be resolved in favor of arbitration.[3] Numerous times since its 1983 decision in *Moses H. Cone,* the Supreme Court has addressed the duty to arbitrate with a party to an arbitration agreement.[4] Each time, the Court required arbitration to proceed,

---

[Section 8:2]

[1]AT&T Mobility LLC v. Concepcion, No. 09-893 (U.S. 2010).

[2]Shearson/American Exp., Inc. v. McMahon, 482 U.S. 220, 226–27, 107 S. Ct. 2332, 96 L. Ed. 2d 185, Fed. Sec. L. Rep. (CCH) P 93265, R.I.C.O. Bus. Disp. Guide (CCH) P 6642 (1987); Dean Witter Reynolds, Inc. v. Byrd, 470 U.S. 213, 220, 105 S. Ct. 1238, 84 L. Ed. 2d 158, Blue Sky L. Rep. (CCH) P 72172, Fed. Sec. L. Rep. (CCH) P 91953 (1985).

[3]Moses H. Cone Memorial Hosp. v. Mercury Const. Corp., 460 U.S. 1, 24–25, 103 S. Ct. 927, 74 L. Ed. 2d 765 (1983).

[4]Examples include AT&T Mobility LLC v. Concepcion, No. 09-893, (U.S. 2010); Rent-A-Center, West, Inc. v. Jackson, 130 S. Ct. 2772, 177 L. Ed. 2d 403, 109 Fair Empl. Prac. Cas. (BNA) 897, 93 Empl. Prac. Dec. (CCH) P 43916 (2010); Southland Corp. v. Keating, 465 U.S. 1, 104 S. Ct. 852, 79 L. Ed. 2d 1 (1984); Mitsubishi Motors Corp. v. Soler Chrysler-Plymouth, Inc., 473 U.S. 614, 105 S. Ct. 3346, 87 L. Ed. 2d 444, 1985-2 Trade Cas. (CCH) ¶ 66669 (1985); Dean Witter Reynolds, Inc. v. Byrd, 470 U.S. 213, 105 S. Ct. 1238, 84 L. Ed. 2d 158, Blue Sky L. Rep. (CCH) P 72172, Fed. Sec. L. Rep. (CCH) P 91953 (1985); Shearson/American Exp., Inc. v. McMahon, 482 U.S. 220, 107 S. Ct. 2332, 96 L. Ed. 2d 185, Fed. Sec. L. Rep. (CCH) P 93265, R.I.C.O. Bus. Disp. Guide (CCH) P 6642 (1987); Perry v. Thomas, 482 U.S. 483, 107 S. Ct. 2520, 96 L. Ed. 2d 426,

even when confronted with a federal statute providing "exclusive" federal court jurisdiction.[5]

Similarly, United States Courts of Appeals have consistently enforced arbitration agreements. For example, the Second Circuit has consistently ordered arbitration and has affirmed a strong federal policy[6] favoring arbitration:

> The FAA, codified at 9 U.S.C. §§ 1 to 14, provides that written provisions to arbitrate controversies in any contract involving interstate commerce "shall be valid, irrevocable, and enforceable, save upon such grounds as exist at law or in equity for the revocation of

---

28 Wage & Hour Cas. (BNA) 137, 106 Lab. Cas. (CCH) P 55735 (1987); Rodriguez de Quijas v. Shearson/American Exp., Inc., 490 U.S. 477, 109 S. Ct. 1917, 104 L. Ed. 2d 526, Fed. Sec. L. Rep. (CCH) P 94407 (1989); Allied-Bruce Terminix Companies, Inc. v. Dobson, 513 U.S. 265, 115 S. Ct. 834, 130 L. Ed. 2d 753 (1995); First Options of Chicago, Inc. v. Kaplan, 514 U.S. 938, 115 S. Ct. 1920, 131 L. Ed. 2d 985, Fed. Sec. L. Rep. (CCH) P 98728 (1995); Vimar Seguros y Reaseguros, S.A. v. M/V Sky Reefer, 515 U.S. 528, 115 S. Ct. 2322, 132 L. Ed. 2d 462, 1995 A.M.C. 1817 (1995); Doctor's Associates, Inc. v. Casarotto, 517 U.S. 681, 116 S. Ct. 1652, 134 L. Ed. 2d 902 (1996); Green Tree Financial Corp.-Alabama v. Randolph, 531 U.S. 79, 121 S. Ct. 513, 148 L. Ed. 2d 373, 84 Fair Empl. Prac. Cas. (BNA) 769 (2000); Circuit City Stores, Inc. v. Adams, 532 U.S. 105, 121 S. Ct. 1302, 149 L. Ed. 2d 234, 85 Fair Empl. Prac. Cas. (BNA) 266, 17 I.E.R. Cas. (BNA) 545, 79 Empl. Prac. Dec. (CCH) P 40401, 143 Lab. Cas. (CCH) P 10939 (2001); Citizens Bank v. Alafabco, Inc., 539 U.S. 52, 123 S. Ct. 2037, 156 L. Ed. 2d 46, 10 A.L.R. Fed. 2d 837 (2003); Green Tree Financial Corp. v. Bazzle, 539 U.S. 444, 123 S. Ct. 2402, 156 L. Ed. 2d 414, 91 Fair Empl. Prac. Cas. (BNA) 1832, 148 Lab. Cas. (CCH) P 59739 (2003); Buckeye Check Cashing, Inc. v. Cardegna, 546 U.S. 440, 126 S. Ct. 1204, 163 L. Ed. 2d 1038 (2006); Preston v. Ferrer, 552 U.S. 346, 128 S. Ct. 978, 169 L. Ed. 2d 917, 27 I.E.R. Cas. (BNA) 257, 28 A.L.R. Fed. 2d 681 (2008). There has been only one case since 1983 where the Supreme Court did not order arbitration. In E.E.O.C. v. Waffle House, Inc., 534 U.S. 279, 122 S. Ct. 754, 151 L. Ed. 2d 755, 12 A.D. Cas. (BNA) 1001, 81 Empl. Prac. Dec. (CCH) P 40850 (2002), the Court held that a government agency with enforcement authority would not be required to arbitrate under a contract to which it was not a party.

[5]*See, Mitsubishi Motors Corp., 476 U.S. at 628–40* (exclusive jurisdiction of the Sherman Act); *Dean Witter, 470 U.S. at 215–17* (exclusive jurisdiction of the Securities Exchange Act of 1934); *Shearson/American Exp., 482 U.S. at 227* (exclusive jurisdiction of the Securities Exchange Act and the Racketeer Influenced and Corrupt Organizations Act); *Rodriguez de Quijas, 490 U.S. at 482–86* (exclusive jurisdiction of the Securities Exchange Act of 1934).

[6]*See,* Garten v. Kurth, 265 F.3d 136, 142 (2d Cir. 2001) ("Under the FAA, courts are required generally to resolve questions of arbitrability in favor of arbitration."); Louis Dreyfus Negoce S.A. v. Blystad Shipping & Trading Inc., 252 F.3d 218, 223, 2001 A.M.C. 1939 (2d Cir. 2001) ("It is familiar law that the Federal Arbitration Act, 9 U.S.C. §§ 1 et seq. (1994) (Arbitration Act), expresses 'a liberal federal policy favoring arbitration agreements' and that 'any doubts concerning the scope of arbitrable issues should be resolved in favor of arbitration.'") (citing *Moses H. Cone Mem'l Hosp., 460 U.S. at 24–25*).

any contract." Id. § 2. "There is a strong federal policy favoring arbitration as an alternative means of dispute resolution." In accordance with that policy, where, as here, the existence of an arbitration agreement is undisputed, doubts as to whether a claim falls within the scope of that agreement should be resolved in favor of arbitrability.[7]

Of course, state courts are also required to enforce arbitration agreements and the FAA pre-empts any state laws that are inconsistent with its mandate. But many states have rules concerning arbitration that supplement the FAA provisions and many states also have a developed body of case law concerning arbitration.[8] Thus, even if an arbitration agreement does not involve interstate commerce, it may very well be subject to the same type of enforcement provisions as the FAA.

§ 8:3 Commencing arbitration

Arbitration is typically commenced when one party to the arbitration agreement, typically referred to as the "Claimant" serves a written demand for arbitration upon another party to

---

[7]ACE Capital Re Overseas Ltd. v. Central United Life Ins. Co., 307 F.3d 24, 29 (2d Cir. 2002) (citing Hartford Acc. and Indem. Co. v. Swiss Reinsurance America Corp., 246 F.3d 219, 226 (2d Cir. 2001)).

[8]For state arbitration provisions supplementing the FAA, *see* Ariz. Rev. Stat. §§ 12-1501 to 12-1518 (2011); Ark. Code Ann. §§ 16-108-101 to 16-108-107 (2011); Colo. Rev. Stat. §§ 13-22-201 to 13-22-230 (2011); Del. Code Ann. tit. 10, §§ 5701 to 5725 (2011); Cal. Civ. Proc. Code §§ 1280 to 1296 (2011); D.C. Code §§ 16-4301 to 16-4319 (2011); Fla. Stat. Ann. §§ 682.01 to 682.22 (2011); Haw. Rev. Stat. Ann. §§ 658A-1 to 658A-29 (2011); Idaho Code Ann. §§ 7-901 to 7-922 (2011); 10 Ill. Comp. Stat. Ann. 710/5 (2011); Ind. Code Ann. §§ 34-57-1-1 to 34-57-2-22 (2011); Iowa Code §§ 679A.1 to 679A.19 (2011); Kan. Stat. Ann. §§ 5-201 to 5-422 (2011); Ky. Rev. Stat. Ann. §§ 417.010 to 417.240 (2011); Me. Rev. Stat. tit. 14, §§ 5927 to 5949 (2011); Md. Code Ann., Courts and Judicial Proceedings §§ 3-201 to 3-234 (2011); Mass. Ann. Laws ch. 251, §§ 1 to 19 (2011); Mich. Comp. Laws Serv. §§ 600.5001 to 600.5035 (2011); Minn. Stat. §§ 572.08 to 572.30 (2011); Mo. Rev. Stat. §§ 435.012 to 435.470 (2011); Mont. Code Ann. §§ 27-5-101 to 27-5-324 (2011); Neb. Rev. Stat. Ann. §§ 25-2601 to 25-2622 (2011); Nev. Rev. Stat. Ann. §§ 38.206 to 38.360 (2011); N.M. Stat. Ann. §§ 44-7A-1 to 44-7A-32 (2011); N.Y.C.P.L.R. 75 Law §§ 7501 to 7514 (Consol. <year>); N.C. Gen. Stat. §§ 1-567.1 to 1-567.20 (2011); N.D. Cent. Code §§ 32-29.3-01 to 32-29.3-29 (2011); Okla. Stat. tit. 15, §§ 801 to 818 (2011); 42 Pa. Cons. Stat. §§ 7301 to 7362 (2011); S.C. Code Ann. §§ 15-48-10 to 15-48-240 (2011); S.D. Codified Laws §§ 21-25A-1 to 21-25B-26 (2011); Tenn. Code Ann. §§ 29-5-101 to 29-5-320 (2011); Tex. Civ. Prac. & Rem. Code Ann. §§ 171.001 to 171.098 (West 2011) (General Arbitration; Texas also has a statute for Seed Arbitration, International Commercial Arbitration, and Arbitration Between Members of Certain Nonprofit Entities); Utah Code Ann. §§ 78B-11-101 to 78B-11-131 (2011); Vt. Stat. Ann. tit. 12, §§ 5651 to 5681 (2011); Va. Code Ann. §§ 8.01-581.01 to 8.01-581.016 (2011); Wyo. Stat. Ann. §§ 1-36-101 to 1-36-119 (2011).

the agreement, referred to as the "Respondent." The manner of service may be specified in the arbitration agreement or may also be specified in state law. In the absence of any specific service mechanism, the demand should be served in the same manner as a lawsuit.

Generally, a third-party that signed the arbitration agreement may be included in the arbitration; however, a party that did not sign the agreement, even if that party may be deemed an indispensible party, cannot be required to arbitrate on the basis that the party is "indispensible."[1] This is because arbitration is solely a function of contract and while courts are instructed to enforce arbitration agreements they cannot enforce agreements against parties who did not sign them or otherwise agree to be bound by them. In furtherance of the FAA policy, the United States Supreme Court has held that arbitration must proceed even if it results in a bifurcated proceeding where arbitrators

---

[Section 8:3]

[1]NORCAL Mutual Ins. Co. v. Newton, 84 Cal. App. 4th 64, 76, 100 Cal. Rptr. 2d 683 (1st Dist. 2000) (In the absence of "an agency or similar relationship between the nonsignatory and one of the parties to an arbitration agreement . . . courts have refused to hold nonsignatories to arbitration agreements."); cf. American Bureau of Shipping v. Tencara Shipyard S.P.A., 170 F.3d 349, 353, 1999 A.M.C. 1858 (2d Cir. 1999) ("A party is estopped from denying its obligation to arbitrate when it receives a 'direct benefit' from a contract containing an arbitration clause."); Specht v. Netscape Communications Corp., 150 F. Supp. 2d 585, 45 U.C.C. Rep. Serv. 2d 1 (S.D. N.Y. 2001), aff'd, 306 F.3d 17, 48 U.C.C. Rep. Serv. 2d 761 (2d Cir. 2002) (quoting County of Contra Costa v. Kaiser Foundation Health Plan, Inc., 47 Cal. App. 4th 237, 242, 54 Cal. Rptr. 2d 628 (1st Dist. 1996), as modified, (Aug. 1, 1996)) (denying Defendant's motion to compel arbitration); County of Contra Costa v. Kaiser Foundation Health Plan, Inc., 47 Cal. App. 4th 237, 244–45, 54 Cal. Rptr. 2d 628 (1st Dist. 1996), as modified, (Aug. 1, 1996) ("Arbitration is consensual in nature. The fundamental assumption of arbitration is that it may be invoked as an alternative to the settlement of disputes by means other than the judicial process solely because all parties have chosen to arbitrate them."); Arthur Andersen LLP v. Carlisle, 556 U.S. 624, 129 S. Ct. 1896, 1902, 173 L. Ed. 2d 832 (2009) (quoting Perry v. Thomas, 482 U.S. 483, 493 n.9, 107 S. Ct. 2520, 96 L. Ed. 2d 426, 28 Wage & Hour Cas. (BNA) 137, 106 Lab. Cas. (CCH) P 55735 (1987)) (internal quotation marks omitted) ("[S]tate law, therefore, is applicable to determine which contracts are binding under § 2 and enforceable under § 3 *if* that law arose to govern issues concerning the validity, revocability, and enforceability of contracts generally."); Arthur Andersen LLP v. Carlisle, 556 U.S. 624, 129 S. Ct. 1896, 1903, 173 L. Ed. 2d 832 (2009) ("[A] litigant who was not a party to the relevant arbitration agreement may invoke § 3 [of the FAA] if the relevant state contract law allows him to enforce the agreement."); In re Rubiola, 334 S.W.3d 220 (Tex. 2011) ("[S]ignatories to an arbitration agreement may identify other parties in their agreement who may enforce arbitration as though they signed the agreement themselves.").

decide disputes between certain parties and a court retains jurisdiction to decide the same dispute as to other parties.[2]

An arbitration demand need not be as specific as a complaint and need not contain the typical formalities of a complaint such as enumerated paragraphs and separate causes of action. Generally, a demand should name the parties to the dispute, state the nature of the dispute, identify (and annex) the arbitration agreement, identify the relief requested, and demand that the other party proceed to arbitrate. If the arbitration agreement provides particulars concerning appointment of one or more arbitrators, the demand should initiate that process. For example, if a contract provides that either party must name an arbitrator or arbitrator candidates, or take some other action to commence the process, the demand for arbitration should include a specific demand that the responding party take such action.

While many Respondents simply proceed to arbitration, some parties object to the demand or simply do nothing. In these cases, the Claimant must seek a court order compelling the Respondent to arbitrate. The Supreme Court has held that the court's role is limited to determining that an arbitration agreement exists. If so, the Court must order arbitration.

Courts that order parties to arbitrate can either dismiss or stay the court proceeding pending the outcome of arbitration. However, in order for an award to be enforced involuntarily, it must ultimately be confirmed in court. It is important to remember that there may be provisions in the agreement or under state law requiring a party to file a motion to compel or stay arbitration within a certain time. For example, Section 7503 of the New York Civil Practice Law and Rules provides that a party seeking arbitration in New York may impose a twenty-day time limit on the Respondent's ability to move to stay the arbitration when serving its demand for arbitration.[3]

The FAA provides that "a party aggrieved by the refusal of an-

---

[2]Dean Witter Reynolds, Inc. v. Byrd, 470 U.S. 213, 217, 105 S. Ct. 1238, 84 L. Ed. 2d 158, Blue Sky L. Rep. (CCH) P 72172, Fed. Sec. L. Rep. (CCH) P 91953 (1985) (the FAA "requires district courts to compel arbitration of pendent arbitrable claims when one of the parties files a motion to compel, even where the result would be the possibly inefficient maintenance of separate proceedings in different forums"); *see also* Rush v. Oppenheimer & Co., 779 F.2d 885, Fed. Sec. L. Rep. (CCH) P 92406 (2d Cir. 1985) (reversing lower court's denial of motion sever arbitrable claim).

[3]N.Y. CPLR § 7503 (McKinney's 2011); Interboro Ins. Co. v. Maragh, 51 A.D.3d 1024, 1025, 858 N.Y.S.2d 391 (2d Dep't 2008) ("An insurer which fails to seek a stay of arbitration within 20 days after being served with a notice of intention or demand to arbitrate under CPLR 7503 (c) is generally precluded

other party to arbitrate may be heard on five days' notice."[4] Generally, such a motion is brought in the United States District Court if diversity of parties is not present or in a state court where the arbitration will proceed. Sometimes the agreement does not state where arbitration will proceed and this can lead to uncertainty. Some parties can thus engage in forum shopping when moving to stay or compel arbitration, but the FAA is designed to ensure uniform results in such event.

> ◆ **PRACTITIONER'S PRACTICE TIP:** Because the FAA contains few specific time limits, a practitioner must review applicable state law to ensure no deadlines are missed. The agreement must also be reviewed to determine if it provides for a particular state's law to govern the dispute. If not, the practitioner should be prepared to litigate choice of law as well, and be sure that all applicable state's laws are reviewed so that no potentially applicable deadlines are missed.

§ 8:4   Scope of arbitration

The arbitration agreement can also provide that the arbitrators will determine all issues of arbitrability. The Supreme Court has enforced this type of agreement.[1] Similarly, the Supreme Court has held that the arbitrators alone are to determine the issue of contract formation.[2] Under *Prima Paint,* contract formation assertions such as duress or fraud concerning the overall agreement do not vitiate the arbitration provision itself, but instead are subject to arbitration. Where a plaintiff's "claims of adhesion, unconscionability, waiver of judicial remedies without knowledge, and lack of mutuality of obligation pertain to the

---

from objecting to the arbitration thereafter."); Matter of Steck (State Farm Ins. Co.), 89 N.Y.2d 1082, 1084, 659 N.Y.S.2d 839, 681 N.E.2d 1285 (1996) ("CPLR 7503(c) requires a party, once served with a demand for arbitration, to move to stay such arbitration within 20 days of service of such demand, else he or she is precluded from objecting."); *but see,* Matarasso v. Continental Cas. Co., 56 N.Y.2d 264, 266, 451 N.Y.S.2d 703, 436 N.E.2d 1305 (1982) (a party may move to stay arbitration under 7503(c) motion outside the 20-day period when "its basis is that the parties never agreed to arbitrate, as distinct from situations in which there is an arbitration agreement which is nevertheless claimed to be invalid or unenforceable because its conditions have not been complied with").

[4]Federal Arbitration Act, 9 U.S.C. § 4 (2011).

[Section 8:4]

[1]Rent-A-Center, West, Inc. v. Jackson, 130 S. Ct. 2772, 177 L. Ed. 2d 403, 109 Fair Empl. Prac. Cas. (BNA) 897, 93 Empl. Prac. Dec. (CCH) P 43916 (2010).

[2]Prima Paint Corp. v. Flood & Conklin Mfg. Co., 388 U.S. 395, 403–04, 87 S. Ct. 1801, 18 L. Ed. 2d 1270, 1969 A.M.C. 222 (1967).

contract as a whole, and not to the arbitration provision alone, then these issues should be resolved in arbitration."[3]

Historically, some courts were reluctant to enforce class action waivers[4] in consumer contracts which are not subject to negotiation. However, the Supreme Court recently upheld a class action waiver in a telephone service contract.[5] By its most recent decision, the Supreme Court added emphasis to its uniform support for the FAA, stating that "[t]he 'principal purpose' of the FAA is the 'ensur[e] that private arbitration agreements are enforced according to their terms.' "[6]

§ 8:5 Selecting arbitrators

The arbitration agreement will typically provide a method for selecting the arbitrator or arbitrators. Once again, the parties are free to agree to a specific procedure as well as specific qualifications. A contract can name a specific individual to be the arbitrator (but in that event should include alternate names), can

---

[3]Benoay v. Prudential-Bache Securities, Inc., 805 F.2d 1437, 1441, Fed. Sec. L. Rep. (CCH) P 93048 (11th Cir. 1986) (citing *Prima Paint, 388 at 404;* Matter of Arbitration Between Nuclear Elec. Ins. Ltd. (Cent. Power and Light Co.), 926 F. Supp. 428, 434–35 (S.D. N.Y. 1996) (same)); *see also* Buckeye Check Cashing, Inc. v. Cardegna, 546 U.S. 440, 449, 126 S. Ct. 1204, 163 L. Ed. 2d 1038 (2006) ("unless the challenge is to the Arbitration Provisions itself, the issue of the contract's validity is considered by the arbitrator in the first instance").

[4]Kristian v. Comcast Corp., 446 F.3d 25, 2006-1 Trade Cas. (CCH) ¶ 75203 (1st Cir. 2006) (finding class action waiver unenforceable as it would severely impair the ability of plaintiffs to enforce antitrust claims; severing portion of arbitration clause containing class action waiver); Miller v. Corinthian Colleges, Inc., 769 F. Supp. 2d 1336, 268 Ed. Law Rep. 235 (D. Utah 2011) (citing Discover Bank v. Superior Court, 36 Cal. 4th 148, 30 Cal. Rptr. 3d 76, 113 P.3d 1100, 1108 (2005) (abrogated by, AT&T Mobility LLC v. Concepcion, 131 S. Ct. 1740, 179 L. Ed. 2d 742, 161 Lab. Cas. (CCH) P 10368 (2011)) ("The California Supreme Court has held that class action waivers are at least sometimes unconscionable under California law."); Discover Bank v. Superior Court, 36 Cal. 4th 148, 30 Cal. Rptr. 3d 76, 79, 113 P.3d 1100 (2005) (abrogated by, AT&T Mobility LLC v. Concepcion, 131 S. Ct. 1740, 179 L. Ed. 2d 742, 161 Lab. Cas. (CCH) P 10368 (2011)) ("at least under some circumstances, the law in California is that class action waivers in consumer contracts of adhesion are unenforceable, whether the consumer is being asked to waive the right to class action litigation or the right to classwide arbitration"); Kinkel v. Cingular Wireless LLC, 223 Ill. 2d 1, 306 Ill. Dec. 157, 857 N.E.2d 250, 278 (2006) (holding that the class action waiver "[i]s unconscionable because it is contained in a contract of adhesion that fails to inform the customer of the cost to her of arbitration, and that does not provide a cost-effective mechanism for individual customers to obtain a remedy for the specific injury alleged in either a judicial or an arbitral forum").

[5]AT&T Mobility, LLC v. Concepcion, No. 09-893 (2011).

[6]AT&T Mobility, LLC v. Concepcion, No. 09-893 (2011).

provide a specific process for nominating or selecting arbitrators, and/or can entitle each side to appoint arbitrators. A contract can also provide specific requirements such as a certain amount of professional experience in a specific field of expertise. Agreements can also provide that the arbitrator be a member of an organization such as AAA or JAMS (see later chapters).

Just as court intervention may be necessary to commence arbitration, in the event one party refuses to engage in the arbitrator selection process, court intervention will be necessary to appoint an arbitrator. Section 5 of the Federal Arbitration Act ("FAA"), 9 U.S.C. § 5, provides that under these circumstances, the Court may designate an arbitrator:

§ 5. Appointment of arbitrators or umpire

If in the agreement provision be made for a method of naming or appointing an arbitrator or arbitrators or an umpire, such method shall be followed; but if no method be provided therein, or if a method be provided and any party thereto shall fail to avail himself of such method, or if for any reasons there shall be a lapse in the naming of an arbitrator or arbitrators or umpire, or in filling a vacancy, then upon the application of either party to the controversy the court shall designate and appoint an arbitrator or arbitrators or umpire, as the case may require, who shall act under the said agreement with the same force and effect as if he or they had been specifically named therein; and unless otherwise provided in the agreement the arbitration shall be by a single arbitrator.

Under 9 U.S.C. § 5, courts will appoint arbitrators.[1] While some courts enforce this provision strictly and have appointed arbitrators where a party missed the contract deadline, other courts have held that appointing an arbitrator is an important right and thus have permitted parties to appoint arbitrators even after deadlines were missed.[2]

[Section 8:5]

[1]Cravens, Dargan & Co. v. Gen. Ins. Co. of Trieste and Venice-U.S. Branch, 1996 U.S. Dist. LEXIS 1051, *4 (S.D.N.Y. Feb. 2, 1996) (court enforcing the agreement "as written" and appointing the defaulting party's arbitrator); Everest Reinsurance Co. v. ROM Reinsurance Management Co., Inc., 303 A.D.2d 243, 756 N.Y.S.2d 739 (1st Dep't 2003) (court enforcing agreement and ruling that other party may appoint defaulting party's arbitrator). See also Certain Underwriters at Lloyd's London v. Argonaut Ins. Co., 500 F.3d 571, 582 (7th Cir. 2007) where the United States Court of Appeals confronted a two-day-late failure to timely-appoint an arbitrator and said that "third days must mean thirty days."

[2]See, e.g., Third Nat. Bank In Nashville v. WEDGE Group, Inc., 749 F. Supp. 851, 855 (M.D. Tenn. 1990) (ordering the parties to submit within thirty

§ 8:6   Discovery and e-discovery in arbitration

Once appointed, an arbitrator or arbitration panel will typically schedule an initial conference with the parties to review the rules that will govern the arbitration and to discuss issues such as scheduling, confidentiality and discovery. As a threshold matter it is important to remember that the arbitration remains governed by the agreement of the parties and the parties remain free to control the process by their own agreements. Generally, the arbitrator must follow the agreements made by the parties and can ultimately, at least in theory, be replaced by the parties' agreement if all parties are inclined to do so. Thus, the parties are generally free to agree to procedures for the entire arbitration, including discovery, and the arbitrator or panel should follow that agreement.

> ◆ **PRACTITIONER'S PRACTICE TIP:** Because arbitration is a function of contract, practitioners have an opportunity to remove the uncertainties concerning electronic discovery by contracting for clear rules. The practitioner can thus select or even create the rules governing all facets of discovery. This can be done by reference to an existing set of rules (AAA, JAMS, etc.) or by simply drafting rules. Thus, an effective practitioner must be familiar with e-discovery rules and should consider them when drafting the arbitration agreement and in the arbitration itself.

Some arbitration agreements will refer to a set of rules that will govern the arbitration such as AAA and JAMS (see later chapters). Parties may also agree to be governed by existing court rules such as the Federal Rules of Civil Procedure. In that circumstance, the arbitrator must look to those rules in making decisions but, as set forth above, arbitrators are not bound to strictly follow the law. In discovery disputes, courts generally have considerable discretion and thus arbitrators have at least as much discretion, and likely more.

The FAA provides no specific rules concerning discovery. Thus, if the parties do not agree to any specific rules, it is up to the arbitrators to establish the parties' procedures and how those procedures will be enforced. The FAA does not authorize courts to intervene on discovery issues, and doing so would make arbitration wholly impractical. In practice, most parties agree to the terms of discovery.

---

(30) days a mutually-acceptable arbitrator notwithstanding although finding that the court had the power, under Section 5 of the FAA, to appoint an arbitrator).

The parties can also agree, or arbitrators can establish, a mechanism to address and resolve discovery disputes. This can include the timing of motions, the form of submissions and an obligation to meet and confer. Courts generally prefer and often require parties to confer before making discovery motions. In arbitration, there is an added incentive because arbitrators are paid by the parties for their work, usually on an hourly basis. Thus, every application to the arbitrator will incur additional fees and, of course, it is likely that at least one party will be unhappy with the outcome. Accordingly, it only makes sense for the parties to make every effort to resolve the dispute, whether required or not.

Moreover, it is well settled that arbitration is a more focused form of dispute resolution, where discovery should be limited to identified issues, and be more controlled and focused than in traditional litigation. For example, the Supreme Court recognized that discovery is more limited in arbitration, stating that in arbitration a party "trades the procedures and opportunity for review of the courtroom for the simplicity, informality, and expedition of arbitration."[1]

One important concept that has impacted e-discovery law should also be applied in arbitration—the concept of proportionality. This concept derives from Federal Rule of Civil Procedure 26(b)(2)(c) which gives a court the power to "limit the frequency or extent of discovery otherwise allowed by these rules or by local rule if it determines that

> . . . (iii) the burden or expense of the proposed discovery outweighs its likely benefit, considering the needs of the case, the amount in controversy, the parties' resources, the importance of the issues at stake in the action, and the importance of the discovery in resolving the issues.

Because arbitration is generally intended to be more streamlined, the proportionality concept should not only be applicable, but perhaps even paramount.

Absent agreement of the parties concerning discovery, it is left to the arbitrator to issue rulings and enforce them. In the event a party does not comply with a discovery requirement (e.g., by fail-

---

[Section 8:6]

[1]Mitsubishi Motors Corp. v. Soler Chrysler-Plymouth, Inc., 473 U.S. 614, 628, 105 S. Ct. 3346, 87 L. Ed. 2d 444, 1985-2 Trade Cas. (CCH) ¶ 66669 (1985); *see also* Gilmer v. Interstate/Johnson Lane Corp., 500 U.S. 20, 31, 111 S. Ct. 1647, 114 L. Ed. 2d 26, 55 Fair Empl. Prac. Cas. (BNA) 1116, 56 Empl. Prac. Dec. (CCH) P 40704 (1991) (arbitration "procedures might not be as extensive as in the federal courts").

ing to produce a witness for deposition), an arbitrator does not have the same authority under the FAA as a court does to compel a witness to appear. In particular, arbitrators do not have the ability, like courts, to hold parties in contempt. However, arbitrators will, of course, issue an award. On this basis, if a party has not complied with the arbitrator's order, the arbitrator may draw inferences from non-compliance and those inferences may very well substantially impact a final decision against the non-appearing party.

§ 8:7 Subpoena discovery

Although the FAA is silent as to the parties' obligations to provide discovery to each other, it contains a specific authorization for an arbitrator to subpoena "any person." Section 7 of the Federal Arbitration Act provides:

> The arbitrators selected either as prescribed in this title or otherwise, or a majority of them, may summon in writing any person to attend before them or any of them as a witness and in a proper case to bring with him or them any book, record, document, or paper which may be deemed material as evidence in the case. The fees for such attendance shall be the same as the fees of witnesses before maters of the United States courts. Said summons shall issue in the name of the arbitrator or arbitrators, or a majority of them, and shall be signed by the arbitrators, or a majority of them, and shall be directed to the said person and shall be served in the same manner as subpoenas to appear and testify before the court; if any person or persons so summoned to testify shall refuse or neglect to obey said summons, upon petition the United States district court for the district in which such arbitrators, or a majority of them, are sitting may compel the attendance of such person or persons before said arbitrator or arbitrators, or punish said person or persons for contempt in the same manner provided by law for securing the attendance of witnesses or their punishment for neglect or refusal to attend in the courts of the United States.

9 U.S.C. § 7 has created a practical problem resulting in a three-way circuit split because read literally it only authorizes the arbitrators to subpoena a witness for hearing, not for pre-trial discovery. Similarly, concerning documents, the statute only states that the witness shall bring them to the hearing. In practice, this would not permit time for the parties to prepare their questions. In fact, merely reviewing the documents could take significant time.

Given the practical concerns of Section 7 of the FAA, the Fourth Circuit Court of Appeals held that a court is authorized to order discovery upon a showing of "special need or hardship" because the arbitration process would be "degraded if the parties are unable to review and digest relevant evidence prior to the arbitration hearing."[1] This holding puts the parties back in Court for a discovery ruling.

In contrast, the Eighth Circuit Court of Appeals held that the arbitrators had "implicit" power to order pre-hearing discovery.[2] This view keeps the dispute before the arbitration panel and gives the arbitrators control over non-party discovery.

The Third Circuit then adopted a third view of the issue when it held that the statute, enacted in 1925 under Federal Rules of Civil Procedures that did not provide for pretrial discovery, simply means that arbitrators may only subpoena a witness for a hearing.[3] The Second Circuit adopted this same approach.[4] One justification for this approach is that the arbitrator can continue the hearing at a later date.

§ 8:8 Conclusion

Arbitration arises from agreement. Because the FAA does not contain specific rules governing discovery between parties, parties should take advantage of the opportunity to agree on rules and procedures and avoid having decisions made by an arbitrator whose findings are not subject to judicial review. In the absence of agreement, the parties must be prepared to argue by analogy to other discovery and e-discovery regimes and principles when discovery disputes arise in arbitration.

[Section 8:7]

[1]COMSAT Corp. v. National Science Foundation, 190 F.3d 269, 276 (4th Cir. 1999).

[2]In re Security Life Ins. Co. of America, 228 F.3d 865, 870–71 (8th Cir. 2000).

[3]Hay Group, Inc. v. E.B.S. Acquisition Corp., 360 F.3d 404, 21 I.E.R. Cas. (BNA) 18 (3d Cir. 2004).

[4]Life Receivables Trust v. Syndicate 102 at Lloyd's of London, 549 F.3d 210, 45 A.L.R. Fed. 2d 727 (2d Cir. 2008).

Chapter 9

E-Discovery in AAA Arbitration

by

Steven C. Bennett[*]

> **KeyCite[R]:** Cases and other legal materials listed in KeyCite Scope can be researched through the KeyCite service on Westlaw[R]. Use KeyCite to check citations for form, parallel references, prior and later history, and comprehensive citator information, including citations to other decisions and secondary materials.

§ 9:1   Introduction

This Chapter discusses how the American Arbitration Association (AAA) addresses discovery and use of ESI in their respective arbitration proceedings.

§ 9:2   General approach to discovery in AAA

Prehearing discovery procedures vary greatly in arbitration

---

[*]Steven Bennett is a partner at Jones Day in New York City and Chair of the firm's e-discovery Committee. He teaches a course on e-discovery at New York Law School. The views expressed are solely those of the Author and should not be attributed to the Author's or its clients.

depending on the agreement of the parties, the sponsoring organization and its rules, the predilections of the arbitrators, and the circumstances of the case. Parties often choose arbitration in part to avoid some of the cost and burden of discovery devices in ordinary civil litigation. Certain discovery devices, such as interrogatories, bill of particulars, or requests for admission, are almost unthinkable in arbitration. Others, like depositions, are possible but rare.

What has become the norm in arbitration, at least in commercial arbitration in the United States (where AAA primarily operates), is the exchange of documents pertinent to a dispute. Essential documents, such as any contract or correspondence between the parties, invoices, and payment records pertaining to the transaction, may be exchanged as a matter of course. More burdensome, time-consuming demands are rare.[1] An arbitrator will weigh cost and delay factors involved in broad discovery more carefully than most judges and magistrates in ordinary litigation.[2]

The arbitration process permits swift identification of key issues and documents pertinent to a dispute.[3] Many arbitrators conduct preliminary conferences, at which the parties are encouraged to outline their positions, to agree upon matters that are not in controversy, and to establish a protocol for exchange of documents.[4] An arbitrator often requires prehearing briefs from the parties. Prehearing process eases preparation for the hear-

---

[Section 9:2]

[1]Thus, wholesale "fishing expeditions" out of all proportion to the needs of the case, may be refused. See, e.g., Rodriguez-Torres v. Government Development Bank of Puerto Rico, 265 F.R.D. 40 (D.P.R. 2010) ("fishing expedition" to determine whether plaintiff can support claims, rejected); Balfour Beatty Rail, Inc. v. Vaccarello, 2007 WL 169628 (M.D. Fla. 2007) (denying request for discovery and characterizing request as "fishing expedition").

[2]See generally Robert B. Davidson & Margaret L. Shaw, Arbitrators Hold Significant Power Over Discovery, N.L.J., Nov. 27, 2006; Thomas L. Aldrich, Arbitration's E Discovery Conundrum, Nat'l L.J., Dec. 16, 2008; John M. Barkett, E Discovery For Arbitrators, 1:2 Dispute Resol. Int'l 129 (2007); Anke Meier, The Production Of Electronically Stored Information In International Commercial Arbitration, 6 Schieds 179 (2008); Charles R. Ragan & Robert F. Copple, Discover New E Worlds, Legal Times, Apr. 21, 2008.

[3]See Leslie Trager, Organizing Documents For Arbitration, Disp. Resol. J. (2006) ("The scope and scheduling of document exchanges are usually discussed at an early preliminary conference.").

[4]See Judith B. Ittig & Michael J. Bayard, Thirty Steps To A Better Arbitration, Disp. Resol. J. (2004) (suggesting use of early conferences to identify issue and focus the arbitration process). Now also at Ch. 3 to AAA Handbook on Arbitration Practice (2010).

ing, encourages early identification of documents and witnesses, and allows parties to respond to arguments from the other side.

Generally, where a party can identify specific documents essential to a fair and rational disposition of the case, an AAA arbitrator will expect those documents to be produced. Failure to produce in circumstances where the need is obvious may even lead the arbitrator to apply an adverse inference: that the missing documents would have been adverse to the party that fails to produce the missing information.[5] The AAA procedures, however, do not contemplate the relatively liberal discovery of all materials potentially relevant to a dispute, as outlined in standard rules of civil procedure.[6]

§ 9:3   The AAA approach

The AAA's "Commercial Arbitration Rules" (the "AAA Rules")[1] do not specifically address the question of e-discovery. Instead, the AAA Rules provide an opportunity for a preliminary conference of the parties, with the tribunal, to discuss the "future conduct of the case," which may include discovery issues.[2] Further, the AAA Rules provide that "[a]t the request of any party or at the discretion of the arbitrator, consistent with the expedited nature of arbitration, the arbitrator may direct... the production of documents and other information;" and "[t]he arbitrator is authorized to resolve any disputes concerning the exchange of information."[3]

Under the "Expedited Procedures" of the AAA Rules, *no* discovery is contemplated. Instead, the Rules merely provide that "[a]t least two business days prior to the hearing, the parties

---

[5]See Irene C. Warshauer, Electronic Discovery In Arbitration: Privilege Issues And Spoliation Of Evidence, 61 Dispute Resol. J. (2007).

[6]Rule 26 of the Federal Rules of Civil Procedure, for example, generally permits discovery of "any nonprivileged matters that is relevant to any party's claim or defense." Relevant information, moreover, "need not be admissible at trial if the discovery appears reasonably calculated to lead to the discovery of admissible evidence." Fed. R. Civ. P. 26(b)(1).

[Section 9:3]

[1]The AAA's Commercial Arbitration Rules, and the other AAA Rule Sets discussed herein, are generally available at www.adr.org.

[2]AAA Rule 20.

[3]AAA Rule 21.

shall exchange copies of all exhibits they intend to submit at the hearing."[4]

The Expedited Procedures generally apply in cases where no claim or counterclaim exceeds \$75,000 in value (or the parties otherwise agree).[5]

Under the AAA "Procedures for Large, Complex Commercial Disputes," a preliminary hearing "shall" be held in every case.[13] One of the issues for the preliminary hearing is "the extent to which discovery shall be conducted."[14] The procedures also call for the tribunal to take steps "to avoid delay and to achieve a just, speedy and cost-effective resolution," and require that parties "shall cooperate[15] in the exchange of documents, exhibits and information within such party's control if the arbitrator(s) consider such production to be consistent with the goal [.]"[16] Further, the procedures permit parties to "conduct such discovery as may be agreed to by all parties," provided that the tribunal "may place such limitations on the conduct of such discovery as the arbitrators shall deem appropriate."[17] If the parties cannot agree, "the arbitrator(s), consistent with the expedited nature of arbitration, may establish the extent of the discovery."[18]

A. AAA Adopts ICDR Guidelines Regarding Exchange of Information

In 2008, recognizing a "genuine concern" about the growing use of conventional litigation procedures in arbitration, the International Centre for Dispute Resolution ("ICDR"), the international arm of the AAA, adopted "ICDR Guidelines for Arbitrators Concerning Exchanges of Information" (the "ICDR Guidelines").[19] The AAA, in announcing the ICDR Guidelines, suggested that these guidelines would be useful both for international matters,

---

[4]AAA Rule E-5.

[5]AAA Rule 1(b).

[13]AAA Rule L-3.

[14]AAA Rule L-3.

[15]In this regard, the AAA procedures largely adopt the approach of the Sedona Conference "Cooperation Proclamation" for e-discovery, which calls for awareness of, and a commitment to, cooperation as an essential value in discovery. See www.thesedonaconference.org.

[16]AAA Rule L-4(a)-(b).

[17]AAA Rule L-4(c).

[18]AAA Rule L-4(c).

[19]International Centre for Dispute Resolution, ICDR Guidelines for Arbitrators Concerning Exchanges of Information, www.adr.org.

under the ICDR's administration, and for "the practice of arbitration as a whole."[20]

The ICDR Guidelines provide that the tribunal "shall" manage the exchange of information "with a view to maintaining efficiency and economy." The tribunal and the parties should "avoid unnecessary delay and expense" while "balancing the goals of avoiding surprise, promoting equality of treatment, and safeguarding each party's opportunity to present its claims and defenses fairly."[21]

Regarding electronic documents, the ICDR Guidelines provide that, when requested, the party in possession of such information "may make them available in the form (which may be paper copies) most convenient and economical for it, unless the Tribunal determines, on application and for good cause, that there is a compelling need for access to the documents in a different form." Requests for electronic information "should be narrowly focused and structured to make searching for them as economical as possible"; the tribunal "may direct testing or other means of focusing and limiting any search."[22]

B. Checklist for AAA Arbitrators in Considering Exchange of Information Issues

The ICDR Guidelines provide that, in resolving any disputes about information exchange, the tribunal "shall require a requesting party to justify the time and expense that its request may involve, and may condition granting such a request on the payment of part or all of the cost by the party seeking the information."[23] Further, the tribunal may "allocate the costs of providing information" among the parties, in an interim order or final award.[24]

---

[20]Claudia T. Salomon, *New ICDR Guidelines Aim to Improve Disclosure of Information*, International Arbitration Newsletter (Aug. 4, 2008) http://www.dla piper.com/new_icdr_guidelines/.

[21]See ICDR Guidelines.

[22]See ICDR Guidelines.

[23]See ICDR Guidelines.

[24]See ICDR Guidelines.

§ 9:4 Additional sources of rules

College Of Commercial Arbitrators [25]

In 2010, the College of Commercial Arbitrators (the "CCA") published "Protocols for Expeditious, Cost-Effective Commercial Arbitration" (the "CCA Protocols"). The CCA Protocols are the product of a national summit of organizations involved in commercial arbitration, including the American Bar Association Section of Dispute Resolution, the AAA, JAMS, the International Institute for Conflict Prevention and Resolution, and the Chartered Institute of Arbitrators. More than 180 participants contributed to the summit, and more than two dozen contributors participated in drafting the CCA Protocols.

The CCA Protocols include more than 70 pages of recommendations for improvement of the arbitration process. The CCA Protocols focus, in particular, on the arbitration discovery process, citing an array of sources, including the ICDR Guidelines and the JAMS Protocols. The CCA Protocols call for actions by business users, arbitration providers, outside counsel and arbitrators. In each instance, the CCA Protocols make specific suggestions for methods to streamline discovery, and e-discovery in particular.

CCA Protocol I, for business users and in-house counsel, suggests that users should "[l]imit discovery to what is essential; do not simply replicate court discovery." Further, the CCA suggests, "[p]lace meaningful limits on discovery in the arbitration agreement or incorporated arbitration procedures," "thoroughly discuss the cost versus benefit of various courses of discovery" with outside counsel," and "memorialize in writing," for the benefit of outside counsel, the decision as to the nature and extent of discovery planned.

CCA Protocol II, for arbitration providers, suggests that providers "[d]envelop and publish rules that provide effective ways of limiting discovery to essential information." The protocol suggests narrowly tailoring the list of electronic disclosure custodians to include only those "whose electronic data may reasonably be expected to contain evidence that is material to the dispute and cannot be obtained from other sources," filtering data "based on file type, date ranges, sender, receiver, search term or other similar parameters," and limiting disclosure to "reasonably acces-

---

[Section 9:4]

[25]Protocols for Expeditious, Cost-Effective Commercial Arbitration are available at www.thecca.net.

sible active data from primary storage facilities." Further, "[i]nformation from back-up tapes or back-up servers, cell phones, PDAs, voicemails and the like should only be subject to disclosure if a particularized showing of exceptional need is made." The CCA Protocol suggests that arbitration providers "address the essential scope and limits of e-discovery," including "handling of the costs of retrieval and review for privilege, the duty to preserve electronic information, spoliation issues and related sanctions," permit a party to make electronic documents "available in the form most convenient and economical for it," relieve parties "of the obligation to conduct a pre-production privilege review of all electronic documents," allow clawback of privileged documents, and have parties identify "likely informational needs" and agree on "what information needs to be preserved, in what format, and for how long."

CCA Protocol III, for outside counsel, suggests the need to "[s]eek to limit discovery in a manner consistent with client goals." On this view, counsel should "cooperate with opposing counsel and the arbitrator in looking for appropriate ways to limit or streamline discovery in a manner consistent with the stated goals of the client."

Finally, CCA Protocol IV, for arbitrators, emphasizes the need to "[s]treamline discovery [and] supervise pre-hearing activities." Thus, arbitrators should "make clear at the preliminary conference that discovery is ordinarily much more limited in arbitration than in litigation," "work with counsel in finding ways to limit or streamline discovery in a manner appropriate to the circumstances," and "keep a close eye on the progress of discovery" and "promptly resolve any problems that might disrupt the case schedule (usually through a conference call preceded by a jointly-prepared email outlining the nature of the parties' disagreements and each side's position with regard to the dispute, rather than formal written submissions)."

International Bar Association[26]

In addition to the AAA, JAMS, and CCA guidance, several other organizations have recently offered guidelines for the conduct of discovery, and e-discovery in particular. In 1998 (updated in 2010), the International Bar Association ("IBA") issued its "Rules On The Taking of Evidence In International Commercial Arbitration." The IBA rules provide that a "document" includes writings of any kind, "whether recorded on paper,

---

[26]Rules On The Taking of Evidence In International Commercial Arbitration are available at www.iba.net.

electronic means, audio or visual recording or any other mechanical or electronic means of storing or recording information." The IBA Rules further provide that a tribunal should "consult the Parties at the earliest appropriate time in the proceedings and invite them to consult each other with a view to agreeing on an efficient, economical and fair process for the taking of evidence," which may include discussion of "the requirements, procedure and format applicable to the production of Documents" (including ESI). The IBA rules, moreover, generally require that any document request must provide a relatively detailed description of any documents requested, and a statement of how the documents are relevant to the case. For ESI, in particular, the IBA rules provide that a party should produce "in the form most convenient or economical to it that is reasonably usable by the recipient," unless otherwise agreed or ordered.

Chartered Institute of Arbitrators[27]

In 2008, the Chartered Institute of Arbitrators (the "CIARB"), a sponsor of international arbitration services, based in London, promulgated a "Protocol For E-Disclosure In Arbitration." The Protocol provides a relatively comprehensive set of guidelines "for use in those cases (not all) in which potentially disclosable documents are in electronic form and in which the time and cost for giving disclosure may be an issue." The CIARB Protocol calls for the tribunal to raise the question of e-discovery "at the earliest opportunity." The parties may then discuss with the tribunal a number of issues related to ESI, including preservation, privilege protection, and techniques to reduce the burden and cost of e-discovery, such as agreement on search terms. The tribunal, in ruling on requests for e-discovery, must pay attention to issues of "reasonableness and proportionality." The "primary source" of disclosure should be "reasonably accessible" data. Documents disclosed are normally to be produced "in the format in which the information is ordinarily maintained or in a reasonably usable form." A party seeking metadata must demonstrate that the relevance and materiality of such information outweighs the costs and burdens of production. The tribunal may allocate costs for e-discovery. It may also obtain "technical guidance" on e-discovery issues, and tax the cost of such guidance as part of the costs of the arbitration.

---

[27]Protocol For E-Disclosure In Arbitration is available at www.ciarb.org.

International Institute for Conflict Prevention and Resolution[28]

In 2009, the International Institute for Conflict Prevention and Resolution ("CPR") issued its "Protocol on Disclosure of Documents and Presentation of Witnesses in Commercial Arbitration." The Protocol divides cases into categories (called "Modes of Disclosure") from A (no pre-hearing discovery, except for the exchange of exhibits to be used by each party at the hearing) to D (relatively full-scale disclosure, which may include discovery of ESI, subject only to limits of reasonableness, avoidance of duplication and undue burden).[29]

The Protocol choices are generally for the parties to agree upon, with the recognition that arbitration is not meant to be a "no stone unturned" exercise. Rather, the CPR Protocol states that "disclosure should be granted only as to those items that are relevant and material, and for which a party has a substantial, demonstrable need in order to present its position."

International Chamber of Commerce[30]

Finally, the International Chamber of Commerce ("ICC"), in its "Techniques for Controlling Time and Costs in Arbitration," generally addressed e-discovery, noting that requests for production "whether in paper or electronic form" should be limited to matters that are "relevant and material to the outcome of the case." The ICC emphasized that "normally" parties will each voluntarily produce all documents upon which they intend to rely in the proceedings. Further, the ICC noted that, once parties have agreed upon "non-controversial facts," no discovery or further documentary evidence should be required to prove the agreed points. Please note that the ICC is covered in greater detail in Chapter 12 of this Book.

---

[28]Protocol on Disclosure of Documents and Presentation of Witnesses in Commercial Arbitration is available at www.cpradr.org.

[29]The CPR modes for discovery are listed in full at the end of this chapter at Appendix B.

[30]Techniques for Controlling Time and Costs in Arbitration are available at www.iccwbo.org.

§ 9:5 Best practices

Guidance from the AAA together with rules and commentary from other arbitration-sponsoring organizations, suggest an array of best practices to consider for use in arbitration.[31]

Some of these practices are discussed below. Other best practices are referenced in the Sample Pre-Hearing Order (attached as Appendix 9C to this Chapter), which can serve as a "road map" to the discovery and other issues that routinely arise in AAA arbitration.

Early Attention to E-Discovery Issues

The AAA rules generally emphasize the importance of early attention to e-discovery issues, as a means to avoid misunderstandings, lower costs and streamline proceedings. Generally, the rules suggest that parties should address e-discovery issues at, or preferably in advance of, the first conference in a case, and that parties and their counsel should come to the first conference prepared to discuss e-discovery issues. This early attention to discovery issues, moreover, reinforces the essential value of cooperation in the discovery process, suggested in the AAA rules, and made explicit in the Sedona Conference "Cooperation Proclamation."

Several important practical points derive from this requirement:

- Advocates must become familiar with the basic language and issues of e-discovery, or be prepared to cede this area of pre-hearing preparation to more tech-savvy colleagues.
- Lawyers and their clients must begin to discuss e-discovery issues almost from the moment that they first learn of the dispute. Even if the client has no e-documents (a very rare case), the discussion must at least concern how the party will receive e-documents from the other side, and which e-documents may be essential to the party's case. Where a

---

[Section 9:5]

[31]Although not directly applicable, guidance from the Sedona Conference with regard to e-discovery in civil proceedings may provide additional useful insights. See, e.g., Commentary on Proportionality (2010); Commentary on Legal Holds (2010); Commentary on Inactive Information Sources (2009); Commentary on Achieving Quality in the E-Discovery Process (2009); Commentary on Preservation, Management and Identification of Sources of Information that are Not Reasonably Accessible (2008); Framework for Analysis of Cross-Border Discovery Conflicts (2008); Best Practices Commentary on Search & Retrieval Methods (2007); The Sedona Principles after the Federal Amendments (2007). All Sedona publications are available at www.thesedonaconference.org.

party has substantial quantities of discoverable e-documents of its own, moreover, an even more concerted discussion of the e-discovery process must be undertaken, as soon as possible.

• Advocates and their clients must bring to the discussion with their adversaries (and ultimately with the tribunal) a good understanding of the client's information and records storage systems. The AAA rules, for example, suggest that the parties should at least discuss the format for discovery (native files, images, or paper). Without some understanding of what documents and information systems the client maintains, the discussion of what is reasonable and possible in the way of e-discovery will suffer, and unnecessary disagreements and misunderstandings (with the tribunal and opposing counsel) may be created.

Preservation and Production

The AAA rules suggest that e-documents should be part of the initial disclosures in a case, and further suggest that questions of data preservation may be a part of the initial conferences with counsel and the tribunal. Among the practical points that flow from these rules:

• Parties and their counsel should be prepared to explain what data preservation policies exist. Ideally, such policies will have been established well in advance of the onset of the dispute. A party should have a system to issue "litigation hold" notices, and to suspend routine destruction of data (such as deletion of e-mails on some fixed, periodic basis). The discussion at the outset of arbitration proceedings should then focus (if necessary) on whether any additional, special preservation efforts (beyond those already embodied in the parties' pre-existing policies) are appropriate.

• The rules generally recognize a distinction between materials used in the ordinary course of business and materials that are not reasonably accessible (such as backup materials, created for emergency purposes only). For a party to obtain discovery of inaccessible materials, some showing of value for the data (cost to retrieve versus benefit to retrieval) must be made. The rules also suggest that cost-shifting may be appropriate in such cases.

Cost and Burden Issues

The AAA rules recognize that the enormous volume of ESI, in many cases, can present significant questions as to the appropriate balance between the costs and burden of producing ESI, versus the benefits of such evidence. The costs of electronic discovery can be crushing. Such costs, moreover, can easily be imposed. All it may take is a few strokes of the word-processing key-board to modify a standard demand for documents and electronically stored information. Some critics fear that e-discovery may be used as a weapon to extract unwarranted settlements to avoid the burdens of e-discovery. The rules suggest several practical steps to avoid inappropriate use of e-discovery.

As noted, the advocate should be prepared to discuss e-discovery issues from the first conference with the tribunal. It may be helpful, in this regard, to set the agenda for the first conference by presenting the tribunal with copies of correspondence between the parties on discovery issues, and an overview of any issues that remain unresolved between the parties.

The practitioner also should be prepared to explain why the requests (or objections) made are necessary and reasonable, and be prepared to negotiate these issues as part of the initial conference—perhaps to offer "fall back" positions or compromises that the tribunal may accept. The practitioner should (if the size of the matter and the complexity of the issues warrants the effort) consider bringing an IT or document management professional to the first conference, to be available to answer questions from the tribunal. The practitioner should seek to avoid adverse "seat of the pants" decisions from the tribunal, which may be difficult to modify once made. As the proceedings progress, the practitioner may occasionally find it necessary to make motions to compel production of one or more items of ESI. To be effective, such requests should be few in number, clearly necessary, and not overstated in scope. The advocate should pursue conciliation with the adversary before making any request to compel production, and couple any request to compel production with an explanation of why the requests are reasonable, and what steps have been taken to resolve the matter amicably. The advocate should stress that the requests are narrow, focused, and limited to highly relevant information.

If necessary or appropriate, the advocate may choose to couple the request to compel with a request for preclusion and adverse inference, in the event that the adversary does not produce the requested information. Such a remedy is essentially self-executing.

Privilege Protection

The AAA rules permit discussion at the outset of a case to address concerns about privilege protection, and the potential for inadvertent production of privileged material (which may occur more frequently when dealing with ESI). This discussion may result in an agreement that inadvertent production will not constitute a waiver of privilege.

One form of privilege-protection agreement is a simple understanding that inadvertent production of privileged material will not constitute a waiver of privilege (as to the particular documents produced, or as to the broader subject matter encompassed by the privileged document). This form is often referred to as a "clawback" agreement (the point being that, in the event of inadvertent production of privileged documents, the producing party may "claw it back," by request to the other side, without waiver of privilege protection).

A more extreme form of clawback agreement (sometimes called the "quick peek" approach) takes as an organizing principle the notion that conventional privilege review takes too long, and costs too much, to be practical in an e-discovery world. Under the quick peek approach, the producing party makes all of its responsive documents available for review by the requesting party, without any initial effort to identify and withhold privileged documents. Instead, only when the requesting party designates specific documents for copying does a privilege review take place. At that point, the responding party, focusing only on the specific requested documents, may seek to withhold some of the documents on grounds of privilege. The quick peek agreement between the parties endorses this procedure, and confirms that no waiver of privilege will occur as a result of voluntary disclosure of privileged material (in the initial review process).

The parties may also address the question of how to deal with allegedly privileged materials once they are in the hands of an adversary. Typically, the parties will agree that, on request by a producing party, a receiving party must segregate (and not use) allegedly privileged materials, and must return such materials to the producing party, or seek direction from the tribunal on the propriety of the privilege invocation. Such an agreement essentially maintains the status quo, pending resolution of the privilege dispute.

Preparation in Advance of Arbitration

Arbitration is generally a creature of contract. Parties may choose the rules of whatever arbitration-sponsoring organization best suits their needs; or they may construct arbitration rules of their own; or they may leave the procedures for arbitration to the discretion of the arbitrators. The AAA rules acknowledge the importance of party autonomy.

Given the growing significance of ESI in business operations, and the increasing recognition that ESI may become critical evidence in dispute resolution, it appears likely that e-discovery will remain an important factor affecting the conduct and outcome of arbitration proceedings. Yet, parties involved in commercial transactions often leave dispute resolution questions to the end of their commercial negotiations. Or, they may incorporate a dispute resolution clause into a contract simply because the clause was accepted in the last deal (or last series of deals).

Parties should be aware, however, that there are many varieties of approaches to dispute resolution, and to e-discovery in arbitration. The choice of arbitrator(s), moreover, may be critical in determining how much (and what forms of) discovery may develop in arbitration. Thus, for the practitioner asked to determine the "best" form of dispute resolution clause to recommend to a client, the list of questions to consider may include the following:[32]

- What position is the client likely to take in the event of a dispute?
- What form(s) of dispute resolution may be most appropriate? (It is possible to specify a series of steps for dispute resolution, each one to proceed if the prior step does not succeed in resolving the dispute).
- If arbitration is preferred, which form is best, and which specific arbitration organization's rules may be desirable? (Keep in mind that arbitration organizations may change their rules, as in the recent addition of e-discovery guidelines, outlined above--and typically those new rules will govern if a dispute arises thereafter).
- Are there any specific terms of arbitration that may be helpful? (In the area of discovery, parties may impose time or monetary limits on the discovery process, specify which forms of discovery may proceed (e.g., no interrogatories or limit of two depositions per side), or require some form of balancing of discovery burdens and benefits—perhaps shifting costs for production in certain instances).
- Who will serve as the arbitrator(s)? Specifying arbitrator national origin or experience may affect the character of the arbitration process.

§ 9:6   Conclusion

Electronic discovery is here to stay in conventional litigation

---

[32]See generally Steven C. Bennett, Arbitration: Essential Concepts (2002) (Chapter 5 on issues in constructing an arbitration clause).

(in the United States, at least). One can easily predict that it will have a significant impact on arbitration as well, in coming years. Practitioners who become familiar with the essential issues that can arise in the course of handling ESI, who have carefully planned their client's approach to arbitration, with e-discovery as one of the significant considerations involved in drafting an ADR clause, and who are prepared to deal with e-discovery issues from the outset of any dispute, will obtain an advantage over their less well-prepared adversaries.

APPENDIX 9A

CPR Protocol on Disclosure of Documents and Presentation of Witnesses in Commercial Arbitration: Schedules of Disclosure

SCHEDULE 1
Modes of Disclosure

Mode A. No disclosure of documents other than the disclosure, prior to the hearing, of documents that each side will present in support of its case.

Mode B. Disclosure provided for under Mode A together with pre-hearing disclosure of documents essential to a matter of import in the proceeding for which a party has demonstrated a substantial need.

Mode C. Disclosure provided for under Mode B together with disclosure, prior to the hearing, of documents relating to issues in the case that are in the possession of persons who are noticed as witnesses by the party requested to provide disclosure.

Mode D. Pre hearing disclosure of documents regarding non-privileged matters that are relevant to any party's claim or defense, subject to limitations of reasonableness, duplication and undue burden.

SCHEDULE 2
Modes of Disclosure of Electronic Information

Mode A. Disclosure by each party limited to copies of electronic information to be presented in support of that party's case, in print-out or another reasonably usable form.

Mode B. (1) Disclosure, in reasonably usable form, by each party of electronic information maintained by no more than [specify number] of designated custodians. (2) Provision only of information created between the date of the signing of the agreement that is the subject of the dispute and the date of the filing of the request for arbitration. (3) Disclosure of information from primary storage facilities only; no information required to be disclosed from back up servers or backup tapes; no disclosure of information from cell phones, PDAs, voicemails, etc. (4) No disclosure of information other than reasonably accessible active data.

Mode C. Same as Mode B, but covering a larger number of custodians [specify number] and a wider time period [to be specified]. The parties may also agree to permit upon a showing of special need and relevance disclosure of deleted, fragmented or other information difficult to obtain other than through forensic means.

Mode D. Disclosure of electronic information regarding non-privileged matters that are relevant to any party's claim or defense, subject to limitations of reasonableness, duplicativeness and undue burden.

Parties selecting Modes B, C, or D agree to meet and confer, prior to an initial scheduling conference with the tribunal, concerning the specific modalities and timetable for electronic information disclosure.

APPENDIX 9B

Chartered Institute of Arbitrators Protocol for E-Disclosure in Arbitration

Early consideration

1. In any arbitration in which issues relating to e-disclosure are likely to arise the parties should confer at the earliest opportunity regarding the preservation and disclosure of electronically stored documents and seek to agree the scope and methods of production.

2. The Tribunal shall raise with the parties the question of whether e-disclosure may arise for consideration in the circumstances of the dispute(s) at the earliest opportunity and in any event no later than the preliminary meeting.

3. The matters for early consideration include:

(i) whether documents in electronic form are likely to be the subject of a request for disclosure (if any) during the course of the proceedings, and if so;

(ii) what types of electronic documents are within each party's power or control, and what are the computer systems, electronic devices, storage systems and media on which they are held;

(iii) what (if any) steps may be appropriate for the retention and preservation of electronic documents, having regard to a party's electronic document management system and data retention policy and practice, provided that it is unreasonable to expect a party to take every conceivable step to preserve every potentially relevant electronic document;

(iv) what rules and practice apply to the scope and extent of disclosure of electronic documents in the arbitration, whether under the agreed arbitration rules, the applicable arbitral law, any agreed rules of evidence (for example, the IBA Rules on the Taking of Evidence in International Commercial Arbitration), this Protocol or otherwise;

(v) whether the parties have made, or wish to make, an agreement to limit the scope;

(vi) what tools and techniques may be usefully considered to reduce the burden and cost of e-disclosure (if any), including:

(a) limiting disclosure of documents or certain categories of documents to particular date ranges or to particular custodians of documents;

(b) the use of agreed search terms;

(c) the use of agreed software tools;

(d) the use of data sampling; and

(e) the format and methods of e-disclosure;

(vii) whether any special arrangements with regard to data privacy obligations, privilege or waiver of privilege in respect of electronic documents disclosed may be agreed; and

(viii) whether any party and/or the Tribunal may benefit from professional guidance on IT issues relating to ediscIosure having regard to the requirements of the case.

Request for disclosure of electronic documents

4. Any request for the disclosure of electronic documents shall contain:

(i) a description of the document or of a narrow and specific requested category of documents;

(ii) a description of how the documents requested are relevant and material to the outcome of the case;

(iii) a statement that the documents are not in the possession or control of the party requesting the documents; and

(iv) a statement of the reason why the documents are assumed to be in the possession or control of the other party.

Order or direction for disclosure of electronic documents

5. In making any order or direction for e-disclosure, or for the retention and preservation of electronic documents, the Tribunal shall have regard to the appropriate scope and extent of disclosure of electronic documents in the arbitration, whether under the agreed arbitration rules, the applicable arbitral law, any agreed rules of evidence (for example, the IBA Rules on the Taking of Evidence in International Commercial Arbitration) and this Protocol. The Tribunal shall have due regard to any agreement between the parties to limit the scope and

extent of disclosure of documents.

6. In making any order or direction for e-disclosure the Tribunal shall have regard to considerations of:

> (i) reasonableness and proportionality;

> (ii) fairness and equality of treatment of the parties; and

> (iii) ensuring that each party has a reasonable opportunity to present its case by reference to the cost and burden of complying with the same. This shall include balancing considerations of the amount and nature of the dispute and the likely relevance and materiality of the documents requested against the cost and burden of giving e-disclosure.

7. The primary source of disclosure of electronic documents should be reasonably accessible data; namely, active data, near-line data or offline data on disks. In the absence of particular justification it will normally not be appropriate to order the restoration of back-up tapes; erased, damaged or fragmented data; archived data or data routinely deleted in the normal course of business operations. A party requesting disclosure of such electronic documents shall be required to demonstrate that the relevance and materiality outweigh the costs and burdens of retrieving and producing the same.

Production of electronic documents

8. Production of electronic documents ordered to be disclosed shall normally be made in the format in which the information is ordinarily maintained or in a reasonably usable form. The requesting party may request that the electronic documents be produced in some other form. In the absence of agreement between the parties the Tribunal shall decide whether production of electronic documents ordered to be disclosed should be in native format or otherwise.

9. A party requesting disclosure of metadata in respect of electronic documents shall be required to demonstrate that the relevance and materiality of the requested metadata outweigh the costs and burdens of producing the same, unless the documents will otherwise be produced in a form that includes the requested metadata.

Procedure and costs

10. The Tribunal shall consider the appropriate allocation of costs in making an order or direction for e-disclosure.

11. The Tribunal shall establish a clear and efficient procedure

for the disclosure of electronic documents, including an appropriate timetable for the submission of and compliance with requests for e-disclosure.

12. The Tribunal shall require that a producing party give advance notice to the requesting party of the electronic tools and processes that it intends to use in complying with any order for disclosure of electronic documents.

13. The Tribunal may, after discussion with the parties, obtain technical guidance on e-disclosure issues. Such discussion shall include the question of who is to be instructed to provide technical guidance and the costs expected to be incurred. The costs of this shall be included in the costs of the arbitration.

14. In the event that a party fails to provide disclosure of electronic documents ordered to be disclosed or fails to comply with this Protocol after its use has been agreed by the parties and the Tribunal or ordered by the Tribunal, the Tribunal shall be entitled to draw such inferences as it considers appropriate when determining the substance of the dispute or any award of costs or other relief.

APPENDIX 9C

Sample pre-hearing oder

The Parties, _____, as Claimant, and _____, as Respondent, stipulate and agree to the following procedures and guidelines in order to facilitate the scheduling and resolution of this arbitration proceeding. This stipulation shall supplement and supersede (in the event of conflict) the contractually specified _____ Rules of the *[Arbitral Institution]*.

I. PRE-ARBITRATION MATTERS

A. General Administrative Procedures:

If and to the extent issues or disputes arise between the parties regarding pre-hearing procedures, the following steps shall be expeditiously taken in order to minimize the potential for delay or disruption of the arbitration hearing:

(a) Counsel will first confer, personally or by telephone, to discuss resolution of the issues or disputes.

(b) All unresolved disputes shall be addressed by a conference call among counsel and the Arbitrators. The conference call will be scheduled by the *[Arbitral Institution]*, at the request of any party, at a mutually agreeable time, as soon as practicable after the dispute arises.

(c) During the conference call, counsel for the parties may make their arguments relative to the dispute. The Arbitrators (or their designated representative) shall then issue a decision regarding the dispute.

B. Pre-Hearing Disclosure

1. Exchange of Relevant Documents:

On or before _____, each of the parties will provide access to the other of all non-privileged documents that relate or refer to the matters at issue and which are in each parties' possession, custody, or control. Each party will be allowed to inspect the other party's documents and designate documents for copying at the requesting party's expense. This obligation to produce documents will be deemed as continuing so as to require notification to the opposing party or counsel that continued inspection and copying of any additional documents relating or referring to the matters at issue coming into a parties' possession, custody, or control after the initial production will be permitted pursuant to this Stipulation.

2. Subpoenas Directed Towards Third Parties:

On or before _____, each of the parties will determine the identities of any known third parties to whom it requests the Arbitrators to issue subpoenas for testimony and/or production of documents. Subpoenas for documents or subpoenas for personal attendance at a deposition or hearing may be requested after _____, with notice to opposing counsel.

3. Exchange Of Tentative Witness Lists:

On or before _____, each party shall provide the other with a tentative list of anticipated witnesses;

(a) With regard to "fact" witnesses, the list shall provide the witness' name, address and telephone number, together with a general synopsis of the anticipated testimony; and

(b) With regard to "expert" witnesses, the list shall include the identity of each anticipated expert witness and a general statement of the subject matter and a general statement of the opinions to which the expert is expected to testify; and

(c) Note: These lists are subject to later revision and refinement (See, e.g. part D, below) upon reasonable advance notice to the other side prior to the arbitration hearing.

4. Preliminary Statement of Claims and Defenses:

On or before _____, the parties shall exchange: (1) a concise written summary of their claims or counterclaims (including claims of offset), and defenses, stating with reasonable particularity concerning each claim or defense, an explanation of the claim or defense and a breakdown of all damages or other relief sought in this Arbitration; and (2) a concise summary on their legal and factual arguments underlying each claim, counterclaim or defense that each party intends to raise at the arbitration hearing. Each party shall be allowed to reply to the other's brief on or before _____.

5. Depositions of Key Witnesses:

On or before _____, the parties will be allowed to depose __ (__) witnesses (e.g., experts and party representatives). No deposition shall exceed a total time (for each deposed party) of __ (__) hours in length.

(6) Stipulation of Uncontested Facts:
(a) The parties shall exchange proposed stipulations of undisputed facts on or before _____.
(b) Each party shall give written notice of objections, if any, to stipulations proposed by any other party by _____.

(c) On or before _____, the parties' counsel shall then confer by conference call (to be initiated by counsel for the Claimant) to review proposed stipulations to which objections have been made to attempt to come to agreement regarding such stipulations.

C. Pre-Hearing Memoranda:

Pre-hearing Memoranda or briefs may be submitted in order to assist the Arbitrators in focusing upon the central issues giving rise to this dispute. The Memoranda or briefs shall not exceed twenty (20) pages (8 × 11, double spaced). Such Memoranda shall be submitted to the *[Arbitral Institution]* for distribution to the Arbitrators on or before _____. The substance of the Pre-Hearing Memoranda shall be limited to the following:

(1) A summary of the factual contentions;

(2) A summary of pertinent legal and contractual issues; and

(3) A final specification of claims, counterclaims (monetary amounts), and defenses.

D. Exchange of Exhibits and Witness List:

On or before _____, the parties shall exchange the following:

(1) A list of witnesses that may be called by the parties regarding their claims and defenses, with a brief summary of the testimony each witness is expected to offer;

(a) This list need not include potential witnesses whose testimony would be purely of a "rebuttal" nature;
(b) This list may be amended by either party upon reasonable advance notice to the other or with the authorization of the Arbitrators (or its presiding member);

(c) With regard to "fact" witnesses, the list shall provide the name, address and telephone number together with a general synopsis of the testimony proposed; and

(d) With regard to "expert" witnesses, the list shall include the identity of each proposed expert witness and a general statement of the subject matter and a general statement of the opinions to which the expert is expected to testify;

(2) A list of the exhibits that may be used by the parties during the hearing;

(a) This list need not include "rebuttal" evidence; and

(b) This list may be amended by either party upon reasonable advance notice (accompanied by immediate production of the exhibit in question to the other parties) and the authorization of the Arbitrators (or its presiding member).

E. Pre-Hearing Consultation of Counsel:

On or before _____, counsel shall meet or confer as necessary in order to accomplish:

(1) An exchange (or to provide access to) all proposed documentary exhibits and witness information;

(2) Compliance with all other hearing procedures;

(3) Finalization of any stipulations of undisputed fact; and

(4) Approximate sequencing and scheduling of witnesses during the hearing. Claimant's counsel shall have the responsibility to schedule and coordinate this conference.

II. ARBITRATION HEARING

A. Witnesses And Evidence:

Except for _____ (__) corporate representative(s) for each party, witnesses shall be sequestered, subject to the further decision of the Arbitrators during the course of the hearing. Subject to the discretion and decision of the Arbitrators, and with the exception of "rebuttal" evidence, a party may only offer, and the Arbitrator may only rely upon, evidence and witnesses that have been timely identified and made available to the opposing party prior to the arbitration hearing as required by this Stipulation.

B. Arbitration Hearing:

(1) The estimated duration of the hearing is ____ (__) days.

(2) Subject to decision by the Arbitrators, the parties suggest that each day's hearing shall run from 9:00 a.m. to 12:30 p.m. and from 1:30 p.m. to 6:00 p.m., with appropriate breaks.

C. Time Allocation:

There is an estimated arbitration hearing time availability of _____ (__) hours. Therefore, unless the parties agree otherwise, this time will be allocated equally (i.e., sixteen (16) hours each) between the parties to use as each party sees fit, subject to the applicable Rules and the discretion of the Arbitrators.

D. Transcription:

The parties have agreed to share equally in the takedown and transcription cost of the hearing.

III. POST-ARBITRATION MATTERS

A. Post-Hearing Brief:

After the close of the hearing, as determined by the Arbitrators, the parties shall be permitted an appropriate amount of time to submit post-hearing memoranda prior to the close of the evidence, the precise timing, scope, content and length of which shall be determined by the Arbitrators.

B. Opinion of the Arbitrator's Award:

The arbitration award shall be in writing and *[shall/shall not]* include an explanation together with a breakdown, if any, of the award.

Respectfully submitted, this __
day of _____, _____.

By: _____
By: _____
_____

Address

ATTORNEYS FOR CLAIMANT

By: _____
By: _____
_____

Address

ATTORNEYS FOR
RESPONDENT

Chapter 10

JAMS And E-Discovery

*by Richard Chernick & Hon. Carl J. West**

§ 10:1   Introduction
Exhibit 10A.   Sample Prehearing Conference Agenda

KeyCiteᴿ: Cases and other legal materials listed in KeyCite Scope can be researched through the KeyCite service on Westlawᴿ. Use KeyCite to check citations for form, parallel references, prior and later history, and comprehensive citator information, including citations to other decisions and secondary materials.

---

§ 10:1   Introduction

The growth of commercial arbitration over the past three decades is principally attributable to the United States Supreme Court's broad embrace of the arbitration process and its rejection of legal doctrines that try to limit the effective use of arbitration. Arbitration was further transformed in the 1980s and 1990s by a series of decisions which have made it more accessible and its enforcement more predictable. These developments in turn have encouraged businesses to consider arbitration for many of their larger and more important disputes and have encouraged indi-

---

*Richard Chernick, Esq. is Vice President and Managing Director of JAMS' Arbitration Practice. He is a nationally recognized expert in the resolution of complex and multi-party matters. Mr. Chernick has conducted hundreds of large and complex arbitrations and mediations employing various rules and before all major administering institutions, both nationally and internationally. He was recently named by the Daily Journal as one of California's top neutrals for 2012.

Hon. Carl J. West (Ret.) joined JAMS following eighteen years on the bench, spending the most recent ten years as a judge with the Los Angeles County Superior Court's complex litigation panel. Judge West held hundreds of settlement conferences for disputes that spanned the legal spectrum, often working closely with parties to bring them together and foster resolution of even the most complex and difficult cases. Judge West is highly regarded as a tech-savvy and hands-on innovator in complex case management, e-discovery, and civil procedure, and is a frequent speaker and lecturer on these topics. The Daily Journal named Judge West as one of California's top neutrals for 2012.

vidual neutrals and providers to promote arbitration as an effective alternative to the court system.

Popularity has not been without drawbacks. As counsel have become more sophisticated in dispute process design, arbitrations now often include many elements of a complicated court trial, and the complexity of managing and conducting arbitrations has increased. Legal issues such as pleadings, broad-based discovery, requests for provisional relief, dispositive motions and application of rules of evidence are more common, as are requests for review of arbitration orders and awards. One only has to consider the number of process issues included in the 2000 revision of the Uniform Arbitration Act (www.upenn.edu/bll/ulc/uarba/arbitrat 1213.htm) to see this dynamic change. This trend also explains why there are so many more decided cases addressing arbitration issues.

One consequence of these changes has been increased expense and delay. Many traditional users of arbitration have realized that they cannot have their cake and eat it too. The more processes parties employ, the longer and the more expensive the arbitration. It is even possible that it will take as much or more time than equivalent court litigation. In these circumstances, where there is no effective right to appeal arbitral awards, the litigation choice may become preferable.

In order to preserve the benefits of arbitration, it is necessary to address the processes that drive expense and delay, such as discovery and motion practice. Each of the stakeholders in the arbitration process (inside counsel and business people, outside counsel, arbitrators and provider organizations) has a role to play in addressing solutions that restore vitality and efficiency to the arbitration process. No element of the process drives cost and delay more than excessive discovery, and the most vexing discovery issue is control of e-discovery. We shall focus here on the opportunities parties, arbitrators and provider organizations have to control this aspect of the process.

As modern commercial arbitration has evolved, so has discovery. Discovery is often the most expensive part of any arbitration, especially now that so much of it involves electronically stored information. In the early days of commercial arbitration, discovery was limited to a broad exchange of relevant and non-privileged documents together with the identification of witnesses expected to testify. Now, counsel often serve elaborate requests for voluminous documents and seek numerous depositions. For arbitration to be truly cost-effective and efficient, it is usually in everyone's interest to rein in costs by establishing a discovery plan that is proportionate to the complexity of the dispute and by managing the agreed process to avoid abuse and undue delay.

Parties control the scope of discovery primarily through careful clause drafting and later by agreeing on discovery limits and procedures that are measured and are proportionate to the complexity of the case, the amount in dispute and the real need for exchange of information. The typical predispute clause usually does not address discovery other than by the selection of an institutional provider (AAA or JAMS). Clause provisions that specify greater discovery than the agreed rules permit are disfavored—both because it is unlikely that the parties will be able to gauge accurately the need for discovery before knowing the exact nature of the dispute and because there is a tendency of counsel to choose greater discovery than will actually be needed. In particular, the adoption of "discovery in accordance with the Federal Rules of Civil Procedure" or incorporation of Cal. Code of Civil Procedure §§ 1283.1 and 1283.05 (authorizing all discovery customarily available in a civil action) are dangerous choices because they contemplate unlimited discovery and prevent any effective control of discovery by the arbitrator.[1]

Provider rules generally contemplate minimal discovery. JAMS Comprehensive Arbitration Rules and Procedures ("Rules"), for example, prescribe an initial informal exchange of "all non-privileged documents and other information (including electronically stored information ("ESI") relevant to the dispute or claim immediately after the commencement of the arbitration."[2] Supplementation of the initial exchange is required by Rule 17(c). Each party is entitled to one deposition, and "the necessity of additional depositions shall be determined by the arbitrator based upon the reasonable need for the requested information, the availability of other discovery options and the burdensomeness of the request on the opposing Parties and the witness."[3] Further guidance is provided in the JAMS Recommended Arbitration Discovery Protocols for Domestic, Commercial Cases ("Protocols") in which relevant factors are listed on Exhibit 9A to the Protocols for determining the appropriate scope of discovery.

[Section 10:1]

[1]In particular, these clause provisions authorize use of interrogatories and requests for admission, which in the authors' experience are invariably expensive and largely ineffective processes when employed in arbitrations.

[2]Rule 17(a). All JAMS Rules and other materials referenced in this chapter are accessible at www.jamsadr.com.

[3]Rule 17(b).

The Protocols can effectively be incorporated into the parties' agreement to arbitrate if they designate not just the Rules in their clause but also the Expedited Procedures embedded in those Rules. The Expedited Procedures may also be chosen by the claimant at the time the Demand for Arbitration is filed. They then become the procedures for the arbitration if the respondent does not object.[4] If there is objection to use of the Expedited Procedures, the arbitrator will take up the issue at the preliminary conference.[5]

Under the Expedited Procedures, document requests shall (1) be limited to documents that are directly relevant to the matter in dispute or to its outcome; (2) be reasonably restricted in terms of time frame, subject matter and persons or entities to which the requests pertain; and (3) not include broad phraseology such as all documents directly or indirectly related to a topic.[6] The Expedited Procedures adopt the specific guidelines in the Protocols as rules of procedure for the arbitration.[7] These procedures are detailed below. The Expedited Procedures also contemplate a timeline for the arbitration that will get the parties to the evidentiary hearing within 150 days of the preliminary conference.

E-discovery is not addressed specifically in the Rules, but is in the Protocols:

• The use of electronic media for the creation, storage and transmission of information has substantially increased the volume of available document discovery. It has also substantially increased the cost of the discovery process.

• To be able to appropriately address issues pertaining to e-discovery, JAMS arbitrators are trained to deal with the technological issues that arise in connection with electronic data.

• While there can be no objective standard for the appropriate scope of e-discovery in all cases, JAMS arbitrators recognize that an early order containing language along the following lines can be an important first step in limiting such discovery in a large number of cases:

  ○ There shall be production of electronic documents only from sources used in the ordinary course of business. Absent a showing of compelling need, no such documents are required to be produced from back-up servers, tapes or other media.

  ○ Absent a showing of compelling need, the production of

---

[4]Rule 16.1.

[5]Rule 16.1.

[6]Rule 16.2.

[7]Rules 16.1 and 16.2.

electronic documents shall normally be made on the basis of generally available technology in a searchable format which is usable by the party receiving the e-documents and convenient and economical for the producing party. Absent a showing of compelling need, the parties need not produce metadata with the exception of header fields for email correspondence.[8]

○ Where the costs and burdens of e-discovery are disproportionate to the nature and gravity of the dispute or to the amount in controversy, or to the relevance of the materials requested, the arbitrator will either deny such requests or order disclosure on condition that the requesting party advance the reasonable cost of production to the other side, subject to the allocation of costs in the final award.

Protocols, pp. 4-5.

These principles reflect an overarching effort to make the arbitration process efficient and economical by making process choices that are proportionate to the real needs of the case (not the parties' or counsel's perceived needs) and to the complexity of the issues and the amount in dispute. The general guidelines reflected in the Protocols are most effectively implemented by early consideration of the need for information exchange, usually at the first preliminary conference (Rule 16) in which the arbitrator meets with counsel to address the procedure that will be followed in the matter. Early identification of the need for exchange of ESI and anticipated issues in that exchange process is essential.

Conduct of the preliminary conference:

The careful arbitrator will prepare fully for the preliminary conference by reading all available pleadings and by paying particular attention to the provisions of the clause or arbitration agreement.[9] Some Arbitrators prepare an "agenda" for transmission to the parties in advance of the preliminary conference and ask counsel to meet and confer as to the issues set out on the agenda. Certain issues will always appear on a pre-conference agenda; other items will be suggested by the issues raised in the

---

[8]Some arbitrators prefer not to limit production of metadata. Metadata fields can be included in the loads that accompany.tiff and /.pdf documents and are recognizable by Concordia and similar programs. They are routinely produced to insure that information regarding the identity of the drafter and the dates of revision are included in the production of Word and other word processing files. This is the same information that is referenced by the Protocols as being included in the email header fields.

[9]In tripartite arbitrations, it is common for arbitrators to confer prior to the preparation of an agenda or for the Chair to prepare a draft agenda and send it to the side arbitrators for their comments.

pleadings or other related documents (such as motions or inquiries directed to the case manager. A sample agenda is annexed as Exhibit 9A.

The following issues should be considered by the Arbitrator for inclusion on the agenda or for discussion at the conference:

- Focus on early identification of key issues of document exchange (Rule 17(a))
- Encourage parties to think "proportionality" in discovery expectations
- Tools which will assist in creating a reasonable discovery process:
  - Rules (especially Expedited Procedures)
  - Development of preservation protocols prior to commencement of the discovery process[10]
  - Consideration of search and production protocols for ESI, specifically addressing the form of production and allocation of the cost of production at the initial stages of the proceedings as opposed to after-the-fact motion practice to determine the sufficiency of productions
  - Need for stipulated protective order
  - Designation of one of arbitrators in tripartite panel to be discovery "referee"
  - Adoption of streamlined motion practice procedures
  - Address "litigation hold" procedure
  - Identify in-house and outside ESI experts and consultants

The Protocols highlight several danger points in the exchange of ESI that the arbitrator will want to focus on in early discussions with counsel. In particular, the scope of requests for documents (paper and electronic) should be limited to those which are directly relevant to the significant issues in the case or to its outcome, not "all documents which relate or refer to. . ." (particularly where "documents," "relate to" and "refer to" are each defined terms with pages of detailed definition). The time frame of requests, their subject matters and the persons or entitles to which the requests pertain should also be judicious in scope.

The sources of production should be limited to those in use in the ordinary course of business that are reasonably accessible to the producing party. The issue of reasonable accessibility should

---

[10]Often the identifying of the scope of the parties' preservation obligation will assist in narrowing and focusing the scope of discovery.

be addressed at the preliminary conference if practical, or in any event, prior to the issuance of any order for production of ESI. To the extent practical, the production of ESI should be an iterative process. The parties and the arbitrators must consider the processing costs associated with the over-production of ESI and seek to control that cost.

The media which is subject to search should ordinarily be limited to computers in active use in the business and reasonably accessible ESI. Generally, legacy systems and back up servers, tapes, or other media that are not easily searchable will not be considered to have reasonably accessible data.

Early identification of custodians likely to have information relevant to the matters at issue is essential to an orderly, efficient, and economical approach to the discovery of ESI. In this regard, a sequential or iterative approach to identification of key custodians that permits the expansion of productions as justified following an initial production by key custodians may be an appropriate means of overproduction of ESI. The initial searches and productions should focus on custodians of such media most directly involved with the claims at issue.

The production of ESI should be made on the basis of generally available technology in a searchable format usable by the recipient and convenient to the producing party. In cases involving sophisticated parties with extensive information technology systems, often the process will benefit from involvement of parties' respective in-house IT personnel or forensic consultants retained by the parties to assist in the collection and production of ESI. Arbitrators and lawyers often will not be informed on the technology at issue, and thus not in a position to make informed decisions regarding search and production protocols without the benefit of input from specialists in the field.

In many cases the parties and the arbitrator should consider the use of sampling techniques to "test" large volumes of ESI prior to compelling production. Often the use of "quick peek" or "claw-back" agreements will permit a less burdensome and more economical approach to large scale ESI productions. The use of innovative technology assisted review of large volumes of ESI may also result in efficiencies and cost savings. JAMS arbitrators seek to work collaboratively with the parties and their counsel to find efficient and economical approaches to the discovery process in general, and to E-Discovery issues in particular.

Arbitrators must also develop a means of monitoring compliance with the agreed or ordered protocols for production of ESI. Historically, some of the most expensive and time consuming disputes in civil cases involve failed discovery of ESI. The cost and burden of motion practice after the fact can and should be avoided by hands-on involvement of the arbitrator on a real time basis. Requiring periodic reports from the parties concerning the progress of their discovery will encourage cooperation among the parties and their counsel. Similarly, the use of joint reports to frame issues concerning the claimed insufficiency of productions will often obviate the need for formal motion practice.

E-Filing and E-Service platform: JAMS Electronic Filing System is a secure, online case management website powered by Case Anywhere. The system is available to parties in a JAMS arbitration proceeding for the purpose of electronically transmitting documents to and communicating with counsel, parties and neutral(s). Case documents and communications are stored in a central repository that can be accessed by all parties and their counsel, and parties can sort and search for case records, calendar events and communications between the arbitrator and counsel. Paper filing and service is replaced with electronic links to documents, and these documents and message board communications are available 24 hours a day, seven days a week from any computer, laptop, iPad or other tablet with Internet access. All records uploaded to JAMS Electronic Filing System are available only to the arbitrator, firms of record, and party representatives. Strong encryption technologies are used to protect data transfer to and from the website.

Techniques for handling voluminous documents in discovery: The use of document/data depositories for the storage of large scale productions in electronic format may often be appropriate for the larger cases. There are several commercial services that provide such capabilities. Case Anywhere, which has partnered with JAMS on its e-filing platform, has capabilities in the document depository area as well.

Motion practice: The parties should adopt efficient means to address disputes early in the exchange process and not rely on traditional noticed motions. They ought to understand that meeting and conferring on points in contention is an essential step in the resolution process and not a pro forma task to check off in order to be entitled to file a motion. The arbitrator should make himself/herself available on an informal basis to address threshold issues before the escalate into disputes. Where technical issues are likely to be important, the parties should be encouraged to involve their technical experts directly rather than to depend on counsel alone to discuss these issues.

Cost shifting: Where the costs and burdens of e-discovery are disproportionate to the nature and gravity of the dispute or to the amount in controversy, or to the relevance of the materials requested, the arbitrator will either deny such requests or order disclosure on condition that the requesting party advance the reasonable cost of production to the other side, subject to the allocation of costs in the final award. This is most important in cases where the resources of the parties are not similar or where one party would be impeded in fair participation in the process by cost constraints. It is less an issue where both sides are well-resourced and can await the end of the case to make cost claims.

The Managerial Arbitrator: None of these techniques for making the document exchange process economical will work unless the arbitrator is experienced, decisive and willing to make the necessary rulings promptly. Arbitrators must be trained to be managerial in their approach to shaping and controlling the arbitration process. That includes setting a schedule for discovery at the preliminary conference and ensuring that the case stays on track. When discovery disputes arise, arbitrators should be available by phone or e-mail—not ex parte of course—to make decisions promptly and on short notice.

International Proceedings: In cases involving cross-border disputes, expectations about the scope of discovery are different. Most civil law jurisdictions do not even recognize the concept of "discovery" in the American sense. Document exchanges are extremely limited, if permitted at all, and this of course would include ESI. For a sense of the general nature of information exchange in international arbitrations see International Bar Association, Rules on the Taking of Evidence in International Arbitrations.[11] Parties should also consider the impact of discovery and privacy laws in the various jurisdictions that may impact the discovery process.

---

[11]See www.ibanet.org.

EXHIBIT 10A

Sample Prehearing Conference Agenda

J A M S ARBITRATION
No. 12200XXXXX

CCCCCCCCCCCCCCC, Claimant and Respondent by Counterclaim

MMMMMMMMMM and HHHHHHHHHHH, Respondents and Counterclaimants

Agenda For Preliminary Conference

Conference Date: 8/17/12

Time: 12:30 p.m.

Call in number: 877/696-5267 (Chernick)

A. <u>Preliminary</u>

1. Parties have stipulated to JAMS arbitration (need copy of stipulation)

2. Demand for Arbitration dated 6/12/12

3. Respondents: M_____ and H_____

4. Each Respondent has filed Answer and Counterclaim (7/9/12 and 7/23/12); Claimant responses dated 7/23/12 and 8/13/12.

5. H_____ parent corp. is not a named Respondent; Claimant intends to file litigation against it in LASC. Does any party contend that H_____ parent is a proper party to this arbitration?

6. Parties have appointed Chernick, West and Ambler as neutral arbitrators. Any issues re appointment?

7. Agreement is dated May 27, 2003 between Claimant and M. Parties' agreement is large and complex. Suggest parties put together agreed, complete version of written agreement including all amendments and attachments and provide to Arbitrators by _____.

8. Clause is Ex. 2 to Demand for Arbitration—¶ 10.4 to Amendment 1 to Amendment 6 to Parties' agreement.

9. Clause requires "written decision within six (6) months after Respondent receives the demand for arbitration." Do parties agree that six month period began to run on 6/25/12?

10. **Brief** summaries by counsel of issues to be decided and parties' positions.

11. Are all claims and defenses identified in Demand and the Answers and Counterclaims arbitrable in this proceeding?

12. Administration by JAMS: Christy Arceo, Senior Case Manager—contact information below).

13. FAA applicability obvious

    a. CAA Applicability (to the extent not inconsistent with FAA)?

14. Applicable Rules: JAMS Comprehensive Arbitration Rules and Procedures ("Rules"); (reference Discovery Protocols)

15. Governing law (assume California law referenced in Agreement)

B. <u>Pre-hearing activities</u> (fix dates as needed)—<u>Information Exchange</u>

1. Document production: See Protocols at ___

2. E-discovery: See Protocols at ___. Parties should meet and confer and develop a plan for discovery of ESI (consider including your IT consultants and employees in the meet and confer). Address the information management system each party employs and the location and custodians of information that is likely to be the subject of production.

    a. Issue: sources of ESI (no back-up servers, tapes or other media)

    b. Identify the network and email servers and hard drives maintained by target custodians

    c. Identify format in which ESI will be produced

    d. Identify types of ESI that will be produced, i.e. data files, emails, etc.

    e. Discuss appropriate search methodology for focused requests

    f. Issue: limit custodians?

    g. Issue: limit time frame of requests?

    h. Issue: limit subject matter?

    i. Issue: phraseology of requests (not "all docs that relate or refer to. . ."

    j. Issue: technology—generally available

    k. Issue: Metadata?

1. Issue: need for cost shifting?

3. Need for third party docs pre-hearing; procedure

4. Need for deposition discovery (counsel to meet and confer re schedule)?

5. Need for depositions *de bene esse* of witnesses unavailable for hearing (or out of subpoena range) *See* CCP § 1283.

6. Other discovery?

7. Resolution of discovery disputes

    a. Should one of arbitrators be designated to hear all discovery disputes (subject to right to ask entire panel to determine a specific dispute)?

    b. Procedure generally (prefer meet and confer followed by joint letter)

    c. Possibility of quick conference call for focused and time-urgent issues (procedure for convening)

8. NB. Parties have agreed to modified CCP § 1283.05 discovery (with arbitrator discretion to allow such discovery as appropriate "in accomplishing fair, speedy and cost-effective resolution of the dispute" Clause ¶ 10.4.2.) In view of six month timeline, arbitrators will be aggressive in limiting discovery to that which will allow that schedule to be achieved.

9. Dispositive motions (discuss)

C. <u>Pre-hearing filings</u> (fix dates as needed)

1. Identify fact witnesses, with brief summary of testimony (issues of telephonic or other presentation of testimony not in person) (date of exchange—H-30 [30 days prior to first hearing day]) Supplemental designation—H-23

2. Exhibits. Agree on efficient marking system. Identify documents to be relied upon at hearing (date of exchange—H-30; Supplemental designation—H-23. Can exhibits be provided electronically? (use Ambler protocol)

3. Experts? If so, identify, and exchange reports? (alt: stipulate to CCP procedure) (designation date?) If no stipulation, experts and reports of experts are designated with other witnesses and documents (¶¶ 1, 23, above) (NB. not much time for expert designation in view of six month timeline)

4. Use witness statements in lieu of direct exam? (filing procedure to be agreed). Can witness statements be provided electronically?

5. Stipulation of uncontested facts? File on H-7. (Electronic also)

6. Pre-hearing memoranda (H-7); motions *in limine* (same)

7. Need for final status conference? (H-7)

8. Agree on use of demonstratives in opening statements

D. <u>Evidentiary hearing</u>

1. Number of days needed

2. Place: Los Angeles Resolution Center (LARC)

3. Start Date:

4. Hours of hearing—9:00 a.m. to 5:00 p.m. with one hour for lunch, subject to accommodating witness and counsel needs

5. Transcript? (Counsel to arrange)

      a. Live Note for arbitrators if they desire

6. Is there an attorney fee provision in Agreement? [need to bifurcate this issue?]

7. Post-hearing briefs? (if so, must be close in time to end of hearing given six month timeline)

8. Argument?

9. Form of award: written decision stating reasons therefor in reasonable detail"; need for interim award?

E. <u>Schedule for all steps in arbitration</u> Counsel to confer and agree)

F. <u>Administrative</u>

1. Confidentiality agreement/stipulated protective order in place?

2. Mode of communications—fax, email, courier, regular mail? Prefer email for non-bulky documents (followed by hard copy by U.S. mail or overnight); OK to send motion or brief by email omitting bulky attachments with later delivery of complete document; copies to opposing counsel always served by same or faster means.

3. Arbitrator cancellation policies

G. <u>Other</u>

[Deleted]

Arbitrators:

Richard Chernick

JAMS

707 Wilshire Boulevard, 46th Floor

Los Angeles, CA 90017

213/253-9790 213/620-0100 (fax)

<u>rchernick@jamsadr.com</u>

Chairman
Hon. Carl ____. West (Ret.)
JAMS
707 Wilshire Boulevard, 46th Floor
Los Angeles, CA 90017
213/253-9790 213/620-0100 (fax)
cwest@jamsadr.com
Hon. Read Ambler (Ret.)
JAMS
160 West Santa Clara Street, Suite 1600
San Jose, CA 95113
408/288-2240 408/295-5267 (fax)
rambler@jamsadr.com

Case Manager:
Christy Arceo
JAMS
707 Wilshire Boulevard, Suite 4600
Los Angeles, CA 90017
213/253-9721 213/620-0100 (fax)
carceo@jamsadr.com

Chapter 11

E-Discovery Under the London Court of International Arbitration

*Richard M. Gelb**

---

*RICHARD M. GELB is a partner and cofounder of the Boston firm of Gelb & Gelb LLP (www.gelbgelb.com) where he represents clients in federal and state court civil and criminal litigation and regulatory proceedings concentrating in the areas of business and securities. He is listed in *The Best Lawyers in America, New England Super Lawyers* and *Massachusetts Super Lawyers (Top 100)*, and is a frequent author and lecturer. He is a co-author of *Massachusetts E-Discovery & Evidence: Preservation through Trial* which is published by Massachusetts Continuing Legal Education, Inc. ("MCLE"), and contributed as an author to *Massachusetts Superior Court Civil Practice Manual and Ethical Lawyering in Massachusetts,* also published by MCLE, and *The Comprehensive Guide to Lost Profits Damages for Experts and Attorneys* (2011 ed.), published by Business Valuation Resources, L.L.C. (BVR). Mr. Gelb is a member of the Leadership Council of the American Inns of Court Foundation and the Massachusetts State Liaison. He is a Fellow of the Massachusetts Bar Foundation, the American Bar Foundation, and The Litigation Counsel of America. Mr. Gelb is a graduate of Boston College Law School (J.D., 1973) and a recipient of *The Reverend James B. Malley, S.J. Award.* He is an undergraduate of New York University (B.A., 1969).

KeyCite®: Cases and other legal materials listed in KeyCite Scope can be researched through the KeyCite service on Westlaw®. Use KeyCite to check citations for form, parallel references, prior and later history, and comprehensive citator information, including citations to other decisions and secondary materials.

§ 11:1 Introduction

Discovery of electronically stored information at the London Court of International Arbitration ("LICA") is not commonplace.[1] Traditionally, litigants in the United Kingdom exchange information on a voluntary basis. However, preserving, harvesting, producing and managing ESI is far more burdensome and costly than the handling of hard copy documents. ESI differs from hard copy documents in the following ways: (1) it is dynamic in nature and can be altered or destroyed if proper procedures for preservation are not put in place; (2) it is significantly more voluminous because of the ease with which it can be distributed (e.g. an email chain) and stored (e.g. daily backups); and (3) an electronic document contains associated information such as dates, modifications and authorship (e.g. metadata). Furthermore, electronic communications continue to proliferate, and technological innovation brings more and varied avenues for electronic communications. Relevant ESI can reside on desktop and laptop computers, on-site and remote servers, digital memory and storage devices, email and electronic facsimile transmissions, PDAs, cell phones, pagers, global positioning services and devices, internet service providers, and web site content. Therefore, the burdens and costs associated with e-discovery can be significant.

Cases which are arbitrated will likely involve e-discovery regardless of whether they are simple or complex. As a result, attorneys cannot effectively advocate for their clients without being conversant with e-discovery.

E-discovery issues must be considered in the context in which they arise. The goal of arbitration is to provide a forum where neutrals are charged with conducting proceedings *fairly*, *efficiently*, and *cost-effectively*. There are variations, however, as to the manner of achieving these goals since they are by nature subjective. Arbitrators and parties coming from different backgrounds may be influenced as to how the proceedings should be conducted. Common law countries have a more litigious ap-

---

[Section 11:1]

[1]Electronic discovery is referred to herein as "e-discovery" and electronically stored information as "ESI."

proach to arbitration than civil law countries. Therefore, the American-style litigation approach would likely be more familiar to the Arbitral Tribunal[2] at the LCIA since the United Kingdom has a common law system.[3] Furthermore, differences in language[4] can create additional burdens and costs during the e-discovery process.

§ 11:2 The LCIA arbitration rules

The LCIA Arbitration Rules[1] address what the arbitrators, counsel and parties are expected to achieve and the procedures for doing so. The LCIA Rules, however, do not specifically address e-discovery, as for example, the United States Federal Rules of Civil Procedure do in their discussion of "electronically stored information." Therefore, as discussed below, other authoritative sources must be considered.

> ◆ **Practitioner Tip:** While the LCIA Rules do not specifically address e-discovery, a LCIA Tribunal has the power to order the production of electronic information. In seeking electronic information, an advocate should focus on how that production will aid the fair, efficient and expeditious conduct of the arbitration.

Article 14 pertains to the *Conduct of the Proceedings*. LCIA recommends the following clause for insertion into parties' agreements:

> Any dispute arising out of or in connection with this contract, including any question regarding its existence, validity or termination, shall be referred to and finally resolved by arbitration under the LCIA Rules, which rules are deemed to be incorporated by reference into this clause.

Article 14 of the LCIA Rules addresses the interactions of the parties with the Arbitral Tribunal when conducting proceedings. The LCIA Rules give deference to the wishes of the parties. Agreements as to procedures must be made by the parties in writing or recorded in writing by the Tribunal at the request and with the

---

[2]Referred to herein as the "Tribunal."

[3]Absent the parties' consent, the LCIA Arbitration Rules require that the arbitrator be of a nationality other than that of either of the parties when the parties are from different countries. See Article 6.

[4]The LCIA Arbitration Rules anticipate the problem of language differences. *See* Article 17.

[Section 11:2]

[1]Referred to herein as the "LCIA Rules."

authority of the parties. Article 14 encourages parties to agree on the conduct of their proceedings so long as their agreement is consistent with the Tribunal's general duties:

- The Tribunal must act fairly and impartially as between all parties.
- Each party is to be given a reasonable opportunity of putting on its case and dealing with its opponent's case.
- The procedures to be adopted must be suitable to the circumstances of the arbitration.
- Unnecessary delay or expense should be avoided.
- The procedures must provide a fair and efficient means for the final resolution of the parties' dispute.

The parties can limit the discretion of the Tribunal under Article 14. Absent such an agreement, the Tribunal has broad discretion to discharge its duties allowed under such laws or rules of law as it determines are applicable.

Article 14 requires that the parties do everything necessary for the *fair*, *efficient*, and *expeditious* conduct of the arbitration. These objectives may be fostered when, in the case of a three-member Tribunal, the chairman, with the prior consent of the other two arbitrators, makes procedural rulings alone.

The issues in dispute are key factors for determining the scope of e-discovery. *Article 15* of the LCIA Rules concerns *written statements and documents.*

The claimant initiates the arbitration through a Request[2] that must include a *brief statement* describing the dispute and the claims involved. The claimant must also submit a Statement of Claim describing the *nature of the dispute*, the *underlying facts* and the *relief sought*. If not contained in the Request, the Statement of Claim must set out in *sufficient detail* the facts and contentions of law on which it relies, as well as the relief claimed against all other parties.[3]

The Statement of Defense is the response to the Statement of Claim. It must also set forth in *sufficient detail* the facts and the law that the respondent admits or denies. The respondent must include the grounds and the other statements and contentions of law upon which it relies.

Counterclaims follow the same rules as Claims and must be contained in the Statement of Defense. The Statement of Reply must include defenses to counterclaims. The LCIA Rules do not

---

[2]*See* Article 1

[3]*See* Article 15.2

provide for a default against the party who fails to comply with the rules. If written statements are not furnished, then the Tribunal may proceed with the arbitration and make an award.

The Tribunal is empowered to **govern** e-discovery by virtue of **Article 22**. Discovery in LCIA proceedings focuses on the relevance of documents.[4] An advocate who requests specific documents rather than categories of documents will be more effective because these types of requests are less likely to be perceived by the Tribunal as a fishing expedition, especially when the specific requests are tied to issues and facts raised in the Statement of Claim or the Statement of Defense.

Article 22 pertains to **Additional Powers**[5] the Tribunal may invoke when directing the parties as to their obligations with respect to conducting e-discovery:

- The Tribunal may itself take the **initiative** in identifying the issues and ascertaining the relevant facts and applicable laws and rules;
- The Tribunal may order the **inspection** of property (e.g. computers) by the other party and its experts;
- The Tribunal may order a party to **produce** to it, and to the other parties, for inspection and copying, all documents and classes of documents including ESI that the Tribunal believes are relevant and in the possession, custody or control of a party;
- The Tribunal may decide whether to apply any strict rules of **evidence** as to admissibility, relevance or weight of materials tendered by a party on any matter of fact or expert opinion (e.g. whether a party must establish a chain of custody with respect to ESI it wishes to present to the Tribunal); and
- The Tribunal may determine the **time**, **manner** and **form** in which materials are to be exchanged between the parties and presented to it (e.g. whether ESI must be produced in native format).

Therefore, although they do not specifically address e-discovery, the LCIA Rules authorize the Tribunal to make those orders with respect to ESI which it deems necessary to advance the objectives[6] of the arbitration.

E-discovery can be extremely costly, and therefore, **Article 28** of the LCIA Rules concerning the **award of arbitration and**

---

[4]*See* Article 22(f).

[5]The complete list of additional powers is set forth in Article 22(a) to (h).

[6]*See* Article 14.

legal costs must be kept in mind. Clients should be forewarned that they might be the party taxed with e-discovery costs at the end of the day.[7] Absent a written agreement of the parties providing otherwise, the Tribunal has the power to render an award in which all or part of the costs incurred by the prevailing party must be paid by the opposing party.

It is important to maintain complete and accurate records of e-discovery costs because the Tribunal must fix the amount of *each item* constituting costs, including legal fees, on a reasonable basis which it thinks fit. Unless the parties otherwise agree in writing, the Tribunal applies the general principle that costs should reflect the parties' relative success and failure in the award or arbitration. The Tribunal may deviate from the general approach, however, when it is inappropriate to the particular circumstances of the arbitration. In any event, awards for costs must set forth the reasons for the taxing of costs and legal fees.[8]

> ◆ **Practitioner Tip:** Clients should be forewarned that, absent a written agreement of the parties providing otherwise, the LCIA Tribunal may tax the non-prevailing party with some or all of the costs of e-discovery.

Article 29 of the LCIA Rules provides *finality* to the arbitration proceedings because:

- The Tribunal's decisions are *conclusive* and *binding*;
- The rights of appeal or review by state court or other judicial authority *shall* be taken as having been *waived*; and
- The Tribunal is not required to express the *reasons* for its decisions.

Article 30 of the LCIA Rules addresses claims that certain ESI contains *confidential information*. Unless the parties agree in writing to the contrary, the parties undertake to hold confidential any awards, materials created for the arbitration, and *documents produced by parties* that are not in the public domain. The forgoing rule allows confidentiality to be breached when:

- A legal duty requires disclosure;
- Disclosure may be required to protect or pursue a legal right; or

---

[7]The United States and the United Kingdom differ notably in their approaches to the costs of litigation. While it is customary in the United States that each party bear its own costs, in the United Kingdom it is customary that the losing party bear the costs of the winning party, as well as its own. The LCIA Rules follow the United Kingdom's custom. *See* Article 28.3.

[8]*See* Article 28.4.

- Disclosure is necessary during bona fide legal proceedings before a state court or other judicial authority to enforce or challenge an award.

The LICA Rules do not guide the Tribunal and parties as to details which must be addressed for handling the arduous task of e-discovery. ESI must be *located*, *preserved*, *retrieved*, *reviewed*, *produced*, *managed*, and *introduced* during the arbitration proceedings. A balance needs to be struck between the relevance of the ESI and the burden of producing the ESI. Early on, the parties should confer about the following topics and, if necessary, present their disputes to the Tribunal:

- The accessibility of the ESI;
- The costs of retrieving the ESI and the allocation of those costs between the parties;
- The search terms to be used for retrieving the ESI;
- Whether metadata must be produced;
- The platform for hosting and managing the ESI;
- The role of computer forensics experts in the e-discovery process; and
- The admissibility of the ESI into evidence.

However, because the LCIA Rules do not fully address the many e-discovery issues that are likely to arise, the parties and Tribunal may look to other sources for guidance, and therefore, e-discovery rules from *other tribunals* are discussed below.

> ◆ **Practitioner Tip:** If the parties cannot reach agreement as to e-discovery issues, the Tribunal may look to other sources for guidance, including the United Kingdom's Rules of Civil Procedure, the ICDR Guidelines, the Chartered Institute of Arbitrator's E-Discovery Protocols, the Rules of the International Bar Association, and The Sedona ConferenceConference®.

§ 11:3   The United Kingdom's Rules of Civil Procedure

The United Kingdom's Ministry of Justice posts on its web site the *Rules of Civil Procedure*[1] which govern judicial proceedings. Counsel familiar with the *Federal Rules of Civil Procedure* will feel quite comfortable navigating within the CPR. Rules used in court are usually not a source for arbitration rules inasmuch as the two forums approach dispute resolution differently. In

---

[Section 11:3]

[1]Available at http://www.justice.gov.uk/civil/procrules_fin/menus/rules.htm (referred to herein as the "CPR").

arbitration, rules which permit extensive discovery are sacrificed for rules which foster expediency, efficiency and cost effectiveness. However, the CPR was recently enacted and will be the most authoritative source for e-discovery among practitioners in the United Kingdom. Additionally, the CPR treatment of e-discovery is detailed and comprehensive. Therefore, counsel who are familiar with the CPR e-discovery rules and are able to apply their principles selectively and appropriately at LCIA will be the more effective advocates.

Part 31 of the CPR addresses overall *Disclosure and Inspection of Documents*. *Practice Direction 31A*[2] supplements Part 31. Paragraph 2A.1 of the Direction which pertains to electronic disclosure directs that the CPR contains a broad definition of "a document" that extends to *Electronic Documents* and includes the following: e-mail and other electronic transmissions; word processed documents and databases; documents that are readily accessible from computer systems and other electronic devices and media; documents stored on servers and back-up systems; Electronic Documents that have been deleted; and additional information stored and associated with Electronic Documents known as metadata.

Effective as of October 1, 2010, CPR Part 31 was supplemented by *Practice Direction 31B*[3] which governs *Disclosure of Electronic Documents*. Particularly noteworthy in guiding the court and parties is the *Electronic Documents Questionnaire*, a copy of which can be found in *Appendix A* to this chapter. This document is an excellent tool for guiding adjudicators and parties in any forum.

Paragraph 2 of Direction 31B fosters the same objectives as Article 14 of the LCIA Rules: "The purpose of this Practice Direction is to encourage and assist the parties to reach agreement in relation to the disclosure of Electronic Documents in a proportionate and cost-effective manner."

Paragraph 5 of Direction 31B sets forth definitions of terms that are applicable to e-discovery: "Data Sampling"; "Disclosure Data"; "Electronic Document"; "Electronic Image"; "Key Word Search"; "Metadata"; "Native Electronic Document" or "Native Format"; and "Optical Character Recognition (OCR)."

The General Principles contained in Paragraph 6 of Direction 31B may guide the Tribunal and parties when addressing e-discovery issues at LCIA:

---

[2]Referred to herein as "Direction 31A."

[3]Referred to herein as "Direction 31B."

- Electronic Documents should be managed efficiently in order to minimize the cost incurred;
- Technology should be used in order to ensure that document management activities are undertaken efficiently and effectively;
- Disclosure should be given in a manner which gives effect to the overriding objective;
- Electronic Documents should generally be made available for inspection in a form which allows the party receiving the documents the same ability to access, search, review and display the documents as the party giving disclosure; and
- Disclosure of Electronic Documents which are of no relevance to the proceedings may place an excessive burden in time and cost on the party to whom disclosure is given.

Paragraph 7 addresses the ***preservation***[4] of documents. Counsel must notify clients as soon as litigation is contemplated of their duty to preserve ESI subject to disclosure, including ESI which would be deleted in the normal course of business (i.e. destruction cycles contained in document retention policies must be suspended).

As discussed above, the LCIA Rules encourage party autonomy. Parts 8 and 9 of Direction 31B, addressing ***discussions*** between the parties before the first Case Management Conference in relation to the use of technology and disclosure, provide excellent guidelines for the parties to follow in resolving e-discovery issues which may arise during LCIA proceedings.

Paragraph 8 requires the parties to prepare for certain e-discovery issues prior to the first case management conference. Similarly, the parties in LCIA arbitrations should consider meeting regarding e-discovery issues. The use of technology in the management of Electronic Documents should be broached as well as how e-discovery will be conducted. Inasmuch as voluntary disclosure is part of the legal tradition in the United Kingdom, counsel should approach the e-discovery issues in the same man-

---

[4]Part 44(1) of the Arbitration Act 1996 (c.23), which applies to arbitrations in the United Kingdom, provides for Court Powers Exercisable in Support of Arbitral Proceedings: "Unless otherwise agreed by the parties, the court has for the purposes of and in relation to arbitral proceedings the same power of making orders about the matters listed below [in part 44(2)] as it has for the purposes of and in relation to legal proceedings." Among those matters is the preservation of evidence (part 44(b)(2)(b)). Therefore, if the parties cannot agree to the terms of the preservation of ESI prior to the formation of the LCIA Tribunal, the parties may go to court on an expeditious basis in order to seek a preservation order.

ner by providing documents in electronic format. Additionally, Paragraph 9 identifies specific e-discovery issues the parties should address, especially in complex cases:

- The categories of Electronic Documents within the parties' control;
- The computer systems, electronic devices and media on which any relevant documents may be held;
- Storage systems and document retention policies; and
- The scope of the reasonable search for Electronic Documents.

The CPR also contemplates the parties considering the use of any tools and techniques which may reduce the burden and cost of disclosure of Electronic Documents such as:

- Limiting disclosure of documents or certain categories of documents to particular date ranges, to particular custodians of documents, or to particular types of documents;
- Use of agreed Keyword Searches;
- Use of agreed software tools;
- Methods to be used to identify duplicate documents;
- Use of Data Sampling;
- The methods to be used to identify privileged documents and other non-disclosable documents, redact documents, and deal with privileged or other documents which have been inadvertently disclosed;
- Use of a staged approach to the disclosure of Electronic Documents;
- Preservation of Electronic Documents with a view to preventing loss of such documents before the trial;
- Exchange of data relating to Electronic Documents in an agreed electronic format using agreed fields;
- Formats in which Electronic Documents are to be provided;
- A basis for charging for or sharing the costs of providing Electronic Documents, and whether any arrangements for charging or sharing of costs are final or are subject to re-allocation by the Tribunal; and
- The use of a neutral electronic repository for storage of Electronic Documents.

Paragraphs 20 and 24 of Direction 31B contemplate a *reasonable search* by addressing the scope of the search, the factors bearing on the reasonableness of the search, and approaches for avoiding or reducing the burdens and costs to the parties of e-discovery. The circumstances of each case should be considered when fixing the extent of the search bearing in mind that the overriding objective includes dealing with the case in ways which are proportionate. The following factors set forth in Paragraph 21 may be relevant when asking the Tribunal to decide whether a request for the discovery of ESI is reasonable:

- The number of documents involved;
- The nature and complexity of the proceedings; and
- The ease and expense of retrieval of any particular document.

The following issues are also relevant:

- The accessibility of Electronic Documents including e-mail communications on computer systems, servers, back-up systems and other electronic devices or media that may contain such documents taking into account alterations or developments in hardware or software systems used by the disclosing party and/or available to enable access to such documents;
- The location of relevant Electronic Documents including computer systems, servers, back-up systems and other electronic devices or media that may contain such documents;
- The likelihood of locating relevant data;
- The cost of recovering Electronic Documents;
- The cost of disclosing and providing inspection of relevant Electronic Documents;
- The likelihood that Electronic Documents will be materially altered in the course of recovery, disclosure or inspection;
- The availability of documents or contents of documents from other sources; and
- The significance of those Electronic Documents which are likely to be located during the search.

If the parties cannot reach agreement as to e-discovery issues, the Tribunal may find the CPR to be instructive. The Tribunal should decide whether all or only some part of a party's electronic storage system should be searched, whether ESI falling outside of a certain date range or in particular categories should be searched, and whether the search should be limited to specified locations. The CPR also directs that the primary source of disclosure of Electronic Documents is normally **reasonably accessible** data, and a party must demonstrate that the relevance and materiality of the Electronic Documents justify the cost and burden of retrieving and producing those Electronic Documents which are not readily accessible.

Direction 31B covers **"Keyword and other automated searches"** in Paragraphs 25 through 27. The CPR advances the following principles:

- It may be reasonable to search for Electronic Documents by means of Keyword Searches or other automated methods of searching if a full review of each and every document would be unreasonable; and
- It will often be insufficient to use simple Keyword Searches or other automated methods of searching alone, and doing so may result in a failure to locate important documents which should be disclosed, and/or may find excessive quantities of irrelevant documents which, if disclosed, would place an excessive burden in time and cost on the party to whom disclosure is given.

Therefore, the CPR directs the parties to consider supplementing Keyword Searches and other automated searches with additional techniques such as individually reviewing certain documents or categories of documents (for example important documents generated by key personnel) and taking such other steps as may be required in order to justify a party's decisions to the Tribunal.

The disclosure of *metadata* is burdensome and costly, especially when privilege reviews are necessary. Paragraphs 28 and 29 of Direction 31B pertain to metadata. The CPR recognizes that some metadata may accompany an Electronic Document produced in its native format. However, a party seeking additional metadata must demonstrate that the relevance and materiality of the requested metadata justify the cost and burden of producing that metadata. Parties may wish to advance the same standards to the LCIA Tribunal.

Paragraphs 32 through 35 of Direction 31B cover the provision of electronic copies of disclosed documents. The CPR directs the parties to co-operate at an early stage about the format in which Electronic Documents are to be provided on inspection, and address the disputed issues with the court. The same approach should be encouraged during arbitrations at LCIA. Electronic Documents should be produced in their Native Format, and redactions or alterations should be disclosed. Available OCR versions of Electronic Documents should also be produced. Counsel in LCIA arbitrations will serve their clients well if they follow a similar approach. Additionally, Paragraph 36 of Direction 31B provides that the party producing Electronic Documents which are best accessed using technology which is not readily available to the opposing party shall co-operate with the opposing party in order to make available such reasonable additional inspection facilities as may be appropriate for affording inspection.

The CPR is detailed and comprehensive, but a LCIA Tribunal

may view the rules as litigious, and not in the spirit of arbitration which encourages cost effectiveness. Moreover, the Tribunal is more sophisticated than a jury, and therefore, may conclude that that burdensome e-discovery is not warranted for a fair adjudication of the case. Therefore, considering e-discovery rules promulgated by other arbitration forums which are discussed below is important.

§ 11:4 The International Centre for Dispute Resolution® guidelines for arbitrators concerning exchanges of information

The International Centre for Dispute Resolution® ("ICDR") is the international arm of the American Arbitration Association. *Guidelines for Arbitrators Concerning Exchanges of Information,*[1] which became effective after May 32, 2008, were promulgated to provide "a simpler, less expensive and more expeditious form of dispute resolution" for international commercial arbitration. The Guidelines relate the following in order to provide context:

> While arbitration must be a fair process, care must also be taken to prevent the importation of procedural measures and devices from different court systems, which may be considered conducive to fairness within those systems, but which are not appropriate to the conduct of arbitrations in an international context and which are inconsistent with an alternative form of dispute resolution that is simpler, less expensive and more expeditious. One of the factors contributing to complexity, expense and delay in recent years has been the migration from court systems into arbitration of procedural devices that allow one party to a court proceeding access to information in the possession of the other, without full consideration of the differences between arbitration and litigation.

In order to effectuate the above goals, the Guidelines inform the arbitrators that they have the authority, the responsibility, and in certain jurisdictions, the mandatory duty to manage arbitration proceedings so as to achieve the goal of providing a simpler, less expensive, and more expeditious process than judicial proceedings.

The Guidelines address the exchange of documents, documents in the possession of another party and inspection of documents, and require that requests for documents contain descriptions of specific documents or classes of documents as well as explana-

---

[Section 11:4]

[1]Available at http://www.adr.org/si.asp?id=5288 (referred to herein as the "ICDR Guidelines").

tions of their relevance and materiality to the outcome of the case.

The Guidelines in Paragraph 4 address Electronic Documents:

> When documents to be exchanged are maintained in electronic form, the party in possession of such documents may make them available in the form (which may be paper copies) most convenient and economical for it, unless the tribunal determines, on application and for good cause, that there is a compelling need for access to the documents in a different form. Requests for documents maintained in electronic form should be narrowly focused and structured to make searching for them as economical as possible. The tribunal may direct testing or other means of focusing and limiting any search.

The ICDR Guidelines achieve the objective of simplicity, but they may be inadequate for complex international arbitrations involving voluminous ESI. To meet the demands of complex arbitrations, the Chartered Institute of Arbitrators promulgated rules that more closely resemble the United Kingdom's Rules of Civil Procedure.

§ 11:5   Chartered Institute of Arbitrators' protocol for E-Disclosure in arbitration

In October 2008, the Chartered Institute of Arbitrators promulgated its *Protocol for E-Disclosure in Arbitration*[1] designed for cases in which potentially disclosable documents are in electronic form and the cost for giving disclosures may be an issue.

The Protocol encourages the early consideration of e-discovery issues, including preservation and disclosure of ESI, by requiring the parties to meet at the earliest opportunity to seek an agreement as to the scope and methods of production. The Protocol also directs the Tribunal to raise e-discovery concerns at the earliest opportunity (in any event, no later than the preliminary meeting). Among the matters to be considered are:

- Determining whether ESI is likely to be the subject of requests for disclosure;
- The locations of ESI;
- The scope of ESI preservation;
- The rules that will be applied to e-discovery;
- Whether the parties can agree to limit ESI disclosure; and

[Section 11:5]

[1]Available at http://www.ciarb.org/ (referred to herein as the "Protocol").

- Tools and techniques for reducing the burden and cost of e-discovery which are available.

The tools and techniques presented in the Protocol include:

- Specification of the categories of ESI;
- Date ranges;
- Identification of custodians;
- Use of agreed-upon search terms and software tools;
- Data privacy obligations, agreements as to waiver of the attorney-client privilege; and
- Whether the Tribunal will benefit from professional guidance as to IT issues.

The Protocol also seeks to avoid requests for ESI that appear to be fishing expeditions. Documents must be described; categories of documents must be specified; the relevance and materiality of the ESI must be stated; and a statement that the requesting party does not have possession or control of the ESI and the reasons why it is assumed that the ESI is in the adverse party's possession or control must be provided.

Absent agreement of the parties regarding e-discovery, the Tribunal should consider the reasonableness and proportionality of a request, fairness and the equal treatment of the parties thereby ensuring that each party has a reasonable opportunity to present its case. The Tribunal must also consider the factors of the burden and cost of complying with a discovery order in light of the amount in controversy, the nature of the dispute, and the relevance and materiality of the ESI in question. Additionally, the primary type of ESI requested should be readily accessible data (e.g. active data).

Although the requesting party may ask for the production in a specific form, ESI should usually be produced in the format in which the information is ordinarily maintained or in a reasonably usable format. Absent an agreement of the parties, the Tribunal must decide whether ESI is required to be produced in native format or otherwise.

Unless the ESI is produced in a form that includes the requested metadata, the party requesting the production of metadata must demonstrate that the relevance and materiality of this data outweigh the burden and cost of its production. The Tribunal must also address cost-allocation and the timetable for production.

If a party fails to comply with the requirements of the Protocol including complying with an order of the Tribunal, the Tribunal is entitled to draw any inferences it considers appropriate.

§ 11:6 International Bar Association's rules on the taking of evidence in international arbitration

The International Bar Association adopted on May 29, 2010 the *IBA Rules on the Taking of Evidence in International Arbitration.*[1] The IBA Rules include in the definition of "document" data of any kind, whether recorded or maintained on paper or by electronic, audio, visual or any other means.

The IBA Rules are also instructive for a LCIA Tribunal confronting situations where parties are attempting to reach an agreement or when orders must be entered due to the absence of an agreement. In any event, the Tribunal's goal is to adopt— hopefully by agreement of the parties—an efficient, economical, and fair process for taking of evidence including e-discovery.

As to ESI, parties may be required to identify specific files, search terms, custodians or other means of searching for ESI in an efficient and economical manner. Parties must show how the requested ESI is relevant and material to the outcome. The IBA Rules require a party to produce ESI in the form most convenient or economical and reasonably usable by the party opponent. The IBA Rules also contemplate the Tribunal setting a schedule for e-discovery.

§ 11:7 The Sedona Conference®

The mission of The Sedona Conference®[1] is as follows:

The Sedona Conference exists to allow leading jurists, lawyers, experts, academics and others, at the cutting edge of issues in the area of antitrust law, complex litigation, and intellectual property rights, to come together—in conferences and mini-think tanks (Working Groups)—and engage in true dialogue, not debate, all in an effort to move the law forward in a reasoned and just way.

Our hallmark is our unique use of the dialogue process to reach levels of understanding and insight not otherwise achievable. Our Working Group Series is designed to focus the dialogue on forward-looking principles, best practices and guidelines in specific areas of the law that may have a dearth of guidance or are otherwise at a "tipping point." The goal is that our Working Groups, the open Working Group Membership Program, and our peer review process, will produce output that is balanced, authoritative, and of immediate benefit to the Bench, Bar and general public.

[Section 11:6]

    [1]Available at http://www.ibanet.org/ (referred to herein as the "IBA Rules").

[Section 11:7]

    [1]Available at http://www.thesedonaconference.org/ (referred to herein as the "TSC").

Among TSC's activities is its Working Group Series:

The Sedona Conference® Working Group Series is the next phase in the evolution of The Sedona Conference® from a forum for advanced dialogue to an open think-tank confronting some of the most challenging issues faced by our legal system today. The Working Group Series was launched in 2002 and is designed as a bridge between our Regular Season Conferences and a pure think-tank model.

TSC, through the efforts of its Working Group on International Electronic Information Management, Discovery & Disclosure (WG6), published two papers that can be obtained through TSC's web site:

- *Framework for Analysis of Cross-Border Discovery Conflicts: A Practical Guide to Navigating the Competing Currents of International Data Privacy and e-Discovery* (August 2008— Public Comment Version); and
- *International Overview of Discovery, Data Privacy & Disclosure Requirements* (September 2009—Public Comment Version).

§ 11:8 E-discovery questions counsel should be prepared to address with clients, opposing counsel and the tribunal

Claimant's counsel should not approach arbitration at LCIA with the objective of using e-discovery as a leverage tool by expanding its scope in order to increase the burden and cost to the opposing party. Likewise, counsel for the respondent should not stonewall the e-discovery process, especially in the LCIA forum which is used to voluntary reciprocal discovery. Moreover, counsel should not assume that a smoking gun will necessarily be found or, on the other hand, that deletion of ESI is preferable to searching for probative evidence.

In light of the above, counsel should be prepared to confer with the opposing party in an attempt to reach agreement as to e-discovery issues, and to effectively advocate with respect to disputed issues the Tribunal is asked to resolve. Among the issues at the preservation stage as to which counsel should be conversant are the following:

- Is a dispute reasonably anticipated?
- If so, should a hold notice be issued to the party's employees?
- Should a preservation notice be sent to the opposing party?
- Will a preservation order be necessary?
- Where does the ESI reside?

- Who are the custodians of the ESI?
- Is the ESI readily accessible?
- What preservation plan should be implemented?
- Is it wise to engage a computer forensics expert?

Next, issues of scope of production and the burden and cost of producing ESI must be resolved. The seminal decision in *Zubulake*[1] is instructive as to what questions the parties and the Tribunal should answer:

- To what extent is each party's request for the production of ESI specifically tailored to the discovery of relevant information?
- How important are the issues at stake?
- Is the information sought available from other sources?
- What is the total cost of production compared to the resources available to each party?
- What is the relative ability of each party to control costs and its incentive to do so?
- What are the relative benefits to the parties of obtaining the information?
- How are attorney-client privilege waiver issues to be handled?

Procedures for harvesting and managing ESI must also be adopted which raise the following questions:

- What tools are available for mining ESI?
- What search terms are necessary?
- Should data culling software be used to eliminate multiple copies of the same documents (i.e. de-duplication)?
- What litigation support tools can be used in order to search and retrieve ESI by issues in the case?
- Should the ESI be hosted in-house or on a web-based platform?

Counsel would be wise to become familiar with computer forensics experts and litigation support vendors who can assist them in formulating strategies, undertaking projects, interacting with opposing counsel and advocating before the LCIA Tribunal.

§ 11:9   Strategies for reducing the burdens and costs of e-discovery in arbitration

Counsel should be sensitive to the culture and norms of the

[Section 11:8]

[1]Zubulake v. UBS Warburg LLC, 217 F.R.D. 309, 91 Fair Empl. Prac. Cas. (BNA) 1574 (S.D. N.Y. 2003).

Tribunal and parties. American style litigation will most likely be frowned upon at LCIA. In addition, advocates should do more than merely follow the LCIA Rules; they should act in accordance with the spirit of the rules. This means striving to be fair and efficient and purposefully avoiding causing unnecessary delay and expense. Counsel will better serve their clients by acting in a professional and civil manner and earning the respect of the Tribunal.

Parties should expect that the LCIA Tribunal will be more available and participatory than would be a judge. The Tribunal may have expertise regarding the matters being decided. Counsel should suggest solutions for e-discovery issues to the Tribunal that demonstrate reasonableness and creativity. For example, parties can reduce e-discovery costs by working together in order to formulate agreeable search terms or request the Tribunal's assistance if necessary prior to performing the searches. Parties should consider sharing the cost of a neutral, web-based, document-hosting platform (especially if the litigation support tool allows electronic files to be passworded).

Once ESI is preserved, the scope of production may more readily be narrowed because additional searches can occur later in the proceedings if necessary. The parties should attempt to reach an agreement or ask the Tribunal for assistance if they cannot agree so that only metadata which is essential for the case need be produced. Privilege reviews will be less burdensome and costly if the parties themselves or with the Tribunal's assistance put in place an order allowing for the claw-back of privileged ESI which is inadvertently produced.

Finally, advocates will be most effective if they are able to explain to the Tribunal why the suggested method of retrieving and producing the ESI is reasonable. Attorneys will more powerfully advance their arguments to the Tribunal if they readily demonstrate knowledge about the attributes of ESI, the e-discovery process, and the available litigation support tools. Lawyers cannot guaranty to clients that arbitration of their cases will be more efficient, cost effective and expeditious than through the judicial system. Lawyers can, however, impress clients by demonstrating their efforts to achieve such results at LICA in a professional manner and by supporting their arguments on e-discovery issues with a strong knowledge base.

Chapter 12

E-Discovery in International Chamber of Commerce (ICC) Arbitrations

*By Antonio Tavares Paes Jr.**

> **KeyCite⚖:** Cases and other legal materials listed in KeyCite Scope can be researched through the KeyCite service on Westlaw⚖. Use KeyCite to check citations for form, parallel references, prior and later history, and comprehensive citator information, including citations to other decisions and secondary materials.

§ 12:1   Introduction

Too often, discovery is not just about uncovering the truth, but also about how much of the truth the parties can afford to disinter . . . [D]iscovery expenses frequently escalate when information is stored in electronic form.[1]

---

*The author is a partner at Costa, Waisberg & Tavares Paes Advogados in Sao Paulo, Brazil. He is a member of Brazilian and New York State Bars. He was assisted in the preparation of this chapter by Claudia Helena Poggio Cortez.

[Section 12:1]

[1]Rowe Entm't, Inc. v. William Morris Agency, Inc., 205 F.R.D.421 (S.D.N.Y. 2002).

Despite recent advances in computer software using linguistic and sociological cues to search electronically stored documents, the citation above is as accurate today as it was when it was made in 2002.[2] A creature of the (relatively) recent societal shift to electronic communications, e-discovery proceedings are a reflection of today's complex relations and the disputes that surround them. Virtually shunned by Civil Law countries, both "traditional" discovery proceedings and e-discovery have also been met with criticism in Common Law countries for the increased level of expenses, time delays and overall complexities that they engender. Nevertheless, both continue to be an integral part of Common Law countries' legal systems, with little evidence that there will be substantial changes to how they are carried on and to the importance attributed to them in these countries.

Much like "traditional" discovery proceedings, which have found acceptance (albeit in a simplified and restricted manner) in international arbitration rules, e-discovery over the past few years has become a necessity in complex international arbitrations and resort to it has become more frequent and prevalent. However, the arbitration rules that preceded the inception of e-discovery, including the ICC, were not necessarily all-encompassing enough to consider the various alternatives of e-discovery and some of its consequences, such as:

(i)   issues relating to the restoration of back-up tapes;

(ii)   the need to access metadata contained in the electronic data;

(iii)   the systems used by the parties to gather electronically stored information (ESI); and

(iv)   the ever-increasing costs associated with the necessary adoption of e-discovery principles.

In some case, arbitration rules have evolved to embody pro active provisions dealing with e-discovery, ranging from specific procedures that should be adopted to retain and produce ESI upon demand, to the shift of the burden to cover the costs associated with the production of such information. In other cases, however, the guidelines have been more general and the ap-

---

[2]Recent technological developments in specialized software in the field of key word search and sociological language usage have exerted downward pressure on the cost of e-discovery, to the point of causing law firm managers to predict downsizing of the market. Experts disagree and indicate that the savings is modest thus far and will only materialize if a law firm has a good retention and destruction policy that is carefully enforced. *See* Greentree Fur Corp v. Randolf, 531 U.S. 79 (2000) on e-discovery and costs.

plicable rules do nothing more than create a broad environment that expands the treatment otherwise given to "pure" discovery (or the simple production of documents and information) to encompass all matters relating to e-discovery.[3]

One set of arbitration rules is not better than the other, but each set impacts parties and counsel differently in specific cases. Likewise, treatment under one set of rules is not better simply because one set is more detailed than the other. Businesses and their counsel, especially those working across borders, need to be aware that compliance with differing sets of rules requires careful planning and clear internal policies to avoid expensive litigation costs.[4] However, in both cases the issue of e-discovery requests and proceedings has raised one distinct concern—that the costs associated with them has escalated in some cases to such a degree that they have become even higher than the amounts in dispute in an arbitration proceeding. And it was exactly for this reason that different bodies of arbitration rules have all, independently, acted with the same concern of encouraging (and even imposing) the reduction of the costs associated with e-discovery matters.

§ 12:2   Conceptual treatment of discovery and e-discovery in arbitrations and litigation

It is often the case that arbitration is referred to as a subcategory of litigation, but this is not the case. Although both kinds of procedures have a lot in common, because the process involved is so different, they may end up sharing fewer similarities in substantial matters than at first glance. For example: (i) litigation procedures are strictly codified or established by case

---

[3]The current ICC Rules are an example of this "all encompassing" body of regulations, where the matter of e-discovery is treated in a general manner. This set of facts has begun to change with the adoption of the ICC Report on Techniques for Controlling Cost in Arbitration, which guidelines were summarized in Appendix IV of ICC Rules in force since January, 2012. There is also a report named Techniques for Managing Electronic Document Production When it is Permitted or Required in International Arbitration. ICC Rules are available at http://www.iccwbo.org/Products-and-Services/Arbitration-and-ADR/Arbitration/Rules-of-arbitration/Download-ICC-Rules-of-Arbitration/ICC-Rules-of-Arbitration-in-several-languages/.

[4]For example, an arbitration proceeding conducted under the aegis of rules of the American Arbitration Association (_http://www.adr.org/commercial_arbitration_) may be expected to contain more instances favorable to e-discovery than a proceeding conducted under the rules of the ICC Rules, given the particular backgrounds of each of such body of rules (AAA—the US; ICC—international) and the expectations of the parties and counsel that select each such rules.

law, whereas an arbitration tends to be more informal, and relies less on specific pre-determined rules than on the determination of arbitral tribunals and the parties themselves; (ii) lawyers in litigation often are more aggressive, where the fulfillment of an absolute duty to the client and the expected zealous representation is *de rigueur*, while in arbitration the overzealous lawyer and the unabashed defense of one's position over all else is often met with skepticism and can be detrimental to the case; and (iii) litigation is a public affair, while arbitration is conducted in private.

In no other area of dispute resolution, however, is the difference between litigation and arbitration as obvious as in the production of evidence and documents. This difference directly reflects the differing approaches to adversarial disputes, driven by counsel to the parties in Common Law countries, and the more intrusive inquisitorial proceedings conducted by judges in Civil Law countries.

Effective evidence gathering is critical to a successful outcome in any dispute and the differences between the US-style discovery and the method of document production in Civil Law countries have carried over to the field of e-discovery in these jurisdictions, where production of ESI has far surpassed traditional document and other evidence production in terms of both volume and relevance for particular types of disputes.[1]

In litigation, despite variations from country to country, the rules affecting document and information production through e-discovery tend to be easy to find and, despite possible discrepancies in interpretation, relatively straightforward.[2]

In arbitration proceedings, however, discovery rules, generally identified as rules of document production, used to be less prevalent but have increased in quantity and relevance as of late. Even now, however, most tend to be general in nature. In jurisdictions where the rules on traditional discovery were already more specific, that trait is generally reflected in connection with e-discovery rules in those jurisdictions. Similarly the rules that have treated the issue of discovery (or document production in

---

[Section 12:2]

[1]In 2003, about 547 billion email messages were transmitted. Daniel B. Garrie & Matthew J. Armstrong, *Electronic Discovery and the Challenge Posed by the Sarbanes-Oxley Act*, 205, UCLA J. L. & TECH. 2, 4 (2005).

[2]It does not mean that there are no disputes or difference in opinions as to the applicability of such rules and changes to them. *See* Daniel B. Garrie et al., *Hiding the Inaccessible Truth: Amending the Federal Rules to Accommodate Electronic Discovery*, 25 REV. litig. 115, 115 (2006).

general) more broadly have tended to take the same approach in dealing with e-discovery issues. The rules of arbitration of the International Chamber of Commerce fall into the latter category.[3]

In fact, arbitration rules have framed the issue of discovery in terms of "document production" rules which will determine how and the extent to which a claimant or respondent will be able to impose on the other party the production of documents and information that are in that party's possession. These rules of "document production" tend to be *in-between* the evidence production rules of Civil Law countries and the provisions of Common Law countries discovery. And because these rules are a middle ground, they can be considered extensive from the perspective of parties and practitioners who are used to less intrusive evidence gathering methods, while at the same time be found lacking by those (parties and counsel as well) who prefer a more defined and proactive approach to evidence gathering.

Likewise, e-discovery issues have received similar treatment, with certain arbitration rules being much more specific in determining the path to be adopted by parties and counsel in ESI production while others remain almost entirely silent about the issue, only touching on the matter of ESI production indirectly and simply determining that, as a general rule, the regulations relating to general document production will necessarily apply, to ESI production and e-discovery.

In this chapter the ICC Rules of Arbitration and its more recent offspring, the Techniques for Controlling Time and Cost in Arbitrations,[4] are examined from the perspective of their treatment of discovery in general and e-discovery in particular.

§ 12:3 E-Discovery in the Context of Existing Rules—The ICC and other similar bodies

E-Discovery may be simply defined as discovery of ESI. More formally, it is *"the collection, review and production of electronically stored information—such as e-mail, word processing documents, spreadsheets, and databases—in accordance with . . .*

---

[3]ICC Rules of Arbitration available at http://www.iccwbo.org/Products-and-Services/Arbitration-and-ADR/Arbitration/Rules-of-arbitration/Download-ICC-Rules-of-Arbitration/ICC-Rules-of-Arbitration-in-several-languages/.

[4]Available in http://www.iccdrl.com/CODE/LevelThree.asp?tocxml=ltoc__CommReportsAll.xml&page=Commission%20Reports&L1=Commission%20Reports&L2=&tocxsl=DoubleToc.xsl&contentxsl=arbSingle.xsl&Locator=9&contentxml=CR__0033.xml&AUTH=&nb=0.

discovery requirements."[1] In principle, thus, it would be fair to state that the traditional rules applicable to discovery as a whole should also apply to e-discovery. If only life were that simple. Nowadays participants to litigation (and to a lesser extent arbitration) see themselves and their counsel immersed in a sea of documents, often stumbling through uncharted territories to comply with orders from judicial courts and arbitration tribunals (again, to a lesser extent), which require them to create new protocols to handle information that is contained in electronic media and no longer in boxes and metal archives full of documents.

Basically, e-discovery consists in the identification and collection of electronically stored information that can be used as evidence, and then in the analysis of this information, to be presented in court. The reality is that e-discovery has brought the task of information and document production to a different level, adding various degrees of complexity to what used to be simply a search for paper documents within paper piles. E-discovery now forces parties and counsel to look for even more data in a virtually infinite, ever changing environment that comprises a myriad of formats of digital data, such as computers, hand-held devices, cell phones, the "Cloud," servers, social networking accounts (Twitter, Facebook, Orkut, Google+, Linkedin, etc.) and other sites. This means that posts, photographs, relationship history, social activities and more can all be assessed in an e-discovery.

Due to an increase in the use of e-discovery in traditional litigation disputes, companies specialized in technology solutions are offering legal technologies in order to facilitate the identification and collection of evidences, in a more agile way.

And while in the past discovery of documents was limited to existing documents, today ESI production encompasses existing and formerly existing documents! According to Sherman Kahn, *"proliferation of electronic media has enabled parties to store massive amounts of information that previously would not have been stored".*[2]

This is akin, figuratively speaking of course, to a party produc-

---

[Section 12:3]

[1]*See* Linda G. Sharp, *Restoration Drama: The Complexity of Electronic Discovery Requires Practitioners to Master New Litigation Skills*, 28 L.A. LAW. 31, 31 (October 2001).

[2]*See* Sherman Kahn, *E-discovery demystified for arbitrators—tips for how to manage e-discovery for efficient proceedings.* http://www.mofo.com/files/Upload s/Images/E-Discovery-Demystified-for-Arbitrators.pdf.

ing a document that has been burned or otherwise destroyed and which had ceased to exist for all purposes. The proposition ceases to sound as ridiculous when we consider the fact that in the e-world, when a document is deleted or otherwise eliminated from the realm of existing things, it does not truly cease to exist but, rather, is transferred to another area of the holding device.[3] This makes a document that was to have been deleted in its entirety (and which would have been destroyed in full in the "paper era") subject to an order of production by an Arbitration Tribunal. This is what makes the new era of E-Discovery potentially dangerous in terms of liability to individuals and corporations, demanding from them a discipline and aforethought yet unheard of.

E-Discovery poses new challenges that were not thought of in the recent past—if all documents are, at least in theory, "discoverable", what are the duties of the parties that hold and store these documents? Do they have an affirmative duty to seek the most accessible system available, irrespective of cost and at the risk of such system being more vulnerable to third party attacks? If so, will a claimant in an arbitration case (or a plaintiff in a litigation matter) have to bear the burden of document production if to do so would require vast sums of money?[4] Are companies obligated to maintain back-up tapes or disks that are no longer readable by more modern applications, rendering virtually impossible the production (at reasonable costs) of legacy data? Who is to bear the costs of retrieving such legacy data?

Despite the generally-broad latitude afforded to ICC Arbitration Tribunals in dealing with issues relating to E-Discovery, the absence of specific ICC-sponsored rules on the issue creates a very clear problem at the outset of an arbitration proceeding: how are the parties supposed to behave at the moment they receive a notice or arbitration in connection with issues such as document retention and destruction, update of e-storage systems, file corruption and restoration, among others, in a way that will not impact that party's ability to provide ESI on its own or upon request and order by an Arbitral Tribunal. Absent such rules, however, these issues should be decided at the outset of the

---

[3]This has serious implications in the case of companies that do not create *and* follow a strict policy for document retention and destruction.

[4]Certain countries, such as Brazil, impose the obligation on the losing party to a judicial proceeding to pay court costs and court-mandated legal fees to the winning party.

arbitration proceeding, at the direction of the Arbitration Tribunal.[5]

The issue of e-discovery has acquired such a level of relevance that the ICC created, in August 2008, a task force comprised of 68 members from 14 different countries, with the express mandate to:

- study and identify the essential features and effects of the disclosure of electronic documents in international arbitration; and
- establish a report, possibly in the form of notes or recommendations for the production of electronic documents in international arbitration.

Althoug the Task Force has produced a report with recommendations (the Techniques for Managing Electronic Document Production When it is Permitted or Required in International Arbitration, which basically describes ESI key features and how they may be managed), these were not encompassed by the new ICC arbitration rules in force as from 1st January 2012, which maintained virtually intact the same rules which were in force until 2011 in connection with the production of evidence.

Despite this, it is important to mention that the main issue of concern relating to the use of e-discovery mechanisms in arbitrations is the potential impact on the cost efficiency and speed of an arbitration proceeding for the single reason that the uncontrolled use of e-discovery proceedings may lead to a collection and analysis of vasts amount of documents (most commercial information today is electronically stored).

In response to this concern, certain arbitral institutions (for example, the Chartered Institute) have already adopted rules and/or protocols to regulate and facilitate the use of e-discovery in arbitration. Regarding e-discovery, ICC only has the Techniques for Managing Electronic Document Production When it is Permitted or Required in International Arbitration.[6] Irrespective of this, there are certain steps that should be observed in any e-discovery realized in an ICC-sponsored arbitration, such as: definition of the scope of the ESI (*i.e.*, the facts that are going to be evidenced through ESI and of the documents that must be analyzed); decision as to whether a particular legal technological

---

[5]ICC Rules Article 25.1.

[6]Available in http://www.iccdrl.com/CODE/LevelThree.asp?tocxml=ltoc__C ommReportsAll.xml&page=Commission%20Reports&L1=Commission%20Repor ts&L2=&tocxsl=DoubleToc.xsl&contentxsl=arbSingle.xsl&Locator=9&contentx ml=CR__0043.xml&AUTH=&nb=0.

solution will to be used or a particular technical expert is going to be hired; and the specific setting of deadlines, if possible.

§ 12:4 ICC Rules of (E-)Document Production

As indicated above, certain rules of arbitration have approached the issue of "document production" in a more general manner, allowing a substantial degree of flexibility to the arbitral tribunal and the parties as to which rules to follow and the procedures to adopt. Within this loosely bound environment, the rules contemplate the possibility of a party asking for, and the tribunal ordering, the production of evidence by the other party (and even third parties), but often without any particular direction as to how the document production is to be accomplished.

The rules created by the International Chamber of Commerce—ICC follow the pattern of broad definitions and scarce impositions, leaving to the parties and the arbitral tribunal the task of determining which rules to apply.[1] The same is true in connection with ESI production/e-discovery (both terms to be used interchangeably herein).

As per the Techniques for Managing Electronic Document Production When it is Permitted or Required in International Arbitration, the inexistence of rules or guidelines regarding e-discovery is deliberate, in order to maintain the parties' and arbitrators' flexibility regarding the production if evidence.

The ICC Rules do not deal specifically with the production of evidence during an arbitral proceeding, but the Rules make clear that the burden of producing evidence rests with the party seeking to prove its allegations. This burden can shift upon request by a party and acceptance by the Arbitral Tribunal.[2]

In addition to the rules of law selected by the parties (and the procedural rules relating to the arbitration), the ICC Rules stipulate that, for the proper resolution of the conflict,

the Arbitral Tribunal shall take account of the provisions of the contract, if any, between the parties and of any relevant trade usages.[3]

The general rule is that no party may demand to have discovery

---

[Section 12:4]

[1]*See* Yves Derains and Eric A. Schwartz, A Guide to the ICC Rules of Arbitration, Second Edition, 272, Kluwer Law International (2005).

[2]ICC Rules Article 25.

[3]ICC Rules Article 21.2.

of documents in an ICC arbitration proceeding, but a party may ask for it and the Arbitral Tribunal may grant such request based on the content of ICC Rule 25(5).[4] This is a case-by-case analysis and there is no guarantee that similar requests will be decided similarly.

The ICC Rules determine that ". . . *any relevant agreements* . . ." are expected to be presented by a party with the Request for Arbitration.[5] This determination applies in principle to the respondent,[6] who is expected to do just that, as provided by ICC Rules Article 25.2.

> *"After studying the written submissions of the* **parties and all documents relied upon** *. . ."* (Emphasis added.).

Although silent in many respects as to the particulars of document production, the ICC Rules contain broad guidance as to how to proceed:

> *. . . where the [ICC] Rules are silent, [the proceedings before an Arbitral Tribunal shall be governed] by any rules which the parties or, failing them, the Arbitral Tribunal may settle on . . . .*[7]

This approach allows the parties (or the Arbitral Tribunal) to determine how to go about producing the documents and information that would be needed in each specific case. Nevertheless, the ICC Rules afford the Arbitral Tribunal the discretion to impose restrictions on the will of the parties for the benefit of the arbitration proceeding overall and, more specifically, for the benefit of each party, as such Rules command the Arbitral Tribunal to proactively act to ". . . *ensure that each party has a reasonable opportunity to present its case.*"[8] This enables the Arbitral Tribunal to keep discovery in check because the acceptability of a party's request to effect discovery is directly dependent on the will of the Arbitral Tribunal.

These same Rules indicate that it behooves the Arbitral Tribunal to ensure the expediency of an arbitration procedure, when it commands it to "*proceed within as short a time as possible to establish the facts of the case by all appropriate means.*"[9] It is this provision of Article 25.1. of the ICC Rules that, in

---

[4]"*At any time during the proceedings, the Arbitral Tribunal may summon any party to provide additional evidence.*"

[5]Rules Article 4.3.e.

[6]ICC Rules Article 5.1.

[7]ICC Rules Article 19.

[8]ICC Rules Article 22.4.

[9]ICC Rules Article 25.1.

combination with Article 19 of the same rules, *"serves as a point of departure whenever decisions need to be taken with respect to matters of arbitral procedure that are not the subject of express provisions in the [ICC] Rules."*[10]

Together with the express direction for the Arbitral Tribunal to act without delay,[11] Article 25 of the ICC rules makes it clear that the truth about the facts of the case may be pursued with the necessary degree of flexibility and *pro-activism* on the part of the Tribunal, as it is expected to adopt *"all appropriate means"* to achieving that goal.[12] This has been welcomed by practitioners and arbitrators as a whole as it allows the Arbitral Tribunal to frame the protocol for document production based on the specific characteristics of a particular arbitration proceeding. This allows for the expansion or retraction of the guidelines for document production depending on whether the parties and their counsel are more aligned with a Common Law or Civil Law system of dispute resolution. This is especially relevant when evidence is to be generated through ESI production, where the parties will have the opportunity to create protocols as to which material is to be produced and by whom, starting, for example, with the determination as to whose information would be available for discovery and production.

This level of flexibility is not without control, however, as such discretion is subject to (i) the remaining ICC Rules; (ii) other rules that may have been selected by the parties under Article 19 of the ICC Rules; and (iii) non-discretionary elements of applicable law,[13] imposing on the Arbitral Tribunal the duty to act appropriately in all circumstances, with constant respect to the "spirit of the [ICC] Rules"[14] and due process.

Article 25 of the ICC Rules can expand the scope of document production from the documents that make up the arbitration proceeding file to encompass those documents and information that may be in the possession of third parties not subject to the particular arbitration. This is the closest to a US-style discovery proceeding that the ICC Rules get, especially when, in order for such a mandate to be enforced, parties to the arbitration may have to resort to judicial action to ensure compliance with the rule and in so doing, may be forced to conduct true discovery

---

[10]*See* Yves Derains and Eric A. Schwartz, *supra*, page 271.

[11]ICC Rules Article 25.1.

[12]ICC Rules Article 25.1.

[13]*See* Yves Derains and Eric A. Schwartz, *supra*, page 271/2.

[14]ICC Rules Article 41.

searches in the jurisdictions where it is allowed.[15] This is true for both "traditional" document production and the gathering and presentation of ESI, based on the general principle that all ICC Rules that apply to paper document production apply as well (*if and when necessary*) to ESI production.

§ 12:5 IBA Rules on Taking of Evidence in ICC Arbitrations—An Overview

It was within the context of Articles 19 and 25 of the ICC Rules that there has been an increase in adoption, by ICC arbitrations, of the 1999 IBA Rules on the Taking of Evidence in International Commercial Arbitration.[1] These rules were updated and ratified in the new IBA rules adopted by the IBA Council on May 29, 2010 (the IBA Rules).[2] The IBA Rules contain a general determination that one party may only be compelled to produce documents in its possession if they are clearly identified in the document production request or if they are of a *"narrow and specific . . . category"* of documents that is *"reasonably believed to exist,"* which are *"relevant and material to the outcome of the case"* and which are not in the possession of the requesting party (who must so state in its request).[3] As (to date) the production of ESI under an ICC Arbitration is regulated in the same manner as the production of paper documents, the same concepts that are applicable to the production of paper documents will apply to the production of ESI. Thus the concepts of reasonableness, relevancy and materiality will apply to ESI production as well as to the substance of the ESI but, also, as to the method of collection and production of such data.' In the era of ESI, the method of

---

[15]*See* Daniel Schimmel and Mesilla E. Byorade, *Does 28 U.S.C. § 1782 Allow U.S. Courts to Order Discovery for Use in Private International Arbitration?*, in International Arbitration 2009, Volume One, Practicing Law Institute.

[Section 12:5]

[1]IBA Rules on the Taking of Evidence in International Commercial Arbitration, June 1, 1999, at http://www.int-bar.org.

[2]IBA Rules on the Taking of Evidence in International Commercial Arbitration, (May 29, 2010), at http://www.ibanet.org/ENews_Archive/IBA_30 June_2010_Enews_Taking_of_Evidence_new_rules.aspx.

[3]IBA Rules on the Taking of Evidence in International Commercial Arbitration, (May 29, 2010), Rules 3(3)(a) and 3(3)(b).

production, not just the content to be produced, is of relevance and subject to prior review by an Arbitral Tribunal.[4]

When the IBA Rules are adopted together with the ICC Rules, the parties and the Arbitral Tribunal are encouraged to move expeditiously on matters related to any production of evidence needed for the settlement of the dispute,[5] including agreeing on a timetable for document production at the earliest possible moment in the arbitration proceeding.[6] The Arbitration Tribunal has a proactive duty to seek the opinion of the parties to the arbitration proceeding in connection with an efficient, economical and fair protocol to produce documents and other information.[7] The expectation is that each of the parties will indicate, at the same time that it provides the Arbitral Tribunal with its first detailed submission in the arbitration proceeding, the list of documents in the possession of the other party that it will seek to obtain, including paper, ESI and other evidence.

A party may oppose a request for the production of evidence under the IBA Rules by indicating that, among other things, the documents requested are not relevant or material or are not in its possession. In addition, a party may oppose such production on the grounds that the document being sought is subject to legal or ethical privilege or commercial confidentiality or because production of such document would place an undue burden on the party based on concepts of fairness or equality of the parties. The Techniques (see below) suggest that document production should adopt the Schedule of Document Production known as the Redfern Schedule, a four-column form of schedule created by the English practitioner Alan Redfern.

§ 12:6 Reducing Time and Expenses in ICC Arbitrations and Applicability to ESI Production

As mentioned before, the most relevant issue in connection with the possible use of e-discovery in arbitration proceedings is the potential increase in costs involved in such proceeding, as well as a possibly longer duration of such proceeding, in view of the fact that e-discovery mechanisms allow for the review of here-

---

[4]For example, production of metadata is often more informative than the actual data, so the result of a request for production of data depends more on what is asked for and what is finally obtained.

[5]ICC Rules Article 25.1.

[6]IBA Rules, Preamble 1—"*the Rules of Evidence are intended to govern in an **efficient and economical manner** the taking of evidence in international commercial arbitrations . . .*" (emphasis added).

[7]ICC Rules Article 25.1 combined with IBA Rules, Article 2.4.

tofore unthinkable amounts of information and documents. This concern lead to responses from arbitration bodies with a goal of reducing costs and providing more efficiency to the arbitration proceeding. This is the case of the International Institute for Conflict Prevention and Resolution,[1] the Chartered Institute[2] and the International Bar Association.[34] These guidelines mostly aim to keep a manageable e-discovery and maintain arbitration faster and cheaper than court.

It was the ever-increasing use of the US-style of discovery proceeding, which encompasses the sometimes unrestricted request for depositions, documents (and more recently ESI) that has prompted a review of the ICC Rules of document production in arbitration proceedings. In mid-2007, the International Chamber of Commerce Commission on Arbitration (ICC Commission) publicized a report on Techniques for Controlling Time and Cost in Arbitration (the Techniques), which guidelines were summarized in Appendix IV of ICC Rules.[5] The Techniques were the result of consultation by the ICC Commission that concentrated on, amongst other issues, the *"unfocused requests for disclosure of documents . . ."*[6] Although not binding, the Techniques are expected to be persuasive in their adoption by Arbitral Tribunals, as they are *"designed to assist arbitral tribunals, parties and their counsel . . . ."*[7]

The Techniques are applicable to various aspects of an arbitra-

---

[Section 12:6]

[1]*See* Fast Track Arbitration Rules, Article 6. http://www.cpradr.org/Resour ces/ALLCPRArticles/tabid/265/ID/609/Fast-Track-Mediation-and-Arbitration-Ru les-of-Procedure.aspx.

[2]*See* Protocol for e-disclosure in arbitration. http://www.ciarb.org/informati on-and-resources/E-Discolusure%20in%20Arbitration.pdf.

[3]*See* IBA Rules on the Taking of Evidence in International Arbitration. ht tp://www.ibanet.org/Publications/publications__IBA__guides__and__free__mater ials.aspx#takingevidence.

[4]*See* Thommas L. Aldrich. Arbitration's E-Discovery Conundrum. http://w ww.law.com/jsp/lawtechnologynews/PubArticleLTN.jsp?id=1202426776050&slre turn=1.

[5]International Chamber of Commerce, Publication No. 843, Techniques for Controlling Time and Cost in Arbitration (2007) (Techniques). http://www.iccdr l.com/CODE/LevelThree.asp?tocxml=ltoc__CommReportsAll.xml&page=Commis sion%20Reports&L1=Commission%20Reports&L2=&tocxsl=DoubleToc.xsl&cont entxsl=arbSingle.xsl&Locator=9&contentxml=CR__0033.xml&AUTH=&nb=0.

[6]International Chamber of Commerce, Publication No. 843, Techniques for Controlling Time and Cost in Arbitration (2007) (Techniques), Introduction.

[7]International Chamber of Commerce, Publication No. 843, Techniques for Controlling Time and Cost in Arbitration (2007) (Techniques).

tion proceeding. Specifically as to document production, they stipulate the advisability of

> *holding a case-management conference . . . as soon as the parties have set out their respective cases in sufficient detail for the arbitral tribunal and the parties to identify the issues in the case and the procedural steps that will be necessary to resolve the case,*[8]

always within the principle that the dispute should be dealt with *as efficiently as possible.*[9]

Based on the principle that the ICC Rules (therein comprised the Techniques) that apply to paper documents also apply to ESI discovery, these recommendations are also extensive to the search for, organization and production of ESI.

And this should be done at the earliest possible moment to enable *"the parties and the arbitral tribunal to understand the key issues at an early stage and adopt procedures to address them in its procedural orders . . ."*[10]

The Techniques impose on each party the duty to produce the documents on which it will rely and recommends that a party *"should consider avoiding requests for production of documents from another party unless such production is relevant and material to the outcome of the case."*[11]

This mandate to only produce documents that have not been presented in the dispute is in synchrony with the IBA Rules[12] that suggest that a document should only be produced if it is actually needed to help prove what is sought to be established.

In a statement of the obvious (that is not always followed), the Techniques also suggest that the parties should avoid seeking documentary evidence to prove what does not need to be proven and what is non-controversial.[13] While this is the kind of common-sense recommendation that is hard to oppose, in practice it does conflict with the often seen situation of discovery requests as a strategic weapon to drive up costs and settlement amounts.

---

[8]International Chamber of Commerce, Publication No. 843, Techniques for Controlling Time and Cost in Arbitration (2007) (Techniques), *Article 31.*

[9]International Chamber of Commerce, Publication No. 843, Techniques for Controlling Time and Cost in Arbitration (2007) (Techniques), *Article 32. "For example, a tribunal that has made itself familiar with the details of the case from the outset can be proactive and give appropriate, tailor-made suggestions as to the issues to be addressed in the documentary and witness evidence."*

[10]Techniques, Article 46.

[11]Techniques, Article 53.

[12]IBA Rules 3(3)(a) and 3(3)(b).

[13]Techniques, Article 53.

The Techniques also bring to the foreground the possibility of an arbitration proceeding among the parties complementing the ICC Rules with other rules that share its principles and spirit. In Article 54, the Techniques indicate that when the parties consider an external rule to regulate the production of documents, *"they could consider referring to Article 3 of the IBA [Rules] . . . for guidance."*[14]

In furtherance of its objective to limit the time and expenses involved in an arbitration proceeding, the Techniques suggest a few steps might be observed by the parties, such as *"limiting requests to the production of documents (whether in paper or electronic form) that are relevant and material to the outcome of the case,"* always taking into consideration *"reasonable time limits for the production of documents"*[15] and the possibility of fixing a cut-off date in advance for the production of documents.[16] This is only one in the many occasions when rules linked to ICC proceedings (whether the ICC Rules or the IBA Rules) have demonstrated particular interest in clarifying that a particular Arbitral Tribunal is expected to decide on the materiality and relevance of any request for documents, including e-documents (note the first explicit reference to e-documents in this portion of the Techiniques).

It is also important to mention the existence of legal technologies solutions developed by technologic companies in order to facilitate e-discovery and make it faster. This is an option that should be taken into consideration by parties in an arbitration.

For example, there are softwares that help companies preserving critical data, softwares that facilitate the management, identification and collection of data that will be used in an arbitration. Besides these technologic solutions, there are companies which render advisory services and information management consulting for e-discovery.

Both the softwares and the companies above mentioned are options in order to provide a cost effective arbitration when an e-discovery must be realized.

§ 12:7 Assistance by Local Courts in ESI Production

The need to produce ESI to be used in an arbitration proceeding, which requires the participation of national judicial courts in the process to compelling third party production of such docu-

---

[14]Techniques, Article 54.

[15]Techniques, Article 55.

[16]Techniques, Article 76.

ments should merit careful consideration by counsel, as moving too fast is no guarantee of production of evidence. Often counsel will be proactive in seeking the assistance of a national tribunal in ESI production proceedings outside of the particular arbitration proceeding even prior to obtaining an approval from the Arbitration Tribunal to such effect. While various national laws will give credence to such requests, claimants may not be successful, because (i) within the same legal system, courts may have differing views as to whether such requests should be accepted,[1] and (ii) local courts may prefer to act only after an arbitration tribunal has opined on the appropriateness of the evidence that a party is seeking to product.[2] And this patterns seems to be more frequent with the ever-expanding acceptability by local courts of arbitration as a proper method of settling disputes. In other words, if an arbitral tribunal has not even passed judgment as to the need and appropriateness of a particular evidence that a party is seeking to produce, why should a local court deem such evidence "needed and appropriate" and order its production? It may even happen that the "hurried" counsel may have his/her request for early production of evidence denied, a situation that may be explored by an astute other party in the dispute. Last but not least, depending on where the judicial courts are located, the party that sought the production of the ESI may be faced with costs to pay and reimburse.[3] As the actual result of such independent evidence gathering effort depends on the substantive laws of a particular country, counsel should review how the courts of the country in question treat such kinds of requests and only then determine whether it is advisable to seek production of third-party evidence even prior to the seating of an arbitration tribunal.

In addition to the restrictions that are normally applicable to production of paper and other "traditional" forms of documents, recent advanced legislation seeking to protect the privacy of individuals in many countries also place constraints on ESI production. As such data is not only contained in corporate computers but, also, in individual handheld devices and other

---

[Section 12:7]

[1]In the US, some circuits allow third-party discovery in an arbitration, but some do not.

[2]See Daniel Schimmel and Melissa E. Byroade, Does 28 U.S.C. § 1782 Allow U. S. Courts to Order Discovery for Use in Private International Arbitration? International Arbitration 2009—Volume One, Practicing Law Institute.

[3]See Daniel Schimmel and Melissa E. Byroade, Does 28 U.S.C. § 1782 Allow U. S. Courts to Order Discovery for Use in Private International Arbitration? International Arbitration 2009—Volume One, Practicing Law Institute.

personal and portable gadgets, production of ESI may raise issues such as invasion of privacy and breach of duty of confidentiality. For example, the European Union Directive 96/46/EC[4] imposes restrictions on the use of third parties' ESI and stipulates that the mishandling of such personal data, or the transfer of such data outside of the boundaries of the particular country, constitute criminal as well as administratively punishable acts, thus creating a situation in which issues of personal concern of a third party directly impact the production of evidence in a case.

§ 12:8   Other Rules

The ICC Rules do not contain reference to particular issues of e-discovery, and neither do the Techniques. Unlike the ICC Rules and the Techniques, other arbitration rules deal directly with the issue of E-Discovery. The International Center for Dispute Resolution (ICDR) and the Institute of Conflict Prevention & Resolution (CPR) have issued guidelines that attempt to control the seemingly boundless activities of e-discovery by subjecting it to certain guidelines, even if not too strict in order to allow the parties to actually seek documents that are indeed relevant to prove their cases.

For example, the ICDR treat e-documents as part of the overall category "documents" and provides that the parties should be cautious in their request for e-documents, which should "be narrowly focused and structured to make searching for them as economical as possible." Also, the rules of the ICDR provide that a party in possession of an e-document "may make them available in the form (which may be paper copies) most convenient and economical for it, unless the Tribunal determines, on application and for good cause, that there is a compelling need for access to the documents in a different form."[1]

§ 12:9   Conclusion

Although a relatively recent legal trend, e-discovery (or production of ESI) has come to stay, for the delight of those practitioners

---

[4]Directive 95/46/EC of the European Parliament and the Council of 24 of October of 1995 on the Protection of Individuals' With Regard to the Processing of Personal data and on the Free Movement of such Data. *See* http://ec.europa.eu/justice/doc_centre/intro/docs/jha_acquis_1009_en.pdf.

[Section 12:8]

[1]The ICDR rules at http://www.adr.org/aaa/faces/rules?_afrLoop=2173000350692492&_afrWindowMode=0&_afrWindowId=gbs17739h_1.

who see the proceeding as a must-have. But those who are not fans of e-discovery are also adhering to it even if ever so slowly in the context of arbitration, and have embraced the concept with a degree of moderation that has done away with excesses and has allowed the parties and the arbitration tribunal to work cooperatively and proactively to use the best of what the concept has to offer.

With broad guidelines and principles, the ICC Rules have endured various changes over the years since arbitrations started to be conducted under its auspices, and by treating e-discovery broadly, it has allowed for customization in each and every arbitration subject to it, ensuring both the use of the method and also the limitation of abuses and expenses.

There is much still to be accomplished, especially through the daily application of the principles contained in the Techniques, which, hopefully, will preserve the best that e-discovery can provide to a dispute settlement mechanism while shunning the parts that may be abusive or overbearing for a proceeding that is not litigation.

Despite all of the recent advances in regulations of arbitration proceedings, at the end of the day it is the individual who is handling a particular arbitration who will have the most important impact on the adoption of the new concepts that are being presented—it will be his/her embrace of the meaning of these new rules that will allow them to start to have a meaningful impact on the parties and practitioners alike.

Chapter 13

Additional Resources in ADR and Electronic Discovery

*by Amy Newman & Candice Lang**

---

*Amy Newman is a well-known expert in the California dispute resolution community. Ms. Newman was invited by the USC Gould School of Law's John Schulman to speak on arbitration and mediation at the school's Entertainment Forum. She served as a judge in the 2011 ABA Section of Dispute Resolution's "Representation in Mediation" Competition held at Pepperdine University. In 2010, she was appointed to a three-year term on the California State Bar Committee on Alternative Dispute Resolution and to the Los Angeles Superior Court A.D.R Committee. Ms. Newman was a featured panelist, along with the vice presidents of AAA and JAMS, at the California Dispute Resolution Council's forum on "ADR Providers: Shaping Our Industry" in 2009. She also spoke to the California Judges Association on "Marketing for Retired Judges." A frequent panel member on legal forums, she has represented dispute resolution firms to the press and presented hundreds of training and MCLE programs to law firms, insurance companies and other organizations. Ms. Newman is a contributing author of the new Westlaw book published in 2011, Dispute Resolution and E-Discovery. She has written numerous articles, including the ADR Resource Guide, published in the March 2010 ADR Edition of California Lawyer; Pick and Choose and New Problems, New Solutions published in the Los Angeles Daily Journal; and Divorce Needn't Be Hateful in the Agoura Hills Acorn. Her entrepreneurial style also resulted in the Friends of Bet Tzedek Fund, an innovative ARC program she developed to support the pro bono legal services of Bet Tzebek House of Justice in the early 1990s. Ms. Newman has been instrumental in making Alternative Resolution Centers (ARC) one of the most successful and longest-standing dispute resolution firms in the United States.

Candice Lang is Senior Associate Counsel with Law & Forensics. Ms. Lang's practice focuses on working with large companies and firms on complex e-discovery, privacy, and forensic investigations and disputes. Prior to joining Law & Forensics, Ms. Lang worked in Central Asia and advised on complex legal and business issues. Ms. Lang is based out of our New York City office and can be reached at clang@lawandforensics.com.

> KeyCite ®: Cases and other legal materials listed in KeyCite Scope can be
> researched through the KeyCite service on Westlaw ®. Use KeyCite to check
> citations for form, parallel references, prior and later history, and comprehen-
> sive citator information, including citations to other decisions and secondary
> materials.

§ 13:1   Introduction

The earlier chapters of this text provided an overview of
electronic discovery practices in alternative dispute resolution,
including mediation, arbitration, special master practice, as well
as proposed and current practices under different arbitral forums.
In this chapter, we discuss and provide the reader with additional
resources that can assist the reader in expanding his or her
knowledge and awareness of alternative dispute resolution and
e-discovery.

The chapter is divided into several sections. *First*, we provide
an overview of selected online resources regarding alternative
dispute resolution, followed by general electronic discovery
resources. *Second*, we provide resources for mediation, arbitration, and special masters. *Third*, we address resources available
from individual courts and additional education programs in
alternative dispute resolution. *Fourth*, please find a number of
appendices containing sample rules, forms, agreements and other
documents to assist the ADR practitioner in understanding and
implementing e-discovery processes.

§ 13:2   General Alternative Dispute Resolution Resources

ADRResources (http://adrresources.com/) is an extensive site
published by Arbitraje y Mediación (ARyME) in both English and
Spanish since 1996 containing directories of ADR providers, biog-
raphies of professionals, a bookstore, a document library, and
more. Certain features of the site, including much of the document library, require an annual subscription.

Hieros Gamos (http://www.hg.org/) was one of the first online
law and government sites and was founded by Lex Mundi, an

international network of independent law firms. HG has information on a wide range of arbitration and mediation associations, ADR service organizations, and individual ADR providers.

The ABA Section of Dispute Resolution (http://www.americanb ar.org/groups/dispute_resolution.html) was established in 1993 to provide information and technical assistance on all aspects of dispute resolution; study existing methods for the prompt and effective resolution of disputes; adapt current legal procedures to accommodate court-annexed and court-directed dispute resolution processes; encourage state and local bar involvement in dispute resolution, conduct public and professional education programs such as the Multi-Door Dispute Resolution Courthouse Centers Project and coordinate a program of research and development including programmatic and legislative models.

LexisNexis (http://law.lexisnexis.com/) allows the user to search areas of law by topic, download treatises and forms, find practitioner directories, and review arbitration rules and procedures. Under the "Alternative Dispute Resolution" topic area additional regulations and arbitral decisions are available.

WestLaw (http://www.westlaw.com) allows the user to search areas of law by topic, download treatises and forms, find practitioner directories, and review arbitration rules and procedures. Awards and decisions from federal agencies are available as are those from International Centre for Settlement of Investment Disputes, the International Chamber of Commerce. Also of interest is the WestLaw ADR-SPECIALIST database of treatises, practice guides, journals, law reviews and arbitration materials covering all aspects of ADR law.

Indisputably, the Alternative Dispute Resolution Professors Blog (http://www.indisputably.org/), is the blog of law professors Andrea Schneider (Marquette), Michael Moffitt (Oregon), Sarah Cole (Moritz), Art Hinshaw (Arizona State), Jill Gross (Pace), and Cynthia Alkon (Texas-Wesleyan). It addresses recent cases, changes in law, opinion pieces, editorial writing, and legal research in the swiftly changing world of ADR.

The Court ADR Resource Center (http://www.courtadr.org/) contains a collection of court ADR resources for state and federal courts throughout the country. Resources are organized into state compilation pages, giving visitors a detailed view of the court ADR system in each state. Their most complete collection is for Illinois, where they are based, however, information is available for several other states as well.

§ 13:3 Electronic Discovery Resources

The Federal Judicial Center ("FJC") (http://www.fjc.gov) has long been providing information on electronic discovery management for federal judges which ADR practitioners will likely find helpful. The FJC is the research and education agency of the federal judicial system to conduct education and training for federal judges and judicial employees, to provide recommendations about the operation and study of the federal courts, and to conduct and promote research on federal judicial procedures and rules. For ADR Practitioners learning about e-discovery, we recommend reviewing the FJC's Materials on Electronic Discovery: Civil Litigation website (http://www.fjc.gov/public/home.nsf/page s/196), which contains these and other materials:

- *Managing Discovery of Electronic Information: A Pocket Guide for Judges*, by Barbara J. Rothstein, Ronald J. Hedges and Elizabeth C. Wiggins. Originally written to assist federal judges in managing the discovery of electronically stored information ("ESI"), the *Pocket Guide* covers issues unique to the discovery of ESI under the Federal Rules of Civil Procedure, including scope, allocation of costs, form of production, waiver of privilege and work-product protection, and data preservation and spoliation.

- *FAQ's Of E-Discovery—The Ten Most FAQ's in the Post-December 1, 2006 World of E-Discovery*, by the Hon. Shira A. Scheinlin. Judge Scheinlin, widely considered the leading light in the federal judiciary on e-discovery issues, wrote this piece just before the 2006 Amendments to the Federal Rules of Civil Procedure as a way to update judges and practitioners on certain changes. Among the topics covered by Judge Scheinlin are inaccessible information, litigation holds and preservation of data.

A good deal of current e-discovery scholarship and leadership comes from the Sedona Conference (http://www.thesedonaconfere nce.org/), a non-profit organization institute dedicated to the advancement of law and policy in the areas of antitrust law, complex litigation and intellectual property rights. The Sedona Conference is made up of a number of Working Groups, of which Working Group 1 develops principles and best practices recommendations for electronic discovery in legal disputes, Working Group 6 addresses issues that arise in the context of e-information management and e-disclosure multi-jurisdictional organizations, and Working Group 7 deals with principles and best practices for Canadian e-discovery. One important publication that the Sedona Conference publishes is the *Sedona Conference Cooperation Proclamation* (http://www.thesedonaconference.org/content/tsc_coope ration_proclamation). The *Proclamation* asks attorneys and judges to rethink the contentious practices that have grown up around civil discovery and refocus litigation toward the substantive resolution of legal disputes.

Another source of education and standard-setting for e-discovery is the *Electronic Discovery Reference Model* (http://www.edrm.net).

The *Colloquium on the Future of Commercial Litigation in New York: Developing a Cost-Efficient Judicial Process for the Electronic Age*, prepared by Maura Grossman (author of Chapter 6 of this text) for the New York State Unified Court system may also be of help. The *Colloquium* is available at http://www.nycourts.gov/ji/commercial-litigation/topics.shtml. Ms. Grossman provides an outline addressing such topics as proportionality and reasonableness in e-discovery, allocation of costs, cooperative versus adversarial e-discovery, rules and procedures, and cross-border e-discovery issues. Each section then contains caselaw, forms, law review articles, court rules and other information to address these topics.

The *K&L Gates Electronic Discovery Law Blog* (http://www.ediscoverylaw.com/), provides a consistently updated collection of the latest rule changes, e-discovery decisions, rules amendments and events affecting the practice of e-discovery. While not solely focused on ADR, the *Electronic Discovery Law Blog* does provide the latest news on e-discovery generally and is an excellent resource.

There are quite a few other blogs dedicated to the topic of e-discovery, the following are just a few of our choices:

- *E-Discovery Team*—http://e-discoveryteam.com/
- *Electronic Discovery and Evidence*—http://arkfeld.blogs.com/
- *E-Discovery Bytes*—http://ediscovery.quarles.com/
- *E-Lessons Learned*—http://ellblog.com/

§ 13:4 Arbitration and Mediation Resources[1]

The United Nations Commission on International Trade Law

The United Nations Commission on International Trade Law (UNCITRAL) (http://www.uncitral.org/) is the primary legal body of the United Nations system to address international trade law.

[Section 13:4]

[1]Editors Garrie and Griver are pleased to provide contact information for the authors of stipulations, rules, forms, and other documents discussed in this chapter upon request.

In late 2010, UNCITRAL provided an updated version of their Rules for Arbitration. The UNCITRAL Rules were originally designed in 1976 to serve as a guide for *ad hoc*, non-institutional, international arbitrations. Usage of the rules in such forums as the London Court of International Arbitration and the Iran-United States Claims Tribunal contributed to the jurisprudence of the UNCITRAL Rules but also revealed weaknesses. Many of these weaknesses were addressed in the 2010 rules, which are reprinted below as **Appendix 13A**.

In 1985, UNCITRAL published the UNCITRAL Model Law on International Commercial Arbitration to address concerns regarding national laws on arbitration, which were felt to be inappropriate for international cases. It was amended in 2006 for further modernization. A copy of the 2006 amendments to the UNCITRAL Model Law may be found on the UNCITRAL website, including a list of over seventy jurisdictions adopting the Model Law at htt p://www.uncitral.org/uncitral/en/uncitral_texts/arbitration/1985 Model_arbitration.html.

To review the UNCITRAL Model Rules, please turn to Appendix 13A. Article 27 of the UNCITRAL Model Rules governs the presentation of evidence and documents.

Federal Arbitration Act

As discussed in a prior chapter, the Federal Arbitration Act ("FAA") is a federal statute that provides for private dispute resolution through arbitration. The FAA applies where the transaction contemplated by the parties "involves" interstate commerce and is predicated on an exercise of the Commerce Clause powers granted to Congress in the U.S. Constitution. Further, the FAA preempts most state laws that disfavor the enforcement of arbitration agreements, as set forth by the Supreme Court in Southland Corp. v. Keating, 465 U.S. 1, 104 S. Ct. 852, 79 L. Ed. 2d 1 (1984).

The FAA is found in Title 9 of the United States Code (9 U.S.C.A. § § 1 et seq.). The complete text of the FAA is reprinted here in **Appendix 13B**.

To review the Federal Arbitration Act, please turn to Appendix 13B.

American Arbitration Association & International Centre for Dispute Resolution

The American Arbitration Association ("AAA") (http://www.adr. org), provides services to individuals and organizations who wish to resolve conflicts out of court. AAA also operates the International Centre for Dispute Resolution ("ICDR") (http://adr.org/sp.a

sp?id=28819), which is charged with administrating all of AAA's international matters. ICDR has numerous cooperative agreements with arbitral institutions throughout the world.

AAA will perform mediation and arbitration services for national and international disputes under its specialized subject matter rules, the UNCITRAL Rules, or any set of rules chosen by the parties. AAA's specialized subject matter rules cover claims programs, class arbitration, commercial disputes, the construction industry, the energy industry, financial services, the healthcare industry, the insurance industry, and the real estate industry. International ADR, as mentioned above, is conducted by the ICDR. **Appendices 13C-1 through 13C-4** contains sample forms provided by AAA for arbitration and mediation.

At the time of publication, AAA/ICDR has also published specific e-discovery rules for international arbitration (http://ww w.adr.org/si.asp?id=5288), which are reprinted below as **Appendix 13D**.

> Many of AAA's individual subject matter rules do not yet address e-discovery or they leave it up to the mediator or arbitrator to determine. For example, AAA's Commercial Arbitration Rules and Mediation Procedures contains the following as "R-21: Exchange of Information":
>
> (a) At the request of any party or at the discretion of the arbitrator, consistent with the expedited nature of arbitration, the arbitrator may direct
>
> i) the production of documents and other information, and
>
> ii) the identification of any witnesses to be called.
>
> (b) At least five business days prior to the hearing, the parties shall exchange copies of all exhibits they intend to submit at the hearing.
>
> (c) The arbitrator is authorized to resolve any disputes concerning the exchange of information.[2]

Also operated by the AAA is the American Arbitration Association University (AAAU) (http://www.aaauonline.org), an extremely valuable resource to assist in learning both basic and advanced skills in alternative dispute resolution. AAAU has a free (registration required) reference center, training courses, and a bookstore. The reference center provides access to numerous publications, guides, FAQs, and online resources, including the AAA's Dispute Resolution Journal.

— To review forms and samples from the American Arbitration Association, please turn to Appendix 13C-1 through 13C-4.

---

[2]American Arbitration Association, *Commercial Arbitration Rules and Mediation Procedures, available at* http://www.adr.org/sp.asp?id=22440 (last accessed March 26, 2011).

- *Appendix 13C-1: Sample Commercial Demand for Arbitration*
- *Appendix 13C-2: Sample General Demand for Arbitration*
- *Appendix 13C-3: Sample Subpoena in Arbitration*
- *Appendix 13C-4: Sample Request for Mediation*

— *To review the ICDR Guidelines For Arbitrations Concerning Exchanges of Information, please turn to Appendix 13D.*

JAMS

JAMS (http://www.jamsadr.com/) is the largest private alternative dispute resolution (ADR) provider in the world. JAMS provides Recommended Arbitration Discovery Protocols (http://www.jamsadr.com/arbitration-discovery-protocols/) and addresses electronically stored information and e-discovery in the JAMS rules as well. The JAMS Protocols for Electronic Discovery are as follows:

- While there can be no objective standard for the appropriate scope of e-discovery in all cases, JAMS arbitrators recognize that an early order containing language along the following lines can be an important first step in limiting such discovery in a large number of cases:
  - There shall be production of electronic documents only from sources used in the ordinary course of business. Absent a showing of compelling need, no such documents are required to be produced from back-up servers, tapes or other media.
  - Absent a showing of compelling need, the production of electronic documents shall normally be made on the basis of generally available technology in a searchable format which is usable by the party receiving the e-documents and convenient and economical for the producing party. Absent a showing of compelling need, the parties need not produce metadata with the exception of header fields for email correspondence.
  - Where the costs and burdens of e-discovery are disproportionate to the nature and gravity of the dispute or to the amount in controversy, or to the relevance of the materials requested, the arbitrator will either deny such requests or order disclosure on condition that the requesting party advance the reasonable cost of produc-

tion to the other side, subject to the allocation of costs in the final award.[3]

Forms used by JAMS may be found in **Appendix 13E** to this chapter.

— *To review forms, procedures, and sample documents from JAMS, please turn to Appendix 13E-1 through 13E-5.*
- *Appendix 13E-1: JAMS California Confidentiality Agreement (Including California Code of Civil Procedure)*
- *Appendix 13E-2: Sample JAMS Arbitration Demand*
- *Appendix 13E-3: Sample JAMS Mediation Submission*
- *Appendix 13E-4: Sample JAMS Stipulation for Arbitration*
- *Appendix 13E-5: JAMS Protocols for Electronic Discovery*

Alternative Resolution Centers

Alternative Resolution Centers ("ARC") (http://www.arc4adr. com) is one of California's first and longest-running private conflict resolution providers and has been on the forefront of alternative dispute resolution since it was founded. ARC is also leading the charge in developing a panel of Electronic Discovery special masters, neutrals, arbitrators and mediators, each highly skilled in technology and law. In fact, ARC may be one of the few organizations that has put forth rules and clauses for Electronic Discovery in arbitration.

ARC provides services and training to alternative dispute resolution providers in numerous formats, including private trials, settlement negotiations, early neutral evaluation, judge *pro tem* services, and, of course, mediation, arbitration, and special master services. ARC is an accredited continuing legal education provider offering courses on many topics ranging from business and entertainment, neutral ethics, and intellectual property to trial practices and premises liability.

Sample ARC forms, clauses and stipulations may be found in **Appendix 13F.**

— *To review forms, procedures, and sample documents from Alternative Resolution Centers, please turn to Appendix 13F-1 through 13F-5.*
- *Appendix 13F-1: ARC Stipulation Regarding Order of Reference*
- *Appendix 13F-2: ARC Stipulation for Temporary Judge*
- *Appendix 13F-3: ARC Stipulation for Binding Arbitration*
- *Appendix 13F-4: ARC Dispute Resolution Clauses (including e-discovery)*

---

[3]JAMS, *JAMS Protocols for Electronic Discovery, available at* http://www.j amsadr.com/arbitration-discovery-protocols/ (last accessed March 08, 2011).

- *Appendix 13F-5: ARC Arbitration Rules (including e-discovery rules)*

International Chamber of Commerce

The International Chamber of Commerce ("ICC") (http://www.iccwbo.org/) is one of the world's leading institutions for resolving international commercial and business disputes. The ICC provides the International Court of Arbitration as well as its own set of rules to govern arbitrations and mediation (http://iccwbo.org/court/arbitration/id4093/index.html).

Appendix 13G contains the ICC Rules of Arbitration.

London Court of Arbitration

The London Court of International Arbitration (LCIA) (http://www.lcia.org/) has been in existence since 1891 and is considered one of the top international institutions for commercial dispute resolution. LCIA offers arbitration, mediation, and other dispute resolution services.

LCIA's Rules for Arbitration are available online at http://www.lcia.org/Dispute__Resolution__Services/LCIA__Arbitration__Rules.aspx. LCIA's Rules for Mediation are available at (http://www.lcia.org/Dispute__Resolution__Services/LCIA__Mediation__Rules.aspx.

The full-text of the LCIA rules can be found in **Appendix 13H.**

— *To review the LCIA Rules for Arbitration, please turn to Appendix 13H-1.*

— *To review the LCIA Rules for Mediation, please turn to Appendix 13H-2.*

The Financial Industry Regulatory Authority, Inc. ("FINRA")

FINRA is the largest independent regulator for all securities firms that do business in the United States, overseeing more than 4,560 brokerage firms, 163,465 branch offices, and 630,820 registered securities representatives. FINRA has a role in nearly every aspect of the securities business, including administering the largest dispute resolution forum for investors and registered securities firms.

FINRA provides substantial information regarding their arbitration and mediation processes on their Arbitration and Mediation website, located at http://www.finra.org/ArbitrationMediation/. The resources provided there include resources for parties, resources for neutrals, and rules for arbitration and for mediation. FINRA also provides training for arbitrators and mediators, the ability to view arbitration awards online, online claim filing, and numerous other resources.

FINRA, being a regulatory agency, has promulgated numerous rules relating to the arbitration process and mediation process, including those related to discovery and encouraging cooperation between parties as they have often dealt with e-discovery issues. FINRA strongly encourages cooperation between parties,[4] provides discovery guides and production lists that parties are presumed to have to produce,[5] and to make[6] and object[7] to further discovery requests. Rules and procedures relating to FINRA arbitration and e-discovery may be found in **Appendix13I.**

— *To review rules and procedures from FINRA, please turn to Appendix 13I-1 through 13I-2.*

- *Appendix 13I-1: FINRA Notice to Parties—Discovery Rules and Procedures*
- *Appendix 13I-2: FINRA Discovery Guide*

National Arbitration Forum

National Arbitration Forum ("FORUM") (http://www.adrforum.com/), founded in 1986, is a national and international administrator of ADR programs. FORUM provides services in arbitration, mediation, domain name disputes, settlement, and no-fault disputes, among others.

FORUM prides itself on providing fair, affordable and accessible neutral panels comprised of more than 1600 neutrals. In addition, they have developed their own independent rules and procedures for ADR. FORUM also provides assistance to parties on procedural and administrative issues, including providing educational services to businesses and individuals.

FORUM also provides a significant amount of information regarding arbitration, mediation, and other ADR programs on their Frequently Asked Question page.

---

[4]FIN. INDUS. REGULATORY AUTHORITY, Cooperation of Parties in Discovery, FINRA MANUAL R. 12505 (2011), *available at* http://finra.complinet.com/en/display/display__main.html?rbid=2403&element__id=4159.

[5]FIN. INDUS. REGULATORY AUTHORITY, Document Production Lists, FINRA MANUAL R. 12506 (2011), *available at http://finra.complinet.com/en/display/display__main.html?rbid=2403&element__id=4160*.

[6]FIN. INDUS. REGULATORY AUTHORITY, Other Discovery Requests, FINRA MANUAL R. 12507 (2011), *available at* http://finra.complinet.com/en/display/display__main.html?rbid=2403&element__id=4161.

[7]FIN. INDUS. REGULATORY AUTHORITY, Objecting to Discovery, Waiver of Objection, FINRA MANUAL R. 12508 (2011), *available at* http://finra.complinet.com/en/display/display__main.html?rbid=2403&element__id=4162.

Appendix 13J contains forms, procedures, and other documents from FORUM.

— *To review forms, procedures, and sample documents from National Arbitration Forum, please turn to Appendix 13J-1 through 13J-5.*

- *Appendix 13J-1: FORUM Code of Procedure*
- *Appendix 13J-2: FORUM Notice of Arbitration*
- *Appendix 13J-3: FORUM Second Notice of Arbitration*
- *Appendix 13J-4: FORUM Mediation Rules*
- *Appendix 13J-5:FORUM Sample Request For Discovery or Other Order*

Special Masters

A leading organization for information regarding special masters is the Academy of Court-Appointed Masters ("ACAM") (http://www.courtappointedmasters.org/). ACAM's mission is to provide judges, lawyers, parties, and other special masters with helpful information regarding the use of special masters and how they help courts, lawyers and parties obtain justice.

The Federal Judicial Center (http://www.fjc.gov) provides information for judges, practitioners, and laypeople regarding special masters. The special masters page, found at http://www.fjc.gov/public/home.nsf/autoframe?openform&url_r=pages/1238, includes studies, guides and reports regarding the use of special masters. These include *Managing Class Action Litigation: A Pocket Guide for Judges, Second Edition*, which discusses case management techniques, such as the use of special masters as well as the *Manual for Complex Litigation*, an extensive text of which several sections discuss the use of special masters.

AskASpecialMaster.Com (http://www.askaspecialmaster.com) is an online resource collecting orders, opinions, cases, and special master reports from federal and state courts. The site also contains a blog of recent special master news and information, with the goal of providing information about special masters that has never before been collected in one place.

Appendix 13K includes sample orders for the appointment of special masters in a variety of cases. Two are previously entered orders from the United States District Court for the Central District of Florida and Western District of Pennsylvania, respectively.

— *To review forms and sample documents regarding Special Masters, please turn to Appendix 13K-1 through 13K-5.*

- *Appendix 13K-1: Sample Appointment Order 1*
- *Appendix 13K-2: Sample Appointment Order 2*

- *Appendix 13K-3: Sample Appointment Order 3*
- *Appendix 13K-4: Order Appointing Special Masters in In re: Toyota Products Liability Litigation*
- *Appendix 13K-5: Order Establishing Panel of Special Masters in Western District of Pennsylvania*
- *Appendix 13K-6: Memorandum and Order of Special Master in Purolite v. Thermax dated July*

§ 13:5 Alternative Dispute Resolution in the United States Court Systems

Throughout the United States, federal and state courts now mandate that litigants attempt ADR as a means to resolve cases prior to trial. The courts are providing and also provide alternative dispute resolution training programs and certification to practitioners as a means of ensuring quality.

For example, in the Los Angeles Superior Court (one of the largest courts in the world), ADR is integrated as a form of case management to move cases towards resolution as early as possible in the course of litigation. Additionally, in many jurisdictions, courts have formed informal partnerships with established ADR providers to provide *pro bono* ADR services, allowing quicker access to justice for litigants of all stripes.

The resources in **Appendix 13L** are a sampling of federal and state court ADR forms.

To review sample documents from State and Federal Alternative Dispute Resolution Programs, please turn to Appendix 13L-1 through 13L-13.

- *Appendix 13L-1: Sample Eastern District of New York Arbitration Award Form*
- *Appendix 13L-2: Sample Eastern District of New York Mediation Agreement*
- *Appendix 13L-3: Sample District of Utah Final Arbitration Agreement*
- *Appendix 13L-4: Multi-Option ADR Form for San Mateo County, California*
- *Appendix 13L-5: Report of Neutral for Western District of Pennsylvania*
- *Appendix 13L-6: ADR Process and Procedure Election Forms for Western District of Pennsylvania*
- *Appendix 13L-7: Western District of Pennsylvania Stipulation to Binding Arbitration*
- *Appendix 13L-8: Superior Court of California, Los Angeles County, Arbitrator Award Form*

- *Appendix 13L-9: Superior Court of California, Stanislaus County, Stipulation and Order to ADR*
- *Appendix 13L-10: Decision and Order of Arbitrator in Eastern District of New York*
- *Appendix 13L-11: Sample Alabama Order of Referral to Mediation*
- *Appendix 13L-12: Sample Alabama Report of Mediator*
- *Appendix 13L-13: Sample Alabama Request for Referral to Mediation*

APPENDIX 13A

Uncitral Arbitration Rules 2010 Revision[*]

Section I. Introductory rules
Scope of application[**]
Article 1

1. Where parties have agreed that disputes between them in respect of a defined legal relationship, whether contractual or not, shall be referred to arbitration under the UNCITRAL Arbitration Rules, then such disputes shall be settled in accordance with these Rules subject to such modification as the parties may agree.

2. The parties to an arbitration agreement concluded after 15 August 2010 shall be presumed to have referred to the Rules in effect on the date of commencement of the arbitration, unless the parties have agreed to apply a particular version of the Rules. That presumption does not apply where the arbitration agreement has been concluded by accepting after 15 August 2010 an offer made before that date.

3. These Rules shall govern the arbitration except that where any of these Rules is in conflict with a provision of the law applicable to the arbitration from which the parties cannot derogate, that provision shall prevail.

Notice and calculation of periods of time
Article 2

1. A notice, including a notification, communication or proposal, may be transmitted by any means of communication that provides or allows for a record of its transmission.

2. If an address has been designated by a party specifically for this purpose or authorized by the arbitral tribunal, any notice shall be delivered to that party at that address, and if so delivered shall be deemed to have been received. Delivery by electronic

---

[*]United Nations Commission on International Trade Law, *2010—UNCITRAL Arbitration Rules (As Revised in 2010)*, *available at* http://www.uncitral.o rg/uncitral/en/uncitral_texts/arbitration/2010Arbitration_rules.html (last visited March 25, 2010).

[**]A model arbitration clause for contracts can be found in the annex to the Rules.

means such as facsimile or e-mail may only be made to an address so designated or authorized.

3. In the absence of such designation or authorization, a notice is:

(a) Received if it is physically delivered to the addressee; or

(b) Deemed to have been received if it is delivered at the place of business, habitual residence or mailing address of the addressee.

4. If, after reasonable efforts, delivery cannot be effected in accordance with paragraphs 2 or 3, a notice is deemed to have been received if it is sent to the addressee's last-known place of business, habitual residence or mailing address by registered letter or any other means that provides a record of delivery or of attempted delivery.

5. A notice shall be deemed to have been received on the day it is delivered in accordance with paragraphs 2, 3 or 4, or attempted to be delivered in accordance with paragraph 4. A notice transmitted by electronic means is deemed to have been received on the day it is sent, except that a notice of arbitration so transmitted is only deemed to have been received on the day when it reaches the addressee's electronic address.

6. For the purpose of calculating a period of time under these Rules, such period shall begin to run on the day following the day when a notice is received. If the last day of such period is an official holiday or a non-business day at the residence or place of business of the addressee, the period is extended until the first business day which follows. Official holidays or non-business days occurring during the running of the period of time are included in calculating the period.

Notice of arbitration

Article 3

1. The party or parties initiating recourse to arbitration (hereinafter called the "claimant") shall communicate to the other party or parties (hereinafter called the "respondent") a notice of arbitration.

2. Arbitral proceedings shall be deemed to commence on the date on which the notice of arbitration is received by the respondent.

3. The notice of arbitration shall include the following:

(a) A demand that the dispute be referred to arbitration;

(b) The names and contact details of the parties;

(c) Identification of the arbitration agreement that is invoked;

(d) Identification of any contract or other legal instrument out of or in relation to which the dispute arises or, in the absence of such contract or instrument, a brief description of the relevant relationship;

(e) A brief description of the claim and an indication of the amount involved, if any;

(f) The relief or remedy sought;

(g) A proposal as to the number of arbitrators, language and place of arbitration, if the parties have not previously agreed thereon.

4. The notice of arbitration may also include:

(a) A proposal for the designation of an appointing authority referred to in article 6, paragraph 1;

(b) A proposal for the appointment of a sole arbitrator referred to in article 8, paragraph 1;

(c) Notification of the appointment of an arbitrator referred to in article 9 or 10.

5. The constitution of the arbitral tribunal shall not be hindered by any controversy with respect to the sufficiency of the notice of arbitration, which shall be finally resolved by the arbitral tribunal.

Response to the notice of arbitration
Article 4

1. Within 30 days of the receipt of the notice of arbitration, the respondent shall communicate to the claimant a response to the notice of arbitration, which shall include:

(a) The name and contact details of each respondent;

(b) A response to the information set forth in the notice of arbitration, pursuant to article 3, paragraphs 3 (c) to (g).

2. The response to the notice of arbitration may also include:

(a) Any plea that an arbitral tribunal to be constituted under these Rules lacks jurisdiction;

(b) A proposal for the designation of an appointing authority referred to in article 6, paragraph 1;

(c) A proposal for the appointment of a sole arbitrator referred to in article 8, paragraph 1;

(d) Notification of the appointment of an arbitrator referred to in article 9 or 10;

(e) A brief description of counterclaims or claims for the purpose of a set-off, if any, including where relevant, an indication of the amounts involved, and the relief or remedy sought;

(f) A notice of arbitration in accordance with article 3 in case the respondent formulates a claim against a party to the arbitration agreement other than the claimant.

3. The constitution of the arbitral tribunal shall not be hindered by any controversy with respect to the respondent's failure to communicate a response to the notice of arbitration, or an incomplete or late response to the notice of arbitration, which shall be finally resolved by the arbitral tribunal.

Representation and assistance

Article 5

Each party may be represented or assisted by persons chosen by it. The names and addresses of such persons must be communicated to all parties and to the arbitral tribunal. Such communication must specify whether the appointment is being made for purposes of representation or assistance. Where a person is to act as a representative of a party, the arbitral tribunal, on its own initiative or at the request of any party, may at any time require proof of authority granted to the representative in such a form as the arbitral tribunal may determine.

Designating and appointing authorities

Article 6

1. Unless the parties have already agreed on the choice of an appointing authority, a party may at any time propose the name or names of one or more institutions or persons, including the Secretary-General of the Permanent Court of Arbitration at The Hague (hereinafter called the "PCA"), one of whom would serve as appointing authority.

2. If all parties have not agreed on the choice of an appointing authority within 30 days after a proposal made in accordance with paragraph 1 has been received by all other parties, any party may request the Secretary-General of the PCA to designate the appointing authority.

3. Where these Rules provide for a period of time within which a party must refer a matter to an appointing authority and no appointing authority has been agreed on or designated, the period is suspended from the date on which a party initiates the procedure for agreeing on or designating an appointing authority until the date of such agreement or designation.

4. Except as referred to in article 41, paragraph 4, if the appointing authority refuses to act, or if it fails to appoint an arbitrator within 30 days after it receives a party's request to do so, fails to act within any other period provided by these Rules, or fails to decide on a challenge to an arbitrator within a reasonable time after receiving a party's request to do so, any party may request the Secretary-General of the PCA to designate a substitute appointing authority.

5. In exercising their functions under these Rules, the appointing authority and the Secretary-General of the PCA may require from any party and the arbitrators the information they deem necessary and they shall give the parties and, where appropriate, the arbitrators, an opportunity to present their views in any manner they consider appropriate. All such communications to and from the appointing authority and the Secretary-General of the PCA shall also be provided by the sender to all other parties.

6. When the appointing authority is requested to appoint an arbitrator pursuant to articles 8, 9, 10 or 14, the party making the request shall send to the appointing authority copies of the notice of arbitration and, if it exists, any response to the notice of arbitration.

7. The appointing authority shall have regard to such considerations as are likely to secure the appointment of an independent and impartial arbitrator and shall take into account the advisability of appointing an arbitrator of a nationality other than the nationalities of the parties.

Section II. Composition of the arbitral tribunal
Number of arbitrators
Article 7

1. If the parties have not previously agreed on the number of arbitrators, and if within 30 days after the receipt by the respondent of the notice of arbitration the parties have not agreed that there shall be only one arbitrator, three arbitrators shall be appointed.

2. Notwithstanding paragraph 1, if no other parties have responded to a party's proposal to appoint a sole arbitrator within the time limit provided for in paragraph 1 and the party or parties concerned have failed to appoint a second arbitrator in accordance with article 9 or 10, the appointing authority may, at the request of a party, appoint a sole arbitrator pursuant to the procedure provided for in article 8, paragraph 2, if it determines that, in view of the circumstances of the case, this is more appropriate.

Appointment of arbitrators (articles 8 to 10)
Article 8

1. If the parties have agreed that a sole arbitrator is to be appointed and if within 30 days after receipt by all other parties of a proposal for the appointment of a sole arbitrator the parties have not reached agreement thereon, a sole arbitrator shall, at the request of a party, be appointed by the appointing authority.

2. The appointing authority shall appoint the sole arbitrator

as promptly as possible. In making the appointment, the appointing authority shall use the following list-procedure, unless the parties agree that the list-procedure should not be used or unless the appointing authority determines in its discretion that the use of the list-procedure is not appropriate for the case:

(a) The appointing authority shall communicate to each of the parties an identical list containing at least three names;

(b) Within 15 days after the receipt of this list, each party may return the list to the appointing authority after having deleted the name or names to which it objects and numbered the remaining names on the list in the order of its preference;

(c) After the expiration of the above period of time the appointing authority shall appoint the sole arbitrator from among the names approved on the lists returned to it and in accordance with the order of preference indicated by the parties;

(d) If for any reason the appointment cannot be made according to this procedure, the appointing authority may exercise its discretion in appointing the sole arbitrator.

Article 9

1. If three arbitrators are to be appointed, each party shall appoint one arbitrator. The two arbitrators thus appointed shall choose the third arbitrator who will act as the presiding arbitrator of the arbitral tribunal.

2. If within 30 days after the receipt of a party's notification of the appointment of an arbitrator the other party has not notified the first party of the arbitrator it has appointed, the first party may request the appointing authority to appoint the second arbitrator.

3. If within 30 days after the appointment of the second arbitrator the two arbitrators have not agreed on the choice of the presiding arbitrator, the presiding arbitrator shall be appointed by the appointing authority in the same way as a sole arbitrator would be appointed under article 8.

Article 10

1. For the purposes of article 9, paragraph 1, where three arbitrators are to be appointed and there are multiple parties as claimant or as respondent, unless the parties have agreed to another method of appointment of arbitrators, the multiple parties jointly, whether as claimant or as respondent, shall appoint an arbitrator.

2. If the parties have agreed that the arbitral tribunal is to be composed of a number of arbitrators other than one or three, the arbitrators shall be appointed according to the method agreed upon by the parties.

3. In the event of any failure to constitute the arbitral tribunal under these Rules, the appointing authority shall, at the request of any party, constitute the arbitral tribunal and, in doing so, may revoke any appointment already made and appoint or reappoint each of the arbitrators and designate one of them as the presiding arbitrator.

Disclosures by and challenge of arbitrators (articles 11 to 13)**

Article 11

When a person is approached in connection with his or her possible appointment as an arbitrator, he or she shall disclose any circumstances likely to give rise to justifiable doubts as to his or her impartiality or independence. An arbitrator, from the time of his or her appointment and throughout the arbitral proceedings, shall without delay disclose any such circumstances to the parties and the other arbitrators unless they have already been informed by him or her of these circumstances.

Article 12

1. Any arbitrator may be challenged if circumstances exist that give rise to justifiable doubts as to the arbitrator's impartiality or independence.

2. A party may challenge the arbitrator appointed by it only for reasons of which it becomes aware after the appointment has been made.

3. In the event that an arbitrator fails to act or in the event of the de jure or de facto impossibility of his or her performing his or her functions, the procedure in respect of the challenge of an arbitrator as provided in article 13 shall apply.

Article 13

1. A party that intends to challenge an arbitrator shall send notice of its challenge within 15 days after it has been notified of the appointment of the challenged arbitrator, or within 15 days after the circumstances mentioned in articles 11 and 12 became known to that party.

2. The notice of challenge shall be communicated to all other parties, to the arbitrator who is challenged and to the other arbitrators. The notice of challenge shall state the reasons for the challenge.

3. When an arbitrator has been challenged by a party, all parties may agree to the challenge. The arbitrator may also, after the challenge, withdraw from his or her office. In neither case

---

**Model statements of independence pursuant to article 11 can be found in the annex to the Rules.

does this imply acceptance of the validity of the grounds for the challenge.

4. If, within 15 days from the date of the notice of challenge, all parties do not agree to the challenge or the challenged arbitrator does not withdraw, the party making the challenge may elect to pursue it. In that case, within 30 days from the date of the notice of challenge, it shall seek a decision on the challenge by the appointing authority.

Replacement of an arbitrator
Article 14

1. Subject to paragraph 2, in any event where an arbitrator has to be replaced during the course of the arbitral proceedings, a substitute arbitrator shall be appointed or chosen pursuant to the procedure provided for in articles 8 to 11 that was applicable to the appointment or choice of the arbitrator being replaced. This procedure shall apply even if during the process of appointing the arbitrator to be replaced, a party had failed to exercise its right to appoint or to participate in the appointment.

2. If, at the request of a party, the appointing authority determines that, in view of the exceptional circumstances of the case, it would be justified for a party to be deprived of its right to appoint a substitute arbitrator, the appointing authority may, after giving an opportunity to the parties and the remaining arbitrators to express their views: (a) appoint the substitute arbitrator; or (b) after the closure of the hearings, authorize the other arbitrators to proceed with the arbitration and make any decision or award.

Repetition of hearings in the event of the replacement of an arbitrator
Article 15

If an arbitrator is replaced, the proceedings shall resume at the stage where the arbitrator who was replaced ceased to perform his or her functions, unless the arbitral tribunal decides otherwise.

Exclusion of liability
Article 16

Save for intentional wrongdoing, the parties waive, to the fullest extent permitted under the applicable law, any claim against the arbitrators, the appointing authority and any person appointed by the arbitral tribunal based on any act or omission in connection with the arbitration.

Section III. Arbitral proceedings
General provisions

Article 17

1. Subject to these Rules, the arbitral tribunal may conduct the arbitration in such manner as it considers appropriate, provided that the parties are treated with equality and that at an appropriate stage of the proceedings each party is given a reasonable opportunity of presenting its case. The arbitral tribunal, in exercising its discretion, shall conduct the proceedings so as to avoid unnecessary delay and expense and to provide a fair and efficient process for resolving the parties' dispute.

2. As soon as practicable after its constitution and after inviting the parties to express their views, the arbitral tribunal shall establish the provisional timetable of the arbitration. The arbitral tribunal may, at any time, after inviting the parties to express their views, extend or abridge any period of time prescribed under these Rules or agreed by the parties.

3. If at an appropriate stage of the proceedings any party so requests, the arbitral tribunal shall hold hearings for the presentation of evidence by witnesses, including expert witnesses, or for oral argument. In the absence of such a request, the arbitral tribunal shall decide whether to hold such hearings or whether the proceedings shall be conducted on the basis of documents and other materials.

4. All communications to the arbitral tribunal by one party shall be communicated by that party to all other parties. Such communications shall be made at the same time, except as otherwise permitted by the arbitral tribunal if it may do so under applicable law.

5. The arbitral tribunal may, at the request of any party, allow one or more third persons to be joined in the arbitration as a party provided such person is a party to the arbitration agreement, unless the arbitral tribunal finds, after giving all parties, including the person or persons to be joined, the opportunity to be heard, that joinder should not be permitted because of prejudice to any of those parties. The arbitral tribunal may make a single award or several awards in respect of all parties so involved in the arbitration.

Place of arbitration

Article 18

1. If the parties have not previously agreed on the place of arbitration, the place of arbitration shall be determined by the arbitral tribunal having regard to the circumstances of the case. The award shall be deemed to have been made at the place of arbitration.

2. The arbitral tribunal may meet at any location it considers

appropriate for deliberations. Unless otherwise agreed by the parties, the arbitral tribunal may also meet at any location it considers appropriate for any other purpose, including hearings.

Language

Article 19

1. Subject to an agreement by the parties, the arbitral tribunal shall, promptly after its appointment, determine the language or languages to be used in the proceedings. This determination shall apply to the statement of claim, the statement of defence, and any further written statements and, if oral hearings take place, to the language or languages to be used in such hearings.

2. The arbitral tribunal may order that any documents annexed to the statement of claim or statement of defence, and any supplementary documents or exhibits submitted in the course of the proceedings, delivered in their original language, shall be accompanied by a translation into the language or languages agreed upon by the parties or determined by the arbitral tribunal.

Statement of claim

Article 20

1. The claimant shall communicate its statement of claim in writing to the respondent and to each of the arbitrators within a period of time to be determined by the arbitral tribunal. The claimant may elect to treat its notice of arbitration referred to in article 3 as a statement of claim, provided that the notice of arbitration also complies with the requirements of paragraphs 2 to 4 of this article.

2. The statement of claim shall include the following particulars:

(a) The names and contact details of the parties;

(b) A statement of the facts supporting the claim;

(c) The points at issue;

(d) The relief or remedy sought;

(e) The legal grounds or arguments supporting the claim.

3. A copy of any contract or other legal instrument out of or in relation to which the dispute arises and of the arbitration agreement shall be annexed to the statement of claim.

4. The statement of claim should, as far as possible, be accompanied by all documents and other evidence relied upon by the claimant, or contain references to them.

Statement of defence

Article 21

1. The respondent shall communicate its statement of defence in writing to the claimant and to each of the arbitrators within a

period of time to be determined by the arbitral tribunal. The respondent may elect to treat its response to the notice of arbitration referred to in article 4 as a statement of defence, provided that the response to the notice of arbitration also complies with the requirements of paragraph 2 of this article.

2. The statement of defence shall reply to the particulars (b) to (e) of the statement of claim (art. 20, para. 2). The statement of defence should, as far as possible, be accompanied by all documents and other evidence relied upon by the respondent, or contain references to them.

3. In its statement of defence, or at a later stage in the arbitral proceedings if the arbitral tribunal decides that the delay was justified under the circumstances, the respondent may make a counterclaim or rely on a claim for the purpose of a set-off provided that the arbitral tribunal has jurisdiction over it.

4. The provisions of article 20, paragraphs 2 to 4, shall apply to a counterclaim, a claim under article 4, paragraph 2 (f), and a claim relied on for the purpose of a set-off.

Amendments to the claim or defence
Article 22

During the course of the arbitral proceedings, a party may amend or supplement its claim or defence, including a counterclaim or a claim for the purpose of a set-off, unless the arbitral tribunal considers it inappropriate to allow such amendment or supplement having regard to the delay in making it or prejudice to other parties or any other circumstances. However, a claim or defence, including a counterclaim or a claim for the purpose of a set-off, may not be amended or supplemented in such a manner that the amended or supplemented claim or defence falls outside the jurisdiction of the arbitral tribunal.

Pleas as to the jurisdiction of the arbitral tribunal
Article 23

1. The arbitral tribunal shall have the power to rule on its own jurisdiction, including any objections with respect to the existence or validity of the arbitration agreement. For that purpose, an arbitration clause that forms part of a contract shall be treated as an agreement independent of the other terms of the contract. A decision by the arbitral tribunal that the contract is null shall not entail automatically the invalidity of the arbitration clause.

2. A plea that the arbitral tribunal does not have jurisdiction shall be raised no later than in the statement of defence or, with respect to a counterclaim or a claim for the purpose of a set-off, in the reply to the counterclaim or to the claim for the purpose of a set-off. A party is not precluded from raising such a plea by the

fact that it has appointed, or participated in the appointment of, an arbitrator. A plea that the arbitral tribunal is exceeding the scope of its authority shall be raised as soon as the matter alleged to be beyond the scope of its authority is raised during the arbitral proceedings. The arbitral tribunal may, in either case, admit a later plea if it considers the delay justified.

3. The arbitral tribunal may rule on a plea referred to in paragraph 2 either as a preliminary question or in an award on the merits. The arbitral tribunal may continue the arbitral proceedings and make an award, notwithstanding any pending challenge to its jurisdiction before a court.

Further written statements

Article 24

The arbitral tribunal shall decide which further written statements, in addition to the statement of claim and the statement of defence, shall be required from the parties or may be presented by them and shall fix the periods of time for communicating such statements.

Periods of time

Article 25

The periods of time fixed by the arbitral tribunal for the communication of written statements (including the statement of claim and statement of defence) should not exceed 45 days. However, the arbitral tribunal may extend the time limits if it concludes that an extension is justified.

Interim measures

Article 26

1. The arbitral tribunal may, at the request of a party, grant interim measures.

2. An interim measure is any temporary measure by which, at any time prior to the issuance of the award by which the dispute is finally decided, the arbitral tribunal orders a party, for example and without limitation, to:

(a) Maintain or restore the status quo pending determination of the dispute;

(b) Take action that would prevent, or refrain from taking action that is likely to cause, (i) current or imminent harm or (ii) prejudice to the arbitral process itself;

(c) Provide a means of preserving assets out of which a subsequent award may be satisfied; or

(d) Preserve evidence that may be relevant and material to the resolution of the dispute.

3. The party requesting an interim measure under paragraphs 2 (a) to (c) shall satisfy the arbitral tribunal that:

(a) Harm not adequately reparable by an award of damages is likely to result if the measure is not ordered, and such harm substantially outweighs the harm that is likely to result to the party against whom the measure is directed if the measure is granted; and

(b) There is a reasonable possibility that the requesting party will succeed on the merits of the claim. The determination on this possibility shall not affect the discretion of the arbitral tribunal in making any subsequent determination.

4. With regard to a request for an interim measure under paragraph 2 (d), the requirements in paragraphs 3 (a) and (b) shall apply only to the extent the arbitral tribunal considers appropriate.

5. The arbitral tribunal may modify, suspend or terminate an interim measure it has granted, upon application of any party or, in exceptional circumstances and upon prior notice to the parties, on the arbitral tribunal's own initiative.

6. The arbitral tribunal may require the pa5rty requesting an interim measure to provide appropriate security in connection with the measure.

7. The arbitral tribunal may require any party promptly to disclose any material change in the circumstances on the basis of which the interim measure was requested or granted.

8. The party requesting an interim measure may be liable for any costs and damages caused by the measure to any party if the arbitral tribunal later determines that, in the circumstances then prevailing, the measure should not have been granted. The arbitral tribunal may award such costs and damages at any point during the proceedings.

9. A request for interim measures addressed by any party to a judicial authority shall not be deemed incompatible with the agreement to arbitrate, or as a waiver of that agreement.

Evidence

Article 27

1. Each party shall have the burden of proving the facts relied on to support its claim or defence.

2. Witnesses, including expert witnesses, who are presented by the parties to testify to the arbitral tribunal on any issue of fact or expertise may be any individual, notwithstanding that the individual is a party to the arbitration or in any way related to a party. Unless otherwise directed by the arbitral tribunal, statements by witnesses, including expert witnesses, may be presented in writing and signed by them.

3. At any time during the arbitral proceedings the arbitral

tribunal may require the parties to produce documents, exhibits or other evidence within such a period of time as the arbitral tribunal shall determine.

4. The arbitral tribunal shall determine the admissibility, relevance, materiality and weight of the evidence offered.

Hearings

Article 28

1. In the event of an oral hearing, the arbitral tribunal shall give the parties adequate advance notice of the date, time and place thereof.

2. Witnesses, including expert witnesses, may be heard under the conditions and examined in the manner set by the arbitral tribunal.

3. Hearings shall be held in camera unless the parties agree otherwise. The arbitral tribunal may require the retirement of any witness or witnesses, including expert witnesses, during the testimony of such other witnesses, except that a witness, including an expert witness, who is a party to the arbitration shall not, in principle, be asked to retire.

4. The arbitral tribunal may direct that witnesses, including expert witnesses, be examined through means of telecommunication that do not require their physical presence at the hearing (such as videoconference).

Experts appointed by the arbitral tribunal

Article 29

1. After consultation with the parties, the arbitral tribunal may appoint one or more independent experts to report to it, in writing, on specific issues to be determined by the arbitral tribunal. A copy of the expert's terms of reference, established by the arbitral tribunal, shall be communicated to the parties.

2. The expert shall, in principle before accepting appointment, submit to the arbitral tribunal and to the parties a description of his or her qualifications and a statement of his or her impartiality and independence. Within the time ordered by the arbitral tribunal, the parties shall inform the arbitral tribunal whether they have any objections as to the expert's qualifications, impartiality or independence. The arbitral tribunal shall decide promptly whether to accept any such objections. After an expert's appointment, a party may object to the expert's qualifications, impartiality or independence only if the objection is for reasons of which the party becomes aware after the appointment has been made. The arbitral tribunal shall decide promptly what, if any, action to take.

3. The parties shall give the expert any relevant information

or produce for his or her inspection any relevant documents or goods that he or she may require of them. Any dispute between a party and such expert as to the relevance of the required information or production shall be referred to the arbitral tribunal for decision.

4. Upon receipt of the expert's report, the arbitral tribunal shall communicate a copy of the report to the parties, which shall be given the opportunity to express, in writing, their opinion on the report. A party shall be entitled to examine any document on which the expert has relied in his or her report.

5. At the request of any party, the expert, after delivery of the report, may be heard at a hearing where the parties shall have the opportunity to be present and to interrogate the expert. At this hearing, any party may present expert witnesses in order to testify on the points at issue. The provisions of article 28 shall be applicable to such proceedings.

Default

Article 30

1. If, within the period of time fixed by these Rules or the arbitral tribunal, without showing sufficient cause:

(a) The claimant has failed to communicate its statement of claim, the arbitral tribunal shall issue an order for the termination of the arbitral proceedings, unless there are remaining matters that may need to be decided and the arbitral tribunal considers it appropriate to do so;

(b) The respondent has failed to communicate its response to the notice of arbitration or its statement of defence, the arbitral tribunal shall order that the proceedings continue, without treating such failure in itself as an admission of the claimant's allegations; the provisions of this subparagraph also apply to a claimant's failure to submit a defence to a counterclaim or to a claim for the purpose of a set-off.

2. If a party, duly notified under these Rules, fails to appear at a hearing, without showing sufficient cause for such failure, the arbitral tribunal may proceed with the arbitration.

3. If a party, duly invited by the arbitral tribunal to produce documents, exhibits or other evidence, fails to do so within the established period of time, without showing sufficient cause for such failure, the arbitral tribunal may make the award on the evidence before it.

Closure of hearings

Article 31

1. The arbitral tribunal may inquire of the parties if they have any further proof to offer or witnesses to be heard or submis-

sions to make and, if there are none, it may declare the hearings closed.

2. The arbitral tribunal may, if it considers it necessary owing to exceptional circumstances, decide, on its own initiative or upon application of a party, to reopen the hearings at any time before the award is made.

Waiver of right to object

Article 32

A failure by any party to object promptly to any non-compliance with these Rules or with any requirement of the arbitration agreement shall be deemed to be a waiver of the right of such party to make such an objection, unless such party can show that, under the circumstances, its failure to object was justified.

Section IV. The award

Decisions

Article 33

1. When there is more than one arbitrator, any award or other decision of the arbitral tribunal shall be made by a majority of the arbitrators.

2. In the case of questions of procedure, when there is no majority or when the arbitral tribunal so authorizes, the presiding arbitrator may decide alone, subject to revision, if any, by the arbitral tribunal.

Form and effect of the award

Article 34

1. The arbitral tribunal may make separate awards on different issues at different times.

2. All awards shall be made in writing and shall be final and binding on the parties. The parties shall carry out all awards without delay.

3. The arbitral tribunal shall state the reasons upon which the award is based, unless the parties have agreed that no reasons are to be given.

4. An award shall be signed by the arbitrators and it shall contain the date on which the award was made and indicate the place of arbitration. Where there is more than one arbitrator and any of them fails to sign, the award shall state the reason for the absence of the signature.

5. An award may be made public with the consent of all parties or where and to the extent disclosure is required of a party by legal duty, to protect or pursue a legal right or in relation to legal proceedings before a court or other competent authority.

6. Copies of the award signed by the arbitrators shall be communicated to the parties by the arbitral tribunal.

Applicable law, *amiable compositeur*
Article 35

1. The arbitral tribunal shall apply the rules of law designated by the parties as applicable to the substance of the dispute. Failing such designation by the parties, the arbitral tribunal shall apply the law which it determines to be appropriate.

2. The arbitral tribunal shall decide as *amiable compositeur* or *ex aequo et bono* only if the parties have expressly authorized the arbitral tribunal to do so.

3. In all cases, the arbitral tribunal shall decide in accordance with the terms of the contract, if any, and shall take into account any usage of trade applicable to the transaction.

Settlement or other grounds for termination
Article 36

1. If, before the award is made, the parties agree on a settlement of the dispute, the arbitral tribunal shall either issue an order for the termination of the arbitral proceedings or, if requested by the parties and accepted by the arbitral tribunal, record the settlement in the form of an arbitral award on agreed terms. The arbitral tribunal is not obliged to give reasons for such an award.

2. If, before the award is made, the continuation of the arbitral proceedings becomes unnecessary or impossible for any reason not mentioned in paragraph 1, the arbitral tribunal shall inform the parties of its intention to issue an order for the termination of the proceedings. The arbitral tribunal shall have the power to issue such an order unless there are remaining matters that may need to be decided and the arbitral tribunal considers it appropriate to do so.

3. Copies of the order for termination of the arbitral proceedings or of the arbitral award on agreed terms, signed by the arbitrators, shall be communicated by the arbitral tribunal to the parties. Where an arbitral award on agreed terms is made, the provisions of article 34, paragraphs 2, 4 and 5, shall apply.

Interpretation of the award
Article 37

1. Within 30 days after the receipt of the award, a party, with notice to the other parties, may request that the arbitral tribunal give an interpretation of the award.

2. The interpretation shall be given in writing within 45 days after the receipt of the request. The interpretation shall form part of the award and the provisions of article 34, paragraphs 2 to 6, shall apply.

Correction of the award
Article 38

1. Within 30 days after the receipt of the award, a party, with notice to the other parties, may request the arbitral tribunal to correct in the award any error in computation, any clerical or typographical error, or any error or omission of a similar nature. If the arbitral tribunal considers that the request is justified, it shall make the correction within 45 days of receipt of the request.

2. The arbitral tribunal may within 30 days after the communication of the award make such corrections on its own initiative.

3. Such corrections shall be in writing and shall form part of the award. The provisions of article 34, paragraphs 2 to 6, shall apply.

Additional award

Article 39

1. Within 30 days after the receipt of the termination order or the award, a party, with notice to the other parties, may request the arbitral tribunal to make an award or an additional award as to claims presented in the arbitral proceedings but not decided by the arbitral tribunal.

2. If the arbitral tribunal considers the request for an award or additional award to be justified, it shall render or complete its award within 60 days after the receipt of the request. The arbitral tribunal may extend, if necessary, the period of time within which it shall make the award.

3. When such an award or additional award is made, the provisions of article 34, paragraphs 2 to 6, shall apply.

Definition of costs

Article 40

1. The arbitral tribunal shall fix the costs of arbitration in the final award and, if it deems appropriate, in another decision.

2. The term "costs" includes only:

(a) The fees of the arbitral tribunal to be stated separately as to each arbitrator and to be fixed by the tribunal itself in accordance with article 41;

(b) The reasonable travel and other expenses incurred by the arbitrators;

(c) The reasonable costs of expert advice and of other assistance required by the arbitral tribunal;

(d) The reasonable travel and other expenses of witnesses to the extent such expenses are approved by the arbitral tribunal;

(e) The legal and other costs incurred by the parties in relation to the arbitration to the extent that the arbitral tribunal determines that the amount of such costs is reasonable;

(f) Any fees and expenses of the appointing authority as well as the fees and expenses of the Secretary-General of the PCA.

3. In relation to interpretation, correction or completion of any award under articles 37 to 39, the arbitral tribunal may charge the costs referred to in paragraphs 2(b) to (f), but no additional fees.

Fees and expenses of arbitrators

Article 41

1. The fees and expenses of the arbitrators shall be reasonable in amount, taking into account the amount in dispute, the complexity of the subject matter, the time spent by the arbitrators and any other relevant circumstances of the case.

2. If there is an appointing authority and it applies or has stated that it will apply a schedule or particular method for determining the fees for arbitrators in international cases, the arbitral tribunal in fixing its fees shall take that schedule or method into account to the extent that it considers appropriate in the circumstances of the case.

3. Promptly after its constitution, the arbitral tribunal shall inform the parties as to how it proposes to determine its fees and expenses, including any rates it intends to apply. Within 15 days of receiving that proposal, any party may refer the proposal to the appointing authority for review. If, within 45 days of receipt of such a referral, the appointing authority finds that the proposal of the arbitral tribunal is inconsistent with paragraph 1, it shall make any necessary adjustments thereto, which shall be binding upon the arbitral tribunal.

4. (a) When informing the parties of the arbitrators' fees and expenses that have been fixed pursuant to article 40, paragraphs 2 (a) and (b), the arbitral tribunal shall also explain the manner in which the corresponding amounts have been calculated;

(b) Within 15 days of receiving the arbitral tribunal's determination of fees and expenses, any party may refer for review such determination to the appointing authority. If no appointing authority has been agreed upon or designated, or if the appointing authority fails to act within the time specified in these Rules, then the review shall be made by the Secretary-General of the PCA;

(c) If the appointing authority or the Secretary-General of the PCA finds that the arbitral tribunal's determination is inconsistent with the arbitral tribunal's proposal (and any adjustment thereto) under paragraph 3 or is otherwise manifestly excessive, it shall, within 45 days of receiving such a referral, make any adjustments to the arbitral tribunal's determination that are necessary to satisfy the criteria in paragraph 1. Any such adjustments shall be binding upon the arbitral tribunal;

(d) Any such adjustments shall either be included by the arbitral tribunal in its award or, if the award has already been issued, be implemented in a correction to the award, to which the procedure of article 38, paragraph 3, shall apply.

5. Throughout the procedure under paragraphs 3 and 4, the arbitral tribunal shall proceed with the arbitration, in accordance with article 17, paragraph 1.

6. A referral under paragraph 4 shall not affect any determination in the award other than the arbitral tribunal's fees and expenses; nor shall it delay the recognition and enforcement of all parts of the award other than those relating to the determination of the arbitral tribunal's fees and expenses.

Allocation of costs

Article 42

1. The costs of the arbitration shall in principle be borne by the unsuccessful party or parties. However, the arbitral tribunal may apportion each of such costs between the parties if it determines that apportionment is reasonable, taking into account the circumstances of the case.

2. The arbitral tribunal shall in the final award or, if it deems appropriate, in any other award, determine any amount that a party may have to pay to another party as a result of the decision on allocation of costs.

Deposit of costs

Article 43

1. The arbitral tribunal, on its establishment, may request the parties to deposit an equal amount as an advance for the costs referred to in article 40, paragraphs 2 (a) to (c).

2. During the course of the arbitral proceedings the arbitral tribunal may request supplementary deposits from the parties.

3. If an appointing authority has been agreed upon or designated, and when a party so requests and the appointing authority consents to perform the function, the arbitral tribunal shall fix the amounts of any deposits or supplementary deposits only after consultation with the appointing authority, which may make any comments to the arbitral tribunal that it deems appropriate concerning the amount of such deposits and supplementary deposits.

4. If the required deposits are not paid in full within 30 days after the receipt of the request, the arbitral tribunal shall so inform the parties in order that one or more of them may make

the required payment. If such payment is not made, the arbitral tribunal may order the suspension or termination of the arbitral proceedings.

5. After a termination order or final award has been made, the arbitral tribunal shall render an accounting to the parties of the deposits received and return any unexpended balance to the parties.

Annex

Model arbitration clause for contracts

Any dispute, controversy or claim arising out of or relating to this contract, or the breach, termination or invalidity thereof, shall be settled by arbitration in accordance with the UNCITRAL Arbitration Rules.

Note. Parties should consider adding:

(a) The appointing authority shall be . . . [name of institution or person];

(b) The number of arbitrators shall be . . . [one or three];

(c) The place of arbitration shall be . . . [town and country];

(d) The language to be used in the arbitral proceedings shall be . . . .

Possible waiver statement

Note. If the parties wish to exclude recourse against the arbitral award that may be available under the applicable law, they may consider adding a provision to that effect as suggested below, considering, however, that the effectiveness and conditions of such an exclusion depend on the applicable law.

Waiver

The parties hereby waive their right to any form of recourse against an award to any court or other competent authority, insofar as such waiver can validly be made under the applicable law.

Model statements of independence pursuant to article 11 of the Rules

No circumstances to disclose

I am impartial and independent of each of the parties and intend to remain so. To the best of my knowledge, there are no circumstances, past or present, likely to give rise to justifiable doubts as to my impartiality or independence. I shall promptly notify the parties and the other arbitrators of any such circumstances that may subsequently come to my attention during this arbitration.

Circumstances to disclose

I am impartial and independent of each of the parties and

intend to remain so. Attached is a statement made pursuant to article 11 of the UNCITRAL Arbitration Rules of (a) my past and present professional, business and other relationships with the parties and (b) any other relevant circumstances. [Include statement.] I confirm that those circumstances do not affect my independence and impartiality. I shall promptly notify the parties and the other arbitrators of any such further relationships or circumstances that may subsequently come to my attention during this arbitration.

Note. Any party may consider requesting from the arbitrator the following addition to the statement of independence:

I confirm, on the basis of the information presently available to me, that I can devote the time necessary to conduct this arbitration diligently, efficiently and in accordance with the time limits in the Rules.

APPENDIX 13B

The Federal Arbitration Act[1]

Arbitration

Chapter 1. General Provisions

Section 1. "Maritime transactions" and "commerce" defined; exceptions to operation of title

"Maritime transactions", as herein defined, means charter parties, bills of lading of water carriers, agreements relating to wharfage, supplies furnished vessels or repairs to vessels, collisions, or any other matters in foreign commerce which, if the subject of controversy, would be embraced within admiralty jurisdiction; "commerce", as herein defined, means commerce among the several States or with foreign nations, or in any Territory of the United States or in the District of Columbia, or between any such Territory and another, or between any such Territory and any State or foreign nation, or between the District of Columbia and any State or Territory or foreign nation, but nothing herein contained shall apply to contracts of employment of seamen, railroad employees, or any other class of workers engaged in foreign or interstate commerce.

Section 2. Validity, irrevocability, and enforcement of agreements to arbitrate

A written provision in any maritime transaction or a contract evidencing a transaction involving commerce to settle by arbitration a controversy thereafter arising out of such contract or transaction, or the refusal to perform the whole or any part thereof, or an agreement in writing to submit to arbitration an existing controversy arising out of such a contract, transaction, or refusal, shall be valid, irrevocable, and enforceable, save upon such grounds as exist at law or in equity for the revocation of any contract.

---

[1] 9 U.S.C.S. §§ 1-307. Title 9, US Code, Section 1-14, was first enacted February 12, 1925 (43 Stat. 883), codified July 30, 1947 (61 Stat. 669), and amended September 3, 1954 (68 Stat. 1233). Chapter 2 was added July 31, 1970 (84 Stat. 692), two new Sections were passed by the Congress in October of 1988 and renumbered on December 1, 1990 (PLS 669 and 702); Chapter 3 was added on August 15, 1990 (PL 101-369); and Section 10 was amended on November 15

Section 3.   Stay of proceedings where issue therein referable to arbitration

If any suit or proceeding be brought in any of the courts of the United States upon any issue referable to arbitration under an agreement in writing for such arbitration, the court in which such suit is pending, upon being satisfied that the issue involved in such suit or proceeding is referable to arbitration under such an agreement, shall on application of one of the parties stay the trial of the action until such arbitration has been had in accordance with the terms of the agreement, providing the applicant for the stay is not in default in proceeding with such arbitration.

Section 4.   Failure to arbitrate under agreement; petition to United States court having jurisdiction for order to compel arbitration; notice and service thereof; hearing and determination

A party aggrieved by the alleged failure, neglect, or refusal of another to arbitrate under a written agreement for arbitration may petition any United States district court which, save for such agreement, would have jurisdiction under Title 28, in a civil action or in admiralty of the subject matter of a suit arising out of the controversy between the parties, for an order directing that such arbitration proceed in the manner provided for in such agreement. Five days' notice in writing of such application shall be served upon the party in default. Service thereof shall be made in the manner provided by the Federal Rules of Civil Procedure. The court shall hear the parties, and upon being satisfied that the making of the agreement for arbitration or the failure to comply therewith is not in issue, the court shall make an order directing the parties to proceed to arbitration in accordance with the terms of the agreement. The hearing and proceedings, under such agreement, shall be within the district in which the petition for an order directing such arbitration is filed. If the making of the arbitration agreement or the failure, neglect, or refusal to perform the same be in issue, the court shall proceed summarily to the trial thereof. If no jury trial be demanded by the party alleged to be in default, or if the matter in dispute is within admiralty jurisdiction, the court shall hear and determine such issue. Where such an issue is raised, the party alleged to be in default may, except in cases of admiralty, on or before the return day of the notice of application, demand a jury trial of such issue, and upon such demand the court shall make an order referring the issue or issues to a jury in the manner provided by the Federal Rules of Civil Procedure, or may specially call a jury for that purpose. If the jury find that no agreement in writing for arbitration was made or that there is no default in proceeding thereunder, the proceeding shall be dismissed. If the jury find that an agreement for arbitration was made in writing and that there is a default in proceeding thereunder, the court shall make an order summarily directing the parties to proceed with the arbitration in accordance with the terms thereof.

Section 5. Appointment of arbitrators or umpire

If in the agreement provision be made for a method of naming or appointing an arbitrator or arbitrators or an umpire, such method shall be followed; but if no method be provided therein, or if a method be provided and any party thereto shall fail to avail himself of such method, or if for any other reason there shall be a lapse in the naming of an arbitrator or arbitrators or umpire, or in filling a vacancy, then upon the application of either party to the controversy the court shall designate and appoint an arbitrator or arbitrators or umpire, as the case may require, who shall act under the said agreement with the same force and effect as if he or they had been specifically named therein; and unless otherwise provided in the agreement the arbitration shall be by a single arbitrator.

Section 6. Application heard as motion

Any application to the court hereunder shall be made and heard in the manner provided by law for the making and hearing of motions, except as otherwise herein expressly provided.

Section 7. Witnesses before arbitrators; fees; compelling attendance

The arbitrators selected either as prescribed in this title or otherwise, or a majority of them, may summon in writing any person to attend before them or any of them as a witness and in a proper case to bring with him or them any book, record, document, or paper which may be deemed material as evidence in the case. The fees for such attendance shall be the same as the fees of witnesses before masters of the United States courts. Said summons shall issue in the name of the arbitrator or arbitrators, or a majority of them, and shall be signed by the arbitrators, or a majority of them, and shall be directed to the said person and shall be served in the same manner as subpoenas to appear and testify before the court; if any person or persons so summoned to testify shall refuse or neglect to obey said summons, upon petition the United States district court for the district in which such arbitrators, or a majority of them, are sitting may compel the attendance of such person or persons before said arbitrator or arbitrators, or punish said person or persons for contempt in the same manner provided by law for securing the attendance of witnesses or their punishment for neglect or refusal to attend in the courts of the United States.

Section 8. Proceedings begun by libel in admiralty and seizure of vessel or property

If the basis of jurisdiction be a cause of action otherwise justiciable in admiralty, then, notwithstanding anything herein to the contrary, the party claiming to be aggrieved may begin his proceeding hereunder by libel and seizure of the vessel or other property of the other party according to the usual course of admiralty proceedings, and the court shall then have jurisdiction to direct the parties to proceed with the arbitration and shall retain jurisdiction to enter its decree upon the award

Section 9. Award of arbitrators; confirmation; jurisdiction; procedure

If the parties in their agreement have agreed that a judgment of the court shall be entered upon the award made pursuant to the arbitration, and shall specify the court, then at any time within one year after the award is made any party to the arbitration may apply to the court so specified for an order confirming the award, and thereupon the court must grant such an order unless the award is vacated, modified, or corrected as prescribed in sections 10 and 11 of this title. If no court is specified in the agreement of the parties, then such application may be made to the United States court in and for the district within which such award was made. Notice of the application shall be served upon the adverse party, and thereupon the court shall have jurisdiction of such party as though he had appeared generally in the proceeding. If the adverse party is a resident of the district within which the award was made, such service shall be made upon the adverse party or his attorney as prescribed by law for service of notice of motion in an action in the same court. If the adverse party shall be a nonresident, then the notice of the application shall be served by the marshal of any district within which the adverse party may be found in like manner as other process of the court.

Section 10. Same; vacation; grounds; rehearing

(a) In any of the following cases the United States court in and for the district wherein the award was made may make an order vacating the award upon the application of any party to the arbitration—

(1) where the award was procured by corruption, fraud, or undue means;

(2) where there was evident partiality or corruption in the arbitrators, or either of them;

(3) where the arbitrators were guilty of misconduct in refusing to postpone the hearing, upon sufficient cause shown, or in refusing to hear evidence pertinent and material to the controversy; or of any other misbehavior by which the rights of any party have been prejudiced; or

(4) where the arbitrators exceeded their powers, or so imperfectly executed them that a mutual, final, and definite award upon the subject matter submitted was not made.

(b) If an award is vacated and the time within which the agreement required the award to be made has not expired, the court may, in its discretion, direct a rehearing by the arbitrators.

(c) The United States district court for the district wherein an award was made that was issued pursuant to section 580 of title 5 may make an order vacating the award upon the application of a person, other than a party to the arbitration, who is adversely affected or aggrieved by the award, if the use of arbitration or the award is clearly inconsistent with the factors set forth in section 572 of title 5.

Section 11. Same; modification or correction; grounds; order

In either of the following cases the United States court in and for the district wherein the award was made may make an order modifying or correcting the award upon the application of any party to the arbitration—

(a) Where there was an evident material miscalculation of figures or an evident material mistake in the description of any person, thing, or property referred to in the award.

(b) Where the arbitrators have awarded upon a matter not submitted to them, unless it is a matter not affecting the merits of the decision upon the matter submitted.

(c) Where the award is imperfect in matter of form not affecting the merits of the controversy.

The order may modify and correct the award, so as to effect the intent thereof and promote justice between the parties.

Section 12. Notice of motions to vacate or modify; service; stay of proceedings

Notice of a motion to vacate, modify, or correct an award must be served upon the adverse party or his attorney within three months after the award is filed or delivered. If the adverse party is a resident of the district within which the award was made, such service shall be made upon the adverse party or his attorney as prescribed by law for service of notice of motion in an action in the same court. If the adverse party shall be a nonresident then the notice of the application shall be served by the marshal of any district within which the adverse party may be found in like manner as other process of the court. For the purposes of the motion any judge who might make an order to stay the proceedings in an action brought in the same court may make an order, to be served with the notice of motion, staying the proceedings of the adverse party to enforce the award.

Section 13.   Papers filed with order on motions; judgment; docketing; force and effect; enforcement

The party moving for an order confirming, modifying, or correcting an award shall, at the time such order is filed with the clerk for the entry of judgment thereon, also file the following papers with the clerk:

(a)   The agreement; the selection or appointment, if any, of an additional arbitrator or umpire; and each written extension of the time, if any, within which to make the award.

(b)   The award.

(c)   Each notice, affidavit, or other paper used upon an application to confirm, modify, or correct the award, and a copy of each order of the court upon such an application.

The judgment shall be docketed as if it was rendered in an action.

The judgment so entered shall have the same force and effect, in all respects, as, and be subject to all the provisions of law relating to, a judgment in an action; and it may be enforced as if it had been rendered in an action in the court in which it is entered.

Section 14.   Contracts not affected

This title shall not apply to contracts made prior to January 1, 1926.

Section 15.   Inapplicability of the Act of State doctrine

Enforcement of arbitral agreements, confirmation of arbitral awards, and execution upon judgments based on orders confirming such awards shall not be refused on the basis of the Act of State doctrine.

Section 16.   Appeals

(a)   An appeal may be taken from—

(1)   an order—

(A)   refusing a stay of any action under section 3 of this title,

(B)   denying a petition under section 4 of this title to order arbitration to proceed,

(C) denying an application under section 206 of this title to compel arbitration,

(D) confirming or denying confirmation of an award or partial award, or

(E) modifying, correcting, or vacating an award;

(2) an interlocutory order granting, continuing, or modifying an injunction against an arbitration that is subject to this title; or

(3) a final decision with respect to an arbitration that is subject to this title.

(b) Except as otherwise provided in section 1292(b) of title 28, an appeal may not be taken from an interlocutory order—

(1) granting a stay of any action under section 3 of this title;

(2) directing arbitration to proceed under section 4 of this title;

(3) compelling arbitration under section 206 of this title; or

(4) refusing to enjoin an arbitration that is subject to this title.

Chapter 2. Convention On The Recognition And Enforcement Of Foreign Arbitral Awards

Section 201. Enforcement of Convention

The Convention on the Recognition and Enforcement of Foreign Arbitral Awards of June 10, 1958, shall be enforced in United States courts in accordance with this chapter.

Section 202. Agreement or award falling under the Convention

An arbitration agreement or arbitral award arising out of a legal relationship, whether contractual or not, which is considered as commercial, including a transaction, contract, or agreement described in section 2 of this title, falls under the Convention. An agreement or award arising out of such a relationship which is entirely between citizens of the United States shall be deemed not to fall under the Convention unless that relationship involves property located abroad, envisages performance or enforcement abroad, or has some other reasonable relation with one or more foreign states. For the purpose of this section a corporation is a citizen of the United States if it is incorporated or has its principal place of business in the United States.

Section 203. Jurisdiction; amount in controversy

An action or proceeding falling under the Convention shall be deemed to arise under the laws and treaties of the United States. The district courts of the United States (including the courts enumerated in section 460 of title 28) shall have original jurisdiction over such an action or proceeding, regardless of the amount in controversy.

Section 204. Venue

An action or proceeding over which the district courts have jurisdiction pursuant to section 203 of this title may be brought in any such court in which save for the arbitration agreement an action or proceeding with respect to the controversy between the parties could be brought, or in such court for the district and division which embraces the place designated in the agreement as the place of arbitration if such place is within the United States.

Section 205. Removal of cases from State courts

Where the subject matter of an action or proceeding pending in a State court relates to an arbitration agreement or award falling under the Convention, the defendant or the defendants may, at any time before the trial thereof, remove such action or proceeding to the district court of the United States for the district and division embracing the place where the action or proceeding is pending. The procedure for removal of causes otherwise provided by law shall apply, except that the ground for removal provided in this section need not appear on the face of the complaint but may be shown in the petition for removal. For the purposes of Chapter 1 of this title any action or proceeding removed under this section shall be deemed to have been brought in the district court to which it is removed.

Section 206. Order to compel arbitration; appointment of arbitrators

A court having jurisdiction under this chapter may direct that arbitration be held in accordance with the agreement at any place therein provided for, whether that place is within or without the United States. Such court may also appoint arbitrators in accordance with the provisions of the agreement.

Section 207. Award of arbitrators; confirmation; jurisdiction; proceeding

Within three years after an arbitral award falling under the Convention is made, any party to the arbitration may apply to any court having jurisdiction under this chapter for an order confirming the award as against any other party to the arbitration. The court shall confirm the award unless it finds one of the grounds for refusal or deferral of recognition or enforcement of the award specified in the said Convention.

Section 208.   Chapter 1; residual application

Chapter 1 applies to actions and proceedings brought under this chapter to the extent that chapter is not in conflict with this chapter or the Convention as ratified by the United States.

Chapter 3. Inter-American Convention On International Commercial Arbitration

Section 301.   Enforcement of Convention

The Inter-American Convention on International Commercial Arbitration of January 30, 1975, shall be enforced in United States courts in accordance with this chapter.

Section 302.   Incorporation by reference

Sections 202, 203, 204, 205, and 207 of this title shall apply to this chapter as if specifically set forth herein, except that for the purposes of this chapter "the Convention" shall mean the Inter-American Convention.

Section 303.   Order to compel arbitration; appointment of arbitrators; locale

(a) A court having jurisdiction under this chapter may direct that arbitration be held in accordance with the agreement at any place therein provided for, whether that place is within or without the United States. The court may also appoint arbitrators in accordance with the provisions of the agreement.

(b) In the event the agreement does not make provision for the place of arbitration or the appointment of arbitrators, the court shall direct that the arbitration shall be held and the arbitrators be appointed in accordance with Article 3 of the Inter-American Convention.

Section 304.   Recognition and enforcement of foreign arbitral decisions and awards; reciprocity

Arbitral decisions or awards made in the territory of a foreign State shall, on the basis of reciprocity, be recognized and enforced under this chapter only if that State has ratified or acceded to the Inter-American Convention.

Section 305.   Relationship between the Inter-American Convention and the Convention on the Recognition and Enforcement of Foreign Arbitral Awards of June 10, 1958

When the requirements for application of both the Inter-American Convention and the Convention on the Recognition and Enforcement of Foreign Arbitral Awards of June 10, 1958, are met, determination as to which Convention applies shall, unless otherwise expressly agreed, be made as follows:

(1) If a majority of the parties to the arbitration agreement are citizens of a State or States that have ratified or acceded to the Inter-American Convention and are member States of the Organization of American States, the Inter-American Convention shall apply.

(2) In all other cases the Convention on the Recognition and Enforcement of Foreign Arbitral Awards of June 10, 1958, shall apply.

Section 306. Applicable rules of Inter-American Commercial Arbitration Commission

(a) For the purposes of this chapter the rules of procedure of the Inter-American Commercial Arbitration Commission referred to in Article 3 of the Inter-American Convention shall, subject to subsection (b) of this section, be those rules as promulgated by the Commission on July 1, 1988.

(b) In the event the rules of procedure of the Inter-American Commercial Arbitration Commission are modified or amended in accordance with the procedures for amendment of the rules of that Commission, the Secretary of State, by regulation in accordance with section 553 of title 5, consistent with the aims and purposes of this Convention, may prescribe that such modifications or amendments shall be effective for purposes of this chapter.

Section 307. Chapter 1; residual application

Chapter 1 applies to actions and proceedings brought under this chapter to the extent chapter 1 is not in conflict with this chapter or the Inter-American Convention as ratified by the United States.

APPENDIX 13C-1

American Arbitration Association Sample Commercial Demand Form[1]

American Arbitration Association
Dispute Resolution Services Worldwide

COMMERCIAL ARBITRATION RULES
DEMAND FOR ARBITRATION

MEDIATION: *If you would like the AAA to contact the other parties and attempt to arrange a mediation, please check this box. ☐ There is no additional administrative fee for this service.*

Name of Respondent			Name of Representative (if known)		
Address			Name of Firm (if applicable)		
			Representative's Address		
City	State	Zip Code	City	State	Zip Code
Phone No.		Fax No.	Phone No.		Fax No.
Email Address:			Email Address:		

The named claimant, a party to an arbitration agreement dated _____, which provides for arbitration under the Commercial Arbitration Rules of the American Arbitration Association, hereby demands arbitration.

THE NATURE OF THE DISPUTE

| Dollar Amount of Claim $ | Other Relief Sought: ☐ Attorneys Fees ☐ Interest ☐ Arbitration Costs ☐ Punitive/ Exemplary ☐ Other _____ |

Amount Enclosed $_____ In accordance with Fee Schedule: ☐ Flexible Fee Schedule ☐ Standard Fee Schedule

PLEASE DESCRIBE APPROPRIATE QUALIFICATIONS FOR ARBITRATOR(S) TO BE APPOINTED TO HEAR THIS DISPUTE:

Hearing locale_____ (check one) ☐ Requested by Claimant ☐ Locale provision included in the contract

| Estimated time needed for hearings overall: _____ hours or _____ days | Type of Business: Claimant _____
Respondent _____ |

Is this a dispute between a business and a consumer? ☐ **Yes** ☐ **No** Does this dispute arise out of an employment relationship? ☐ **Yes** ☐ **No**

If this dispute arises out of an employment relationship, what was/is the employee's annual wage range? Note: This question is required by California law. ☐ Less than $100,000 ☐ $100,000 - $250,000 ☐ Over $250,000

You are hereby notified that a copy of our arbitration agreement and this demand are being filed with the American Arbitration Association with a request that it commence administration of the arbitration. The AAA will provide notice of your opportunity to file an answering statement.

Signature (may be signed by a representative) Date:	Name of Representative		
Name of Claimant	Name of Firm (if applicable)		
Address (to be used in connection with this case)	Representative's Address		
City	State	Zip Code	City	State	Zip Code
Phone No.		Fax No.	Phone No.		Fax No.
Email Address:			Email Address:		

To begin proceedings, please send a copy of this Demand and the Arbitration Agreement, along with the filing fee as provided for in the Rules, to: American Arbitration Association, Case Filing Services, 1101 Laurel Oak Road, Suite 100 Voorhees, NJ 08043. Send the original Demand to the Respondent.

Please visit our website at www.adr.org if you would like to file this case online. AAA Case Filing Services can be reached at 877-495-4185.

---

[1]American Arbitration Association, *AAA Commercial Arbitration Filing Form—Commercial Demand Form*, available at http://www.adr.org/sp.asp?id= 29042 (last accessed March 25, 2011).

APPENDIX 13C-2

American Arbitration Association Sample General Demand Form[1]

American Arbitration Association
Dispute Resolution Services Worldwide

_____ **ARBITRATION RULES**
(ENTER THE NAME OF THE APPLICABLE RULES)
Demand for Arbitration

MEDIATION: *If you would like the AAA to contact the other parties and attempt to arrange mediation, please check this box.* ☐ *There is no additional administrative fee for this service.*	

Name of Respondent	Name of Representative (if known)
Address:	Name of Firm (if applicable):
	Representative's Address

City	State	Zip Code	City	State	Zip Code
Phone No.		Fax No.	Phone No.		Fax No.
Email Address:			Email Address:		

The named claimant, a party to an arbitration agreement dated _____, which provides for arbitration under the _____ Arbitration Rules of the American Arbitration Association, hereby demands arbitration.

THE NATURE OF THE DISPUTE:

Dollar Amount of Claim $	Other Relief Sought: ☐ Attorneys Fees ☐ Interest
	☐ Arbitration Costs ☐ Punitive/ Exemplary ☐ Other _____

Amount Enclosed $_____   In accordance with Fee Schedule: ☐ Flexible Fee Schedule   ☐ Standard Fee Schedule

PLEASE DESCRIBE APPROPRIATE QUALIFICATIONS FOR ARBITRATOR(S) TO BE APPOINTED TO HEAR THIS DISPUTE:

Hearing locale_____ (check one) ☐ Requested by Claimant   ☐ Locale provision included in the contract

Estimated time needed for hearings overall:	Type of Business: Claimant _____
_____hours or _____days	Respondent_____

Is this a dispute between a business and a consumer?   ☐ Yes   ☐ No
Does this dispute arise out of an employment relationship?   ☐ Yes   ☐ No

If this dispute arises out of an employment relationship, what was/is the employee's annual wage range? Note: This question is required by California law. ☐ Less than $100,000 ☐ $100,000 - $250,000 ☐ Over $250,000

> You are hereby notified that a copy of our arbitration agreement and this demand are being filed with the American Arbitration Association with a request that it commence administration of the arbitration. The AAA will provide notice of your opportunity to file an answering statement.

Signature (may be signed by a representative) Date:	Name of Representative
Name of Claimant	Name of Firm (if applicable)
Address (to be used in connection with this case):	Representative's Address:

City	State	Zip Code	City	State	Zip Code
Phone No.		Fax No.	Phone No.		Fax No.
Email Address:			Email Address:		

To begin proceedings, please send a copy of this Demand and the Arbitration Agreement, along with the filing fee as provided for in the Rules, to Case Filing Services at 1101 Laurel Oak Road, Suite 100, Voorhees, NJ 08043. Send the original Demand to the Respondent. Please visit our website at www.adr.org if you would like to file this case online. AAA Case Filing Services can be reached at 877-495-4185

---

[1]American Arbitration Association, AAA Commercial Arbitration Filing Form—General Demand Form, available at http://www.adr.org/sp.asp?id=29042 (last accessed March 25, 2011).

APPENDIX 13C-3

American Arbitration Association Sample Subpoena[1]

**The Arbitration Tribunals of the
American Arbitration Association**

In the Matter of the Arbitration between

Subpoena

FROM THE PEOPLE OF THE STATE OF

to

GREETING:

WE COMMAND YOU that, all business and excuses being laid aside, you and each of you appear and attend before

, arbitrator(s)

acting under the arbitration law of this state, at

_____
(address)

on the _____ day of _____ , 20 ___ , at _____ o'clock, to testify and give evidence in a certain arbitration, then and there to be held between the above entitled parties.

Signed: _____

Signed: _____
Arbitrator(s)

Requested by: _____

_____
Name of Representative

Address _____ Zip Code _____

_____
Telephone

Dated: _____

Form G9-11/89

---

[1]American Arbitration Association, AAA Employment Arbitration Filing Forms—Sample Subpoena, available at http://www.adr.org/sp.asp?id=32501 (last accessed March 25, 2011).

APPENDIX 13C-4

American Arbitration Association Sample Request for Mediation[1]

American Arbitration Association
Dispute Resolution Services Worldwide

REQUEST FOR MEDIATION

* Required items are indicated with an asterisk (*)

NOTE: Only use this form to file a mediation if there is a CONTRACT that provides for mediation by the AAA. If there is no contract providing for mediation or if the mediation clause does not specify the AAA, please file using the Submission to Mediation form. Please send a copy of the contract's mediation clause along with this form at the time of filing.

The information you provide is solely for the purpose of managing your mediation. If you are using Acrobat Reader 8.0 or higher, you should be able to save the form once completed. After completing the form please save it to the hard drive on your computer BEFORE navigating away from the form. If you navigate away from the form before saving it your data will be lost. Once you have completed and saved the form, send it simultaneously to us and the opposing party/parties.
You may file this form via email at casefiling@adr.org, via fax at 1-877-304-8457, or via U.S. mail at
American Arbitration Association, Case Filing Services, 1101 Laurel Oak Road, Suite 100, Voorhees, NJ 08043.
If you have any questions please email us at mediationservices@adr.org.

* Name of Requesting Party (Company, Organization, or Person's Name if an individual.)	Name of Representative (if applicable) Select "YES" if Self-Represented: __ _Yes
* Email Address:	Firm (if applicable):
* Confirm Email Address:	
* Address Line 1:	Email Address:
Address Line 2:	Confirm Email Address:
Address Line 3:	Address Line 1:
* City:	Address Line 2:
* State:	Address Line 3:
* Zip Code:	City:
* Telephone:	State:
Fax:	Zip Code:
	Telephone:
	Fax:

* Name of Person Submitting this Request:

* Please indicate the category that best describes the nature of your dispute:

☐ Commercial   ☐ Construction   ☐ Employment   ☐ Other (specify)

Does this matter involve more than two parties?   ☐ Yes   ☐ No
(If "Yes", please attach an additional page listing the names and contact information of any parties beyond two.)

* Requested Mediation Locale (city & state):

* Have parties mutually agreed to a mediator?   ☐ Yes   ☐ No   If "Yes" enter name of mediator:

Summary of Dispute:

Page 1 of 2

---

[1]American Arbitration Association, AAA Mediation Filing Form—Request for Mediation, available at http://www.adr.org/sp.asp?id=29026 (last accessed March 25, 2011).

Claim or Relief Sought:
(amount, if any)

* Please indicate your preference for when you   Within 7 business days   Within two weeks
  would like the actual mediation conference to   Within 30 days   Later than 30 days
  be conducted: Specific Date(s)

* Name of Responding Party   Name of Representative (if known)
  (Company, Organization, or Person's Name if an individual.)

* Email Address: Firm (if applicable):

* Confirm Email Address:

* Address Line 1:   Email Address:

  Address Line 2:   Confirm Email Address:

  Address Line 3:   Address Line 1:

* City: Address Line 2:

* State: Address Line 3:

* Zip Code: City:

* Telephone: State:

  Fax: Zip Code:

                                                       Telephone:

                                                       Fax:

APPENDIX 13D

ICDR Guidelines For Arbitrations Concerning Exchanges of Information[1]

Introduction

The American Arbitration Association (AAA) and its international arm, the International Centre for Dispute Resolution® (ICDR) are committed to the principle that commercial arbitration, and particularly international commercial arbitration, should provide a simpler, less expensive and more expeditious form of dispute resolution than resort to national courts.

While arbitration must be a fair process, care must also be taken to prevent the importation of procedural measures and devices from different court systems, which may be considered conducive to fairness within those systems, but which are not appropriate to the conduct of arbitrations in an international context and which are inconsistent with an alternative form of dispute resolution that is simpler, less expensive and more expeditious. One of the factors contributing to complexity, expense and delay in recent years has been the migration from court systems into arbitration of procedural devices that allow one party to a court proceeding access to information in the possession of the other, without full consideration of the differences between arbitration and litigation.

The purpose of these guidelines is to make it clear to arbitrators that they have the authority, the responsibility and, in certain jurisdictions, the mandatory duty to manage arbitration proceedings so as to achieve the goal of providing a simpler, less expensive, and more expeditious process. Unless the parties agree otherwise in writing, these guidelines will become effective in all international cases administered by the ICDR commenced after May 31, 2008, and may be adopted at the discretion of the tribunal in pending cases. They will be reflected in amendments incorporated into the next revision of the International Arbitration Rules. They may be adopted in arbitration clauses or by

---

[1]American Arbitration Association/International Centre for Dispute Resolution, ICDR Guidelines For Arbitrations Concerning Exchanges of Information, available at http://www.adr.org/si.asp?id=5288 (last accessed March 26, 2011).

agreement at any time in any other arbitration administered by the AAA.

1. **In General**

a. The tribunal shall manage the exchange of information among the parties in advance of the hearings with a view to maintaining efficiency and economy. The tribunal and the parties should endeavor to avoid unnecessary delay and expense while at the same time balancing the goals of avoiding surprise, promoting equality of treatment, and safeguarding each party's opportunity to present its claims and defenses fairly.

b. The parties may provide the tribunal with their views on the appropriate level of information exchange for each case, but the tribunal retains final authority to apply the above standard. To the extent that the Parties wish to depart from this standard, they may do so only on the basis of an express agreement among all of them in writing and in consultation with the tribunal.

2. **Documents on which a Party Relies**.

Parties shall exchange, in advance of the hearing, all documents upon which each intends to rely.

3. **Documents in the Possession of Another Party**.

a. In addition to any disclosure pursuant to paragraph 2, the tribunal may, upon application, require one party to make available to another party documents in the party's possession, not otherwise available to the party seeking the documents, that are reasonably believed to exist and to be relevant and material to the outcome of the case. Requests for documents shall contain a description of specific documents or classes of documents, along with an explanation of their relevance and materiality to the outcome of the case.

b. The tribunal may condition any exchange of documents subject to claims of commercial or technical confidentiality on appropriate measures to protect such confidentiality.

4. **Electronic Documents**.

When documents to be exchanged are maintained in electronic form, the party in possession of such documents may make them available in the form (which may be paper copies) most convenient and economical for it, unless the Tribunal determines, on application and for good cause, that there is a compelling need for access to the documents in a different form. Requests for documents maintained in electronic form should be narrowly focused and structured to make searching for them as economical as possible. The Tribunal may direct testing or other means of focusing and limiting any search.

5. **Inspections**.

The tribunal may, on application and for good cause, require a party to permit inspection on reasonable notice of relevant premises or objects.

6. **Other Procedures**.

   a. Arbitrators should be receptive to creative solutions for achieving exchanges of information in ways that avoid costs and delay, consistent with the principles of due process expressed in these Guidelines.

   b. Depositions, interrogatories, and requests to admit, as developed in American court procedures, are generally not appropriate procedures for obtaining information in international arbitration.

7. **Privileges and Professional Ethics**.

The tribunal should respect applicable rules of privilege or professional ethics and other legal impediments. When the parties, their counsel or their documents would be subject under applicable law to different rules, the tribunal should to the extent possible apply the same rule to both sides, giving preference to the rule that provides the highest level of protection.

8. **Costs and Compliance**.

   a. In resolving any dispute about pre-hearing exchanges of information, the tribunal shall require a requesting party to justify the time and expense that its request may involve, and may condition granting such a request on the payment of part or all of the cost by the party seeking the information. The tribunal may also allocate the costs of providing information among the parties, either in an interim order or in an award.

   b. In the event any party fails to comply with an order for information exchange, the tribunal may draw adverse inferences and may take such failure into account in allocating costs.

APPENDIX 13E-1

JAMS California Confidentiality Agreement[1]

Re: Mediation of _____
       JAMS Reference Number _____

In order to promote communication among the parties and to facilitate resolution of the dispute, the participants agree as follows:

1. This mediation process is to be considered settlement negotiations for the purpose of all state and federal rules protecting disclosures made during such process from later discovery and/or use in evidence.

2. The provisions of California Evidence Code §§ 1115 to 1128 and 703.5, as attached hereto, apply to this mediation. THIS CONFIDENTIALITY AGREEMENT ("AGREEMENT") EXTENDS TO ALL PRESENT AND FUTURE CIVIL, JUDICIAL, QUASI-JUDICIAL, ARBITRAL, ADMINISTRATIVE OR OTHER PROCEEDINGS.

3. The participants' sole purpose in conducting or participating in mediation is to compromise, settle or resolve their dispute, in whole or in part.

4. The privileged character of any information or documents is not altered by disclosure to the mediator. The mediation process may continue after the date appearing below. Therefore, the mediator's subsequent oral and written communications with the mediation participants in a continuing effort to resolve the dispute are subject to this Agreement. This Agreement may be signed before, during or after the mediation.

5. ANY WRITTEN SETTLEMENT AGREEMENT PREPARED DURING OR AT THE CONCLUSION OF THE MEDIATION IS SUBJECT TO DISCLOSURE, BINDING, ENFORCEABLE, AND ADMISSIBLE to prove the existence of and/or to enforce the agreement under California Code of Civil Procedure § 664.6, if applicable, or otherwise.

---

[1]JAMS, California Confidentiality Agreement, available at http://www.jamsadr.com/mediation-forms/, (last accessed March 25, 2011).

6. Because the participants are disclosing information in reliance upon this Agreement, any breach of this Agreement would cause irreparable injury for which monetary damages would be inadequate. Consequently, any party to this Agreement may obtain an injunction to prevent disclosure of any such confidential information in violation of this Agreement.

7. The mediator is serving as a neutral intermediary and settlement facilitator and may not act as an advocate for any party. THE MEDIATOR'S STATEMENTS DO NOT CONSTITUTE LEGAL ADVICE TO ANY PARTY. ACCORDINGLY, THE PARTIES ARE STRONGLY ENCOURAGED TO SEEK LEGAL ADVICE FROM THEIR OWN COUNSEL. If the mediator assists in preparing a settlement agreement, each participant is advised to have the agreement independently reviewed by their own counsel before executing the agreement.

Executed on _____

for	for
for	for
for	for
for	for
for	for

CALIFORNIA EVIDENCE CODE

Mediation

§ 1115. For purposes of this chapter:

(a) "Mediation" means a process in which a neutral person or persons facilitate communication between the disputants to assist them in reaching a mutually acceptable agreement.

(b) "Mediator" means a neutral person who conducts a mediation. "Mediator" includes any person designated by a mediator either to assist in the mediation or to communicate with the participants in preparation for a mediation.

(c) "Mediation consultation" means a communication between a person and a mediator for the purpose of initiating, considering, or reconvening a mediation or retaining the mediator.

§ **1116.** (a) Nothing in this chapter expands or limits a court's authority to order participation in a dispute resolution proceeding. Nothing in this chapter authorizes or affects the enforceability of a contract clause in which parties agree to the use of mediation.

(b) Nothing in this chapter makes admissible evidence that is inadmissible under Section 1152 or any other statute.

§ **1117.** (a) Except as provided in subdivision (b), this chapter applies to a mediation as defined in Section 1115.

(b) This chapter does not apply to either of the following:

(1) A proceeding under Part 1 (commencing with Section 1800) of Division 5 of the Family Code or Chapter 11 (commencing with Section 3160) of Part 2 of Division 8 of the Family Code.

(2) A settlement conference pursuant to Rule 222 of the California Rules of Court.

§ **1118.** An oral agreement "in accordance with Section 1118" means an oral agreement that satisfies all of the following conditions:

(a) The oral agreement is recorded by a court reporter, tape recorder, or other reliable means of sound recording.

(b) The terms of the oral agreement are recited on the record in the presence of the parties and the mediator, and the parties express on the record that they agree to the terms recited.

(c) The parties to the oral agreement expressly state on the record that the agreement is enforceable or binding or words to that effect.

(d) The recording is reduced to writing and the writing is signed by the parties within 72 hours after it is recorded.

§ **1119.** Except as otherwise provided in this chapter:

(a) No evidence of anything said or any admission made for the purpose of, in the course of, or pursuant to, a mediation or a mediation consultation is admissible or subject to discovery, and disclosure of the evidence shall not be compelled, in any arbitration, administrative adjudication, civil action, or other noncriminal proceeding in which, pursuant to law, testimony can be compelled to be given.

(b) No writing, as defined in Section 250, that is prepared

for the purpose of, in the course of, or pursuant to, a mediation or a mediation consultation, is admissible or subject to discovery, and disclosure of the writing shall not be compelled, in any arbitration, administrative adjudication, civil action, or other noncriminal proceeding in which, pursuant to law, testimony can be compelled to be given.

(c) All communications, negotiations, or settlement discussions by and between participants in the course of a mediation or a mediation consultation shall remain confidential.

§ **1120.** (a) Evidence otherwise admissible or subject to discovery outside of a mediation or a mediation consultation shall not be or become inadmissible or protected from disclosure solely by reason of its introduction or use in a mediation or a mediation consultation.

(b) This chapter does not limit any of the following:

(1) The admissibility of an agreement to mediate a dispute.

(2) The effect of an agreement not to take a default or an agreement to extend the time within which to act or refrain from acting in a pending civil action.

(3) Disclosure of the mere fact that a mediator has served, is serving, will serve, or was contacted about serving as a mediator in a dispute.

§ **1121.** Neither a mediator nor anyone else may submit to a court or other adjudicative body, and a court or other adjudicative body may not consider, any report, assessment, evaluation, recommendation, or finding of any kind by the mediator concerning a mediation conducted by the mediator, other than a report that is mandated by court rule or other law and that states only whether an agreement was reached, unless all parties to the mediation expressly agree otherwise in writing, or orally in accordance with Section 1118.

§ **1122.** (a) A communication or writing, as defined in Section 250, that is made or prepared for the purpose of, or in the course of, or pursuant to, a mediation or a mediation consultation, is not made inadmissible, or protected from disclosure, by provisions of this chapter if either of the following conditions is satisfied:

(1) All persons who conduct or otherwise participate in the mediation expressly agree in writing, or orally in accordance with Section 1118, to disclosure of the communication, document, or writing.

(2) The communication, document, or writing was pre-

pared by or on behalf of fewer than all the mediation participants, those participants expressly agree in writing, or orally in accordance with Section 1118, to its disclosure, and the communication, document, or writing does not disclose anything said or done or any admission made in the course of the mediation.

(b) For purposes of subdivision (a), if the neutral person who conducts a mediation expressly agrees to disclosure, that agreement also binds any other person described in subdivision (b) of Section 1115.

§ **1123.** A written settlement agreement prepared in the course of, or pursuant to, a mediation, is not made inadmissible, or protected from disclosure, by provisions of this chapter if the agreement is signed by the settling parties and any of the following conditions are satisfied:

(a) The agreement provides that it is admissible or subject to disclosure, or words to that effect.

(b) The agreement provides that it is enforceable or binding or words to that effect.

(c) All parties to the agreement expressly agree in writing, or orally in accordance with Section 1118, to its disclosure.

(d) The agreement is used to show fraud, duress, illegality that is relevant to an issue in dispute.

§ **1124.** An oral agreement made in the course of, or pursuant to, a mediation is not made inadmissible, or protected from disclosure, by the provisions of this chapter if any of the following conditions are satisfied:

(a) The agreement is in accordance with Section 1118.

(b) The agreement is in accordance with subdivisions (a), (b), and (d) of Section 1118, and all parties to the agreement expressly agree, in writing or orally in accordance with Section 1118, to disclosure of the agreement.

(c) The agreement is in accordance with subdivisions (a), (b), and (d) of Section 1118, and the agreement is used to show fraud, duress, or illegality that is relevant to an issue in dispute.

§ **1125.** (a) For purposes of confidentiality under this chapter, a mediation ends when any one of the following conditions is satisfied:

(1) The parties execute a written settlement agreement that fully resolves the dispute.

(2) An oral agreement that fully resolves the dispute is reached in accordance with Section 1118.

(3) The mediator provides the mediation participants with a writing signed by the mediator that states that the mediation is terminated, or words to that effect, which shall be consistent with Section 1121.

(4) A party provides the mediator and the other mediation participants with a writing stating that the mediation is terminated, or words to that effect, which shall be consistent with Section 1121. In a mediation involving more than two parties, the mediation may continue as to the remaining parties or be terminated in accordance with this section.

(5) For 10 calendar days, there is no communication between the mediator and any of the parties to the mediation relating to the dispute. The mediator and the parties may shorten or extend this time by agreement.

(b) For purposes of confidentiality under this chapter, if a mediation partially resolves a dispute, mediation ends when either of the following conditions is satisfied:

(1) The parties execute a written settlement agreement that partially resolves the dispute.

(2) An oral agreement that partially resolves the dispute is reached in accordance with Section 1118.

(c) This section does not preclude a party from ending a mediation without reaching an agreement. This section does not otherwise affect the extent to which a party may terminate a mediation.

§ **1126.** Anything said, any admission made, or any writing that is inadmissible, protected from disclosure, and confidential under this chapter before a mediation ends, shall remain inadmissible, protected from disclosure, and confidential to the same extent after the mediation ends.

§ **1127.** If a person subpoenas or otherwise seeks to compel a mediator to testify or produce a writing, as defined in Section 250, and the court or other adjudicative body determines that the testimony or writing is inadmissible under this chapter, or protected from disclosure under this chapter, the court or adjudicative body making the determination shall award reasonable attorney's fees and costs to the mediator against the person seeking the testimony or writing.

§ **1128.** Any reference to a mediation during any subsequent trial is an irregularity in the proceedings of the trial for the purposes of Section 657 of the Code of Civil Procedure. Any reference to a mediation during any other subsequent noncriminal proceeding is grounds for vacating or modifying the decision in that proceeding, in whole or in part, and granting a new or further hearing on all or part of the issues, if the reference materially affected the substantial rights of the party requesting relief.

§ **703.5.** Judges, arbitrators or mediators as witnesses; subsequent civil proceeding.

No person presiding at any judicial or quasi-judicial proceeding, and no arbitrator or mediator, shall be competent to testify, in any subsequent civil proceedings, as to any statement, conduct, decision, or ruling, occurring at or in conjunction with the prior proceeding, except as to a statement or conduct that could (a) give rise to civil or criminal contempt, (b) constitute a crime, (c) be the subject of investigation by the State Bar or Commission on Judicial Performance, or (d) give rise to disqualification proceedings under paragraph (1) or (6) of subdivision (a) of Section 170.1 of the Code of Civil Procedure. However, this section does not apply to a mediator with regard to any mediation under Chapter 11 (commencing with Section 3160) of Part 2 of Division 8 of the Family Code.

APPENDIX 13E-2

JAMS Arbitration Demand[1]

THE RESOLUTION EXPERTS

Demand for Arbitration Before JAMS

Instructions for Submittal of Arbitration to JAMS

Demand for Arbitration Based on Pre-Dispute Provision

If you wish to proceed with an arbitration by executing and serving a Demand for Arbitration on the appropriate party, please submit the following items to JAMS:

A. Two (2) copies of the **Demand for Arbitration**

B. **Proof of service** of the Demand on the appropriate party
   E.g., copy of certified mail receipt signed by recipient or sworn statement of service by a non-party over 18 years of age.

C. **Two (2) copies of the entire contract containing the arbitration clause**

D. **Initial non-refundable $400 Case Management Fee (CMF) per party**
   Each party may submit its own CMF, or to expedite the commencement of the proceedings one party may elect to submit both or all CMFs. In lengthier, more complex cases additional CMF may be billed. For cases involving consumers, see JAMS Policy on Consumer Arbitrations Pursuant to Pre-Dispute Clauses.

OR

Arbitration Based on Post-Dispute Fully Executed Arbitration Agreement, Oral Stipulation or Court Order Compelling Arbitration

Whether or not a certain arbitrator has been designated, if the parties have agreed to arbitrate at JAMS or the court has ordered that the parties arbitrate at JAMS, kindly forward the following items:

A. Two (2) copies of **Executed Arbitration Agreement OR Court Order appointing arbitrator/JAMS**
   Please contact JAMS to obtain the appropriate form (e.g., Arbitration Agreement)

B. Two (2) copies of the **entire contract, if any, containing an applicable arbitration clause**

C. **Initial non-refundable $400 Case Management Fee (CMF) per party**
   Each party may submit its own CMF, or to expedite the commencement of the proceedings one party may elect to submit both or all CMFs. In lengthier, more complex cases additional CMF may be billed. For cases involving consumers, see JAMS Policy on Consumer Arbitrations Pursuant to Pre-Dispute Clauses.

Please submit to your local JAMS Resolution Center.

Once the above items are received, JAMS will contact all parties to commence the arbitration process, including the appointment of an arbitrator and scheduling of a hearing date.

---

[1]JAMS, JAMS Arbitration Demand, available at http://www.jamsadr.com/arbitration-forms/ (last accessed March 25, 2011).

THE RESOLUTION EXPERTS®

Demand for Arbitration Before JAMS

TO RESPONDENT: _____
(Name of the Party on whom Demand for Arbitration is made)

(Address) _____

(City)	(State)	(Zip)
(Telephone)	(Fax)	(E-Mail)

Representative/Attorney (if known): _____
(Name of the Representative/Attorney of the Party on whom Demand for Arbitration is made)

(Address) _____

(City)	(State)	(Zip)
(Telephone)	(Fax)	(E-Mail)

FROM CLAIMANT (Name): _____

(Address) _____

(City)	(State)	(Zip)
(Telephone)	(Fax)	(E-Mail)

Representative/Attorney of Claimant (if known): _____
(Name of the Representative/Attorney for the Party Demanding Arbitration)

(Address) _____

(City)	(State)	(Zip)
(Telephone)	(Fax)	(E-Mail)

NATURE OF DISPUTE
Claimant hereby demands that you submit the following dispute to final and binding arbitration (a more detailed statement of the claim(s) may be attached):

ARBITRATION AGREEMENT
This demand is made pursuant to the arbitration agreement which the parties made as follows (cite location of arbitration provision & attach two (2) copies of entire agreement).

THE RESOLUTION EXPERTS®

Demand for Arbitration Before JAMS

CLAIM & RELIEF SOUGHT BY CLAIMANT

Claimant asserts the following claim and seeks the following relief (include amount in controversy, if applicable):

RESPONSE

Respondent may file a response and counter-claim to the above-stated claim according to the applicable arbitration rules. Send the original response and counter-claim to the claimant at the address stated above with two (2) copies to JAMS.

REQUEST FOR HEARING

JAMS is requested to set this matter for hearing at:_____

(Preferred Hearing Location)

ELECTION FOR EXPEDITED PROCEDURES (COMPREHENSIVE RULE 16.1)

By checking this box ☐ Claimant requests that the Expedited Procedures described in JAMS Comprehensive Rules 16.1 and 16.2 be applied in this matter. Respondent shall indicate not later than 7 days from the date this Demand is served whether it agrees to the Expedited Procedure.

Signed (Claimant): _____   Date: _____

(may be signed by an attorney)

Print Name: _____

Please include a check payable to JAMS for the required initial, non-refundable $400 per party deposit to be applied toward your Case Management Fee and submit to your local JAMS Resolution Center.

Effective 10/01/2010
Resolution Centers Nationwide • 1.800.352.5267 • www.jamsadr.com

THE RESOLUTION EXPERTS®

Demand for Arbitration Before JAMS

COMPLETION OF THIS SECTION IS REQUIRED FOR CLAIMS INITIATED IN CALIFORNIA

A. **Please check here if this** ☐ **IS** or ☐ **IS NOT** a CONSUMER ARBITRATION as defined by California Rules of Court Ethics Standards for Neutral Arbitrators, Standard 2(d) and (e):

"Consumer arbitration" means an arbitration conducted under a pre-dispute arbitration provision contained in a contract that meets the criteria listed in paragraphs (1) through (3) below. "Consumer arbitration" excludes arbitration proceedings conducted under or arising out of public or private sector labor-relations laws, regulations, charter provisions, ordinances, statutes, or agreements.

    1) The contract is with a consumer party, as defined in these standards;

    2) The contract was drafted by or on behalf of the non-consumer party; and

    3) The consumer party was required to accept the arbitration provision in the contract.

"Consumer party" is a party to an arbitration agreement who, in the context of that arbitration agreement, is any of the following:

    1) An individual who seeks or acquires, including by lease, any goods or services primarily for personal, family, or household purposes including, but not limited to, financial services, insurance, and other goods and services as defined in section 1761 of the Civil Code;

    2) An individual who is an enrollee, a subscriber, or insured in a health-care service plan within the meaning of section 1345 of the Health and Safety Code or health-care insurance plan within the meaning of section 106 of the Insurance Code;

    3) An individual with a medical malpractice claim that is subject to the arbitration agreement; or

    4) An employee or an applicant for employment in a dispute arising out of or relating to the employee's employment or the applicant's prospective employment that is subject to the arbitration agreement.

If Respondent disagrees with the assertion of Claimant regarding whether this IS or IS NOT a CONSUMER ARBITRATION, Respondent should communicate this objection in writing to the JAMS Case Manager and Claimant within seven (7) calendar days of service of the Demand for Arbitration.

B. **If this is an EMPLOYMENT matter, Claimant must complete the following information:**

Effective January 1, 2003, private arbitration companies are required to collect and publish certain information at least quarterly, and make it available to the public in a computer-searchable format. In employment cases, this includes the amount of the employee's annual wage. The employee's name will not appear in the database, but the employer's name will be published. Please check the applicable box below:

Annual Salary:

    ☐ Less than $100,000   ☐ More than $250,000

    ☐ $100,000 to $250,000   ☐ Decline to State

C. **In California, consumers (as defined above) with a gross monthly income of less than 300% of the federal poverty guidelines are entitled to a waiver of the arbitration fees.** In those cases, the respondent must pay 100% of the fees. Consumers must submit a declaration under oath stating the consumer's monthly income and the number of persons living in his or her household. Please contact JAMS at 1-800-352-5267 for further information.

Effective 10/01/2010
Resolution Centers Nationwide • 1.800.352.5267 • www.jamsadr.com

APPENDIX 13E-3

JAMS Mediation Submission Form[1]

CASE SUBMISSION FORM

Resolution Centers Nationwide · 1.800.352.JAMS · www.jamsadr.com

Please submit this form to your local JAMS Resolution Center.
A JAMS professional will contact all parties to coordinate the ADR process.
To file an Arbitration, please use the *Demand for Arbitration* form at www.jamsadr.com.

CASE CAPTION   vs.

Additionally, submit caption page, if available.

PLAINTIFF/CLAIMANT   Name

Representative/Attorney

Law Firm

Address

City/State/Zip

Telephone   Fax   Email

File Number

DEFENDANT/RESPONDENT   Name

Representative/Attorney

Law Firm

Address

City/State/Zip

Telephone   Fax   Email

File or Claim Number

INSURANCE CARRIER   Name

Address

City/State/Zip

Telephone   Fax   Email

File or Claim Number

If multiple parties are involved, attach a service list.

---

[1]JAMS, Mediation Submission Form, available at http://www.jamsadr.com/mediation-forms/, (last accessed March 25, 2011).

348

CASE SUBMISSION FORM continued

NATURE OF DISPUTE

Attach a brief description of the case including issues in controversy and case history.

CLAIMS & RELIEF SOUGHT BY CLAIMANT

Attach the claims asserted by Plaintiff/Claimant and requested relief (including amount in controversy, if applicable).

CASE INFORMATION

Has suit been filed?   Case Number   Trial Date

Mediation deadline (if applicable)

SESSION INFORMATION

____ Mediation   ____ Neutral Evaluation   ____ Discovery Referee/Special Master   ____ Judge Pro Tem

____ Other

Requested JAMS Resolution Center

Requested session dates

Estimated session duration

Fee Split   % Plaintiff/Claimant   % Defendant/Respondent

NEUTRAL INFORMATION

Have the parties mutually agreed to a neutral?   If so, whom?

Submitted By   Date

APPENDIX 13E-4

JAMS Stipulation for Arbitration[1]

Arbitration Matter between: [Claiming Party] v. [Responding Party]	Reference Number:

STIPULATION FOR ARBITRATION

It is stipulated and agreed by the Parties to submit all disputes, claims or controversies to neutral, binding arbitration at JAMS, pursuant to the JAMS Arbitration Administrative Policies and, unless otherwise agreed in writing by the parties, to the applicable JAMS Arbitration Rules and Procedures. For cases proceeding under the JAMS Comprehensive Rules, the parties agree that the Expedited Procedures set forth in Rules 16.1 and 16.2 shall be employed. The Parties hereby agree to give up any rights they might possess to have this matter litigated in a court or jury trial.

BY: _____   BY: _____

FOR: _____   FOR: _____

DATE: _____   DATE: _____

BY: _____   BY: _____

FOR: _____   FOR: _____

DATE: _____   DATE: _____

---

[1]JAMS, JAMS Arbitration Demand, available at http://www.jamsadr.com/arbitration-forms/ (last accessed March 25, 2011).

COMPLETION OF THIS SECTION IS REQUIRED FOR CLAIMS INITIATED IN CALIFORNIA

A. Please check here if this   [   ] IS   or   [   ] IS NOT   a CONSUMER ARBITRATION as defined by California Rules of Court Ethics Standards for Neutral Arbitrators, Standard 2(d) and (e):

"Consumer arbitration" means an arbitration conducted under a pre-dispute arbitration provision contained in a contract that meets the criteria listed in paragraphs (1) through (3) below. "Consumer arbitration" excludes arbitration proceedings conducted under or arising out of public or private sector labor-relations laws, regulations, charter provisions, ordinances, statutes, or agreements.

    (1)   The contract is with a consumer party, as defined in these standards;

    (2)   The contract was drafted by or on behalf of the non-consumer party; and

    (3)   The consumer party was required to accept the arbitration provision in the contract.

"Consumer party" is a party to an arbitration agreement who, in the context of that arbitration agreement, is any of the following:

    (1)   An individual who seeks or acquires, including by lease, any goods or services primarily for personal, family, or household purposes including, but not limited to, financial services, insurance, and other goods and services as defined in section 1761 of the Civil Code;

    (2)   An individual who is an enrollee, a subscriber, or insured in a health-care service plan within the meaning of section 1345 of the Health and Safety Code or health-care insurance plan within the meaning of section 106 of the Insurance Code;

    (3)   An individual with a medical malpractice claim that is subject to the arbitration agreement; or

    (4)   An employee or an applicant for employment in a dispute arising out of or relating to the employee's employment or the applicant's prospective employment that is subject to the arbitration agreement.

If Respondent disagrees with the assertion of Claimant regarding whether this IS or IS NOT a CONSUMER ARBITRATION, Respondent should communicate this objection in writing to the JAMS Case Manager and Claimant within seven (7) calendar days of service of the Demand for Arbitration.

B. If this is an EMPLOYMENT matter, Claimant must complete the following information:

Effective January 1, 2003, private arbitration companies are required to collect and publish certain information at least quarterly, and make it available to the public in a computer-searchable format. In employment cases, this includes the amount of the employee's annual wage. The employee's name will not appear in the database, but the employer's name will be published. Please check the applicable box below:

Annual Salary:

    ___ Less than $100,000   ___ More than $250,000

    ___ $100,000 to $250,000   ___ Decline to State

C. **In California, consumers (as defined above) with a gross monthly income of less than 300% of the federal poverty guidelines are entitled to a waiver of the arbitration fees.** In those cases, the respondent must pay 100% of the fees. Consumers must submit a declaration under oath stating the consumer's monthly income and the number of persons living in his or her household. Please contact JAMS at 1-800-352-5267 for further information.

APPENDIX 13E-5

JAMS Recommended Arbitration Discovery Protocols For Domestic Commercial Cases Effective January 6, 2010[1]

Effective January 6, 2010

Introduction

JAMS is committed to providing the most efficient, cost-effective arbitration process that is possible in the particular circumstances of each case. Its experienced, trained and highly qualified arbitrators are committed to: (1) Being sufficiently assertive to ensure that an arbitration will be resolved much less expensively and in much less time than if it had been litigated in court; and (2) At the same time, being sufficiently patient and restrained to ensure that there is enough discovery and evidence to permit a fair result.

The JAMS Recommended Arbitration Discovery Protocols ("Protocols"), which are set forth below, provide JAMS arbitrators with an effective tool that will help them exercise their sound judgment in furtherance of achieving an efficient, cost-effective process which affords the parties a fair opportunity to be heard.

The Key Element—Good Judgment of the Arbitrator

- JAMS arbitrators understand that while some commercial arbitrations may have similarities, for the most part each case involves unique facts and circumstances. As a result, JAMS arbitrators adapt arbitration discovery to meet the unique characteristics of the particular case, understanding that there is no set of objective rules which, if followed, would result in one "correct" approach for all commercial cases.
- JAMS appreciates that the experience, talent and preferences brought to arbitration will vary with the arbitrator. It follows that the framework of arbitration discovery will always be

---

[1]JAMS, JAMS Protocols for Electronic Discovery, available at http://www.jamsadr.com/arbitration-discovery-protocols/ (last accessed March 08, 2011).

based on the judgment of the arbitrator, brought to bear in the context of variables such as the applicable rules, the custom and practice for arbitrations in the industry in question, and the expectations and preferences of the parties and their counsel.

- Attached as Exhibit A is a list of factors which JAMS arbitrators take into consideration when addressing the type and breadth of arbitration discovery.

Early Attention to Discovery by the Arbitrator

- JAMS understands the importance of establishing the ground rules governing an arbitration in the period immediately following the initiation of the arbitration. Therefore, following appointment, JAMS arbitrators promptly study the facts and the issues and become prepared to preside effectively over the early stages of the case in a way that will ultimately lead to an expeditious, cost-effective and fair process.
- Depending upon the provisions of the parties agreement, JAMS arbitrations may be governed by the JAMS Comprehensive Arbitration Rules and Procedures or by the arbitration rules of another provider organization. Such rules, for good reason, lack the specificity that one finds, for example, in the Federal Rules of Civil Procedure. That being so, JAMS arbitrators seek to avoid uncertainty and surprise by ensuring that the parties understand at an early stage the basic ground rules for discovery. This early attention to the scope of discovery increases the chance that parties will adopt joint principles of fairness and efficiency before partisan positions arise in concrete discovery disputes.
- JAMS arbitrators place the type and breadth of arbitration discovery high on the agenda for the first pre-hearing conference at the start of the case. If at all possible, in-house counsel should attend the pre-hearing conference at which discovery will be discussed.
- JAMS arbitrators strive to enhance the chances for limited, efficient discovery by acting at the first pre-hearing conference to set hearing dates and interim deadlines which, the parties are told, will be strictly enforced, and which, in fact, are thereafter strictly enforced.
- Where appropriate, JAMS arbitrators explain at the first pre-hearing conference that document requests:
  - should be limited to documents which are directly relevant to significant issues in the case or to the case's outcome,
  - should be restricted in terms of time frame, subject matter and persons or entities to which the requests pertain, and

- should not include broad phraseology such as "all documents directly or indirectly related to."

Party Preferences

- Overly broad arbitration discovery can result when all of the parties seek discovery beyond what is needed. This unfortunate circumstance may be caused by parties and/or advocates who are inexperienced in arbitration and simply conduct themselves in a fashion which is commonly accepted in court litigation. In any event, where all participants truly desire unlimited discovery, JAMS arbitrators will respect that decision, since arbitration is governed by the agreement of the parties.
- Where one side wants broad arbitration discovery and the other wants narrow discovery, the arbitrator will set meaningful limitations.

e-discovery

- The use of electronic media for the creation, storage and transmission of information has substantially increased the volume of available document discovery. It has also substantially increased the cost of the discovery process.
- To be able to appropriately address issues pertaining to e-discovery, JAMS arbitrators are trained to deal with the technological issues that arise in connection with electronic data.
- While there can be no objective standard for the appropriate scope of e-discovery in all cases, JAMS arbitrators recognize that an early order containing language along the following lines can be an important first step in limiting such discovery in a large number of cases:
  - There shall be production of electronic documents only from sources used in the ordinary course of business. Absent a showing of compelling need, no such documents are required to be produced from back-up servers, tapes or other media.
  - Absent a showing of compelling need, the production of electronic documents shall normally be made on the basis of generally available technology in a searchable format which is usable by the party receiving the e-documents and convenient and economical for the producing party. Absent a showing of compelling need, the parties need not produce metadata with the exception of header fields for email correspondence.
  - Where the costs and burdens of e-discovery are disproportionate to the nature and gravity of the dispute or to the amount in controversy, or to the relevance of the materials requested,

the arbitrator will either deny such requests or order disclosure on condition that the requesting party advance the reasonable cost of production to the other side, subject to the allocation of costs in the final award.

Artfully Drafted Arbitration Clauses

- JAMS recognizes that there is significant potential for dealing with time and other limitations on discovery in the arbitration clauses of commercial contracts. An advantage of such drafting is that it is much easier for parties to agree on such limitations before a dispute has arisen. A drawback, however, is the difficulty of rationally providing for how best to arbitrate a dispute that has not yet surfaced. Thus, the use of such clauses may be most productive in circumstances in which parties have a good idea from the outset as to the nature and scope of disputes that might thereafter arise.
- JAMS understands that in order for rational time and other discovery limitations to be effectively included in an arbitration clause, it is necessary that an attorney with a good understanding of arbitration be involved in the drafting process.

Depositions

- Rule 17(c) of the JAMS Rules provides that in a domestic arbitration, each party is entitled to one deposition of an opposing party or an individual under the control of an opposing party and that each side may apply for the taking of additional depositions, if necessary.
- JAMS recognizes that the size and complexity of commercial arbitrations have now grown to a point where more than a single deposition can serve a useful purpose in certain instances. Depositions in a complex arbitration, for example, can significantly shorten the cross-examination of key witnesses and shorten the hearing on the merits.
- If not carefully regulated, however, deposition discovery in arbitration can become extremely expensive, wasteful and time-consuming. In determining what scope of depositions may be appropriate in a given case, a JAMS arbitrator balances these considerations, considers the factors set forth in Exhibit A and confers with counsel for the parties. If a JAMS arbitrator determines that it is appropriate to permit multiple depositions, he/she may attempt to solicit agreement at the first pre-hearing conference on language such as the following:

Each side may take 3* discovery depositions. Each side's depositions are to consume no more than a total of 15* hours. There are to be no speaking objections at the depositions, except to preserve privilege. The total period for the taking of depositions shall not exceed 6* weeks.[2]

Discovery Disputes

- Discovery disputes must be resolved promptly and efficiently. In addressing discovery disputes, JAMS arbitrators consider use of the following practices which can increase the speed and cost-effectiveness of the arbitration:
  - Where there is a panel of three arbitrators, the parties may agree, by rule or otherwise, that the Chair or another member of the panel is authorized to resolve discovery issues, acting alone.
  - Lengthy briefs on discovery matters should be avoided. In most cases, a prompt discussion or submission of brief letters will sufficiently inform the arbitrator with regard to the issues to be decided.
  - The parties should negotiate discovery differences in good faith before presenting any remaining issues for the arbitrator's decision.
  - The existence of discovery issues should not impede the progress of discovery where there are no discovery differences.

Discovery & Other Procedural Aspects of Arbitration

Other aspects of arbitration have interplay with, and impact on, discovery in arbitration, as discussed below.

Requests for Adjournments

- Where parties encounter discovery difficulties, this circumstance often leads to a request for adjournment and the possible delay of the hearing. While the arbitrator may not reject a joint application of all parties to adjourn the hearing, the fact is that such adjournments can cause inordinate disruption and delay by needlessly extending unnecessary discovery and can substantially detract from the cost-effectiveness of the arbitration. If the request for adjournment is by all parties and is based on a perceived need for further discovery (as opposed to personal considerations), a JAMS arbitrator ensures that the parties understand the implications in time and cost of the adjournment they seek.
- If one party seeks a continuance and another opposes it, then

---

[2]*The asterisked numbers can of course be changed to comport with the particular circumstances of each case.*

the arbitrator has discretion to grant or deny the request. Factors that affect the exercise of such discretion include the merits of the request and the legitimate needs of the parties, as well as the proximity of the request to the scheduled hearing and whether any earlier requests for adjournments have been made.

Discovery and Dispositive Motions

- In arbitration, "dispositive" motions can cause significant delay and unduly prolong the discovery period. Such motions are commonly based on lengthy briefs and recitals of facts and, after much time, labor and expense, are generally denied on the ground that they raise issues of fact and are inconsistent with the spirit of arbitration. On the other hand, dispositive motions can sometimes enhance the efficiency of the arbitration process if directed to discrete legal issues such as statute of limitations or defenses based on clear contractual provisions. In such circumstances, an appropriately framed dispositive motion can eliminate the need for expensive and time consuming discovery. On balance, a JAMS arbitrator will consider the following procedure with regard to dispositive motions:
  - Any party wishing to make a dispositive motion must first submit a brief letter (not exceeding five pages) explaining why the motion has merit and why it would speed the proceeding and make it more cost-effective. The other side would have a brief period within which to respond.
  - Based on the letters, the arbitrator would decide whether to proceed with more comprehensive briefing and argument on the proposed motion.
  - If the arbitrator decides to go forward with the motion, he/she would place page limits on the briefs and set an accelerated schedule for the disposition of the motion.
  - Under ordinary circumstances, the pendency of such a motion should not serve to stay any aspect of the arbitration or adjourn any pending deadlines.

Note: These Protocols are adapted from the April 4, 2009 Report on Arbitration Discovery by the New York Bar Association.

Exhibit A

Relevant Factors Considered By JAMS Arbitrators In Determining The Appropriate Scope Of Domestic Arbitration Discovery

Nature of The Dispute
- The factual context of the arbitration and of the issues in question with which the arbitrator should become conversant before making a decision about discovery.
- The amount in controversy.
- The complexity of the factual issues.
- The number of parties and diversity of their interests.
- Whether any or all of the claims appear, on the basis of the pleadings, to have sufficient merit to justify the time and expense associated with the requested discovery.
- Whether there are public policy or ethical issues that give rise to the need for an in depth probe through relatively comprehensive discovery.
- Whether it might be productive to initially address a potentially dispositive issue which does not require extensive discovery.

Agreement of The Parties
- Agreement of the parties, if any, with respect to the scope of discovery.
- Agreement, if any, by the parties with respect to duration of the arbitration from the filing of the arbitration demand to the issuance of the final award.
- The parties' choice of substantive and procedural law and the expectations under that legal regime with respect to arbitration discovery.

Relevance and Reasonable Need For Requested Discovery
- Relevance of the requested discovery to the material issues in dispute or the outcome of the case.
- Whether the requested discovery appears to be sought in an excess of caution, or is duplicative or redundant.
- Whether there are necessary witnesses and/or documents that are beyond the tribunal's subpoena power.
- Whether denial of the requested discovery would, in the arbitrator's judgment (after appropriate scrutinizing of the issues), deprive the requesting party of what is reasonably necessary to allow that party a fair opportunity to prepare and present its case.
- Whether the requested information could be obtained from another source more conveniently and with less expense or other burden on the party from whom the discovery is requested.
- To what extent the discovery sought is likely to lead, as a

practical matter, to a case-changing "smoking gun" or to a fairer result.

• Whether broad discovery is being sought as part of a litigation tactic to put the other side to great expense and thus coerce some sort of result on grounds other than the merits.

• The time and expense that would be required for a comprehensive discovery program.

• Whether all or most of the information relevant to the determination of the merits is in the possession of one side.

• Whether the party seeking expansive discovery is willing to advance the other side's reasonable costs and attorneys' fees in connection with furnishing the requested materials and information.

• Whether a limited deposition program would be likely to: (i) streamline the hearing and make it more cost-effective; (ii) lead to the disclosure of important documents not otherwise available; or (iii) result in expense and delay without assisting in the determination of the merits.

Privilege and Confidentiality

• Whether the requested discovery is likely to lead to extensive privilege disputes as to documents not likely to assist in the determination of the merits.

• Whether there are genuine confidentiality concerns with respect to documents of marginal relevance. Whether cumbersome, time-consuming procedures (attorneys' eyes only, and the like) would be necessary to protect confidentiality in such circumstances.

Characteristics and Needs of The Parties

• The financial and human resources the parties have at their disposal to support discovery, viewed both in absolute terms and relative to one another.

• The financial burden that would be imposed by a broad discovery program and whether the extent of the burden outweighs the likely benefit of the discovery.

• Whether injunctive relief is requested or whether one or more of the parties has some other particular interest in obtaining a prompt resolution of all or some of the controversy.

• The extent to which the resolution of the controversy might have an impact on the continued viability of one or more of the parties.

APPENDIX 13F-1

Alternative Resolution Centers Stipulation Regarding Order of Reference[1]

STIPULATION RE ORDER OF REFERENCE

The parties intend this general reference agreement to be specifically enforceable in accordance with California Code of Civil Procedure sec. 638. The parties hereby agree that, subject to disqualification pursuant to California Code of Civil Procedure secs. 641 and 170.1 – 170.5 and California Rules of Court Rule 2.831, the referee shall be

_____.

Should he/she be unable for any reason to act as referee, the parties shall attempt to agree on an alternative referee from the ARC panel. If the parties are unable to do so, then a retired judge or justice on the ARC panel shall be appointed to act as referee by the Presiding Judge of the Superior Court of the county in which the Order of Reference is sought by any of the parties hereto.

Fees and Expenses. A non – refundable administration filing fee per party will be charged when the first hearing/trial date is scheduled.

The compensation of the referee shall be at the usual hourly rate established by ARC for his/her services and shall include all the time spent on the case, including but not limited to the reading of memoranda, review of records, research, deliberation time, and the preparation of a statement of decision. Unless modified by prior request all scheduled time shall be paid in advance as a retainer fee and shall be applied toward any final billing. All statements rendered by ARC shall be due and payable upon receipt. Any sums due and unpaid to ARC by any party to this cause shall be included in and ordered paid in the final order or judgment of the court.

Continuance, Cancellation and Refunds. Continuances of a hearing or trial date are strongly disfavored. If a hearing or trial is cancelled or continued more than 14 days before the scheduled date, the retainer fee will be refunded, less any time expended in preparation. If the matter settled, continued or cancelled is scheduled for 8 hours or longer, a minimum of thirty (30) days advance notice is required to receive a refund unless the hearing or trial can be rescheduled for a date no less than fourteen (14) days before the original hearing or trial date. If the retainer fee has not yet been paid it becomes due and payable upon notice of the continuance or cancellation.

Further Stipulations (Optional). The parties hereby incorporate by reference into this agreement those additional Stipulations which are attached hereto as Exhibits and initialed by the parties.

Dated: _____

_____
Plaintiff

_____
Attorney for Plaintiff

_____
Defendant

_____
Attorney for Defendant

_____

[1]Alternative Resolution Centers, Stipulation Regarding Order of Reference, available at http://www.arc4adr.com/rulesforms.html (last accessed March 25, 2011).

360

COURT CASE NO.: _____

_____

Plaintiff

v.

_____

Defendant

STIPULATION FOR HEARING/TRIAL ON ORDER OF REFERENCE

The undersigned parties hereby agree to submit to [a two-step dispute resolution process to be administered by ARC, first using mediation before judge, justice or other neutral, from the ARC panel, followed, if necessary, by] a hearing/trial on an Order of Reference before a member of the State Bar, retired judge, justice or other neutral, from the ARC panel, to be appointed pursuant to the provisions of California Code of Civil Procedure (CCP) sec. 638, as to the following:

[ ]   all issues remaining in dispute after mediation, whether of fact of law
[ ]   all discovery matters
[ ]   all law and motion matters
[ ]   all pre-trial motions of any kind
[ ]   trial of issues of fact and law
[ ]   all post motions including motions for reconsideration,
       motions for new trial and motions to tax costs, including attorney
       fees and prejudgment interest
[ ]   only the issues of [specify]

The parties understand that the decision of the referee will stand as the decision of the Court, and upon filing of the statement of decision on any of the issues presented with the clerk of the Court, an order or a judgment will be entered thereon in the same manner as if the action had been tried by the Court. The parties hereby waive and give up the right to a jury trial with respect to any and all of the issues submitted to the referee.

The referee shall apply California rules of procedure, evidence, and substantive law in deciding the issues submitted herein.

Dated: _____

_____   _____
Plaintiff   Attorney for Plaintiff(s)

_____   _____
Defendant   Attorney for Defendant(s)

APPENDIX 13F-2

Alternative Resolution Centers Stipulation and Order for Appointment of Temporary Judge According to California Constitution[1]

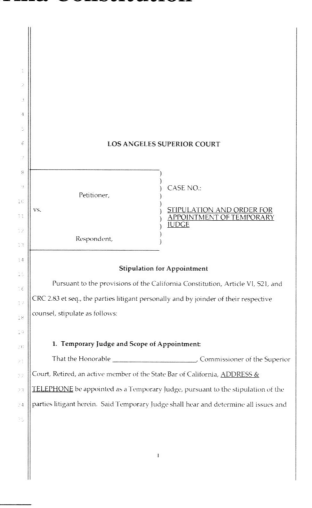

LOS ANGELES SUPERIOR COURT

	)
	) CASE NO.:
Petitioner,	)
	)
vs.	) STIPULATION AND ORDER FOR
	) APPOINTMENT OF TEMPORARY
	) JUDGE
	)
Respondent,	)

Stipulation for Appointment

Pursuant to the provisions of the California Constitution, Article VI, S21, and CRC 2.83 et seq., the parties litigant personally and by joinder of their respective counsel, stipulate as follows:

1. Temporary Judge and Scope of Appointment:

That the Honorable _____, Commissioner of the Superior Court, Retired, an active member of the State Bar of California, <u>ADDRESS &</u> <u>TELEPHONE</u> be appointed as a Temporary Judge, pursuant to the stipulation of the parties litigant herein. Said Temporary Judge shall hear and determine all issues and

---

[1]Alternative Resolution Centers, Stipulation for Temporary Judge, available at http://www.arc4adr.com/rulesforms.html (last accessed March 25, 2011).

1   motions relating to the above matter, and shall continue to act in said capacity until the

2   conclusion of all matters which may be determined within the trial jurisdiction of the

3   Superior Court related thereto, including, but not limited to, all post-trial motions

4   relating to the Judgment filed or to be filed herein.

5   2. **Parties Litigant and Attorneys:**   The parties to this cause and their

6   attorneys are:

7   Parties: Attorneys:

8

9

10

11

12

13

14   3. **Trial Date:**

15

16   (a) The Temporary Judge and the parties have set the trial date(s) as follows:

17

18   (b) The time estimate is:

19   (c) The place of Trial is offices of:

20

21   (d) Completion date of appointment is :

22   (e) Telephone number at which the Court may be reached at during trial is:

23

24

25

2

1

2

3

4

5

6

7

8

9

10

11

12

13

14

15

16

17

18

19

20

21

22

23

24

25

Joinder by Counsel of Record

The foregoing stipulation is approved as to form and content and counsel of record for the respective parties join therein, and on behalf of their respective clients do hereby so stipulate.

Dated: _____   _____

                                             Attorneys for Petitioner

Dated: _____   _____

                                             Attorneys for Respondent

Joinder by the Parties

The parties hereby authorize their attorneys of record to enter into the foregoing stipulation and hereby approve said stipulation and agree to be bound by all of the terms thereof.

Dated: _____   _____

                                             Petitioner

Dated: _____   _____

                                             Respondent

3

Consent and Certification

I, _____, Commissioner of the Superior Court, Retired, an active member of the State Bar of California, hereby consent to act as Temporary Judge until final determination of this matter as set forth in the above Stipulation and I certify that I am aware of and will comply with the applicable provisions of Canon 6 of the Code of Judicial Ethics and California Rule of Court 2.831 et seq.

I, _____, do solemnly swear that I will support and defend the Constitution of the United States and the Constitution of the State of California against all enemies, foreign and domestic; that I will bear true faith and allegiance to the Constitution of the United States and the Constitution of the State of California; that I take this obligation freely, without any mental reservation or purpose of evasion; and that I will well and faithfully discharge the duties upon which I am about to enter.

My original oath dated _____, is on file in Department _____ of the Los Angeles Superior Court

Dated: _____   _____

                               HON. _____, RET.

4

1

Approval and Order Designating Temporary Judge

2

Good cause appearing therefore, it is ordered:

3

    1. The stipulation of the parties that the Honorable _____,

4

Commissioner of the Superior Court, Retired, and an active member of the State Bar of

5

California, act as Temporary Judge in this cause is hereby approved.

6

    2. Commissioner _____, Retired, having consented to so

7

act, is hereby appointed and designated as Temporary Judge to hear and determine this

8

matter until its final determination in the Superior Court, her oath of office having been

9

filed _____.

10

    3. Said appointment shall remain in full force and effect until _____.

11

If there is no final disposition of this case within 30 days of the completion date, this

12

order is subject to revocation by this Court.

13

The terms of the Minute Order of this date are incorporated herein by reference.

14

15

Dated: _____   _____

16

                                    Judge of the Los Angeles Superior Court

17

18

19

20

21

22

23

24

25

5

APPENDIX 13F-3

Alternative Resolution Centers Stipulation for Binding Arbitration[1]

ALTERNATIVE RESOLUTION CENTERS, LLC

STIPULATION TO BINDING ARBITRATION

The undersigned parties hereby agree to submit the following dispute to binding arbitration under ARC Arbitration Rules and request that ARC serve as administrator of the arbitration:

The parties further agree that there shall be a single, neutral arbitrator and, subject to disqualification under the Rules, the arbitrator shall be _____.

The parties understand that by agreeing to binding arbitration, they give up the right to a trial on the merits by judge or jury, the right to a trial de novo, and the right to appeal.

The parties agree that they will faithfully observe this agreement and the Rules, that they will abide by and perform any award rendered by the arbitrator, and that a judgment of the court having jurisdiction may be entered on the award.

[Further Stipulations. The parties hereby incorporate by reference into this agreement those additional Stipulations which are attached hereto as Exhibits and initialed by the parties].

Dated: _____   _____
Plaintiff/Claimant

Dated: _____   _____
Defendant/Respondent

APPROVED:

Dated: _____   _____
Plaintiff/Claimant's Attorney (or
Representative)

APPROVED:

Dated: _____   _____
Defendant/Respondent's Attorney (or
Representative)

Copyright © ARC 2008

---

[1]Alternative Resolution Centers, Stipulation For Binding Arbitration, available at http://www.arc4adr.com/rulesforms.html (last accessed March 25, 2011).

APPENDIX 13F-4

Alternative Resolution Centers Dispute Resolution Clauses (Including e-discovery Clauses)[1]

The parties can provide for the mediation and/or arbitration by inserting the following clauses into their contract(s).

Mediation Clause: "If any controversy or claim arises out of or relates to this contract, or the breach thereof, and if said dispute cannot be settled through direct discussions, the parties agree to attempt to settle the dispute by mediation under the ARC Mediation Rules, before having recourse to arbitration or a judicial forum."

Arbitration Clause: "Any Controversy or claim arising out of or relating to this contract, or the breach thereof, shall be settled by binding arbitration under the ARC Arbitration Rules."

Two-Step Dispute Resolution Clause: "Any controversy or claim arising out of this contract, or the breach thereof, shall be submitted to a two-step dispute resolution process to be administered by ARC. This two-step dispute resolution shall begin with mediation under ARC Mediation Rules, followed immediately, should any dispute remain after mediation is terminated, by the procedure indicated below:

———— final and binding arbitration under ARC Arbitration Rules. Judgment upon an award rendered by the arbitrator may be entered in any court having jurisdiction.

———— hearing/trial by an Order of Reference pursuant to the provisions of California Code of Civil Procedure sec. 638 and in accordance with the ARC Stipulation for Hearing/Trial on Order of Reference executed by the parties, attached hereto as Exhibit ———— and incorporated herein by reference. [Note: The parties should execute the Stipulation at the same time that they execute the underlying agreement; they should check the first box in the first paragraph of the Stipulation.]

Good Faith: "Upon the commencement of any controversy or

---

[1]Alternative Resolution Centers, ARC Dispute Resolution Clauses, available at http://www.arc4adr.com/rulesforms.html (last accessed March 25, 2011).

claim arising out of this contract, or the breach thereof, the parties thereto agree to cooperate in good faith in the voluntary and informal exchange of all non-privileged documents and other information (including electronically stored information relevant to the dispute or claim immediately after commencement of the Arbitration."

Limiting Discovery of Electronically Stored Informat ion: "The production of electronically stored information resulting from any controversy or claim arising out of this contract, or the breach thereof, shall be limited to sources used in the ordinary course of business and made available using generally available technology in a searchable format usable by the receiving party and convenient and cost-effective for the producing party. Absent a showing of compelling need, backup servers, tapes or other sources not used in the ordinary course of business shall not be discoverable."

Limiting Discovery of Metadata: "The discovery of metadata resulting from any controversy or claim arising out of this contract, or the breach thereof, shall be limited to header fields for email correspondence and, absent a showing of compelling need, additional metadata shall not be discoverable."

APPENDIX 13F-5

Alternative Resolution Centers Arbitration Rules—Including e-discovery Rules (March 8, 2011 Version)[1]

ALTERNATIVE RESOLUTION CENTERS (ARC)

ARBITRATION RULES

1.   **Agreement of the Parties.**   These rules shall apply whenever the parties have agreed to arbitrate in accordance with ARC Arbitration Rules and/or whenever the parties agree that ARC shall serve as the administrator of an arbitration.

2.   **Initiation of Arbitration Proceeding.**   The arbitration may be initiated in one of the following ways:

    a.   **By ARC Stipulation.**   The parties may initiate an arbitration by executing an ARC Stipulation to Binding Arbitration.

    b.   **By Submission Agreement.**   The parties, having agreed to submit a pending dispute to arbitration, may request, either orally or in writing, that ARC administer the arbitration. The parties should inform ARC as to the names, addresses, and telephone numbers of all the parties and their attorneys or other representative, if any; the issues to be determined by the arbitrator; the amount of money involved, if any; and the remedies requested.

    c.   **By Pre-Dispute Agreement.**   Where the dispute arises under the terms of a contract in which the parties have agreed to binding arbitration to be administered by ARC or in accordance with ARC Rules, arbitration may be initiated by one party's serving all other parties with notice of the nature of the claim and a demand for arbitration. The claimant shall file two (2) copies of the notice and demand, together with two (2) copies of the contract, with ARC. The party may file a response, which may include a counterclaim. Failure to respond to the demand will not delay the arbitration, and lack of response will be considered a denial of the claim. Any response must be served on the claimant and two (2) copies filed with ARC within thirty (30) days of service of the notice and demand.

3.   **Selection of the Arbitrator.**   ARC shall maintain a special panel of neutrals qualified to serve as arbitrators. The case shall be submitted to a single arbitrator chosen by the parties from the ARC panel. If the parties' stipulation, submission agreement, or pre-dispute agreement names an arbitrator on the panel or specifies a method for selecting an arbitrator from the ARC panel, the arbitrator named shall be appointed or the method specified utilized. Otherwise, the parties may select any mutually agreeable ARC panel member to hear the case. If the parties have not notified ARC of their selection within thirty (30) days from the date of initiating arbitration, ARC shall furnish each party with a list of panel members numbering one more than the number of parties; each party shall strike one name from the list and return the list to ARC within seven (7) days; and ARC shall appoint a name from those names remaining on the list as arbitrator. If a party does not return the list to ARC within the specified time period, all names on the list shall be deemed acceptable to that party.

---

[1]Alternative Resolution Centers, Alternative Resolution Centers Arbitration Rules, available at http://www.arc4adr.com/rulesforms.html (last accessed March 25, 2011).

4.　　**Disclosure and Disqualification.**　The proposed arbitrator shall make disclosures as required by law, including California Code of Civil Procedure (CCP) sec. 1281.9 or its successor statute and the Ethics Standards, in writing within 10 days after notice of the proposed appointment. The disclosures shall be served upon the parties and ARC. Party responses, if any, shall be in accordance with the CCP with a copy served on ARC. After the time for any response has passed, and no timely objection has been received, ARC will deem that the proposed arbitrator has been appointed.

Disqualification of the proposed arbitrator shall be as required by law, including CCP sec. 1281.91 or its successor statute and the Ethics Standards.

5.　　**Vacancy.**　If the proposed arbitrator is disqualified or otherwise cannot serve or if a vacancy occurs after appointment because the arbitrator withdraws, becomes disqualified, or is otherwise determined by ARC to be unable to serve, a substitute arbitrator shall be selected in the manner set forth herein for selection of the original arbitrator.

6.　　**Communications with Arbitrator.**　After the arbitrator is appointed, there shall be no direct communication between the parties and the arbitrator other than at oral hearings. Any other communications from the parties shall be directed to ARC.

7.　　**Time and Place of Hearing.**　After consultation with the parties and the arbitrator, ARC shall fix the date and time of the first hearing. The arbitrator shall fix the date and time of any adjourned hearing at the time of adjournment after conferring with the ARC Administrator.

The parties shall select a mutually agreeable place where the arbitration is to be held, provided the site is acceptable to the arbitrator, and shall notify ARC of the place selected. If a place is not designated at least three (3) days before the date set for hearing, ARC may determine the site, which determination shall be final and binding.

8.　　**Service of Notice.**　Any papers or process necessary or proper for the initiation or continuation of an arbitration under these Rules, for any court action in connection therewith, or for the entry of judgment on an award made thereunder, may be served upon a party by facsimile or mail addressed to such party or its attorney at the last known address for service, or by personal service, or in any other manner permitted by law. ARC may be served by facsimile or mail addressed to its main office (1875 Century Park East, Suite 450, Los Angeles, California, 90067; FAX (310-284-8229), or in any other manner permitted by law.

9.　　**Pre-hearing Conference/Case Management Meeting.**　Once an arbitrator is selected, the parties may request, or the arbitrator may require, that a pre-hearing conference or case management meeting be scheduled to arrange for the exchange of information, stipulations as to uncontested facts, or other matters which will expedite the arbitration proceeding. The arbitrator may recommend non-binding mediation or a settlement conference at this time.

10.   **Mediation or Settlement Conference.**   A mediation or settlement conference may be scheduled at any time with the agreement of the parties and the concurrence of the arbitrator. The mediation or settlement conference may be presided over by the designated arbitrator with the consent of the parties or by such other ARC panel member as the parties may select.

11.   **Stenographic Record.**   Any party wishing a stenographic record shall make arrangements directly with a stenographer and shall notify the other parties of such arrangement in advance of the hearing. After the hearing at which a stenographic record is made, a copy of the transcript shall be made available to the arbitrator and to any other party for inspection. In the absence of a stenographer, the arbitrator may, on his or her own motion, cause the hearing to be tape recorded, and the recording will remain an informal record of the proceeding to serve as an aid to the arbitrator. In no event is ARC obligated to preserve any of the records so made.

12.   **Arbitration in Absence of Party.**   The arbitration may proceed in the absence of any party or representative who, after due notice, fails to appear of fails to obtain an adjournment or continuance. Even if a party defaults, the arbitrator shall require the appearing party to submit such evidence as is necessary for the making of an award.

13.   **Conduct of the Proceedings.**   Except as otherwise provided in these Rules or by agreement of the parties not inconsistent with these Rules, the conduct of the arbitration proceedings shall be governed by the provisions of CCP secs. 1282 - 1284.2.

14.   **Time of Award.**   The award shall be rendered promptly by the arbitrator and, unless otherwise agreed upon by the parties, not more then forty-five (45) days from the date of the closing of the hearing.

15.   **Award Upon Settlement.**   If the parties settle their dispute during the course of the arbitration, the arbitrator, upon their request, may set forth the terms of the agreed settlement in an award or in a mediation consent agreement.

16.   **Delivery of Award to the Parties.**   The parties shall accept as legal delivery of the award the placing of the award or a true copy thereof in the mail by ARC, addressed to a party or to its attorney at the last known address for service, or by personal service of the award, or by the filing of the award in any manner that may be permitted by law.

17.   **Retention, Return and Release of Documents.**   The arbitrator will maintain custody of the exhibits and documents filed during the course of the hearing. After the expiration of 30 days from service of the arbitrator's award, the arbitrator will return to each party those documents and exhibits which the party introduced. ARC has no obligation to preserve copies of any such exhibits or documents.

ARC shall, upon the written request of a party, furnish to such party, at the party's expense, certified facsimiles of any papers in the possession of ARC that may be required in judicial proceedings relating to the arbitration.

18.   **Waiver of Rules.**   Any party who proceeds with the arbitration after knowing that any provision or requirement of these Rules has not been complied with, and fails to state objections thereto in writing, shall be deemed to have waived the right to object.

19.   **Extension of Time.**   ARC may extend any period of time established by these Rules, except the time of making the award. ARC shall notify the parties of any such extension and the reason for it.

20.   **Exclusion of Liability.**   Neither ARC nor any arbitrator shall be liable to any party for any act or omission in connection with any arbitration conducted under these Rules.

21.   **Interpretation and Application of Rules.**   The arbitrator shall interpret and apply these Rules insofar as they relate to the arbitrator's powers and duties. All other Rules shall be interpreted and applied by ARC.

22.   **Fees and Expenses.**   A non-refundable administration/filing fee per party is charged when a hearing is placed on calendar.

The compensation of the arbitrator shall be at the usual hourly rate established by ARC for his/her services and shall include all the time spent on the case, including, but not limited to, pre-hearing conferences or case management meetings, the reading of briefs, review of records, research, and deliberation time. Unless modified by prior agreement of the parties, counsel and/or claims representatives, each party shall bear his/her pro rata share of the arbitration fees. The hourly fee for the scheduled time shall be paid in advance as a retainer fee and shall be applied toward any final billing. All statements rendered by ARC shall be due and payable upon receipt. ARC's agreement to render services is not only with the party, but also with the attorney or other representative in attendance at the hearing.

Each party shall pay its own attorney fees, witness fees, and other expenses incurred for its own benefit, unless otherwise provided by contract, or by statute other than CCP sec. 1032 et seq. Except where the parties specifically agree to the contrary, allowable costs under CCP sec. 1032 et seq. shall not be awarded to the prevailing party, but shall be borne by the party incurring them.

Unless the parties agree otherwise, the cost of the stenographic record, if any is made, and all transcripts thereof, shall be paid by the requesting party. Payment shall be made directly to the reporting agency.

23.   **Continuance, Cancellation and Refund Policy.**   The parties may stipulate to a continuance of a hearing date. CONTINUANCES ARE STRONGLY DISFAVORED. If a hearing date is continued or canceled more than 14 days before the scheduled hearing, the retainer fee will be refunded, less any time expended in preparation for the hearing. However, if the matter continued or cancelled is scheduled for 8 hours or longer, a minimum of thirty days (30) advance notice is required to receive a refund. If the retainer fee has not yet been paid, it becomes due and payable upon notice of the continuance or cancellation.

ELECTRONIC DISCOVERY RULES*

24.   **Preliminary Conference on Electronic Discovery.**   Prior to the pre-hearing conference the parties shall confer regarding steps they can take to facilitate discovery of electronically stored information, preserve and make available potentially relevant data and metadata, limit discovery costs and delay, and avoid discovery disputes. In the event that a party will seek to establish a compelling need to discover media sources other than those used in the ordinary course of business or metadata other than the header section of an email, that party shall put other parties on notice of such need prior to the peliminary conference on electronic discovery.

25.   **The Description of Custodians of Electroncially Stored Information.**
Descriptions of custodians shall specify only custodians who may be reasonably be expected to possess or control electronically stored information that is material to the dispute.

26.   **Limiting the Cost and Burden of Discovery.**   If the cost or burden of a discovery request is disproportionate to the nature of the dispute, the amount in controversy, or the relevance of the materials requested, the arbitrator shall either deny such request or order production on condition that the requesting party advance the reasonable cost of production to the other side, subject to the allocation of costs in the final award.

APPENDIX 13G

2010 ICC Rules of Arbitration[1]

INTRODUCTORY PROVISIONS

Article 1
International Court of Arbitration

1. The International Court of Arbitration (the "Court") of the International Chamber of Commerce (the "ICC") is the arbitration body attached to the ICC. The statutes of the Court are set forth in Appendix I.

Members of the Court are appointed by the World Council of the ICC. The function of the Court is to provide for the settlement by arbitration of business disputes of an international character in accordance with the Rules of Arbitration of the International Chamber of Commerce (the "Rules"). If so empowered by an arbitration agreement, the Court shall also provide for the settlement by arbitration in accordance with these Rules of business disputes not of an international character.

2. The Court does not itself settle disputes. It has the function of ensuring the application of these Rules. It draws up its own Internal Rules (Appendix II).

3. The Chairman of the Court or, in the Chairman's absence or otherwise at his request, one of its Vice-Chairmen shall have the power to take urgent decisions on behalf of the Court, provided that any such decision is reported to the Court at its next session.

4. As provided for in its Internal Rules, the Court may delegate to one or more committees composed of its members the power to take certain decisions, provided that any such decision is reported to the Court at its next session.

5. The Secretariat of the Court (the "Secretariat") under the direction of its Secretary General (the "Secretary General") shall have its seat at the headquarters of the ICC.

---

[1]International Chamber of Commerce, ICC Rules of Arbitration, available at http://iccwbo.org/court/arbitration/id4093/index.html (last accessed March 25, 2011).

Article 2
Definitions

In these Rules:

(i) "Arbitral Tribunal" includes one or more arbitrators.

(ii) "Claimant" includes one or more claimants and "Respondent" includes one or more respondents.

(iii) "Award" includes, inter alia, an interim, partial or final Award.

Article 3
Written Notifications or Communications; Time Limits

1. All pleadings and other written communications submitted by any party, as well as all documents annexed thereto, shall be supplied in a number of copies sufficient to provide one copy for each party, plus one for each arbitrator, and one for the Secretariat. A copy of any communication from the Arbitral Tribunal to the parties shall be sent to the Secretariat.

2. All notifications or communications from the Secretariat and the Arbitral Tribunal shall be made to the last address of the party or its representative for whom the same are intended, as notified either by the party in question or by the other party. Such notification or communication may be made by delivery against receipt, registered post, courier, facsimile transmission, telex, telegram or any other means of telecommunication that provides a record of the sending thereof.

3. A notification or communication shall be deemed to have been made on the day it was received by the party itself or by its representative, or would have been received if made in accordance with the preceding paragraph.

4. Periods of time specified in or fixed under the present Rules shall start to run on the day following the date a notification or communication is deemed to have been made in accordance with the preceding paragraph. When the day next following such date is an official holiday, or a non-business day in the country where the notification or communication is deemed to have been made, the period of time shall commence on the first following business day. Official holidays and non-business days are included in the calculation of the period of time. If the last day of the relevant period of time granted is an official holiday or a non-business day in the country where the notification or communication is deemed to have been made, the period of time shall expire at the end of the first following business day.

COMMENCING THE ARBITRATION

Article 4
Request for Arbitration

1. A party wishing to have recourse to arbitration under these Rules shall submit its Request for Arbitration (the "Request") to the Secretariat, which shall notify the Claimant and Respondent of the receipt of the Request and the date of such receipt.

2. The date on which the Request is received by the Secretariat shall, for all purposes, be deemed to be the date of the commencement of the arbitral proceedings.

3. The Request shall, inter alia, contain the following information:
   a) the name in full, description and address of each of the parties;
   b) a description of the nature and circumstances of the dispute giving rise to the claim(s);
   c) a statement of the relief sought, including, to the extent possible, an indication of any amount(s) claimed;
   d) the relevant agreements and, in particular, the arbitration agreement;
   e) all relevant particulars concerning the number of arbitrators and their choice in accordance with the provisions of Articles 8, 9 and 10, and any nomination of an arbitrator required thereby; and
   f) any comments as to the place of arbitration, the applicable rules of law and the language of the arbitration.

4. Together with the Request, the Claimant shall submit the number of copies thereof required by Article 3(1) and shall make the advance payment on administrative expenses required by Appendix III ("Arbitration Costs and Fees") in force on the date the Request is submitted. In the event that the Claimant fails to comply with either of these requirements, the Secretariat may fix a time limit within which the Claimant must comply, failing which the file shall be closed without prejudice to the right of the Claimant to submit the same claims at a later date in another Request.

5. The Secretariat shall send a copy of the Request and the documents annexed thereto to the Respondent for its Answer to the Request once the Secretariat has sufficient copies of the Request and the required advance payment.

6. When a party submits a Request in connection with a legal relationship in respect of which arbitration proceedings between the same parties are already pending under these Rules, the

Court may, at the request of a party, decide to include the claims contained in the Request in the pending proceedings provided that the Terms of Reference have not been signed or approved by the Court. Once the Terms of Reference have been signed or approved by the Court, claims may only be included in the pending proceedings subject to the provisions of Article 19.

Article 5
Answer to the Request; Counterclaims

1. Within 30 days from the receipt of the Request from the Secretariat, the Respondent shall file an Answer (the "Answer") which shall, inter alia, contain the following information:
   a) its name in full, description and address;
   b) its comments as to the nature and circumstances of the dispute giving rise to the claim(s);
   c) its response to the relief sought;
   d) any comments concerning the number of arbitrators and their choice in light of the Claimant's proposals and in accordance with the provisions of Articles 8, 9 and 10, and any nomination of an arbitrator required thereby; and
   e) any comments as to the place of arbitration, the applicable rules of law and the language of the arbitration.
2. The Secretariat may grant the Respondent an extension of the time for filing the Answer, provided the application for such an extension contains the Respondent's comments concerning the number of arbitrators and their choice and, where required by Articles 8, 9 and 10, the nomination of an arbitrator. If the Respondent fails to do so, the Court shall proceed in accordance with these Rules.
3. The Answer shall be supplied to the Secretariat in the number of copies specified by Article 3(1).
4. A copy of the Answer and the documents annexed thereto shall be communicated by the Secretariat to the Claimant.
5. Any counterclaim(s) made by the Respondent shall be filed with its Answer and shall provide:
   a) a description of the nature and circumstances of the dispute giving rise to the counterclaim(s); and
   b) a statement of the relief sought, including, to the extent possible, an indication of any amount(s) counterclaimed.
6. The Claimant shall file a reply to any counterclaim within 30 days from the date of receipt of the counterclaim(s) communicated by the Secretariat. The Secretariat may grant the Claimant an extension of time for filing the reply.

Article 6
Effect of the Arbitration Agreement

1. Where the parties have agreed to submit to arbitration under the Rules, they shall be deemed to have submitted ipso facto to the Rules in effect on the date of commencement of the arbitration proceedings, unless they have agreed to submit to the Rules in effect on the date of their arbitration agreement.

2. If the Respondent does not file an Answer, as provided by Article 5, or if any party raises one or more pleas concerning the existence, validity or scope of the arbitration agreement, the Court may decide, without prejudice to the admissibility or merits of the plea or pleas, that the arbitration shall proceed if it is prima facie satisfied that an arbitration agreement under the Rules may exist. In such a case, any decision as to the jurisdiction of the Arbitral Tribunal shall be taken by the Arbitral Tribunal itself. If the Court is not so satisfied, the parties shall be notified that the arbitration cannot proceed. In such a case, any party retains the right to ask any court having jurisdiction whether or not there is a binding arbitration agreement.

3. If any of the parties refuses or fails to take part in the arbitration or any stage thereof, the arbitration shall proceed notwithstanding such refusal or failure.

4. Unless otherwise agreed, the Arbitral Tribunal shall not cease to have jurisdiction by reason of any claim that the contract is null and void or allegation that it is non-existent, provided that the Arbitral Tribunal upholds the validity of the arbitration agreement. The Arbitral Tribunal shall continue to have jurisdiction to determine the respective rights of the parties and to adjudicate their claims and pleas even though the contract itself may be non-existent or null and void.

THE ARBITRAL TRIBUNAL

Article 7
General Provisions

1. Every arbitrator must be and remain independent of the parties involved in the arbitration.

2. Before appointment or confirmation, a prospective arbitrator shall sign a statement of independence and disclose in writing to the Secretariat any facts or circumstances which might be of such a nature as to call into question the arbitrator's independence in the eyes of the parties. The Secretariat shall

provide such information to the parties in writing and fix a time limit for any comments from them.

3. An arbitrator shall immediately disclose in writing to the Secretariat and to the parties any facts or circumstances of a similar nature which may arise during the arbitration.

4. The decisions of the Court as to the appointment, confirmation, challenge or replacement of an arbitrator shall be final and the reasons for such decisions shall not be communicated.

5. By accepting to serve, every arbitrator undertakes to carry out his responsibilities in accordance with these Rules.

6. Insofar as the parties have not provided otherwise, the Arbitral Tribunal shall be constituted in accordance with the provisions of Articles 8, 9 and 10.

Article 8
Number of Arbitrators

1. The disputes shall be decided by a sole arbitrator or by three arbitrators.

2. Where the parties have not agreed upon the number of arbitrators, the Court shall appoint a sole arbitrator, save where it appears to the Court that the dispute is such as to warrant the appointment of three arbitrators. In such case, the Claimant shall nominate an arbitrator within a period of 15 days from the receipt of the notification of the decision of the Court, and the Respondent shall nominate an arbitrator within a period of 15 days from the receipt of the notification of the nomination made by the Claimant.

3. Where the parties have agreed that the dispute shall be settled by a sole arbitrator, they may, by agreement, nominate the sole arbitrator for confirmation. If the parties fail to nominate a sole arbitrator within 30 days from the date when the Claimant's Request for Arbitration has been received by the other party, or within such additional time as may be allowed by the Secretariat, the sole arbitrator shall be appointed by the Court.

4. Where the dispute is to be referred to three arbitrators, each party shall nominate in the Request and the Answer, respectively, one arbitrator for confirmation. If a party fails to nominate an arbitrator, the appointment shall be made by the Court. The third arbitrator, who will act as chairman of the Arbitral Tribunal, shall be appointed by the Court, unless the parties have agreed upon another procedure for such appointment, in which case the nomination will be subject to confirmation pursuant to Article 9. Should such procedure not result in

a nomination within the time limit fixed by the parties or the Court, the third arbitrator shall be appointed by the Court.

Article 9
Appointment and Confirmation of the Arbitrators

1. In confirming or appointing arbitrators, the Court shall consider the prospective arbitrator's nationality, residence and other relationships with the countries of which the parties or the other arbitrators are nationals and the prospective arbitrator's availability and ability to conduct the arbitration in accordance with these Rules. The same shall apply where the Secretary General confirms arbitrators pursuant to Article 9(2).

2. The Secretary General may confirm as co-arbitrators, sole arbitrators and chairmen of Arbitral Tribunals persons nominated by the parties or pursuant to their particular agreements, provided they have filed a statement of independence without qualification or a qualified statement of independence has not given rise to objections. Such confirmation shall be reported to the Court at its next session. If the Secretary General considers that a co-arbitrator, sole arbitrator or chairman of an Arbitral Tribunal should not be confirmed, the matter shall be submitted to the Court.

3. Where the Court is to appoint a sole arbitrator or the chairman of an Arbitral Tribunal, it shall make the appointment upon a proposal of a National Committee of the ICC that it considers to be appropriate. If the Court does not accept the proposal made, or if the National Committee fails to make the proposal requested within the time limit fixed by the Court, the Court may repeat its request or may request a proposal from another National Committee that it considers to be appropriate.

4. Where the Court considers that the circumstances so demand, it may choose the sole arbitrator or the chairman of the Arbitral Tribunal from a country where there is no National Committee, provided that neither of the parties objects within the time limit fixed by the Court.

5. The sole arbitrator or the chairman of the Arbitral Tribunal shall be of a nationality other than those of the parties. However, in suitable circumstances and provided that neither of the parties objects within the time limit fixed by the Court, the sole arbitrator or the chairman of the Arbitral Tribunal may be chosen from a country of which any of the parties is a national.

6. Where the Court is to appoint an arbitrator on behalf of a

party which has failed to nominate one, it shall make the appointment upon a proposal of the National Committee of the country of which that party is a national. If the Court does not accept the proposal made, or if the National Committee fails to make the proposal requested within the time limit fixed by the Court, or if the country of which the said party is a national has no National Committee, the Court shall be at liberty to choose any person whom it regards as suitable. The Secretariat shall inform the National Committee, if one exists, of the country of which such person is a national.

Article 10
Multiple Parties
1. Where there are multiple parties, whether as Claimant or as Respondent, and where the dispute is to be referred to three arbitrators, the multiple Claimants, jointly, and the multiple Respondents, jointly, shall nominate an arbitrator for confirmation pursuant to Article 9.
2. In the absence of such a joint nomination and where all parties are unable to agree to a method for the constitution of the Arbitral Tribunal, the Court may appoint each member of the Arbitral Tribunal and shall designate one of them to act as chairman. In such case, the Court shall be at liberty to choose any person it regards as suitable to act as arbitrator, applying Article 9 when it considers this appropriate.

Article 11
Challenge of Arbitrators
1. A challenge of an arbitrator, whether for an alleged lack of independence or otherwise, shall be made by the submission to the Secretariat of a written statement specifying the facts and circumstances on which the challenge is based.
2. For a challenge to be admissible, it must be sent by a party either within 30 days from receipt by that party of the notification of the appointment or confirmation of the arbitrator, or within 30 days from the date when the party making the challenge was informed of the facts and circumstances on which the challenge is based if such date is subsequent to the receipt of such notification.
3. The Court shall decide on the admissibility and, at the same time, if necessary, on the merits of a challenge after the Secretariat has afforded an opportunity for the arbitrator concerned, the other party or parties and any other members of the Arbitral Tribunal to comment in writing within a suit-

able period of time. Such comments shall be communicated to the parties and to the arbitrators.

Article 12
Replacement of Arbitrators

1. An arbitrator shall be replaced upon his death, upon the acceptance by the Court of the arbitrator's resignation, upon acceptance by the Court of a challenge, or upon the request of all the parties.
2. An arbitrator shall also be replaced on the Court's own initiative when it decides that he is prevented *de jure* or *de facto* from fulfilling his functions, or that he is not fulfilling his functions in accordance with the Rules or within the prescribed time limits.
3. When, on the basis of information that has come to its attention, the Court considers applying Article 12(2), it shall decide on the matter after the arbitrator concerned, the parties and any other members of the Arbitral Tribunal have had an opportunity to comment in writing within a suitable period of time. Such comments shall be communicated to the parties and to the arbitrators.
4. When an arbitrator is to be replaced, the Court has discretion to decide whether or not to follow the original nominating process. Once reconstituted, and after having invited the parties to comment, the Arbitral Tribunal shall determine if and to what extent prior proceedings shall be repeated before the reconstituted Arbitral Tribunal.
5. Subsequent to the closing of the proceedings, instead of replacing an arbitrator who has died or been removed by the Court pursuant to Articles 12(1) and 12(2), the Court may decide, when it considers it appropriate, that the remaining arbitrators shall continue the arbitration. In making such determination, the Court shall take into account the views of the remaining arbitrators and of the parties and such other matters that it considers appropriate in the circumstances.

THE ARBITRAL PROCEEDINGS

Article 13
Transmission of the File to the Arbitral Tribunal

The Secretariat shall transmit the file to the Arbitral Tribunal as soon as it has been constituted, provided the advance on costs requested by the Secretariat at this stage has been paid.

Article 14
Place of the Arbitration
1. The place of the arbitration shall be fixed by the Court unless agreed upon by the parties.
2. The Arbitral Tribunal may, after consultation with the parties, conduct hearings and meetings at any location it considers appropriate unless otherwise agreed by the parties.
3. The Arbitral Tribunal may deliberate at any location it considers appropriate.

Article 15
Rules Governing the Proceedings
1. The proceedings before the Arbitral Tribunal shall be governed by these Rules and, where these Rules are silent, by any rules which the parties or, failing them, the Arbitral Tribunal may settle on, whether or not reference is thereby made to the rules of procedure of a national law to be applied to the arbitration.
2. In all cases, the Arbitral Tribunal shall act fairly and impartially and ensure that each party has a reasonable opportunity to present its case.

Article 16
Language of the Arbitration

In the absence of an agreement by the parties, the Arbitral Tribunal shall determine the language or languages of the arbitration, due regard being given to all relevant circumstances, including the language of the contract.

Article 17
Applicable Rules of Law
1. The parties shall be free to agree upon the rules of law to be applied by the Arbitral Tribunal to the merits of the dispute. In the absence of any such agreement, the Arbitral Tribunal shall apply the rules of law which it determines to be appropriate.
2. In all cases the Arbitral Tribunal shall take account of the provisions of the contract and the relevant trade usages.
3. The Arbitral Tribunal shall assume the powers of an amiable compositeur or decide ex aequo et bono only if the parties have agreed to give it such powers.

Article 18
Terms of Reference; Procedural Timetable

1. As soon as it has received the file from the Secretariat, the Arbitral Tribunal shall draw up, on the basis of documents or in the presence of the parties and in the light of their most recent submissions, a document defining its Terms of Reference. This document shall include the following particulars:

   a) the full names and descriptions of the parties;

   b) the addresses of the parties to which notifications and communications arising in the course of the arbitration may be made;

   c) a summary of the parties' respective claims and of the relief sought by each party, with an indication to the extent possible of the amounts claimed or counterclaimed;

   d) unless the Arbitral Tribunal considers it inappropriate, a list of issues to be determined;

   e) the full names, descriptions and addresses of the arbitrators;

   f) the place of the arbitration; and

   g) particulars of the applicable procedural rules and, if such is the case, reference to the power conferred upon the Arbitral Tribunal to act as amiable compositeur or to decide ex aequo et bono.

2. The Terms of Reference shall be signed by the parties and the Arbitral Tribunal. Within two months of the date on which the file has been transmitted to it, the Arbitral Tribunal shall transmit to the Court the Terms of Reference signed by it and by the parties. The Court may extend this time limit pursuant to a reasoned request from the Arbitral Tribunal or on its own initiative if it decides it is necessary to do so.

3. If any of the parties refuses to take part in the drawing up of the Terms of Reference or to sign the same, they shall be submitted to the Court for approval. When the Terms of Reference have been signed in accordance with Article 18(2) or approved by the Court, the arbitration shall proceed.

4. When drawing up the Terms of Reference, or as soon as possible thereafter, the Arbitral Tribunal, after having consulted the parties, shall establish in a separate document a provisional timetable that it intends to follow for the conduct of the arbitration and shall communicate it to the Court and the parties. Any subsequent modifications of the provisional timetable shall be communicated to the Court and the parties.

Article 19
New Claims

After the Terms of Reference have been signed or approved by the Court, no party shall make new claims or counterclaims which fall outside the limits of the Terms of Reference unless it has been authorized to do so by the Arbitral Tribunal, which shall consider the nature of such new claims or counterclaims, the stage of the arbitration and other relevant circumstances.

Article 20
Establishing the Facts of the Case

1. The Arbitral Tribunal shall proceed within as short a time as possible to establish the facts of the case by all appropriate means.
2. After studying the written submissions of the parties and all documents relied upon, the Arbitral Tribunal shall hear the parties together in person if any of them so requests or, failing such a request, it may of its own motion decide to hear them.
3. The Arbitral Tribunal may decide to hear witnesses, experts appointed by the parties or any other person, in the presence of the parties, or in their absence provided they have been duly summoned.
4. The Arbitral Tribunal, after having consulted the parties, may appoint one or more experts, define their terms of reference and receive their reports. At the request of a party, the parties shall be given the opportunity to question at a hearing any such expert appointed by the Tribunal.
5. At any time during the proceedings, the Arbitral Tribunal may summon any party to provide additional evidence.
6. The Arbitral Tribunal may decide the case solely on the documents submitted by the parties unless any of the parties requests a hearing.
7. The Arbitral Tribunal may take measures for protecting trade secrets and confidential information.

Article 21
Hearings

1. When a hearing is to be held, the Arbitral Tribunal, giving reasonable notice, shall summon the parties to appear before it on the day and at the place fixed by it.
2. If any of the parties, although duly summoned, fails to appear without valid excuse, the Arbitral Tribunal shall have the power to proceed with the hearing.
3. The Arbitral Tribunal shall be in full charge of the hearings,

at which all the parties shall be entitled to be present. Save with the approval of the Arbitral Tribunal and the parties, persons not involved in the proceedings shall not be admitted.

4. The parties may appear in person or through duly authorized representatives. In addition, they may be assisted by advisers.

Article 22
Closing of the Proceedings

1. When it is satisfied that the parties have had a reasonable opportunity to present their cases, the Arbitral Tribunal shall declare the proceedings closed. Thereafter, no further submission or argument may be made, or evidence produced, unless requested or authorized by the Arbitral Tribunal.

2. When the Arbitral Tribunal has declared the proceedings closed, it shall indicate to the Secretariat an approximate date by which the draft Award will be submitted to the Court for approval pursuant to Article 27. Any postponement of that date shall be communicated to the Secretariat by the Arbitral Tribunal.

Article 23
Conservatory and Interim Measures

1. Unless the parties have otherwise agreed, as soon as the file has been transmitted to it, the Arbitral Tribunal may, at the request of a party, order any interim or conservatory measure it deems appropriate. The Arbitral Tribunal may make the granting of any such measure subject to appropriate security being furnished by the requesting party. Any such measure shall take the form of an order, giving reasons, or of an Award, as the Arbitral Tribunal considers appropriate.

2. Before the file is transmitted to the Arbitral Tribunal, and in appropriate circumstances even thereafter, the parties may apply to any competent judicial authority for interim or conservatory measures. The application of a party to a judicial authority for such measures or for the implementation of any such measures ordered by an Arbitral Tribunal shall not be deemed to be an infringement or a waiver of the arbitration agreement and shall not affect the relevant powers reserved to the Arbitral Tribunal. Any such application and any measures taken by the judicial authority must be notified without delay to the Secretariat. The Secretariat shall inform the Arbitral Tribunal thereof.

AWARDS

Article 24
Time Limit for the Award
1. The time limit within which the Arbitral Tribunal must render its final Award is six months. Such time limit shall start to run from the date of the last signature by the Arbitral Tribunal or by the parties of the Terms of Reference or, in the case of application of Article 18(3), the date of the notification to the Arbitral Tribunal by the Secretariat of the approval of the Terms of Reference by the Court.
2. The Court may extend this time limit pursuant to a reasoned request from the Arbitral Tribunal or on its own initiative if it decides it is necessary to do so.

Article 25
Making of the Award
1. When the Arbitral Tribunal is composed of more than one arbitrator, an Award is given by a majority decision. If there be no majority, the Award shall be made by the chairman of the Arbitral Tribunal alone.
2. The Award shall state the reasons upon which it is based.
3. The Award shall be deemed to be made at the place of the arbitration and on the date stated therein.

Article 26
Award by Consent
   If the parties reach a settlement after the file has been transmitted to the Arbitral Tribunal in accordance with Article 13, the settlement shall be recorded in the form of an Award made by consent of the parties if so requested by the parties and if the Arbitral Tribunal agrees to do so.

Article 27
Scrutiny of the Award by the Court
   Before signing any Award, the Arbitral Tribunal shall submit it in draft form to the Court. The Court may lay down modifications as to the form of the Award and, without affecting the Arbitral Tribunal's liberty of decision, may also draw its attention to points of substance. No Award shall be rendered by the Arbitral Tribunal until it has been approved by the Court as to its form.

Article 28
Notification, Deposit and Enforceability of the Award

1. Once an Award has been made, the Secretariat shall notify to the parties the text signed by the Arbitral Tribunal, provided always that the costs of the arbitration have been fully paid to the ICC by the parties or by one of them.

2. Additional copies certified true by the Secretary General shall be made available on request and at any time to the parties, but to no one else.

3. By virtue of the notification made in accordance with Paragraph 1 of this Article, the parties waive any other form of notification or deposit on the part of the Arbitral Tribunal.

4. An original of each Award made in accordance with the present Rules shall be deposited with the Secretariat.

5. The Arbitral Tribunal and the Secretariat shall assist the parties in complying with whatever further formalities may be necessary.

6. Every Award shall be binding on the parties. By submitting the dispute to arbitration under these Rules, the parties undertake to carry out any Award without delay and shall be deemed to have waived their right to any form of recourse insofar as such waiver can validly be made.

Article 29
Correction and Interpretation of the Award

1. On its own initiative, the Arbitral Tribunal may correct a clerical, computational or typographical error, or any errors of similar nature contained in an Award, provided such correction is submitted for approval to the Court within 30 days of the date of such Award.

2. Any application of a party for the correction of an error of the kind referred to in Article 29(1), or for the interpretation of an Award, must be made to the Secretariat within 30 days of the receipt of the Award by such party, in a number of copies as stated in Article 3(1). After transmittal of the application to the Arbitral Tribunal, the latter shall grant the other party a short time limit, normally not exceeding 30 days, from the receipt of the application by that party, to submit any comments thereon. If the Arbitral Tribunal decides to correct or interpret the Award, it shall submit its decision in draft form to the Court not later than 30 days following the expiration of the time limit for the receipt of any comments from the other party or within such other period as the Court may decide.

3. The decision to correct or to interpret the Award shall take the form of an addendum and shall constitute part of the Award. The provisions of Articles 25, 27 and 28 shall apply mutatis mutandis.

COSTS

Article 30
Advance to Cover the Costs of the Arbitration

1. After receipt of the Request, the Secretary General may request the Claimant to pay a provisional advance in an amount intended to cover the costs of arbitration until the Terms of Reference have been drawn up.

2. As soon as practicable, the Court shall fix the advance on costs in an amount likely to cover the fees and expenses of the arbitrators and the ICC administrative costs for the claims and counterclaims which have been referred to it by the parties. This amount may be subject to readjustment at any time during the arbitration. Where, apart from the claims, counterclaims are submitted, the Court may fix separate advances on costs for the claims and the counterclaims.

3. The advance on costs fixed by the Court shall be payable in equal shares by the Claimant and the Respondent. Any provisional advance paid on the basis of Article 30(1) will be considered as a partial payment thereof. However, any party shall be free to pay the whole of the advance on costs in respect of the principal claim or the counterclaim should the other party fail to pay its share. When the Court has set separate advances on costs in accordance with Article 30(2), each of the parties shall pay the advance on costs corresponding to its claims.

4. When a request for an advance on costs has not been complied with, and after consultation with the Arbitral Tribunal, the Secretary General may direct the Arbitral Tribunal to suspend its work and set a time limit, which must be not less than 15 days, on the expiry of which the relevant claims, or counterclaims, shall be considered as withdrawn. Should the party in question wish to object to this measure, it must make a request within the aforementioned period for the matter to be decided by the Court. Such party shall not be prevented, on the ground of such withdrawal, from reintroducing the same claims or counterclaims at a later date in another proceeding.

5. If one of the parties claims a right to a set-off with regard to either claims or counterclaims, such set-off shall be taken into account in determining the advance to cover the costs of arbitration in the same way as a separate claim insofar as it may require the Arbitral Tribunal to consider additional matters.

Article 31
Decision as to the Costs of the Arbitration

1. The costs of the arbitration shall include the fees and expenses of the arbitrators and the ICC administrative expenses fixed by the Court, in accordance with the scale in force at the time of the commencement of the arbitral proceedings, as well as the fees and expenses of any experts appointed by the Arbitral Tribunal and the reasonable legal and other costs incurred by the parties for the arbitration.
2. The Court may fix the fees of the arbitrators at a figure higher or lower than that which would result from the application of the relevant scale should this be deemed necessary due to the exceptional circumstances of the case. Decisions on costs other than those fixed by the Court may be taken by the Arbitral Tribunal at any time during the proceedings.
3. The final Award shall fix the costs of the arbitration and decide which of the parties shall bear them or in what proportion they shall be borne by the parties.

MISCELLANEOUS

Article 32
Modified Time Limits

1. The parties may agree to shorten the various time limits set out in these Rules. Any such agreement entered into subsequent to the constitution of an Arbitral Tribunal shall become effective only upon the approval of the Arbitral Tribunal.
2. The Court, on its own initiative, may extend any time limit which has been modified pursuant to Article 32(1) if it decides that it is necessary to do so in order that the Arbitral Tribunal or the Court may fulfil their responsibilities in accordance with these Rules.

Article 33
Waiver

A party which proceeds with the arbitration without raising its objection to a failure to comply with any provision of these Rules, or of any other rules applicable to the proceedings, any direction given by the Arbitral Tribunal, or any requirement under the arbitration agreement relating to the constitution of the Arbitral Tribunal, or to the conduct of the proceedings, shall be deemed to have waived its right to object.

Article 34
Exclusion of Liability

Neither the arbitrators, nor the Court and its members, nor the ICC and its employees, nor the ICC National Committees shall be liable to any person for any act or omission in connection with the arbitration.

Article 35
General Rule

In all matters not expressly provided for in these Rules, the Court and the Arbitral Tribunal shall act in the spirit of these Rules and shall make every effort to make sure that the Award is enforceable at law.

APPENDIX 13H-1

London Court of International Arbitration Arbitration Rules[1]

LCIA ARBITRATION RULES

Effective 1 January 1998

Where any agreement, submission or reference provides in writing and in whatsoever manner for arbitration under the rules of the LCIA or by the Court of the LCIA ("the LCIA Court"), the parties shall be taken to have agreed in writing that the arbitration shall be conducted in accordance with the following rules ("the Rules") or such amended rules as the LCIA may have adopted hereafter to take effect before the commencement of the arbitration. The Rules include the Schedule of Costs in effect at the commencement of the arbitration, as separately amended from time to time by the LCIA Court.

CONTENTS

---

[1]London Court of International Arbitration, LCIA Arbitration Rules, available at http://www.lcia.org/Dispute__Resolution__Services/LCIA__Arbitration__Rules.aspx (last accessed March 25, 2011).

Article 1   The Request for Arbitration

1.1   Any party wishing to commence an arbitration under these Rules ("the Claimant") shall send to the Registrar of the LCIA Court ("the Registrar") a written request for arbitration ("the Request"), containing or accompanied by:

(a)   the names, addresses, telephone, facsimile, telex and e-mail numbers (if known) of the parties to the arbitration and of their legal representatives;

(b)   a copy of the written arbitration clause or separate written arbitration agreement invoked by the Claimant ("the Arbitration Agreement"), together with a copy of the contractual documentation in which the arbitration clause is contained or in respect of which the arbitration arises;

(c)   a brief statement describing the nature and circumstances of the dispute, and specifying the claims advanced by the Claimant against another party to the arbitration ("the Respondent");

(d)   a statement of any matters (such as the seat or language(s) of the arbitration, or the number of arbitrators, or their qualifications or identities) on which the parties have already agreed in writing for the arbitration or in respect of which the Claimant wishes to make a proposal;

(e)   if the Arbitration Agreement calls for party nomination of arbitrators, the name, address, telephone, facsimile, telex and e-mail numbers (if known) of the Claimant's nominee;

(f)   the fee prescribed in the Schedule of Costs (without which the Request shall be treated as not having been received by the Registrar and the arbitration as not having been commenced);

(g)   confirmation to the Registrar that copies of the Request (including all accompanying documents) have been or are being served simultaneously on all other parties to the arbitration by one or more means of service to be identified in such confirmation.

1.2   The date of receipt by the Registrar of the Request shall be treated as the date on which the arbitration has commenced for all purposes. The Request (including all accompanying documents) should be submitted to the Registrar in two copies where a sole arbitrator should be appointed, or, if the parties have agreed or the Claimant considers that three arbitrators should be appointed, in four copies.

Article 2   The Response

2.1   Within 30 days of service of the Request on the Respondent, (or such lesser period fixed by the LCIA Court), the Respondent shall send to the Registrar a written response to the Request ("the Response"), containing or accompanied by:

(a)   confirmation or denial of all or part of the claims advanced by the Claimant in the Request;

(b)   a brief statement describing the nature and circumstances of any counterclaims advanced by the Respondent against the Claimant;

(c)   comment in response to any statements contained in the Request, as called for under Article 1.1(d), on matters relating to the conduct of the arbitration;

(d)   if the Arbitration Agreement calls for party nomination of arbitrators, the name, address, telephone, facsimile, telex and e-mail numbers (if known) of the Respondent's nominee; and

(e)   confirmation to the Registrar that copies of the Response (including all accompanying documents) have been or are being served simultaneously on all other parties to the arbitration by one or more means of service to be identified in such confirmation.

2.2   The Response (including all accompanying documents) should be submitted to the Registrar in two copies, or if the parties have agreed or the Respondent considers that three arbitrators should be appointed, in four copies.

2.3   Failure to send a Response shall not preclude the Respondent from denying any claim or from advancing a counterclaim in the arbitration. However, if the Arbitration Agreement calls for party nomination of arbitrators, failure to send a Response or to nominate an arbitrator within time or at all shall constitute an irrevocable waiver of that party's opportunity to nominate an arbitrator.

Article 3   The LCIA Court and Registrar

3.1   The functions of the LCIA Court under these Rules shall be performed in its name by the President or a Vice-President of the LCIA Court or by a division of three or five members of the LCIA Court appointed by the President or a Vice-President of the LCIA Court, as determined by the President.

3.2   The functions of the Registrar under these Rules shall be performed by the Registrar or any deputy Registrar of the LCIA Court under the supervision of the LCIA Court.

3.3   All communications from any party or arbitrator to the LCIA Court shall be addressed to the Registrar.

Article 4   Notices and Periods of Time

4.1   Any notice or other communication that may be or is required to be given by a party under these Rules shall be in writing and shall be delivered by registered postal or courier service or transmitted by facsimile, telex, e-mail or any other means of telecommunication that provide a record of its transmission.

4.2   A party's last-known residence or place of business during the arbitration shall be a valid address for the purpose of any notice or other communication in the absence of any notification of a change to such address by that party to the other parties, the Arbitral Tribunal and the Registrar.

4.3   For the purpose of determining the date of commencement of a time limit, a notice or other communication shall be treated as having been received on the day it is delivered or, in the case of telecommunications, transmitted in accordance with Articles 4.1 and 4.2.

4.4   For the purpose of determining compliance with a time limit, a notice or other communication shall be treated as having been sent, made or transmitted if it is dispatched in accordance with Articles 4.1 and 4.2 prior to or on the date of the expiration of the time-limit.

4.5   Notwithstanding the above, any notice or communication by one party may be addressed to another party in the manner agreed in writing between them or, failing such agreement, according to the practice followed in the course of their previous dealings or in whatever manner ordered by the Arbitral Tribunal.

4.6   For the purpose of calculating a period of time under these Rules, such period shall begin to run on the day following the day when a notice or other communication is received. If the last day of such period is an official holiday or a non-business day at the residence or place of business of the addressee, the period is extended until the first business day which follows. Official holidays or non-business days occurring during the running of the period of time are included in calculating that period.

4.7   The Arbitral Tribunal may at any time extend (even where the period of time has expired) or abridge any period of time prescribed under these Rules or under the Arbitration Agreement for the conduct of the arbitration, including any notice or communication to be served by one party on any other party.

3

Article 5   Formation of the Arbitral Tribunal

5.1   The expression "the Arbitral Tribunal" in these Rules includes a sole arbitrator or all the arbitrators where more than one. All references to an arbitrator shall include the masculine and feminine. (References to the President, Vice-President and members of the LCIA Court, the Registrar or deputy Registrar, expert, witness, party and legal representative shall be similarly understood).

5.2   All arbitrators conducting an arbitration under these Rules shall be and remain at all times impartial and independent of the parties; and none shall act in the arbitration as advocates for any party. No arbitrator, whether before or after appointment, shall advise any party on the merits or outcome of the dispute.

5.3   Before appointment by the LCIA Court, each arbitrator shall furnish to the Registrar a written resume of his past and present professional positions; he shall agree in writing upon fee rates conforming to the Schedule of Costs; and he shall sign a declaration to the effect that there are no circumstances known to him likely to give rise to any justified doubts as to his impartiality or independence, other than any circumstances disclosed by him in the declaration. Each arbitrator shall thereby also assume a continuing duty forthwith to disclose any such circumstances to the LCIA Court, to any other members of the Arbitral Tribunal and to all the parties if such circumstances should arise after the date of such declaration and before the arbitration is concluded.

5.4   The LCIA Court shall appoint the Arbitral Tribunal as soon as practicable after receipt by the Registrar of the Response or after the expiry of 30 days following service of the Request upon the Respondent if no Response is received by the Registrar (or such lesser period fixed by the LCIA Court). The LCIA Court may proceed with the formation of the Arbitral Tribunal notwithstanding that the Request is incomplete or the Response is missing, late or incomplete. A sole arbitrator shall be appointed unless the parties have agreed in writing otherwise, or unless the LCIA Court determines that in view of all the circumstances of the case a three-member tribunal is appropriate.

5.5   The LCIA Court alone is empowered to appoint arbitrators. The LCIA Court will appoint arbitrators with due regard for any particular method or criteria of selection agreed in writing by the parties. In selecting arbitrators consideration will be given to the nature of the transaction, the nature and circumstances of the dispute, the nationality, location and languages of the parties and (if more than two) the number of parties.

5.6   In the case of a three-member Arbitral Tribunal, the chairman (who will not be a party-nominated arbitrator) shall be appointed by the LCIA Court.

Article 6   Nationality of Arbitrators

6.1   Where the parties are of different nationalities, a sole arbitrator or chairman of the Arbitral Tribunal shall not have the same nationality as any party unless the parties who are not of the same nationality as the proposed appointee all agree in writing otherwise.

6.2   The nationality of parties shall be understood to include that of controlling shareholders or interests.

6.3   For the purpose of this Article, a person who is a citizen of two or more states shall be treated as a national of each state; and citizens of the European Union shall be treated as nationals of its different Member States and shall not be treated as having the same nationality.

Article 7   Party and Other Nominations

7.1   If the parties have agreed that any arbitrator is to be appointed by one or more of them or by any third person, that agreement shall be treated as an agreement to nominate an arbitrator for all purposes. Such nominee may only be appointed by the LCIA Court as arbitrator subject to his prior compliance with Article 5.3. The LCIA Court may refuse to

4

appoint any such nominee if it determines that he is not suitable or independent or impartial.

7.2   Where the parties have howsoever agreed that the Respondent or any third person is to nominate an arbitrator and such nomination is not made within time or at all, the LCIA Court may appoint an arbitrator notwithstanding the absence of the nomination and without regard to any late nomination. Likewise, if the Request for Arbitration does not contain a nomination by the Claimant where the parties have howsoever agreed that the Claimant or a third person is to nominate an arbitrator, the LCIA Court may appoint an arbitrator notwithstanding the absence of the nomination and without regard to any late nomination.

Article 8   Three or More Parties

8.1   Where the Arbitration Agreement entitles each party howsoever to nominate an arbitrator, the parties to the dispute number more than two and such parties have not all agreed in writing that the disputant parties represent two separate sides for the formation of the Arbitral Tribunal as Claimant and Respondent respectively, the LCIA Court shall appoint the Arbitral Tribunal without regard to any party's nomination.

8.2   In such circumstances, the Arbitration Agreement shall be treated for all purposes as a written agreement by the parties for the appointment of the Arbitral Tribunal by the LCIA Court.

Article 9   Expedited Formation

9.1   In exceptional urgency, on or after the commencement of the arbitration, any party may apply to the LCIA Court for the expedited formation of the Arbitral Tribunal, including the appointment of any replacement arbitrator under Articles 10 and 11 of these Rules.

9.2   Such an application shall be made in writing to the LCIA Court, copied to all other parties to the arbitration; and it shall set out the specific grounds for exceptional urgency in the formation of the Arbitral Tribunal.

9.3   The LCIA Court may, in its complete discretion, abridge or curtail any time-limit under these Rules for the formation of the Arbitral Tribunal, including service of the Response and of any matters or documents adjudged to be missing from the Request. The LCIA Court shall not be entitled to abridge or curtail any other time-limit.

Article 10   Revocation of Arbitrator's Appointment

10.1   If either (a) any arbitrator gives written notice of his desire to resign as arbitrator to the LCIA Court, to be copied to the parties and the other arbitrators (if any) or (b) any arbitrator dies, falls seriously ill, refuses, or becomes unable or unfit to act, either upon challenge by a party or at the request of the remaining arbitrators, the LCIA Court may revoke that arbitrator's appointment and appoint another arbitrator. The LCIA Court shall decide upon the amount of fees and expenses to be paid for the former arbitrator's services (if any) as it may consider appropriate in all the circumstances.

10.2   If any arbitrator acts in deliberate violation of the Arbitration Agreement (including these Rules) or does not act fairly and impartially as between the parties or does not conduct or participate in the arbitration proceedings with reasonable diligence, avoiding unnecessary delay or expense, that arbitrator may be considered unfit in the opinion of the LCIA Court.

10.3   An arbitrator may also be challenged by any party if circumstances exist that give rise to justifiable doubts as to his impartiality or independence. A party may challenge an arbitrator it has nominated, or in whose appointment it has participated, only for reasons of which it becomes aware after the appointment has been made.

10.4   A party who intends to challenge an arbitrator shall, within 15 days of the formation of the Arbitral Tribunal or (if later) after becoming aware of any circumstances referred to in Article 10.1, 10.2 or 10.3, send a written statement of the reasons for its challenge to the LCIA Court, the Arbitral Tribunal and all other parties. Unless the challenged arbitrator withdraws or all other parties agree to the challenge within 15 days of receipt of the written statement, the LCIA Court shall decide on the challenge.

Article 11   Nomination and Replacement of Arbitrators

11.1   In the event that the LCIA Court determines that any nominee is not suitable or independent or impartial or if an appointed arbitrator is to be replaced for any reason, the LCIA Court shall have a complete discretion to decide whether or not to follow the original nominating process.

11.2   If the LCIA Court should so decide, any opportunity given to a party to make a re-nomination shall be waived if not exercised within 15 days (or such lesser time as the LCIA Court may fix), after which the LCIA Court shall appoint the replacement arbitrator.

Article 12   Majority Power to Continue Proceedings

12.1   If any arbitrator on a three-member Arbitral Tribunal refuses or persistently fails to participate in its deliberations, the two other arbitrators shall have the power, upon their written notice of such refusal or failure to the LCIA Court, the parties and the third arbitrator, to continue the arbitration (including the making of any decision, ruling or award), notwithstanding the absence of the third arbitrator.

12.2   In determining whether to continue the arbitration, the two other arbitrators shall take into account the stage of the arbitration, any explanation made by the third arbitrator for his non-participation and such other matters as they consider appropriate in the circumstances of the case. The reasons for such determination shall be stated in any award, order or other decision made by the two arbitrators without the participation of the third arbitrator.

12.3   In the event that the two other arbitrators determine at any time not to continue the arbitration without the participation of the third arbitrator missing from their deliberations, the two arbitrators shall notify in writing the parties and the LCIA Court of such determination; and in that event, the two arbitrators or any party may refer the matter to the LCIA Court for the revocation of that third arbitrator's appointment and his replacement under Article 10.

Article 13   Communications between Parties and the Arbitral Tribunal

13.1   Until the Arbitral Tribunal is formed, all communications between parties and arbitrators shall be made through the Registrar.

13.2   Thereafter, unless and until the Arbitral Tribunal directs that communications shall take place directly between the Arbitral Tribunal and the parties (with simultaneous copies to the Registrar), all written communications between the parties and the Arbitral Tribunal shall continue to be made through the Registrar.

13.3   Where the Registrar sends any written communication to one party on behalf of the Arbitral Tribunal, he shall send a copy to each of the other parties. Where any party sends to the Registrar any communication (including Written Statements and Documents under Article 15), it shall include a copy for each arbitrator; and it shall also send copies direct to all other parties and confirm to the Registrar in writing that it has done or is doing so.

Article 14   Conduct of the Proceedings

14.1   The parties may agree on the conduct of their arbitral proceedings and they are encouraged to do so, consistent with the Arbitral Tribunal's general duties at all times:

(i) to act fairly and impartially as between all parties, giving each a reasonable opportunity of putting its case and dealing with that of its opponent; and

(ii) to adopt procedures suitable to the circumstances of the arbitration, avoiding

6

unnecessary delay or expense, so as to provide a fair and efficient means for the final resolution of the parties' dispute.

Such agreements shall be made by the parties in writing or recorded in writing by the Arbitral Tribunal at the request of and with the authority of the parties.

14.2   Unless otherwise agreed by the parties under Article 14.1, the Arbitral Tribunal shall have the widest discretion to discharge its duties allowed under such law(s) or rules of law as the Arbitral Tribunal may determine to be applicable; and at all times the parties shall do everything necessary for the fair, efficient and expeditious conduct of the arbitration.

14.3   In the case of a three-member Arbitral Tribunal the chairman may, with the prior consent of the other two arbitrators, make procedural rulings alone.

Article 15   Submission of Written Statements and Documents

15.1   Unless the parties have agreed otherwise under Article 14.1 or the Arbitral Tribunal should determine differently, the written stage of the proceedings shall be as set out below.

15.2   Within 30 days of receipt of written notification from the Registrar of the formation of the Arbitral Tribunal, the Claimant shall send to the Registrar a Statement of Case setting out in sufficient detail the facts and any contentions of law on which it relies, together with the relief claimed against all other parties, save and insofar as such matters have not been set out in its Request.

15.3   Within 30 days of receipt of the Statement of Case or written notice from the Claimant that it elects to treat the Request as its Statement of Case, the Respondent shall send to the Registrar a Statement of Defence setting out in sufficient detail which of the facts and contentions of law in the Statement of Case or Request (as the case may be) it admits or denies, on what grounds and on what other facts and contentions of law it relies. Any counterclaims shall be submitted with the Statement of Defence in the same manner as claims are to be set out in the Statement of Case.

15.4   Within 30 days of receipt of the Statement of Defence, the Claimant shall send to the Registrar a Statement of Reply which, where there are any counterclaims, shall include a Defence to Counterclaim in the same manner as a defence is to be set out in the Statement of Defence.

15.5   If the Statement of Reply contains a Defence to Counterclaim, within 30 days of its receipt the Respondent shall send to the Registrar a Statement of Reply to Counterclaim.

15.6   All Statements referred to in this Article shall be accompanied by copies (or, if they are especially voluminous, lists) of all essential documents on which the party concerned relies and which have not previously been submitted by any party, and (where appropriate) by any relevant samples and exhibits.

15.7   As soon as practicable following receipt of the Statements specified in this Article, the Arbitral Tribunal shall proceed in such manner as has been agreed in writing by the parties or pursuant to its authority under these Rules.

15.8   If the Respondent fails to submit a Statement of Defence or the Claimant a Statement of Defence to Counterclaim, or if at any point any party fails to avail itself of the opportunity to present its case in the manner determined by Article 15.2 to 15.6 or directed by the Arbitral Tribunal, the Arbitral Tribunal may nevertheless proceed with the arbitration and make an award.

Article 16   Seat of Arbitration and Place of Hearings

16.1   The parties may agree in writing the seat (or legal place) of their arbitration. Failing such a choice, the seat of arbitration shall be London, unless and until the LCIA Court determines in view of all the circumstances, and after having given the parties an opportunity to make written comment, that another seat is more appropriate.

16.2 The Arbitral Tribunal may hold hearings, meetings and deliberations at any convenient geographical place in its discretion; and if elsewhere than the seat of the arbitration, the arbitration shall be treated as an arbitration conducted at the seat of the arbitration and any award as an award made at the seat of the arbitration for all purposes.

16.3 The law applicable to the arbitration (if any) shall be the arbitration law of the seat of arbitration, unless and to the extent that the parties have expressly agreed in writing on the application of another arbitration law and such agreement is not prohibited by the law of the arbitral seat.

Article 17   Language of Arbitration

17.1 The initial language of the arbitration shall be the language of the Arbitration Agreement, unless the parties have agreed in writing otherwise and providing always that a non-participating or defaulting party shall have no cause for complaint if communications to and from the Registrar and the arbitration proceedings are conducted in English.

17.2 In the event that the Arbitration Agreement is written in more than one language, the LCIA Court may, unless the Arbitration Agreement provides that the arbitration proceedings shall be conducted in more than one language, decide which of those languages shall be the initial language of the arbitration.

17.3 Upon the formation of the Arbitral Tribunal and unless the parties have agreed upon the language or languages of the arbitration, the Arbitration Tribunal shall decide upon the language(s) of the arbitration, after giving the parties an opportunity to make written comment and taking into account the initial language of the arbitration and any other matter it may consider appropriate in all the circumstances of the case.

17.4 If any document is expressed in a language other than the language(s) of the arbitration and no translation of such document is submitted by the party relying upon the document, the Arbitral Tribunal or (if the Arbitral Tribunal has not been formed) the LCIA Court may order that party to submit a translation in a form to be determined by the Arbitral Tribunal or the LCIA Court, as the case may be.

Article 18   Party Representation

18.1 Any party may be represented by legal practitioners or any other representatives.

18.2 At any time the Arbitral Tribunal may require from any party proof of authority granted to its representative(s) in such form as the Arbitral Tribunal may determine.

Article 19   Hearings

19.1 Any party which expresses a desire to that effect has the right to be heard orally before the Arbitral Tribunal on the merits of the dispute, unless the parties have agreed in writing on documents-only arbitration.

19.2 The Arbitral Tribunal shall fix the date, time and physical place of any meetings and hearings in the arbitration, and shall give the parties reasonable notice thereof.

19.3 The Arbitral Tribunal may in advance of any hearing submit to the parties a list of questions which it wishes them to answer with special attention.

19.4 All meetings and hearings shall be in private unless the parties agree otherwise in writing or the Arbitral Tribunal directs otherwise.

19.5 The Arbitral Tribunal shall have the fullest authority to establish time-limits for meetings and hearings, or for any parts thereof.

8

Article 20   Witnesses

20.1   Before any hearing, the Arbitral Tribunal may require any party to give notice of the identity of each witness that party wishes to call (including rebuttal witnesses), as well as the subject matter of that witness's testimony, its content and its relevance to the issues in the arbitration.

20.2   The Arbitral Tribunal may also determine the time, manner and form in which such materials should be exchanged between the parties and presented to the Arbitral Tribunal; and it has a discretion to allow, refuse, or limit the appearance of witnesses (whether witness of fact or expert witness).

20.3   Subject to any order otherwise by the Arbitral Tribunal, the testimony of a witness may be presented by a party in written form, either as a signed statement or as a sworn affidavit.

20.4   Subject to Article 14.1 and 14.2, any party may request that a witness, on whose testimony another party seeks to rely, should attend for oral questioning at a hearing before the Arbitral Tribunal. If the Arbitral Tribunal orders that other party to produce the witness and the witness fails to attend the oral hearing without good cause, the Arbitral Tribunal may place such weight on the written testimony (or exclude the same altogether) as it considers appropriate in the circumstances of the case.

20.5   Any witness who gives oral evidence at a hearing before the Arbitral Tribunal may be questioned by each of the parties under the control of the Arbitral Tribunal. The Arbitral Tribunal may put questions at any stage of his evidence.

20.6   Subject to the mandatory provisions of any applicable law, it shall not be improper for any party or its legal representatives to interview any witness or potential witness for the purpose of presenting his testimony in written form or producing him as an oral witness.

20.7   Any individual intending to testify to the Arbitral Tribunal on any issue of fact or expertise shall be treated as a witness under these Rules notwithstanding that the individual is a party to the arbitration or was or is an officer, employee or shareholder of any party.

Article 21   Experts to the Arbitral Tribunal

21.1   Unless otherwise agreed by the parties in writing, the Arbitral Tribunal:

(a)   may appoint one or more experts to report to the Arbitral Tribunal on specific issues, who shall be and remain impartial and independent of the parties throughout the arbitration proceedings; and

(b)   may require a party to give any such expert any relevant information or to provide access to any relevant documents, goods, samples, property or site for inspection by the expert.

21.2   Unless otherwise agreed by the parties in writing, if a party so requests or if the Arbitral Tribunal considers it necessary, the expert shall, after delivery of his written or oral report to the Arbitral Tribunal and the parties, participate in one or more hearings at which the parties shall have the opportunity to question the expert on his report and to present expert witnesses in order to testify on the points at issue.

21.3   The fees and expenses of any expert appointed by the Arbitral Tribunal under this Article shall be paid out of the deposits payable by the parties under Article 24 and shall form part of the costs of the arbitration.

Article 22   Additional Powers of the Arbitral Tribunal

22.1   Unless the parties at any time agree otherwise in writing, the Arbitral Tribunal shall have the power, on the application of any party or of its own motion, but in either case only after giving the parties a reasonable opportunity to state their views:

(a)   to allow any party, upon such terms (as to costs and otherwise) as it shall determine, to amend any claim, counterclaim, defence and reply;

(b)   to extend or abbreviate any time-limit provided by the Arbitration Agreement or these Rules for the conduct of the arbitration or by the Arbitral Tribunal's own orders;

(c)   to conduct such enquiries as may appear to the Arbitral Tribunal to be necessary or expedient, including whether and to what extent the Arbitral Tribunal should itself take the initiative in identifying the issues and ascertaining the relevant facts and the law(s) or rules of law applicable to the arbitration, the merits of the parties' dispute and the Arbitration Agreement;

(d)   to order any party to make any property, site or thing under its control and relating to the subject matter of the arbitration available for inspection by the Arbitral Tribunal, any other party, its expert or any expert to the Arbitral Tribunal;

(e)   to order any party to produce to the Arbitral Tribunal, and to the other parties for inspection, and to supply copies of, any documents or classes of documents in their possession, custody or power which the Arbitral Tribunal determines to be relevant;

(f)   to decide whether or not to apply any strict rules of evidence (or any other rules) as to the admissibility, relevance or weight of any material tendered by a party on any matter of fact or expert opinion; and to determine the time, manner and form in which such material should be exchanged between the parties and presented to the Arbitral Tribunal;

(g)   to order the correction of any contract between the parties or the Arbitration Agreement, but only to the extent required to rectify any mistake which the Arbitral Tribunal determines to be common to the parties and then only if and to the extent to which the law(s) or rules of law applicable to the contract or Arbitration Agreement permit such correction; and

(h)   to allow, only upon the application of a party, one or more third persons to be joined in the arbitration as a party provided any such third person and the applicant party have consented thereto in writing, and thereafter to make a single final award, or separate awards, in respect of all parties so implicated in the arbitration;

22.2   By agreeing to arbitration under these Rules, the parties shall be treated as having agreed not to apply to any state court or other judicial authority for any order available from the Arbitral Tribunal under Article 22.1, except with the agreement in writing of all parties.

22.3   The Arbitral Tribunal shall decide the parties' dispute in accordance with the law(s) or rules of law chosen by the parties as applicable to the merits of their dispute. If and to the extent that the Arbitral Tribunal determines that the parties have made no such choice, the Arbitral Tribunal shall apply the law(s) or rules of law which it considers appropriate.

22.4   The Arbitral Tribunal shall only apply to the merits of the dispute principles deriving from "ex aequo et bono", "amiable composition" or "honourable engagement" where the parties have so agreed expressly in writing.

Article 23   **Jurisdiction of the Arbitral Tribunal**

23.1   The Arbitral Tribunal shall have the power to rule on its own jurisdiction, including any objection to the initial or continuing existence, validity or effectiveness of the Arbitration Agreement. For that purpose, an arbitration clause which forms or was intended to form part of another agreement shall be treated as an arbitration agreement independent of that other agreement. A decision by the Arbitral Tribunal that such other agreement is non-existent, invalid or ineffective shall not entail ipso jure the non-existence, invalidity or ineffectiveness of the arbitration clause.

23.2   A plea by a Respondent that the Arbitral Tribunal does not have jurisdiction shall be treated as having been irrevocably waived unless it is raised not later than the Statement of Defence; and a like plea by a Respondent to Counterclaim shall be similarly treated unless it is raised no later than the Statement of Defence to Counterclaim. A plea that the Arbitral Tribunal is exceeding the scope of its authority shall be raised promptly after the Arbitral Tribunal has indicated its intention to decide on the matter alleged by any party to be beyond the scope of its authority, failing which such plea shall also be treated as having been waived irrevocably. In any case, the Arbitral Tribunal may nevertheless admit an untimely plea if it considers the delay justified in the particular circumstances.

23.3   The Arbitral Tribunal may determine the plea to its jurisdiction or authority in an award as to jurisdiction or later in an award on the merits, as it considers appropriate in the circumstances.

23.4   By agreeing to arbitration under these Rules, the parties shall be treated as having agreed not to apply to any state court or other judicial authority for any relief regarding the Arbitral Tribunal's jurisdiction or authority, except with the agreement in writing of all parties to the arbitration or the prior authorisation of the Arbitral Tribunal or following the latter's award ruling on the objection to its jurisdiction or authority.

Article 24   Deposits

24.1   The LCIA Court may direct the parties, in such proportions as it thinks appropriate, to make one or several interim or final payments on account of the costs of the arbitration. Such deposits shall be made to and held by the LCIA and from time to time may be released by the LCIA Court to the arbitrator(s), any expert appointed by the Arbitral Tribunal and the LCIA itself as the arbitration progresses.

24.2   The Arbitral Tribunal shall not proceed with the arbitration without ascertaining at all times from the Registrar or any deputy Registrar that the LCIA is in requisite funds.

24.3   In the event that a party fails or refuses to provide any deposit as directed by the LCIA Court, the LCIA Court may direct the other party or parties to effect a substitute payment to allow the arbitration to proceed (subject to any award on costs). In such circumstances, the party paying the substitute payment shall be entitled to recover that amount as a debt immediately due from the defaulting party.

24.4   Failure by a claimant or counterclaiming party to provide promptly and in full the required deposit may be treated by the LCIA Court and the Arbitral Tribunal as a withdrawal of the claim or counterclaim respectively.

Article 25   Interim and Conservatory Measures

25.1   The Arbitral Tribunal shall have the power, unless otherwise agreed by the parties in writing, on the application of any party:

(a)   to order any respondent party to a claim or counterclaim to provide security for all or part of the amount in dispute, by way of deposit or bank guarantee or in any other manner and upon such terms as the Arbitral Tribunal considers appropriate. Such terms may include the provision by the claiming or counterclaiming party of a cross-indemnity, itself secured in such manner as the Arbitral Tribunal considers appropriate, for any costs or losses incurred by such respondent in providing security. The amount of any costs and losses payable under such cross-indemnity may be determined by the Arbitral Tribunal in one or more awards;

(b)   to order the preservation, storage, sale or other disposal of any property or thing under the control of any party and relating to the subject matter of the arbitration; and

(c)   to order on a provisional basis, subject to final determination in an award, any relief which the Arbitral Tribunal would have power to grant in an award, including a provisional order for the payment of money or the disposition of property as between any parties.

11

25.2   The Arbitral Tribunal shall have the power, upon the application of a party, to order any claiming or counterclaiming party to provide security for the legal or other costs of any other party by way of deposit or bank guarantee or in any other manner and upon such terms as the Arbitral Tribunal considers appropriate. Such terms may include the provision by that other party of a cross-indemnity, itself secured in such manner as the Arbitral Tribunal considers appropriate, for any costs and losses incurred by such claimant or counterclaimant in providing security. The amount of any costs and losses payable under such cross-indemnity may be determined by the Arbitral Tribunal in one or more awards. In the event that a claiming or counterclaiming party does not comply with any order to provide security, the Arbitral Tribunal may stay that party's claims or counterclaims or dismiss them in an award.

25.3   The power of the Arbitral Tribunal under Article 25.1 shall not prejudice howsoever any party's right to apply to any state court or other judicial authority for interim or conservatory measures before the formation of the Arbitral Tribunal and, in exceptional cases, thereafter. Any application and any order for such measures after the formation of the Arbitral Tribunal shall be promptly communicated by the applicant to the Arbitral Tribunal and all other parties. However, by agreeing to arbitration under these Rules, the parties shall be taken to have agreed not to apply to any state court or other judicial authority for any order for security for its legal or other costs available from the Arbitral Tribunal under Article 25.2.

Article 26   The Award

26.1   The Arbitral Tribunal shall make its award in writing and, unless all parties agree in writing otherwise, shall state the reasons upon which its award is based. The award shall also state the date when the award is made and the seat of the arbitration; and it shall be signed by the Arbitral Tribunal or those of its members assenting to it.

26.2   If any arbitrator fails to comply with the mandatory provisions of any applicable law relating to the making of the award, having been given a reasonable opportunity to do so, the remaining arbitrators may proceed in his absence and state in their award the circumstances of the other arbitrator's failure to participate in the making of the award.

26.3   Where there are three arbitrators and the Arbitral Tribunal fails to agree on any issue, the arbitrators shall decide that issue by a majority. Failing a majority decision on any issue, the chairman of the Arbitral Tribunal shall decide that issue.

26.4   If any arbitrator refuses or fails to sign the award, the signatures of the majority or (failing a majority) of the chairman shall be sufficient, provided that the reason for the omitted signature is stated in the award by the majority or chairman.

26.5   The sole arbitrator or chairman shall be responsible for delivering the award to the LCIA Court, which shall transmit certified copies to the parties provided that the costs of arbitration have been paid to the LCIA in accordance with Article 28.

26.6   An award may be expressed in any currency. The Arbitral Tribunal may order that simple or compound interest shall be paid by any party on any sum awarded at such rates as the Arbitral Tribunal determines to be appropriate, without being bound by legal rates of interest imposed by any state court, in respect of any period which the Arbitral Tribunal determines to be appropriate ending not later than the date upon which the award is complied with.

26.7   The Arbitral Tribunal may make separate awards on different issues at different times. Such awards shall have the same status and effect as any other award made by the Arbitral Tribunal.

26.8   In the event of a settlement of the parties' dispute, the Arbitral Tribunal may render an award recording the settlement if the parties so request in writing (a "Consent Award"), provided always that such award contains an express statement that it is an award made by the parties' consent. A Consent Award need not contain reasons. If the parties do not require a consent award, then on written confirmation by the parties to the LCIA Court that a settlement has been reached, the Arbitral Tribunal shall be discharged and

12

the arbitration proceedings concluded, subject to payment by the parties of any outstanding costs of the arbitration under Article 28.

26.9   All awards shall be final and binding on the parties. By agreeing to arbitration under these Rules, the parties undertake to carry out any award immediately and without any delay (subject only to Article 27); and the parties also waive irrevocably their right to any form of appeal, review or recourse to any state court or other judicial authority, insofar as such waiver may be validly made.

Article 27   Correction of Awards and Additional Awards

27.1   Within 30 days of receipt of any award, or such lesser period as may be agreed in writing by the parties, a party may by written notice to the Registrar (copied to all other parties) request the Arbitral Tribunal to correct in the award any errors in computation, clerical or typographical errors or any errors of a similar nature. If the Arbitral Tribunal considers the request to be justified, it shall make the corrections within 30 days of receipt of the request. Any correction shall take the form of separate memorandum dated and signed by the Arbitral Tribunal or (if three arbitrators) those of its members assenting to it; and such memorandum shall become part of the award for all purposes.

27.2   The Arbitral Tribunal may likewise correct any error of the nature described in Article 27.1 on its own initiative within 30 days of the date of the award, to the same effect.

27.3   Within 30 days of receipt of the final award, a party may by written notice to the Registrar (copied to all other parties), request the Arbitral Tribunal to make an additional award as to claims or counterclaims presented in the arbitration but not determined in any award. If the Arbitral Tribunal considers the request to be justified, it shall make the additional award within 60 days of receipt of the request. The provisions of Article 26 shall apply to any additional award.

Article 28   Arbitration and Legal Costs

28.1   The costs of the arbitration (other than the legal or other costs incurred by the parties themselves) shall be determined by the LCIA Court in accordance with the Schedule of Costs. The parties shall be jointly and severally liable to the Arbitral Tribunal and the LCIA for such arbitration costs.

28.2   The Arbitral Tribunal shall specify in the award the total amount of the costs of the arbitration as determined by the LCIA Court. Unless the parties agree otherwise in writing, the Arbitral Tribunal shall determine the proportions in which the parties shall bear all or part of such arbitration costs. If the Arbitral Tribunal has determined that all or any part of the arbitration costs shall be borne by a party other than a party which has already paid them to the LCIA, the latter party shall have the right to recover the appropriate amount from the former party.

28.3   The Arbitral Tribunal shall also have the power to order in its award that all or part of the legal or other costs incurred by a party be paid by another party, unless the parties agree otherwise in writing. The Arbitral Tribunal shall determine and fix the amount of each item comprising such costs on such reasonable basis as it thinks fit.

28.4   Unless the parties otherwise agree in writing, the Arbitral Tribunal shall make its orders on both arbitration and legal costs on the general principle that costs should reflect the parties' relative success and failure in the award or arbitration, except where it appears to the Arbitral Tribunal that in the particular circumstances this general approach is inappropriate. Any order for costs shall be made with reasons in the award containing such order.

28.5   If the arbitration is abandoned, suspended or concluded, by agreement or otherwise, before the final award is made, the parties shall remain jointly and severally liable to pay to the LCIA and the Arbitral Tribunal the costs of the arbitration as determined by the LCIA Court in accordance with the Schedule of Costs. In the event that such arbitration costs are less than the deposits made by the parties, there shall be a refund by the LCIA in such proportion as the parties may agree in writing, or failing such agreement, in the same proportions as the deposits were made by the parties to the LCIA.

Article 29   Decisions by the LCIA Court

29.1   The decisions of the LCIA Court with respect to all matters relating to the arbitration shall be conclusive and binding upon the parties and the Arbitral Tribunal. Such decisions are to be treated as administrative in nature and the LCIA Court shall not be required to give any reasons.

29.2   To the extent permitted by the law of the seat of the arbitration, the parties shall be taken to have waived any right of appeal or review in respect of any such decisions of the LCIA Court to any state court or other judicial authority. If such appeals or review remain possible due to mandatory provisions of any applicable law, the LCIA Court shall, subject to the provisions of that applicable law, decide whether the arbitral proceedings are to continue, notwithstanding an appeal or review.

Article 30   Confidentiality

30.1   Unless the parties expressly agree in writing to the contrary, the parties undertake as a general principle to keep confidential all awards in their arbitration, together with all materials in the proceedings created for the purpose of the arbitration and all other documents produced by another party in the proceedings not otherwise in the public domain - save and to the extent that disclosure may be required of a party by legal duty, to protect or pursue a legal right or to enforce or challenge an award in bona fide legal proceedings before a state court or other judicial authority.

30.2   The deliberations of the Arbitral Tribunal are likewise confidential to its members, save and to the extent that disclosure of an arbitrator's refusal to participate in the arbitration is required of the other members of the Arbitral Tribunal under Articles 10, 12 and 26.

30.3   The LCIA Court does not publish any award or any part of an award without the prior written consent of all parties and the Arbitral Tribunal.

Article 31   Exclusion of Liability

31.1   None of the LCIA, the LCIA Court (including its President, Vice-Presidents and individual members), the Registrar, any deputy Registrar, any arbitrator and any expert to the Arbitral Tribunal shall be liable to any party howsoever for any act or omission in connection with any arbitration conducted by reference to these Rules, save where the act or omission is shown by that party to constitute conscious and deliberate wrongdoing committed by the body or person alleged to be liable to that party.

31.2   After the award has been made and the possibilities of correction and additional awards referred to in Article 27 have lapsed or been exhausted, neither the LCIA, the LCIA Court (including its President, Vice-Presidents and individual members), the Registrar, any deputy Registrar, any arbitrator or expert to the Arbitral Tribunal shall be under any legal obligation to make any statement to any person about any matter concerning the arbitration, nor shall any party seek to make any of these persons a witness in any legal or other proceedings arising out of the arbitration.

Article 32   General Rules

32.1   A party who knows that any provision of the Arbitration Agreement (including these Rules) has not been complied with and yet proceeds with the arbitration without promptly stating its objection to such non-compliance, shall be treated as having irrevocably waived its right to object.

32.2   In all matters not expressly provided for in these Rules, the LCIA Court, the Arbitral Tribunal and the parties shall act in the spirit of these Rules and shall make every reasonable effort to ensure that an award is legally enforceable.

APPENDIX 13H-2

London Court of International Arbitration Mediation Rules[1]

Arbitration and ADR worldwide

LCIA MEDIATION RULES

effective 1 June 2010

Where any agreement provides for mediation of existing or future disputes under the rules of the LCIA, the parties shall be taken to have agreed that the mediation shall be conducted in accordance with the following rules (the "Rules") or such amended rules as the LCIA may have adopted hereafter to take effect before the commencement of the mediation. The Rules includes the Schedule of Mediation Costs (the "Schedule") in effect at the commencement of the mediation, as separately amended from time to time by the LCIA Court.

CONTENTS

Article

1

---

[1]London Court of International Arbitration, LCIA Mediation Rules, available at http://www.lcia.org/Dispute__Resolution__Services/LCIA__Mediation__Rules.aspx (last accessed March 25, 2011).

Article 1

Commencing Mediation - Prior existing agreements to mediate

1.1   Where there is a prior existing agreement to mediate under the Rules (a "Prior Agreement"), any party or parties wishing to commence a mediation shall send to the Registrar of the LCIA Court ("the Registrar") a written request for mediation (the "Request for Mediation"), which shall briefly state the nature of the dispute and the value of the claim, and should include, or be accompanied by a copy of the Prior Agreement, the names, addresses, telephone, facsimile, telex numbers and e-mail addresses (if known) of the parties to the mediation, and of their legal representatives (if known) and of the mediator proposed (if any) by the party or parties requesting mediation.

1.2   If the Request for Mediation is not made jointly by all parties to the Prior Agreement, the party commencing the mediation shall, at the same time, send a copy of the Request for Mediation to the other party or parties.

1.3   The Request for Mediation shall be accompanied by the registration fee prescribed in the Schedule.

1.4   The LCIA Court shall appoint a mediator as soon as practicable after receipt by the Registrar of the Request for Mediation, with due regard for any nomination, or method or criteria of selection agreed in writing by the parties, and subject always to Article 8 of the Rules.

1.5   Where there is a Prior Agreement, the date of commencement of the mediation shall be the date of receipt by the Registrar of the Request for Mediation.

Article 2

Commencing Mediation – no Prior Agreement

2.1   Where there is no Prior Agreement, any party or parties wishing to commence a mediation under the Rules shall send to the Registrar a Request for Mediation, which shall briefly state the nature of the dispute and the value of the claim, and should include, or be accompanied by, the names, addresses, telephone, facsimile, telex numbers and e-mail addresses (if known) of the parties to the mediation, and of their legal representatives (if known) and of the mediator proposed (if any) by the party or parties requesting mediation.

2.2   The Request for Mediation shall be accompanied by the registration fee prescribed in the Schedule.

2.3   If the Request for Mediation is not made jointly by all parties to the dispute,

a)   the party wishing to commence the mediation shall, at the same time, send a copy of the Request for Mediation to the other party or parties; and

b)   the other party or parties shall, within 14 days of receiving the Request for Mediation, advise the Registrar in writing whether or not they agree to the mediation of the dispute.

2

2.4   In the event that the other party or parties either declines mediation, or fails to agree to mediation within the 14 days referred to at Article 2.3(b), there shall be no mediation under the Rules and the Registrar shall so advise the parties, in writing.

2.5   The LCIA Court shall appoint a mediator as soon as practicable after agreement to mediate has been reached between the parties, with due regard for any nomination, or method or criteria of selection agreed in writing by the parties, and subject always to Article 8 of the Rules.

2.6   Where there is no Prior Agreement, the date of commencement of the mediation shall be the date that agreement to mediate is reached in accordance with Article 2.3(b).

Article 3

Appointment of Mediator

3.1   Before appointment by the LCIA Court, pursuant to Article 1.4 or Article 2.5, the mediator shall furnish the Registrar with a written résumé of his or her past and present professional positions; and he or she shall sign a declaration to the effect that there are no circumstances known to him or her likely to give rise to any justified doubts as to his or her impartiality or independence, other than any circumstances disclosed by him or her in the declaration. A copy of the mediator's résumé and declaration shall be provided to the parties.

3.2   Where the mediator has made a disclosure, pursuant to Article 3.1, or where a party independently knows of circumstances likely to give rise to justified doubts as to his or her impartiality or independence, a party shall be at liberty to object to his or her appointment; in which case the LCIA Court shall appoint another mediator.

Article 4

Statements by the Parties

4.1   The parties are free to agree how, and in what form, they will inform the mediator of their respective cases, provided that, unless they have agreed otherwise, each party shall submit to the mediator, no later than 7 days before the date agreed between the mediator and the parties for the first scheduled mediation session, a brief written statement summarising his case; the background to the dispute; and the issues to be resolved.

4.2   Each written statement should be accompanied by copies of any documents to which it refers.

4.3   Each party shall, at the same time, submit a copy of his written statement and supporting documents to the other party or parties.

Article 5

Conduct of the Mediation

5.1 The mediator may conduct the mediation in such manner as he or she sees fit, having in mind at all times the circumstances of the case and the wishes of the parties.

5.2 The mediator may communicate with the parties orally or in writing, together, or individually, and may convene a meeting or meetings at a venue to be determined by the mediator after consultations with the parties.

5.3 Nothing which is communicated to the mediator in private during the course of the mediation shall be repeated to the other party or parties, without the express consent of the party making the communication.

5.4 Each party shall notify the other party and the mediator of the number and identity of those persons who will attend any meeting convened by the mediator.

5.5 Each party shall identify a representative of that party who is authorised to settle the dispute on behalf of that party, and shall confirm that authority in writing.

5.6 Unless otherwise agreed by the parties, the mediator will decide the language(s) in which the mediation will be conducted.

Article 6

Conclusion of the Mediation

The mediation will be at an end when, either

(a)   a settlement agreement is signed by the parties; or

(b)   the parties advise the mediator that it is their view that a settlement cannot be reached and that it is their wish to terminate the mediation; or

(c)   the mediator advises the parties that, in his or her judgement, the mediation process will not resolve the issues in dispute; or

(d)   the time limit for mediation provided in a Prior Agreement has expired and the parties have not agreed to extend that time limit.

Article 7

Settlement Agreement

7.1 If terms are agreed in settlement of the dispute, the parties, with the assistance of the mediator if the parties so request, shall draw up and sign a settlement agreement, setting out such terms.

7.2 By signing the settlement agreement, the parties agree to be bound by its terms.

4

Article 8

Costs

8.1   The costs of the mediation (the "Costs") shall include the fees and expenses of the mediator and the administrative charges of the LCIA, as set out in the Schedule.

8.2   The Costs shall be borne equally by the parties (or in such other proportions as they have agreed in writing).

8.3   As soon as practicable after receipt of the Request for Mediation, pursuant to Article 1 of the Rules, or after the parties have agreed to mediate, pursuant to Article 2 of the Rules, the LCIA will request the parties to file a deposit to be held on account of the Costs ("the Deposit"). The Deposit shall be paid by the parties in equal shares (or in such other proportions as they have agreed) prior to the appointment of the mediator.

8.4   In the event that a party fails to pay its share of the Deposit, another party may make a substitute payment to allow the mediation to proceed.

8.5   A mediator shall not be appointed and the mediation shall not proceed until and unless the Deposit has been paid in full.

8.6   At the conclusion of the mediation, the LCIA, in consultation with the mediator, will fix the Costs of the mediation.

8.7   If the Deposit exceeds the Costs, the excess will be reimbursed to the parties in the proportions in which they paid the deposit. If the Costs exceed the Deposit, the shortfall will be invoiced to the parties for immediate payment in equal shares (or in such other proportions as they have agreed).

8.8   Any other costs incurred by the parties, whether in regard to legal fees, experts' fees or expenses of any other nature will not be part of the Costs for the purposes of the Rules.

Article 9

Judicial or Arbitral Proceedings

Unless they have agreed otherwise, and notwithstanding the mediation, the parties may initiate or continue any arbitration or judicial proceedings in respect of the dispute which is the subject of the mediation.

Article 10

Confidentiality and Privacy

10.1   All mediation sessions shall be private, and shall be attended only by the mediator, the parties and those individuals identified pursuant to Article 5.4.

10.2   The mediation process and all negotiations, and statements and documents prepared for the purposes of the mediation, shall be confidential and covered by "without prejudice" or negotiation privilege.

5

10.3   The mediation shall be confidential.   Unless agreed among the parties, or required by law, neither the mediator nor the parties may disclose to any person any information regarding the mediation or any settlement terms, or the outcome of the mediation.

10.4   All documents or other information produced for or arising in relation to the mediation will be privileged and will not be admissible in evidence or otherwise discoverable in any litigation or arbitration, except for any documents or other information which would in any event be admissible or discoverable in any such litigation or arbitration.

10.5   There shall be no formal record or transcript of the mediation.

10.6   The parties shall not rely upon, or introduce as evidence in any arbitral or judicial proceedings, any admissions, proposals or views expressed by the parties or by the mediator during the course of the mediation.

Article 11

Exclusion of Liability

11.1   None of the LCIA, the LCIA Court (or any of their respective officers, members or directors), the Registrar, any Deputy Registrar, and any mediator shall be liable to any party howsoever for any act or omission in connection with any mediation conducted by reference to the Rules, save where the act or omission is shown by that party to constitute conscious and deliberate wrongdoing committed by the body or person alleged to be liable to that party.

11.2   None of the LCIA, the LCIA Court (or any of their respective officers, members or directors), the Registrar, any Deputy Registrar, or the Mediator shall be under any legal obligation to make any statement to any person about any matter concerning the mediation, nor shall any party seek to make any of these persons a witness in any legal or other proceedings arising out of the mediation.

6

APPENDIX 13I-1

FINRA Notice to Parties—Discovery Rules and Procedures (1/6/2010)[1]

Notice to Parties—Discovery Rules and Procedures

The timely exchange of relevant documents and information between parties to FINRA arbitrations is vital to the efficient, cost-effective resolution of disputes. Recently, complaints from parties regarding possible abuses of the discovery process in FINRA arbitrations have been on the rise. This trend suggests that some parties believe that noncompliance with the discovery process is a routine and acceptable part of arbitration strategy. It is not.

The purpose of this Notice is to remind all parties—claimants and respondents—that failure to comply with the forum's discovery rules and procedures can result in sanctions, including dismissal of a claim, defense or proceeding.

Possible sanctions include:

- Assessing monetary penalties payable to one or more parties;
- Precluding a party from presenting evidence;
- Making an adverse inference against a party;
- Assessing postponement and/or forum fees;
- Assessing attorneys' fees, costs and expenses; and
- Dismissal of a claim, defense or proceeding.

In addition, members and associated persons who fail to comply with a discovery order of the panel may be referred to FINRA Enforcement for possible disciplinary action, which can include suspension or termination of FINRA membership or registration. You may contact the FINRA Investor Complaint Center for more information.

Exchange of Documents in Customer Dispute Cases

Rule 12505 of the Customer Code requires that parties to FINRA arbitrations cooperate to the fullest extent practicable in the exchange of documents and information to expedite the arbitration.

---

[1]FINRA, Notice to Parties—Discovery Rules and Procedures, available at http://www.finra.org/ArbitrationMediation/Parties/ArbitrationProcess/NoticesTo Parties/P009517 (last accessed March 25, 2011).

The Discovery Guide and Document Production Lists are designed for customer disputes with firms and Associated Person(s). The Document Production Lists specifically identify which documents parties to customer disputes should exchange before the hearing. Document Production Lists 1 and 2 apply to all customer disputes, while Lists 3 through 14 apply to specific types of customer dispute claims. (For example, Lists 4 and 5 apply to cases involving churning allegations.)

Unless the parties agree otherwise, they must give each other copies of all documents in their possession or control that are on Document Production Lists 1 or 2, and any other lists applicable to the dispute, within 60 days of the date that the answer to the claim is due. This exchange should happen automatically, without arbitrator or staff intervention. See Rules 12506 and 12507 of the Customer Code for more information on time frames for turning over documents.

If any party objects to the production of any document listed in the relevant Document Production Lists, the party must file a written objection on or before the date that the exchange of documents is due to occur. Objections should set forth the reasons the party objects to producing the documents. An objection to the production of a document or a category of documents is not an acceptable reason to delay the production of any document not covered by the objection. The arbitrators will decide whether disputed documents must be exchanged, and resolve any other issues, including requests for confidential treatment of documents. See Rule 12508 of the Customer Code for more information on objections.

Rule 12506(b)(2) of the Customer Code establishes a good faith standard for the exchange of documents and information; requiring that a party must use its best efforts to produce all documents required or agreed to be produced.

Parties may also request documents or information not on the Document Production Lists. Parties must either produce requested documents or information within 60 days of the time the request was received, or file a written objection in the manner described above. See Rule 12507 of the Customer Code for more information on additional discovery.

Exchange of Documents in Industry Dispute Cases

Rule 13505 of the Industry Code requires that parties to FINRA arbitrations cooperate to the fullest extent practicable in the exchange of documents and information to expedite the arbitration.

Parties may request documents or information from any party by serving a written request directly on the party. Requests for information are generally limited to identification of individuals, entities, and time periods related to the dispute; such requests should be reasonable in number and not require narrative answers or fact finding. Standard interrogatories are generally not permitted in arbitration. See Rule 13506 of the Industry Code for more information on requesting documents and information.

Rule 13507 provides that—unless the parties agree otherwise—within 60 days from the date a discovery request is received, the party receiving the request must either:

- Produce the requested documents or information to all other parties;
- Identify and explain the reason that specific requested documents or information cannot be produced within the required time, and state when the documents will be produced; or
- Object as provided in Rule 13508.

Objections should set forth the reasons the party objects to producing the documents. An objection to the production of a document or a category of documents is not an acceptable reason to delay the production of any document not covered by the objection. The arbitrators will decide whether disputed documents must be exchanged, and resolve any other issues, including requests for confidential treatment of documents. See Rule 13508 of the Industry Code for more information on objections.

Rule 13507(b) of the Industry Code establishes a good faith standard for the exchange of documents and information; requiring that a party must use its best efforts to produce all documents required or agreed to be produced.

Sanctions for Noncompliance

As noted above, failure to comply with the forum's discovery rules and procedures, or orders of the arbitrators, can, and does, result in sanctions. The following is a partial list of cases in which arbitrators issued sanctions for discovery abuse:

- A member was ordered to pay $10,000 a day for each day that the firm continued to withhold documents that the panel ordered the firm to produce;
- A claimant was ordered to reimburse the respondent costs in the amount of $1,500 for failing to respond in a timely manner to ordered discovery requests;
- A member was assessed over $10,000 in sanctions and $2,500

in attorney's fees when a panel found that the member intentionally concealed documents and delayed the discovery process;

- A panel awarded a claimant over $7,000 due to a member firm's failure to cooperate in the discovery process;
- A claimant was ordered to pay to a respondent $1,475 as a sanction for failing to comply with discovery procedures;
- A panel awarded a claimant $2,750 in attorney's fees as a sanction for the member's failure to provide discoverable material.
- A panel awarded a claimant $3,000 in sanctions for a respondent's failure to provide discoverable material as ordered by the panel;
- Claimants were ordered to pay a respondent $1,000 as a sanction for failing to provide copies of expert witness exhibits; and
- A panel sanctioned a member $10,000 for failure to produce documents required by the chairperson of the panel.

In addition, arbitrators have dismissed claims with prejudice when claimants failed to comply with discovery orders after previous sanctions proved ineffective. Arbitrators in several other cases referred members or associated persons for disciplinary review for discovery abuse.

To avoid discovery sanctions, parties should familiarize themselves with the forum's discovery rules and procedures, and make every attempt to cooperate in the exchange of documents and information within the designated time frames. In customer cases, parties should assume that documents on Document Production Lists 1 and 2, and any other applicable lists, are discoverable, and, absent a written objection, should exchange such documents without waiting for an arbitrator order to do so.

Other Arbitrator and Staff Actions to Deal with Discovery Abuse

In addition to reminding parties of their obligation to comply with the forum's discovery rules and procedures, FINRA reminds arbitrators about what they can do to manage the discovery process effectively, including what sanctions are available when parties violate either the forum's rules or arbitrator orders. Among other things, FINRA offers an online discovery "mini-course" to all arbitrators. FINRA Dispute Resolution staff has also initiated a practice of bringing all alleged discovery abuses to the attention of the Director of Arbitration and the President of FINRA Dispute Resolution. These cases will be carefully reviewed and, when appropriate, FINRA Dispute Resolution will refer such cases to FINRA Enforcement for disciplinary review.

Discovery Arbitrator Pilot Program

FINRA Dispute Resolution is discontinuing its Discovery Arbitrator Pilot Program. Effective January 1, 2010, the procedures under the pilot will no longer apply, unless the parties stipulate to their use under Rule 12105 of the Customer Code or Rule 13105 of the Industry Code.

The Discovery Guide and the rules addressing discovery under FINRA's Codes of Arbitration Procedure will continue to govern discovery issues in arbitration claims.

Conclusion

FINRA hopes that these measures will lead to a significant reduction in the instances of discovery abuse in the forum, and alleviate the need for future rule changes or other additional steps to deter such abuse.

APPENDIX 13I-2

FINRA Discovery Guide and Document Production Lists for Claims Filed On or After April 16, 2007[1]

DISCOVERY GUIDE

This Discovery Guide and Document Production Lists supplement the discovery rules contained in NASD Code of Arbitration Procedure for Customer Disputes ("NASD Customer Code.") (See Rules 12505-12511.)

No requirement under the Discovery Guide supersedes any record retention requirement of any federal or state law or regulation or any rule of a self-regulatory organization.

The Discovery Guide, including the Document Production Lists serves as a guide for the parties and the arbitrators; it is not intended to remove flexibility from arbitrators or parties in a given case. Arbitrators can order the production of documents not provided for by the Document Production Lists or alter the production schedule described in the Discovery Guide. Nothing in the Discovery Guide precludes the parties from voluntarily agreeing to an exchange of documents in a manner different from that set forth in the Discovery Guide. NASD encourages the parties to agree to the voluntary exchange of documents and information and to stipulate to various matters. The fact that an item appears on a Document Production List does not shift the burden of establishing or defending any aspect of a claim.

The arbitrators and the parties should consider the documents described in Document Production Lists 1 and 2 presumptively discoverable. Absent a written objection, documents on Document Production Lists 1 and 2 shall be exchanged by the parties within the time frames set forth in the NASD Customer Code. The arbitrators and parties also should consider the additional documents identified in Document Production Lists 3 through 14, respectively, discoverable, as indicated, for cases alleging the following causes of action: churning, failure to supervise, misrepresentation/omission, negligence/breach of fiduciary duty, unauthorized trading, and unsuitability. For the general document production and for each of these causes of action, there are separate Document Production Lists for firms/Associated Person(s) and for customers.

Confidentiality

---

[1] FINRA, Discovery Guide and Document Production List (post April 16, 2007), available at http://www.finra.org/ArbitrationMediation/Rules/RuleGuidance/DiscoveryGuide/index.htm (last accessed March 25, 2011).

If a party objects to document production on grounds of privacy or confidentiality, the arbitrator(s) or one of the parties may suggest a stipulation between the parties that the document(s) in question will not be disclosed or used in any manner outside of the arbitration of the particular case, or the arbitrator(s) may issue a confidentiality order. The arbitrator(s) shall not issue an order or use a confidentiality agreement to require parties to produce documents otherwise subject to an established privilege. Objections to the production of documents, based on an established privilege, should be raised in accordance with the time frame for objections set forth in the NASD Customer Code.

Affirmation In The Event That There Are No Responsive Documents or Information

If a party responds that no responsive information or documents exist, the customer or the appropriate person in the brokerage firm who has personal knowledge (i.e., the person who has conducted a physical search), upon the request of the requesting party, must: 1) state in writing that he/she conducted a good faith search for the requested information or documents; 2) describe the extent of the search; and 3) state that, based on the search, no such information or documents exist.

Admissibility

Production of documents in discovery does not create a presumption that the documents are admissible at the hearing. A party may state objections to the introduction of any document as evidence at the hearing to the same extent that any other objection may be raised in arbitration.

* * *

DOCUMENT PRODUCTION LISTS

* * *

LIST 1

DOCUMENTS TO BE PRODUCED IN ALL CUSTOMER CASES[1]

FIRM/ASSOCIATED PERSON(S):

1) All agreements with the customer, including, but not limited to, account opening documents, cash, margin, and option agreements, trading authorizations, powers of attorney, or discretionary authorization agreements, and new account forms.

2) All account statements for the customer's account(s) during the time period and/or relating to the transaction(s) at issue.

3) All confirmations for the customer's transaction(s) at issue. As an alternative, the firm/Associated Person(s) should ascertain from the claimant and produce those confirmations that are at issue and are not within claimant's possession, custody, or control.

4) All "holding (posting) pages" for the customer's account(s) at issue or, if not available, any electronic equivalent.

5) All correspondence between the customer and the firm/Associated Person(s) relating to the transaction(s) at issue.

6) All notes by the firm/Associated Person(s) or on his/her behalf, including entries in any diary or calendar, relating to the customer's account(s) at issue.

7) All recordings and notes of telephone calls or conversations about the customer's account(s) at issue that occurred between the Associated Person(s) and the customer (and any person purporting to act on behalf of the customer), and/or between the firm and the Associated Person(s).

8) All Forms RE-3, U-4, and U-5, including all amendments, all customer complaints identified in such forms, and all customer complaints of a similar nature against the Associated Person(s) handling the account(s) at issue.

9) All sections of the firm's Compliance Manual(s) related to the claims alleged in the statement of claim, including any separate or supplemental manuals governing the duties and responsibilities of the Associated Person(s) and supervisors, any bulletins (or similar notices) issued by the compliance department, and the entire table of contents and index to each such Manual.

10) All analyses and reconciliations of the customer's account(s) during the time period and/or relating to the transaction(s) at issue.

---

[1]   Only named parties must produce documents pursuant to the guidelines set forth herein. However, non-parties may be required to produce documents pursuant to a subpoena or an arbitration panel order to direct the production of documents (see Rule 12513). In addition, the arbitration chairperson may use the Document Production Lists as guidance for discovery issues involving non-parties.

11) All records of the firm/Associated Person(s) relating to the customer's account(s) at issue, such as, but not limited to, internal reviews and exception and activity reports which reference the customer's account(s) at issue.

12) Records of disciplinary action taken against the Associated Person(s) by any regulator or employer for all sales practices or conduct similar to the conduct alleged to be at issue.

* * *

LIST 2

DOCUMENTS TO BE PRODUCED IN ALL CUSTOMER CASES

CUSTOMER:

1) All customer and customer-owned business (including partnership or corporate) federal income tax returns, limited to pages 1 and 2 of Form 1040, Schedules B, D, and E, or the equivalent for any other type of return, for the three years prior to the first transaction at issue in the statement of claim through the date the statement of claim was filed.

2) Financial statements or similar statements of the customer's assets, liabilities and/or net worth for the period(s) covering the three years prior to the first transaction at issue in the statement of claim through the date the statement of claim was filed.

3) Copies of all documents the customer received from the firm/Associated Person(s) and from any entities in which the customer invested through the firm/Associated Person(s), including monthly statements, opening account forms, confirmations, prospectuses, annual and periodic reports, and correspondence.

4) Account statements and confirmations for accounts maintained at securities firms other than the respondent firm for the three years prior to the first transaction at issue in the statement of claim through the date the statement of claim was filed.

5) All agreements, forms, information, or documents relating to the account(s) at issue signed by or provided by the customer to the firm/Associated Person(s).

6) All account analyses and reconciliations prepared by or for the customer relating to the account(s) at issue.

7) All notes, including entries in diaries or calendars, relating to the account(s) at issue.

8) All recordings and notes of telephone calls or conversations about the customer's account(s) at issue that occurred between the Associated Person(s) and the customer (and any person purporting to act on behalf of the customer).

9) All correspondence between the customer (and any person acting on behalf of the customer) and the firm/Associated Person(s) relating to the account(s) at issue.

10) Previously prepared written statements by persons with knowledge of the facts and circumstances related to the account(s) at issue, including those by accountants, tax advisors, financial planners, other Associated Person(s), and any other third party.

11) All prior complaints by or on behalf of the customer involving securities matters and the firm's/Associated Person(s') response(s).

12) Complaints/Statements of Claim and Answers filed in all civil actions involving securities matters and securities arbitration proceedings in which the customer has been a party, and all final decisions and awards entered in these matters.

13) All documents showing action taken by the customer to limit losses in the transaction(s) at issue.

* * *

LIST 3

CHURNING

FIRM/ASSOCIATED PERSON(S)

1)   All commission runs relating to the customer's account(s) at issue or, in the alternative, a consolidated commission report relating to the customer's account(s) at issue.

2)   All documents reflecting compensation of any kind, including commissions, from all sources generated by the Associated Person(s) assigned to the customer's account(s) for the two months preceding through the two months following the transaction(s) at issue, or up to 12 months, whichever is longer. The firm may redact all information identifying customers who are not parties to the action, except that the firm/Associated Person(s) shall provide at least the last four digits of the non-party customer account number for each transaction.

3)   Documents sufficient to describe or set forth the basis upon which the Associated Person(s) was compensated during the years in which the transaction(s) or occurrence(s) in question occurred, including: a) any bonus or incentive program; and b) all compensation and commission schedules showing compensation received or to be received based upon volume, type of product sold, nature of trade (e.g., agency v. principal), etc.

* * *

LIST 4

CHURNING

CUSTOMER

No additional documents identified.

* * *

LIST 5

FAILURE TO SUPERVISE

FIRM/ASSOCIATED PERSON(S):

1)   All commission runs and other reports showing compensation of any kind relating to the customer's account(s) at issue or, in the alternative, a consolidated commission report relating to the customer's account(s) at issue.

2)   All exception reports and supervisory activity reviews relating to the Associated Person(s) and/or the customer's account(s) that were generated not earlier than one year before or not later than one year after the transaction(s) at issue, and all other documents reflecting supervision of the Associated Person(s) and the customer's account(s) at issue.

3)   Those portions of internal audit reports at the branch in which the customer maintained his/her account(s) that: (a) focused on the Associated Person(s) or the transaction(s) at issue; and (b) were generated not earlier than one year before or not later than one year after the transaction(s) at issue and discussed alleged improper behavior in the branch against other individuals similar to the improper conduct alleged in the statement of claim.

4)   Those portions of examination reports or similar reports following an examination or an inspection conducted by a state or federal agency or a self-regulatory organization that focused on the Associated Person(s) or the transaction(s) at issue or that discussed alleged improper behavior in the branch against other individuals similar to the improper conduct alleged in the statement of claim.

* * *

LIST 6

FAILURE TO SUPERVISE

CUSTOMER

No additional documents identified.
* * *

LIST 7

MISREPRESENTATION/OMISSIONS

FIRM/ASSOCIATED PERSON(S)

Copies of all materials prepared or used by the firm/Associated Person(s) relating to the transactions or products at issue, including research reports, prospectuses, and other offering documents, including documents intended or identified as being "for internal use only," and worksheets or notes indicating the Associated Person(s) reviewed or read such documents. As an alternative, the firm/Associated Person(s) may produce a list of such documents that contains sufficient detail for the claimant to identify each document listed. Upon further request by a party, the firm/Associated Person(s) must provide any documents identified on the list.

* * *

LIST 8

MISREPRESENTATION/OMISSIONS

CUSTOMER

    1)   Documents sufficient to show the customer's ownership in or control over any business entity, including general and limited partnerships and closely held corporations.

    2)   Copy of the customer's resume.

    3)   Documents sufficient to show the customer's complete educational and employment background or, in the alternative, a description of the customer's educational and employment background if not set forth in a resume produced under item 2.

* * *

LIST 9

NEGLIGENCE/BREACH OF FIDUCIARY DUTY

FIRM/ASSOCIATED PERSON(S)

    Copies of all materials prepared or used by the firm/Associated Person(s) relating to the transactions or products at issue, including research reports, prospectuses, and other offering documents, including documents intended or identified as being "for internal use only," and worksheets or notes indicating the Associated Person(s) reviewed or read such documents. As an alternative, the firm/Associated Person(s) may produce a list of such documents that contains sufficient detail for the claimant to identify each document listed. Upon further request by a party, the firm/Associated Person(s) must provide any documents identified on the list.

LIST 10

NEGLIGENCE/BREACH OF FIDUCIARY DUTY

CUSTOMER

    1)   Documents sufficient to show the customer's ownership in or control over any business entity, including general and limited partnerships and closely held corporations.

    2)   Copy of the customer's resume.

    3)   Documents sufficient to show the customer's complete educational and employment background or, in the alternative, a description of the customer's educational and employment background if not set forth in a resume produced under item 2.

* * *

LIST 11

UNAUTHORIZED TRADING

FIRM/ASSOCIATED PERSON(S)

1) Order tickets for the customer's transaction(s) at issue.

2) Copies of all telephone records, including telephone logs, evidencing telephone contact between the customer and the firm/Associated Person(s).

3) All documents relied upon by the firm/Associated Person(s) to establish that the customer authorized the transaction(s) at issue.

LIST 12

UNAUTHORIZED TRADING

CUSTOMER

1. Copies of all telephone records, including telephone logs, evidencing telephone contact between the customer and the firm/Associated Person(s).

2. All documents relied upon by the customer to show that the transaction(s) at issue was made without his/her knowledge or consent.

* * *

LIST 13

UNSUITABILITY

FIRM/ASSOCIATED PERSON(S)

1) Copies of all materials prepared, used, or reviewed by the firm/Associated Person(s) related to the transactions or products at issue, including but not limited to research reports, prospectuses, other offering documents, including documents intended or identified as being "for internal use only," and worksheets or notes indicating the Associated Person(s) reviewed or read such documents. As an alternative, the firm/Associated Person(s) may produce a list of such documents. Upon further request by a party, the firm/Associated Person(s) must provide any documents identified on the list.

2) Documents sufficient to describe or set forth the basis upon which the Associated Person(s) was compensated in any manner during the years in which the transaction(s) or occurrence(s) in question occurred, including, but not limited to: a) any bonus or incentive program; and b) all compensation and commission schedules showing compensation received or to be received based upon volume, type of product sold, nature of trade (e.g., agency v. principal), etc.

LIST 14

UNSUITABILITY

CUSTOMER

1) Documents sufficient to show the customer's ownership in or control over any business entity, including general and limited partnerships and closely held corporations.

2) Written documents relied upon by the customer in making the investment decision(s) at issue.

3) Copy of the customer's resume.

4) Documents sufficient to show the customer's complete educational and employment background or, in the alternative, a description of the customer's educational and employment background if not set forth in a resume produced under item 3.

APPENDIX 13J-1

Code of Procedure for National Arbitration Forum[1]

NATIONAL ARBITRATION FORUM
Code of Procedure
August 1, 2008

i

---

[1]National Arbitration Forum, Code of Procedure (August 1, 2008), available at http://www.adrforum.com/resource.aspx?id=1423 (last accessed March 29, 2011).

PART I

SCOPE

RULE 1. Arbitration Agreement.

A. Parties who contract for or agree to arbitration provided by the Forum or this Code of Procedure agree that this Code governs their arbitration proceedings, unless the Parties agree to other procedures. This Code shall be deemed incorporated by reference in every Arbitration Agreement, which refers to the National Arbitration Forum, the International Arbitration Forum, the Arbitration Forum, adrforum.com, Forum or this Code of Procedure, unless the Parties agree otherwise. This Code shall be administered only by the National Arbitration Forum or by any entity or individual providing administrative services by agreement with the National Arbitration Forum.

B. Parties may agree to submit any matter, including any Claim for legal or equitable relief, to arbitration unless prohibited by applicable law.

2

C. Arbitrations will be conducted in accord with the applicable Code of Procedure in effect at the time the Claim is filed, unless the law or the agreement of the Parties provides otherwise. A case that has been Stayed, extended or Adjourned for more than one hundred-eighty (180) days may be subject to the Code of Procedure and Fee Schedule in effect at the time the case proceeds.

D. Parties may modify or supplement these rules as permitted by law. Provisions of this Code govern arbitrations involving an appeal or a review de novo of an arbitration by other Arbitrators.

RULE 2. Definitions.

For purposes of this Code, the following definitions apply:

A. Affidavit: A Written statement of a person who asserts the statement to be true under penalty of perjury or who makes the statement under oath before a notary public or other authorized individual.

B. Adjournment: A continuance or delay for a specific period of time requested after the appointment of an Arbitrator. See Time Extension and Stay.

C. Amendment: A change made to a Claim after it has been served on the Respondent and any change made to a Response after it has been filed and Delivered to all Parties.

D. Appearance: Any filing by a Party or Party's Representative under Rules 12, 13, 19B, 41A or 44H.

E. Arbitration Agreement: Any Written provision in any agreement between or among the Parties to submit any dispute, controversy or Claim to the Forum or to arbitration under this Code.

F. Arbitrator: An individual selected in accord with the Code or an Arbitration Agreement to render Orders and Awards, including a sole Arbitrator and all Arbitrators of an arbitration panel. No Arbitrator may be a director or officer of the Forum. A Party Arbitrator is an Arbitrator selected by a Party to serve as a member of a panel of Arbitrators in accord with the agreement of the Parties.

G. Award: Any Award establishing the final rights and obligations of the Parties or as otherwise provided by this Code or by law.

H. Claim: Any Claim submitted by any Party including an Initial Claim, Cross-claim, Counter Claim, and Third Party Claim.

I. Claimant: Any individual or Entity making any Claim under this Code.

3

J. Claim Amount: The total value of all relief sought. A Claimant seeking non-monetary relief states a monetary value for this relief for purposes of establishing the Claim Amount.

K. Common Claim: A Claim Amount less than $75,000.

L. Consumer: An individual, who is not a business or other Entity, whose Claim or Response against a business or other Entity arises:

(1) From a transaction or event entered into primarily for personal, family or household purposes;

(2) From an existing, past or prospective employment relationship with an employer Party; or

(3) From a transaction or event involving any aspect of health care.

M. Delivery: Delivery to the address of a Party, the Forum or an Arbitrator by the postal service of the United States or any country, or by a reliable private service, or by facsimile, e-mail, electronic or computer transmission.

N. Director: The Director of Arbitration and the Forum staff administer arbitrations under this Code or under other rules agreed to by the Parties.

O. Document: Any Writing or data compilation containing information in any form, including an agreement, record, correspondence, summary, electronically stored information, tape, e-mail, video, audio, disk, computer file, electronic attachment, notice, memorandum or other Writings or data compilations.

P. E-commerce Transaction: All contracts and agreements entered into, in whole or in part, by electronic or computer communication and all transactions consummated through electronic or computer communication.

Q. Entity: Any association, business, company, cooperative, corporation, country, governmental unit, group, institution, organization, partnership, sole proprietorship, union or other establishment.

R. Fee Schedule: The Fee Schedule appears in a supplement to this Code.

S. Forum: The National Arbitration Forum, the International Arbitration Forum, the Arbitration Forum, arbitration-forum.com, and adrforum.com constitute the administrative organizations conducting arbitrations under this Code. The Forum or an entity or individual providing administrative services by agreement with the Forum administers arbitrations in accord with this Code.

T. Hearing: Hearings include:

4

(1) Document Hearing: A proceeding in which an Arbitrator reviews documents or property to render an Order or Award and the Parties do not attend.

(2) Participatory Hearing: Any proceeding in which an Arbitrator receives testimony or arguments and reviews documents or property to render an Order or Award. The types of Participatory Hearings include:

    a. In-person Hearing – A Hearing at which the participants may appear before the Arbitrator in person;

    b. Telephone Hearing – A Hearing at which the participants may appear before the Arbitrator by telephone; and,

    c. On-line Hearing – A Hearing at which the participants may appear before the Arbitrator on-line, by e-mail or by other electronic or computer communication.

U. Interim Order: Any Order providing temporary or preliminary relief pending a final Award.

V. Large Claim: A Claim Amount of $75,000 or more.

W. Order: Any Order establishing specific rights and obligations of the Parties.

(1) A Dispositive Order results in a final Award or dismissal of any Claim or Response.

(2) All other Orders are Non-dispositive.

X. Party: Any individual or Entity who makes a Claim or against whom a Claim is made including Claimants, Respondents, Cross-claimants, and Third Parties.

Y. Party Witness: Any person who is an individual Party or who is an employee of an entity Party at the time of the service of the subpoena.

Z. Proof of Service: An Affidavit stating how and where service was made.

AA. Receive or Receipt: The Delivery or other effective notice to the Forum, or to a Party at the address of the Party or Party Representative.

BB. Representative: Any individual, including an attorney, who makes an appearance on behalf of a Party.

CC. Request: Any Request by a Party directed to an Arbitrator or the Forum for an Order or other relief, including any motion, petition or other type of Request.

DD. Respondent: Any Party against whom a Claim is made.

EE. Response: Any Written Response by a Party or Representative to any Claim.

5

FF. Sanctions: Sanctions include dismissal of the arbitration or the Claims or Responses; preclusion of evidence; admission of facts; payment of costs; payment of fees including reasonable attorney fees, Arbitrator fees, and arbitration fees; the rendering of an Order or Award; and other Sanctions deemed appropriate. Sanctions may be imposed against a Party, a Representative or both.

GG. Signature or Signed: Any mark, symbol or device intended as an attestation, produced by any reliable means, including an electronic transcription intended as a Signature.

HH. Stay: A delay for an indefinite period of time requested by a Claimant before an Arbitrator is appointed. See Time Extension and Adjournment.

II. Time Extension: A continuance or delay for a specific period of time requested before the appointment of an Arbitrator. See Adjournment and Stay.

JJ. With Prejudice: The case cannot be brought again. The Claimant cannot subsequently bring the same Claim against the Respondent.

KK. Without Prejudice: The case may be brought again. The Claimant can subsequently file the same Claim against the same Respondent.

LL. Writing or Written: Any form intended to record information, including symbols on paper or other substance, recording tape, computer disk, electronic recording, and video recording and all other forms.

RULE 3. Representation.

A. Parties may act on their own behalf or may be represented by an attorney or by a person who makes an appearance on behalf of a Party.

B. Parties, their Representatives, and all participants shall act respectfully toward the Forum staff, the Arbitrator, other Parties, Representatives, witnesses, and participants in the arbitration.

RULE 4. Confidentiality.

Arbitration proceedings are confidential unless all Parties agree or the law requires arbitration information to be made public. Arbitration Orders and Awards are not confidential and may be disclosed by a Party. The Arbitrator and Forum may disclose case filings, case dispositions, and other case information filed with the Forum as required by a Court Order or the applicable law.

6

PART II

COMMENCEMENT OF
ARBITRATION

RULE 5. Summary of Procedures.

A. Claim. A Party begins an arbitration by filing with the Forum a properly completed copy of the Initial Claim described in Rule 12, accompanied by the appropriate filing fee which appears in the Fee Schedule. The Forum reviews the Claim, opens a file, assigns a file number, and notifies the Claimant, who then serves the Respondent in accord with Rule 6.

B. Response. A Respondent may file a Response as explained in Rule 13 or respond otherwise as explained in these rules and the Notices of Arbitration, which appear in Appendices A and B. If there is no timely Response, the arbitration proceeds in accord with Rule 36.

C. After a Response. The arbitration proceeds in accord with a Scheduling Notice issued by the Forum or by action by the Parties.

D. Hearing. A Party may select a Document Hearing under Rule 25 or a Participatory Hearing under Rule 26 and pay the fee, if any, listed in the Fee Schedule. Parties have a full and equal right to present relevant and reliable direct and cross examination testimony, documents, exhibits, evidence, and arguments. A record may be made of Participatory Hearings.

E. Arbitrator. The Parties select an Arbitrator(s) by mutual agreement in accord with Rules 21, 22, and 23. Forum arbitrators are neutral, independent, experienced, and knowledgeable about the applicable law.

F. Arbitrator Qualifications. A neutral Arbitrator shall not serve if circumstances exist that create a conflict of interest or cause the Arbitrator to be unfair or biased in accord with Rules 21 and 23. A Forum Arbitrator may also be removed similar to the ways a judge or juror may be stricken.

G. Arbitrator Powers. An Arbitrator decides issues in a case including questions of fact and law. An Arbitrator follows the applicable substantive law and may grant any remedy or relief provided by law or equity, including monetary and injunctive relief, in accord with Rules 20, 27, 37, and 38.

H. Discovery. Before a Hearing is held, Parties shall cooperate in the discovery process and may exchange and obtain discovery in accord with Rule 29.

I. Requests. Parties may seek appropriate relief or remedies in accord with Rule 18.

7

J. Fee Schedules. The Fee Schedules appear in a supplement to this Code. The Forum Fee Schedules are a model of fair cost and fee allocation. The Common Claim Fee Schedule governs amounts under $75,000, and the Large Claim Fee Schedule governs all other Claim Amounts.

K. Consumers. See Rule 2L. Consumers include Consumers, employees, and patients. Consumers pay only reasonable arbitration fees as explained in these Rules and the Fee Schedule, and as required by the applicable law. Other Parties may have to pay fees for Consumers.

L. Indigent Parties. In accord with Rule 45, Consumers who meet the United States Federal poverty standards need not pay arbitration fees.

M. Substantive Law and Remedies. All types of legal and equitable remedies and relief available in court are available in arbitration. Claims, Responses, remedies or relief cannot be unlawfully restricted, and Parties may effectively pursue any remedy or relief in arbitration including statutory, common law, injunctive, equitable, and all other lawful remedies and relief.

N. Award or Order. After a Hearing, an Arbitrator shall promptly issue an Award or Order in accord with Rule 37 or 38. Reasons, findings of fact, and conclusions of law shall be in accord with Rule 37 or 38.

O. Review and Enforcement. An Award may be enforced in any court of competent jurisdiction, as provided by applicable law. An Award or Order may be reviewed by a court with jurisdiction to determine whether the Arbitrator properly applied the applicable substantive law and whether the arbitration complied with applicable arbitration laws.

P. Public Information. Arbitration information may be made public in accord with Rule 4 or as required by Court Order.

Q. Access to Justice. This Code shall be interpreted to provide all Parties with a fair and impartial arbitration and with reasonable access to civil justice. Arbitrations under the Code are governed by the Federal Arbitration Act in accord with Rule 48B.

RULE 6. Service of Claims, Responses, Requests, and Documents.

A. After being notified by the Forum that a Claim has been accepted for filing in accord with Rules 7 and 12, and a file number has been provided, the Claimant shall promptly serve on each Respondent one (1) copy of the Initial Claim Documents, containing the Forum file number, together with a Notice of Arbitration substantially conforming to Appendix A of this Code, including notice that the Respondent may obtain a copy of the Code, without cost, from the Claimant or the Forum.

B. Service of Initial Claims and Third Party Claims shall be effective if done by:

    (1) United States Postal Service Certified Mail Signed return receipt or equivalent service by the national postal service of the country where the Respondent resides or does business;

8

(2) Delivery by a private service with the Delivery receipt Signed by a person of suitable age and discretion who Received the Documents;

(3) Delivery with a Written acknowledgment of Delivery by the Respondent or a Representative;

(4) In accord with the Federal Rules of Civil Procedure of the United States or the rules of civil procedure of the jurisdiction where the Respondent entered into the Arbitration Agreement;

(5) In accord with any agreement of the Party served;

(6) For Claims related to or arising from an E-commerce Transaction, Delivery to the e-mail address of the Party served, Receipt confirmed; or

(7) Service is complete upon Receipt by the Party served or the filing of a Response with the Forum by a Respondent.

C. Service of Responses, Counter Claims, Cross-claims, Requests, notices, and Documents shall be by Delivery, as defined in Rule 2M, to the address of all Parties or their Representatives at their addresses of record with the Forum, or by using service methods for an Initial Claim in Rule 6B. Amended Claims shall be served or Delivered as provided in Rule 17D.

D. The Party serving or Delivering a Claim, Response, Request, notice or Document shall timely Deliver copies to all Parties not required to be served. This rule does not apply to a Rule 45 Request.

E. Parties and Representatives shall immediately notify the Forum and all other Parties of their mail, facsimile and e-mail address and any changes in their addresses. If they fail to do so, Parties and their Representatives agree to Receive service at the previous address provided to the Forum.

RULE 7. Filing.

A. A Party who serves a Claim or Response shall timely file these and all other Documents and Proof of Service with the Forum. The filing of Proof of Service constitutes a certification that the service conforms to Rule 6. A Party who files paper Documents with the Forum shall file two (2) copies. A Party who files Documents online need only file one set of Documents.

B. Parties may file by Delivery as defined in Rule 2M, in person, or by other methods of filing authorized by the Forum at:

P.O. Box 50191
Minneapolis, Minnesota USA 55405-0191
or

9

www.adrforum.com
or
file@adrforum.com
or
Fax: 952-345-1160

C. Upon Proof of Service of an Initial Claim, where no Response has been filed, the Forum shall mail to Respondent the Second Notice of Arbitration, substantially conforming to Appendix B of this Code.

D. The Forum may distribute copies of Documents filed with the Forum to Parties or their Representatives who have entered an Appearance with the Forum.

E. Filing is complete upon Receipt by the Forum of all required Documents and fees. Claims, Responses, Requests, Notices, and all other Documents Received by the Forum are not considered filed until all required Documents are Received together with all applicable fees.

F. The effective date of filing is the business day the Forum Receives all required Documents and fees. A submission is due before Midnight, United States Central time, on its due date.

RULE 8. Notices and Conferences.

A. The Forum may notify and communicate with a Party or Parties by Writing, facsimile, e-mail, telex, telegram, telephone, in person or by other means of communication.

B. The Forum or Arbitrator may conduct a conference with a Party or Parties to discuss procedural matters on the initiative of the Forum or at the Request of a Party or Arbitrator.

C. The Forum may issue a Scheduling Notice regarding the Hearing process, including preliminary Hearings.

RULE 9. Time Periods, Time Extensions, Adjournments, and Stays.

A. **Time Periods.** In computing any period of time under this Code, the day of the act or event from which the designated period of time begins to run shall not be included.

B. **Holidays.** Saturdays, Sundays, and federal holidays of the United States are included in the computation of time, except when they fall on the last day of a period.

C. Enforcement. The time periods established in this Code are to be strictly enforced and a Party's untimely Claim, Response, Request, Notice, Document or submission may be denied solely because it is untimely.

D. **Time Extensions.** The Forum may extend time periods in this Code. A Request for a Time Extension must be filed with the Forum and delivered on all other Parties at least five (5) days before the time period ends or no later than a deadline established by a Scheduling Notice, whichever is earlier, and must be accompanied by a fee, if any, as provided in the Fee Schedule.

10

A Request submitted after the time period has ended will not be considered unless extraordinary circumstances exist.

E. **Adjournments.** An Arbitrator may Adjourn the arbitration process or a Hearing to a later date. A Rule 18 Request for an Adjournment must be filed with the Forum and served on the other Parties at least seven (7) days before the scheduled event and must be accompanied by a fee, if any, as provided in the Fee Schedule. A Request submitted after the time period has ended will not be considered unless extraordinary circumstances exist. Any other Party may object to a Request by filing with the Forum and serving on all other Parties an objection within three (3) days of the Request being filed with the Forum.

F. **Stays.**

(1) A Claimant may obtain a Stay of a case for an indefinite period of time by filing with the Forum and serving on all other Parties a Stay Notice prior to the appointment of an Arbitrator. An opposing Party may end a Stay by filing with the Forum and serving on all Parties an objection which ends the Stay. Claimant may file only one (1) Stay Notice and may seek a subsequent Stay by submitting a Rule 18 Request. A Stay suspends the time when proceedings and hearings occur and when Documents and Fees are due.

(2) By submitting a Notice at any time, Parties may mutually agree to Stay a matter based on a settlement agreement. Upon receipt of the Notice, the Forum shall stay the matter for the duration of the settlement agreement. Any Party may end such a Stay by filing with the Forum and serving on all Parties an objection seeking to end the Stay.

(3) The Forum shall Stay a case if ordered by a court of competent jurisdiction, and may Stay a case when reasonably necessary.

G. **International.** For arbitration Hearings to be held outside of the United States, an additional thirty (30) days shall be added to the time periods in Rule 13 of this Code. Additional time for other proceedings will be made available at the determination of the Forum or at the Request of a Party.

RULE 10. Time Limitations.

A. No Claim may be brought after the passage of time which would preclude a Claim regarding the same or similar subject matter being brought in court. This time limitation shall be suspended for the period of time a court of competent jurisdiction exercises authority over the Claim or dispute. This rule shall not extend nor shorten statutes of limitation or time limits agreed to by the Parties, nor shall this rule apply to any case that is directed to arbitration by a court of competent jurisdiction.

B. An arbitration shall commence on the date the Respondent is served with the Initial Claim Documents or the date a Response is filed with the Forum, whichever is earlier.

11

PART III

DOCUMENTS

RULE 11. Form and Parties.

A. Every Claim, Response, Amendment, and Request shall be in Writing and Signed by a Party or Representative.

B. Parties and Representatives shall provide the Forum and all Parties with their names, current address, an address where service will be accepted, telephone numbers, and available facsimile numbers and e-mail addresses. Respondents shall provide the Forum with the address of their residence or business for determination of the proper location of the Hearing in accord with Rule 32.

C. Statements in Claims, Responses, Amendments, and Requests may be made in separate or numbered sentences, paragraphs or sections, and may refer to exhibits attached to Claims, Responses, Requests or Documents.

D. English is the language used in Forum proceedings unless the Parties agree to use another language. The Forum or Arbitrator may Order the Parties to provide translations at their own cost unless the Forum has agreed in advance to the use of another language.

E. A Party may be:

    (1) An executor, administrator, guardian, bailee, trustee, or

    (2) An assignee, a successor in interest, a recipient of a transfer of interest, or

    (3) A guardian, conservator, fiduciary, or other legal Representative for an infant or incompetent person.

Proof of the status of a Party under this rule must be made by an Affidavit filed with the Forum. A Party who contests the status of another Party may file a Rule 18 Request for relief with the fee, if any, as provided in the Fee Schedule.

RULE 12. Initial Claim.

A. An Initial Claim, which begins an arbitration in accord with Rule 6 of this Code, shall include:

    (1) A statement in plain language of the dispute or controversy, the facts and the law (if known) supporting the Claim, the specific relief requested and the reasons supporting the

relief, the specific amount and computation of any money or damages, the specific value of non-monetary or other relief, the specific amount and computation of any interest, costs, and attorney fees under Rule 12B, and other relevant and reliable information supporting the Claim;

(2) A copy of the Arbitration Agreement, or, if not in the possession of the Claimant, notice of the location of a copy of the Arbitration Agreement;

(3) A copy of available Documents that support the Claim;

(4) An Affidavit asserting that the information in the Claim is accurate; and

(5) The appropriate Filing Fee as provided in the Fee Schedule.

B. A Claimant who seeks costs and attorney fees must include this statement in the Claim and may either:

(1) State the specific amount sought in the Claim; or

(2) Amend the Claim to state the specific amount sought:

    a. For Document Hearings no later than ten (10) days from the date of the Notice of the Selection of an Arbitrator; or

    b. For Participatory Hearings no later than seven (7) days from the close of the Hearing; or

    c. For prevailing Parties, by Order of the Arbitrator.

C. After service of the Initial Claim on the Respondent, the Claimant shall promptly file with the Forum Proof of Service of the Initial Claim on the Respondent. A Claim shall not proceed to arbitration until the Forum has received a copy of the Proof of Service of the Initial Claim or a Response has been filed with the Forum.

D. An Arbitrator may reject, in whole or in part, an Initial Claim that does not substantially conform to this rule.

E. A Claimant may seek any remedy or relief allowed by applicable substantive law.

RULE 13. Response.

A. Upon service of an Initial Claim, Counter Claim, Cross-claim, or Third Party Claim on a Respondent, the Respondent shall Deliver to the Claimant and file with the Forum, within thirty (30) days from Receipt of service or fourteen (14) days from the date of the Second Notice of Arbitration, whichever is later, a Response which shall include:

(1) A Written Document stating in plain language a Response to the Claim or stating the Respondent has insufficient information to affirm or deny a statement. A Response shall

also include any defenses to each Claim made, the facts and the law (if known) supporting the defenses, including affirmative defenses and set offs;

(2) An objection to the arbitration of the Claim, if the Respondent so objects. A Response that does not assert this objection is an agreement to the arbitration of the Claim and a waiver of this objection which cannot be asserted in an Amendment;

(3) A copy of available Documents that support the Response;

(4) Any Counter Claim the Respondent has against the Claimant in accord with Rule 14 of this Code, including the Counter Claim filing fee;

(5) Proof of Delivery of the Response to all other Parties; and

(6) Any fees as provided in the Fee Schedule or as required by the agreement of the Parties.

B. A Party may obtain ten (10) additional days to respond to an Initial Claim by filing with the Forum and Delivering to all other Parties an extension Notice before the Response is due. Only one (1) extension by Notice is available.

C. A Respondent who responds but does not state available replies, defenses or Claims may be barred by the Arbitrator from presenting such replies, defenses or Claims at the Hearing. The failure of a Respondent to deny a statement in a Claim may be considered by the Arbitrator as an admission of that statement.

D. An Arbitrator may reject, in whole or in part, a Response that does not substantially conform to this rule.

RULE 14. Counter Claim.

A. A Respondent may assert a Counter Claim against a Claimant by Delivering to the Claimant, as part of the Response in accord with Rule 13, Counter Claim Documents which include:

(1) A Counter Claim stating in plain language the dispute or controversy, the facts and the law (if known) supporting the Counter Claim, the specific relief requested and the reasons supporting the relief, the specific amount and computation of any money or damages, the specific value of non-monetary or other relief, the specific amount and computation of any interest, costs, and attorney fees under Rule 12B, and other relevant and reliable information supporting the Counter Claim;

(2) A copy of available Documents that support the Counter Claim; and

(3) An Affidavit asserting that the information in the Counter Claim is accurate.

B. The Respondent shall also pay the filing fee for a Counter Claim as provided in the Fee Schedule at the time of filing the Counter Claim with the Forum.

14

C. An Arbitrator may reject, in whole or in part, Counter Claim Documents that do not substantially conform to this rule.

RULE 15. Cross-claim.

A. A Party may assert a Claim against a co-Party arising out of the same or related transaction or occurrence of the dispute or controversy by Delivering to the co-Party the Cross-claim Documents which include:

> (1) A Cross-claim setting forth in plain language the dispute or controversy, the facts and the law (if known) supporting the Cross-claim, the specific relief requested and the reasons supporting the relief, the specific amount and computation of any money or damages, the specific value of non-monetary or other relief, the specific amount and computation of any interest, costs, and attorney fees under Rule 12B, and other relevant and reliable information supporting the Cross-claim;

> (2) A copy of available Documents that support the Cross-claim; and

> (3) An Affidavit asserting that the information in the Cross-claim is accurate.

B. A Party shall Deliver a Cross-claim on all Parties and shall file copies with the Forum within fifteen (15) days of the date of service of a Response.

C. The Cross-claimant shall file with the Forum, promptly after Delivery of the Cross-claim, the proof of Delivery of the Cross-claim on all Parties, with the fee for filing a Cross-claim, if any, and the fee for a Hearing, if selected, as provided in the Fee Schedule.

D. An Arbitrator may reject, in whole or in part, Cross-claim Documents that do not substantially conform to this Rule.

RULE 16. Third Party Claim.

A. If a Respondent asserts that a non-Party, who has entered into an Arbitration Agreement but was not served by the Claimant, is responsible for the Award demanded, the Respondent may serve a Third Party Claim on this Party, which shall include:

> (1) All information required in an Initial Claim in Rule 12 of this Code, including a copy of the Claim Documents that gave rise to the Third Party Claim; and

> (2) A copy of the Arbitration Agreement, or notice of the location of a copy of the Arbitration Agreement.

B. The Third Party Claim shall be Delivered to all other Parties and a copy shall be filed with the Forum within thirty (30) days of the date of service of the Initial Claim, as required by Rule 16A.

15

C. The Third Party Claimant shall file with the Forum, promptly after service of the Third Party Claim the Proof of Service of the Third Party Claim on Third Party Respondent and proof of Delivery on all other Parties, with the fee for a Third Party Claim, and the fee for a Hearing, if selected, as provided in the Fee Schedule.

D. An Arbitrator may reject, in whole or in part, Third Party Claim Documents that do not substantially conform to this rule.

RULE 17. Amendment.

A. A Claim or Response may be Amended:

    (1) By agreement of the Parties at any time;

    (2) By Request, not later than the Scheduling Notice deadline or ten (10) days from the date of the Notice of Selection of an Arbitrator for a Document Hearing or thirty (30) days before the earliest date set for a Participatory Hearing, if the Amendment does not delay the arbitration and promotes fairness, efficiency, or economy, which Request shall be promptly decided by an Arbitrator; or

    (3) By Request during or within three (3) days following a Document or Participatory Hearing, if the Arbitrator finds the Amendment conforms to the evidence received.

B. An Amendment of a Claim or Response, or a Request for an Amendment, shall be designated as such and promptly served on all Parties and filed with the Forum. Any Party may object to the Amendment Request by filing with the Forum and Delivering to all Parties a Written objection(s) within ten (10) days of Delivery of the Request. An amended Claim which increases the Claim Amount shall also be accompanied by the additional filing fee in the Fee Schedule. An amended Claim, excluding Amendments agreed to by all Parties, shall also be accompanied by the Amendment Request Fee as provided in the Fee Schedule.

C. A Respondent shall respond to an amended Claim within the time remaining for a Response to the Initial Claim or within fifteen (15) days after service of the amended Claim, whichever time is longer, unless the Parties agree or an Arbitrator orders otherwise.

D. After service of the Initial Claim, an Amendment of a Claim that increases the monetary amount of the value of relief sought in the Initial Claim must be served in accord with Rule 6B. All other Amendments may be Delivered in accord with Rule 2M.

E. Any change to the Claim before service is made on Respondent is not an Amendment. After service, a reduction of the Claim Amount, a change of address of a Party, and the substitution of a successor in interest are not Amendments.

F. An Amendment of a Claim shall relate back to the time the Initial Claim was commenced unless otherwise provided by applicable law.

16

RULE 18. Request to Arbitrator or Forum.

A. A Party may Request an Order or other relief from an Arbitrator or the Forum by filing with the Forum:

    (1) A Document stating in plain language:

        a. The Request;
        b. The specific rule, if any, relied on for an Order or other relief;
        c. The specific relief or Order sought;
        d. The facts and law supporting the Request; and
        e. Any other relevant and reliable information.

    (2) All Documents that support the Request, Order or relief;

    (3) Proof of Delivery of the Request Documents on all Parties; and

    (4) The fee, as provided in the Fee Schedule.

B. The Party shall Deliver the Rule 18A(1) and (2) Documents to all Parties at the time of filing.

C. Any other Party may object to a Request by filing with the Forum and Delivering to all Parties a Written objection(s) within ten (10) days of Delivery of the Request, unless another time is provided by rule or is necessary based on the relief requested.

D. Requests directed to the Forum are decided by the Forum as permitted by the Code. Requests directed to an Arbitrator are decided by an Arbitrator. Prior to the appointment of an Arbitrator, Requests may be granted by the Forum as permitted by this Code.

E. All Requests or motions made by a Party are Rule 18 Requests. A Party filing a Request or objection must pay the fee, if any, as provided in the Fee Schedule. A Request or motion to reconsider is usually not granted, unless the controlling law has changed. The Fee Schedule lists fees that may accompany Rule 18 Requests, objections, procedures, and proceedings.

F. No Request may be filed later than the Scheduling Notice deadline or fifteen (15) days before a Participatory Hearing or for Document Hearings later than ten (10) days from the date of the Notice of the Selection of an Arbitrator, unless another time is provided by rule or is necessary based on the relief requested.

RULE 19. Joinder, Intervention, Consolidation, and Separation.

A. Any individual or Entity may, as agreed to by the Parties or as required by applicable law, join any dispute, controversy, Claim or Response in an arbitration by filing a Claim Document stating the grounds. An Arbitrator has no authority to issue an Order or Award binding any

17

individual or Entity not a Party, unless that individual or Entity agrees or as required by applicable law. The Forum may require a Party to pay a fee.

B. Any individual or Entity that entered into the Arbitration Agreement between Claimant and Respondent may intervene in an arbitration if a common question of fact or law arising from the same or related transaction or occurrence exists and such a proceeding promotes fairness, efficiency or economy. The Forum may require a Party to pay a fee.

C. Separate arbitrations involving the same named Parties and a common question of fact or law arising from the same or related transaction or occurrence shall be consolidated at the Request of a Party or at the determination of the Forum if the consolidation promotes fairness, efficiency or economy. A Party may challenge this consolidation by filing a Rule 18 Request for severance, and an Arbitrator shall promptly decide this Request by determining whether consolidation or severance promotes fairness, efficiency or economy. The Forum may require a Party to pay a fee.

D. An arbitration involving multiple Claims or Responses or Parties may be separated into individual Hearings if such proceedings promote fairness, efficiency or economy. The Forum may require the Party or Parties to pay Hearing fees for separate Hearings.

E. A Request by an individual or Entity to join or intervene or a Request by a Party for separation must be filed in accord with Rule 18.

F. An Arbitrator shall promptly decide Requests for joinder, intervention, severance or separation. Any decision by an arbitrator joining, consolidating or aggregating parties or claims is an Award under 9 U.S.C. Section 9.

18

PART IV

ARBITRATORS

RULE 20. Authority of Arbitrators.

A. Arbitrators have the powers provided by this Code, the agreement of the Parties, and the applicable law.

B. Arbitrators selected in accord with Rule 21A(3) shall take an oath prescribed by the Director and shall be neutral and independent.

C. Arbitrators shall decide all factual, legal, and other arbitrable issues submitted by the Parties and do not have the power to decide matters not properly submitted under this Code.

D. An Arbitrator shall follow the applicable substantive law and may grant any legal, equitable or other remedy or relief provided by law in deciding a Claim, Response or Request properly submitted by a Party under this Code. Claims, Responses, remedies or relief cannot be unlawfully restricted.

E. An Arbitrator shall have the power to rule on all issues, Claims, defenses, questions of arbitrability, and objections relating to the existence, scope, and validity of the contract, transaction, or relationship of the Parties.

F. An Arbitrator shall have the power to rule on all issues, Claims, Responses, questions of arbitrability, and objections regarding the existence, scope, and validity of the Arbitration Agreement including all objections relating to jurisdiction, unconscionability, contract law, and enforceability of the Arbitration Agreement.

RULE 21. Selection of Arbitrators.

A. Parties select an Arbitrator(s):

    (1) By selecting an Arbitrator or a panel of Arbitrators on mutually agreeable terms; or

    (2) By each Party selecting an Arbitrator and those Arbitrators selecting another Arbitrator for a panel of Arbitrators; or

    (3) In the absence of an election of Rule 21A(1) or (2), by using the selection process in Rules 21B through 23 of this Code.

Parties must notify the Forum of their election of Rule 21A(1) or (2), or other agreement for Arbitrator selection, no later than thirty (30) days after the filing of a Response with the Forum.

19

B. For Large Claim Hearings, the Forum shall provide to each Party making an Appearance a list of Arbitrator candidates equal in number to the number of Parties plus the number of Arbitrators required under Rule 22. Each Party making an Appearance may strike one of the candidates and may Request disqualification of any candidate in accord with Rule 23C by notifying the Forum in Writing, within ten (10) days of the date of the strike list.

C. For Common Claim Hearings, the Forum shall submit one Arbitrator candidate to all Parties making an Appearance. A Party making an Appearance may remove one Arbitrator candidate by filing a notice of removal with the Forum within ten (10) days from the date of the notice of Arbitrator selection. A Party making an Appearance may request disqualification of any subsequent Arbitrator in accord with Rule 23.

D. Upon Request for an Expedited Hearing or if the need for an Arbitrator arises before an Arbitrator is designated in accord with Rule 21A, the Forum shall promptly designate an Arbitrator and the issues to be decided.

E. A Party is prohibited from striking or removing an Arbitrator or an Arbitrator candidate based on race, gender, nationality, ethnicity, religion, age, disability, marital status, family status, or sexual orientation. <u>A party may only strike or remove an arbitrator in good faith and not for the purpose of delay or to gain an unfair advantage.</u>

F. A Party may request Receipt of the Notice of Arbitrator selection by notifying the Forum, in Writing, within ten (10) days from the date Claimant files Proof of Service of the Initial Claim. Notices related to Arbitrator selection need not be provided to a Party who has failed to respond to a Claim or otherwise appear or defend or pay fees as provided by this Code.

RULE 22. Number of Arbitrators.

Unless the Parties agree otherwise, for all Hearings, one (1) Arbitrator shall conduct the Hearing and issue an Award. Where the Parties have agreed to more than one (1) Arbitrator, that number of Arbitrators will serve and the Forum shall designate the chair of the panel, unless the Parties agree otherwise.

RULE 23. Disqualification of Arbitrator.

A. An Arbitrator shall be disqualified if circumstances exist that create a conflict of interest or cause the Arbitrator to be unfair or biased, including but not limited to the following:

(1) The Arbitrator has a personal bias or prejudice concerning a Party, or personal knowledge of disputed evidentiary facts;

(2) The Arbitrator has served as an attorney to any Party or Representative, the Arbitrator has been associated with an attorney who has represented a Party during that association, or the Arbitrator or an associated attorney is a material witness concerning the matter before the Arbitrator;

(3) The Arbitrator, individually or as a fiduciary, or the Arbitrator's spouse or minor child residing in the Arbitrator's household, has a direct financial interest in a matter before the Arbitrator;

(4) The Arbitrator, individually or as a fiduciary, or the Arbitrator's spouse or minor child residing in the Arbitrator's household, has a direct financial interest in a Party;

(5) The Arbitrator or the Arbitrator's spouse or minor child residing in the Arbitrator's household has a significant personal relationship with any Party or a Representative for a Party; or

(6) The Arbitrator or the Arbitrator's spouse:

    a. Is a Party to the proceeding, or an officer, director, or trustee of a Party; or,
    b. Is acting as a Representative in the proceeding.

B. An Arbitrator shall provide the Forum with a complete and accurate resume, a copy of which the Forum shall provide the Parties at the time of the selection process. An Arbitrator shall disclose to the Forum circumstances that create a conflict of interest or cause an Arbitrator to be unfair or biased. The Forum shall disqualify an Arbitrator or shall inform the Parties of information disclosed by the Arbitrator if the Arbitrator is not disqualified.

C. A Party making an Appearance may request that an Arbitrator be disqualified by filing with the Forum a Written Request stating the circumstances and specific material reasons for the disqualification. A Party who knows or has reason to know of circumstances that may disqualify an Arbitrator must immediately disclose those circumstances to the Arbitrator, the Forum, and all other Parties. A Party who fails to timely and properly disclose disqualifying circumstances agrees to accept the Arbitrator and waives any subsequent objection to the Arbitrator in the pending arbitration or any other legal proceeding.

D. A Request to disqualify an Arbitrator must be filed with the Forum within ten (10) days from the date of the Notice of Arbitrator selection. The Forum shall promptly review the Request and shall disqualify the Arbitrator if there exist circumstances requiring disqualification in accord with Rule 23A or other material circumstances creating bias or the appearance of bias.

E. If an Arbitrator is disqualified or becomes unable to arbitrate before the issuance of an Award, the Forum shall designate a new Arbitrator or panel or re-schedule the hearing, unless the Parties agree otherwise.

RULE 24. Communications with Arbitrators.

A. No Party or Party Representative shall directly communicate with an Arbitrator except at a Participatory Hearing, by providing Documents in accord with this Code, or during a conference with the Arbitrator scheduled by the Forum.

B. No Party or Party Representative shall communicate with a Party Arbitrator after the complete panel of Arbitrators has been selected, except at a Participatory Hearing, by providing Documents in accord with this Code, or during a conference with the Arbitrator scheduled by the Forum.

22

PART V

HEARING

RULE 25. Selection of a Document Hearing.

A. In Common Claim cases, a Document Hearing shall be scheduled upon the filing of a Response and Receipt of the Administrative Fee.

B. In Large Claim cases, a Party may select a Document Hearing by filing a Written selection with the Forum, served on all other Parties by Delivery as defined in Rule 2M, and accompanied by a Written estimate of the number of hours or days required for the hearing and the fee for the Document Hearing provided in the Fee Schedule.

C. The Forum shall provide Written notice of a Document Hearing to all Parties not later than fifteen (15) days before the Document Hearing.

D. If another Party selects a Participatory Hearing, the Document Hearing shall be part of the Participatory Hearing.

E. For sufficient reason, the Forum or Arbitrator may postpone a Document Hearing at the Request of a Party or on the initiative of the Arbitrator or Forum.

RULE 26. Selection of a Participatory Hearing.

A. A Party may select a Participatory Hearing of any type by:

(1) Filing a Written selection for a Participatory Hearing containing the information required in Rule 26B;

(2) Designating the type of Participatory Hearing requested: In-person, Telephone, or On-line; and

(3) Serving by Delivery, as defined by Rule 2M, the selection on all other Parties.

(4) For Common Claim cases, a selection of a Participatory Hearing must be filed with the Forum not later than fifteen (15) days after the Delivery of a Response. A Request for a Participatory Hearing made after this time may be filed in accord with Rule 18.

(5) The failure to timely select a Participatory Hearing is a waiver of the right to a Participatory Hearing.

B. Parties to a Participatory Hearing shall provide:

(1) The Party's estimate of the number of hours or days required, taking into account the rights of all Parties under Rules 34B and 35A;

(2) The names of witnesses proposed to offer evidence at the Hearing;

(3) The number of exhibits to be offered at the Hearing and their description;

(4) Any Request or requirement for a Written Award accompanied by the appropriate fee; and

(5) The fee for the Hearing as provided in the Fee Schedule.

No selection for a Participatory Hearing session is effective without payment of the appropriate fee, unless a waiver under Rule 45 has been granted.

C. The Forum shall set the date, time, place, and length of the Participatory Hearing and notify all Parties of the Hearing at least thirty (30) days before the beginning of the Participatory Hearing.

D. Before or after the beginning of a Participatory Hearing, if it is determined that the Participatory Hearing requires additional sessions, the Forum or Arbitrator shall require that the responsible Party pay for additional sessions in accord with Rule 44, or may suspend the Hearing until the additional sessions are properly scheduled.

E. For sufficient reason, the Forum or Arbitrator may postpone a Participatory Hearing at the Request of a Party or on the initiative of the Arbitrator or Forum.

RULE 27. Request for an Expedited Hearing.

A. A Party may Request an Expedited Hearing to obtain expedited relief in an Order or Award. A Request for an Expedited Hearing may be brought when the Respondent is served with Claim Documents or at any time before an Award becomes final and shall be accompanied by an explanation of the reasons for the expedited relief and the applicable law and by the fee as provided in the Fee Schedule.

B. An Arbitrator shall promptly decide the Request.

C. The requesting Party shall serve Notice of the Expedited Hearing on all Parties not less than forty-eight (48) hours before the time set for the Expedited Hearing. Proof of Service of this Notice shall be filed with the Forum before the Expedited Document Hearing or shall be presented at the Expedited Participatory Hearing.

D. A Party may seek a temporary restraining Order or a preliminary injunction to prevent irreparable injury by requesting an Expedited Hearing and filing with the Forum and serving on the Respondent and any other Parties the following:

(1) An Initial Claim in accord with Rule 12 or a Counter Claim or Third Party Claim;

(2) A Request that explains the irreparable injury and the specific reasons and Documents supporting the Request;

(3) An Affidavit from a person with personal knowledge describing the irreparable injury and specific facts;

(4) The proposed security for the relief sought;

(5) A proposed Order stating the specific relief sought, including a Hearing for a preliminary injunction if a temporary restraining Order is sought; and

(6) The fee as provided in the Fee Schedule.

E. Any Party may immediately file with the Forum and Deliver to all Parties an objection to the Request and a fee as provided in the Fee Schedule.

F. A temporary restraining Order may be granted without Written or oral notice to the Respondent or that Party's Representative only if:

(1) It clearly appears from specific facts shown by Affidavit that immediate and irreparable injury, loss or damage will result to the Requesting Party before the Respondent or that Party's Representative can be heard in opposition; and

(2) The Requesting Party or Representative of the Requesting Party certifies in writing the efforts, if any, which have been made to give the notice and the reasons supporting the claims that notice should not be required.

(3) A temporary restraining Order granted without notice shall be immediately served on all Parties by the Requesting Party.

G. A preliminary injunction shall only be issued upon notice to all Parties.

H. An Expedited Telephone, Document or In-person Hearing shall be scheduled as soon as possible by the Forum. A Hearing for a temporary restraining Order shall be scheduled no later than forty-eight (48) hours from the time of filing or notice, whichever is later. If a temporary restraining Order is issued without notice, a Party may request that a Hearing with notice be held within forty-eight (48) hours of the issuance of the temporary restraining Order.

I. An Arbitrator will conduct the Hearing and issue an Order promptly, and the Forum will enter the Order promptly.

25

J. Every Order granting relief shall state the time and date of issuance, the reasons for the issuance including the irreparable injury, the specific conduct to be restrained, the duration of the Order, the security required, and, if applicable, the reason why it was issued without notice.

K. A temporary restraining Order shall expire within the time fixed in the Order, not to exceed ten (10) days, unless the Parties agree to a longer period of time or an Arbitrator issues a preliminary injunction.

L. If a Party who receives a temporary restraining Order fails to timely proceed with the Hearing for a preliminary injunction, the Arbitrator shall dissolve the temporary restraining Order.

M. A Hearing on a Request for a preliminary injunction may be consolidated by the Arbitrator with the final Hearing in the case upon a Request by a Party.

N. No temporary restraining Order or preliminary injunction shall be issued unless the Requesting Party provides security as deemed proper by the Arbitrator for the payment of costs and damages as may be incurred or suffered by a Party wrongfully restrained or enjoined.

O. Where security is given in the form of a bond, stipulation or other undertaking with a surety or sureties, each surety agrees to submit to the jurisdiction of the Forum and the arbitration and agrees to be bound by all Orders issued by the Arbitrator in the case including Orders affecting the liability of each surety on the bond, stipulation or undertaking.

RULE 28. Document Hearing.

A. A Party may submit any Document or property for consideration by the Arbitrator in a Document Hearing by filing with the Forum two (2) copies of the Document or property description and Delivering to all other Parties copies of the Document and property description.

B. Documents and property offered for consideration at a Document Hearing must be Received by the Forum and Delivered to all other Parties no later than ten (10) days from the date of the Notice of Selection of an Arbitrator as provided in Rule 21. Documents or property submitted after that date will be considered by Request of the submitting Party and granted by the Arbitrator for sufficient reason.

C. The Arbitrator shall determine the admissibility and weight of evidence and shall not be bound by rules of evidence.

D. During a Document Hearing, the Arbitrator may Request that the Parties submit additional information or Documents, including legal memoranda. Documents submitted in response to an Arbitrator's Request shall be filed with the Forum and Delivered to all other Parties no later than thirty (30) days after the date of the Request. A Party may obtain forty-five (45) additional days to respond to an Arbitrator's Request by filing with the Forum and Delivering to all other Parties an extension notice before the initial thirty (30) day time period expires. Only one (1) extension by notice is available.

26

E. The Arbitrator may visit a site to examine a matter relating to the arbitration.

F. The close of a Document Hearing occurs when the Arbitrator completes reviewing the Documents or property.

G. The presence or involvement of a Party in a Hearing results in the waiver of any objections to the notice of the Hearing.

RULE 29. Discovery.

A. Cooperative Discovery. After a Response is filed, Parties shall cooperate in the exchange of Documents and information. A Party seeking discovery shall contact other Parties and discuss discovery information and any objections and arrange for the exchange of Documents and information.

B. Seeking Discovery.

  (1) If the Parties are unable to resolve discovery matters under Rule 29A, a Party may seek the disclosure of Documents, sworn answers to not more than twenty-five (25) Written questions, and one or more depositions before a Hearing where:

  a. The information sought is relevant to a Claim or Response, reliable, and informative to the Arbitrator; and
  b. The production of the information sought is reasonable and not unduly burdensome and expensive.

  (2) The Party seeking discovery shall Deliver to all other Parties a Notice identifying the Documents to be produced, Written questions to be answered, or the Notice of deposition identifying the deponent, the proposed length of time for the deposition, and the scope of the deposition, no later than thirty (30) days before the date of a Participatory Hearing or for a Document Hearing ten (10) days from the date of the Notice of the Selection of an Arbitrator.

  (3) A Party may seek other discovery, including Requests for admissions and Requests for physical or mental examinations, before a Hearing, where:

  a. The information sought is relevant to a Claim or Response, reliable, and essential to a fair hearing of the matter; and

  b. The production of the information is reasonable and not unduly burdensome or expensive.

  (4) The Party seeking discovery shall Deliver to all other Parties a copy of the Notice identifying the discovery sought no later than thirty (30) days before the date of a Participatory Hearing or for a Document Hearing ten (10) days from the date of the Notice of Selection of an Arbitrator.

27

C. Responding to Discovery. A Party Receiving a Notice shall Deliver to the Requesting Party:

(1) Within five (5) days after Receipt of the Notice of a deposition, a Written reply agreeing to the deposition or objecting to the deposition, including an explanation of the objections.

(2) Within twenty (20) days of the Receipt of the Notice for other discovery, a copy of the Documents Requested or a statement permitting an examination of the original Documents or property at a convenient time and place, sworn answers to the Written questions, or a Written agreement to provide other Requested discovery, or a Written objection explaining why all or some of the Documents, property or other discovery has not been provided.

D. Request for Discovery. If a Party objects in accord with this Rule, the Requesting Party may file with the Forum and Deliver to all Parties, no later than the Scheduling Notice deadline or ten (10) days after Receiving the objection:

(1) A Rule 18 Request for a Discovery Order;

(2) A copy of the Written objections; and

(3) A Written statement of reasons why the Requesting Party needs the discovery.

E. Decision. An Arbitrator shall promptly determine whether sufficient reason exists for the discovery and issue an Order.

F. Consequences. An Arbitrator may draw an unfavorable, adverse inference or presumption from the failure of a Party to provide discovery. An Arbitrator may impose Sanctions and costs and fees related to seeking or resisting discovery under Rule 29, including reasonable attorney fees, Arbitrator fees, and administrative fees against the non-prevailing Party.

RULE 30. Subpoena for In-person Participatory Hearing.

A. A Party may obtain a subpoena from an Arbitrator for a Participatory Hearing ordering a non-Party witness or other person permitted by law to produce Documents or property at the Hearing or ordering a witness to testify at the Hearing by filing with the Forum and serving on all other Parties a Rule 18 Request.

B. The Request shall state reasons for the relevancy and reliability of the Documents, property or testimony and shall identify the witness and describe the Documents or property.

C. A Request for a Rule 30 subpoena must be Received by the Forum no later than twenty (20) days before the In-person Participatory Hearing, unless the Scheduling Notice provides otherwise.

28

D. The subpoena shall be issued by an Arbitrator if the Request conforms to Rules 30A, 30B, and 30C and demonstrates the relevancy and reliability of the Documents, property or testimony. No Party, lawyer or Representative of a Party may issue a subpoena.

E. The subpoena shall be served:

    (1) By a person who is not a Party and is not less than eighteen (18) years of age if served upon a non-Party witness, or

    (2) By Delivery or personal service if served upon a Party witness or the Party. The subpoena must be Received by the person subpoenaed no later than five (5) days before the Hearing, unless the Arbitrator Orders otherwise.

F. A subpoena may be served on a non-Party witness at any place allowed by applicable law.

G. A subpoena served on a non-Party witness shall be accompanied by a witness fee of twenty-five dollars ($25) and reasonable travel reimbursement to and from the Hearing location and the residence or place of business of the non-Party. A subpoena for the production of Documents or property served on a non-Party witness shall also be accompanied by payment of the reasonable costs of producing the Documents and property.

H. Within five (5) days after being served with the subpoena or before the time specified in the subpoena to appear at the Hearing, if less than five (5) days, the witness or a Party may Request an Order that the subpoena be dismissed or modified. The Request shall conform to Rule 18 and shall state why the subpoena should be dismissed or modified.

I. If a witness or Party makes a Request under Rule 30H, an Arbitrator shall promptly determine whether sufficient reason exists for the Order, or enforce the subpoena.

J. The Party having the subpoena served shall provide the Arbitrator with the Proof of Service of the subpoena if the witness fails to appear at the Hearing.

K. Subpoenas issued under this Code may be enforced in accord with the applicable law. A subpoena not issued by an Arbitrator under this Rule is unenforceable.

L. An Arbitrator may draw an unfavorable, adverse inference or presumption from the failure of a Party to produce a Party witness, in addition to imposing any other Sanction.

RULE 31. Exchange of Information Before a Participatory Hearing.

A. Before all Participatory Hearings, each Party shall Deliver to all other Parties and file with the Forum two (2) copies of:

    (1) A list of all witnesses expected to testify and a summary of their testimony;

    (2) A list and description of all exhibits to be introduced;

(3) A copy of all Documents and a detailed description of any property to be introduced at the Hearing;

(4) An Affidavit establishing the authenticity of any Document proposed to be introduced at the Hearing; and

(5) Any Request for additional Participatory Hearing sessions, accompanied by the fee as provided in the Fee Schedule.

B. All Parties and the Forum shall Receive the lists, Documents, and Affidavits provided for in Rule 31A no later than ten (10) days before the Participatory Hearing, unless a Notice from the Forum or Arbitrator provides otherwise. Lists, Documents, and Affidavits may be submitted after that date only by Request of the submitting Party. Such Requests may be granted by the Arbitrator for sufficient reason.

C. The Arbitrator may exclude witnesses, testimony or Documents sought to be introduced by a Party who fails to comply with Rules 31A and 31B.

RULE 32. Location of an In-person Participatory Hearing.

A. An In-person Participatory Hearing shall be held where the Arbitration Agreement designates or where the Parties agree or, in the absence of an agreement and for all Consumer cases, at a reasonably convenient location within the United States federal judicial district or other national judicial district where the Respondent to the Initial Claim resides or does business. A Respondent Entity does business where it has minimum contacts with a Consumer.

B. Unless the Parties agree otherwise, if there is more than one Respondent to an Initial Claim, an In-person Participatory Hearing shall be held in the United States federal judicial district or other national judicial district where the majority of the Respondents to the Initial Claim resides or does business. If there is no United States federal judicial district or other national judicial district where a majority of Respondents resides or does business, the Forum shall select a reasonably convenient location for the In-person Participatory Hearing.

RULE 33. Participatory Hearing.

A. A Participatory Hearing may include:

(1) An introduction by the Arbitrator.

(2) Opening statements by each of the Parties. The Respondent and other Parties have the option of reserving the opening statement until the presentation of their evidence.

(3) Claimant's case. The Claimant may introduce evidence, examine witnesses, and submit exhibits. The Respondent and other Parties may also examine the witnesses and submit exhibits.

30

(4) Respondent's case. The Respondent may introduce evidence, examine witnesses, and submit exhibits. The Claimant and other Parties may also examine the witnesses and submit exhibits.

(5) Additional cases. Other Parties may present their case.

(6) Rebuttal. A Party may introduce additional evidence, examine witnesses, and submit exhibits to rebut an opposing Party's case if the submissions are not repetitive, cumulative or otherwise inadmissible.

(7) Summation. Each Party may present a closing statement.

(8) Concluding remarks by the Arbitrator.

B. The close of a Participatory Hearing occurs when either the Arbitrator announces the Hearing closed or more than twenty (20) days elapse from the final session.

RULE 34. Participatory Hearing Proceedings.

A. A Participatory Hearing may consist of one or more sessions. A Hearing may be conducted on any business day unless the Parties and Arbitrator agree otherwise.

B. Hearing Sessions: Parties shall select sufficient time and sessions for Participatory Hearings in accord with Rule 26B. For Common Claim cases, a Hearing session is scheduled for the following length of time, unless more time or sessions are selected and the fees are paid:

A one hundred eighty-minute (180) session is scheduled for cases in which the amount in controversy exceeds $35,000.

A one hundred twenty-minute (120) session is scheduled for cases in which the amount in controversy is between $13,001 and $35,000.

A ninety-minute (90) session is scheduled for cases in which the amount in controversy is between $3,501 and $13,000.

A sixty-minute (60) session is scheduled for cases in which the amount in controversy is $5,000 or less.

C. The Arbitrator shall conduct a Participatory Hearing in an orderly, efficient, and economic manner, and shall determine the order and presentation of evidence and oral arguments.

D. All Parties to the arbitration and their Representatives shall be entitled to attend or be involved in the Participatory Hearing. Other persons may not attend unless the Parties agree or the Arbitrator Orders otherwise. The Arbitrator may sequester witnesses.

E. The Arbitrator may request Documents and information from the Parties, and may question any witness or Party to clarify evidence or arguments.

F. An Arbitrator may Request Parties to submit additional information or Documents, including legal memoranda, which the Forum, the Arbitrator, and the Parties shall Receive no later than thirty (30) days after the final Participatory Hearing session.

G. A Party may Request permission to submit a post-hearing memorandum, which may be granted by the Arbitrator. The responsible Party shall pay the fee provided by the Fee Schedule.

H. The presence or involvement of a Party in a Hearing results in the waiver of any objections to the Notice and scheduling of the Hearing.

RULE 35. Evidence in a Participatory Hearing.

A. Presentation. Parties shall have a full and equal opportunity to present relevant and reliable evidence and oral and written arguments in support of their positions. Parties may present evidence and arguments in any reasonable form and by any means of communication.

B. Oath. The Arbitrator shall administer an oath or affirmation before a witness testifies.

C. Admissibility. The Arbitrator shall determine the admissibility and weight of evidence, and shall not be bound by rules of evidence.

D. Objections. A Party may object to the introduction of evidence by another Party or a Request or question by an Arbitrator, and the Arbitrator shall rule on the objection.

E. Site Examination. An Arbitrator may visit a site to examine a matter relating to the arbitration accompanied by the Parties or their Representatives, if they so choose.

F. Record. No record of a Hearing shall be kept unless agreed by all Parties or Ordered by the Arbitrator. The responsible Party or Parties Requesting a record shall arrange and pay for the record, and promptly provide a copy of the transcript or recording to the Arbitrator and the Forum at no cost to the Arbitrator or the Forum, and, if Requested by another Party, to that Party, at that Party's expense.

G. Interpreter. A Party who requires an interpreter shall arrange and pay for the interpreter. An Arbitrator may have an interpreter present, with a fee assessed to a Party or Parties as determined by the Forum.

RULE 36. Arbitration Proceedings in Absence of a Party.

A. An Arbitrator may issue an Award or Order when any Party has failed to respond, appear, or proceed at a Hearing, or otherwise defend as provided in this Code.

32

B. If a Party does not respond to a Claim, an Arbitrator will timely review the merits of the Claim for purposes of issuing an Award or Order. The Claimant need not submit an additional Request for an Award.

C. An Arbitrator may require an Affidavit, information or Documents from Parties who have appeared or conduct a Hearing to Receive evidence necessary to issue an Award or Order. Documents submitted in Response to an Arbitrator's Request shall be filed with the Forum no later than thirty (30) days after the date of the Request. A Party may obtain forty-five (45) additional days to respond to an Arbitrator's Request by filing with the Forum and Delivering to all other Parties an extension notice before the initial thirty (30) day time period expires. Only one (1) extension by notice is available.

D. Each Party making an Appearance shall be provided notices relating to a Hearing.

E. No Award or Order shall be issued against a Party solely because that Party failed to respond, appear or defend.

33

PART VI

AWARDS AND
ORDERS

RULE 37. Awards.

A. An Award or Dispositive Order establishes the rights and obligations of all Parties named in the Award or Order and is final and binding, unless those Parties agree otherwise.

B. An Award shall not exceed the money or relief requested in a Claim or amended Claim and any amount awarded under Rule 37C.

C. An Award may include fees and costs awarded by an Arbitrator in favor of any Party only as permitted by law. A Party with a Claim for attorney fees or costs may seek to recover those expenses by bringing a timely Request in accord with Rules 18 and 12B. An opposing Party may object in accord with Rule 18. The Arbitrator may include attorney fees and costs in the final Award or in a separate Award.

D. An Award may include arbitration fees awarded by an Arbitrator or in favor of the Forum for fees due.

E. An Arbitrator shall endeavor to render an Award within twenty (20) days after the date of the close of the Hearing.

F. All Awards and Orders shall be in Writing, dated, and Signed by the Arbitrator or by a majority of the panel, and filed with the Forum.

G. An Award of an arbitration panel shall be by a majority of the Arbitrators. The chair of an arbitration panel may issue Orders, make rulings, and conduct proceedings.

H. An Award is a summary Award unless: (1) a Written notice is filed by a Party seeking reasons, findings of fact or conclusions of law, or (2) a prior Written agreement of the Parties requires reasons, findings of fact or conclusions of law and at least one Party files a Written notice requesting reasons, findings or conclusions. This Written agreement or notice must be filed with the Forum within ten (10) days of the date of the Notice of Selection of an Arbitrator and must be accompanied by a fee, if any, as provided in the Fee Schedule.

I. Awards shall be based upon a preponderance of the evidence presented, unless an agreement of the Parties or the applicable law provides otherwise.

J. An Arbitrator or the Forum may issue an Award or Order based upon a Written settlement Signed by the Parties.

34

RULE 38. Orders.

A. An Arbitrator or the Forum, where permitted by the Code, may issue an Order at the Request of a Party or on the initiative of the Arbitrator or the Forum.

B. At any time following the filing of a Claim, upon a Request by a Party and after a Hearing, the Arbitrator may issue an Interim Order and may require security as a condition of the Interim Order.

C. An Arbitrator who dismisses a Claim because there was no Arbitration Agreement or because the Arbitrator does not have the power to decide a Claim shall state the reason in the dismissal Order.

RULE 39. Entry and Service of Awards and Orders.

A. An Award or Order shall be entered in the state, country, or other jurisdiction provided for a Hearing in Rule 32, which shall appear on the Award or Order.

B. An Award or Order becomes final when entered. An Award or Order may not be entered if fees required by the Fee Schedule remain unpaid.

C. The Forum shall Deliver a copy of the Award or Order to all Parties or their Representatives or as directed by any Party.

D. Parties consent to service of the Award or Order and of all Documents, notices, and Orders necessary to confirm an Award or Order or to enter a judgment based on an Award or Order by Delivery, as defined by Rule 2M, at any address of the Party or Representative of record with the Forum.

E. An Award or Order may be confirmed, entered or enforced as a judgment in any court of competent jurisdiction. The Forum may disclose necessary Award information in connection with the confirmation, entering, enforcement or challenge of an Award or Order or otherwise as required by law.

F. Parties may request a duplicate original of an Award or Order or a copy of other filed Documents and pay the fee as determined by the Forum.

RULE 40. Voluntary Dismissal.

A. A Claimant may dismiss a Claim after it is filed and before the Respondent is served with the Claim by filing with the Forum a notice of dismissal.

B. A Claimant may dismiss a Claim after it is served and before the Respondent Delivers a Response to Claimant by Delivering to all Parties and filing with the Forum a notice of dismissal.

35

C. A Claimant may dismiss a Claim after a Respondent Delivers a Response that contains no Counter Claim within forty-five (45) days of the date the Response has been delivered to the Claimant or no later than a deadline established by a Scheduling Notice, whichever is later, by delivering to all Parties and filing with the Forum a notice of dismissal.

D. Any other Claim may be dismissed at the Request of the Claimant in accord with Rule 18. Before the selection of an Arbitrator, the Forum may dismiss the Claim. After the selection of the Arbitrator, the Arbitrator may dismiss the Claim.

E. A Claim shall be dismissed upon agreement of the Parties filed with the Forum.

F. Unless stated otherwise, the first voluntary dismissal of a Claim is Without Prejudice, and the Claim may be brought again.

G. A Claim voluntarily dismissed more than once is dismissed With Prejudice, and cannot be brought again.

RULE 41. Involuntary Dismissal.

A. A Claim or Response may be dismissed by an Arbitrator at the Request of the Forum or a Party or on the initiative of the Arbitrator for one or more of the following reasons:

   (1) It is not supported by evidence.

   (2) It is not supported by existing law.

   (3) It is frivolous.

   (4) It has been presented or maintained for an improper purpose, such as to harass, cause unnecessary delay or needlessly increase the cost of arbitration.

   (5) It is brought by a Party who has been declared to be a vexatious litigant by a court or Arbitrator.

   (6) A Party has violated any provision of the Code, or any Order or notice from an Arbitrator or the Forum.

B. A Claim or Response may be dismissed by an Arbitrator or the Forum at the Request of a Party in accord with Rule 18 or on the initiative of the Arbitrator or the Forum for one or more of the following reasons:

   (1) A Party has failed to proceed with an arbitration or Claim.

   (2) A Party has failed to pay fees as provided in the Fee Schedule.

36

(3) More than one hundred twenty (120) days have elapsed between the filing date of the Claim and the date the Forum receives a Response or Proof of Service of the Initial Claim.

(4) More than sixty (60) days have elapsed since a Hearing has been postponed or an arbitration case has been placed on inactive status.

(5) More than twelve (12) months have elapsed since a case has been stayed under Rule 9F1 and no notification has been received from the Claimant to extend the stay.

C. The Forum shall Deliver notice of an involuntary dismissal to all Parties who have made an Appearance.

D. Unless stated otherwise, an involuntary dismissal by an Arbitrator is With Prejudice and the Claim may not be brought again.

E. An involuntary dismissal by the Forum is Without Prejudice and the Claim may be brought again.

F. If a Claimant again brings a Claim against a Respondent that was dismissed Without Prejudice, the Forum or Arbitrator may Order the costs incurred by the Respondent in the previous case to be paid to the Respondent, and may Stay the proceedings of the arbitration until the Claimant has complied with this Order.

G. If a Request for an Involuntary Dismissal is the only Request for a dispositive Order, that Request may be determined at the Document or Participatory Hearing.

RULE 42. Correction.

The Forum or an Arbitrator may correct clerical or administrative mistakes or errors arising from oversight or omission in the administration of cases or in the issuance of an Order or Award.

RULE 43. Reopening and Reconsideration.

A. An Arbitrator may reopen a Hearing or reconsider an Order or Award within a reasonable time from the date the Order or Award is entered if:

(1) Service of Process or Proof of Service of Process of a Claim was not complete as required by this Code;

(2) The Order or Award is ambiguous or contains evident material mistakes; or

(3) If all Parties agree.

B. An Arbitrator may reopen a Hearing or reconsider an Order or Award within forty-five (45) days from the date the Order or Award is entered if:

37

    (1) The Arbitrator failed to timely disclose material circumstances or material reasons for disqualification in accord with Rule 23A; or

    (2) The Arbitrator did not decide a submitted issue.

C. Otherwise, neither the Arbitrator nor the Forum has the power to vacate an Order or Award after the Order or Award becomes final, unless all Parties agree.

D. Requests that an Arbitrator reopen a Hearing or reconsider an Order or Award must be timely filed with the Forum in accord with Rule 18 and Delivered to all Parties. A Party cannot make a second Request.

E. An Order or Award is reviewable by a court of competent jurisdiction as provided by applicable law.

38

PART VII

FEES

RULE 44. Fees.

A. Fee Recovery. The prevailing Party may recover fees paid in the arbitration in accord with Rule 37C.

B. Prepaid Fees. All fees for the filing of a Claim, Response, Request, objection, and any other Document and Hearing fees must be paid at the time the Document is filed or the Hearing is selected. These fees include fees required by this Code, the Forum Fee Schedule, the Parties' contract, an Order of an Arbitrator, or as required by law.

C. Non-Monetary Relief Fees. A Respondent may file a Rule 18 Request to review the value of injunctive, declaratory or other non-monetary relief sought in a Claim. An Arbitrator shall promptly determine the value of the Claim, which determines the amount of the fees to be paid in accord with the Fee Schedule.

D. Hearing Fees. The Party selecting the type of Hearing prepays the Hearing fee unless the agreement of the Parties, this Code or the applicable law provides otherwise. The Forum may proceed with an arbitration in a case involving a Consumer Party who Requests that the case proceed even after another Party required to pay the Hearing fee fails to pay. The Arbitrator may Award the Forum the amount of the unpaid Hearing fees.

E. Advance Fees. During the course of any Participatory Hearing, the Forum or an Arbitrator may require any Party, who is not a Consumer in a Common Claim case, to pay in advance a fee for necessary Participatory Hearing sessions in addition to those requested under Rules 26 and 27.

F. Arbitrators. Fees for Arbitrators selected in accord with Rules 21A(1) and (2) are paid by the Parties to the Forum. Fees for Arbitrators selected in accord with Rule 21A(3) are paid to the Forum by the Parties as provided for in the Forum Fee Schedule. In cases where the Parties select a number of Arbitrators in addition to those provided by the Code or select Arbitrators with qualifications different than those required by the Forum, a fee for each Arbitrator will be determined by the Forum to be paid by the responsible Party or Parties.

G. Consumer Request. A Consumer Claimant or a Consumer Respondent in a Large Claim who asserts that arbitration fees prevent the Consumer Party from effectively vindicating the Consumer's case in arbitration may, at the time of filing of the Consumer's Initial Claim or Consumer's Response to a Large Claim and prior to paying any filing fee, file a Request that another Party or Parties pay all or part of the arbitration fees or that the arbitration provision be

39

declared unenforceable, permitting the Consumer to litigate the case instead of arbitrating the case. This Request shall be processed without a fee and must be filed with the Forum and Delivered to all Parties together with the Initial Claim or Response and proof of Delivery.

    (1) Within fifteen (15) days of the filing and Delivery of the Request, another Party may:

        a. Agree to pay all or part of the fees required of the Consumer, or

        b. Agree to litigate instead of arbitrate the case, or

        c. File an objection to the Request.

    (2) If there is no agreement by the Parties, an Arbitrator shall promptly decide the Request and objection, if any, based on the applicable law.

    (3) The arbitration is suspended during this process.

H. Respondent Request. In cases where a Consumer Claimant brings a Large Claim and a Respondent is obligated to pay the fees by agreement or by law, the Respondent may, before or reasonably after the time of filing a Response, file with the Forum and serve on all Parties a Rule 18 Request that an Arbitrator determine whether there is a prima facie Claim of $75,000 or more. If the Arbitrator determines the Claim is a Common Claim, the Common Claim Fee Schedule shall apply. Otherwise, the Large Claim Fee Schedule shall apply.

I. International Cases. The Forum may assess additional fees for arbitrations conducted outside the United States or involving Parties from more than one country.

J. United States Dollars. Forum Fee Schedule fees are listed in United States Dollars. Fees shall be paid to the Forum in United States Dollars, unless the Forum agrees to accept other currency based on the exchange rate in effect on the required date of the fee payment as determined by the Forum.

K. Refunds. Fees are not refundable, except as otherwise provided by the Code or Fee Schedule.

L. Other Fees. The Forum may establish reasonable fees for proceedings not covered by the Fee Schedule and may assess appropriate, additional fees for Code proceedings as permitted by law or in accord with this Code. Parties may obtain the amount of a fee by contacting the Forum.

RULE 45. Waiver of Fees.

A. An indigent Consumer Party may Request a waiver of Common Claim filing fees, Request Fees, Hearing Fees, or security for any arbitration, by filing with the Forum a Written Request for a waiver at the time payment is due. The Request for a waiver shall be accompanied by an Affidavit including:

(1) The Party's family size;

(2) All of the Party's income and sources, property and assets, expenses and costs, liabilities and debts;

(3) A statement that there is no agreement providing for any other person or Entity to either pay the costs or share in the proceeds of the Claim or a copy of the agreement and the financial information described in Rule 45A(2) for any person or Entity that has agreed to pay the costs or share in the proceeds of the Claim; and

(4) All other relevant information, including releases for credit information, as requested by the Forum.

Neither the Request nor Affidavit need be sent to the other Parties.

B. The Forum shall promptly issue a full or partial waiver to a Consumer Party eligible under this Rule and under the United States federal poverty standards or the applicable law. The Forum may also Order another Party to pay all or part of the waived fees as permitted or required by law.

C. If another Party has agreed to pay fees, a Rule 45 Request is unnecessary and the fee paying Party is obligated to pay the fees.

D. The Consumer Party must file an amended Affidavit of Poverty within thirty (30) days of a material change in the financial condition or circumstances described in the Consumer Party's initial Affidavit of Poverty. A separate Request must be filed by the indigent Consumer Party for each subsequent fee waiver requested.

E. If the statements in the Rule 45 Affidavit are untrue or incomplete, or if the Consumer Party is later determined to be able to pay the fees, the Forum shall Order the Consumer Party to pay the fees waived.

PART VIII

CODE PROVISIONS

RULE 46. Compliance with Rules.

An Arbitrator may Sanction a Party or Representative, or both, for violating any Rule, notice, ruling, or Order or for asserting an unsupportable Claim or Response. A Party may be Sanctioned on the initiative of the Arbitrator or at the Request of the Forum or a Party. An Arbitrator shall Sanction a Party who refuses to pay fees as required by agreement, these Rules, an Arbitrator Order, or the applicable law, unless the offending Party establishes reasonable neglect. A Sanction Order may require an offending Party to pay for fees and costs incurred by another Party, unpaid fees, and other appropriate monetary Sanctions, and may require payment to another Party or the Forum.

RULE 47. Legal Proceedings.

A. The Arbitrator, the Director, the Forum, and any individual or Entity associated with the Forum are immune from liability and shall not be liable to any Party for any act or omission in connection with any arbitration conducted under this Code.

B. No Party or prospective Party, before or during the arbitration of any matter eligible for submission under this Code, shall commence or pursue any lawsuit, administrative proceeding, or other action against any other Party, prospective Party, the Forum, or individual or Entity associated with the Forum relating to any of the matters subject to arbitration under this Code or the agreement of the Parties. Any Party commencing or pursuing such a proceeding agrees to pay and indemnify all such Parties, the Forum, individuals, and Entities for all expenses and costs incurred, including attorney fees as permitted by applicable law.

C. No Arbitrator, Director or any individual associated with the Forum shall be a witness in any legal proceeding arising out of the arbitration.

D. Any Party commencing or pursuing any lawsuit, administrative proceeding, arbitration or other action against the Forum, an Arbitrator or individual or Entity associated with the Forum, after an Award is final, agrees to pay and indemnify the Forum, an Arbitrator, individuals and Entities for all expenses and costs incurred, including attorney fees.

E. Every Party to any arbitration administered by the Forum or to an Arbitration Agreement as described in Rules 1 or 2E and the Forum agree that any Claim or dispute of any nature against the Forum or any agent, officer, employee, or affiliate of the Forum or any Arbitrator shall be resolved by final, binding arbitration conducted by a panel of three (3) Arbitrators. The Party or Parties shall select one Arbitrator; the Forum shall select a second Arbitrator; and these two Arbitrators shall select a third Arbitrator who is neutral and independent and who shall be the chair of the panel. The Arbitrators shall conduct the arbitration pursuant to the Code of

42

Procedure in effect at the time the arbitration is brought. The chair shall have the powers of the Forum and perform the responsibilities of the Director. All fees payable under the Fee Schedule shall be assessed by the chair and paid to the panel of Arbitrators. Neither the Forum, nor its Director, nor any employee or agent of the Forum shall administer the arbitration.

RULE 48. Interpretation and Application of Code.

A. This Code shall be interpreted in conformity with 9 U.S.C. §§ 1-16 and 9 U.S.C. §§ 201 - 208 in the United States or the applicable law of other countries in order to provide all participants in the arbitration with a fair and impartial proceeding and an enforceable Award or Order.

B. Unless the Parties agree otherwise, any Arbitration Agreement as described in Rules 1 and 2E and all arbitration proceedings, Hearings, Awards, and Orders are to be governed by the Federal Arbitration Act, 9 U.S.C. §§ 1-16.

C. The Forum shall stay a case if a court with jurisdiction has issued an order staying arbitration and may stay a case in appropriate circumstances.

D. In the event a court of competent jurisdiction shall find any portion of this Code or Fee Schedule to be in violation of the law or otherwise unenforceable, that portion shall not be effective and the remainder of the Code shall remain effective.

E. The Director or Arbitrator may decline the use of arbitration for any dispute, controversy, Claim, Response or Request that is not a proper or legal subject matter for arbitration or where the agreement of the Parties has substantially modified a material portion of the Code. If Parties are denied the opportunity to arbitrate a dispute, controversy or Claim before the Forum, the Parties may seek legal and other remedies in accord with applicable law.

F. In the event of a cancellation of this Code, any Party may seek legal and other remedies regarding any matter upon which an Award or Order has not been entered.

G. The Forum Code Committee, appointed by the Board of Directors, shall have the power and authority to effectuate the purposes of this Code, including establishing appropriate rules and procedures governing arbitrations and altering, amending or modifying this Code in accord with the law.

43

APPENDIX 13J-2

National Arbitration Forum Notice of Arbitration[1]

NOTICE OF ARBITRATION

Dear Respondent:

AN ARBITRATION CLAIM HAS BEEN FILED AGAINST YOU.

Enclosed and served upon you is the Initial Claim. You may obtain a copy of the Code of Procedure, without cost, from the Claimant or from the Forum at www.adrforum.com or 800-474-2371.

IF YOU DO NOT DELIVER TO THE CLAIMANT AND FILE WITH THE FORUM A WRITTEN RESPONSE, AN AWARD MAY BE ENTERED AGAINST YOU. AN ARBITRATION AWARD MAY BE ENFORCED IN COURT AS A CIVIL JUDGMENT.

YOU HAVE THIRTY (30) DAYS TO RESPOND FROM RECEIPT OF SERVICE.

You have a number of options at this time. You may:

1. *Submit a written Response to the Claim,* stating your reply and defenses to the Claim, together with documents supporting your position. Your Response must be delivered to the Claimant and filed with the Forum. See National Arbitration Forum [NAF] Code of Procedure Rules 13 and 6C.

   Proof of delivery of the Response on the Claimant must also be filed with the Forum. See NAF Rules 2A, 2M, and 2Z. Proof of delivery can be a statement: "Respondent, under penalty of perjury, states that the Response was delivered to Claimant by [explain how delivered, such as mail or other methods in NAF Rule 6C]".

   A Counter Claim, Cross-claim or Third Party Claim must also be delivered and filed with the Forum, and accompanied by the fee as provided in the Fee Schedule. See NAF Rules 14, 15, and 16. Forms for such Response and Claims may be obtained from the Forum.

   If you fail to respond in writing to the Claim, an Award may be entered against you and in favor of the Claimant. See NAF Rule 36.

2. *Select a Document Hearing or a Participatory Hearing.* You may request a Hearing in your Response or in a separate writing. You may select a Document or Participatory Hearing, and you may also request a Hearing on-line or by telephone. If an In-person Participatory Hearing is selected, it will be held in the federal Judicial District where you reside or do business, unless you have agreed otherwise. Parties have a full and equal right to present relevant and reliable direct and cross examination testimony, documents, exhibits, evidence and arguments. Parties also have the right to subpoena witnesses. Your written Request for a Hearing must be filed with the Forum. You must also deliver a copy of your Request to the Claimant and any other Parties. See NAF Rules 5D, 25, 26, 29, 30, 31, and 33.

3. *Have other options.* You may seek the advice of an attorney or any person who may assist you regarding this arbitration. See NAF Rule 3. You should seek this advice promptly so that your Response can be delivered and filed within the time required by the Code of Procedure. Parties have the right to adjournment for good cause within the time period allowed in Rule 9E. See NAF Rule 5 for a Summary of Arbitration Procedures. If you have any questions about responding, you may contact the Forum.

The Forum is an independent and impartial arbitration organization, which does not give legal advice or represent parties. THIS SUMMARY IS NOT A SUBSTITUTE FOR READING AND UNDERSTANDING THE CODE OF PROCEDURE WHICH GOVERNS THIS ARBITRATION.

National Arbitration Forum
P.O. Box 50191, Minneapolis, MN USA 55405-0191
(800) 474-2371
info@adrforum.com
adrforum.com

---

[1]National Arbitration Forum, Code of Procedure—Notice of Arbitration, available at http://www.adrforum.com/resource.aspx?id=1423 (last accessed March 29, 2011).

APPENDIX 13J-3

National Arbitration Forum Second Notice of Arbitration[1]

SECOND NOTICE OF ARBITRATION

Date

Name of Case
File Number

Dear Respondent,

We have received notice that you have been served with an Arbitration Claim in the above case. If you want to respond to the Claim, the Code of Procedure requires you to respond in writing.

If you have not yet responded, YOU MAY STILL SUBMIT A WRITTEN RESPONSE to the Claimant and the Forum. YOU HAVE THIRTY (30) DAYS FROM THE DATE OF SERVICE OR FOURTEEN (14) DAYS FROM THE DATE OF THIS NOTICE, whichever is later, to respond.

The First Notice of Arbitration you received with the Initial Claim documents stated that you could:

1. *Submit a written Response to the Claim, stating your reply and defenses to the Claim, together with documents supporting your position.* Proof of delivery of the Response on the Claimant must also be filed with the Forum. Proof of delivery can be a statement: "Respondent, under penalty of perjury, states that the Response was delivered to Claimant by [explain how delivered, such as by mail or other methods in NAF Rule 6C]".

2. *Request a Document Hearing, an In-Person Participatory Hearing where you reside or do business, or an On-Line or Telephone Hearing as provided in the Forum Code of Procedure.* Parties have a full and equal right to present relevant and reliable direct and cross examination testimony, documents, exhibits, evidence and arguments. Parties also have the right to subpoena witnesses. See NAF Rules 5, 25, 26, 29, 30, 31, and 33.

3. *Seek the advice of an attorney or any person who may assist you regarding this arbitration.* See NAF Rule 3. *You should seek this advice immediately.* Parties have the right to adjournment for good cause within the time period allowed in NAF Rule 9. *You should also read the National Arbitration Forum Code of Procedure which explains what you must and can do.* See NAF Rules 5, 6C, 13, 14, 15, 16, 24, and 25.

You still have these options. If you have any questions or need a copy of the Initial Claim Documents or the Forum Code of Procedure, or have any questions about responding, you may contact the National Arbitration Forum:

P.O. Box 50191, Minneapolis, MN USA 55405-0191
Telephone: (800) 474-2371; Fax (866) 743-4517; info@adrforum.com; www.adrforum.com

The Forum is an independent and impartial arbitration organization, which does not give legal advice or represent parties. Furthermore, any Arbitrator appointed to this proceeding is an independent and impartial Neutral who hears the matter and arrives at decisions. The Arbitrator does not represent you and does not serve as your attorney, therefore no attorney-client privilege exists between you and the Arbitrator.

Notice of Proceeding

If you do not deliver to the Claimant and file with the Forum a written response, an Award may be entered against you in favor of the Claimant. An arbitration Award may be enforced in court as a civil judgment. NAF Rule 36B states in part: "If a Party does not respond to a Claim, an Arbitrator will timely review the merits of the Claim for purposed of issuing an Award or Order ...." This Notice informs you that an Arbitrator will conduct a Rule 36 Proceeding after the time has passed for you to submit a written response. If you do not respond, you will not receive any additional notice about this hearing.

THIS SUMMARY IS NOT A SUBSTITUTE FOR READING AND UNDERSTANDING THE FORUM CODE OF PROCEDURE WHICH GOVERNS THIS ARBITRATION.

---

[1]National Arbitration Forum, Code of Procedure—Second Notice of Arbitration, available at http://www.adrforum.com/resource.aspx?id=1423 (last accessed March 29, 2011).

APPENDIX 13J-4

National Arbitration Forum Rules for Mediation[1]

National Arbitration Forum Mediation Rules

The National Arbitration Forum (FORUM) encourages disputing parties to use mediation to resolve their differences. Mediation is a consensual process whereby a neutral third party helps disputing parties resolve their dispute by working toward and achieving a mutually satisfactory solution. The neutral party, known as a mediator, assists the parties with settlement negotiations but does not have authority to impose a decision on the parties.

Part I – Initiation of a Mediation Proceeding

A. Mediation Agreement
The National Arbitration Forum Mediation Rules may be adopted by the agreement of the parties before or after a dispute has arisen. Where the parties have not agreed to mediate, a party or parties may request that the FORUM invite another party or parties involved in the dispute to mediate. The FORUM will contact the other party or parties and attempt to facilitate a mediation agreement.

B. Request for Mediation
1. A party or parties may request mediation by contacting the FORUM by telephone, facsimile, or mail including electronic mail. The requesting party shall at the same time notify the other party or parties of the request. Parties may use the FORUM's Request For Mediation form, or simply provide a written request for mediation that contains the information listed in subsection 1 below.

2. The request for mediation shall contain or be accompanied by:

> a. the names, addresses and telephone, fax, e-mail or other contact information for the parties to the dispute and their authorized representatives;

> b. a copy of the mediation agreement or a statement that the party seeks to mediate a dispute with another party or parties;

> c. a brief statement of the nature of the dispute;

> d. the Mediation Filing Fee of $50 per party.

3. All submissions to the FORUM may be made through the FORUM's website at www.arbitrationforum.com, by facsimile, telephone, or by mail to:

> National Arbitration Forum
> PO Box 50191
> Minneapolis, MN 55405
> Attention: Mediation Coordinator

> Telephone 800.474.2371, ext. 6460; Facsimile 952.345.1160

1

---

[1]National Arbitration Forum, Mediation Rules, available at http://www.ad rforum.com/users/naf/resources/200609MediationRules2.pdf (last accessed March 29, 2011).

4. The FORUM will notify the parties of the acceptance of the mediation. The FORUM reserves the right to decline a mediation request.

C. Selection of the Mediator
1. The parties may agree on a mediator from the appropriate panel of FORUM mediators who have experience with the type of dispute needing mediation. The FORUM will provide the names, resumes, and compensation rates of FORUM mediators after the parties submit a Request for Mediation and the appropriate fee. If one of these mediators is used by the parties, the parties agree that the FORUM will administer the mediation, and the parties will not privately use any mediator listed by the FORUM.

2. The parties may also select a mediator who is not listed as a FORUM mediator, and request that the FORUM administer that mediation. The FORUM will contact that mediator and determine if that mediator is available and whether the FORUM can appoint that person as mediator.

3. If the parties are unable to agree upon a mediator or the FORUM is unable to appoint the mediator proposed by the parties, a mediator shall be appointed by the FORUM as follows:

> a. Two-party mediation. In cases where there are two parties in interest, the FORUM may submit a list of three potential candidates. Within five business days, each party may provide the FORUM with its preference by submitting a writing to the FORUM by which that party may strike one of the mediators and rank the other mediators in order of preference. The remaining mediator, or the mediator with the lowest combined score, will be appointed by the FORUM. If more than one mediator has the same score, the FORUM will appoint one of those mediators. A party who fails to timely notify the FORUM is deemed to accept all the listed candidates.

> b. Multiple-party mediation. In cases where are there are three or more parties in interest, the FORUM may submit a list of three or more potential candidates, depending upon the number of parties, their common interests, the damages or remedies at stake, the factual and legal issues in dispute, and related matters. The FORUM will inform the parties of the available candidates and how they are to be selected, including how mediators may be ranked, stricken, or accepted, by the parties.

> c. Parties in Interest. The FORUM shall determine how many parties in interest appear in a mediation in relation to mediators appointed pursuant to Rule I.C.3.b.

4. By accepting an appointment, the mediator agrees to remain impartial and asserts that there is no known conflict of interest or circumstance that would cause the mediator to be unfair or biased. The mediator and the FORUM shall comply with all disclosure requirements pursuant to applicable laws. Any party who knows or should know of any

2

conflict of interest or material circumstance that would cause the mediator to be unfair, biased, or prejudiced shall immediately disclose the information immediately on its discovery to the mediator, the parties, and the FORUM. A party who fails to immediately disclose this information waives any claim to assert the mediator had a conflict or was unfair, biased, or prejudiced. The FORUM may appoint another qualified mediator if the initially appointed mediator is unwilling or unable to serve.

5. The mediator also agrees to make sufficient time available to conduct the mediation efficiently and fairly.

6. In the event that parties to a mediation administered by the FORUM also enter into arbitration before the FORUM, and absent agreement of the parties to the contrary, a different individual will be appointed by the FORUM to serve as the arbitrator than that which served as the mediator.

Part II – Conduct of the Mediation

A. Authority and Representation
Each party shall be represented at mediation sessions by individuals with full authority to settle the dispute. The parties may be represented by legal counsel at any stage of the mediation.

B. Cooperation
Each party is expected to cooperate in good faith with the mediator to advance the mediation efficiently and fairly and shall spend as much time as necessary until the case is settled or until an impasse is declared or the parties elect to pursue an alternative procedure. Mediation is a voluntary process and any party may withdraw at any time, either by notifying the mediator and other parties in writing or by leaving the mediation hearing. The parties may be represented by legal counsel at any stage of the mediation. Perseverance and steadfastness often contribute to the success of a mediation, and the mediator shall continue with a mediation until it is clear that no settlement may be reached. The mediator is authorized to end the mediation session whenever, in the judgment of the mediator, the parties have reached impasse in their attempts to forge a resolution. A party who wishes to withdraw from a mediation may do so by requesting that the mediator declare an impasse or may notify the mediator and other parties in writing or by leaving the mediation hearing.

C. Impasse
An impasse may occur if a party withdraws from mediation, the parties fail to arrive at a settlement, or a mediator declares an impasse. An impasse may affect the parties' rights and remedies and may trigger the provisions of other agreements between the parties. If the parties to mediation are also parties to an agreement to arbitrate before the FORUM, an impasse may allow a party to immediately pursue arbitration before the FORUM.

D. Role of Mediator

The function of the mediator is to promote and facilitate voluntary resolution of the issues. The mediator has no authority to impose a settlement on the parties. The mediator does not legally represent any of the parties. The mediator has no responsibility concerning the fairness or legality of the resolution. Mediators are independent contractors and not employees or agents of the FORUM. The mediator will determine the procedural aspects of the mediation hearing including the timing and occurrence of separate caucus sessions. At no time shall the mediator reveal confidential information without the specific consent of the parties. The mediator is authorized to end the mediation session whenever, in the judgment of the mediator, the parties have reached impasse in their attempts to forge a resolution.

E. Exchange of Information

1. Information may be exchanged through written and confidential submissions, telephone conference calls, meetings prior to the mediation or a combination of these methods. The mediator may establish which methods will be used and their timing, and parties may offer suggestions to the mediator.

2. At least ten (10) business days prior to the first scheduled mediation session, each party shall provide the mediator with a written brief not to exceed five pages summarizing the
background and present status of the dispute, including any settlement efforts that have occurred. Parties may also submit copies of documents and other written submissions that will assist the mediator in understanding the case and their position. The mediator may at any time during the mediation request that a party provide such additional information or materials, as the mediator deems useful. The mediator shall not, without authorization of the party submitting the brief or disclosing information, disclose such information to other parties or non-parties.

3. Any party may at any time submit to the mediator, for consideration by the mediator only, written information or materials that it considers to be confidential. The mediator shall not, without the authorization of that party, disclose such information or materials to other parties or non-parties.

4. The parties may have entered into agreements, including the applicability of supplemental rules and/or procedures, or the exchange of information, that relate to the mediation but are external to these Rules. The parties are directed to meet the terms of such agreements.

F. Mediation Sessions

1. Unless otherwise agreed to by the parties, the mediation session will be held at a time and place established by the FORUM in consultation with the mediator and the parties. Requests for changes of the scheduling of such a mediation session must be handled through the FORUM, with copies to all parties.

2. Requests to reschedule a session may result in the assessment of a rescheduling fee by

4

the FORUM.

3. The FORUM may assess fees against any party who fails to attend a mediation session.

G. Settlement
1. If a settlement is reached prior to the initial mediation session, the parties shall immediately notify the FORUM. The FORUM will assess additional fees, if any, based on the FORUM expenses and any fees due the mediator. Unless otherwise agreed to by the parties, these expenses will be borne equally by the parties.

2. If a settlement is reached during the mediation, the parties or their representatives, in conjunction with the mediator and prior to the conclusion of the mediation, may complete a document listing the points agreed upon by the parties. The mediator will inform the FORUM that a settlement has been reached, without revealing details of the settlement.

H. Confidentiality
1. The mediator shall not, without the authorization of that party, disclose privileged or confidential information or materials to other parties or non-parties.

2. The following provisions shall apply to all mediations, and the mediator may ask the parties to sign a confidentiality agreement prior to the commencement of mediation. If any provision below conflicts with the laws of the applicable jurisdiction, these provisions shall apply unless the parties agree otherwise.

    a. No evidence of the mediation session or any fact concerning the mediation may be admitted in a subsequent arbitration, hearing, or trial or any other subsequent proceeding involving any of the issues or parties to the mediation.

    b. Statements made and documents produced during mediation, which are not otherwise discoverable, are not subject to discovery or other disclosure and are not admissible as evidence for any purpose at trial, including impeachment.

    c. Notes, records, and recollections of the mediator and the FORUM are confidential and shall not be disclosed to anyone, including the parties and the public.

    d. All copies of materials produced during the mediation will be returned to the originator upon request at the termination of the mediation.

    e. All individuals involved in the mediation, including the mediator, the parties and their representatives, and any other persons present during the mediation, shall respect the confidentiality of the mediation and may not, unless otherwise agreed by the parties and the mediator, use or disclose to any outside party any information concerning, or obtained in the course of, the mediation and which may be included in a confidentiality statement to that effect.

5

Part III – Mediation Fees

All fees described in this section shall be based on the fees in effect on the date the mediation is accepted by the FORUM. Unless otherwise agreed by the parties, the FORUM will divide the fees equally among the parties.

A. Filing Fee

A non-refundable Mediation Filing Fee of $50 per party shall be submitted at the same time as the Request for Mediation. The Mediation Filing Fee covers the administrative costs associated with preparing a case for mediation. The FORUM will not take any action on the request until the Mediation Filing Fee is received.

B. Mediator Compensation Rates

The mediator's compensation rate will be communicated to the parties prior to appointment of the mediator.

C. Deposits

1. The FORUM may require that parties deposit with the FORUM amounts as an advance on the costs of the mediation, based on the FORUM's estimate of the mediation fees and expenses. The FORUM will provide an estimate the total costs of the mediation. The estimated time necessary for the mediation shall be determined by the FORUM. The FORUM will provide that estimate and seek the deposits from the parties prior to commencement of the mediation. Unless agreed otherwise by the parties, the parties will contribute in equal shares. All deposits will be accounted for and credited to a party in the amount that party paid. In the event that deposits are not used at all or in total for the mediation, remaining balances will be refunded. In the event that the deposit is exhausted, parties may be billed for additional charges and/or requested to make additional deposits for further proceedings.

2. The FORUM will maintain an ongoing accounting of expenses and, if the incurred expenses sufficiently deplete the deposited funds, additional contributions may be required of the parties.

3. Failure by a party to make a required deposit may result in termination or suspension of the mediation. Mediation Fees are based on the total time spent by the mediator to prepare for and conduct the mediation. Preparation time shall be reasonable, taking into account the nature and complexity of the case. The parties and mediator will discuss any special circumstance that calls for more extensive preparation time.

4. Upon termination of the mediation, the FORUM will provide to the parties a statement of expenses and fees. Unless otherwise agreed, any amount remaining of the initial or subsequent deposits will be returned to the parties according to the ratio contributed by the parties. Any balance due or additional fees and expenses will be billed to the parties on the same basis.

6

D. Additional Fees

The FORUM may assess additional fees to parties that have agreed to supplemental rules and/or procedures, or the exchange of information, that relate to the mediation but are external to these Rules.

E. Expenses

All expenses not covered by the fees above, including, but not limited to, mediator travel expenses, conference calls, facility charges and session expenses will be shared equally by the parties unless otherwise agreed. Parties shall be individually responsible for their own costs.

F. Collection and Disbursement of Fees and Expenses

Parties and parties' counsel are responsible for the prompt payment of all fees and expenses. The FORUM has the sole responsibility for collecting and disbursing payment to the mediator, and retains a portion of the Mediation Fees for its services. Parties agree to pay FORUM within thirty (30) days of their receipt of a final fee and expense invoice. Counsel, as well as the parties, are responsible for the payment of fees. FORUM may assess additional fees and costs for late payments and for expenses, including legal expenses and reasonable attorney fees to arbitrate or litigate a case to collect payment.

G. Cancellation Fees

Parties are strongly encouraged to meet and confer at least fifteen (15) days before the scheduled mediation session to ensure readiness for the matter and to request postponement or cancellation of any scheduled mediation session. Due to demands on the calendar and the reality of turning away other matters because dates are reserved, if the parties fail to appear at a mediation session, or a mediation session is cancelled or rescheduled at party request less than ten (10) days prior to the scheduled mediation session, the parties may be assessed a cancellation fee of an amount no greater than the time reserved for that mediation session.

Part IV – Limitations for Mediation

A. Exclusion of Liability

Neither the FORUM nor the mediator shall be liable to any party for any act or omission in connection with any mediation administered under these Rules. Neither the FORUM nor any mediator is a necessary party in any judicial proceeding related to the mediation. The mediator, the FORUM and its employees are incompetent to testify as witnesses in any proceeding relating to the mediation or the subject matter of the dispute. The parties release and agree to indemnify the FORUM and the mediator jointly and severally against all claims the parties may have arising out of or in any way referable to any act or omission in the performance of any obligation under this agreement, including all expenses, costs, and attorney fees incurred by the mediator and the FORUM.

7

B. Defamation

No statements or comments, whether written or oral, made or used by the parties, their representatives, or the mediator either in preparation for or in the course of the mediation shall be relied upon to found or maintain any action for defamation, libel, slander, or any related complaint.

C. Claims

Any claim or dispute between the FORUM and any party or between the FORUM and any mediator arising out of or related to these rules or related to any mediation administered by the FORUM shall be resolved by binding arbitration under the rules then in effect of a national arbitration administrator agreed to by the disputing parties. Any award of the arbitrator(s) may be entered in any Court of competent jurisdiction. This arbitration provision shall be governed by and interpreted under the United States Federal Arbitration Act, 9 U.S.C. Sections 1-16.

8

APPENDIX 13J-5

National Arbitration Forum Sample Request by a Party[1]

Name, address and phone number for **Claimant(s):**	REQUEST BY A PARTY
_____ _____ _____	
Telephone:_____ Fax:_____ E-Mail Address:_____	
Name, address and phone number for **Respondent(s):**	File Number:_____ *(As it appears on Initial Claim)*
_____ _____ _____	
Telephone:_____ Fax:_____ E-Mail Address:_____	

For a Request for an Order or other relief, _____ states:
(Print Name of Party)

_____

_____

_____

_____

_____

_____

_____

_____

_____

1. Attach accurate and correct copies of all Documents that support the Request, Order or relief **(see Rule 18).**

2. Attach Proof of Delivery of the Request Documents on all Parties.

P.O. Box 50191, Minneapolis, MN 55405-0191 • Tel. 800-474-2371 • Fax. 866-743-4517 • www.adrforum.com

---

[1]National Arbitration Forum, Request by a Party, available at http://www. adrforum.com/resource.aspx?id=586 (last accessed March 29, 2011).

APPENDIX 13K-1

Sample Appointment Order 1[1]

This matter was submitted to the undersigned upon *[choose one:* the joint request of the parties / the consent of the parties / the motion of _____ / the Court's own initiative]. Counsel appearances were:

Based upon the *[recite in some detail the basis of the Court's authority for appointment, such as the consent of the parties, the press of business, the unusual needs of the case, or other unusual circumstances]:*

IT IS HEREBY ORDERED:

1. [Name of Special Master] of [Address] is appointed Special Master for the purpose of *[specify scope of Special Master's role in detail; options include the following:*

    a. Directing, managing, and facilitating settlement negotiations among the parties. *[Settlement Master]*

    b. Managing and supervising discovery and resolving discovery disputes. *[Discovery Master]*

    c. Coordinating activity on the case as follows _____ *[Coordinating Master]*

    d. Hearing evidence on [specify issue(s)] and issuing [choose one: findings and recommendations / a final decision *NOTE: The second option is available only with the parties' consent]. [Trial Master]*

    e. Compiling and interpreting *[specify the technical, voluminous, or complex evidence that is in need of review]* and issuing findings and recommendations for the Court regarding _____. *[Trial Master*

    f. Advising the Court on the subject of _____ . *[Expert Master]*

    g. Managing and supervising discovery involving electronic information or data. *[Technology Master]*

    h. Serving as Monitor as described in paragraph _ of *[choose one:* the Consent Decree / this Court's Order dated _____]. *[Monitor]*

    i. [Drafting / implementing] a notice to the class. *[Class Action Master]*

    j. Supervising a hearing regarding the fairness of the Settlement Agreement to the class and issuing findings and recommendations for the Court. *[Class Action Master]*

    k. Administering the distribution of [settlement / damage] payments to Plaintiffs. *[Claims Administrator]*

    l. Providing an accounting of *[sped evidence]. [Auditor]*

    m. Acting as a receiver for *[identify the subject of the receivership]* pending the resolution of this dispute. *[Receiver]*

[The following provision is required in federal court:] The Special Master is directed to proceed with all reasonable diligence to complete the tasks assigned by this order.

2. [Special Master's Name] shall have the sole discretion to determine the appropriate procedures for resolution of all assigned matters and shall have the authority to take all appropriate measures to perform the assigned duties. The Special Master may by order impose upon a party any sanction other than contempt and may recommend a contempt sanction against a party and contempt or any other sanction against a non-party.

---

[1]Academy of Court Appointed Masters, Sample Appointment Order- Form Order: Includes Language to fit most situations, available at http://www.courtap pointedmasters.org/SampleApptOrders.asp (last accessed March 25, 2011).

3a. Alternative 1: No ex parte contact. The parties shall not engage in any ex parte discussions with the Special Master and the Special Master shall not engage in any ex parte discussions with any of the parties. [Fed. R. Civ. P. 53(b)(2)(B)]

3b. Alternative 2: Limited ex parte contact permitted. Because *[specify reasons]*, the Special Master shall be allowed to engage in ex parte conversations with counsel for the parties only in conjunction with duly convened settlement conferences.

3c. Alternative 3: Ex parte contact on the record. Because *[specify reasons]*, the Special Master shall be allowed to engage in ex parte conversations with counsel for the parties in order to permit full consideration of the issues. Any ex parte conversation will be conducted on the record in order to permit appropriate review by the undersigned or the appellate courts.

4. The parties shall file with the Clerk all papers filed for consideration by the Master. The Special Master shall also file with the Clerk all reports or other communications with the undersigned. [Fed. R. Civ. P. 53(b)(2)(C)].

5. Any party seeking review of any ruling of the Special Master shall [specify appeal procedure and timing; in the absence of special considerations, the default procedures of Rule 53(g) may be implemented, either by reference to the rule or incorporation of them].

5a. Alternative 1: comply with the procedures and within the time limits specified in Fed. R. Civ. P. 53(g).

5b. Alternative 2: object to any provision of such a ruling or may move the court to adopt or modify the Special Master's order, report or recommendations within 20 days from the date of such ruling is served on the parties. Fact findings of the Special Master *[Choose one:* will be reviewed for clear error / will be final *NOTE: The second option is available only with the parties' consent.].* All legal conclusions of the Special Master will be reviewed de novo and all procedural rulings of the Special Master will be reviewed only for an abuse of discretion.

6. The Special Master shall be paid $ ____ per hour for work done pursuant to this Order, and shall be reimbursed for all reasonable expenses incurred. The Special Master shall bill the parties on a monthly basis for fees and disbursements, and those bills shall be promptly paid [50% by the plaintiffs and 50% by the defendants / *or identify an alternative arrangement].* As to any particular portion of the proceedings necessitated by the conduct of one party or group of parties, the Special Master can assess the costs of that portion of the proceedings to the responsible party or parties. The Court will determine at the conclusion of this litigation whether the amounts paid to the Special Master will be borne on the 50/50 basis or will be reallocated.

7. The Special Master is authorized to hire _____ to assist in completion of the matters referred to the Special Master by this Order. The reasonable fees of _____ shall be paid by the parties in accordance with the procedure set forth in Paragraph 6, above.

Dated this ____ day of _____, 20___.

_____
Judge

APPENDIX 13K-2

Sample Appointment Order 2: Where Special Master Will Serve as Mediator and Was Previously Serving as Mediator Through an ADR Administrator[1]

Sample Appointment Order 1:
Where Special Master Will Serve as
Mediator and Was Previously Serving as
Mediator Through an ADR Administrator

After reviewing the progress of mediation in this action before _____, and with the consent of all parties, this Court finds that the appointment of a Special Master for purposes of further mediation and settlement is justified and necessary.

Pursuant to Federal Rule of Civil Procedure 53 it is **ORDERED** that the current mediator, _____, is appointed as Special Master for purposes of mediation and settlement.

The Special Master shall have the following authority, which he shall exercise with all reasonable diligence in accordance with Rule 53:

1. To direct and facilitate the settlement negotiations among the parties and their insurers.

2. To schedule mediation sessions, telephone conference calls, and other forms of communication among the parties, and to require the parties, counsel, expert consultants, and insurers to attend and participate in mediation sessions and/or other communications. The Special Master will make reasonable efforts to take into consideration the convenience of attendees when selecting locations for mediation sessions.

3. To require that parties and their insurers appear at and participate in mediation sessions with full authority to negotiate in a good faith effort to reach a settlement.

4. To take all appropriate measures to perform fairly and efficiently the responsibilities of a mediator in an effort to effectuate a complete settlement of this action.

5. To report to the Court at regularly scheduled status conferences the progress and status of the settlement negotiations.

[ADR administrator] shall charge $__/hour for _____'s services as Special Master, plus the normal [ADR administrator] administrative fee of 10% of the professional charges. [Add details about what the master will/will not charge for.]

Pursuant to the parties' agreement, the parties shall pay the charge for the Special Master's service [add details about how the parties will share responsibility for paying these charges.] If any party is added to or removed from the case, the pro rata shares shall be reallocated as the parties agree or by order of the Court. At the request of any party, the Court shall review and approve the charges for the Special Master's services.

The parties may have *ex parte* communications with the Special Master as to all matters related in any way to the mediation process. The Special Master may communicate *ex parte* with the Court as he and the Court deem necessary concerning the status of the mediation process, but shall not disclose to the Court the specifics of any party's settlement position without the consent of that party.

The Special Master need not preserve any record of his activities.

The clerk is directed to add Special Master _____ to the court's electronic service list at _____.

IT IS SO ORDERED.

---

[1]Academy of Court Appointed Masters, Sample Appointment Order- Where Special Master Will Serve as Mediator and Was Previously Serving as Mediator Through an ADR Administrator, available at http://www.courtappointedmasters.org/SampleApptOrders.asp (last accessed March 25, 2011).

APPENDIX 13K-3

Sample Appointment Order 3: Where Special Master Will Serve Various Roles in Multi-District Litigation[1]

Sample Appointment Order 5:
Where Special Master Will Serve Various Roles
in Multi-District Litigation

On [date], [parties] in this matter filed a motion for appointment of a Special Master. The parties having had notice and an opportunity to be heard, that motion is GRANTED and, with the advice and consent of the parties, the Court now APPOINTS as Special Master [name and address].

This appointment is made pursuant to Fed. R. Civ. P. 53 and the inherent authority of the Court.[1] As Rule 53 requires, the Court sets out below the duties and terms of the Special Master and reasons for appointment, and ORDERS the Special Master to "proceed with all reasonable diligence," Rule 53(b)(2).

I. BACKGROUND

[Description of how Multi-District Litigation came into being and the specific reasons that appointment of a Special Master is appropriate].

It is clear that this MDL presents many difficult issues and will require an inordinate amount of attention and oversight from the Court. Other MDL courts, facing similar challenges, have easily concluded that appointment of a Special Master was appropriate to help the Court with various pretrial, trial, and post-trial tasks.[2] Indeed, the appointment of a

---

[1] "Beyond the provisions of [Fed. R. Civ. P. 53] for appointing and making references to Masters, a Federal District Court has 'the inherent power to supply itself with this instrument for the administration of justice when deemed by it essential.'" *Schwimmer v. United States*, 232 F.2d 855, 865 (8th Cir. 1956) (quoting *In re: Peterson*, 253 U.S. 300, 311 (1920)); *see Ruiz v. Estelle*, 679 F.2d 1115, 1161 n.240 (5th Cir. 1982), *cert. denied*, 460 U.S. 1042 (1983) (same); *Reed v. Cleveland Bd. of Educ.*, 607 F.2d 737, 746 (6th Cir. 1979) (the authority to appoint "expert advisors or consultants" derives from either Rule 53 or the Court's inherent power). The Court's inherent power to appoint a Special Master, however, is not without limits. *See Cobell v. Norton*, 334 F.3d 1128, 1142 (D.C. Cir. 2003) (in the absence of consent by the parties, the inherent authority of the court does extend to allow appointment of Special Master to exercise "wide-ranging extrajudicial duties" such as "investigative, quasi-inquisitorial, quasi-prosecutorial role[s]").

This Court first discussed with the parties the advisability of appointing a Special Master during a case management conference on [date]. *See* Fed. R. Civ. P. 16(c)(8, 12) ("At any conference under this rule consideration may be given, and the court may take appropriate action, with respect to . . . (8) the advisability of referring matters to a magistrate judge or master; [or] . . . (12) the need for adopting special procedures for managing potentially difficult or protracted actions that may involve complex issues, multiple parties, difficult legal questions, or unusual proof problems").

[2] *See, e.g., In re: Diet Drugs (Phentermine, Fenfluramine, Dexfenfluramine) Products Liab. Litig.*, 1999 WL 782560 at *2 (E.D. Pa. Sept. 27, 1999) (MDL No. 1203) (noting that the court had earlier appointed a Special Master to oversee discovery matters and "facilitate the timely remand of individual civil actions to their respective transferor courts;" the court later broadened the Special Master's duties to include oversight and administration of the settlement trust funds); *In re: Bridgestone Firestone Inc., ATX, ATX II, and Wilderness Tires Products Liab. Litig.*, Order at 3-5, docket no. 14 (MDL No. 1373) (S.D. Ind. Nov. 1, 2000) (available at

1

---

[1] Academy of Court Appointed Masters, Sample Appointment Order- Where Special Master Will Serve Various Roles in Multi-District Litigation, available at http://www.courtappointedmasters.org/SampleApptOrders.asp (last accessed March 25, 2011).

Special Master in cases such as this is common. The 2003 amendments to Rule 53 specifically recognize the pretrial, trial, and post-trial functions of masters in contemporary litigation. Thus, the Court agrees with the parties that appointment of a Special Master to assist the Court in both effectively and expeditiously resolving their disputes.

II. RULE 53(B)(2).

Rule 53 was amended on December 1, 2003, and now requires an order of appointment to include certain contents. *See* Fed. R. Civ. P. 53(b)(2). The following discussion sets forth the matters required.

A. Master's Duties.

Rule 53(a)(1)(A) states that the Court may appoint a master to "perform duties consented to by the parties." [If applicable: The parties in this case consented to

> having a Special Master: 1) assist the Court with legal analysis of the parties' submissions; and 2) perform any and all other duties assigned to him by the Court (as well as any ancillary acts required to fully carry out those duties) as permitted by both the Federal Rules of Civil Procedure and Article III of the Constitution. The parties [further] request, however, that the Court retain sole authority to issue final rulings on matters formally submitted for adjudication.

Motion for appointment at 2.][3] The Court has reviewed recent legal authority addressing the duties of a Special Master that are permitted under the "Federal Rules of Civil Procedure and Article III of the Constitution."[4] Consonant with this legal authority, the

---

www.insd.uscourts.gov/Firestone) (appointing a Special Master to assist the court with all phases of the litigation, from "formulating a governance structure of [the] MDL" in its earliest stage to assisting with "attorneys fees" issues and "settlement negotiations" during the latter stages of the litigation); *In re: Baycol Products Liab. Litig.,* 2004 WL 32156072 (D. Minn. Mar. 25, 2002) (MDL No. 1431) (appointing a Special Master early in the case and assigning him all available "rights, powers, and duties provided in Rule 53;" the court has since appointed two additional masters to assist the first Special Master); *In re: Propulsid Products Liab. Litig.,* 2004 WL 1541922 (E.D. La. June 25, 2004) (MDL No. 1355) (appointing a Special Master and setting out a variety of duties).

[3] In addition, the Court may appoint a master to: (1) "address pretrial and post-trial matters that cannot be addressed effectively and timely by an available district judge or magistrate judge of the district;" and (2) "hold trial proceedings and make or recommend findings of fact on issues to be decided by the court without a jury," if warranted by certain conditions. Rule 53(a)(1)(B, C).

[4] *See, e.g.,* Fed. R. Civ. P. 53, advisory committee's notes (discussing the range of duties and authority of the Special Master). *See also* Mark Fellows & Roger Haydock, *Federal Courts Special Masters: A Resource in the Era of Complex Litig.* 31:3 Wm. Mitchell L. Rev. __ (forthcoming Spring 2005); David Ferleger, *Masters in Complex Litigation and Amended Rule 53,* Special Masters Conference 2004 Course Materials (Nat'l Arbitr. Forum ed., 2004) (unpublished); Margaret Farrell, *Special Masters in the Federal Courts Under Revised Rule 53: Designer Roles,* Special Masters Conference 2004 Course Materials (Nat'l Arbitr. Forum ed., 2004) (unpublished). These three articles, written by federal-court-appointed Special Masters, note the increasing use and need for such appointments, and discuss the range of duties and limits of appointment. The articles are on file with the Advanced Dispute Resolution

currently-anticipated needs of the court, and the parties' broad consent, the Court states that the Special Master in these proceedings shall have the authority to:[5]

1.   assist with preparation for attorney conferences (including formulating agendas), court scheduling, and negotiating changes to the case management order;

2.   establish discovery and other schedules, review and attempt to resolve informally any discovery conflicts (including issues such as privilege, confidentiality, and access to medical and other records), and supervise discovery;

3.   oversee management of docketing, including the identification and processing of matters requiring court rulings;

4.   compile data and assist with, or make findings and recommendations with regard to, interpretation of scientific and technical evidence;

5.   assist with legal analysis of the parties' motions or other submissions, whether made before, during, or after trials, and make recommended findings of fact and conclusions of law;

6.   assist with responses to media inquiries;

7.   help to coordinate federal, state and international litigation;

8.   direct, supervise, monitor, and report upon implementation and compliance with the Court's Orders, and make findings and recommendations on remedial action if required;

9.   interpret any agreements reached by the parties;

10.   propose structures and strategies for settlement negotiations on the merits, and on any subsidiary issues, and evaluate parties' class and individual claims, as may become necessary;

11.   propose structures and strategies for attorneys fee issues and fee settlement negotiations, review fee applications, and evaluate parties' individual claims for fees, as may become necessary;

12.   administer, allocate, and distribute funds and other relief, as may become necessary;

13.   adjudicate eligibility and entitlement to funds and other relief, as may become necessary;

14.   monitor compliance with structural injunctions, as may become necessary;

15.   make formal or informal recommendations and reports to the parties, and make recommendations and reports to the Court, regarding any matter pertinent to these proceedings; and

16.   communicate with parties and attorneys as needs may arise in order to permit

---

Institute at the William Mitchell College of Law, and are contained in reference materials distributed at the October, 2004 National Special Masters Conference.

[5] This list is meant to be illustrative, not comprehensive.

the full and efficient performance of these duties. *See* discussion below.

B. Communications with the Parties and the Court.

Rule 53(b)(2)(B) directs the Court to set forth "the circumstances—if any—in which the master may communicate ex parte with the court or a party." The Special Master may communicate ex parte with the Court at the Special Master's discretion, without providing notice to the parties, in order to "assist the Court with legal analysis of the parties' submissions" (e.g., the parties' motions). Motion for appointment at 2. The Special Master may also communicate ex parte with the Court, without providing notice to the parties, regarding logistics, the nature of his activities, management of the litigation, and other appropriate procedural matters. The Court may later limit the Special Master's ex parte communications with the Court with respect to certain functions, if the role of the Special Master changes.[6]

The Special Master may communicate ex parte with any party or his attorney, as the Special Master deems appropriate, for the purposes of ensuring the efficient administration and management of this MDL, including the making of informal suggestions to the parties to facilitate compliance with Orders of the Court; such ex parte communications may, for example, address discovery or other procedural issues. Such ex parte communications shall not, however, address the merits of any substantive issue, except that, if the parties seek assistance from the Special Master in resolving a dispute regarding a substantive issue, the Special Master may engage in ex parte communications with a party or his attorney regarding the merits of the particular dispute, for the purpose of mediating or negotiating a resolution of that dispute, only with the prior permission of those opposing counsel who are pertinent to the particular dispute.[7]

C. Master's Record.

Rule 53(b)(2)(c) states that the Court must define "the nature of the materials to be preserved and filed as a record of the master's activities." The Special Master shall maintain normal billing records of his time spent on this matter, with reasonably detailed descriptions of his activities and matters worked upon. See also section II.E of this Order, below. If the Court asks the Special Master to submit a formal report or recommendation regarding any matter, the Special Master shall either submit such report or recommendation in writing, for electronic filing

---

[6] If, for example, the Court later finds it desirable to use the Special Master as a mediator regarding the merits of a particular dispute, which mediation would require disclosure of information by the parties to the Special Master that the parties would prefer to keep from a final adjudicator, the Court may redefine the scope of allowed ex parte communications with the Court regarding that dispute. *See, e.g., In re: Propulsid Products Liab. Litig.,* 2002 WL 32156066 (E.D. La. Aug. 28, 2002) (after the Special Master was given additional mediation duties, the scope of his ex parte communications with the parties and the Court, as well as his record-keeping obligations, changed); Rule 53(b)(4) (noting that an order of appointment may be amended). On the other hand, such imposition of different limits on ex parte communications does not necessarily require amendment of this Order.

[7] To the extent it may be considered a "substantive issue," the Special Master may engage in ex parte communications with a party or counsel, without first obtaining the prior permission of opposing counsel, to resolve privilege or similar questions and in connection with in camera inspections.

4

on the case docket. The Special Master need not preserve for the record any documents created by the Special Master that are docketed in this or any other court, nor any documents received by the Special Master from counsel or parties in this case. The Court may later amend the requirements for the Special Master's record if the role of the Special Master changes.[8]

D. Review of the Special Master's Orders.

Rule 53(b)(2)(D) directs the Court to state "the time limits, method of filing the record, other procedures, and standards for reviewing the master's orders, findings, and recommendations." The Special Master shall either: (1) reduce any formal order, finding, report, or recommendation to writing and file it electronically on the case docket via Electronic Case Filing ("ECF"); or (2) issue any formal order, finding, report, or recommendation on the record, before a court reporter. Pursuant to Rule 53(g)(2), any party may file an objection to an order, finding, report, or recommendation by the Special Master within 14 calendar days of the date it was electronically filed; failure to meet this deadline results in permanent waiver of any objection to the Special Master's orders, findings, reports, or recommendations.[9] Absent timely objection, the orders, findings, reports, and recommendations of the Special Master shall be deemed approved, accepted, and ordered by the Court, unless the Court explicitly provides otherwise.

As provided in Rule 53(g)(4, 5), the Court shall decide de novo all objections to conclusions of law made or recommended by the Special Master; and the Court shall set aside a ruling by the Special Master on a procedural matter only for an abuse of discretion. The Court shall retain sole authority to issue final rulings on matters formally submitted for adjudication, unless otherwise agreed by the parties, and subject to waiver of objection to written orders or recommendations as noted above. To the extent the Special Master enters an order, finding, report, or recommendation regarding an issue of fact, the Court shall review such issue de novo, if any party timely objects pursuant to the Rules and within the 14 calendar day time period set forth herein; see Rule 53(g)(3). Failure to meet this deadline results in permanent waiver of any objection to the Special Master's findings of fact.

E. Compensation.

Rule 53(b)(2)(E) states that the Court must set forth "the basis, terms, and procedure for

---

[8] *See, e.g., In re: Propulsid Products Liab. Litig.,* 2004 WL 1541922 (E.D. La. June 25, 2004) (setting out additional record-keeping requirements after the Special Master was charged with new duties of administering a settlement program).

[9] Rule 53(g)(2) provides that parties may file objections "no later than 20 days from the time the master's order, report, or recommendations are served, unless the court sets a different time." The Court chooses to set a period of 14 calendar days (NOT business days) in order to expedite final resolution of matters formally reported upon by the Special Master. Motions for extensions of time to file objections will not normally be granted unless good cause is shown. The Special Master may, however, provide in his order, finding, report, or recommendation that the period for filing objections to that particular document is some period longer than 14 calendar days, if a longer period appears warranted.

5

fixing the master's compensation;" see also Rule 53(h) (addressing compensation). The Special Master shall be compensated at the rate of [$ per hour], with the parties bearing this cost equally (50% by the plaintiffs and 50% by the defendants). The Special Master shall incur only such fees and expenses as may be reasonably necessary to fulfill his duties under this Order, or such other Orders as the Court may issue. Within 14 days of the date of this Order, the parties shall **REMIT** to the Special Master an initial, one-time retainer of [$___] (50% by the plaintiffs and 50% by the defendants); the Court will not order additional payments by the parties to the Special Master until the retainer is fully earned. The Court has "consider[ed] the fairness of imposing the likely expenses on the parties and [has taken steps to] protect against unreasonable expense or delay." Rule 53(a)(3).

From time to time, on approximately a monthly basis, the Special Master shall submit to the Court an Itemized Statement of fees and expenses, which the Court will inspect carefully for regularity and reasonableness. Given that, at this juncture in the litigation, one of the duties of the Special Master is to assist the Court with legal analysis of the parties' submissions, the Court expects these Itemized Statements will reveal confidential communications between the Special Master and the Court. Accordingly, the Court shall maintain these Itemized Statements under seal, and they shall not be made available to the public or counsel. The Special Master shall attach to each Itemized Statement a Summary Statement, which shall not reflect any confidential information and shall contain a signature line for the Court, accompanied by the statement "approved for disbursement." If the Court determines the Itemized Statement is regular and reasonable, the Court will sign the corresponding Summary Statement and transmit it to the parties. The parties shall then remit to the Special Master their half-share of any Court-approved amount, within 20 calendar days of Court approval.[10]

Finally, the Special Master shall not seek or obtain reimbursement or compensation for support personnel, absent approval by the Court.[11]

F. Other Matters.

1. Affidavit.

Rule 53(b)(3) notes that the Court may enter an Order of appointment "only after the master has filed an affidavit disclosing whether there is any ground for disqualification under 28

---

[10] The Court adopts this procedure from Judge Sarah Evans Barker, who used it in *In re: Bridgestone Firestone*. *See* www.insd.uscourts.gov/Firestone/, docket no. 593 ("Entry concerning fees of Special Master").

[11] *Cf. Triple Five of Minnesota, Inc. v. Simon*, 2003 WL 22859834 at *2 (D. Minn. Dec. 1, 2003) (authorizing the Special Master to "hire accountants, real estate consultants, attorneys, or others as necessary to assist him in carrying out his duties under this Order" and further stating: "The special master shall be compensated at the rate of $400.00 per hour. Additionally, the parties shall pay the usual and customary rates for work which the special master delegates to others."). In light of the complexity of this litigation, and depending on how it proceeds, it may become appropriate for the Special Master to retain consultants or otherwise obtain assistance.

6

U.S.C. §455." <u>See also</u> Rule 53(a)(2) (discussing grounds for disqualification). Attached to this Order is the affidavit earlier submitted to the Court by the Special Master.

2. <u>Cooperation</u>.

The Special Master shall have the full cooperation of the parties and their counsel. Pursuant to Rule 53(c), the Special Master may, if appropriate, "impose upon a party any noncontempt sanction provided by Rule 37 or 45, and may recommend a contempt sanction against a party and sanctions against a nonparty." As an agent and officer of the Court, the Special Master shall enjoy the same protections from being compelled to give testimony and from liability for damages as those enjoyed by other federal judicial adjuncts performing similar functions.[12] The parties will make readily available to the Special Master any and all facilities, files, databases, and documents which are necessary to fulfill the Special Master's functions under this Order.

IT IS SO ORDERED.

---

[12] <i>See Atkinson-Baker & Associates, Inc. v. Kolts</i>, 7 F.3d 1452, 1454-55 (9th Cir. 1993) (applying the doctrine of absolute quasi-judicial immunity to a Special Master).

<u>AFFIDAVIT OF [NAME]</u>
<u>TENDERED PURSUANT TO FED. R. CIV. P. 53</u>

STATE OF _____)
) ss.   AFFIDAVIT
COUNTY OF _____)

[name], being first duly sworn according to law, states the following:

1. I am an attorney at law, duly licensed to practice law in the States of [___]. My bar admissions are as follows:

[list]

2. I have thoroughly familiarized myself with the issues involved in the Multi-District Litigation captioned [ ]. As a result of my knowledge of that case, I can attest and affirm that there are no non-disclosed grounds for disqualification under 28 U.S.C. §455 that would prevent me from serving as the Special Master in the captioned matter.

FURTHER AFFIANT SAYETH NAUGHT.

_____

Sworn to before me and subscribed in my presence this day of , 20 .

_____
Notary Public

8

APPENDIX 13K-4

Order Appointing Special Masters Pursuant to Stipulation in the United States District Court for the Central District of Florida

In re Toyota Motor Corp., Case No. 8:10ML2151-JVS (C.D.Fl. August 13, 2010)[1]

UNITED STATES DISTRICT COURT

CENTRAL DISTRICT OF CALIFORIA

IN RE: TOYOTA MOTOR CORP. UNINTENDED ACCELERATION MARKETING, SALES PRACTICES, AND PRODUCTS LIABILITY LITIGATION	Case No.: 8:10ML2151 JVS (FMOx)
This documents relates to:	ORDER NO. 6: APPOINTING SPECIAL MASTERS (PURSUANT TO STIPULATION)
ALL CASES	

WHEREAS the parties agree that the volume of discovery in this litigation warrants special masters to resolve discovery disputes and allow the Court to focus primarily on substantive pre-trial matters in this litigation;

WHEREAS the Court agrees that appointing special masters will assist the Court in effectively and expeditiously resolving the parties' discovery disputes;

WHEREAS all parties to this litigation have stipulated and consented to the appointment of the Honorable _____ (ret.) and the Honorable _____ (ret.) to serve as the Special Masters in these proceedings; and

WHEREAS the Court appointed the Special Masters in these proceedings by order dated July 1, 2010,

IT IS HEREBY ORDERED, pursuant Fed. R. Civ. P. 53 and by the consent of the parties that the Special Masters shall proceed with all reasonable diligence to fulfill their duties and responsibilities, as follows:

I. **DUTIES AND RESPONSIBILITIES**

A.   The Special Masters are empowered and charged with the duties outlined below, subject to and consistent with Fed. R. Civ. P. 53:

1.   Rule on legal and factual disputes arising from discovery issues under Fed. R. Civ. P. 26(b) including, but not limited to, issues of discoverability, privilege, and attorney work product.

2

---

[1]Order Appointing Special Masters Pursuant to Stipulation in the United States District Court for the Central District of Florida, In re Toyota Motor Corp., Case No. 8:10ML2151-JVS (C.D.Fl. August 13, 2010).

2.   Resolve disputes between the parties relating to depositions, including but, not limited to:

    a.   Fixing the time and place of depositions if counsel are not able to reach agreement.

    b.   Attending depositions as necessary or by agreement of the parties. When the Special Masters are requested to be available for a deposition, but cannot attend the deposition in person, one of the Special Masters shall make himself available to be consulted by telephone to rule on disputes arising during the deposition. The Special Masters shall confer, determine which Special Master will be available for consultation during the deposition and notify the parties of such determination prior to the start of the deposition.

    c.   Ruling, if requested, on any objection, refusal to answer, failure to provide a responsive answer to a question at a deposition, or failure to produce documents for deposition. If a party objects to and seeks Court review of (i) a ruling made by the Special Master at the deposition or (ii) any matter arising in a deposition, then the witness is relieved from proceeding as directed by the Special Master pending review by the Court, and the Special Master may order completion of the deposition pending Court review of the Special Master's ruling. If no party requests review of the ruling when made by the Special Master, then the witness shall proceed as directed by the Special Master. With respect to any such Special Master ruling that relates specifically to a deponent who resides outside the United States, a party challenging such ruling of the Special Master

Case 8:10-ml-02151-JVS -FMO   Document 278   Filed 08/13/10   Page 4 of 12   Page ID
#:6585

1   shall present its request for review, including any supporting

2   legal or factual showing, within two Court days of the ruling

3   challenged. Any response to the challenge shall be filed

4   within three Court days of the ruling. With this procedure

5   for foreign deponents, it is the Court's goal to obviate the

6   need for a second trip to the foreign country where the

7   deposition is held if the deposition is held outside the United

8   States and the need for the deponent to return to the United

9   States if the deposition is held in the United States.

10   3.   Rule upon all motions related to discovery, including but, not

11   limited to:

12   a.   All applications for protective orders in this litigation and

13   requests for modification of, or exceptions to, such

14   protective orders.

15   b.   All requests for an order compelling discovery pursuant to

16   Fed. R. Civ. P. 37 and for costs or expenses related thereto.

17   The parties may object to assessments ordered by the

18   Special Masters pursuant to the procedures detailed in

19   Section IV of this Order.

20   c.   All issues relating to the manner and format of document

21   production.

22   B.   To resolve a discovery dispute, the Special Masters may set a hearing,

23   which may take place in person at a JAMS office, may be conducted telephonically, or

24   as otherwise agreed to by the parties and as approved by the Special Master. A court

25   reporter shall be present at any hearing before the Special Masters, and the court

26   reporter shall submit bills as provided in Section VI of this Order.

27   C.   The Special Masters' adjudicatory powers are limited to discovery

28   matters. Rulings on substantive legal issues are within the exclusive jurisdiction of

LEGAL02/32108852v2   4

the Court.

II.   ALLOCATION OF DUTIES AND RESPONSIBILITIES

A.   The Special Masters shall allocate all of the work prescribed under this Order between themselves, at their own discretion.

B.   All matters within the scope of Section I of this Order may be decided in writing by a single Special Master, provided that the other Special Master shall review and indicate his concurrence in the order. If there is no concurrence by the second Special Master, the matter shall be referred directly to the Court for review. Rulings by the Special Master(s) are subject to review as provided in Section IV, *infra*.

C.   On all procedural matters to which there is no disagreement between the parties, the signature of a single Special Master shall be sufficient.

D.   The Special Masters are authorized to carry out their duties and responsibilities using Commissioner Greer Stroud (Ret.) and Derek Scott, J.D., for limited research and administrative work, respectively. The fees for Stroud and Scott, who are affiliated with JAMS, shall be billed by the Special Masters under the procedures set forth in Section VII.

E.   If the Special Masters deem it necessary to consult with an e-discovery expert, they are authorized to use a JAMS Neutral with expertise in that area after first providing the parties with 5 days' written notice and an opportunity to object. If the Special Master denies an objection, then the objecting party may request formalization of the ruling and also seek judicial review under Section IV. The charges for any JAMS Neutral used for e-discovery shall be billed by the Special Masters under the procedures set forth in Section VII.

F.   In accordance with Fed. R. Civ. P. 53(b)(3), the Special Masters have submitted affidavits to the Court stating that there are no grounds for disqualification under 28 U.S.C. § 455, copies of which are attached hereto collectively as Exhibit A.

III.   BRIEFING AND HEARING OF MOTIONS

A.   The timing and procedure for resolving discovery disputes, including

LEGAL02/32108852v2   5

1   briefing of motions, should comply with the Federal Rules of Civil Procedure, and the

2   Court's Local Rules and case management orders.

3   B.   Nonetheless, the Special Masters may resolve discovery disputes by

4   informal procedures when both parties consent, such consent not to be unreasonably

5   withheld, or if the Court has authorized the use of such procedures generally or for the

6   specific matter after the parties have had an opportunity to be heard. Under such

7   procedures, the parties may brief the issues orally or by letters or e-mail, and the

8   Special Masters may issue orders by letters or e-mail.

9   C.   Absent extraordinary circumstances, the Special Masters shall resolve all

10 disputes within 30 days of submission of a motion or letter by the parties.

11

12

13

14

15

16

17

18

19

20

21

22

23

24

25

26

27

28

IV.   JUDICIAL REVIEW OF RULINGS BY THE SPECIAL MASTER

A.   After concurring on a ruling, the Special Masters shall either:

1.   Reduce their formal order, finding, report or recommendation to writing and file it electronically on the case docket via Electronic Case Filing ("ECF"); or

2.   Issue any formal order, finding, report, or recommendation on the record before a court reporter.

B.   If the Special Masters issue an informal order or finding that is not made part of the record via ECF or the court reporter, and a party wishes to object to that order or finding, then the party shall ask the Special Masters to formalize the order by reducing the order or finding to writing, and filing it on the docket via ECF. Such request shall be made within 5 days of issuance of the informal order or finding. The Special Master shall formalize the order or finding within 3 days of the party's request. After formalization, the other procedures and deadlines outlined in this Section shall apply. If no party requests formalization within 5 days of the Special Masters issuing the informal order or finding, then the opportunity to object shall be permanently waived and the informal order or finding shall be deemed approved, accepted and ordered by the Court, unless the Court expressly provides otherwise.

C.   Pursuant to Fed. R. Civ. P. 53(f)(2), any party may file an objection to any formal order, finding, report, or recommendation by the Special Masters with the Court within 12 days of ECF date. Failure to meet this deadline results in permanent waiver of any objection to the Special Masters' specific order, finding, report, or recommendation.

D.   Absent an objection within 12 days, the formal orders, findings, reports and recommendations of the Special Masters shall be approved, accepted and ordered by the Court, unless the Court expressly provides otherwise. Motions for extensions of time to file objections will only be granted upon a showing of good cause. The Special Masters may, however, provide in their formal order, finding, report or recommendation that the period for filing objections to that particular document is a period longer or shorter than 12 days if warranted under the circumstances.

E.   The party seeking review shall, at its own expense, provide the Court with a transcript of the proceedings before the Special Masters (if a court reporter was present), together with a concise statement of the issues and authorities that does not exceed 10 pages. The other party shall have an opportunity to file a responsive statement that does not exceed 10 pages.

F.   As provided in Fed. R. Civ. P. 53(f), the Court shall review all orders, findings, reports or recommendations by the Special Masters, including any findings of fact and conclusions of law, under the *de novo* standard.

V.   ***EX PARTE* COMMUNICATION**

A.   Except until further order of the Court, *ex parte* communications between the Special Masters and the Court shall be governed by the Court's Minutes from July 9, 2010, which provide that: "[t]he Court shall not communicate with the Special Masters, and the Special Masters shall not communicate with the Court, on substantive matters except in writing with service upon the parties or in the presence of the parties. The Court and the Special Masters may communicate with each other on procedural matters without restriction."

B.   The Special Masters may not communicate *ex parte* with the parties regarding pending matters requiring adjudication by the Special Masters, unless the parties have consented in writing. Otherwise, the Special Masters may only communicate *ex parte* with the parties concerning purely administrative matters, such as availability for hearing dates.

VI.   **MAINTENANCE OF RECORDS**

A.   The Special Masters shall preserve billing records of time spent on this litigation, with reasonably detailed descriptions of the activities worked on.

B.   The Special Masters shall preserve all documents which they generate or receive during this litigation, including but not limited to the documents which they consider when making orders, findings, reports, or recommendations, until such time that the Court grants permission to destroy the documents.

VII. COMPENSATION

A.   Special Masters Trotter and Stone shall each be compensated at their reasonable and customary   rates, which are set forth in the JAMS fee schedule attached hereto as Exhibit B:

> o $8,000 for a full day, including up to 10 hours of hearing time;
>
> o $5,000 for a half day, including up to 4 hours of hearing time; and
>
> o $750 per hour other professional time.

The Special Masters shall incur only such reasonable fees and expenses as may be reasonably necessary to fulfill their duties under this Order. The Special Masters' reasonable expenses shall include any applicable JAMS Case Management fees listed in Exhibit B.

B.   If the Special Masters use Commissioner Stroud or Mr. Scott for limited research or administrative work, respectively, then the Special Masters shall bill for Stroud's and Scott's time at the reasonable rates of $400 and $125 per hour, respectively, as set forth in Exhibit B.

C.   If the Special Masters consult with a JAMS neutral on e-discovery issues, they shall also bill for the JAMS neutral's time. The JAMS neutral's hourly rate shall not exceed $400.

D.   Any court reporter retained by the Special Masters or the parties shall be compensated at rates which are reasonable and customary for the geographic market in which the testimony is taken. The court reporters shall only incur such fees and expenses as may be reasonably necessary to fulfill their duty of acting as stenographers.

E.   On the first business day of each month, the Special Masters (through JAMS) and any court reporters shall submit to the Court *ex parte* their respective itemized statements of fees and expenses that the Court will inspect carefully for

LEGAL02/32108852v2

9

reasonableness.

F.   The Special Masters (through JAMS) and any court reporters shall attach to each itemized statement a "Summary Statement," which shall not reflect any confidential information and shall contain a signature line for the Court, accompanied by the statement "approved for disbursement."

G.   Once approved, the Court shall send the executed Summary Statements to the parties. The parties shall bear the cost equally and submit payments to the Special Masters (through JAMS) and any court reporters, respectively, within 30 days of receiving the Summary Statements.

IT IS SO ORDERED.

Dated: August 13, 2010

_____
James V. Selna
United State District Judge

APPENDIX 13K-5

Order Creating Panel of E-Discovery Special Masters[1]

IN THE UNITED STATES DISTRICT COURT
FOR THE WESTERN DISTRICT OF PENNSYLVANIA

IN RE: ESTABLISHMENT OF
A PANEL OF SPECIAL MASTERS
FOR ELECTRONIC DISCOVERY

10 - mc - 324

WHEREAS, on November 16, 2010 the Board of Judges approved the establishment of a list of attorneys with expertise in electronic discovery to serve as Special Masters upon appointment by the Court.

WHEREAS, the criteria for appointment as an Electronic Discovery Special Master for the United States District Court for the Western District of Pennsylvania will be:

1. Active Bar Admission,
2. Demonstrated litigation experience,
3. Demonstrated electronic discovery knowledge, training and experience,
4. Mediation and/or other Alternative Dispute Resolution (ADR) training and/or experience.

WHEREAS, an electronic mail message will be sent through the Court's CM/ECF system notifying qualified attorneys that applications will be available on the Court's web site, beginning November 30, 2010 and ending on January 14, 2011.

WHEREAS, applications will be reviewed by members of the Court's CM/ADR Committee for approval.

WHEREAS, approved special masters for electronic discovery will be required to attend a four-hour Orientation in February, 2011, as detailed in their notice of selection.

IT IS HEREBY ORDERED, that effective March 15, 2011, the Court will maintain on its web site a list of qualified attorneys to serve as Electronic Discovery Special Masters.

FOR THE COURT:

11 | 16 | 10
Date

Gary L. Lancaster
Chief Judge

---

[1] Order Creating Panel of E-Discovery Special Masters, In re: Establishment of a Panel of Special Masters for Electronic Discovery (W.D.PA Nov. 16, 2010).

APPENDIX 13L-1

Sample Eastern District of New York Arbitration Award Form[1]

```
UNITED STATES DISTRICT COURT,
EASTERN DISTRICT OF NEW YORK
-------------------------------

                -Plaintiff
        -v-                                CV

                -Defendant
-------------------------------------X
```

AWARD OF ARBITRATOR

I, the undersigned, having been certified and designated as arbitrator in the above captioned matter, and having been duly sworn and having heard the civil action on _____ 200__ do hereby render the following AWARD pursuant to the Local Arbitration Rules of the U.S. District Court, Eastern District of New York: (The Award will not be entered on the ECF Docket)

1. _____   AWARD in favor of the Plaintiff(s) in the sum of

    $_____ with interest from_____

2. _____   AWARD in favor of the Defendant(s) dismissing the complaint on the merits.

3. _____   AWARD_____

    _____

_____   _____
                                            DATED
ARBITRATOR

IMPORTANT NOTICE

The Arbitration Award will become a final Judgment of this Court, without the right to appeal, unless a party files with THE ARBITRATION CLERK a demand for a TRIAL-DE-NOVO within 30 days after entry of this Arbitration Award. **Please do not disclose the nature of this Award to any District Court Judge or Magistrate Judge or forward copies of the Award to any District Court Judge or Magistrate. If you request a TRIAL-DE-NOVO, DO NOT SUBMIT THE AWARD WITH THE REQUEST.

---

[1]United States District Court for the Eastern District of New York, Arbitration Documents—Arbitration Award Form, available at https://www.nyed.uscourts.gov/adr/Arbitration/Arbiration_Documents/arbiration_documents.html (last accessed March 25, 2011).

```
UNITED STATES DISTRICT COURT,
EASTERN DISTRICT OF NEW YORK
-------------------------------
                 -Plaintiff
        -v-                                    CV
                 -Defendant
-----------------------------------X
```

CERTIFICATION OF SERVICES RENDERED

I,_____, member of the bar of the United

States District Court for the Eastern District of New York, having been

appointed by the Court as arbitrator in the subject legal action

above, hereby certify that on:_____

       / /   The arbitration hearing was held.
       / /   The case settled before the hearing.
       / /   The case settled during the hearing.
       / /   Other (describe briefly)

         _____
         _____

     I also reviewed the Complaint and Answer and read the
various statutes cited by the parties in support of the respective
claim

    Taxpayer Id:_____
    Address: _____
               _____
               _____
    Email: _____

    Signature:_____

```
UNITED STATES DISTRICT COURT,
EASTERN DISTRICT OF NEW YORK
--------------------------------
                    -Plaintiff
          -v-                              CV

                    -Defendant
------------------------------------X
```

OATH OF ARBITRATOR

I,_____do hereby solemnly swear (or affirm)

that I will administer justice without respect to persons, and do equal rights to the poor

and the rich, and that I will faithfully and impartially discharge and perform all the duties

incumbent upon me as arbitrator according to the best of my abilities and understanding,

agreeably to the Constitution and laws of the United States.   So Help Me. God.

_____
Signature

Sworn to and subscribed before me this_____day of_____20____

at_____

_____   _____
Signature   **Title**

UNITED STATES DISTRICT COURT,
EASTERN DISTRICT OF NEW YORK

```
            -Plaintiff
     -v-                                        CV

            -Defendant
------------------------------------X
```

OATH OF WITNESS
<u>AT THE ARBITRATION HEARING</u>

DO YOU SWEAR (OR AFFIRM) THAT THE TESTIMONY

YOU ARE ABOUT TO GIVE ON THE MATTER NOW BEFORE

THE ARBITRATOR OF THIS COURT IS THE TRUTH, THE

WHOLE TRUTH, AND NOTHING BUT THE TRUTH, SO HELP

YOU GOD

```
UNITED STATES DISTRICT COURT,
EASTERN DISTRICT OF NEW YORK
-------------------------------
                -Plaintiff
         -v-                                    CV
                -Defendant
-------------------------------------X
```

NOTICE OF APPEARANCE

DATE_____

      PLEASE NOTICE THAT I,_____,
                           (Print Name)

have been retained by (Plaintiff/Defendant)_____

_____

NAME AND ADDRESS OF FIRM

_____

_____

_____   TELEPHONE_____

Email:_____

SIGNATURE OF ATTORNEY_____

UNITED STATES DISTRICT COURT,
EASTERN DISTRICT OF NEW YORK

                    -Plaintiff
           -v-   CV

                    -Defendant
------------------------------------X

                    <u>NOTICE OF APPEARANCE</u>

DATE_____

        PLEASE NOTICE THAT I,_____,
                              (Print Name)

have been retained by (Plaintiff/Defendant)_____

_____

NAME AND ADDRESS OF FIRM

_____

_____

_____   TELEPHONE_____

Email:_____

SIGNATURE OF ATTORNEY_____

UNITED STATES DISTRICT COURT,
EASTERN DISTRICT OF NEW YORK

　　　　　　　　-Plaintiff

　　　-v-　　　　　　　　　　　　　　　　　CV

　　　　　　　　-Defendant
-------------------------------------X

APPENDIX 13L-2

Sample Eastern District of New York Mediation Agreement[1]

UNITED STATES DISTRICT COURT
EASTERN DISTRICT OF NEW YORK

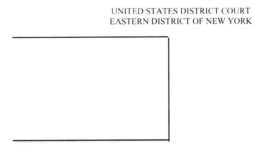

IT IS HEREBY STIPULATED AND AGREED by and between the undersigned parties:

1.   No party shall be bound by anything said or done during the Mediation, unless either a written and signed stipulation is entered into or the parties enter into a written and signed agreement.

2.   The Mediator may meet in private conference with less than all of the parties.

3.   Information obtained by the Mediator, either in written or oral form, shall be confidential and shall not be revealed by the Mediator unless and until the party who provided that information agrees to its disclosure.

4.   The Mediator shall not, without the prior written consent of both parties, disclose to the Court any matters which are disclosed to him or her by either of the parties or any matters which otherwise relate to the Mediation.

5.   The mediation process shall be considered a settlement negotiation for the purpose of all federal and state rules protecting disclosures made during such conferences from later discovery or use in evidence. The entire procedure shall be confidential, and no stenographic or other record shall be made except to memorialize a settlement record. All communications, oral or written, made during the Mediation by any party or a party's agent, employee, or attorney are confidential and, where appropriate, are to be considered work product and privileged. Such communications, statements, promises, offers, views and opinions shall not be subject to any discovery or admissible for any purpose, including impeachment, in any litigation or other proceeding involving the parties. Provided, however, that evidence otherwise subject to discovery or admissible is not excluded from discovery or admission in evidence simply as a result of it having been used in connection with this mediation process.

6.   The Mediator and his or her agents shall have the same immunity as judges and

---

[1]United States District Court for the Eastern District of New York, Mediation Documents—Mediation Confidentiality Form, available at https://www.nyed.uscourts.gov/adr/Mediation/Mediation___Documents/mediation___documents.html (last accessed March 25, 2011).

509

court employees have under Federal law and the common law from liability for any act or omission in connection with the Mediation, and from compulsory process to testify or produce documents in connection with the Mediation.

7. The parties (i) shall not call or subpoena the Mediator as a witness or expert in any proceeding relating to: the Mediation, the subject matter of the Mediation, or any thoughts or impressions which the Mediator may have about the parties in the Mediation, and (ii) shall not subpoena any notes, documents or other material prepared by the Mediator in the course of or in connection with the Mediation, and (iii) shall not offer into evidence any statements, views or opinions of the Mediator.

8. The Mediator's services have been made available to the parties through the dispute resolution procedures sponsored by the Court. In accordance with those procedures, the Mediator represents that he has taken the oath prescribed by 28 U.S.C. 453.

9. Any party to this Stipulation is required to attend at least one session and as many sessions thereafter as may be helpful in resolving this dispute.

10. An individual with final authority to settle the matter and to bind the party shall attend the Mediation on behalf of each party.

Dated: _____

_____   _____
Plaintiff   Defendant

_____   _____
Attorneys for Plaintiff   Attorneys for Defendant

Consented to: _____
     Mediator

APPENDIX 13L-3

Sample District of Utah Final Arbitration Agreement[1]

SAMPLE FORM OF FINAL ARBITRATION AGREEMENT

Attorney Submitting and Utah State Bar Number
Attorney for |Plaintiff/Defendant|
Address
Telephone

IN THE UNITED STATES DISTRICT COURT
FOR THE DISTRICT OF UTAH

	:	
	:	
	:	**FINAL ARBITRATION**
	:	**AGREEMENT**
Plaintiff,	:	
vs.	:	
	:	**Civil Case No.**
	:	
	:	
Defendant.	:	

The parties hereto agree that this matter will be arbitrated in accordance with the provisions of the ADR Plan, Rule 16-2 of the District of Utah Civil Rules of Practice, and applicable federal statutes.

The parties further agree:

      1.   That the following arbitrator(s) will oversee the arbitration process:

List each arbitrator by name.

---

[1]United States District Court for the District of Utah, ADR Program Documents, available at http://www.utd.uscourts.gov/documents/adrpage.html (last accessed March 25, 2011).

2.   The arbitrator(s), while acting in the official capacity of court-appointed arbitrator in this matter, shall have the same immunity from liability accorded to United States district judges while acting in their official capacity.

3.   *Select Alternative (A) or (B):*

(A)   Pursuant to ADR Plan Section 5(n), any party may file a demand for trial de novo within thirty (30) days after the filing of the arbitration award. *Where timely demand has been made, the clerk of court will vacate the award, and the case will be returned to the regular trial calendar. Where no timely trial de novo demand is made, the clerk will enter judgment on the award in accordance with Fed. R. Civ. P. 58, unless the award involves equitable or other relief, in which case the award will be submitted to the court for the entry of the judgment.*

(B)   The parties agree that the arbitration award will be final and binding. The parties hereby agree to waive the right, under ADR Plan Section 5(n), to file a demand for trial de novo.

4.   The factual and legal issues on which the parties agree are: *The parties and their counsel, under the guidance of the arbitrator(s), should agree on as many facts and/or issues as possible in order to focus and maximize the vaule of the arbitration hearing.*

5.   The factual and legal issues that remain to be decided are: *List clearly and concisely. Because the arbitrator(s) may determine only the facts and decide only the issues set forth in this agreement as stated in the ADR Plan Section 5(i), due care should be taken to frame them properly. Where, during the proceedings, other issues not set forth*

2

in this agreement emerge that must be decided in order for the arbitrator(s) to render an award, the arbitrator(s) must seek the parties' agreement before proceeding. If the parties cannot agree, the arbitration may be terminated without result.

6.   The parties' respective positions on the factual and legal issues that remain to be decided are: *List clearly and concisely by party.*

7.   The scope of discovery conducted by the parties is limited to: *Parties should minimize discovery (i) pursuant to DUCivR 16-2(f), and (ii) because arbitration hearings must be conducted within one-hundred-twenty (120) days of the date of the pre-hearing conference. Protective orders, if any are to be imposed, should be described in this section.*

8.   The names of the witnesses will be exchanged between the parties no later than: *Live testimony in ADR proceedings should be limited to resolution of factual disputes and witness credibility issues. Parties should use stipulations, affidavits, proffers of testimony, written submission of expert opinions, and other time-saving evidentiary procedures. Parties may utilize the subpoena process under Fed. R. Civ. P. 45 to compel the presence of witnesses or the production of documents or other evidence at the arbitration hearing.*

9.   Each party will designate its expert witnesses no later than: *All such designations should be served on all counsel or pro se parties and the arbitrator(s). Counsel should bear in mind the court's recommendation that expert opinion should be submitted in writing unless the arbitrator(s) determine that live testimony is required to resolve conflicts in expert opinion through direct- and cross-examination.*

3

10.   The parties will exchange hearing exhibits no later than: *Must be served at least twenty (20) days prior to the scheduled arbitration hearing date.* Objections to such exhibits will be served no later than: *Must be served at least seven (7) days prior to the scheduled arbitration hearing date.* Pursuant to ADR Plan Section 5(e), objections based upon any issue of evidentiary foundation, authentication, or hearsay that are not served by this date will be deemed to be waived. All original exhibits and copies must be pre-marked before the arbitration hearing as required in DUCivR 83-5. At the arbitration hearing, the party must retain the original exhibit, and the arbitrator (or each panel member) and each opposing party shall be furnished a marked copy.

11.   The arbitration hearing has been scheduled for the _____ day of _____, 199__ at _____.m. in Room _____ of _____. *Must be within 120 days of the pre-hearing conference.* Each side will have _____ hours in which to present its evidence and make its argument, unless the time is enlarged by the arbitrator(s) with the agreement of all parties. *Absent unusual circumstances, the hearing should completed in one day.*

12.   This agreement and all proceedings thereunder shall be subject to the provisions of ADR Plan Section 5(o). No stipulation or admission made in this agreement or in the course of the arbitration proceeding will be admissible in any trial de novo in this case unless (i) the evidence is independently admissible pursuant to the Federal Rules of Evidence, or (ii) the parties otherwise stipulate.

4

13.   Until a judgment has been entered or an award or a demand for trial de novo has been filed, neither a party nor counsel may reveal any information about or related to the arbitration proceedings.

14.   Any party desiring to record the hearing by stenographic or electronic means must arrange to do so prior to the hearing at its expense. Any such record shall be subject to ADR Plan Section 5(o). Video recording shall not be permitted. *All other parties to the matter will have the option of ordering copies at reasonable expense. Copies of transcripts, if any are ordered, shall be provided to the panel members at the arranging party's expense.*

15.   This agreement may be signed in counterparts by the parties hereto with the same effect as though each had executed the same document.

DATED this _____ day of _____, 199__.

_____
Plaintiff

_____
Attorney for Plaintiff

_____
Defendant

_____
Attorney for Defendant

h:\adrforms\agreemnt.arb

5

APPENDIX 13L-4

Multi-Option ADR Form For San Mateo County, California[1]

<table>
<tr><td></td><td>Print Form</td><td>Save A Copy</td></tr>
</table>

Send to:
Multi-Option ADR Project - SMC127AM
400 County Center
Redwood City, CA 94063-1655

San Mateo County Superior Court, Multi-Option ADR Project, MAP

CONFIDENTIAL EVALUATION BY NEUTRAL

In accordance with **Local Rule 2.3(i)(5)**, please submit evaluation by mail or fax within 10 days of completion of the ADR process. Telephone: (650) 599-1070   Fax: (650) 599-1754

MAP staff and committees use this *confidential* information to assess the impact on the court, to track quality, and to inform our decisions regarding redesign of program procedures. Other staff and trial judges do not see specific evaluations. This information will be aggregated for blind statistical reports to the Judicial Council, the Court and the community.

Case Name: Case Number:

Name of Neutral: _____

1. Are you a member of the MAP panel?   ☐ Yes ☐ No

2. Did attorney/clients meet with MAP staff?   ☐ Yes ☐ No ☐ Unknown

3. Agreement reached?   ☐ Yes   ☐ No   ☐ Partial

4. Process used in case – indicate if more than one:
   - ☐ Mediation   ☐ Neutral Evaluation   ☐ Special Master/Discovery Referee
   - ☐ Arbitration   ☐ Private Settlement Conference   ☐ Other: _____

5. Type of case:
   - ☐ Business   ☐ Malpractice   ☐ Real Estate/Eminent Domain
   - ☐ Construction   ☐ Neighborhood   ☐ Restraining Order/Injunction
   - ☐ Employment   ☐ Personal Injury   ☐ Will Contest/Trust
   - ☐ Insurance   ☐ Public Agency   ☐ Other: _____

6. At what phase in the dispute did the ADR session occur?
   - ☐ Before filing   ☐ Within 4 months of filing
   - ☐ After some discovery   ☐ After significant discovery
   - ☐ Trial was imminent   ☐ Other: _____

7. Describe primary style used in this case:

   Facilitative   Directive
   1 ☐   2 ☐   3 ☐   4 ☐   5 ☐

8. Did you discuss the law? ☐ Yes ☐ No   Did disputants ask about the law? ☐ Yes ☐ No

9. Approximate total # of hours _____ Total # of sessions _____ Total # of follow-up calls ____

11. In this case, did the ADR process: ☐ Reduce costs   ☐ Increase costs
    - ☐ Under $5,000   ☐ $5—$10,000   ☐ $10—$25,000   ☐ $25—$50,000
    - ☐ $50—$100,000   ☐ $100—$250,000   ☐ $250—$500,000   ☐ Other_____

12. In this case, did the ADR process: ☐ Reduce court time ☐ Increase court time
    - ☐ 1-3 days   ☐ 3-5 days   ☐ 5-10 days   ☐ 10-20 days   ☐ 20+ days

13. Any court procedures averted? _____

14. Do you have any comments or suggestions regarding the administration of MAP? _____

---

[1] Superior Court of California, County of San Mateo, Appropriate Dispute Resolution Programs—Civil ADR, available at https://www.sanmateocourt.org/court_divisions/adr/civil/ (last accessed March 25, 2011).

APPENDIX 13L-5

Report of Neutral for Western District of Pennsylvania[1]

IN THE UNITED STATES DISTRICT COURT
FOR THE WESTERN DISTRICT OF PENNSYLVANIA

_____)	
_____)	
_____)	
Plaintiff(s))	
v.)	Civil Action No. _____
_____)	
_____)	
_____)	
Defendant(s))	

REPORT OF NEUTRAL

A _____ session was held in the above captioned matter _____

The case (please check one):
_____ has resolved
_____ has resolved in part (see below)
_____ has not resolved.

A follow up session, if applicable:
_____ is scheduled for date _____

_____ will be held with the neutral within _____ days

_____ parties agree that a follow up conference with the Court should be scheduled within

_____ days.

If the case has resolved in part, please indicate the part that has resolved and/or the claim(s)/parties that remain.

_____

_____

_____

Dated: _____   _____
                              Signature of Neutral

Rev.03/09

---

[1]United States District Court for the Western District of Pennsylvania, ADR Neutrals—Neutral Report, available at http://www.pawd.uscourts.gov/Applications/pawd_adr/Pages/ADRNeutral.cfm (last accessed March 25, 2011).

APPENDIX 13L-6

ADR Process and Procedure Election Form for Western District of Pennsylvania[1]

```
..................................... )
..................................... )
..................................... )
            Plaintiff(s),             )        Civil Action No. .............................
     v.                               )
..................................... )
..................................... )
..................................... )
            Defendant(s).             )
```

STIPULATION SELECTING ADR PROCESS

Counsel report that they have met and conferred regarding Alternative Dispute Resolution (ADR) and have reached the following stipulation pursuant to L.R. 16.2 and the Court's ADR Policies and Procedures.

I. PROCESS

Select one of the following processes:

_____ Mediation
_____ Early Neutral Evaluation (ENE)
_____ Court sponsored Binding‡ Arbitration
_____ Court sponsored Non-binding Arbitration
_____ Private ADR (please identify process and provider)

_____ Other (please identify process and provider)_____
_____

*If you are utilizing a private process, be advised that the case is still governed by the Court's ADR Policies and Procedures. It is the responsibility of counsel to ensure that all of the proper forms are timely submitted and filed, as required by Polices and Procedures.

II. COSTS

The parties have agreed to share the ADR costs as follows (do not complete percentages for court sponsored arbitration. For that process costs are paid by the court in accordance with 28 USC §658.):

_____ % by Plaintiff
_____ % by Defendant

If a dispute arises as to compensation and costs for the mediator/neutral evaluator/private arbitrator, the Court will set reasonable compensation and costs.

III. NEUTRAL

‡ For binding arbitration, please complete form "Stipulation to Binding Arbitration" located on the Court's website at www.pawd.uscourts.gov

---

[1]United States District Court for the Western District of Pennsylvania, ADR Program Information—Stipulation Selecting ADR Process, available at http://www.pawd.uscourts.gov/Applications/pawd_adr/Pages/ADRInfo.cfm (last accessed March 25, 2011).

The parties hereby designate by agreement the following individual to serve as a Neutral in the above-styled action:

Name of Neutral: _____

Address of Neutral: _____

Telephone & FAX Numbers: _____

Email address of Neutral: _____

The parties represent that they have contacted the selected prospective neutral and have determined that the neutral is available to conduct the ADR session within the time prescribed by the Court's Policies and Procedures and that the neutral does not have a conflict.

IV. PARTICIPANTS

Name of the individual(s) who will be attending the mediation or early neutral evaluation session in accordance with Sections 3.8A and 4.10A of the Court's ADR Policies and Procedures:

For Plaintiff(s):_____   _____

                                                   Name and title

For Defendant _____   _____

                                                   Name and title

For Defendant _____   _____

                                                   Name and title

For 3d party Deft _____   _____

                                                   Name and title

If there is insufficient space to list all parties who will be attending the session, please add additional sheets as necessary.

Each party certifies that the representative(s) attending the ADR session on its behalf has full and complete settlement authority.

V. ACKNOWLEDGMENT

We, the undersigned parties to this action, declare that this stipulation is both consensual and mutual.

Dated:_____   _____

                                          Attorney for Plaintiff

Dated:_____   _____

                                          Attorney for Defendant

     4/15/09

APPENDIX 13L-7

Western District of Pennsylvania Stipulation to Binding Arbitration[1]

	)	
	)	
Plaintiff(s)	)	
	)	
v.	)	Civil Action No.
	)	
	)	
Defendant(s)	)	

STIPULATION TO BINDING ARBITRATION

Pursuant to Section 5.12 of the Court's Alternative Dispute Resolution Policies and Procedures, the parties in the above captioned matter do hereby stipulate that the parties waive their rights to request a trial de novo.

We, the undersigned parties to this action, declare that this stipulation is both consensual and mutual.

Date: _____ Attorney for Plaintiff: _____

Date: _____ Attorney for Defendant: _____

200609

---

[1]United States District Court for the Western District of Pennsylvania, ADR Program Information—Stipulation to Binding Arbitration, available at http://www.pawd.uscourts.gov/Applications/pawd_adr/Pages/ADRInfo.cfm (last accessed March 25, 2011).

APPENDIX 13L-8

Superior Court of California, Los Angeles County, Arbitrator Award Form[1]

ARBITRATOR NAME, ADDRESS, TELEPHONE, FAX AND E-MAIL	STATE BAR NUMBER	Reserved for Clerk's File Stamp
		To keep other people from seeing what you entered on your form, please press the Clear This Form button at the end of this form when finished.

SUPERIOR COURT OF CALIFORNIA, COUNTY OF LOS ANGELES

COURTHOUSE ADDRESS
Click on the button to select the appropriate court address.

PLAINTIFF

DEFENDANT

AWARD OF ARBITRATOR

CASE NUMBER

INSTRUCTIONS TO ARBITRATOR *In order that this Award may be entered as Judgment, all information must be clear, complete and accurate. Please specify the full names of all parties (as they appear on the complaint) in the body of the Award: for whom and against whom the award is rendered; precise dollar amounts for all money awards; and a disposition as to each party named on the complaint and any cross-complaint(s).*

The undersigned Arbitrator, appointed pursuant to Section 1141.10, Code of Civil Procedure and Rule 3.815, California Rules of Court, having been duly sworn, and having heard the above cause on *(date)* _____, and considered the evidence, awards as follows:

IN FAVOR OF: (Show FULL names)	AND AGAINST: (Show FULL names)
1.	
2.	
3.	
4.	

MONEY AWARD FOR ABOVE PARTIES	PRINCIPAL	INTEREST	ATTORNEY FEES	COSTS	TOTAL
1.	$	$	$	$	$
2.	$	$	$	$	$
3.	$	$	$	$	$
4.	$	$	$	$	$

☐ Pages attached for additional parties: _____   Total volunteer hours (including travel time): _____

Dated:

_____   _____
(TYPE OR PRINT NAME)   (SIGNATURE OF ARBITRATOR)

IMPORTANT!
PURSUANT TO CALIFORNIA RULES OF COURT, RULE 3.826, THIS AWARD WILL BECOME A JUDGMENT THIRTY (30) DAYS AFTER ITS FILING IF NO PARTY HAS FILED A REQUEST FOR TRIAL (DE NOVO) WITH PROOF OF SERVICE.

SATISFACTION OF JUDGMENT MUST BE FILED WITH THE CLERK OF THE COURT WHEN PAID IN FULL.

☐ Trial de Novo filed by: JOHN A. CLARKE, Executive Officer/Clerk
    ☐ Plaintiff ☐ Defendant ☐ Other _____ on: _____

☐ 30 days having passed and no Request for Trial de Novo filed,
    AWARD ENTERED AS JUDGMENT ON: _____   By: _____
                                                                              Deputy Clerk

(See reverse for Proof of Service by Mail)

LAADR 014 10-03
LASC Approved
(Rev. 01-07)

AWARD OF ARBITRATOR

Code of Civil Procedure, §1141.23
Page 1 of 2

---

[1]Superior Court of California, Los Angeles County, ADR Forms—Award of Arbitrator, available at http://www.lasuperiorcourt.org/adr/UI/forms.aspx?source= (last accessed March 25, 2011).

Short Title	Case Number

PROOF OF SERVICE BY MAIL

1. I am over the age of 18 and not a party to this action. I am a resident of or employed in the county where the mailing occurred. My residence or business address is:

2. I served a true and correct copy of this Award of Arbitrator on all interested parties by enclosing it in an envelope and:
   a. ☐ **depositing** the sealed envelope with the United States Postal Service with the postage fully prepaid.
   b. ☐ **placing** the envelope for collection and mailing on the date and the place shown in items 4 and 5 following our ordinary business practices. I am readily familiar with this business's practices for collecting and processing correspondence for mailing. On the same day that correspondence is placed for collection and mailing, it is deposited in the ordinary course of business with the United States Postal Service in a sealed envelope with the postage fully prepaid.

3. The envelopes were addressed as follows:
   (If additional space is needed, attach a separate list.)

4. Date of mailing:

5. Place of mailing *(city and state)*:

6. I declare under penalty of perjury under the laws of the State of California that the foregoing, including any attachment, is true and correct.

Dated:

_____   _____
(TYPE OR PRINT NAME)   (SIGNATURE)

Print This Form	To protect your privacy, please press the Clear This Form button after you have printed this form.	Clear This Form

LAADR 014 10-03
LASC Approved
(Rev. 01-07)

AWARD OF ARBITRATOR

Code of Civil Procedure, §1141.23
Page 2 of 2

APPENDIX 13L-9

Stanislaus County, California, Stipulation and Order to ADR[1]

STAN-100

ATTORNEY FOR PLAINTIFF *(name, bar card, and address)*:	FOR COURT USE ONLY
TELEPHONE NO. FAX NO. *(Optional)* E-MAIL ADDRESS *(Optional)*	

SUPERIOR COURT OF CALIFORNIA, STANISLAUS COUNTY

MAILING ADDRESS   **1100 I. Street**
CITY AND ZIP CODE: **MODESTO, CA 95354**
BRANCH NAME: **MODESTO**

CASE NAME:	
STIPULATION AND ORDER TO ADR	CASE NUMBER:

The parties and their attorneys stipulate that the claims in this action shall be submitted to the following alternative dispute resolution process:

☐ Voluntary Mediation
☐ Private Mediation
☐ Judicial Arbitration

☐ Private Arbitration
☐ Neutral Evaluation
☐ Voluntary Mediation in lieu of Judicial Arbitration

This box is to be filled out for or Voluntary Mediation and Neutral Evaluation only.

In accordance with Stanislaus County Rule of Court 3.10(D)(4) and 3.11(C)(2) this form must be signed by the agreed upon mediator or neutral-evaluator. If both parties agree the court will select a mediator for the case.

☐ It is Stipulated that _____ (name of mediator/neutral evaluator) shall serve as the neutral for this case.

_____   _____
Signature of Neutral   Date

☐ It is Stipulated that the Court select a mediator for this case.

• For Voluntary Mediation this form must be completed and returned with $400 ($200 from the plaintiffs and $200 from the defendants).

► _____   ► _____
        (PLAINTIFF)   (DEFENDANT)

_____   _____
(SIGNATURE)   (DATE)   (SIGNATURE)   (DATE)

► _____   ► _____
    (PLAINTIFF'S ATTORNEY)   (DEFENDANT'S ATTORNEY)

_____   _____
(SIGNATURE)   (DATE)   (SIGNATURE)   (DATE)

July 1, 2006 (mandatory)   **STIPULATION AND ORDER TO ADR**

---

[1]Superior Court of California, Stanislaus County, Local Forms—Stipulation and Order to ADR, available at https://www.stanct.org/Content.aspx?page=local_forms (last accessed March 25, 2011).

APPENDIX 13L-10

Decision and Order of Arbitrator in Eastern District of New York[1]

UNITED STATES DISTRICT COURT
EASTERN DISTRICT OF NEW YORK
_____ARBITRATION PART_____   Case 1:10-cv-01957-JBW-VVP

DOROTHY GRIFFITH,

               Plaintiff,

   - Against -   DECISION and ORDER

MELALEUCA, INC.,

               Defendant.

In a compulsory arbitration case whereby the Plaintiff claims to have contracted salmonella after eating the Defendant's product, the arbitrator holds that he has the authority under Local Rule 83.10 to direct an expedited deposition of the Plaintiff's expert witness, limited to the issue of causal connection, although the text of the Rule neither prohibits, nor provides for pre-hearing depositions of non-party witnesses.

The within action was assigned to the undersigned by Order of Senior Judge Jack B. Weinstein on December 28, 2010. By agreement of the parties, the arbitration hearing is scheduled for March 11, 2011, at 10AM, at the United States District Court, Eastern District of New York, 225 Cadman Plaza East, Brooklyn, NY 11201.

On January 14, 2011, the attorney for the Defendant moved by email submissions, for an Order granting the Defendant an oral deposition of the Plaintiff's treating physician or other expert. On January 15, 2011, the attorney for the Plaintiff, by email submission, opposed the Defendant's application.

The parties have failed to submit copies of their pleadings, although an email request for same was made on December 21, 2010. Thus, the arbitrator is not fully apprised of the all of the claims and defenses raised in said pleadings. Nevertheless, from the various emails exchanged between the attorneys for the parties and the arbitrator it is gleaned that the action is for personal injuries due to the Plaintiff's alleged contraction of salmonella from the Defendant's product, when the Plaintiff ate a candy bar prior to the receipt of a Notice of Recall.

In order to be prepared for trial, the Defendant seeks a pre-hearing oral deposition of the Plaintiff's treating physician or whomever the Plaintiff intends to present at trial to testify regarding the question, "Did the Plaintiff contract salmonella from the defendant's product?" The Defendant does not seek to depose any other person involved in the case. The Defendant agrees to pay for the witness's reasonable hourly rate during the deposition, which the Defendant estimates would be a low cost, due to the limited inquiry. The Defendant correctly states that nothing in the compulsory arbitration rules as

---

[1]Griffith v. Melaleuca, Inc., Decision & Order of Arbitrator, Case. No. 1:10-cv-01957-JBW-VVP (E.D.NY. Arb. Part., Jan. 25, 2011).

contained in Local Rule 83.10 <u>prohibits</u> discovery depositions, as provided for in Rule 30 of the Federal Rules of Civil Procedure, which permits oral depositions of "any person".

The Plaintiff opposes the application, contending that the granting of such application would be contrary to the intended purpose of arbitration, that is, a forum meant to be a quicker and less expensive alternative to a trial before a judge or a magistrate. Further contending that such deposition is unnecessary, the Plaintiff offers that before the trial, the Plaintiff will supply the Defendant with a copy of the report and credentials of the expert, the sum and substance of the expert's opinions and the facts upon which the expert relies. The Plaintiff correctly states that nothing in the compulsory arbitration rules contained in Local Rule 83.10 <u>provides</u> for expert depositions prior to arbitration.

Neither party has submitted any reported court decisions or administrative rulings concerning Local Rule 83.10, addressing the issues and contentions of the parties. Nor has the arbitrator found any such decisions or rulings in his own research.

In the classic movie, "Fiddler on the Roof", there was a dispute between villagers Perchic and Mordcha, and each one presented his arguments on what the good book says. In deciding who was right, Tevya, the milkman, ruled:

> TEVYA: "He is right (turning to Perchic) ....and he is right" (turning to Mordcha).

> AVRAM: "He is right and he is right? They can't both be right".

> TEVYA: "You know, you are also right".
>   (Fiddler On The Roof Script – Script-O-Rama Movie Scripts, 1971)

In the within application, the argument of the Defendant is right. The compulsory arbitration rules contained in Local Rule 83.10 do not <u>prohibit</u> pre-hearing oral depositions of expert witnesses. The argument of the Plaintiff is right. The compulsory arbitration rules contained in Local Rule 83.10 do not <u>provide</u> for pre-hearing oral depositions. Accordingly, the arbitrator must determine the issue from sources other than the said arbitration rules. Thus, the arbitrator is also right.

COMPULSORY ARBITRATION UNDER LOCAL RULE 83.10

The objective of compulsory arbitration of civil cases mandated by Local Rule 83.10 of the United States District Court, Eastern District of New York, is to relieve court congestion and to provide litigants in cases concerning damages of up to $150, 000, exclusive of interest and costs, with a forum to resolve their disputes in a more timely, efficient and less costly manner than trials before judges and magistrates. (Local Rule 83.10 (d) (1)) The damages in all civil cases are presumed to be not in excess of $150,000 (Local Rule 83.10 (d) (3)), unless counsel for the Plaintiff or the Defendant

Page 2

timely files a certification that the damages in the complaint or counter-claim, respectively, exceed $150.000, exclusive of interest and costs (Local Rule 83.10 (d) (3) (A) and (B)). Counsel have 90 days from the date of the clerk's notice of arbitration to complete discovery (Local Rule 83.10 (e) (1)). A Single arbitrator hears the cases, unless a party requests a panel of three arbitrators, but cases concerning damages of $5,000 or less, are heard only by a single arbitrator (Local Rule 83.10 (e) (4)).

"Rule 45 of the Federal Rules of Civil Procedure shall apply to subpoenas for attendance of witnesses and the production of documentary evidence at an arbitration hearing under this Rule" (Emphasis supplied) (Local Rule 83.10 (f) (4)). Interestingly, the Guidelines for Arbitrators regarding the compulsory arbitration process omit the words, "at an arbitration hearing". There is no mention in the Local Rule 83.10 or in the Guidelines for Arbitrators of any specific rules of discovery, other than the aforementioned requirement that counsel for the parties have 90 days from the date of the clerk's notice of arbitration to complete discovery (Local Rule 83.10 (e) (1), Emphasis supplied). There is no indication of what specific type or types of "discovery" is referred to.

The Federal Rules of Evidence shall apply to such arbitration proceedings as guides to the admissibility of evidence (Local Rule 83.10 (f) (5)).

In summary, Local Rule 83.10 does refer to the Federal Rules of Evidence, and to the subpoena provisions of the Federal Rules of Civil Procedure, and to non-specified "discovery". The word "discovery", following the word "complete", was not written in a vacuum. It must have substantial meaning. The arbitrator is of the opinion that the "discovery" mentioned in Local Rule 83.10 (e) (1) could only mean the discovery rules contained in the Federal Rules of Civil Procedure. The court is urged to amend Local Rule 83.10 (e) (1) so as to add, "as provided in the Federal Rules of Civil Procedure" after the words "complete discovery".

FEDERAL ARBITRATION ACT (FAA)

A review of the court decisions regarding Section 7 of the Federal Arbitration Act (FAA) as to non-party depositions would be helpful in determining the Defendant's application to depose the Plaintiff's expert witness under the compulsory arbitration process.

Section 7 of the Federal Arbitration Act (9 U.S.C. Section 7) provides:

> "The arbitrators selected either as prescribed in this title (9 U.S.C. Section 1 et seq.) or otherwise, or a majority of them, may summon in writing any person to attend before them or any of them as a witness and in a proper case to bring with him or them any book, record, document or paper which may be deemed material as evidence in the case. .....if any person or persons so summoned to testify shall refuse or neglect said summons,.....the United States district court.....may compel the attendance of such

Page 3

person or persons <u>before said arbitrators</u> .....". (Emphasis supplied)

The words "attend before them" and "before said arbitrators" in FAA Section 7 are similar in nature to the words "at an arbitration hearing" in Local Rule 83.10 (f) (4). Do these word mean that an arbitrator under FAA Section 7 or under Local Rule 83.10 can compel a non-party witness to appear for a deposition only before the arbitrator or at an arbitration hearing, as opposed to compel the non-party witness to appear at a pre-hearing oral deposition in the absence of the arbitrator? This arbitrator could find no case on point as to the Local Rule 83.10 compulsory arbitration process. There are cases on point as to FAA Section 7.

The following are some of the cases, using a broad interpretation, that hold that an arbitrator under FAA Section 7 may compel a non-party witness to appear and give testimony at a pre-hearing oral deposition: <u>Stanton v. Paine Webber Jackson & Curtis, Inc.</u>, 685 F. Supp. 1241 (S.D. Fla 1988); <u>Amgen, Inc. v. Kidney Center of Delaware County, Ltd.</u>, 879 F. Supp. 878 (N.D. Ill 1995); <u>Liberty Securities Corp. v. Fetchco</u>, 114 F. Supp 2d 1319 (S.D. Fla 2000; <u>In re Arbitration Between Scandinavian Reinsurance Co., Ltd and Continental Casualty Co.</u>, No. 04-C-7020 (S.D. Ill Dec. 10, 2004).

The following are some of the cases, using a narrow or strict interpretation, that hold that an arbitrator may not compel a non-party witness to appear and testify at a pre-hearing oral deposition: <u>Integrity Insurance Co. v. American Continental Insurance Co.</u>, 885 F. Supp. 69 (S.D.N.Y. 1995); <u>In the Matter of the Arbitration Between Hawaiian Electric Industries, Inc. and Hei Power Corp</u>, 2004 WC 1542254 (S.D.N.Y. 2004); <u>SchlumbergerSerma, Inc. v. Xcel Energy, Inc.</u>, 2004 WL 67647 (D. Minn Jan. 9, 2004); <u>Odfjelll ASA v. Celanese AG</u>, 328 F. Supp.805 (S.D.N.Y 2004); <u>Life Receivables Trust v. Snydicate 102 at Lloyd's of London</u>, 549 F. 3d 210 (2nd Cir. 2008).

None of the above cases involve the pre-hearing oral deposition of a non-party expert witness whom a party intends to call to prove causal connection in a personal injury negligence or products liability suit.

PRIVATE ARBITRATION FORUMS

A review of arbitration rules of private arbitration forums, not court annexed, reveals the following sample rules for depositions:

"At the discretion of the arbitrator(s), upon good cause shown, and consistent with the expedited nature of arbitration, the arbitrator(s) may order depositions of ..... such persons who may possess information determined by the arbitrator(s) to be necessary to (sic) determination of the matter." American Arbitration Association (AAA), Rule L-4 (d)

Page 4

"Expert Depositions, if any, shall be limited as follows: Where written expert reports are produced to the other side in advance of the Hearing (Rule 17 (a)), expert depositions may be conducted by agreement of the Parties or by order of the Arbitrator for good cause shown." JAMS, Inc (JAMS), Rule 16.2 (e)

"NAM's Arbitrations do not entail comprehensive discovery. Unlimited discovery would be contrary to NAM's goal of efficient and economical resolutions. The parties shall have the right to take depositions and to request documents on an expedited and limited basis subject to the approval of the Hearing Officer." National Arbitration and Mediation (NAM), Rule 11

In summary, private arbitration forums, not court annexed, provide for limited expedited and economical depositions at the sound discretion of the arbitrator, upon good cause shown.

DISCUSSION

Arbitration, of whatever form, compulsory or by agreement or contract, and of whatever forum, court annexed or private, is designed to achieve expedited, efficient and cost effective resolution of civil disputes, and to relieve the courts of the overburdence of a multitude of cases in our modern litigious society. Discovery is generally discouraged, although permitted under certain limited circumstances.

Local Rule 83.10 of the United States District Court, Eastern District of New York, and similar rules of other United States District Courts, provide for compulsory arbitration of civil cases of a value of up to $150,000. The rule does not specifically prohibit or provide for pre-hearing depositions, although reference is made therein for the completion of unspecified "discovery".

Rule 30 of the Federal Rules of Civil Procedure provides a procedure for depositions of "any person", meaning parties and non-party witnesses. It does not prohibit such depositions in compulsory arbitration cases.

Section 7 of the Federal Arbitration Act authorizes arbitrators to compel "any person" to appear as a witness before them and to produce material documents "in a proper case", without any guidelines or standards as to what is a proper case. The use of the words "any person" includes parties and not-parties. It makes no differentiation as to a witness's appearance before the arbitrators at a pre-hearing conference or deposition, or at the fact determination hearing, itself. Several cases decisions fall on both sides of the argument as to whether an arbitrator may compel non-party witnesses to appear at a pre-hearing deposition, where the arbitrator is not present.

The rules of private arbitration forums, not court annexed, allow arbitrators to compel or authorize limited pre-hearing depositions of parties and non-parties, upon good cause

Page 5

shown.

The within case involves a Plaintiff who alleges that she contracted salmonella after ingesting the Defendant's product, a candy bar, before receiving a Notice of Recall. This type of claim requires the testimony of an expert in order for the Plaintiff to recover. The Plaintiff announced that she has such an expert, and has offered to deliver to the Defendant before trial the report and credentials of the expert, and the sum and substance of the expert's opinion and the facts upon which the expert relies.

The Defendant wishes to conduct a pre-hearing deposition of the expert on the limited issue of whether the Plaintiff contracted salmonella from the Defendant's product. This issue is the crux of the case. Without the connection of the injury to the product, the Plaintiff cannot recover. The Defendant seeks the deposition in order to prepare for the hearing. The Defendant does not seek to depose any other person. The Defendant offers to absorb the expenses of the deposition, including the reasonable compensation of the witness.

Such a pre-hearing deposition would shorten the hearing, but it could also lead to a settlement before the hearing, should the Defendant be of the opinion that the expert witness' testimony would make the required causal connection, or should the Plaintiff be of the opposite opinion.

The limitation of the scope of the pre-hearing deposition of the expert witness will make the arbitration process quicker, more efficient, and cost effective.

CONCLUSION

After analyzing the provisions of Local Rule 83.10, Rules 30 and 45 of the Federal Rules of Civil Procedure, Section 7 of the Federal Arbitration Act (and the cases interpreting it), and the rules of private arbitration forums, not court annexed, the arbitrator finds that there is good cause for the requested limited deposition. Accordingly, the application of the Defendant is granted.

Upon receipt of this Decision, the parties are directed to communicate with the expert witness to arrange for the expedited and limited deposition, whether by agreement of the parties and the expert, or by the timely service of a proper Notice of Deposition. The deposition shall take place not later than February 15, 2011. The arbitrator shall be notified of the date, time and place of the deposition, so that the arbitrator may be available for telephone rulings, should the need arise. The Defendant shall pay for the cost of the deposition, including the reasonable fee of the witness. Before the deposition, the Plaintiff shall supply the Defendant with copies of the report and credentials of the witness, including the sum and substance of the opinion of the expert and facts upon

Page 6

which the expert relies. The Defendant shall supply the Plaintiff with a copy of the deposition transcript not later than 10 days before the March 11, 2011 hearing. Within 5 days after the conclusion of the deposition, the parties shall hold a pre-hearing telephone conference with the arbitrator.

(s)

Dated: January 25, 2011   _____

APPENDIX 13L-11

Sample Alabama Order of Referral to Mediation[1]

IN THE CIRCUIT COURT FOR THE

———— JUDICIAL CIRCUIT OF ALABAMA

Plaintiff(s)

v.   Civil Action No. ————

Defendant(s)

ORDER OF REFERRAL TO MEDIATION

Plaintiff(s) and/or defendant(s) ————————, *(hereafter the "parties")* through their undersigned counsel, have *[has]* requested *[have agreed to the suggestion of the Court]* that the Court enter an order referring this civil action to mediation. The Court concludes this matter is appropriate for mediation pursuant to the Alabama Civil Court Mediation Rules. [This cause is before the Court upon motion for mediation filed by plaintiff(s)/ defendant(s) pursuant to Ala. Code § 6-6-20 (1975). Having considered said motion, the Court concludes that this matter is appropriate for mediation pursuant to the Alabama Civil Court Mediation Rules.

Accordingly, it is ORDERED as follows:

1. By agreement of the parties *[At the discretion of the Court]* *[The motion for mediation filed by plaintiffs/defendants is hereby GRANTED, and] (Name of Mediator)* of *(Address)* is appointed as Mediator in this matter.
2. The fees and expenses of the Mediator shall be paid [equally by the parties] [by plaintiff(s) [by defendant(s)], and in the manner required by the Mediator.

---

[1]Alabama Center for Dispute Resolution, Mediation Forms—Order of Referral to Mediation, available at http://www.alabamaadr.org/index.php?optio n=com__content&task=view&id=33&Itemid=48 (last accessed March 25, 2011).

3. The first mediation session shall commence with in *(Number)* days from the date of this order. The Mediator shall set the initial mediation session with due regard to the schedules and other commitments of the parties and counsel, and may continue or adjourn a mediation session in his or her discretion, so long as such continuance or adjournment is within the time constraints set out herein.

4. A representative of each party, which may be counsel, having full authority to settle the entire case for the party must attend the mediation conferences.

5. At least ten (10) days before the initial mediation session, the parties shall deliver to the Mediator all materials requested by the Mediator relating to the parties' respective claims and defenses.

6. The Mediator shall have the authority to control the procedures to be followed in mediation; may adjourn a mediation session and set times for reconvening; and may suspend or terminate the mediation whenever, in the opinion of the Mediator, the matter is not appropriate for further mediation.

7. The Mediator may meet and consult privately with any party with its counsel, or privately with counsel, at any time. (The mediator should not consult with any party without the presence of the party's counsel without the knowledge of counsel.) Counsel may consult privately with counsel's client at any time during mediation.

8. All discussions, representations, and statement made at the mediation conferences, or with the Mediator privately, shall be confidential and deemed privileged by both the Mediator and all parties as settlement negotiations and thus inadmissible in a court of law. Each party shall have the right to instruct the Mediator not to disclose to the other parties certain information or facts furnished by that party to the Mediator. The mediation proceedings shall not be recorded by a court reporter or by an electronic recording device, except as necessary to memorialize any settlement reached. The Mediator shall not be called as a witness, nor shall the Mediator's records be subpoenaed or used as evidence in any adversary proceeding or judicial forum.

9. The pre-trial schedule currently set in this case is rescheduled as follows: (_____).

10. The parties are encouraged to resolve as many issues as possible during mediation. Partial or complete settlements should be immediately reduced to writing in the presence of the Mediator and should be signed by all parties or their counsel.

11. The parties shall provide a joint status report concerning the progress of mediation on or before *(date)*. Within ten (10) days of the termination of mediation, either be settlement or otherwise, the Mediator shall file a final status report, with copies to all parties, stating that mediation is completed and whether settlement was reached.

12. All proceedings in this civil action with respect to the mediating parties which pertain to the dispute mediation are stayed during the pendency of the mediation process which process shall terminate upon the filing of the Mediator's final status report or upon the filing of any party's notice of termination as provided for by Rule 13 of the Alabama Civil Court Mediation Rules.

ORDERED this ———— day of ————————, 20—.

————————————————
Circuit Judge

APPENDIX 13L-12

Sample Alabama Report of Mediator[1]

IN THE CIRCUIT COURT FOR THE

——— JUDICIAL CIRCUIT OF ALABAMA

_____
Plaintiff(s)

v.   Civil Action No. ———
_____
_____
Defendant(s)

REPORT OF MEDIATOR

To: Judge ———, Circuit Court for the ——— Judicial Circuit.

1. The above civil action was mediated by the undersigned, commencing on the ——— day of ———, 20 —.
2. This civil action was settled by mediation with the request by the parties that the terms of the settlement not be disclosed. *[This civil action was settled by mediation on the following terms: (outline terms).]*
3. *(If applicable)* Attorneys for the parties will file with the Court within the next ten (10) days appropriate settlement documents for the Court's approval and appropriate order, with a request that the civil action be dismissed.

or, alternatively

2. The civil action was not resolved at this mediation session.

_____

[1]Alabama Center for Dispute Resolution, Mediation Forms—Report of Mediator, available at http://www.alabamaadr.org/index.php?option=com_content&task=view&id=33&Itemid=48 (last accessed March 25, 2011).

_____

(Name of Mediator)
(Address)
(Telephone Number)

CERTIFICATE OF SERVICE

I hereby certify that a true and correct copy of the foregoing Report of Mediation was served by U.S. Mail, First Class postage prepaid, upon the attorneys for the parties to the mediation proceeding, on this ____ day of _____, 20__.

_____

(Name of Mediator)

APPENDIX 13L-13

Sample Alabama Request for Referral to Mediation[1]

IN THE CIRCUIT COURT FOR THE

_____ JUDICIAL CIRCUIT OF ALABAMA

_____
Plaintiff(s)

v.   Civil Action No. _____
_____
Defendant(s)

REQUEST FOR REFERRAL TO MEDIATION BY PLAINTIFF(S) [OR DEFENDANTS(S)]

Pursuant to Rule 16(c)(7) of the Ala. R. Civil Proc., and Ala. Code § 6-6-20 (1975), plaintiff(s) and defendant(s) request the Court to enter an order referring this civil action to mediation pursuant to the Alabama Civil Court Mediation Rules.

1. This civil action is not presently set for trial [or this civil action is set for trial on *(date)*].
2. The dispute in this civil action is appropriate for the mediation process.

_____
Attorney for Plaintiff(s) or Defendant (s)

(Name of Attorney)
(Address)
(Telephone Number)

---

[1]Alabama Center for Dispute Resolution, Mediation Forms—Request for Referral to Mediation by Plaintiff(s) or Defendant(s), available at http://www.ala bamaadr.org/index.php?option=com__content&task=view&id=33&Itemid=48 (last accessed March 25, 2011).

[CERTIFICATE OF SERVICE]

Glossary[2]

Access: To read or get data from memory, or some mass storage device.

Active Data: Currently in-use data files that may be stored on any computing device, not just the hard disks of a network server. In a Windows-type environment, active also refers to the Window that is currently the subject of input from a computer user. If there are several Windows visible on a computer screen, often the active or in focus window will have a colored bar across the top of the window, whereas the other windows will have a gray bar across the top of the window. An active window is the one which can receive mouse action and keystrokes. See CEDR and TCP/IP.

Address: Identification by name, label, or number of a location in a computer memory or other storage device where data or program instructions are stored. Also an IP address, a 32-bit numeric identifier of a computer on a TCP/IP network, written as four numbers separated by periods. See TCP/IP and IPv6.

ADF Scanner: A scanner with an automatic document feeder (ADF) will allow a computer operator with an appropriate computer and scanning software to scan in multi-page documents at one time. For example, with a 25–page ADF scanner, one can place a 25–page brief on the feeder and the document will automatically be fed through the scanner and a digital image, or picture, of the document will be transferred to the computer. This method of importing paper documents into a computer is often referred to as the process of digitizing paper documents. One popular software used with ADF scanners is Adobe Acrobat. See Adobe Acrobat and Scanner.

Adobe Acrobat: Versatile and inexpensive software capable of creating, managing and searching a wide variety of digital documents. This software is well known for its ability to create and work with PDFs, or "portable document format" data. PDFs have become the standard for digital documents on the Internet and by many government agencies and court systems. One can use Adobe Acrobat (not to be confused with the ubiquitous

---

[2]Reprinted with permission from Jay E. Grenig and William C. Gleisner, III, eDiscovery & Digital Evidence (West). Sources for the Grenig and Gleisner glossary include Computer Technology in Civil Litigation, 71 Am. Jur. Trials 111 §§ 172 to 173; Thomson, The Paper Trail Has Gone Digital: Discovery in the Age of Electronic Information, J. Kan. B.A., Mar. 2002, at 16; Webopedia, at <u>www.webopedia.com</u>.

Acrobat Reader) to create PDFs on a Windows platform that then can be read on UNIX or Macintosh platforms with no difficulty.

Alphanumeric Character Set: Letters, numerals, punctuation, and other symbols used by a computer.

Analyst: A person skilled in the techniques of computer and business problem solving.

ANSI: American National Standards Institute. Many of the large computer companies belong to ANSI, which sets standards for a wide variety of computer operations.

Application: Software program used to accomplish a specific task such as word processing, database management, or spreadsheet planning. Distinguished from software that performs only tasks related to the computer itself and from computer games.

Architecture: The physical and logical arrangement of a computer.

ASCII: American Standard Code for Information Interchange, a basic standard code for exchanging information between computers. ASCII provides a standard format for representing characters to permit the sharing of data between programs. ASCII text is a rudimentary format for documents containing words or sentences. Unlike a Microsoft Word document, an ASCII document may contain little or no formatting or metadata, and can usually be opened by a very simple program such as Windows WordPad. See metadata.

ASP: "Application service provider." Generally a provider that rents software for use by an individual or company and making it available over the Internet. ASP software is often very sophisticated and designed for use over a VPN. For example, the Mi8 Corporation, offers large companies a hosted Exchange approach that transforms Exchange Server 2003 from software and hardware an organization must purchase and maintain into a pay-as-you-go service delivered over public and private networks, utilizing Internet and web technologies.

Assembly Language: A low-level, symbolic language used for programming a computer.

Automated Litigation Support System (ALSS): Any operation combining people, machines, and methods for processing information for use by attorneys or expert consultants in preparation for and trial of lawsuit.

Auxiliary Storage: Memory units outside of the computer's main internal memory, such as disk drives, and memory expansion cards.

Backup Data: Information copied to removable media to be used to reestablish the system in the event of a failure.

Backup File: Duplicate copy of another file created for data recovery in the event of a malfunction or loss of data.

Backup Tapes: The media one uses to backup or safeguard a computer system. The entire concept of backup tapes takes on a special significance in the case of digital discovery. When backup tapes exist to restore electronic files lost because of system failures or through disasters such as fires or tornadoes, their contents are duplicative of the contents of active computer systems at a specific point in time.

Bandwidth: Amount of information or data that can be sent over a network connection in a given period of time.

Banner: A posted notice informing users as they log on to a network that their use may be monitored, and that subsequent use of the system will constitute consent to the monitoring.

Batch: An accumulation of data or documents to be processed. In batch processing, one subjects a group of files to a single command simultaneously through an automated process. For example, there is a "batch conversion wizard" in Microsoft Word 2002 allowing a user to automate the conversion of a number of documents to or from Word format.

Batch Control: Designation of several consecutively numbered documents as a batch to be handled as a unit during document analysis.

Bates Stamp: A method of automatically numbering documents consecutively by affixing a unique number to each document. It is the best way to organize documents in a large litigation file because it is possible to affix a standard and unique identifier to each document in a file that is not dependent on the content of the document and that will allow all parties in a lawsuit and the court to have a uniform "language" to keep track of documents. Software allowing the use of Bates stamps on electronic documents can be purchased. Sophisticated litigation support software, such as Summation, can automatically affix Bates stamps to digital documents. Some less sophisticated programs can do likewise, if one is prepared to purchase an add on, or "plug-in" piece of software. For example, Adobe Acrobat sells a plug-in called IntelliPDF BATES that provides the user with the possibility of the automatic numbering of the document.

Baud: Unit of measurement, usually bits per second, relating to the rate of speed for the transmission of data between two computer devices. Baud indicates the number of bits per second transmitted. For example, 300 baud means that 300 bits are transmitted each second (abbreviated 300 bps).

Binary: A numbering system that has just two unique digits; a circuit that can assume one of two possible states.

Binary Code: System for representing information by a combination of numbers, such as the digits 1 and 0. Computers are based on a binary numbering system, which consists of just two unique numbers, 0 and 1.

Bit: "Binary digit." A single digit of a binary number—a one or a zero. The basic unit of computer memory and the smallest unit of information recognized by a computer. A single bit can hold only one of two values: 0 or 1. Eight consecutive bits form one "byte."

BMP: "Bitmap." One of the standard graphical formats used in Windows. Files in this format have a .bmp extension. See GIF, JPG, and PNG.

Boards: Printed circuit boards used to hold microchips.

Bookmarks: Network addresses stored as shortcuts marking a location on a network to which the computer can quickly return. Many digital programs also create "bookmarks," allowing a user to return quickly to a place within a digital document. For example, Word and Adobe Acrobat both have sophisticated book marking capabilities, as do web browsers.

Boolean Logic: Search method using terms and connectors. Anyone who has conducted a "terms and connector search" in Westlaw has used a type of Boolean logic. Many programs allow for Boolean searches. For example, litigation software such as Summation permits users to search the document database using a number of Boolean operators. At its most complex, Boolean searches involve a type of algebra. At its simplest, Boolean logic permits a user to search large amounts of word-searchable data using complex terms joined together by connecting terms such as "and," "or," "not," "but not," etc. to form a very precise search for documents in a database. Boolean searches also permit a user to search for documents containing specific words that are within so many words, sentences or paragraphs of one another (called "proximity searching" in Summation). See relational database, database, and SQL.

Boot: To start the computer or to interrupt an operation in a fashion causing the computer to respond as though it had been physically turned off and turned on again. "Booting the system" refers to bringing the operating system into the computer's memory in order to allow the user to begin using the computer.

Browsing: Review of the records in a retrieval set during interactive searching to determine whether to modify the search argument. Also, method of reviewing web pages.

Buffer: Temporary storage area used to accumulate a burst of data transmitted from one device to another at a rate faster than the receiving device can process it. A temporary storage area, usually in RAM. The purpose of most buffers is to act as a holding area, enabling the CPU to manipulate data before transferring it to a device.

Bug: Programming or hardware logic error.

Bundling: Software sold with a computer to add value to the computer, as in "that computer is being sold bundled with word processing and spreadsheet software."

Burn: Make a CD-ROM or DVD copy of data.

Bus: Set of wires carrying signals through a computer. All buses consist of two parts—an address bus and a data bus. The data bus transfers actual data whereas the address bus transfers information about where the data should go.

Byte: Unit of measurement denoting the amount of space needed to store data. A byte usually consists of eight bits. A computer's memory capacity is measured in bytes. A single bit can hold only one of two values: 0 or 1. Eight consecutive bits form one "byte." See bit.

Cable: Group of bundled electrical wires used to connect a computer and its peripherals.

Cache Files: Files recording Internet addresses visited by the user and graphic elements of the web pages visited. Cache files are created and stored automatically by the user's computer, identifying the path the user has traveled on the Internet. Also, a mechanism that allows for high speed storage of information. It can be either a reserved section of main memory or an independent high-speed storage device. The system cache is responsible for a great deal of the system performance improvement of today's PCs."

CAD: "Computer-Aided Drafting" or "Computer-Aided Design." Also referred to as "CAD-CAM"). It often consists of a hardware-software combination system used by architects and engineers to create three-dimensional models. A user can zoom in and out of a model, view all sides of a model and otherwise make the model perform just like the device it models. Very sophisticated CADs can even be displayed in layers of drawings approximating how a device will be constructed or deconstructed. Automobile manufacturers make extensive use of CAD drawings in designing automobiles.

Card: Printed circuit boards can be conveniently and easily slid into a computer's expansion slots to enhance or strengthen an existing. A basic computer might be turned into a high powered graphics machine with the proper video expansion board, or a SCSI card might be used to attach additional peripherals to a computer. Also called an "expansion board." See SCSI card.

Cataloging: Method of analyzing and processing documents for litigation support. See coding.

Cathode Ray Tube (CRT): A vacuum tube or picture tube used to convert an electronic signal into a visual image, used as a computer monitor, video monitor, or television Screen of a video display using; a monitor used to display information to a computer operator.

CD-ROM: "Compact Disk-Read Only Memory." removable data storage medium using compact disks. CDs today hold roughly 770 megabytes (abbreviated "MB") of data. One can purchase CDs that can be used with a CD-R, which is a device that allows for the writing of data to a CD by an ordinary user. One can also purchase CD-RWs, which refer to disks that are rewritable. Today, one can purchase DVDs which have the same characteristics as CDs.

Cell: Memory location. Also where a single piece of data is entered in a spreadsheet.

Central Processing Unit (CPU): Brain of a computer interpreting and executing instructions by performing the system's arithmetic, logic, and control operations. In a microcomputer, the CPU is usually located on a single chip that is the center of all activity inside the system unit. It carries out instructions and processes information stored in memory.

Character: Letter, number, punctuation mark, symbol, or space in document or document record, or coded representation of letter, number, punctuation mark, symbol, or space.

Character String: Unique group of consecutive letters, digits, symbols, or spaces in computer record.

Chip: Device containing thousands of transistors and other electronic components formed on surface of tiny square of silicon enabling computer system to process information. At its most basic, a chip is a small piece of semiconducting material (usually silicon) on which an integrated circuit is embedded.

CIDR: "Classless Inter-Domain Routing." Current Internet addresses are running out and this refers to the next generation of IP addressing. Also called supernetting. See IP addresses and IPv6.

Circuit: Electronic network through which current flows.

Circuit Board: Board on which electronic components are mounted.

Civil Discovery Standards: Discovery standards adopted by the American Bar Association. In August 2004, the ABA added electronic discovery to the ABA's Civil Discovery Standards. The Standards can be downloaded from www.abanet.org/litigat ion/discoverystandards/2004civildiscoverystandards.pdf. The Standards contain five standards relating to electronic discovery.

Clock: Device coordinating computer's operations; circuit providing synchronizing signals for the different elements of computer system. The CMOS clock keeps track of basic computer functions, such as the date and time in a Windows computer, when the computer is powered off.

Clip Art: Desktop publishing term referring to ready-made illustrations that can be inserted into computer document.

Clipping: Process of removing portions of graphic image beyond limits of display screen; also called cropping.

Clone: Computer that imitates another computer.

COBOL: "Common Business-Oriented Language." High-level computer language, or programming language, particularly suited for business data processing. See programming language.

Coder: Person who processes document text for litigation support; document analyst.

Coding: Instructions of program; process by which document is analyzed and information extracted from document formatted or standardized for retrieval. Also, the art of entering data into a database one field at a time, either by keying the data or by means of an automated system, for example by means of a dii file utilized by Summation coders in building a document database.

Concordance: Alphabetical index of terms. Also, sophisticated litigation support software made by Dataflight Software, Inc., located at www.dataflight.com/.

Confidential Document: Document protected from discovery in litigation because it contains trade secrets or proprietary information.

Command: An order given to a computer system by a user, such as "copy" or "print," setting in motion preprogrammed response or set of instructions.

Command Language: Specific computer instructions operator must use to conduct on-line retrieval.

Communications: Data transmission link between computers, or between computer and output device such as printer or plotter.

Compatible: Things that work together.

Compatibility: Ability of program or hardware component to operate on different computers.

Compiler: Method of converting high-level language program into a lower, more user friendly language, such as either machine code or assembly language. Programmers write programs in a form called source code. The source code consists of instructions in a particular language, like C or FORTRAN. Computers, however, can only execute instructions written in a low-level language called machine language. To get from source code to machine language, the programs must be transformed by a compiler. See machine language and programming language.

Computer: Device that receives, processes, and produces information.

Computer Record: Record corresponding to document record form and its contents.

Computer Word: Group of bits or bytes that can be stored in single computer memory location.

Configuration: Arrangement of working elements of computer system.

Connect Time: Time on-line information providers charge their customers, frequently computed from moment user logs onto system until customer logs off the system.

Console: Computer terminal containing keyboard, video display, and printer, from which programs can be entered, used, and output data received.

Control Character: Any command created by pressing key while simultaneously holding down the control (Ctrl) key.

Control Unit: Circuits in a CPU used to carry out instructions.

Controller: Hardware mechanism controlling transfer of data to and from peripheral storage devices.

Conversational: Retrieval software utilizing commands in English rather than programming language.

Cookie: File containing bits of information about the user and/or the use of the computer, such as the user ID, details the user may have filled out on a form, past purchases and other personal data. The files are placed on the hard drive by website operators. Information is sent back to the website every time the computer returns there, so the website can track the user's patterns and preferences. Basically, a message given to a user's web browser by a remote web server. The browser stores the message in a text file. The message is then sent back to the server each time the browser requests a page from the server.

Coordinate Data: Set of two (x, y) or three (x, y, z) measurements establishing location of point relative to reference point, called the origin.

Cursor: Small, flashing symbol used on video display to show operator's current position in a program or text file. Sometimes used to prompt user for input data during interactive program.

DAT: "Digital audio tape." Medium used as storage medium in some systems.

Data: Basic elements of information.

Database: Collection of data in computer organized for rapid search and retrieval. A database program stores and organizes information on variety of subjects in variety of ways and provides access to information in all of files quickly and easily. Information is most often displayed in a spreadsheet consisting of columns and rows. Traditional databases are organized by fields, records, and files. A field is a single piece of information, a record is one complete set of fields, and a file is a collection of records.

Database Maintenance: Housekeeping required to keep database in good operating order by adding or deleting records and updating existing records or fields.

Database Review: review of database to determine conformance of data to document analysis procedures and vocabulary control tools.

Data Entry: Process of entering information into a computer.

Data Management: Programs and procedures connected with the planning, organization, maintenance, and control of a database.

Debug: To track down an error in programming or hardware logic.

Decoding: Translation of coded data back into natural language.

De-duplication: The process whereby documents that appear in a user's mailbox on multiple days are not counted as multiple hits. For example, if the same email appeared in an inbox over a period of several months, only one copy of the document would be produced.

Default: Value or option that is assumed when none is specified. This may be program data (default data) or system information flow (default disk drive).

Deleted File: File with disk space designated as available for reuse; deleted file remains intact until it has been overwritten with a new file.

Deletion: Process by which data are removed from active files and other data storage structures on computers and rendered inaccessible except by means of special data recovery tools.

Desktop: A desktop personal computer that is not portable or easily transportable; what is visible on the monitor of a computer using a GUI when the computer is at rest. See GUI.

Device: Individual computer accessory performing useful function, such as display or printer.

Diagnostic Routine: Test program used to determine operating condition of computer system.

Digit: Symbol representing a number.

Digital: Any information expressed through a string of ones and zeros.

Digitizer: Electronic input device resembling tablet from which scaled coordinate data may be entered into computer. Frequently used by CAD programs.

Digital Cassette: High-quality audio cassette used for storing computer data.

Directory: Grouping of files into a single storage unit. Directories are typically either root directories or subdirectories.

Disk: Storage device for programs and data. See also CD-ROM, magnetic disk, and optical disk.

Diskette: Another term for floppy disk. A thin, low-volume magnetic medium enclosed in jacket which, unlike a hard disk, can be inserted and removed from the computer and transported between computers.

Disk Drive: A computer component that reads data from and writes data on a disk. A disk drive rotates the disk very fast and has one or more heads that read and write data. A disk drive may be internally installed in computer, or an auxiliary disk drive may be used as external peripheral device.

Disk Mirroring: (1) Redundancy. A type of backup system. Most large organizations have the need for optimal redundancy; their data must always be available to them, regardless of the emergency. Redundancy is accomplished by building servers with multiple disks to which data are written simultaneously and by interlocking or clustered servers so that if one fails another to which data have been written simultaneously will automatically go online. If only two disks are used, the process of simultaneously writing data to the two disks is called "mirroring." (2) Discovery preservation. The process of preserving the content of a computer's hard drive in anticipation of discovery during litigation. See redundancy, RAID, and disk striping.

Disk Striping: A technique for spreading data over multiple disk drives. Disk striping can speed up operations that retrieve data from disk storage. The computer system breaks a body of data into units and spreads these units across the available disks. Systems that implement disk striping generally allow the user to select the data unit size or stripe width. Disk striping is available in two types. Single user striping uses relatively large data units, and improves performance on a single-user workstation by allowing parallel transfers from different disks. Multi-user striping uses smaller data units and improves performance in a multi-user environment by allowing simultaneous (or overlapping) read operations on multiple disk drives. Because disk striping stores each data unit in only one place, it does not offer protection from disk failure. See disk mirroring, redundancy, and RAID.

Display: Video display.

Display Adapter: Computer component, usually contained on an expansion card, providing communication between computer and its display. It determines whether computer is capable of displaying graphics, and graphic resolution. See card.

Distributed Data: Information belonging to an organization residing in multiple locations, usually by means of a network, existing on portable media or remote devices such as home computers, laptop computers, floppy disks, CD-ROMs, personal digital assistances, wireless communication devices, zip drives, Internet repositories such as mail hosted by Internet service providers; data held by third parties such as application service providers or data warehouses.

Document: Collection of information, such as a contract, report, memorandum, or book. A source document is the original record from which computer-stored information is derived. A document may also be a file opened in a computer for the storage of information or for word processing. In the digital world, "document" often refers to all digital copies of drafts of a collection of data.

Document Analysis: Extraction of specified information from source documents and recording it on worksheets or marking it on the documents themselves for loading into a computer database.

Document Analyst: See coder.

Document Control: System of identifying, storing, and locating source documents.

Document Retrieval: Searching for and finding document in database by matching computer record with search argument.

Document Surrogate: Computer substitute for source document.

Documentation: User's guide or reference manual for software programs.

DOS: "Disk Operating System." Operating system for personal computers. An early operating system of the Microsoft Corporation. Early versions of Windows were built upon a DOS foundation.

DOS Prompt: Characters displayed by disk operating system when awaiting user input. Normally, DOS prompt is an "A" or "C" followed by a colon and a backslash. It may also include the pathname of the current subdirectory (for example, "C:/ [subdirectory name]").

Dot-Matrix Printer: Type of impact printer that uses block of pins to form characters in pattern of dots.

Downtime: Period of time a machine is inoperable.

Drive: Component of computer that spins disk or diskette and reads or writes information. Depending on computer configuration, each drive is specified by drive letter, such as "A," "B," or "C."

Driver: Not really a program but instead a small piece of software containing commands that mediate the translation of commands from a computer to an internal or external peripheral, like a printer or external storage device. Drivers are external to a program, allowing changes in hardware technology to minimally affect changes in application.

DXF: "Drawing Interchange File." DXF is a standard ASCII text file functionally describing contents of AutoCAD file and may be used to provide compatibility between drawing files of different CAD programs.

Edit: Rearrangement of data in a computer.

Electronic Data Processing (EDP): Using computer to process data.

Email: Electronic mail. Electronic messages exchanged among persons on an intranet or on the Internet. Also e-mail. Popular proprietary email management systems include Microsoft Exchange, Outlook, Outlook Express, Lotus Notes, and Eudora.

Embedded Data: Information contained in an electronic version of a document that is not usually apparent on screen or in the printed hard copy, including the date the document was created, the identity of the author, the identity of subsequent editors, the distribution route for the document, and even the history of editorial changes (for example, pieces of the drafts leading up to the latest version of the document may be invisibly and automatically saved by the computer and hidden in the files). This information is also called metadata, which see.

Encryption: Procedure rendering contents of a message or file unintelligible to anyone that does not have the key for decryption. Encryption is an effective way to achieve data security. One must have access to a secret key or password to read encrypted data. Unencrypted data is called plain text; encrypted data is referred to as cipher text.

Enhancement: Converting data in text of document into more accurately retrievable form; that is, substituting specific for general term.

Enterprise: A business organization. In the computer industry, any large organization utilizing computers. An intranet is an example of an enterprise computing system."

Entity: Most basic drawing elements, such as a circle, arc, or line.

Error: Value difference between actual and intended responses.

Ethernet: Common method of networking PCs to create a local area network, or LAN.

Execute: To run program or to enter command instructing the computer to perform a program or set of commands.

Extranet: An intranet partially accessible to authorized outsiders. Typically used in cases of joint venture and vendor-client relationships. An intranet resides behind a firewall and is accessible only to people who are members of the same organization.

Family: A phenomenon whereby a document related to a document containing a hit is counted as two separate hits even if the related document does not contain a search term. For example, an email containing a search term with an attachment that does not contain a search term is counted as two hits even if the attachment did not contain a hit.

Fault Tolerance: A type of redundancy or backup system. See disk mirroring, disk striping, redundancy, and RAID.

Fetch: Act of bringing a program portion or data record into main memory.

Field: Individual data values within file; location in computer storage of specific information, such as names, addresses, telephone numbers, or anything user desires.

File: Unit or collection of a finite amount of related data stored in computer memory, either on floppy disk or a hard disk. File can be in the form of text, data, or programs; usually identified by a unique file name. Units within subdirectories are also called files; collection of documents.

File Extension: A tag of three or four letters, preceded by a period (dot), identifying a data file's format or the application used to create the file.

File Maintenance: Generating, correcting, adding, or deleting records in a file.

File Server: When several computers are networked together, as in a local area network (LAN), one computer may be used as a storage location for files of the group. They may be used to store email, financial data, word processing information, or backup files. Servers on a large distributed network often are assigned names that correspond to their job tasks: a file server manages files, a print server manages printers, a network server manages network traffic, etc.

File Sharing: Sharing of files stored on a server by users of any network.

Firewall: Software and hardware devices used to protect resources of a private network from persons not on network.

Flag: Data bit used to indicate the state of a device or the result of an operation.

Floppy Disk: Flexible piece of plastic coated with magnetic material and used to store programs and data.

Fonts: Character typefaces on video display, plotter, or printer.

Forensic Copy: An exact bit-by-bit copy of the entire physical hard drive of a computer system, including slack and unallocated space. See disk mirroring.

Format: Preparing a storage medium for the reading or writing of data. Also, specific style and form of data stored in computer, particularly for word processing; Also, particular arrangement of data on device such as diskette; and also DOS command initializing new diskette and preparing diskette for storage of information.

Formatting: Preprogrammed or on-line arrangement of data fields in retrieval set so as to position data in visually helpful manner.

FTP: "File Transfer Protocol." Older method of Internet protocol enabling person to transfer files between computers on the Internet.

Full Text: Complete document rather than representation of contents of the document unit (a document surrogate).

Genlock: "Generator locking device." A device enabling a composite video machine, such as a TV, to accept two signals simultaneously. A genlock locks one set of signals while it processes the second set. A gunlock one to combine graphics from a computer with video signals from a second source such as a video camera.

GIF: "Graphic Interchange Format." Files in this format end in the extension .gif. A compression format for pictures. One of the common image formats used on the web, it only supports 256 colors. See BMP, JPG, and PNG.

Graphical User Interface (GUI): Graphical manner in which computer programs present themselves to a user in an environment where computer commands and computer operations are displayed as visual displays instead of as command lines and mathematical equations, and which relies on hand-operated devices, such as a mouse, that points to objects or words on screen and executes computer command when an operator depresses button. It is a modern innovation, characteristic for many years of Microsoft Windows and Apple Macintosh systems.

Graphics: Computer-generated data expressed as pictures.

GUI: See Graphical User Interface.

Hardcopy: Computer output data or information reproduced by a printer or plotter.

Hard Disk: Rigid disk made from aluminum or plastic and coated with magnetic medium used to store programs and data; also known as "fixed disk." See disk.

Hard Drive: Primary storage unit on personal computers, consisting of one or more magnetic media platters on which digital data can be written and erased magnetically.

Hardware: Computer equipment; computer system's electrical and mechanical components used to run programs or software

Head: Part of disk or tape drive that reads and writes information on magnetic surface.

Header: Preliminary record identifying file.

Hit: Finding a digital document containing a search term. Counting the number of hits in a search can be somewhat misleading. For example, an email containing a search term that exists in a user's outbox and also exists in another user's inbox counts as two hits, although it is really one document. A document containing a search term that is sent from one user to another and returned under the "reply" option may count as two hits. The process of de-duplication attempts to prevent an email from being counted multiple times.

Housekeeping: Steps keeping system functional.

HTML: "Hypertext Markup Language." Tag-based ASCII language used to create pages on the web. HTML is both a language that maps the structure and layout of a web document by using tags and attributes, and also the method by which links (called hyperlinks) are created containing an embedded web address, so that one need only click on a hyperlink to be taken from the viewed web page to an entirely different web page.

Image: There are many formats that support pictures, "images," on the web and in computers, such as BMP, GIF, JPG, and PNG.

Impact Printer: Printer that uses hammer-like device to form characters in same manner as a conventional typewriter.

Icon: Symbol on display screen used to identify computer file, program, or procedure.

Image: To make an identical copy of a drive, including empty sectors.

Index: Use of same field or fields from collection of records to reference locations of entire record.

Information: Collection of data.

Information Retrieval: Technology and methodology of storing and searching from large amounts of information.

Input: Data entered into computer's processing area.

Instruction: Coded program step telling computer to perform an operation; set of instructions forms a program.

Integrated Circuit: Complex of electronic components and their connections formed on tiny piece of semiconductor material, usually silicon.

Integrated Software: Package of two or more applications programs sharing central database.

Interactive: On-line programming in which computer terminal displays results of executing operator commands so that operator can modify instructions to computer.

Interactive File: Computer file, similar to a library card catalog, containing indices to records in linear file.

Interface: Place where two systems meet and interact.

Internet: The worldwide network of networks using the TCP/IP protocol to facilitate information exchange.

Interoperability: Capability of software and hardware on different computers from different vendors to share data.

Interpreter: Program that translates high-level language into machine language and performs program steps as soon as each operation is translated.

Interrupt: Signals that stop ordinary program flow and demand attention.

Intranet: A network not connected to other networks.

IP Address: A 32 bit numeric identifier of a computer on a TCP/IP network, isolated networks and the Internet, which is written as four numbers separated by periods. See IPv6.

IP Spoofing: A technique used to gain unauthorized access to computers. An intruder sends messages to a computer with an

IP address indicating the message is coming from a trusted host. Firewalls can protect against IP spoofing.

IPv6: Internet addresses are running out. This is the next generation of IP addressing, and will allow for the continued growth of the Internet. See IP address.

IS: "Information Systems." People responsible for networks and computers in an enterprise. See Enterprise and IT.

ISP: "Internet Service Provider." In civil discovery, counsel may wish to learn the identity of relevant ISPs early in litigation and send them letters requesting that they preserve relevant records relating to target defendants for a specified period of time until a subpoena can be issued for production of those records.

IT: "Information technology." People responsible for networks and computers in an enterprise. See Enterprise and IS.

JPG: A common image format used on the web, which supports 16 million colors. Files in this format have a .jpg extension. See BMP, GIF, and PNG.

Job: Individual computer program or task.

Jump: Transfer in memory; break in program sequence, moving execution to another place in program.

K: Abbreviation for kilo, meaning 1,000.

Key: Field or fields used in record identifying it.

Keyboard: Typewriter-like keyboard on computer or terminal used to enter information.

Key Entry: Typing of data on keyboard that coverts keystrokes to machine-readable code; keyboarding.

Key Verification: System of proofreading consisting of double keyboarding same data and then reading both products electronically to identify any keystrokes that differ.

Keyword: Word chosen from document text to represent portion of its intellectual content.

Keyword Search: Search for documents using one or more keywords specified by user.

Kilobyte (KB): 1,000 bytes of information or storage space.

Label: Symbol used to describe file, record, item, message, or location in memory.

LAN: "Local area network." A network of computers located within a small area. LANs usually connect workstations and personal computers. Each individual computer) in a LAN has its own CPU with which it executes programs, but it also is able to access data and devices anywhere on the LAN. See WAN.

Language: Method people use to communicate with computers.

Laser Printer: High-resolution printer that produces typeset text and graphics.

Legacy Applications: Older applications, the data of which can no longer be read using current software or hardware.

Library: Collection of related data files.

Line Feed: Terminal or printer control code used to advance printed output by one line.

Linear File: Computer file containing all document records in sequence in which they were loaded.

LINUX: Operating system popular for many minicomputer applications. See UNIX.

Liquid Crystal Display (LCD): Digital display of characters formed by liquid crystal material between pieces of glass, often used on laptops.

Listing: Hardcopy reproduction of program statements and data.

Load: To transfer data or application programs into computer's random access memory.

Loading: Electronic transmission of data to or from computer memory. Downloading is transfer of data from one computer to memory of another computer.

Location: Memory storage position.

Machine Code: Binary instructions to the processor for given program and that can be understood by computer without translation.

Machine Language: Computer's native language, consisting of binary ones and zeros. Machine language is the only language understood by computers.

Macro: Series of keystrokes, usually forming frequently used commands or expressions, executed automatically by computer usually at the press of two-key combination.

Magnetic Disk: Type of storage medium. Data are encoded by microscopic, magnetized needles on the disk's surface. Magnetic disks can be reused many times. See also optical disk.

Magnetic Tape: Type of storage medium representing data by means of tiny magnetized spots on very thin layer of ferrous material. See backup tapes.

Main Memory: Computer's internal, central memory storage area.

Mainframe: Very large and expensive computer capable of supporting hundreds, or even thousands, of users simultaneously.

Mass Memory: Large memory storage area, usually external.

Master File: Main reference file containing permanent data.

Medium: Material holding computer-readable data, such as magnetic disks or tapes or CD-ROMs.

Megabyte (MB): 1,048,576 bytes of information or storage space, usually expressed as M or MB.

Memory: Internal storage section of a computer where data are stored and from which date can be retrieved. Data on disks or tapes are in external storage; portion of computer containing sequence of machine instructions to be executed.

Menu: List of available options, such as commands, functions, or programs, displayed on monitor screen from which user can select.

Merge: Combining two or more sequenced files into a single-sequenced file.

Metadata: Data about data. Hidden data that can only be seen when a digital document is viewed in its native format using the program that originally produced the document. Often even the user of a program may not know it is there unless he or she knows how to find it. When a document is created by a particular program (such as MS Word) there is hidden information (metadata) about that document that can only be viewed if the data is opened by that program. Examples include the modification history of a document or the date and time when the document was first created. Metadata can be a small problem, or a very serious problem, depending on the type of document and metadata involved. For example, email created in Lotus Notes, MS Outlook or Outlook Express, may contain metadata that can only be viewed within those programs. This metadata may include references to blind copies of mail, date stamps, routing information, and the like. See embedded data.

MHz: Megahertz, or 1,000,000 hertz. One MHz represents one million cycles per second. Unit of frequency equal to one cycle per second. Commonly referred to as "clock speed" of computer, representing number of bits that can be processed by computer in one second.

Microcomputer: Computer system integrated on a single chip or a computer system composed of single chips.

Microprocessor: CPU contained on a single silicon chip.

Microsecond: Millionth of a second.

Migrated data: Information that has been moved from one database or format to another, usually as a result of a change from one hardware of software technology to another.

Minicomputer: Midsize computer more powerful than a microcomputer but not as powerful as a mainframe.

MIPS: "Million instructions per second."

Mirroring: Simultaneous duplication of data among several computers for purposes of backup or to distribute network traffic. See, especially, disk mirroring.

MIS: Manager of information systems.

Modem: Modulate and Demodulate. Telecommunications device attached to computer allowing it to communicate with other computers over ordinary telephone lines.

Monitor: Output device visually displaying computer data.

Mouse: Electronic input device used for selecting menu options and entering data into computer; small hand-held device that, when rolled across surface, controls the movement of cursor on video display screen.

MS-DOS: "Microsoft-Disk Operating System."

Multiprocessor: Computer having two or more central processing units under integrated control.

Network: Group of computers connected together; the system used to connect computers. See LAN and WAN.

NIC Card: An expansion card used to connect computers to a network.

Node: Any device connected to a network, such as PCs, servers, and printers.

Object Code: Machine-readable binary instructions produced by compiler or assembler.

OCR: "Optical character recognition." Technology that takes data from a paper document and turns it into editable and searchable text data.

Offline: Related to a computer but not having direct operator control; noted connected to a network.

Online: In direct communication with central processing unit; having direct connection to computer via communications such as telephone line.

Operating System: Program controlling or supervising computer's use of programs as well as how information is sent to screen, printer, disk drives, and other devices; basic system software that runs computer and enables it to perform fundamental tasks such as loading programs, copying files, keeping track of files, and using various storage devices such as disk drives.

Optical Disk: Storage device for programs and data. An optical disk records data by burning microscopic holes in the surface of the disk with a laser. To read the disk, another laser beam shines on the disk and detects the holes by changes in the reflection pattern. A CD-ROM is an example of an optical disk. See CD-ROM and magnetic disk.

OS/2: Operating system for IBM PS/2 computer systems.

Output: Information generated by computer to outside source; processed information leaving computer and going to screen or printer.

Overflow: Error condition occurring when amount of data is too large for system's memory.

Parallel: Processing of several bits of data or instructions at one time.

Parity: The quality of being either odd or even. All numbers used in data communications have a parity to assure the validity of data. This is called parity checking. Parity is frequently used to ensure the validity of data that is the subject of some type of RAID arrangement of redundant disks. See disk mirroring, disk striping, fault tolerance, RAID, and redundancy.

Password: String of characters used as security device to inhibit unauthorized access to a computer or computer database.

PC: "Personal computer."

PDA: "Personal digital assistant."

PDF: "Portable document format." Technology for formatting documents so they can be viewed and printed using Adobe Acrobat Reader. See Adobe Acrobat.

Plain Text: Least formatted and most portable form of text for computerized documents.

Peripheral: Physically separate piece of hardware, such as printer, plotter, or modem, attached to computer to add more capability to system.

Phishing: The act of sending an email to a user falsely claiming to be a legitimate business in an effort to scam the user into surrendering private information.

Pixel: Picture element; smallest addressable area on computer's screen; used to define display resolution.

Plotter: Output device that draws graphs and other line images and produces graphics with better resolution than dot-matrix printer.

Plug-in: Many software programs allow users to purchase a piece of software, called a plug-in, that will enhance or expand the power of a software program.

PNG: Another image format supported on the web, known for its transparency capacity. See BMP, GIF, and JPG.

Port: Connecting point between computer and various input and output peripherals; provides outlet into which is plugged device, such as printer, plotter, or mouse; sometimes referred to as "communication port."

Printer: Output device allowing computer to create printed documents such as letters, briefs, and reports.

Printout: Form of output from computer printed on paper; also referred to as hardcopy.

Procedure: Step-by-step method of solving a problem.

Processing: Manipulation of information according to program's instructions.

Program: Set of instructions carried out by computer in sequence to perform given tasks or solve specific problems; software applications.

Programming: Task of developing program.

Programming Language: Words, codes, or symbols used in specific syntax to describe program to computer. A programming language such as C, FORTRAN, or Pascal enables a programmer to write programs that are independent of a particular type of computer.

Prompt: Message presented by computer telling user system is ready for further commands; question computer asks when it requires further information.

Query: Question addressed to a computer database.

RAID: "Redundant Array of Independent (or Inexpensive) Disks." A category of disk drives employing two or more drives in combination for fault tolerance and performance. RAID disk drives are used frequently on servers but are not generally necessary for personal computers. There are a number of different RAID levels: **Level 0** (Striped Disk Array without Fault Tolerance) provides data striping (spreading out blocks of each file across multiple disk drives) but no redundancy. While this improves performance, it does not deliver fault tolerance. If one drive fails, then all data in the array is lost. **Level 1** (Mirroring and Duplexing) provides disk mirroring. It provides twice the read transaction rate of single disks and the same write transaction rate as single disks. **Level 2** (Error-Correcting Coding) is not a typical implementation, and it is rarely used. Level 2 stripes data at the bit level rather than the block level. **Level 3** (Bit-Interleaved Parity: Provides byte-level striping with a dedicated parity disk. This level cannot service simultaneous multiple requests. It is rarely used. **Level 4** (Dedicated Parity Drive) is a commonly used implementation of RAID, This level provides block-level striping (like Level 0) with a parity disk. If a data disk fails, the parity data is used to create a replacement disk. **Level 5** (Block Interleaved Distributed Parity) provides data striping at the byte level and also stripe error correction information. Level 5 provides excellent performance and good fault tolerance. It is one of the most popular implementations of RAID. **Level 6** (Independent Data Disks with Double Parity) provides block-level striping with parity data distributed across all disks. **Level 7** is a trademark of Storage Computer Corporation. It adds caching to Levels 3 or 4. **Level 0+1** (A Mirror of Stripes) is not one of the original RAID levels. Two RAID 0 stripes are created, and a RAID 1 mirror is created over them. This level is used for both replicating and sharing data among disks. **Level 10** (A Stripe of Mirrors) is not one of the original RAID levels. Multiple RAID 1 mirrors are created, and a RAID 0 stripe is created over these. RAID S is EMC Corporation's proprietary striped parity RAID system used in its Symmetrix storage systems. See disk striping, disk mirroring, fault tolerance parity and redundancy.

RAM: Random access memory. Portion of computer memory where information can be read from or written to; temporary storage location for program while it is in use. It is erased when system's power is shut off. RAM storage is expressed in kilobytes and represents amount of open memory computer has available to run programs.

RAM Disk: Feature found in some multifunction boards and disk operating systems using random access memory as extra disk drive. RAM disk usually saves time by allowing high-speed access of frequently used files normally stored on the disk drive. Sometimes referred to as a "virtual disk."

Read: Process of taking information from a memory device.

Read Only Memory (ROM): Portion of the computer memory allowing information to be read from, but not written to or modified; area of computer memory used to permanently store data necessary for computer to operate. ROM can be read but not changed.

Real Time: Graphic presentation or simulation in which moving image is displayed at its actual speed, according to display scale.

Record: Group of data items or fields.

Redundancy: The quest for security on a computer network by providing one or more copies of data as a backup. See disk mirroring.

Relational Databases: Method of storing data in the form of related tables. Relational databases are powerful because they require few assumptions about how data is related or how it will be extracted from the database. The same database can be viewed in many different ways.

Replicant Data: Files automatically created as part of redundant system designed to eliminate system failures or downtime.

Resident: Program that "resides" in computer's internal memory.

Residual Data: Information including the entirety or remnants of deleted files to which the file reference has been removed from the directory listings, making the information invisible to most application programs.

Response Time: In interactive searching, elapsed time between generation of message at computer terminal and receipt of reply from computer.

Retrieve: To search and find specific information from file or database; steps taken in searching database in batch or on-line mode and evaluating the search product.

RGB: "Red-Green-Blue," the primary colors used by electronic video equipment, including computer displays.

Routers: A device that forwards data packets along networks. A router is connected to at least two networks. Routers are located at gateways, the places where two or more networks connect. They use headers and forwarding tables to determine the best path for forwarding the packets, and protocols to communicate with each other and configure the best route between any two hosts.

Routine: Sequence of machine language instructions.

Run: Command to execute a program.

Scale: Ratio of object's actual size to its drawn size.

Scanner: A peripheral device, most often attached to a computer by means of a SCSI or USB cable, enabling a user of a computer with appropriate software to import paper documents into a computer, often referred to as the process of "digitizing" paper documents. See ADF scanner.

Scroll: Moving information up and down the length of a video display.

SCSI Cards: SCSI interfaces provide for faster data transmission rates (up to 80 megabytes per second) than standard serial and parallel ports. In addition, you can attach many devices to a single SCSI port, so that SCSI is really an I/O bus rather than simply an interface. See www.scsi4me.com/.

Sector: Section of disk's recording track.

Sedona Principles: Best Practices, Recommendations, and Principles for Addressing Electronic Document Production. Principles regarding digital discovery promulgated by The Sedona Conference regarding digital discovery, located on Westlaw at 5 Sedona Conf. J. 151 (2004). See Appendix A. The Sedona Principles are the product of the Sedona Conference Working Group on Best Practices for Electronic Document

Retention and Production. The Sedona Conference is an organization that allows leading jurists, lawyers, experts, academics and others, at the cutting edge of issues in the areas of antitrust law, complex litigation, and intellectual property rights, to come together—in conferences and mini-think tanks (Working Groups)—and engage in true dialogue, not debate, all in an effort to move the law forward in a reasoned and just way.

Semiconductor: Principle behind computer chips allowing thousands of microscopic switches to be placed on a single sliver of silicon.

Serial: Processing of single bits of data or instructions sequentially.

Server: Any computer on a network containing data or applications shared by network users on the users' PCs.

Silicon: Semiconductor element from which computer chips are made.

Software: Program that runs a computer; collection of machine instructions directing computer to perform predetermined series of computations or commands. Software usually consists of a series of instructions electromagnetically coded as a program that directs the system to perform a task.

Sorting: Process of arranging data into desired order.

Source Code: Computer program written and recorded in high-level computer language ready for processing by compiler or assembler. See compiler.

SPAM: Electronic junk mail or junk newsgroup postings.

Specifications: List of measurements or requirements.

Spline: Mathematical model for drawing smooth, but irregular, curved lines used by CAD programs.

Spreadsheet: Representation of data as series of columns and rows related by functions and operations. When either the values or the operations are changed, the resulting values in other cells can be recalculated. A spreadsheet application program can solve a variety of mathematical problems and can provide forecasts based on resulting data. An electronic spreadsheet allows a business to experiment with a large number of figures which can be recalculated with lightning speed when new data is entered. A presentation graphic package can take the spreadsheet data and transform it into an assortment of bar charts, pie graphics, graphs, and other presentations. Spreadsheet programs are particularly suitable for accounting, financial analysis, and modeling.

SQL: "Structured query language." (Pronounced either see-kwell or as separate letters.) A standardized query language for requesting information from a database. IBM designed the original version called SEQUEL in the mid-1970s. SQL was introduced as a commercial database system in 1979 by Oracle Corporation.

Stand-Alone Computer: Personal computer not connected to any other computer or network, except possibly through a modem.

Storage: Device in which data can be held and from which data can be retrieved at later time; memory.

Subdirectory: Group of related files (a directory) within a directory.

Surrogate: Substitute for document; computer record of contents of document.

Surrogation: Creation of document surrogate, such as bibliographic cataloging and subject indexing or abstracting.

System: Computer, its peripheral devices, and software.

System Administrator: Person in charge of keeping a network working; also sysadmin and sysop.

Systems Programs: Set of general purpose programs, including compilers, assemblers and executive programs needed to operate applications programs on computer system.

TCP/IP: "Transmission Control Protocol." (Pronounced as separate letters.) TCP is one of the main protocols in today's networks, including the Internet. The IP protocol deals only with packets, while TCP enables two hosts to establish a connection and exchange streams of data. TCP assures delivery of data and also assures that packets will be delivered in the same order in which they were sent. See active data.

Tape: Storage system, using magnetic tape storing information sequentially. See backup tapes.

Tape Drive: Electromechanical device that stores information to and recalls information from tape.

Taxonomy: Comprehensive classification of broad subject into major categories and narrow subcategories.

Telecommunication: Exchange of information at distance using telephone line, radio, or cable media.

Teleprocessing: Access to computer from remote location, usually by terminal connected to Internet.

Terminal: Device permitting people and computers to communicate, usually through some telecommunications medium; workstations.

Text Editor: Software enabling users to manipulate alphanumeric information.

Text Processing: Treatment of document text to improve its retrievability.

TIFF: "Tagged image file format." Widely supported file format for storing bit-mapped images. TIFF files end with .tif extension. See BMP, JPG, PNG, PDF, and Adobe Acrobat.

Time-sharing: Program or software allowing number of users to execute programs simultaneously.

Track Ball: Stationary mouse controlling cursor movement by thumb- or finger-operated roller ball that is partially exposed on top surface of unit.

Tractor Feed: Device guiding continuous-form paper through a printer.

Transistor: Electrical switch used in computer logic.

Unit Record: Card image containing one complete record or transaction.

UNIX: Operating system popular for many minicomputer applications.

Updating: Adding, changing, or deleting information in database.

Upgrade: Updating computer by adding devices that make system work faster or more efficiently.

User Friendly: Hardware or software not requiring extensive computer knowledge to use.

Utility Program: Program performing tasks related to computer, such as sorting, copying, setting screen colors, or managing files.

Value: Data in data field or computer record.

Video Display: Video screen that prints messages by which system communicates with operator.

Virtual Disk: See RAM disk.

VPN: "Virtual private network." A network constructed over the Internet to connect nodes, using encryption and other security mechanisms to ensure that only authorized users can access the network and that the data cannot be intercepted.

WAN: "Wide-area network." A computer network spanning a relatively large geographical area, usually consisting of two or more local-area networks (LANs). Computers connected to a wide-area network are often connected through public networks. See LAN.

Window: Partitioned section of display screen in which data of one program is displayed while data from another program is displayed simultaneously in another window or in the background; technique of simultaneously displaying information about another subject on a computer screen without corrupting or destroying background information already displayed.

Word: Group of data treated as single entity; basic unit of storage of computer operations. A "word" is generally a sequence of 8, 16, or 32 bits processed as a unit.

Word Length: Number of bits in a word.

Word Processing: Computer application allowing users to create, edit, manipulate, and print text in variety of configurations.

Workstation: Computer terminal connected to data processing or word processing network.

World Wide Web: The web is made up of all computers on the Internet using HTML-capable software to exchange data.

Write: Store data in internal or external memory.

Zoom: Enlargement or reduction of an on-screen image.

Table of Laws and Rules

AMERICANS WITH DISABILITIES ACT OF 1990

ARBITRATION ACT

FEDERAL ARBITRATION ACT

UNITED STATES CODE ANNOTATED

UNITED STATES PUBLIC LAWS

FEDERAL RULES OF CIVIL PROCEDURE

FEDERAL RULES OF CRIMINAL PROCEDURE

FEDERAL RULES OF EVIDENCE

ARIZONA STATUTES

ARKANSAS CODE ANNOTATED

CALIFORNIA CODE OF CIVIL PROCEDURE

CALIFORNIA RULES OF COURT

CALIFORNIA STATE BAR RULES, CODE OF JUDICIAL ETHICS

CALIFORNIA RULES AND REGULATIONS OF THE STATE BAR

COLORADO REVISED STATUTES

DELAWARE CODE

DISTRICT OF COLUMBIA CODE

FLORIDA STATUTES

HAWAII REVISED STATUTES

IDAHO CODE

ILLINOIS COMPILED STATUTES

INDIANA CODE

IOWA CODE

KANSAS STATUTES

KENTUCKY REVISED STATUTES

MAINE REVISED STATUTES ANNOTATED

MARYLAND CODE, COURTS AND JUDICIAL PROCEEDINGS

MICHIGAN COMPILED LAWS ANNOTATED

MINNESOTA STATUTES

MISSOURI STATUTES

MONTANA CODE

NEBRASKA REVISED STATUTES

NEVADA REVISED STATUTES

NEW MEXICO STATUTES

NEW YORK CIVIL PRACTICE LAW AND RULES

Table of Cases

nologies, Inc., 2010 WL 2500301 (D. Colo. 2010)—6:2

Medtronic Sofamor Danek, Inc. v. Michelson, 229 F.R.D. 550, 56 Fed. R. Serv. 3d 1159 (W.D. Tenn. 2003)—6:7

Micron Technology, Inc. v. Rambus Inc., 645 F.3d 1311 (Fed. Cir. 2011)—7:2

Miller v. Corinthian Colleges, Inc., 769 F. Supp. 2d 1336, 268 Ed. Law Rep. 235 (D. Utah 2011)—8:4

v. Holzmann, 2007 U.S. Dist. LEXIS 2987 (D.D.C. Jan. 17, 2007)—2:1, 2:5

Mitsubishi Motors Corp. v. Soler Chrysler-Plymouth, Inc., 473 U.S. 614, 105 S. Ct. 3346, 87 L. Ed. 2d 444 (1985)—8:2, 8:6

Mobil Oil Corp. v. Altech Industries, Inc., 117 F.R.D. 650 (C.D. Cal. 1987)—6:8

Montana v. Wyoming, 130 S. Ct. 1753, 176 L. Ed. 2d 210 (2010)—6:2

Moore v. Publicis Groupe, 287 F.R.D. 182 (S.D. N.Y. 2012)—6:2

Moreno v. Ostly, 2011 WL 598931 (Cal. App. 1st Dist. 2011)—5:2

Moses v. Halstead, 236 F.R.D. 667 (D. Kan. 2006)—4:3

Moses H. Cone Memorial Hosp. v. Mercury Const. Corp., 460 U.S. 1, 103 S. Ct. 927, 74 L. Ed. 2d 765 (1983)—8:2

MSC.Software Corp. v. Altair Engineering, Inc., 2009 WL 4726588 (E.D. Mich. 2009)—6:5

Multiven, Inc. v. Cisco Systems, Inc., 2010 WL 2813618 (N.D. Cal. 2010)—6:2

Munshani v. Signal Lake Venture Fund II, LP, 60 Mass. App. Ct. 714, 805 N.E.2d 998 (2004)—4:1

N

National Security Agency Telecommunications Records Litigation, In re, 2007 WL 3306579 (N.D. Cal. 2007)—2:4

National Tank Co. v. Brotherton, 851 S.W.2d 193 (Tex. 1993)—7:2

Nat'l Century Fin. Enterprises, Inc. Fin. Inv. Litig., In re, 2009 WL 2160174 (S.D. Ohio July 16, 2009)—2:4

Nebraska, State of v. State of Wyoming, 515 U.S. 1, 115 S. Ct. 1933, 132 L. Ed. 2d 1 (1995)—6:2

Newman v. Borders, Inc., 257 F.R.D. 1 (D.D.C. 2009)—6:1

NORCAL Mutual Ins. Co. v. Newton, 84 Cal. App. 4th 64, 100 Cal. Rptr. 2d 683 (1st Dist. 2000)—8:3

Northington v. H & M Intern., 2011 WL 663055 (N.D. Ill. 2011)—5:1

Nuclear Elec. Ins. Ltd. (Cent. Power and Light Co.), Matter of Arbitration Between, 926 F. Supp. 428 (S.D. N.Y. 1996)—8:4

Nursing Home Pension Fund v. Oracle Corp., 254 F.R.D. 559 (N.D. Cal. 2008)—2:4

Nycomed U.S. Inc. v. Glenmark Generics Ltd., 2010 WL 3173785 (E.D. N.Y. 2010)—5:1

O

Oracle Corp. v. SAP AG, 566 F. Supp. 2d 1010 (N.D. Cal. 2008)—2:4, 6:1

Ovitz v. Schulman, 133 Cal. App. 4th 830, 35 Cal. Rptr. 3d 117 (2d Dist. 2005)—8:1

P

P&G Co. v. S.C. Johnsom & Son, Inc., 2009 U.S. Dist. LEXIS

Index